Sou Fujimoto
Architecture Works 1995-2015

藤 本 壮 介 建 築 作 品 集

Sou Fujimoto Architecture Works 1995-2015

1st edition published in Japan on April 16, 2015
1st edition, 6th printing published on June 30, 2025

Author: Sou Fujimoto
Publisher: Akira Watai
TOTO Publishing （TOTO LTD.)
TOTO Nogizaka Bldg., 2F
1-24-3 Minami-Aoyama, Minato-ku
Tokyo 107-0062, Japan
[Sales]Telephone: +81-3-3402-7138 Facsimile: +81-3-3402-7187
[Editorial]Telephone: +81-3-3497-1010
URL: https://jp.toto.com/publishing
Printer: TOPPAN Colorer Inc.

Except as permitted under copyright law, this book may not be reproduced, in whole or in part, in any form or by any means, including photocopying, scanning, digitizing, or otherwise, without prior permission. Scanning or digitizing this book through a third party, even for personal or home use, is also strictly prohibited.
The list price is indicated on the cover.

ISBN978-4-88706-349-5

Sou Fujimoto

Architecture Works 1995-2015

藤 本 壮 介 建 築 作 品 集

Introduction

Twenty years have gone by since I graduated from university and began my explorations as an architect. Now, by compiling the collection of works in this book, I have attempted to give an inclusive overview of the trial and error and experimentation of these last two decades.

The concepts I explored at first, guided only by faint inklings and presentiments, gradually came to bear relation to actually completed projects, and evolved, split off, or merged in a variety of ways, giving rise to new ideas. In recent years there have been more overseas projects, and as a result the primal, core ideas I keep in mind are subjected to unexpected stimuli in the form of different climates, cultures, histories and environments. These have begun producing surprising mutations and ever-increasing diversity.

That is why this look back over the past 20 years seems like both a motley collection of all different sorts of endeavors, or a consistent pursuit of one single direction. It is in fact both, and I believe the marriage of these two brings about an architecture that blends simplicity and complexity, the primordial and the futuristic.

This book presents 107 projects over 20 years, in chronological order. These are not necessarily well-known projects, and some of them are shown here for the first time, including conceptual models I have never presented and competition proposals that were not selected. I hope that by appearing alongside many other projects, each one is contextualized in a way it could not be when simply described on its own, and the evolution and deepening of concepts, the turning points and fusions will become visible. I believe it will become evident that beneath even the boldest, most daring proposals lie many years of patient trial and error.

The indexes on black bands attached to each project description contain numbers of other projects that seem to bear a relation to that project, and are intended to function like links. They enable the reader to get a different angle on the body of work by tracing it not only chronologically but also as a web of interrelated concepts.

Twenty years as an architect represents a milestone, but also a new beginning. As this book shows, in recent years there have been more projects and they are growing more diverse, the range of concepts and ideas expanding dramatically. While rooted in architecture's fundamental and primordial values, these projects entail new and unexpected ideas and forms, and I hope that they will sow seeds for the future and some of them will serve in some small way to forge the value systems of tomorrow. These value systems will in turn generate the future of the future, in ways we can scarcely imagine.

Below I list some of the fundamental concepts that underlie all of these projects. When read as words alone, they may at first glance be as cryptic as Zen koans, but when the collection of works based on these concepts is viewed, I believe the issues explored in them will take on more tangible form. In the future, where will we live, how, and in what kind of society? What is the nature of the relationships between bodies and spaces, interior and exterior, nature and artifice, the individual and the group? As we explore these questions, we come to have premonitions and visions of the future of architecture itself.

1   Place of both separation and connection

2   Architecture as gradation between interior and exterior

3   House as city, City as house

4   Interior items / furniture / room / architecture / street / city / landscape

5   Living within a chiaroscuro of infinite floating matters

6   Architecture as forest

7   Many many many

8   Stratified terrain / Undulated architecture

9   Architecture as variety of flow

10 Soft order born from local interrelationships

11 Architecture – connecting past, present, and future

12 Between nature and artifice

序

大学を卒業してすぐにひとりで建築家としての思索を始めてからもう20年になる。この作品集をまとめるにあたって、その20年間の試行錯誤の流れを一覧できるような本をつくることができないだろうかと考えた。最初期の、本当にかすかな予感だけを頼りに手探りで模索していたコンセプチュアルな思考が、徐々に現実のプロジェクトに出合ってさまざまな形で変化し、分化し、あるいは融合して、新しいアイデアが生まれてくる。ここ最近は、海外のプロジェクトも増えてきて、そうすると、芯で考えている根源的な思考が、さまざまな気候や文化、歴史や周辺環境によって思いもよらない刺激を受けて、驚くような変異と多様な展開が始まっている。

だからこうやって20年を振り返ってみると、実にまったくばらばらなことをやっているようにも見えるし、ひとつのことをやり続けているようにも見える。その両方が混ざり合って、単純さと多様さ、根源性と未来性が融合した建築が生まれてきているに違いない。

この本では、20年間、107におよぶプロジェクトを、ひたすらに時系列に並べた。その中には、よく知られたプロジェクトばかりでなく、今までに発表してこなかったコンセプチュアルなモデルや、コンペに応募したが敗れた案など、初めて発表するものも多く含まれる。そのようなほかの多くのプロジェクトと並ぶことで、個々のプロジェクトをただ説明するだけでは見えてこないような、コンセプトの進化や深化、転機や融合などが見えてくるのではないかと期待している。鮮やかな提案の裏に、何年にもおよぶ試行錯誤が繰り返されているのが見て取れると思う。各プロジェクトの冒頭に付けた黒帯のインデックスには、そのプロジェクトと関連がありそうなプロジェクトの番号を、リンクのように提示した。時系列に追っていくだけではなく、このリンクをたどることで、また違った全体像が見えてくるに違いない。

20年は節目ではあるが、また新たな始まりでもある。見ていただくと分かる通り、近年ますます多くのプロジェクトが、多様な形で展開して、それにつれてコンセプトやアイデアもどんどん広がっている。建築の原初的で根源的な価値に根差しながらも、思いもよらない新しい思考と形が生まれてくる。それが未来の種となって蒔かれ、そのいくつかは、僕たちの未来の価値観にかすかにでも役に立ってほしいと思う。そこからまた、未来の未来が生まれてくるはずだ。

ここに、すべてのプロジェクトの背後に流れている、原初的で根源的なコンセプトを並べてみたい。それは文章で読んだだけでは一見謎めいた禅の問答のように聞こえるかもしれない。しかしこれらをふまえた上で作品群を見ると、そこに込められた問いを感じてもらえると思う。　未来に、僕たちはどんな場所に、どんな社会に、どのように住むのだろうか？　身体と空間、内部と外部、自然と人工、個と共同体の関係とは？　その先に、未来の建築の予感が広がっている。

1　離れていて同時に繋がっている場所

2　内部と外部の間のグラデーションとしての建築

3　家であり同時に街である

4　雑貨／家具／部屋／建築／路／街／ランドスケープ

5　無数のモノたちが浮遊してつくり出す密度感の中に住む

6　森のような建築

7　many many many

8　積層された地形／起伏をもった建築

9　流れとその滞留としての建築

10　局所的な関係性から緩やかな秩序が生まれる

11　建築とは、過去と現在と未来を繋げるものである

12　自然と人工の間

Contents

Introduction			*4*
Collected Works 1995-2015			
1995	001	House of Gradation	*12*
1996	002	Seidai Hospital Occupational Therapy Ward	*14*
1997	003	Network by Walk	*16*
1998	004	Seidai Hospital Annex	*18*
2000	005	Art Museum in Aomori	*20*
	006	Day-care Center	*22*
2001	007	Primitive Future House	*24*
2002	008	Oura Town Hall	*26*
	009	Glass Cloud	*28*
	010	Hana Café	*30*
	011	Shijima Lodge	*32*
2003	012	House N (Preliminary version)	*34*
	013	Dormitory in Date	*36*
	014	Annaka Environmental Art Forum	*40*
2005	015	T house	*42*
	016	Atelier in Hokkaido	*48*
2006	017	House in Hayama	*50*
	018	Residential treatment center for emotionally disturbed children	*52*
	019	7/2 House	*58*
2007	020	House O	*60*
	021	Spiral House	*64*
2008	022	House Inside-Out Tree	*66*
	023	Dubai Skyscraper	*68*
	024	Kumamoto station plaza	*70*
	025	Empty House	*72*
	026	House/Garden	*74*
	027	House N	*76*
	028	house/trees in Basel	*84*
	029	Final Wooden House	*86*
	030	House before House	*92*
2009	031	Benetton Building	*98*
	032	Sumida Hokusai Museum	*102*
	033	City as Architecture, Architecture as Mountain, Mountain as City	*104*
	034	Peak-Oslo National Museum	*110*
	035	House as water way	*114*
	036	House H	*116*
	037	Art Museum in China	*122*
	038	Another Island	*124*
	039	1000㎡ House -ORDOS 100	*126*
	040	Gunma Agricultural Technology Center	*128*
	041	Taipei Pop Music Center	*130*
	042	Kogakuin University Hachioji campus	*132*
2010	043	Tokyo Apartment	*134*
	044	Musashino Art University Museum & Library	*138*
	045	House OM	*146*
	046	House as Cloud	*152*
	047	Cloud Bridge	*154*
	048	Inside Outside Tree	*156*
	049	House B	*160*
	050	Vertical Forest	*162*
	051	UNIQLO Shinsaibashi	*164*
	052	Nube Arena	*166*
2011	053	Kultur Projekte Berlin	*168*
	054	LA Small House	*172*
	055	House NA	*174*
	056	Tree Skyscraper	*180*
	057	Louisiana Cloud	*182*
	058	Layered Plaza	*184*
	059	Garden Gallery	*186*
	060	sacai Minamiaoyama	*188*
	061	Beton Hala Waterfront Center	*190*
	062	Jyoshutomioka Station	*196*
	063	Taiwan Tower	*198*
	064	Geometric Forest -SOLO Houses Project	*202*
	065	FOREST OF SILENCE	*206*
2012	066	Toilet in Nature	*210*
	067	House K	*214*
	068	Home-for-All in Rikuzentakata	*220*
	069	No Dog, No Life -ARCHITECTURE FOR DOGS	*224*
	070	Smallest/Largest Art Museum	*226*
2013	071	MINKA Japanese Traditional Houses: Yukio Futagawa and the Origins of His Architectural Photography, 1955	*228*
	072	Mirrored Gardens -Vitamin Creative Space	*230*
	073	Energy Forest	*234*
	074	Catalunya House	*236*
	075	Setonomori Houses	*238*
	076	Connecticut Pool House	*240*
	077	Serpentine Gallery Pavilion 2013	*244*
	078	Taiwan Cafe	*256*
	079	Souk Mirage/Particles of Light	*260*
	080	Kunsthalle Bielefeld Annex	*266*
	081	Media Forest -Axel Springer Campus	*270*
	082	Museum in the Forest	*276*
	083	Salford Sphere	*280*
	084	Amakusa City Hall	*282*
	085	Ginza Building	*284*
	086	JJ99 Youth Hostel	*286*
	087	Taipei Apartment	*288*
	088	Omotesando Branches	*290*
	089	Fuke Nursery School	*294*
	090	House in Guangzhou	*296*
2014	091	L'Arbre Blanc	*298*
	092	bus stop in Krumbach	*304*
	093	Naoshima Pavilion	*308*
	094	TAINAN MUSEUM OF FINE ARTS	*312*
	095	São Paulo House - Branch	*318*
	096	São Paulo House - Cave	*320*
	097	São Paulo House - Louver Cloud	*324*
	098	Stacked Rock House	*326*
	099	Many Small Cubes -Small Nomad House	*330*
	100	House of sliding doors	*334*
	101	The Miami Design District Palm Courtyard	*336*
	102	OPEN ART MUSEUM -HELSINKI GUGGENHEIM MUSEUM	*338*
	103	Beijing Cultural and Art Center	*342*
	104	Forest of Music	*346*
	105	Art Museum in Shiga	*354*
	106	House I	*358*
2015	107	Skyscraper/Forest	*360*

Sou Fujimoto Chronology	*362*
Data on Works	*368*
Profile, Staff List, Credits	*374*

目次

序 *6*
Collected Works 1995-2015

1995	001	House of Gradation	*12*
1996	002	聖台病院作業療法棟	*14*
1997	003	Network by Walk	*16*
1998	004	聖台病院新病棟	*18*
2000	005	青森県立美術館	*20*
	006	Day-care Center	*22*
2001	007	Primitive Future House	*24*
2002	008	邑楽町役場	*26*
	009	Glass Cloud	*28*
	010	Hana Café	*30*
	011	しじま山荘	*32*
2003	012	House N (Preliminary version)	*34*
	013	伊達の援護寮	*36*
	014	安中環境アートフォーラム	*40*
2005	015	T house	*42*
	016	Atelier in Hokkaido	*48*
2006	017	House in Hayama	*50*
	018	児童心理治療施設	*52*
	019	7/2 House	*58*
2007	020	House O	*60*
	021	Spiral House	*64*
2008	022	House Inside-Out Tree	*66*
	023	Dubai Skyscraper	*68*
	024	熊本駅前広場	*70*
	025	Empty House	*72*
	026	House/Garden	*74*
	027	House N	*76*
	028	house/trees in Basel	*84*
	029	Final Wooden House	*86*
	030	House before House	*92*
2009	031	Benetton Building	*98*
	032	墨田区北斎会館	*102*
	033	建築のような都市、都市のような山、山のような建築	*104*
	034	Peak-Oslo National Museum	*110*
	035	House as water way	*114*
	036	House H	*116*
	037	Art Museum in China	*122*
	038	もう一つの島	*124*
	039	1000㎡ House -ORDOS 100	*126*
	040	群馬県農業技術センター	*128*
	041	Taipei Pop Music Center	*130*
	042	工学院大学八王子キャンパス	*132*
2010	043	Tokyo Apartment	*134*
	044	武蔵野美術大学美術館・図書館	*138*
	045	House OM	*146*
	046	House as Cloud	*152*
	047	Cloud Bridge	*154*
	048	Inside Outside Tree	*156*
	049	House B	*160*
	050	Vertical Forest	*162*
	051	UNIQLO 心斎橋店	*164*
	052	Nube Arena	*166*
2011	053	Kultur Projekte Berlin	*168*
	054	LA Small House	*172*
	055	House NA	*174*
	056	Tree Skyscraper	*180*
	057	Louisiana Cloud	*182*
	058	Layered Plaza	*184*
	059	Garden Gallery	*186*
	060	sacai 南青山店	*188*
	061	Beton Hala Waterfront Center	*190*
	062	上州富岡駅舎	*196*
	063	台湾タワー	*198*
	064	Geometric Forest -SOLO Houses Project	*202*
	065	FOREST OF SILENCE	*206*
2012	066	Toilet in Nature	*210*
	067	House K	*214*
	068	陸前高田みんなの家	*220*
	069	No Dog, No Life -ARCHITECTURE FOR DOGS	*224*
	070	Smallest/Largest Art Museum	*226*
2013	071	日本の民家　一九五五年　二川幸夫・建築写真の原点	*228*
	072	Mirrored Gardens -Vitamin Creative Space	*230*
	073	Energy Forest	*234*
	074	Catalunya House	*236*
	075	せとの森住宅	*238*
	076	Connecticut Pool House	*240*
	077	Serpentine Gallery Pavilion 2013	*244*
	078	Taiwan Cafe	*256*
	079	Souk Mirage/Particles of Light	*260*
	080	Kunsthalle Bielefeld Annex	*266*
	081	Media Forest -Axel Springer Campus	*270*
	082	Museum in the Forest	*276*
	083	Salford Sphere	*280*
	084	天草本庁舎	*282*
	085	Ginza Building	*284*
	086	JJ99 Youth Hostel	*286*
	087	Taipei Apartment	*288*
	088	Omotesando Branches	*290*
	089	守山市浮気保育園	*294*
	090	House in Guangzhou	*296*
2014	091	L'Arbre Blanc	*298*
	092	bus stop in Krumbach	*304*
	093	直島パヴィリオン	*308*
	094	TAINAN MUSEUM OF FINE ARTS	*312*
	095	São Paulo House - Branch	*318*
	096	São Paulo House - Cave	*320*
	097	São Paulo House - Louver Cloud	*324*
	098	Stacked Rock House	*326*
	099	Many Small Cubes -Small Nomad House	*330*
	100	House of sliding doors	*334*
	101	The Miami Design District Palm Courtyard	*336*
	102	OPEN ART MUSEUM -HELSINKI GUGGENHEIM MUSEUM	*338*
	103	Beijing Cultural and Art Center	*342*
	104	Forest of Music	*346*
	105	滋賀県立近代美術館	*354*
	106	House I	*358*
2015	107	Skyscraper/Forest	*360*

藤本壮介年表 *362*

作品データ *368*

略歴、スタッフリスト、クレジット *374*

Collected Works 1995-2015

House of Gradation

1995

Inside / Outside – the infinite gradations in between

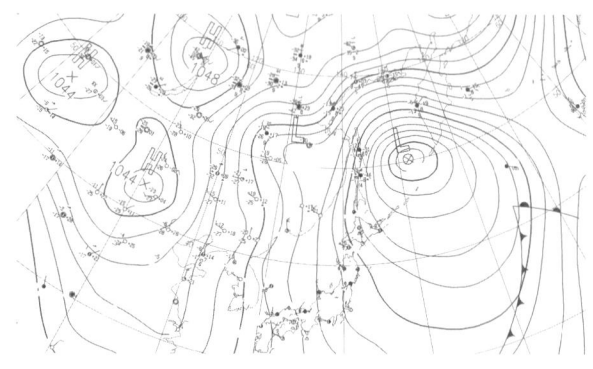 

Shortly after graduation, I set myself in search of something that challenges the very essence of architecture. Notably, a quest to re-define the most fundamental concept within architecture: the demarcation of inside and outside space, not simply by a single wall, but by somehow manifesting the gradation of this change itself as a tangible territory. By doing so, I imagined architecture might be able to come to a turning point in which it would be liberated from its rigid and solid form, surrounded by walls, and become something more ambiguous like a territory. Architecture inevitably manifests itself in a solid form, however supple one's perception of it is. I sought the new possibilities of architecture veiled within this difference. This endeavour has since extended to *House N* and also to the *Serpentine Gallery Pavilion 2013*.

大学を卒業して間もなくの頃、建築を根底から問い直すような何かを模索していた。建築においてもっとも根源的な概念である内部と外部というものを、壁1枚で切り分けるのではなく、少しずつ変化していく領域のグラデーションとして捉えることはできないだろうか、という問いであった。そうすることで、壁で囲まれた硬く強い建築というものから、揺らぎながら変化していく領域としての建築という大きな転換が生まれるのではないかと考えたのだ。建築は硬い。しかし体験はどこまでも柔らかい。その狭間に新しい建築の可能性を模索した。その思考は「House N」を経由して「Serpentine Gallery Pavilion 2013」まで連続していく。

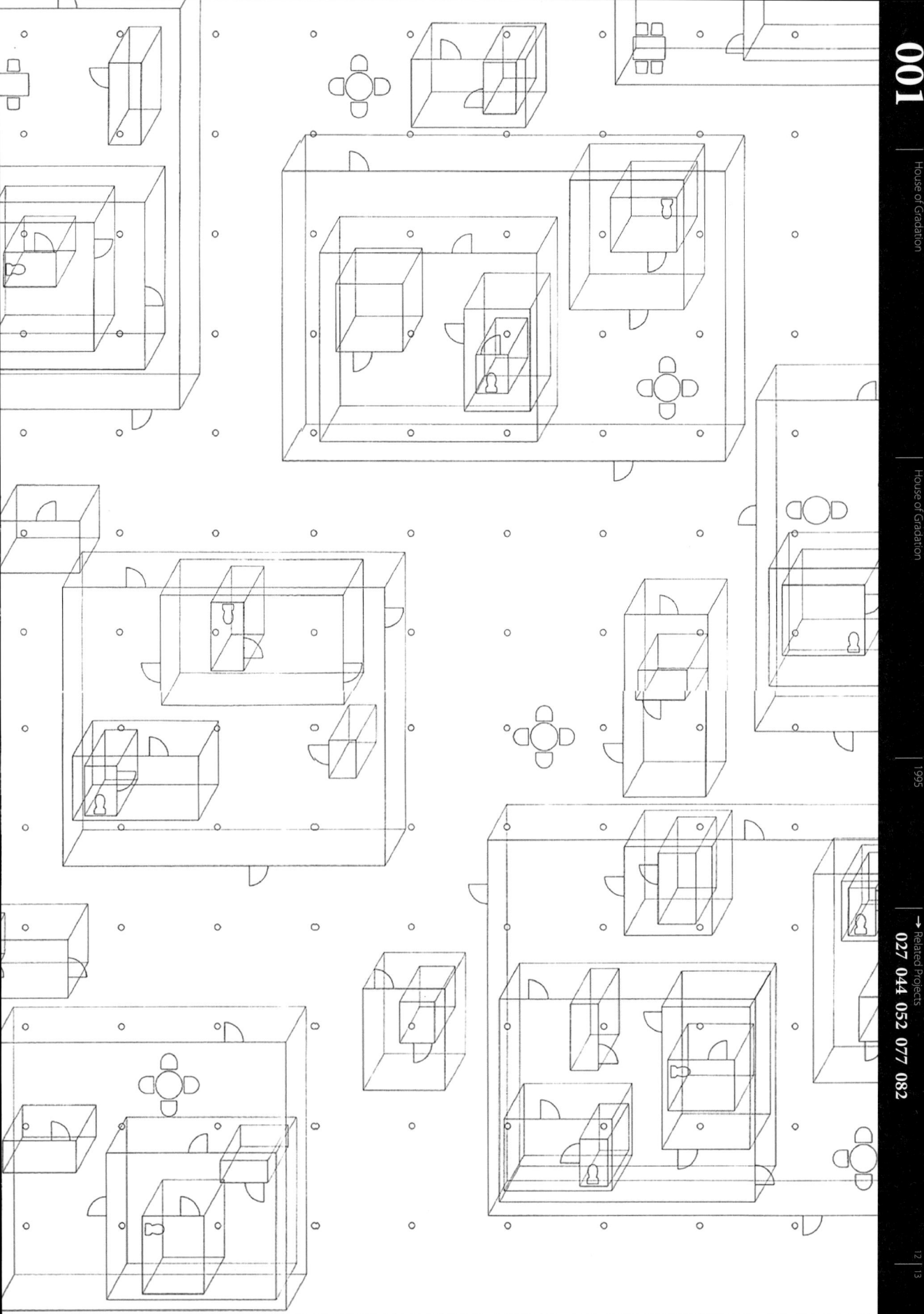

Seidai Hospital Occupational Therapy Ward
HOKKAIDO, JAPAN 1996

Obscure space / To be connected, to be separate

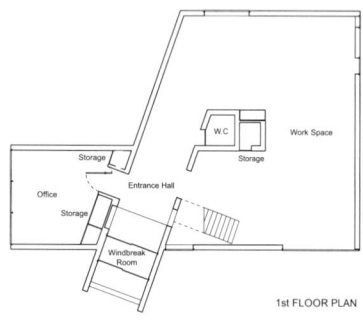

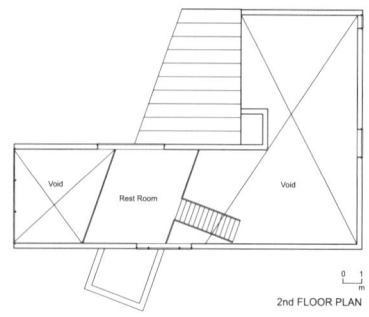

Could the quintessential purpose of architecture be to make space understood in a more fundamental manner, as something that generates various relationships between people? In this day and age, such relationships are becoming increasingly complex. This workspace for a small medical institute was my first architectural design to be realized. Here, by forming a simple space into a distorted ring like a Klein bottle, I imagined a space that was both singular and diverse, connected yet separated synchronously, as if occupants shared the space with others whilst simultaneously occupying spaces of their own. This was the first step in my endeavour for fundamental architectural space where simplicity and diversity coexist.

建築とは空間をつくること以上に、人と人とのさまざまな関係をつくり出すものではないだろうか？ そして現代において、その関係性はとても複雑だ。この小さな医療施設のためのワークスペースは、僕が実現した最初の建築だ。ここでは、単純な一つひとつの空間が、クラインの壺のようにねじれた円環の形をとることで、一つひとつでありながら無数であるような、繋がっていながら離れているような、皆と場所を共有しながら自分一人ひとりの場所をもつことができるような、そんな空間を構想した。それは単純さと多様さが同居する根源的な建築空間への探求の最初の一歩となった。

Roof
Work Space
Rest Room
Office
Entrance

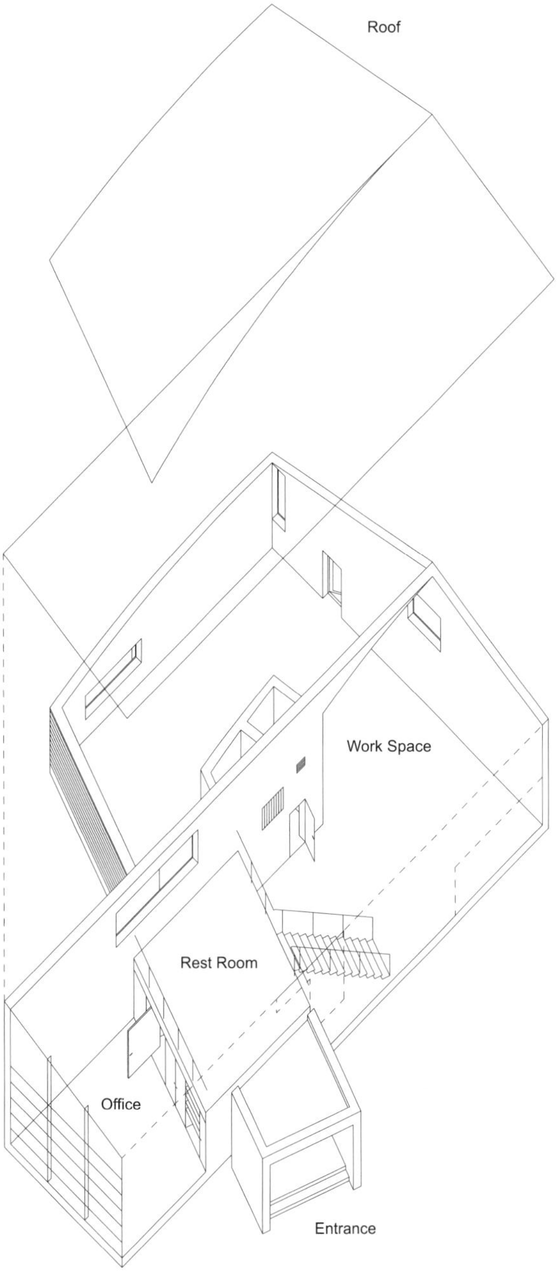

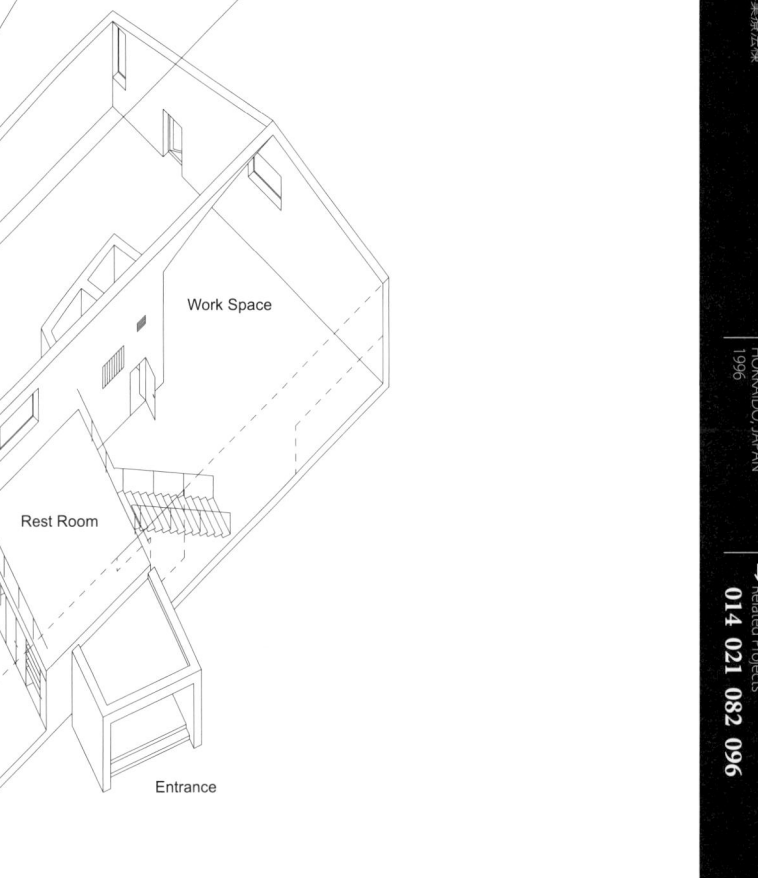

Network by Walk

TOKYO, JAPAN 1997

Architecture and the city fuse together in network

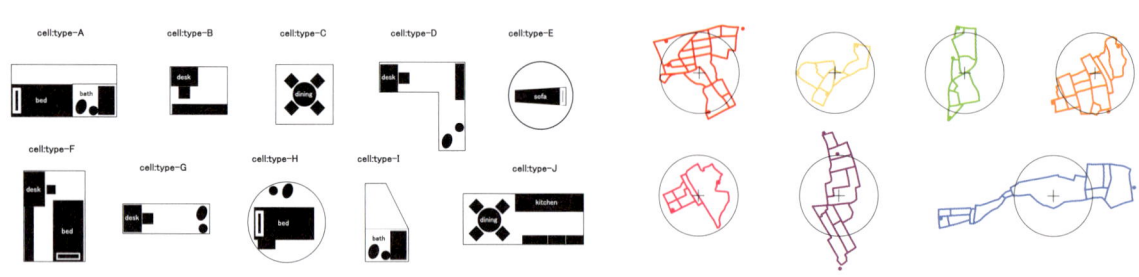

What exists in between architecture and the city, or between a dwelling and urbanity? These questions aim to re-address the relationship between the house and the city. In this project, houses depart from their existence as exclusive objects, and are construed rather as fragments of a greater complex network subsumed within the city. As such, the threshold between architecture and the city becomes ambiguous, and the diverse and complex milieu of the city and the physical human scale inherent in each unit of architecture becomes a singular phenomenon. All architecture is in a sense a city, and every city is a large and complex piece of architecture. I believe the richness of architecture emanates from such contradictions, uniting serendipities and order so that they coexist in the process. This method of fragmenting architectural elements and then re-assembling them, whilst engulfing all kinds of incongruous matters, has been explored in several projects such as the *Residential treatment center for emotionally disturbed children* and *House-before-House*, before being applied to the *Media Forest -Axel Springer Campus*.

建築と都市の間には何があるだろうか？ あるいは家と都市の間には？ この問いは家と都市との関係を問い直すことを意図している。このプロジェクトでは、とてもシンプルに、家が単体の物体としての存在を離れて無数の断片となり、そのまま都市へと溶け出して複雑なネットワークを成していくことを想像した。そこでは建築と都市の境界はもはや曖昧であり、都市的な複雑で多様な体験と、建築的で身体的なスケールが融合している。すべての建築は都市であり、またすべての都市は家である。その矛盾の中にこそ、建築の豊かさがあるに違いない。その過程で、予測不可能性と秩序が両立する。建築を分節し、異物を内包しながら再結合していくというこの方法は、「児童心理治療施設」から「House before House」を経て「Media Forest -Axel Springer Campus」へと展開していく。

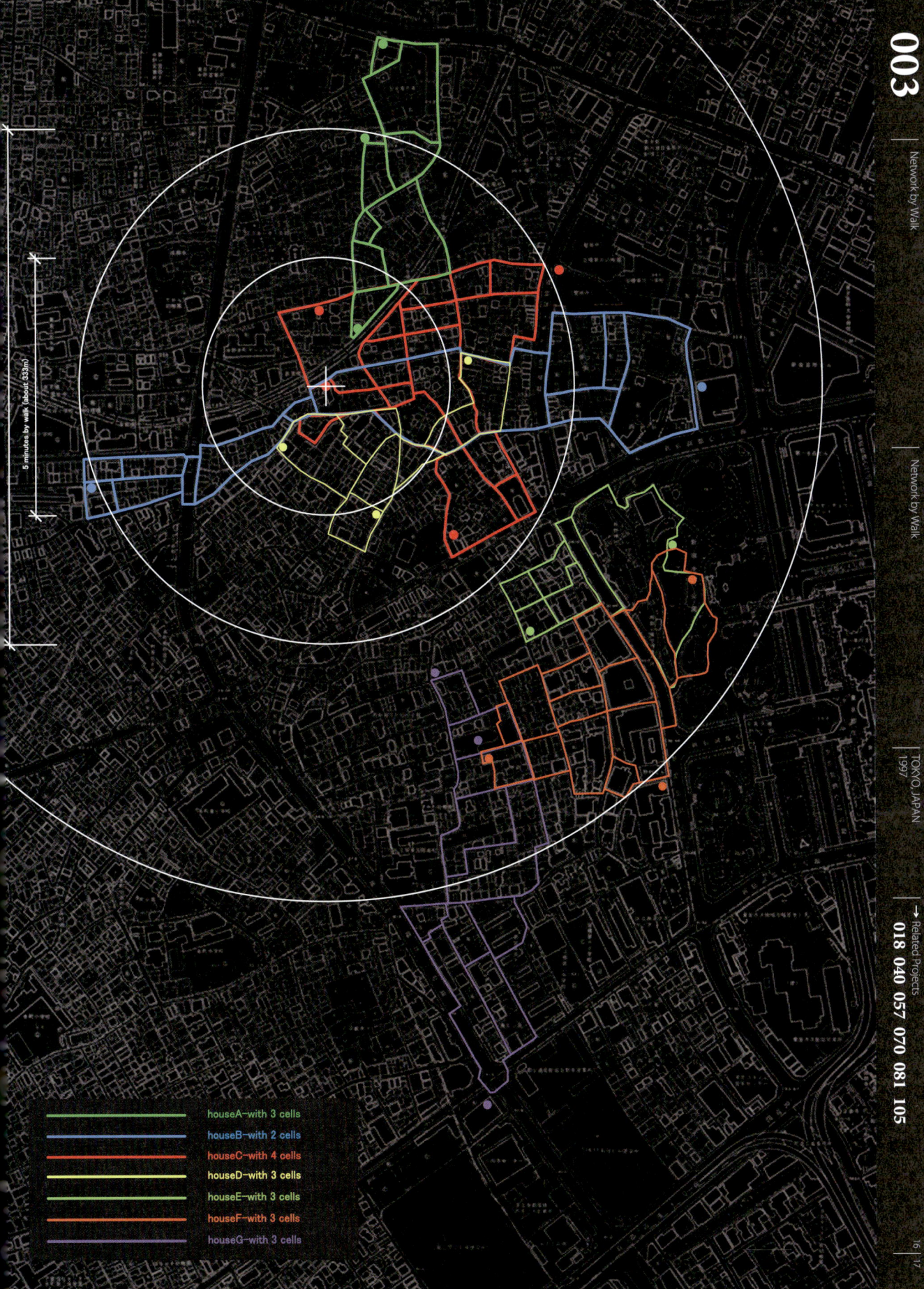

Seidai Hospital Annex

HOKKAIDO, JAPAN 1999

A house, and simultaneously a City

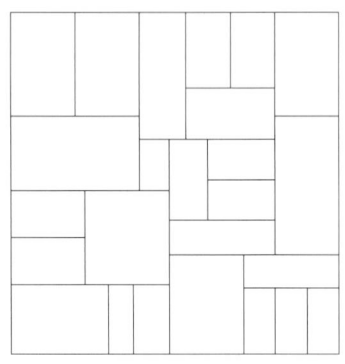 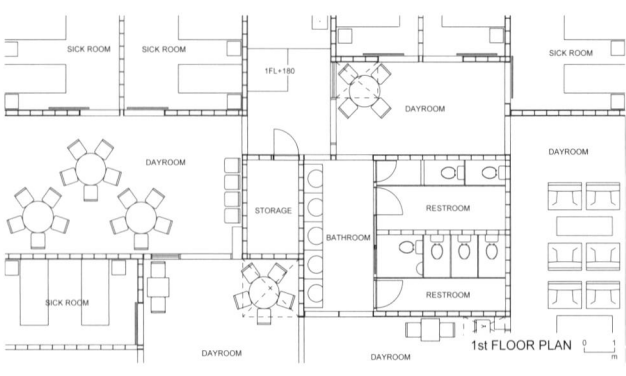

In retrospect, having designed quite a number of medical facilities during the early part of my career was a significant influence on my architectural theory(s). A medical facility is a place that needs to possess qualities of both a house and a city–to encompass intimate and very personal spaces, and yet accommodate the city-like conditions of unexpected occurrences. The proposal seeks a form of architecture that ties together both facets of these diametric opposites to coexist in harmony: simplicity and complexity, privacy and communication, the personal and the social. With the assembly of an innumerable spectrum of small rooms, minute spatial entities attain alley-like scale, and further gain the multifarious complexities of cities. In doing so we break down the heartless central corridor and instead connect the rooms with an intimate but city-like network. Such examples, where minute parts are mutually intertwined in the vast web of interrelationships to form a complex field of order, developed from the *Network by Walk* project, later setting the framework for many future projects. It is also worthy to note that this project set the direction towards a concept of living that traverses and challenges the common architectural codes.

キャリアの最初期に医療施設を多く手がけたことは、自分の建築思考に決定的な影響を与えた。医療施設とは、家であり同時に街である。とてもパーソナルで親密な空間と、さまざまな出来事が起こり得る都市的な空間。これらふたつが両立するような建築形式を構想した。単純さと複雑さ、プライバシーとコミュニケーション、パーソナルとソーシャル、身体スケールと都市スケール。ここでは、家に近い小さな部屋を無数に繋ぎ合わせることで、小さなスケールから路地的なスケール、そして街のもつ広がり感と複雑さを獲得する平面を構想した。機能的とされてきた巨大な中廊下の非人間性を排し、身体スケールのネットワークによって親密さと都市性の両立を実現する。小さな部分が相互に関係し合って複雑な秩序を形づくるこの方法は、「Network by Walk」からの発展形であり、その後のさまざまなプロジェクトへと繋がっていくとともに、建築プログラムを横断して居住環境の原型を思考するきっかけとなった。

Art Museum in Aomori

AOMORI, JAPAN 2000

Simplicity / Complexity – Making architecture as a forest

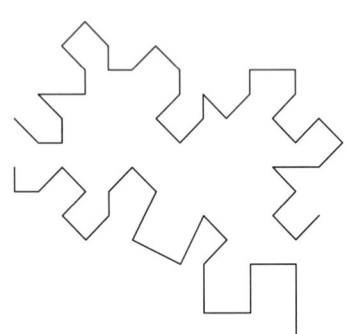
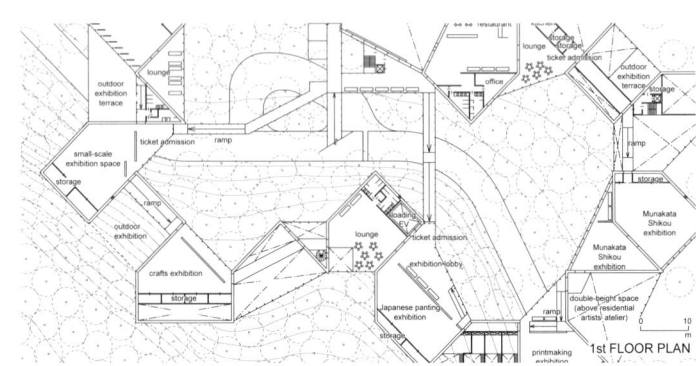

How can one make architecture akin to a forest? The crucial point is conceiving an existence between nature and artificiality. The natural order is beautifully simple, yet its appearance is diversely complex. On the other hand, architectural order is crudely robust, rigid, and at the same time frail. This proposal for an art museum set in the forest was an attempt to impart form to the diverse possibilities hidden between simplicity/complexity, and nature/artificiality. Using the Cartesian grid – an inherently artificial creation – as the base, the fortuitous line loosely defines the plan as if conversing with the surrounding forest for guidance. Would such geometric yet almost unpredictably conceived forms engender a key to an experience neither artificial nor natural? To this day, this never-ending search and journey towards a locus between man-made order and the natural is a theme both well trod and brand new for us, most recently explored in the *Serpentine Gallery Pavilion 2013*.

森のような建築をつくることはできないだろうか？ それは自然と人工の間を問うことだ。自然の秩序はとても美しく単純でありながら、そのあらわれはとても多様で複雑だ。それに比べて建築の秩序は大雑把で荒く、強すぎ、また弱すぎる。この森の中の美術館では、単純さと複雑さ、自然と人工の間に広がる可能性を空間化しようと試みた。グリッドという極めて人工的な秩序をベースとしながら、プランの線はその碁盤目の上を半ば偶然に任せて、周囲の森と対話するように移動していく。そうして出来た幾何学的でありながら予測不可能な形は、森と建築の間のような体験を生み出すのではないだろうか？この人工の秩序と自然の秩序の終わりのない対比と融合は、「Serpentine Gallery Pavilion 2013」においてもなお現在進行形で試みられている古くて新しいテーマである。

Day-care Center
HOKKAIDO, JAPAN 2000

Nebulous field

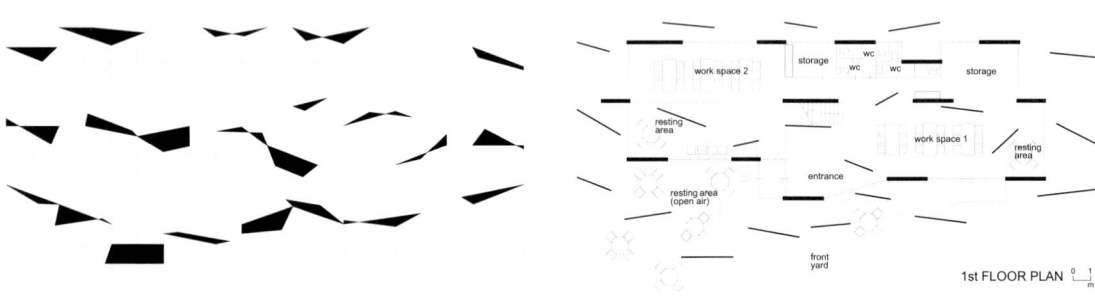

I wonder if architecture can be realized not as an enclosure but as something more like a territory, where the boundary becomes nebulous. Varying densities of a place colour its qualities like chiaroscuro in space, prompting the uses and activities of the people. I find this to be one image of what an ideal architecture might look like. This project marks the first manifestation of such an idea. Randomly layered walls engender spaces of gradual depth, where layers get deeper within, and the spaces are not entirely cut off. Various places existing between the walls are used heuristically in dialogue with the quality of the space–its openness, relativity to its neighbours, and so on. This project is a distinct and conceptual heir to the Architecture as Forest experiment in the *Aomori Museum of Art* proposal.

建築を、たんなる箱ではなく、ぼんやりとした境界をもった領域のようなものとしてつくることはできないだろうか？　場の粗密によって、それぞれの領域が特徴をもち、人びとの活動や使い方を誘発する。そんな＜曖昧な領域としての建築＞は、僕にとって夢の建築だ。このプロジェクトはその最初のあらわれである。ランダムに配置された壁が幾重にも重なることによって、徐々に奥まっていく空間が生まれる。奥はより囲まれ守られた場所であり、しかし閉じてはいない。無数の壁と壁の間に生まれる＜居場所＞は、その開き具合や他の場所との繋がり具合に応じてさまざまに使われるであろう。「青森県立美術館」で試みた＜森のような建築＞を空間的により発展させたものだと言えるかもしれない。

Day-care Center

Day-care Center

HOKKAIDO, JAPAN
2000

→ Related Projects
009 012 027 061 063 101

Primitive Future House
2001

Body / Space – Interaction between body and space

What lies in between the body and space? The 20th century labelled and systemized this under "function." Functionalism was the relationship between the body and space. However, in the 21st century, our contemporary notion of function is sustained through spatial qualities with enriching experiences to accommodate a myriad of activities, and perhaps in this very interrelationship itself. This visionary project was an attempt to dismantle architecture to its limits and re-orchestrate it solely as a diverse relationship between the body and space. In this context, diverse activities are stimulated and facilitated by how one acts or relate to the space. Function is found within the oscillations between the body and place, and architectural space is endlessly reinterpreted by its users. This heuristic conception of space has since evolved and surfaced in many forms, such as the *Serpentine Gallery Pavilion 2013*. Fragmented and thus spatialized floors also embody the relationship between matter and space.

身体と空間の間とはなんだろうか？ 20世紀にはそれは機能と呼ばれた。機能とは身体と空間の関係性のことであった。21世紀には、機能の意味は拡張し＜さまざまな身体の振る舞いを許容し刺激するようなさまざまな空間の様相、またその相互作用的な関係性＞と言えるのではないだろうか？ この初期のプロジェクトでは建築というものをいったん徹底的に解体し、ただ身体と空間の関係性のみからもう一度組み立て直すという試みである。ここでは人びとの振る舞いによって同じ地形からもまったく異なる意味や機能が導き出される。機能は身体と空間の相互作用の揺らぎの中にあり、建築空間そのものも人間の振る舞いによって随時規定され直す。この思考は「Serpentine Gallery Pavilion 2013」に至るまで、さまざまに変奏と進化を繰り返していく。またここでは、床が細分化されて空間化されている、という意味において、物体と空間の間が顕在化されてもいるのである。

Oura Town Hall

GUNMA, JAPAN 2002

Relationship through interdependency of trees and architecture

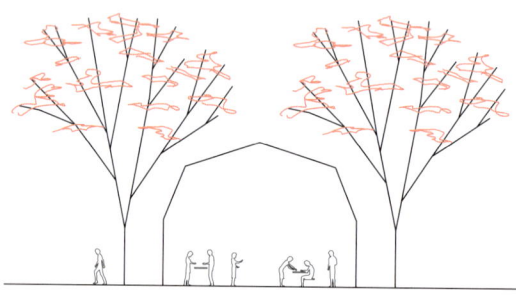

This proposal was for a competition to design a town hall in Oura-machi, Gunma. The entire site was covered with a forest and I positioned the building as if it was woven into the trees. Along with the leaves, the glass roof, with a vaulted form that corresponds to the shape of the trees, functions to obstruct sunlight. By dealing with the building and the trees on equal terms, I attempted to create a new living environment. Though the proposal did not win the competition, it was an extremely important step that marked the beginning of the tree concept I later developed in everything from *House N* and *House before House* to the *Benetton Building* and *Omotesando Branches*.

群馬県邑楽町の役場を設計するコンペの応募案。敷地全体を森とし、その森に編み込むように建築を配置していった。樹形にそってボールト状につくられたガラス屋根は、木々の葉と組み合わさることによって日差しを遮る屋根として機能する。建築と樹木を対等に扱って新しい居住環境をつくり出す試み。コンペでは敗れたが、後の「House N」や「House before House」、「Benetton Building」や「Omotesando Branches」へと至る樹木系のコンセプトの最初のものとして、とても重要な一歩であった。

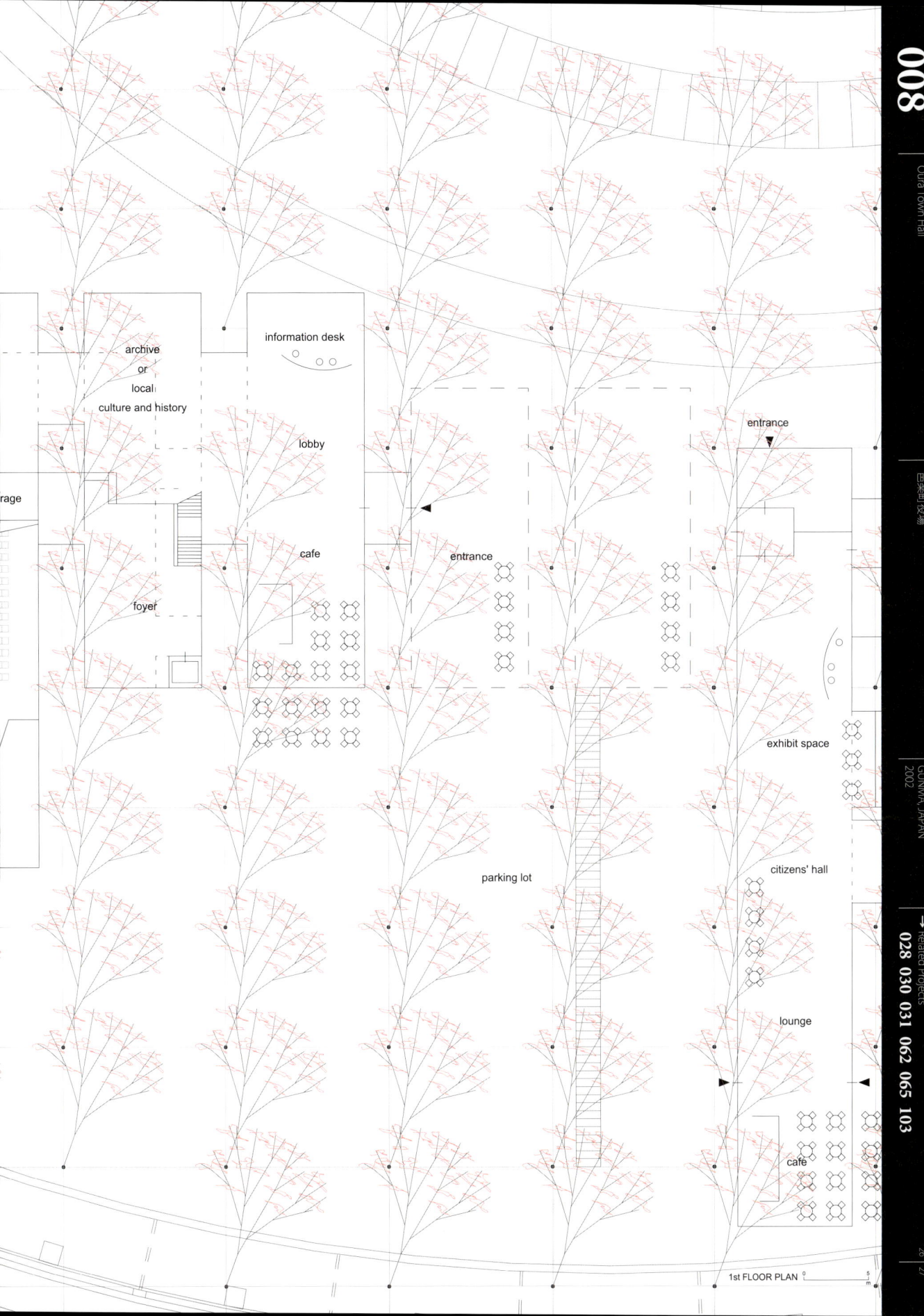

Glass Cloud

TOKYO, JAPAN 2002

To live between architecture and street
- A cloud-like space made of glass

 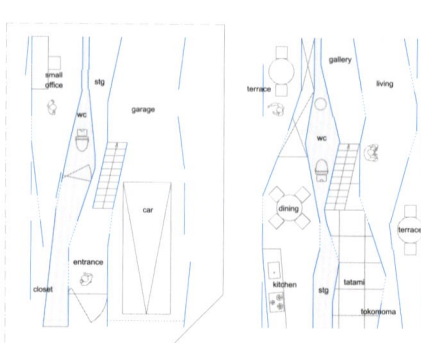 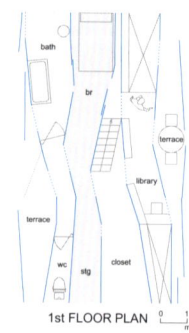

1st FLOOR PLAN

After moving to Tokyo from Hokkaido, where most of the land is essentially occupied by nature, the dense artificial environment of Tokyo was a big change and thus deeply captivating. In Hokkaido, one step outside the door lies a domain of harsh, unforgiving nature, whereas in Tokyo, after passing through the front door, a corridor which is only marginally open extends out further, and it feels as if there is very slight differentiation between interior and exterior. And further beyond the corridor, the route opens up only slightly again into a narrow and intimate alleyway. Here interior and exterior, house and city are neither antithetical nor divided, rather it is as if both phenomena gradually expand and progressively metamorphose into each other. I sought to render this remarkable impression as an architectural concept. The idea of using semi-transparent glass to create an amorphous gradation initially dates back to the *House of Gradation (1995)* but is rediscovered here as an instrument to foster such relationship between house and city. A further five years was spent in deliberation before *House N* was created.

北海道という自然の中で育った後に東京の高密人工環境で生活し始めた僕にとって、東京の街はとても興味深かった。北海道ではドアを開ければ強大な自然が待ち構えている。しかし東京では、ドアを開けても少し開けた人工環境が続いているだけで、室内と室外の間にそれほど大きな違いがないように思えた。さらにマンションの共用廊下を下っていくと、また少しだけ開けた、しかしほとんど室内のスケールと変わらない狭い街路に出る。ここでは内部と外部、都市と家の間は断絶しているのではなくむしろ徐々に変化しながらも連続しているのだった。それが僕には面白く感じられ、なんとか建築に置き換えられないものかと考えていた。半透明なガラスによって徐々に変化するグラデーションというアイデアは1995年の「House of Gradation」にまで遡るが、それが都市と住宅の関係として再発見されたのがこの計画である。そこから「House N」まで、さらに5年を要する。

Hana Café
2002

Adaptable terrain

There was a period of time when I had great interest in the notion of a loose order born from interrelationships among minute parts. I was awestruck by Ilya Prigogine's books and papers about complex theories, which I encountered shortly after graduation, and amidst this fever I was certain that this was the key to a new concept of order beyond modernism: geometric order which is not encompassed by grand arterial axes or grids, but rather a loose and nebulous order consisting of diverse networks of localities. This furniture project was a smaller by-product born out of this design process. A single form possesses various meanings depending on its interaction with the body. When the furniture is turned to its side, or even upside down, it can be used in new and unique ways. When multiple pieces are used collectively, some become tables and others may become sofas or stools, and an archipelago of furniture becomes animated by a network of interaction and function. Although this furniture was not realized at the time, it is one of the projects that one day I would like to see in material form.

当時僕は、部分と部分が関係し合うことで生まれる緩やかな秩序、というものにとても大きな興味をもっていた。大学を卒業してすぐに読んだプリゴジンの著書や複雑系の理論に触発されて、これこそが近代を超える新しい秩序の在り方だと熱狂していたのだ。巨大な軸線やグリッドの幾何学ではなく、部分と部分がネットワーク的に関係し合うことで生まれる局所的で緩やかな秩序。そしてたまたま当時集中的に取り組んでいた精神医療施設の設計を通して、形とプログラムの両面からこの新しい秩序の建築を形にしていった。この家具のプロジェクトは、そんな思考の過程から生まれた小さな試みである。ひとつの形が、人の関わり方によって3つの異なる意味をもつ。横に倒したり、転がしたりすることで、身体と家具との新しい関係が生まれる。さらにそれらの家具が無数に集まって関係し合うことで、あるものはテーブルとなり、あるものは椅子やソファとなり、家具の群れの中に機能の揺らぎが生まれる。いつか実現したいプロジェクトのひとつだ。

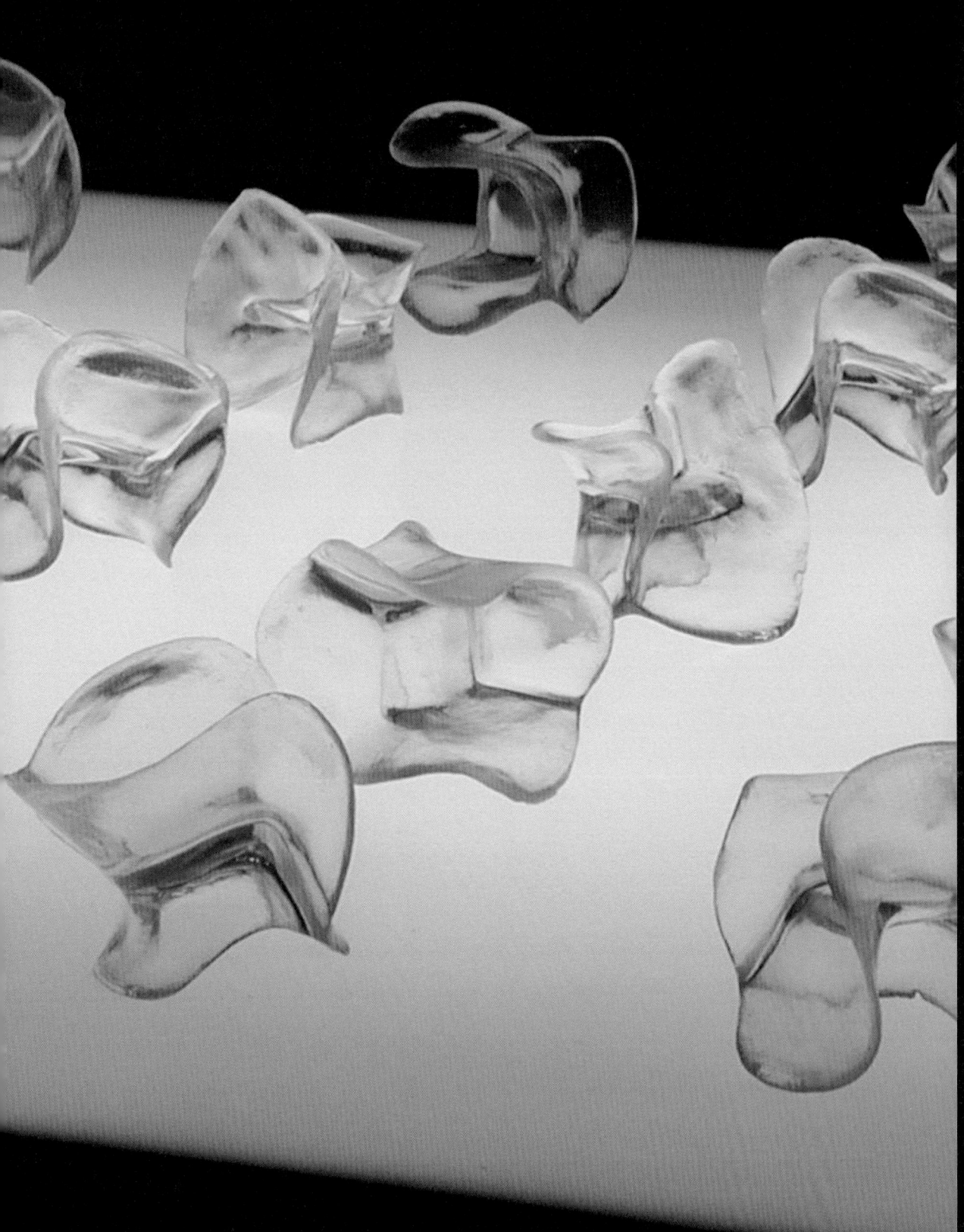

Shijima Lodge

NAGANO, JAPAN 2002

Sculpturing places from space

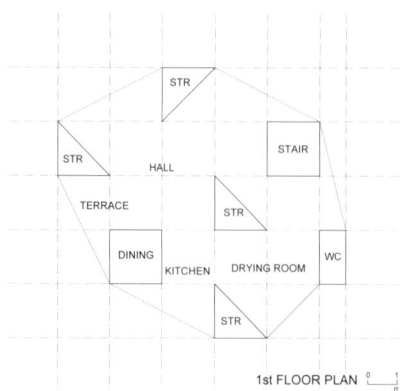

1st FLOOR PLAN

In the mountains of Hakuba, Nagano, I designed this villa for a university alpine club. The lot is located in an area of heavy snowfall, and the winter weather conditions are severe. I attempted to create a structure that would protect people from the snow load and the cold without being closed. The interior space is supported by several columns with huge volumes. Because they are like giant trees, they create comfortable hollows between them in the room. Huge trees are strong enough structurally to support the snow, and by creating various kinds of openings, it was possible to control the proportion of window space while making use of full-height glass walls. The toilet and storage functions are contained in the volume of huge trees. The irregular shape of the room, created by placing the trees there, produces a number of comfortable nooks, allowing the place to naturally accommodate various numbers of people, from one or two to ten or more. The grid base was based on my earlier work for the *Art Museum in Aomori* and I later developed its potential further in my plan for the *Residential treatment center for emotionally disturbed children*.

長野県白馬の山中に、大学の山岳サークルのための山荘を設計した。敷地は豪雪地帯であり、冬の気候は厳しい。ここでは、雪の荷重や寒さから守られながらも閉鎖的ではない構造を模索した。内部空間は、数本の巨大なボリューム状の柱によって支えられている。それらは巨樹のようであり、室内は巨樹の間に生まれた快適な凹みのようである。巨樹は十分な構造強度で積雪を支え、また開口のメリハリをつけることで、フルハイトのガラス壁を使いながらも開口の比率は低く抑えられる。巨樹のボリュームの中にはトイレや収納などの機能が収められている。さらに巨樹の配置によって生まれる室内のイレギュラーな形状は、いくつもの居心地の良い隅っこをつくり出し、ひとりから2、3人、10人以上など、ここに集まる人びとのさまざまなスケール感を自然に受け止めることができる。グリッドベースの巨樹は「青森県立美術館」からの展開であり、その後の「児童心理治療施設」へと展開する可能性を見ることができる。

House N (Preliminary version)
OITA, JAPAN 2003

The field between past and future equally becomes the field between architecture and the street

  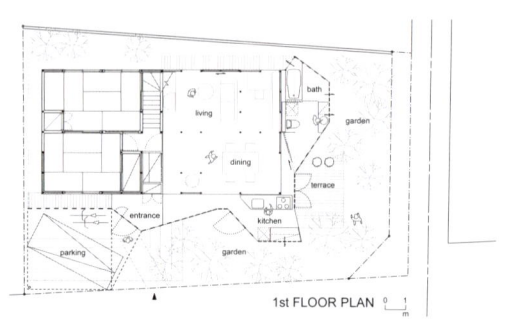

1st FLOOR PLAN

This was a renovation project for a private residence, a preliminary scheme for a project which would later be realized as *House N*. Initially the project began as a renovation/extension design, which sought to add new functions while preserving the house the client had lived for several decades. Confronting the brief for an extension, the first idea I had was that of injecting the house with new functions–a house inflating like a balloon. The term inflating particularly felt right in the sense that it would literally be expanding whilst maintaining the original attributes of the house, and depicting the new and the old in a continuum. I imagined perhaps this might open up a new window for how we could approach renovation projects. Eventually, by designing an outer shell as though the house had inflated, I created genial ma/in-between spaces where the series of new functions were housed. In hindsight, the execution was perhaps more like envelop than inflate. As the client changed his request from a renovation to an entirely new building halfway during the project, we inevitably had to make a fresh start. However, this idea of the ma-space enveloping the space was inventively re-discovered in the final design of *House N* in a very different manner.

個人住宅の増築のプロジェクト。後に実現する「House N」の初期バージョンである。もともとは、クライアントが数十年住み続けてきた住宅本体を残しながら、新たな機能を増築するプロジェクトとしてスタートした。家を増築するということは風船のように＜家が膨らむ＞ような感じではないだろうか？　というのが最初のアイデアだった。膨らむという考え方は、もともともっている性質を保ちながら拡大するという意味において、既存建物と新しくなった建物を連続的に捉えるものである。それは増築における新しいタイポロジーになるのではないだろうか？最終的には、家の外装が膨らむことによって、既存との間に魅力的な＜間の空間＞をつくり出し、そこに新しく求められた機能を配置した。膨らむというよりも、かぶせる、という感じである。クライアントが改築よりも新築を求めたことによって、プロジェクトは再出発することになったが、この＜かぶせる＞あるいは＜間の空間＞というアイデアは、最終形である「House N」に発明的に展開されることとなった。

012

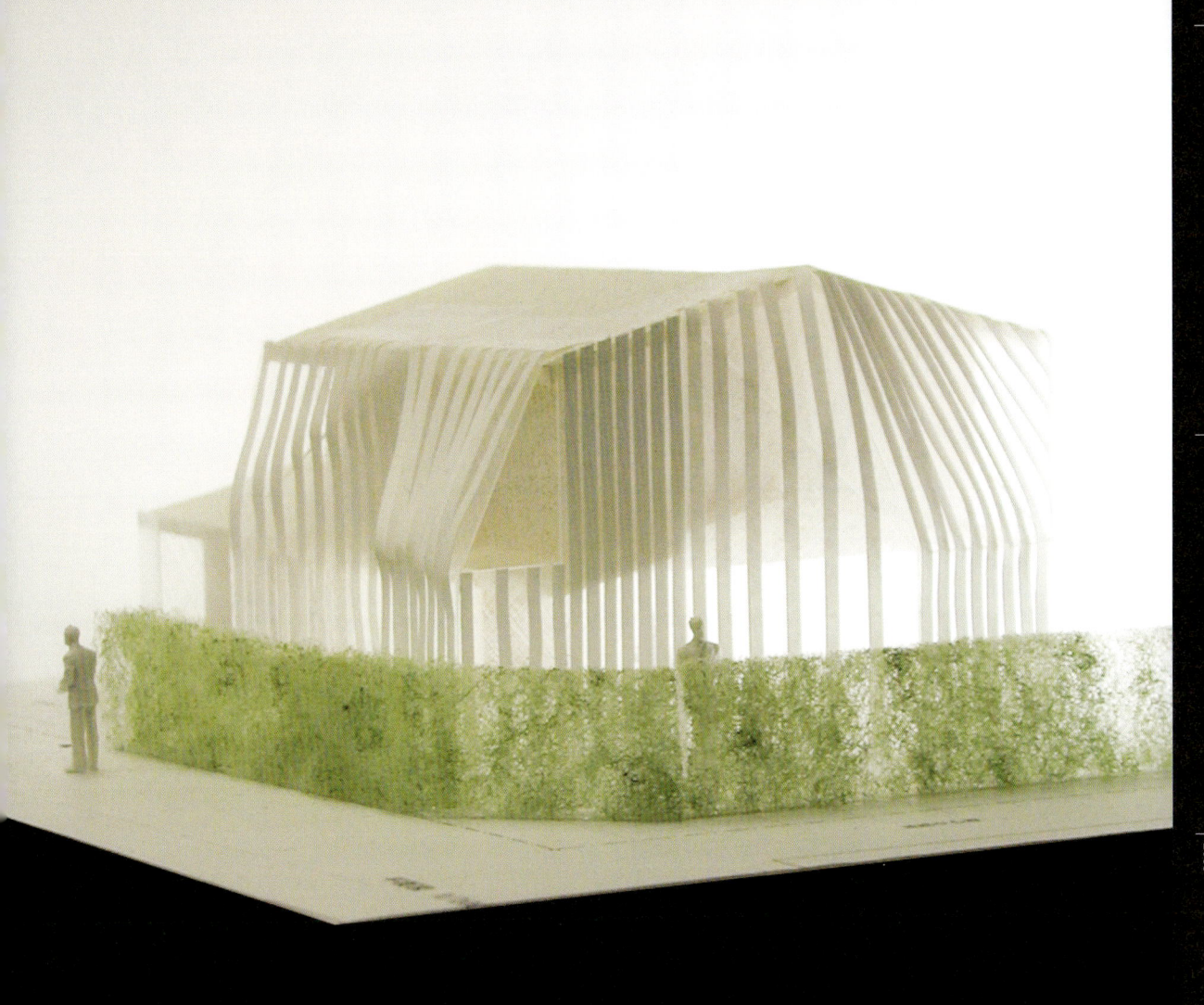

House N (Preliminary version)

OITA, JAPAN
2003

→ Related Projects
006 027 094 101

Dormitory in Date
HOKKAIDO, JAPAN 2003

Soft order born from local interrelationships

This was the first real building project to manifest the idea of conceiving loose order from local interrelationships. Medical facilities are required to accommodate various territories, from personal intimate ones to those for large groups, and for this very reason such facilities can be related to both house and city. By linking the corners of 5.4m-square units like a chain, unique triangular ma-spaces (in-between spaces) formed by various angles of the square volumes emerge within an alley-like corridor like a small plaza or an alcove. A series of rooms aligned across a single corridor is itself a ubiquitous format, but the insertion of unique urban-quality spaces through the contorted angles within the elastic pulsating corridor transforms it into a rich and colourful place(s). Residents stop and rest in these semi-open alcove spaces, meet neighbours for conversation, or unwind and read books. Since it was first conceived in the early *Seidai-Hospital Annex* project, this conception of "city-like architecture where simplicity and complexity coexist" has been translated into many forms including the *Residential treatment center for emotionally disturbed children* in 2006, and has become one of the vital frameworks of my architectural thoughts.

局所的な関係性から緩やかな秩序が生まれる、という考え方を現実の建物として実現した最初の例が、このプロジェクトだった。医療施設とは、個と集団とその間のさまざまな領域を扱うという意味において、家であり同時に街であると言える。この小さな村のような建物は、5.4m角のユニットをボリュームの角で接続しながら次々に継いでいく、という方法でつくられている。接続の角度がさまざまに変化することを利用して、この三角形の＜間の空間＞を、街路的な廊下の途中途中に現れる小さな広場、あるいはアルコーブのような場所とした。ひと繋がりの片廊下に個室が連なる形式はとてもシンプルだが、この角度の変化と廊下が脈動するように伸び縮みする小さな街角空間によって、とても変化に富んだ場所がつくられている。入居者はこの路の半ばに位置する半個室のようなアルコーブに足を止め、隣人と会話し、また本を読んだりもする。この＜複雑さと単純さをあわせもった街のような建築＞という構想は、初期の「聖台病院新病棟」から、2006年の「児童心理治療施設」に至るまでさまざまに試みられ、その後の僕の建築のひとつの骨格となっていく。

013

Dormitory in Date
伊達の風連幕
HOKKAIDO, JAPAN
2003

→ Related Projects
018 019 043 070 075 105

1st FLOOR PLAN

2nd FLOOR PLAN

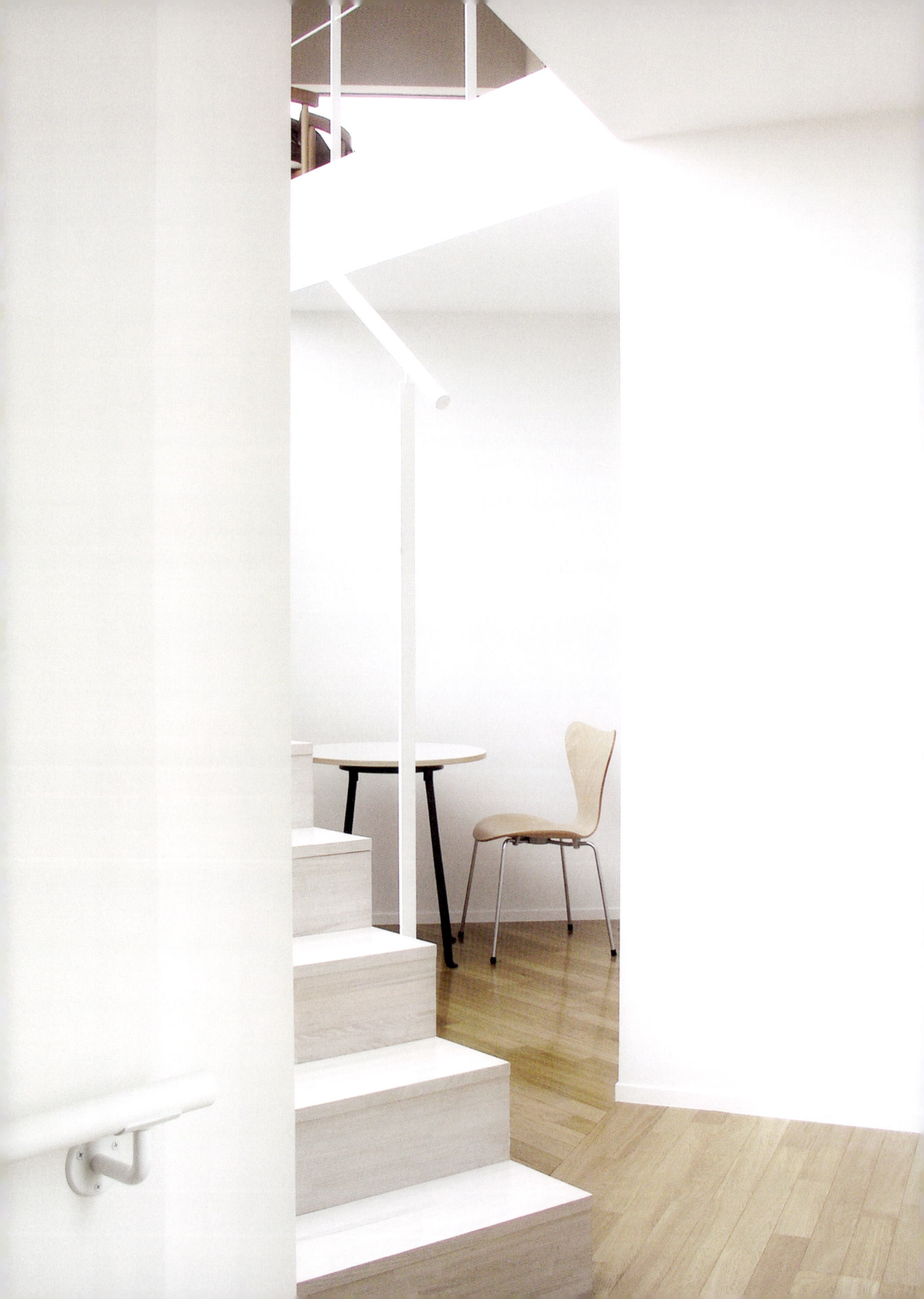

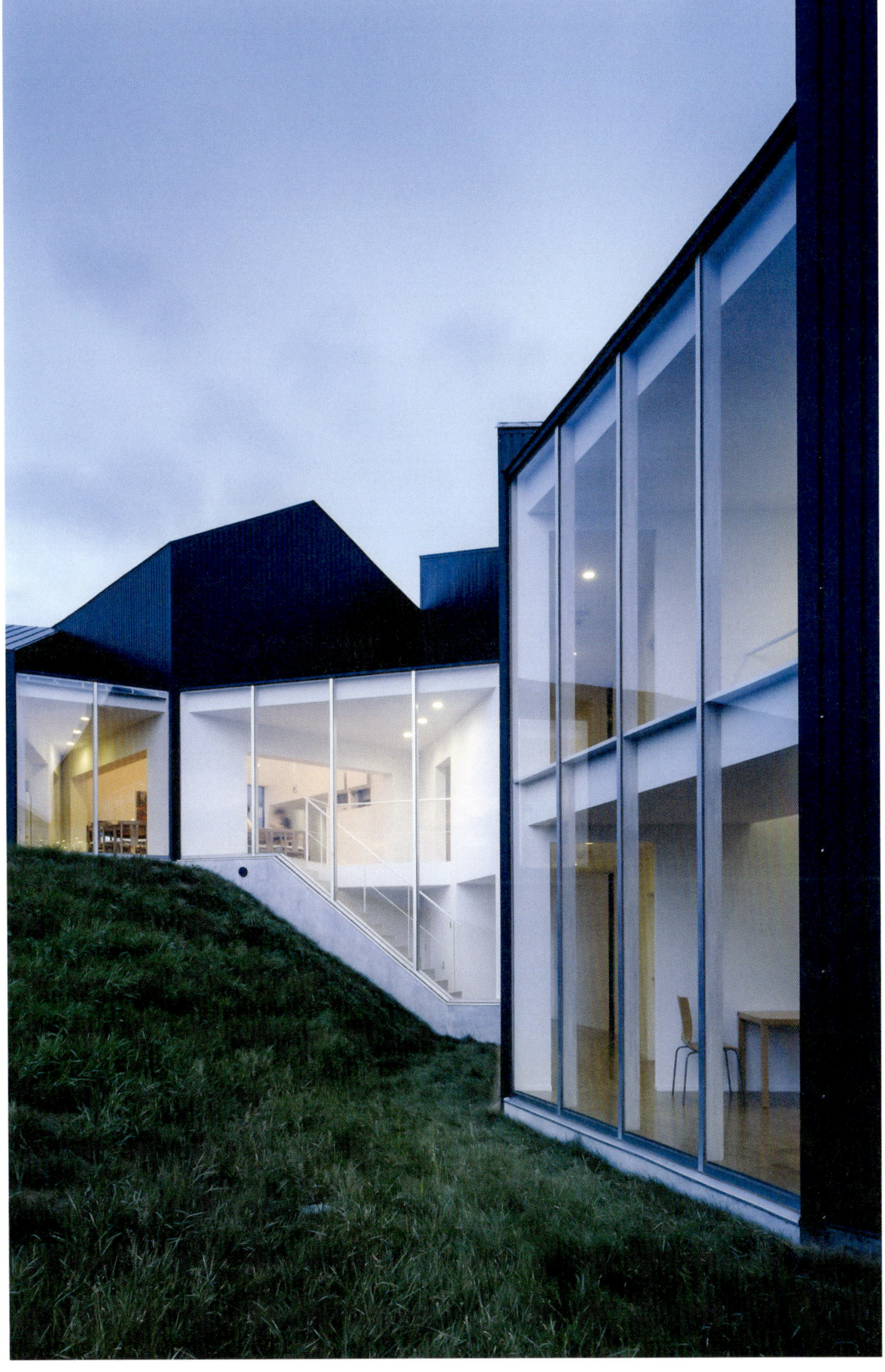

Annaka Environmental Art Forum

GUNMA, JAPAN 2003

One / Many – Simultaneously separated and connected

Being in one space, yet belonging to many places. A place unique for one, and a place for many to gather, in between which lies a field of diverse places for diverse people. Can we think of architectural space as born from rich layers of diverse groups of people? As if sketching an infinite field of rings of various sizes on top of one another, I imagine an amorphous network oscillating in space. This project was one that interiorized an entire urban square, which would allow diverse activities to take place. I sought to create a diverse place where space for one and many would synchronously coexist by means of a single undulating wall. The inflexions and depressions of the wall would enfold spaces of different scale – simultaneously distant and connected – engendering an infinite spectrum of propinquities between separation and connection. Here, both public and private – and simplicity and complexity – coalesce in a proposal for the most elementary form of public space.

ひとつの場所でありながら、たくさんの場所であること。ひとりのための場所であることと、たくさんの人が集まる場所であること。そしてその間に広がる、多様な人のための多様な場所。建築とは、いろいろな人数の集団の多様な重なりの場に他ならないのではないだろうか？ それはさまざまな大きさの円がさまざまに重なり合うスケッチで表現されるような、脈動とネットワークと揺らぎの場であろう。これは多様な活動が行われるであろう都市広場を屋内化するようなプロジェクトであった。そしてここでは＜ひとつ＞と＜たくさん＞が同居する複雑で多様な場所を、ただひとつの波打つ壁の抑揚によってつくり出そうと試みた。揺らめく壁はスケールの異なるさまざまな場所を囲い取り、またこの場所とあの場所との距離感の違いによって、繋がりと分節の無限のグラデーションをつくり出す。公共性とプライベート、単純さと複雑さが融合した、公共空間の原型的な提案。

014

Annaka Environmental Art Forum
International Design Competition for the Environment Art Forum for Annaka, first prize

安中環境アートフォーラム
安中環境アートフォーラム国際設計競技 1等受賞

GUNMA, JAPAN
2003

→ Related Projects
005 015 025 061 081 102

1st FLOOR PLAN

T house
GUNMA, JAPAN 2005

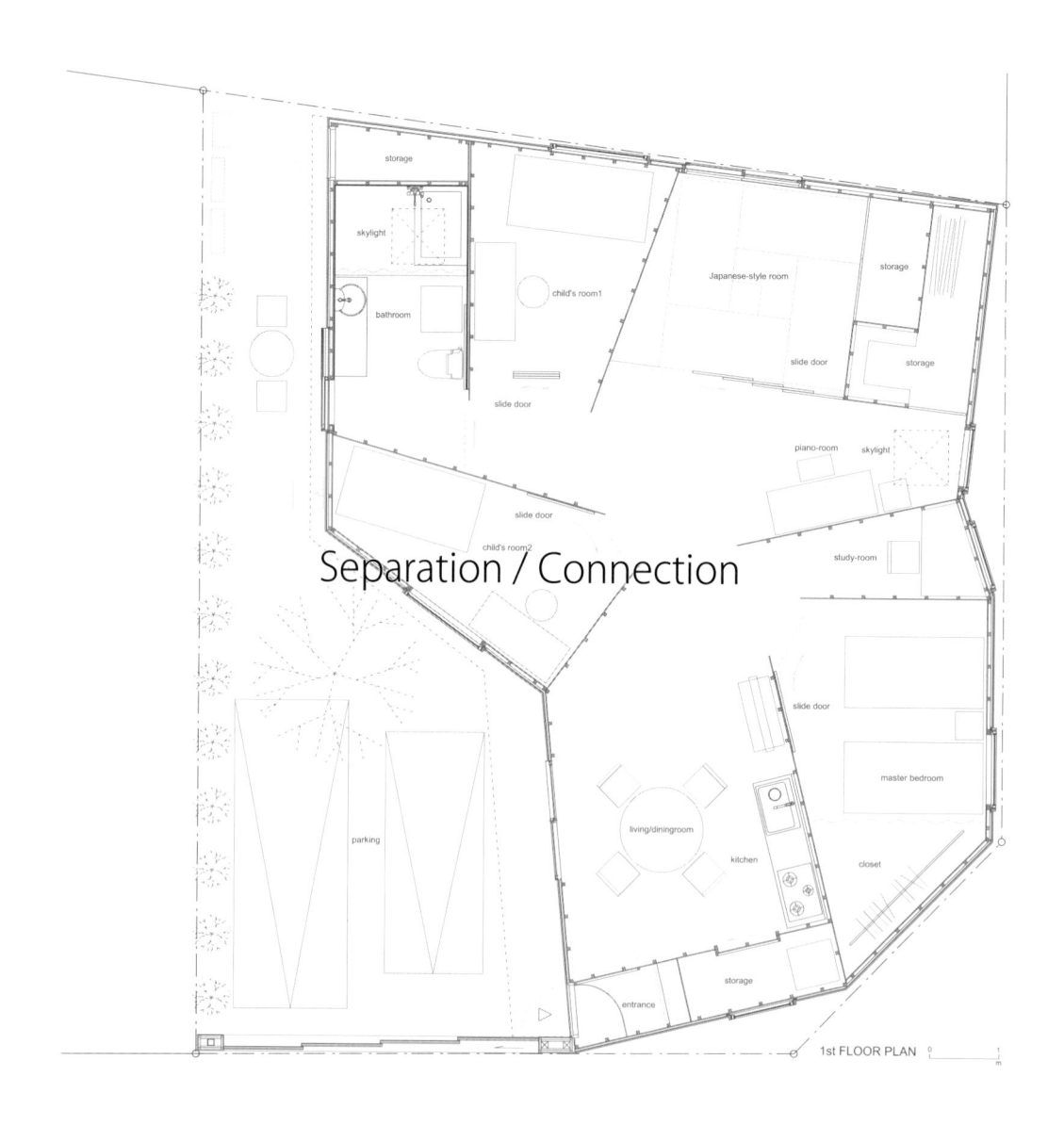

Separation / Connection

1st FLOOR PLAN

At its most basic, a house is a place of separation and connection, and the vast field of interrelationships within. People and people, people and objects, and people and the surroundings, connect and separate, fostering diverse forms of relationships. If a dynamic order can be produced that is simultaneously distant and connected, can a state of dynamic equilibrium be seen through the ever-changing relationships of people and their surrounding environments? In this house for a family of four, various places within the house are made so that they all become corner(s) of the radially arranged space. Travelling deeper and outwards within the space, it becomes more private and intimate, and moving closer towards the centre the space gradually opens up, connecting to the other spaces. Within this depth of modulation, each of the occupants begins to discover his or her space and its relationship with the autres (others). Being synchronously separated and connected, weaving the infinite lattice of relationships: this is an essential subject for the "contemporary space."

家とは、突き詰めれば、離れていることと繋がっていること、その間の無数の関係性の場のことである。人と人、人とモノ、人と周辺環境などが、繋がり、離れ、そして関係し合っている。そして離れていながら同時に繋がっているという中間的な状態において、人と人との関係や人と周辺環境との関係性などが、さまざまに変化して動的な均衡が生まれてくるのではないだろうか？ この4人家族のための住宅では、家の中のさまざまな居場所が、緩やかな放射状の空間のいくつもの揺らぎの隅っことしてつくられている。より奥まれば、より離れてプライベートな場となり、中央に近づけば、より他の場所と繋がりながら開いていく。この奥まりの抑揚の中に、住み手は自分の居場所と他者との関係性を見つけ出していく。離れていて同時に繋がっていること。その間の無限の関係性の編み目ということは、＜現代的な空間＞の本質をついているはずだ。

T house

GUNMA, JAPAN
2005

→ Related Projects
002 014 021 044 060

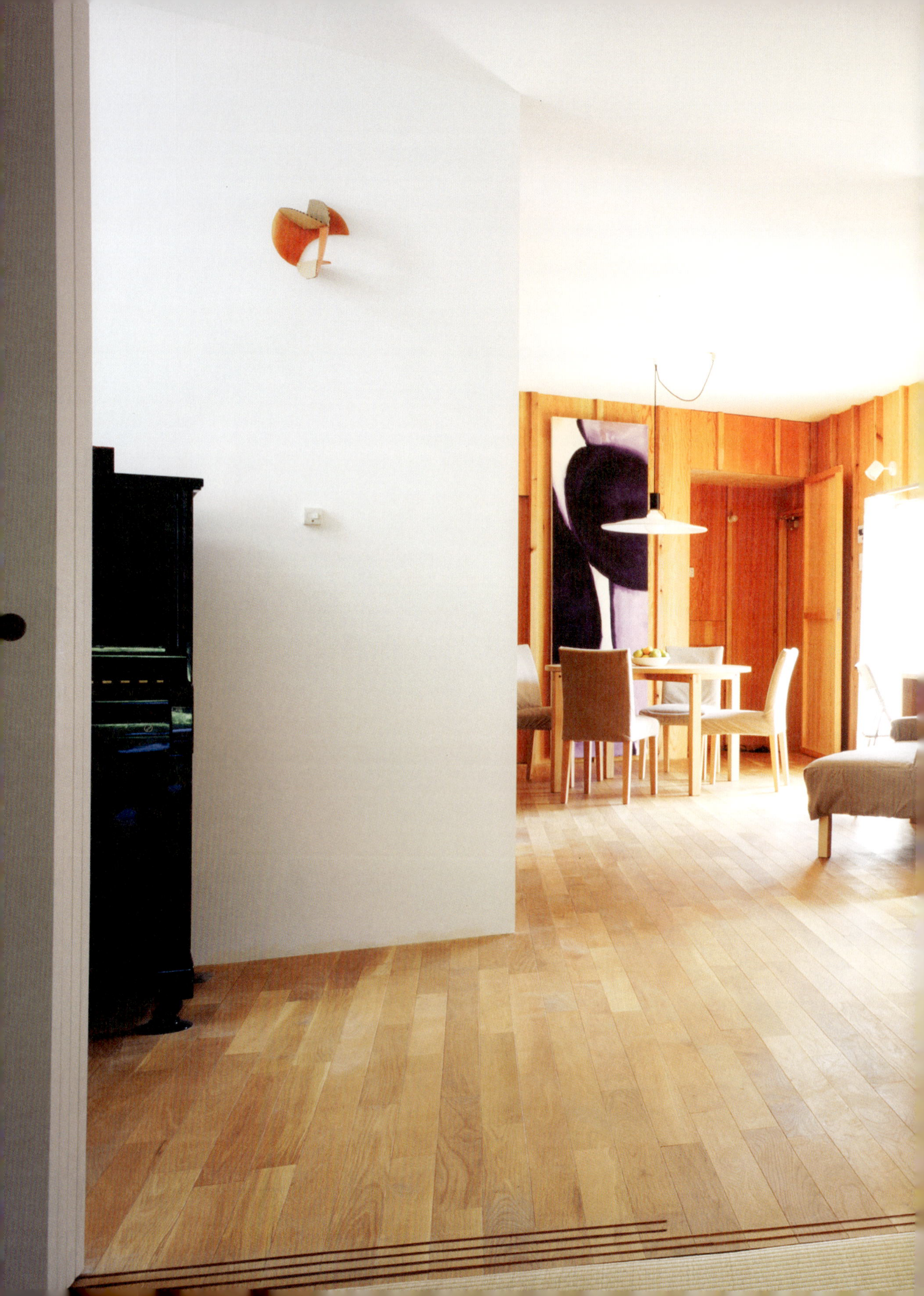

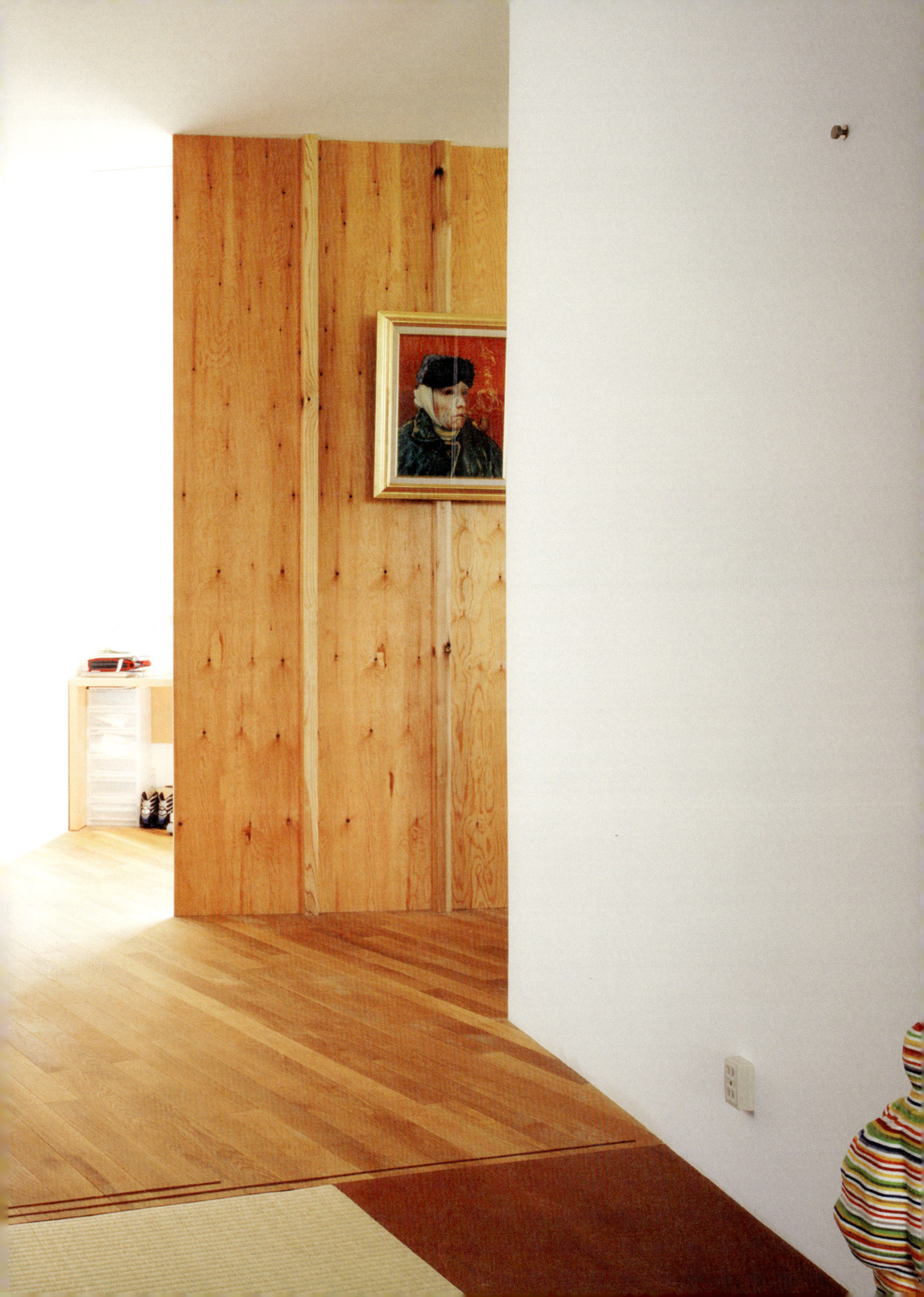

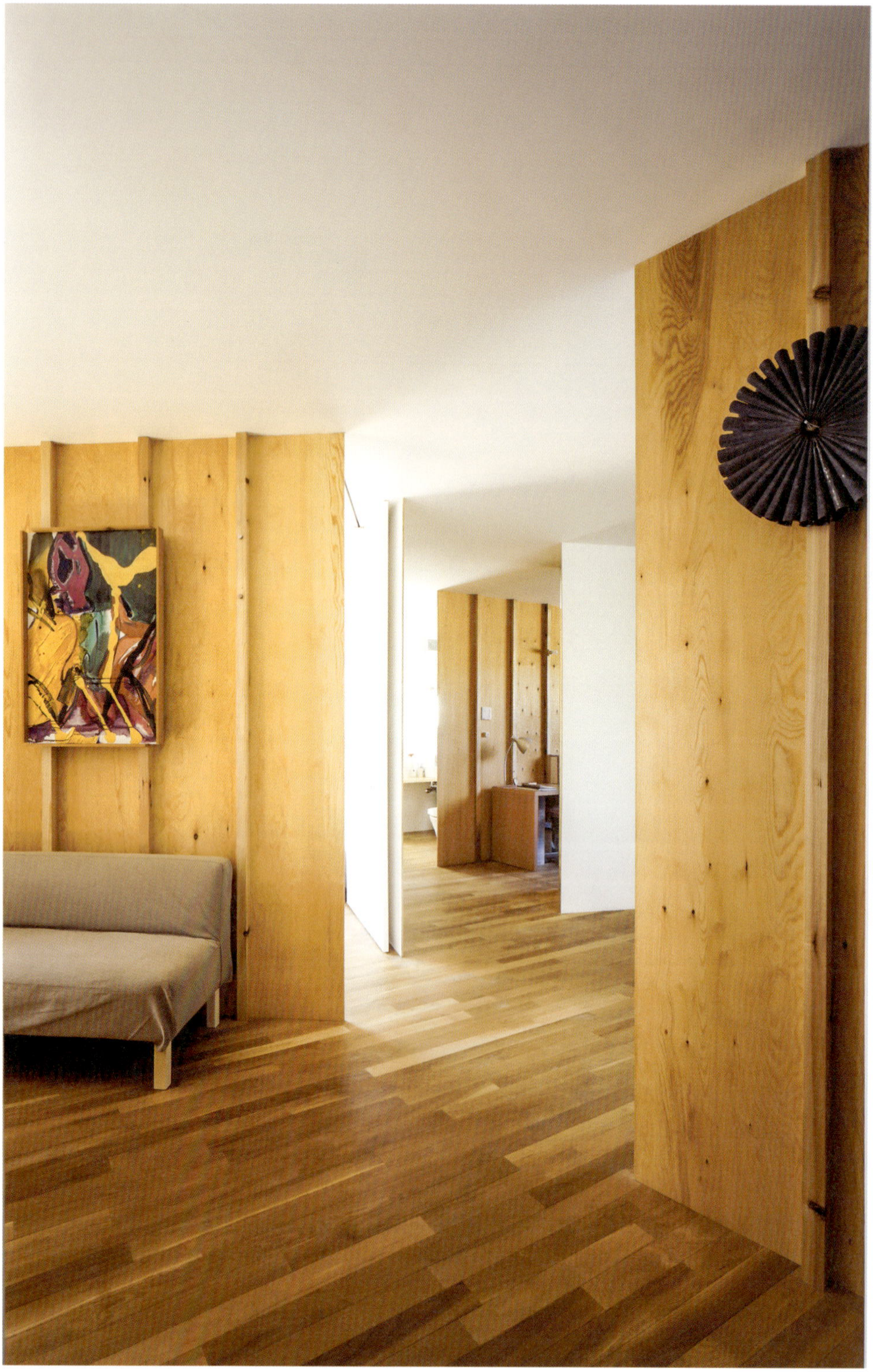

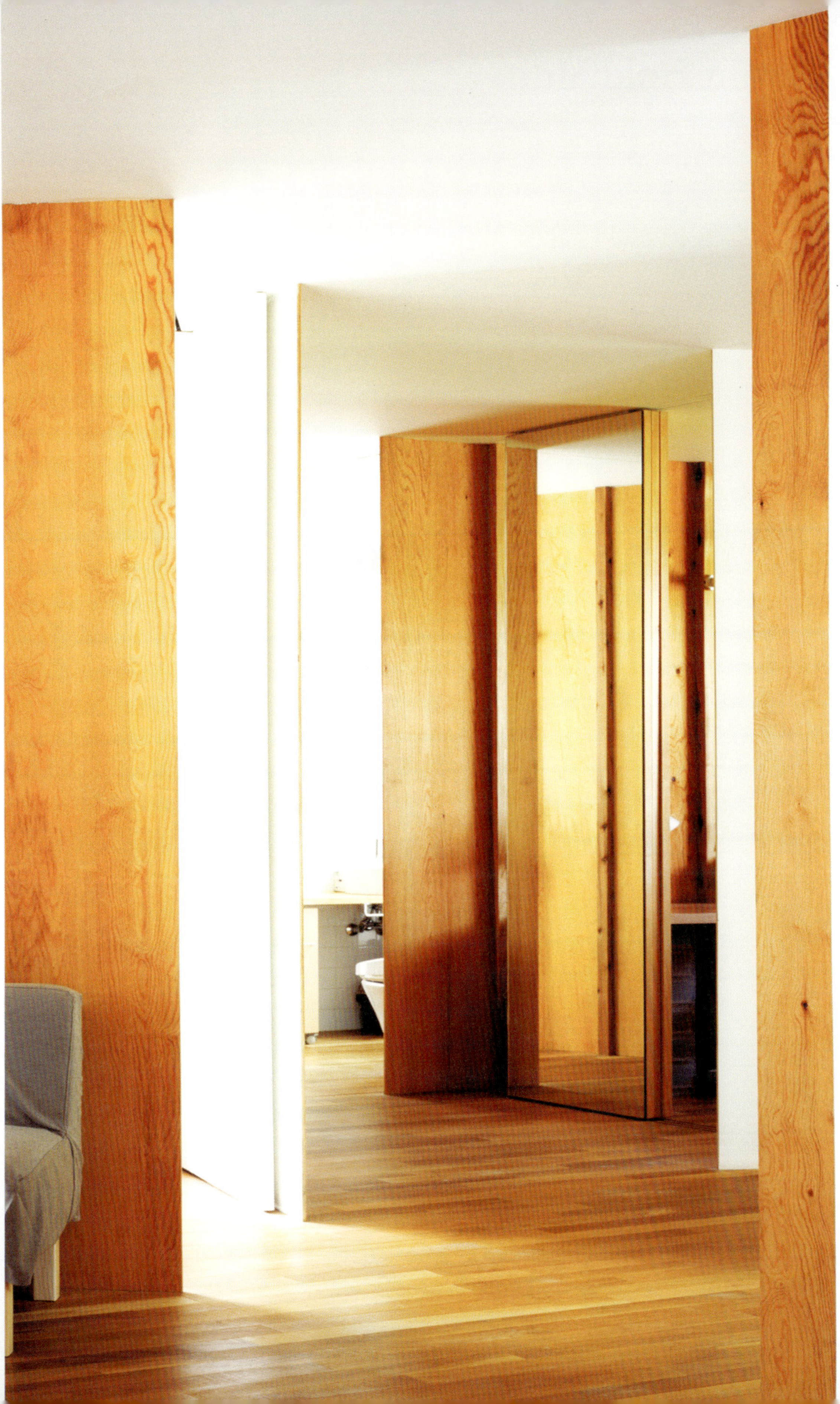

Atelier in Hokkaido

HOKKAIDO, JAPAN 2005

Bigger than furniture / Smaller than a building
New spaces hidden between the floors

Since presenting Primitive Future House in 2001, I had been thinking about a new type of architectural scale––one that traverses the definitions of architecture/building and furniture. What is bigger than furniture but smaller than a building? I imagined it might become a new locus for interaction between architecture and the body.In this half-studio, half-dwelling project for an artist, I started to think about how to articulate but at the same time associate the dissimilar functions required in the brief: garage, storage, art studio, and living quarters. This antithetical relationship of each program was realized by first stratifying each program and then shifting it off-centre at mid-layer as if it were sliced horizontally. By slicing and shifting the layers in the middle, architectural scale begins to disintegrate into smaller furniture-like scales, yet still spatially retains the quality of being part of a much bigger space. A series of acts, such as differentiating interior materials like white plaster and timber along the horizontal shifting bands, and designing shelves and other joineries around the edges of the layers, all impart a multitude of meanings to these shifting volumes.It was a critical project that led to House NA several years later.

2001年に発表した「Primitive Future House」以降、家具と建築の両方を行き来するような新しい建築のスケール感について考えていた。家よりも小さく、家具よりも大きい何か。それは建築と身体の新しい場所となる予感があった。この画家のためのアトリエ住居のプロジェクトでは、車庫、倉庫、アトリエ、住居という異なるプログラムが要求されたため、それぞれ関係し合いながら緩やかに分節することを考えた。その分節と融合を実現するのが、半層ずつズレながら重なり合うこの形式である。半層ズレることで、建築のスケールより小さく、しかも家具のスケールよりも大きな場が生まれる。内部を白と木など異なる素材で分け、また吹き抜け開口の小口を本棚とすることで、このズレ自体がさまざまに意味をもち始める。この先の「House NA」へと繋がるプロジェクトである。

016

Atelier in Hokkaido

HOKKAIDO, JAPAN
2005

→ Related Projects
007 016 017 055 095

House in Hayama

KANAGAWA, JAPAN 2006

Large space, Medium cavities, Small notches

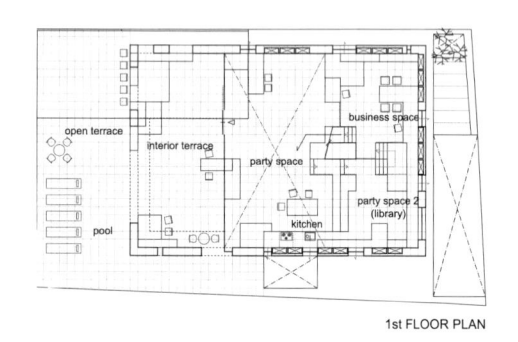

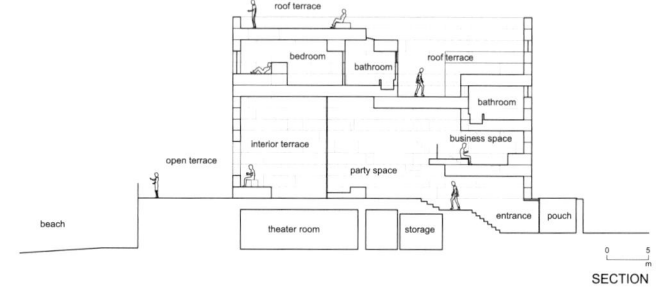

1st FLOOR PLAN

SECTION

This was a project to build a mansion along the coast in Hayama. Mansions have lots of bedrooms. As an architect who has been thinking primarily about how to link and connect spaces, it was extremely difficult for me to deal with so many bedrooms and bathrooms as separate rooms. The final plan called for a place that was like a huge artificial, seaside cave. The topography was made by stacking up numerous precast concrete volumes. A terrace surrounded by walls and roof opens up to the oceanside, of which is connected to the living space. The bedrooms were designed as if they were nested within the shadow of rocks or as small caves, and are linked to the large living area. The stone-like architecture attained the independence of the protected bedrooms and at the same time captured the topographically-linked ambiguity of the living spaces that extended from there. Segmentation and connection: As I have become involved in more and more residential projects abroad in recent years, it becomes more evident that this question of how to divide and connect bedrooms is a vital and fundamental theme.

葉山の海際に豪邸をつくるというプロジェクト。豪邸には寝室が多い。それまでいかに空間を連続し関係づけるかということを考えてきた僕にとって、＜切り離された部屋＞としてのたくさんの寝室と浴室はとても難しいものだった。最終案は、いわば人工的につくられた海辺の巨大な洞窟のような場所だ。プレキャストコンクリートの塊を無数に積み上げて地形をつくる。海側には壁と屋根によって囲まれたテラスが開き、リビングスペースがそこに連続する。寝室群は岩陰や別の小さな洞窟としてつくられ、いろいろな場所でリビングエリアの大空間へと連続していく。岩的な建築とすることで、守られた寝室群の独立性を確保し、そこからリビングなどの生活空間が地形的に連続する両義性を獲得した。分節と連続。近年海外での住宅プロジェクトが増えてくるにつれ、この寝室の分節と連続の問題は、やはり根源的なテーマとして浮かび上がってくる。

017

House in Hayama

KANAGAWA, JAPAN
2006

→ Related Projects
022 029 079 096

Residential treatment center for emotionally disturbed children

HOKKAIDO, JAPAN 2006

City as a house / House as a city

1st FLOOR PLAN

When thinking of a house, to imagine it as a city, and when thinking of a city, to imagine it as a house. In this light, would it not be correct to say that architecture for the public, such as this medical institute, is both a house and a city-like place? Here the physical tranquillity of the house and the serendipitous richness of the city harmoniously coexist. It is by encompassing the ability to discover both a homely place of your own, and one that embraces diverse ambiguities, that we are able to engender a public space for the complex age we call "contemporary." Here, uniform cubic-volume units are dispersed, randomly at first glance, in essence infusing order and chaos. This is done so that many irregular recesses and corners endow space with uniquely intimate scales, and at the same time series of angular facets entice unforeseen spatial territories beyond, like meandering through a forest.

家を考える時には、それは街であると考え、街を考える時には、それは家であると考える。その意味において、この医療施設をはじめとする公共建築というものは、家であり、同時に街であるような場所だと言えないだろうか？ 家のもつ身体的な落ち着き感と、街のもつ多様で予測不可能な豊かさの感覚が両立する。さまざまな不確定性を受け入れる都市的な性格と、その中において常に居心地の良い居場所を見つけられるような家的な性格をあわせもつことで、この複雑な現代という時代にふさわしい公共空間が生まれてくるはずだ。ここではキューブ状の同じユニットの繰り返しがランダムさをあわせもつことで、秩序と乱雑さの同居を実現した。

018

Residential treatment center for emotionally disturbed children | 児童心理治療施設

HOKKAIDO, JAPAN
2006

→ Related Projects
004 013 030 038 071 081

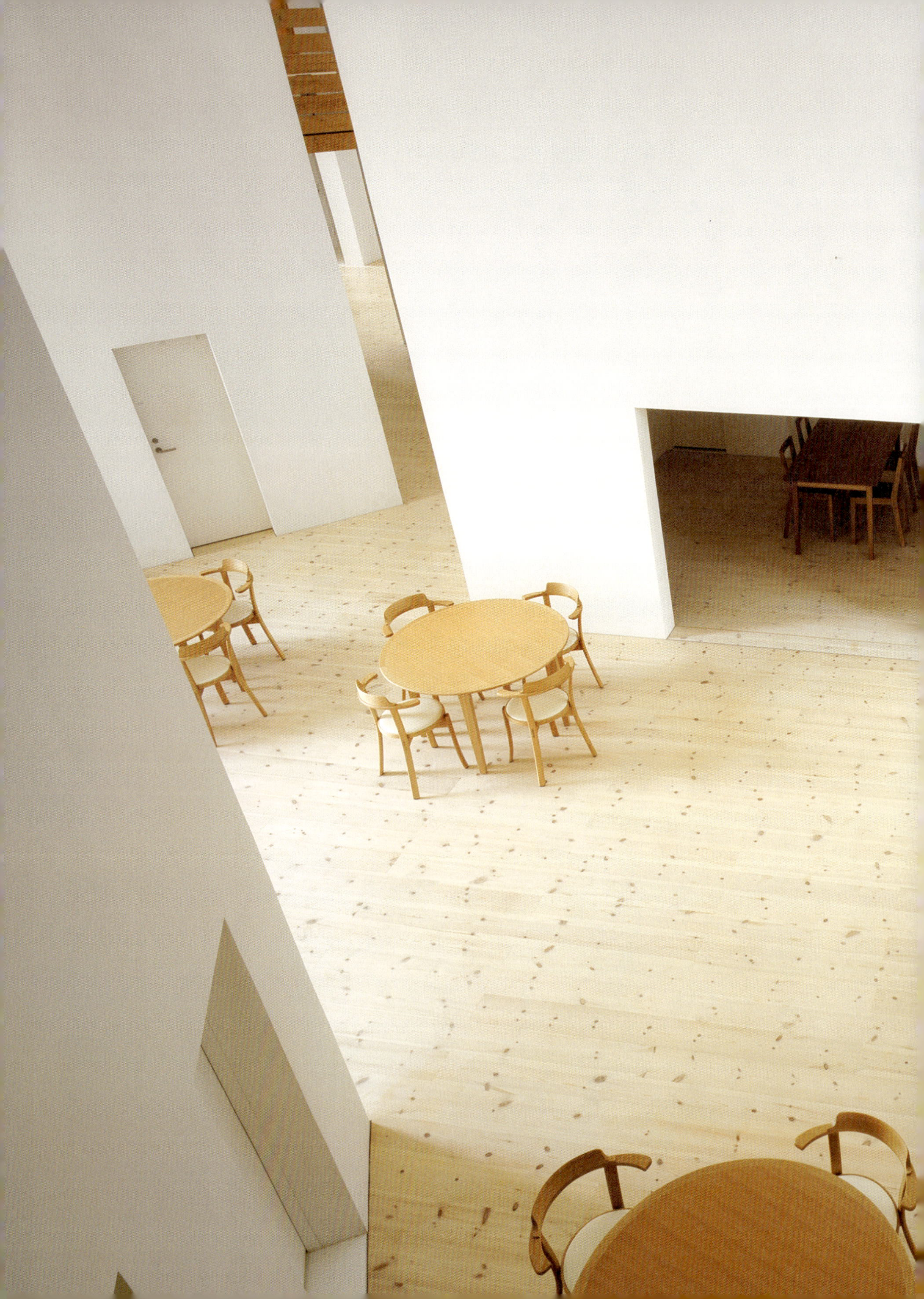

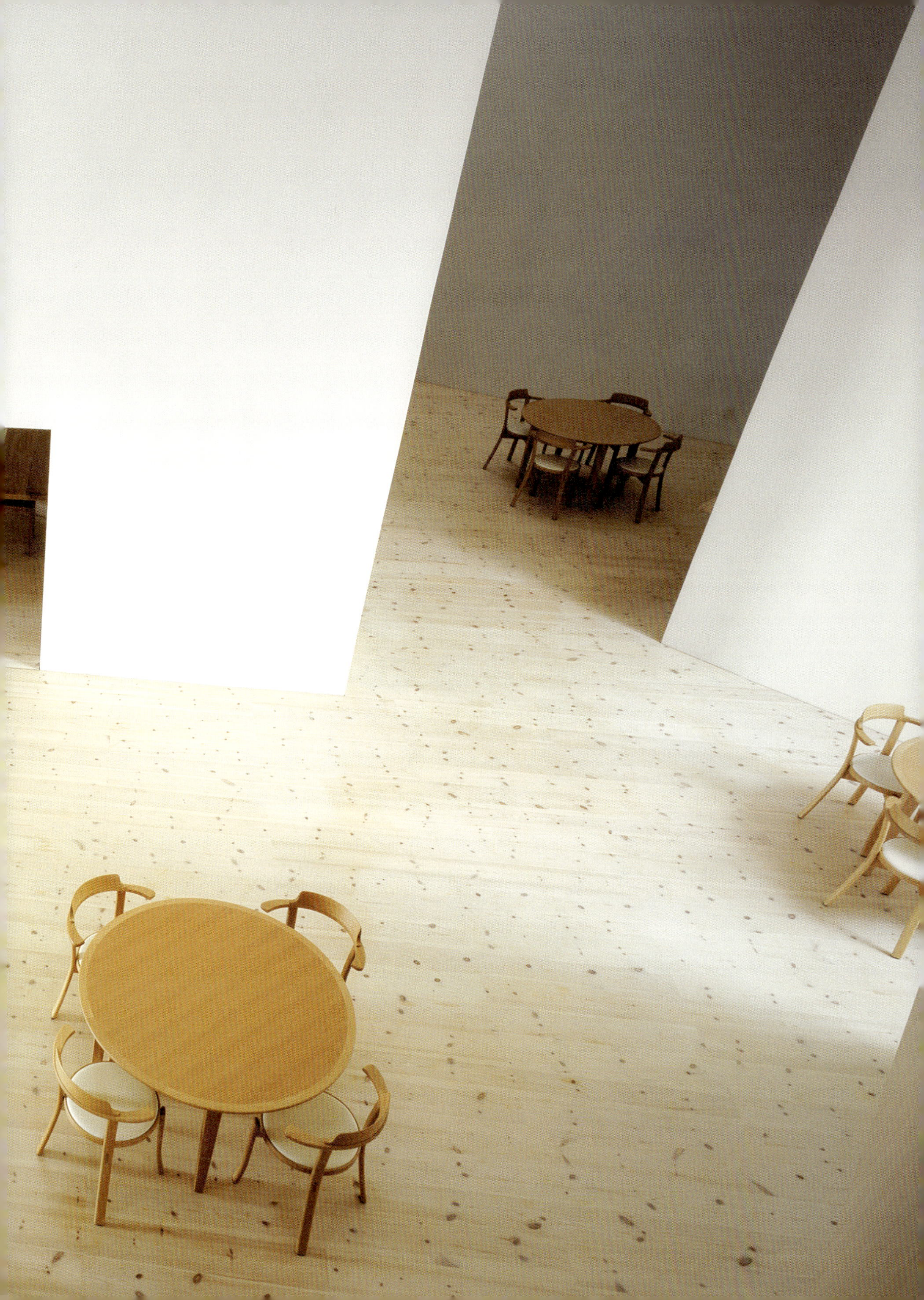

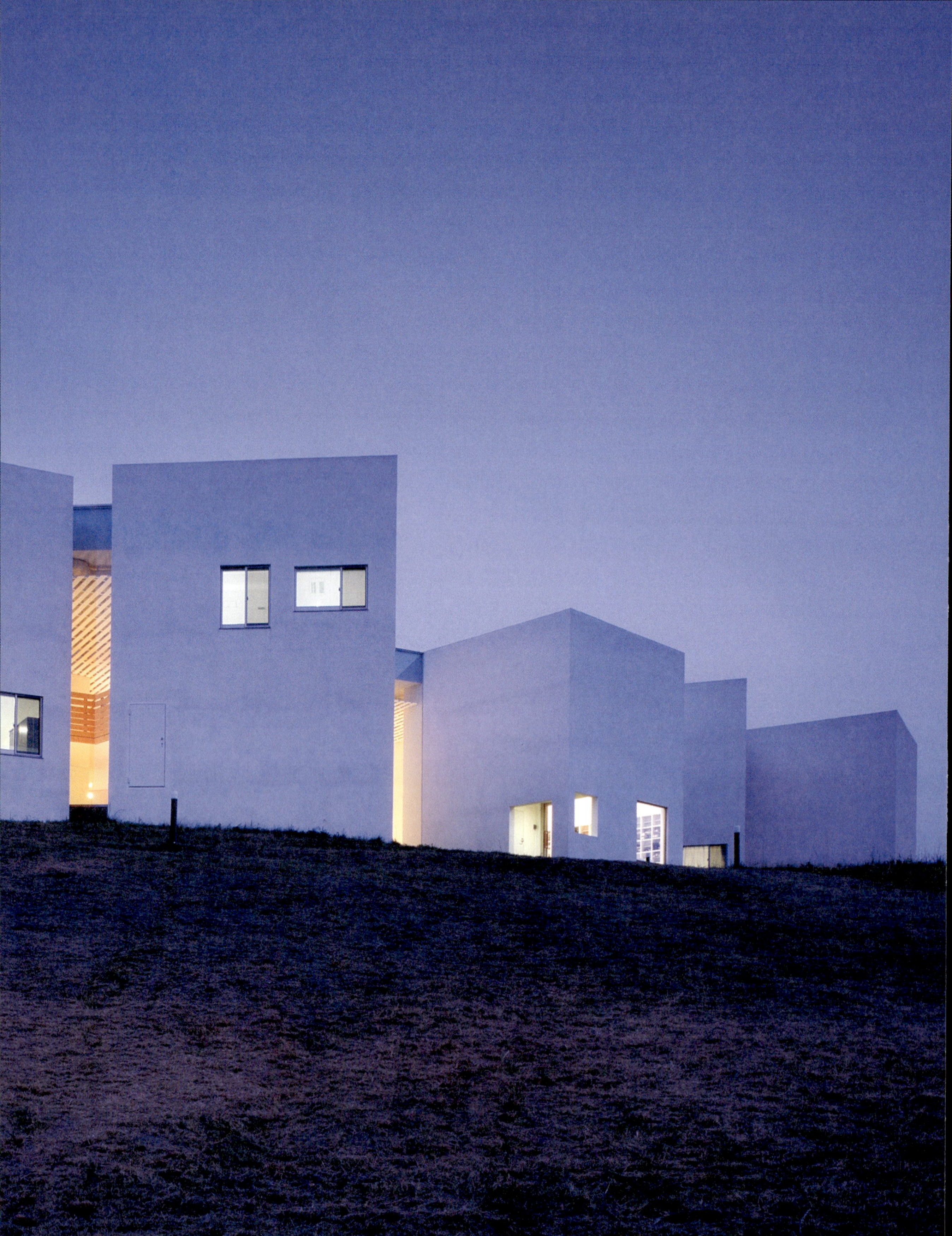

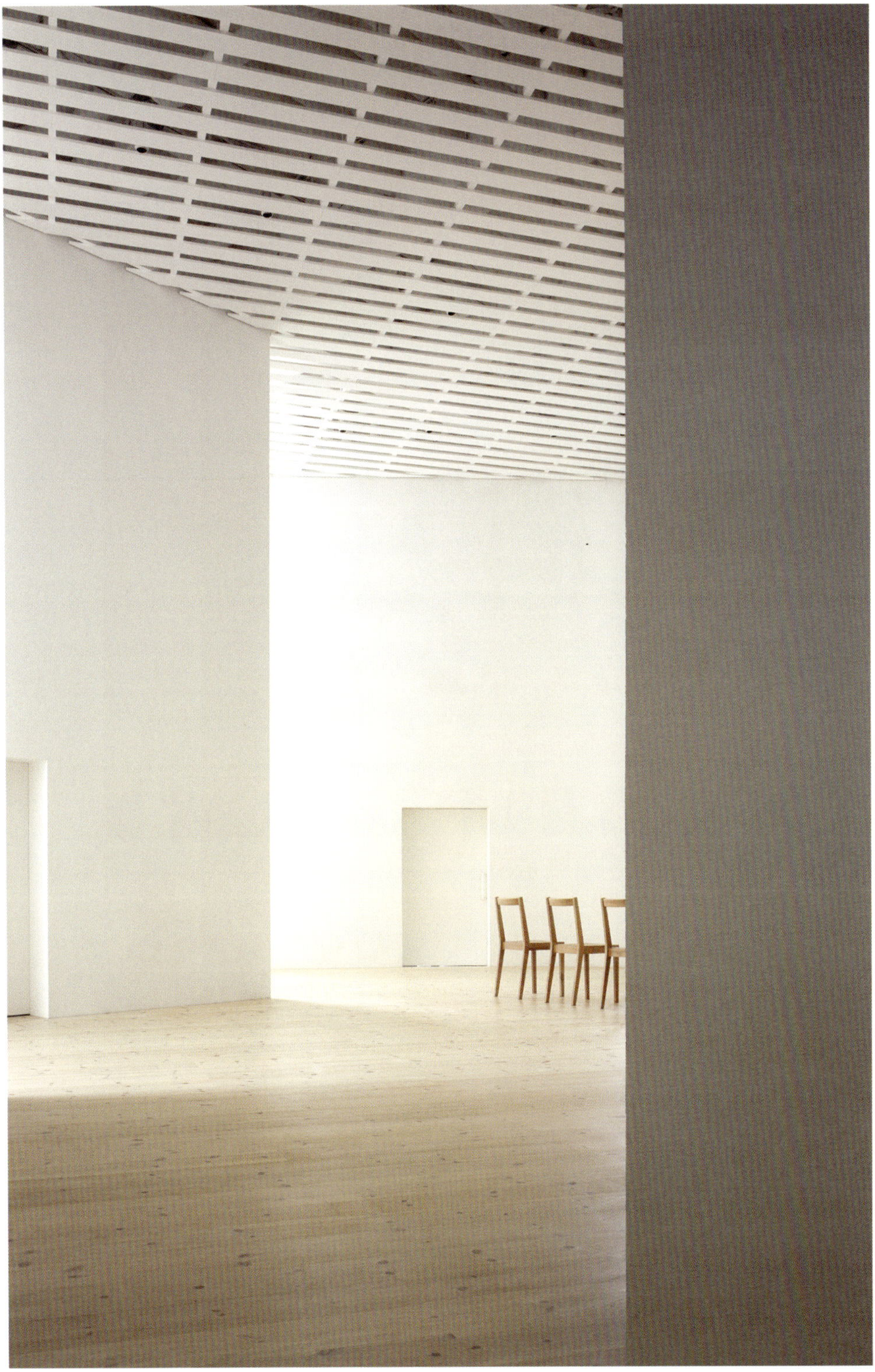

7/2 House

HOKKAIDO, JAPAN 2006

Unexpected spaces from the gaps

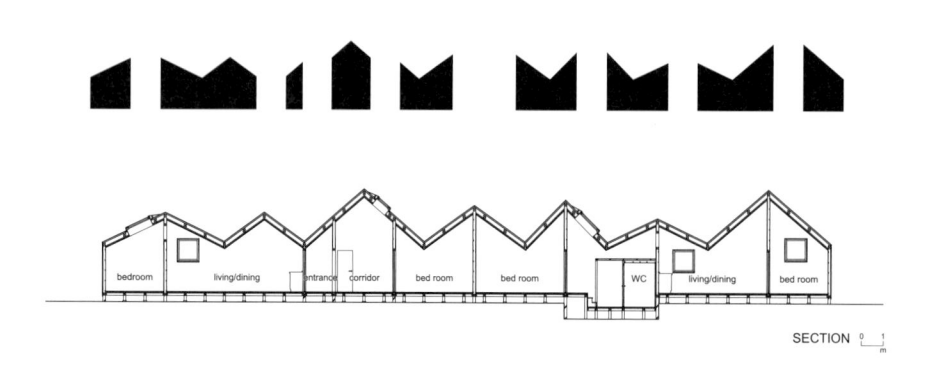

SECTION

bedroom | living/dining | entrance | corridor | bed room | bed room | WC | living/dining | bed room

This building is a combination of two houses. Although there are only two, it looks as if there are countless houses, but also appear as a single house with a collection of rooms. By slightly staggering the spatial segmentation of the gabled roof and the walled segmentation of the rooms, the segmentation of the rooms and the gradient of the roof that links them resonate with each other, creating a rich exchange between segmentation and fusion. The unexpected and unique shape of the ceiling that appears in each room engender a spatial chiaroscuro within simple shaped rooms.

住居がふたつ組み合わさった建物。ふたつの家なのだが、無数の家があるようにも見え、またいくつもの部屋が集まったひとつの家のようにも見える。切妻屋根による内部空間の分節と、壁による部屋の分節が少しずつズレるように設計することで、部屋の分節とそれを繋げる屋根の勾配が共鳴し合って豊かな分節と融合のやりとりが生まれる。またそれぞれの部屋に予期せぬ不思議な天井の形が現れることで、単純な形の部屋の中に場所の濃淡をつくり出す。

019

7/2 House

7/2 House

HOKKAIDO, JAPAN
2006

→ Related Projects
013 043 072 075

House O

CHIBA, JAPAN 2007

One space, many places

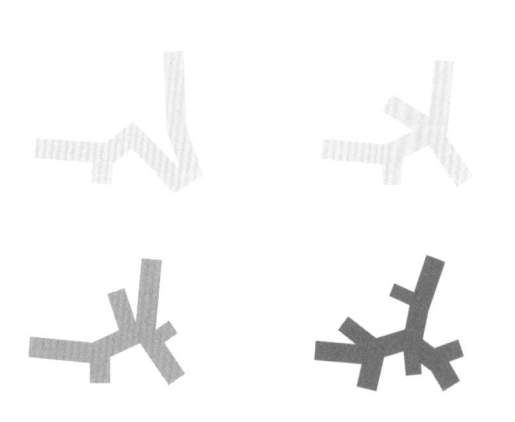

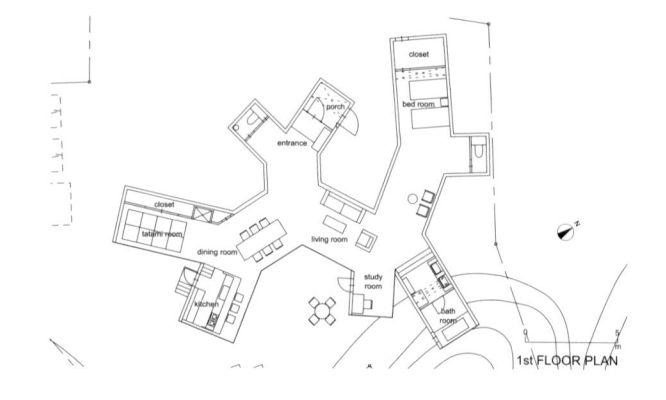

What will occur when a house and a street come together? Over a stretch of street, there are many corners and pockets of space for people to simply loiter, meet or even carry out a discussion over a cup of tea. Diverse spaces, views and relationships are all captured within the continuity of this one space, and the dynamic dimensions of the space are made perceptible through the co-occurrence of activity and tranquillity. For this project site overlooking the ocean, I aspired to create a space akin to a route meandering the coastline. This route or street is contorted and branches off to create places for living. The angular route alludes to a variety of framed views of the ocean. Here again we search for something between the simple and the complex, or rather a place where a street and a house coalesce.

家と路とが融合すると何が起こるだろうか？　ひと続きの曲がりくねった路にも、いくつもの隅があり、立ち話ができたり机をもち出してお茶を飲むような場所が生まれる。ひとつの空間でありながら、無数の居場所を内包し、無数の視線と関係性が生まれる。それは動きと落ち着きの同居する動的な場所であろう。海に面したこの敷地で、海沿いを散策する路のような場所をつくり出した。路は折れ曲がり枝分かれすることで、日々の生活のためのさまざまな居場所が生まれていく。折れ曲がる路は海へのさまざまな視点を提供する。単純さと複雑さの間を、また路という都市的な要素と家の間を模索していく。

020 | House O | House O | CHIBA, JAPAN 2007 | Related Projects 003 014 037 056 088 095

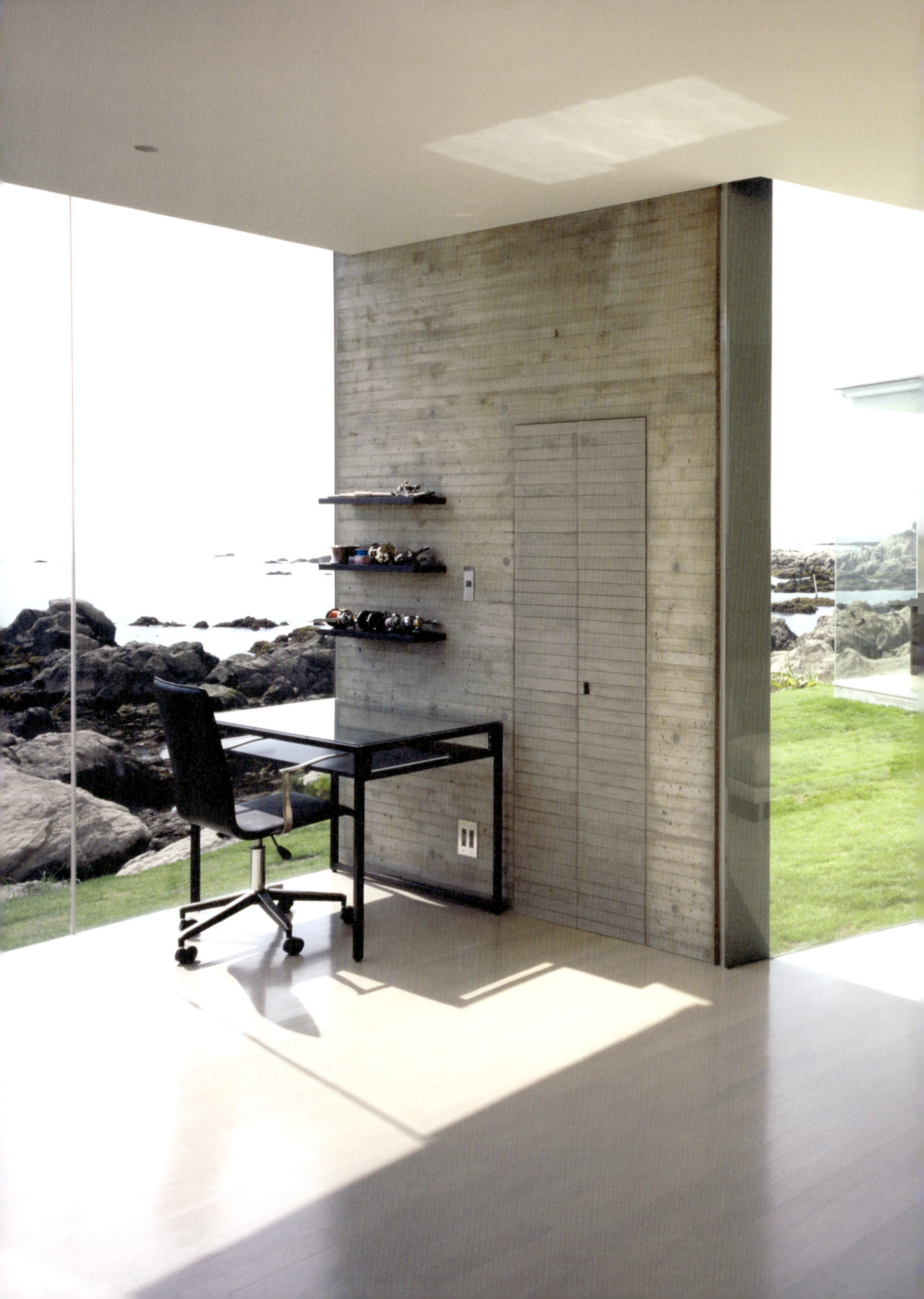

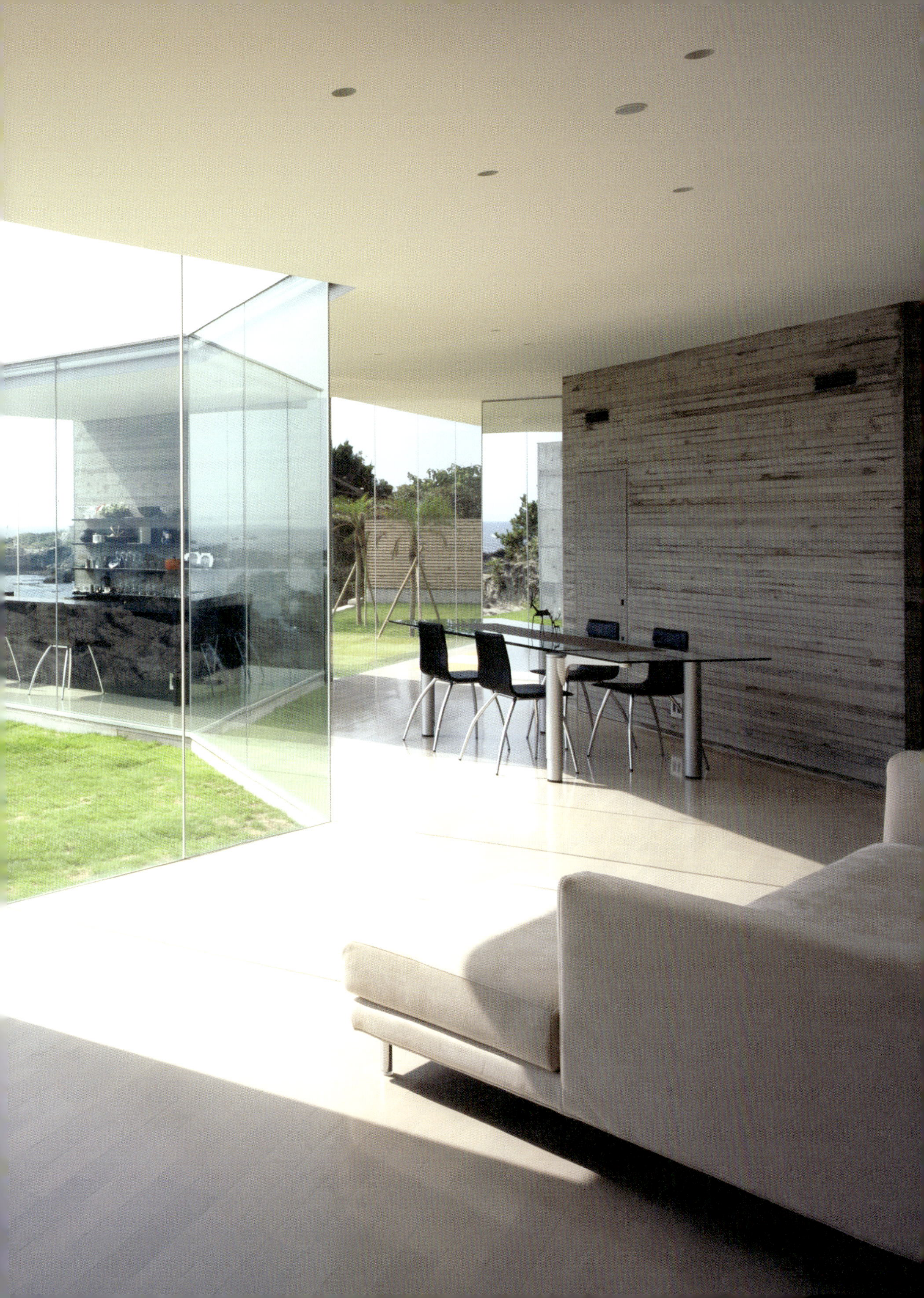

Spiral House

TOKYO, JAPAN 2007

Perhaps there is no differentiation between a house and the city, only the depth

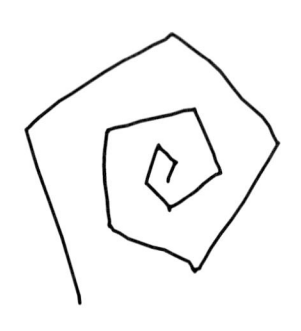

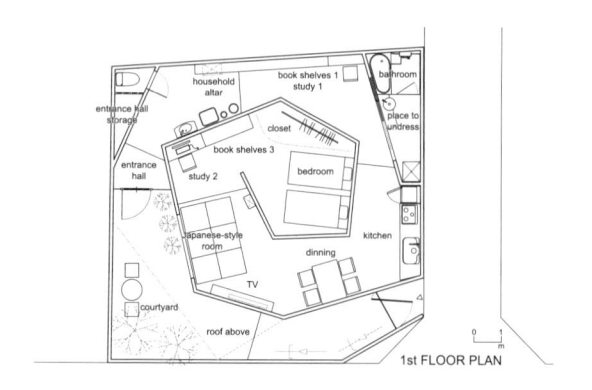

After moving to Tokyo, I began to think about the distance between house and the city. The more I thought, the more it felt increasingly clear that it was not only a single door that we are separated by. For example can we not consider a room within a house the inmost depth of the city? This residential project is an attempt to make a house solely following this notion of depth. From the large aperture opening out to the city on the outer most wall of the spiral, the depth is created by the curves of a single wall that invites one to move deeper within. As a result, essentially all space within this house is connected. The deeper the space, the more personal it becomes, and its openness to the city allows the quality of the space to transform. The many openings in the walls also allow shortcuts into the space of varying depth. The design of this house inherits the concept of gradational territory proposed in the *Glass Cloud* project and *House N*. The geometric composition of the spiral will appear again in the *Musashino University Museum & Library* project, but in this, the adaptation departs from a unidirectional perception of depth into multi-faceted and more complex layers of space.

東京に住むようになってから、街と家の中との距離について考えるようになった。それはドア1枚で隔てられるものではないかもしれない。むしろ家というのは、街の一部がどんどんと奥まっていった状態だと言えないだろうか？ そんな奥まりだけでできた家がこの住宅である。渦巻き状の壁によって、街に開いた最外周の前庭から、徐々に奥へと引き込まれる。ひと繋がりの空間でできたこの家は、より奥にはよりプライベートな場所があり、徐々に街に開いていくに従ってそれぞれの場所の性格が変化していく。壁にはいくつも開口が開いているので、奥まり具合をショートカットもできる。グラデーションの領域を試みた「Glass Cloud」のコンセプトを引き継ぎながら、この当時すでに設計が進んでいた「House N」の入れ子の考え方をさらに押し進めた計画である。この渦巻きの幾何学は、後に「武蔵野美術大学美術館・図書館」で再び現れるが、そこでは一方向の単純な奥まりではなく、より多焦点で複雑な空間の重なりを生み出すこととなった。

021

Spiral House

TOKYO, JAPAN
2007

→ Related Projects
026 027 044 061

House Inside-Out Tree
2008

Artificial cave

The segmentation of a place using a branch-shaped space, which was explored in *House O*, embodies the potential for a more three-dimensional form. Within this branch-shaped void space, people live by alternatively climbing, sitting, and moving from branch to branch. By letting light in from the ends of the branches, a huge amount of light shines in through the countless skylights, reflecting and pouring into the space. The branch-shaped space is both an open cave and a place in which narrowness and width, segmentation and connection are constantly shifting back and forth between each other.

「House O」で試みた枝状の空間による場所の分節は、3次元的に試してみたくなるポテンシャルをもっている。枝状のヴォイド空間を、時にはよじ上り、また腰掛け、枝から枝へと移動しながら生活する。枝の端部から光が差すことで、無数のスカイライトから無数の光が反射し合いながら降り注ぐ場所となる。枝状の空間は同時に開いた洞窟でもあり、狭さと広さ、分節と連続が絶えず入れ替わり続ける場所である。

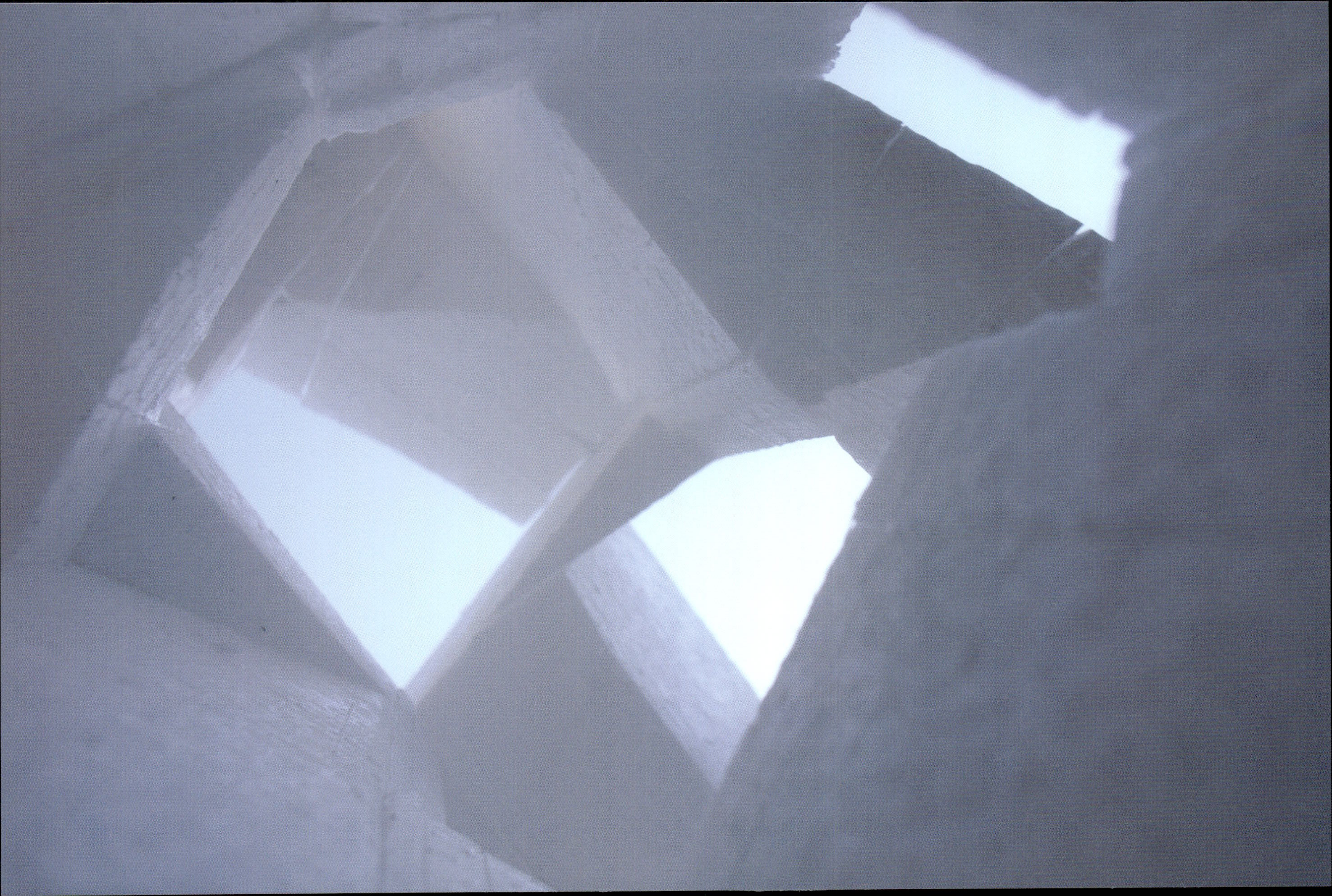

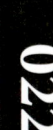

Dubai Skyscraper
DUBAI, UAE 2008

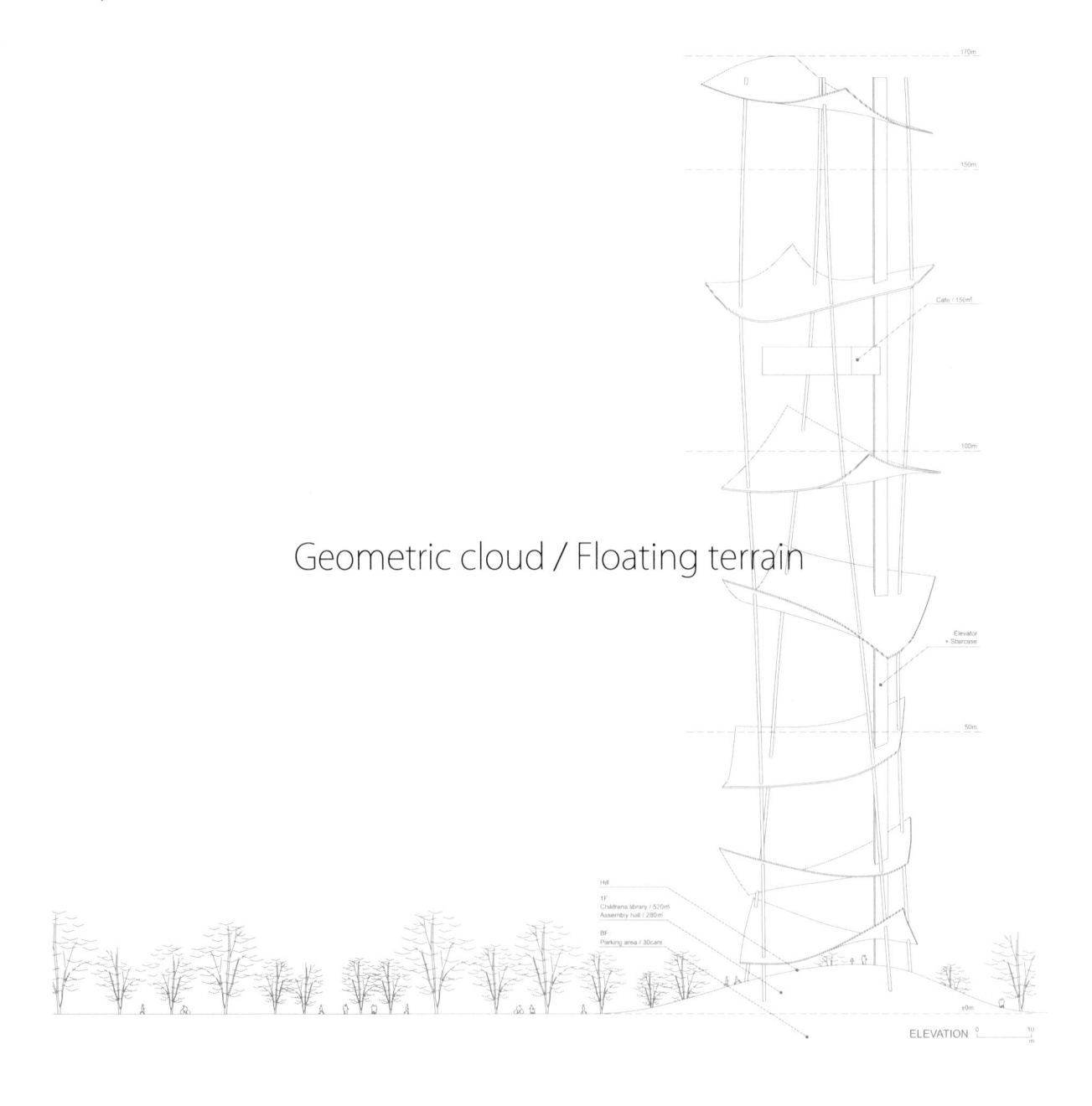

Geometric cloud / Floating terrain

The tower as a typology in itself signifies a symbol of some kind, and due to the clarity of its existence, it has challenged architects to redefine it since antiquity. This competition proposal is a simple thought-experiment comparing things like matter and antimatter, strength and fragility, object and landscape, and precise and wavering forms. At the time I had no idea that I would win the *Taiwan Tower* competition several years later, but I am convinced that the ideas inherent in this unrealistic proposal provided the foundation for that project.

何かのシンボルとなるようなタワーというタイポロジーは、それがとても古くからあり明瞭であるゆえに、建築家による再定義の挑戦をかき立てるものである。このコンペ案では物体に対する非物体、強さに対するはかなさ、オブジェクトに対するランドスケープ、明瞭な形に対する揺らいだ形、など、比較的単純な思考実験が行われた。数年後に「台湾タワー」のコンペに勝利することになるとは想像だにしなかったが、おそらくこの非現実的な提案で思考したことが伏流水となっていたことは確かであろう。

023

Dubai Skyscraper

DUBAI, UAE
2008

→ Related Projects
035 047 050 104

Kumamoto station plaza

KUMAMOTO, JAPAN 2008

Paths forming a three-dimensional plaza
Architectural hill / Roof as a terrain

SITE PLAN

This was a competition proposal to redesign the Kumamoto Station plaza. A station plaza is a place where diverse movements and speeds coalesce. Would it be possible to render form to resemble such a diverse flow of movements, with multifarious layers superimposed above one another? An idea like this brought forth a scheme of diverse interwoven bridges covering the entirety of the station plaza. These bridges form a roof but can also be seen as a diaphanous ground-plane, with each appearing as lines but also as a surface. It is also a nexus where countless relationships are made and fostered. The supple hill-like shape formed by thin members loosely woven together emerges transparent and ill defined, yet as a whole strongly expresses its existence as a landmark. This approach of an accumulating multitude of thin members or paths to form substantial planes or volume-like masses has later been appropriated in projects such as *Serpentine Gallery Pavilion 2013* and *Taiwan Tower*. In retrospect, the competition scheme itself was a rather crude one. However it did set a firm foundation for the various developments that followed.

熊本駅の駅前広場をデザインするコンペ案。駅前広場というのはいろいろな動きや速度が混ざりあう場所である。それらの多様な動きをあたかも透明なレイヤーを重ねるように重ねあわせることは出来ないだろうか？　そのようなアイデアから、この無数のブリッジが網の目をなして広場を覆う案が生まれてきた。それは屋根でもあり透明な地面でもあり、線でもあり面でもあり また無数の関係性を生み出すネットワークでもある。無数の線によって編み上げられた緩やかな丘のような形状は、透明でありながら同時にランドマークともなる。この無数の線やパスが生み出す面的なもの、ボリューム的なものへの次元の移行のアイデアは、後の「台湾タワー」や「Serpentine Gallery Pavilion 2013」と展開していくこととなった。コンペ案としては稚拙であったがその後の展開を考えると、意義のある最初の一歩だったと言える。

024 | Kumamoto station plaza | 熊本駅前広場 | KUMAMOTO, JAPAN 2008 | Related Projects 003 040 041 063 078 084

Empty House
2008

Architecture is superposing territories over one another

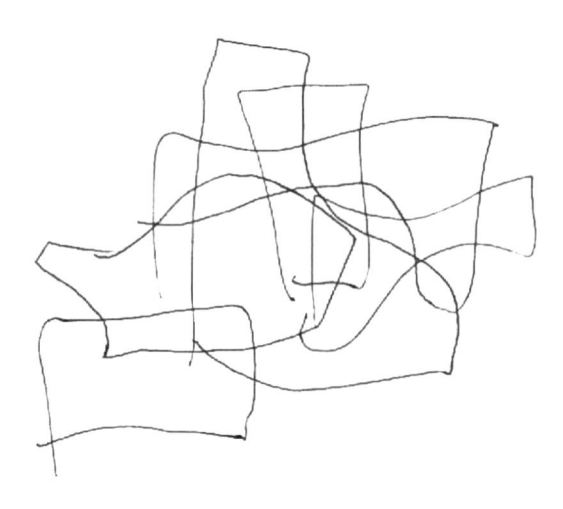

If architecture is something that deals with territories, every architect probably hopes to create an ambiguous realm through the layering of multiple territories. This simple model is meant to give form to this idea. This concept, rather than applying to a building in a closed site, may prove to be effective in programs that encompass everything from the city and architecture to open areas and landscape. This model, small enough to fit in the palm of one's hand, is a genesis of architecture waiting to bloom in the future. It is also the legitimate heir to projects like *Beton Hala Waterfront Center*, but heirs tend to take other forms when other discoveries are made.

建築が領域を扱うものであるとするなら、その領域のリングをいくつも重ねて、曖昧な領域を生み出したいというのは建築家の夢ではないだろうか？　この簡単な模型は、そのアイデアに形を与えたものである。おそらくこの方法は、閉じられた敷地の中の建築に適用するよりも、むしろ都市と建築、広場やランドスケープまでも含み込んだプログラムにおいて力を発揮するに違いない。この手の平に載るくらいの小さな模型は、未来において花開くのを待つ建築の種である。「Beton Hala Waterfront Center」のプロジェクトなどは、このプロジェクトの正統的な継承者であろう。しかし継承者はいつも、発見を伴って異なるものへと変化していく。

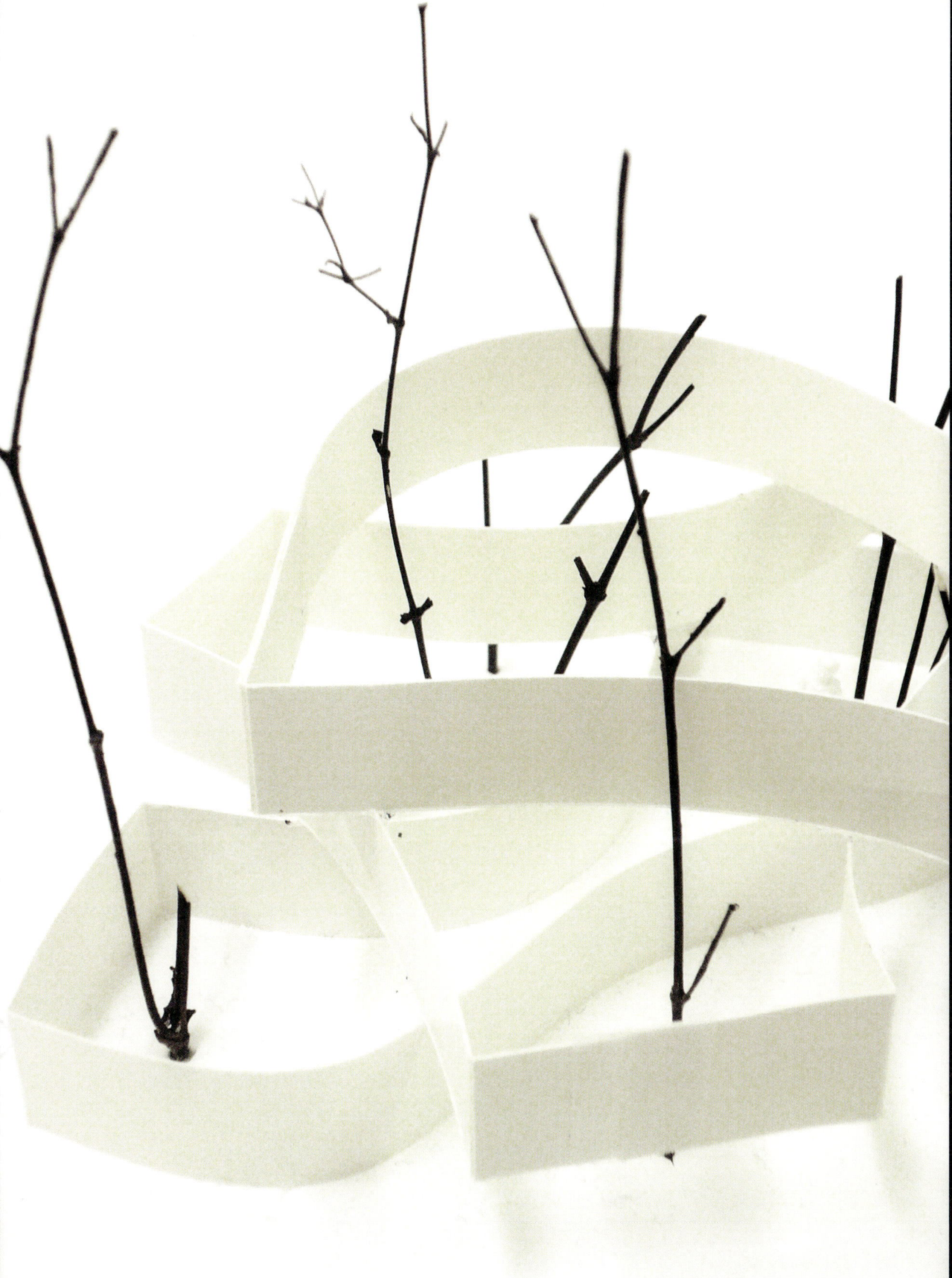

House/Garden

TOCHIGI, JAPAN 2008

Enclosed nature / Architecture without roof

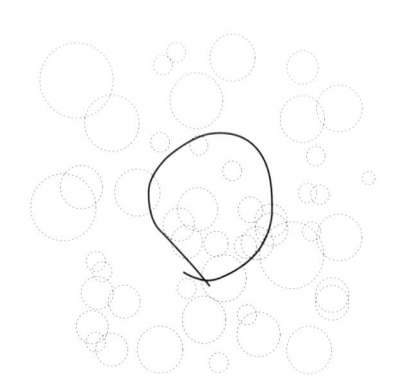

When considering building a house within the forest, in a sense, does the forest already exist as a kind of architecture in its own right? Simply framing this forest with walls epitomizes the ultimate house in the forest. Enclosed nature can be seen equally as architecture devoid of a roof, or as a ruin. It manifests architecture's end and also its origin. Here nature and artificiality are intertwined in a meticulous friction with one another.

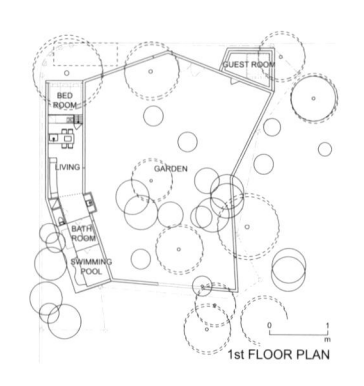

森の中に家を建てるとき、そもそもそこにある森は既に建築ではないだろうか？だとするなら、その森を壁で囲い取るだけで、それは究極の＜森の中の家＞となり得るに違いない。囲まれた自然はまた同時に、屋根のない建築であり、それは廃墟のようにも見え、建築の原初／終焉の姿でもある。そこには自然と人工物の間のぎりぎりのせめぎ合いがある。

026

House N

OITA, JAPAN 2008

Between transparency and opaque
– Architecture as a geometric forest

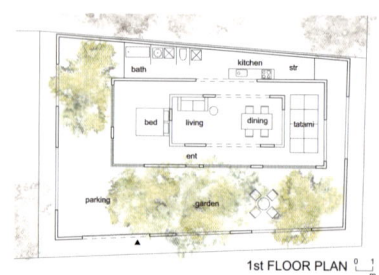

SECTION

1st FLOOR PLAN

Can we not state that architecture is a field where the transparent and the opaque are intricately woven together? And furthermore, that the quintessential place where opacity and transparency are vividly interspersed is the forest? Under such a premise, I imagine that ultimately architecture will evolve to be something like a forest. Here, although the house is composed of white box form with rectangular openings of an artificial order, the effervescent layers endow the space with an amorphous and organic richness. The concrete box recedes in the perpetual cycle of transparency and opacity, and in this moment space and perception transcends the object. The preliminary idea conceived in the *House of Gradation* became more than an idea and was realized as a different space. This inquiry into the conception of inside/outside, transparency and opacity, later takes a more substantial form in projects such as *Serpentine Gallery Pavilion 2013* and beyond.

建築とは、透明性と不透明性の複雑な混ざり合いの場のことではないだろうか？そして透明性と不透明性がもっとも鮮やかに多様に融合する場所とは森である。その意味において、僕は建築とは究極的には森のような場所になるのではないかと考えている。この住宅は白い四角い箱と無数の四角い開口という、完全に人工的な秩序によってつくられながら、それらが幾重にも揺らぎながら関係し合うことで、とても有機的な、捉えがたい、豊かな奥行きをもった空間が建ち現れる。四角いコンクリートの箱が、透明性と不透明性の終わりのない連鎖の場の中に溶けていく。空間と体験が物質を超えていく。初期の「House of Gradation」の計画案が、コンセプトを超えて、新しい空間として実現した。この内部と外部、透明性と不透明性の問いは、その後「Serpentine Gallery Pavilion 2013」を経てさらに本質的に展開するであろう。

027 House N

House N

OITA, JAPAN
2008

→ Related Projects
001 012 044 077 100 104

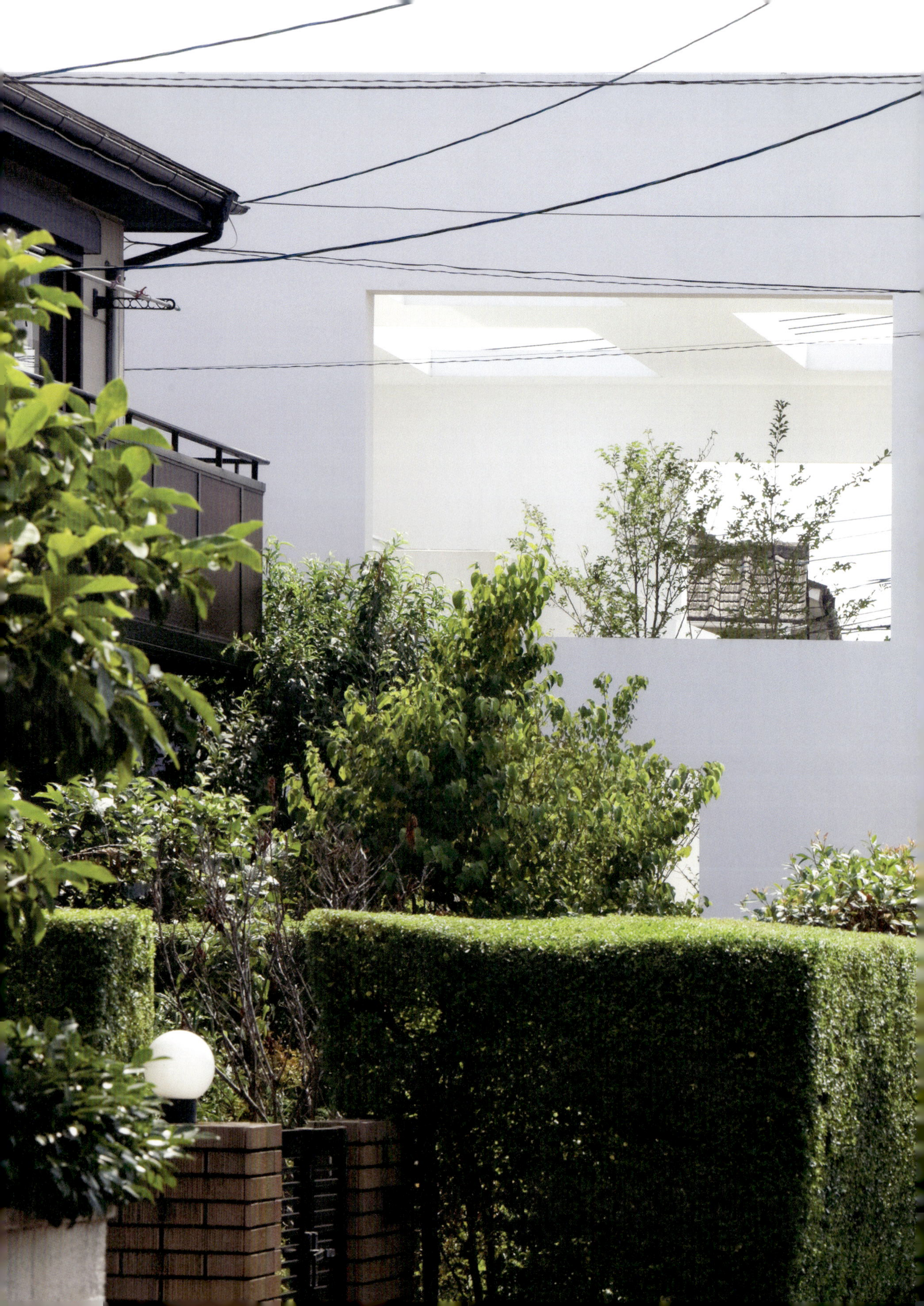

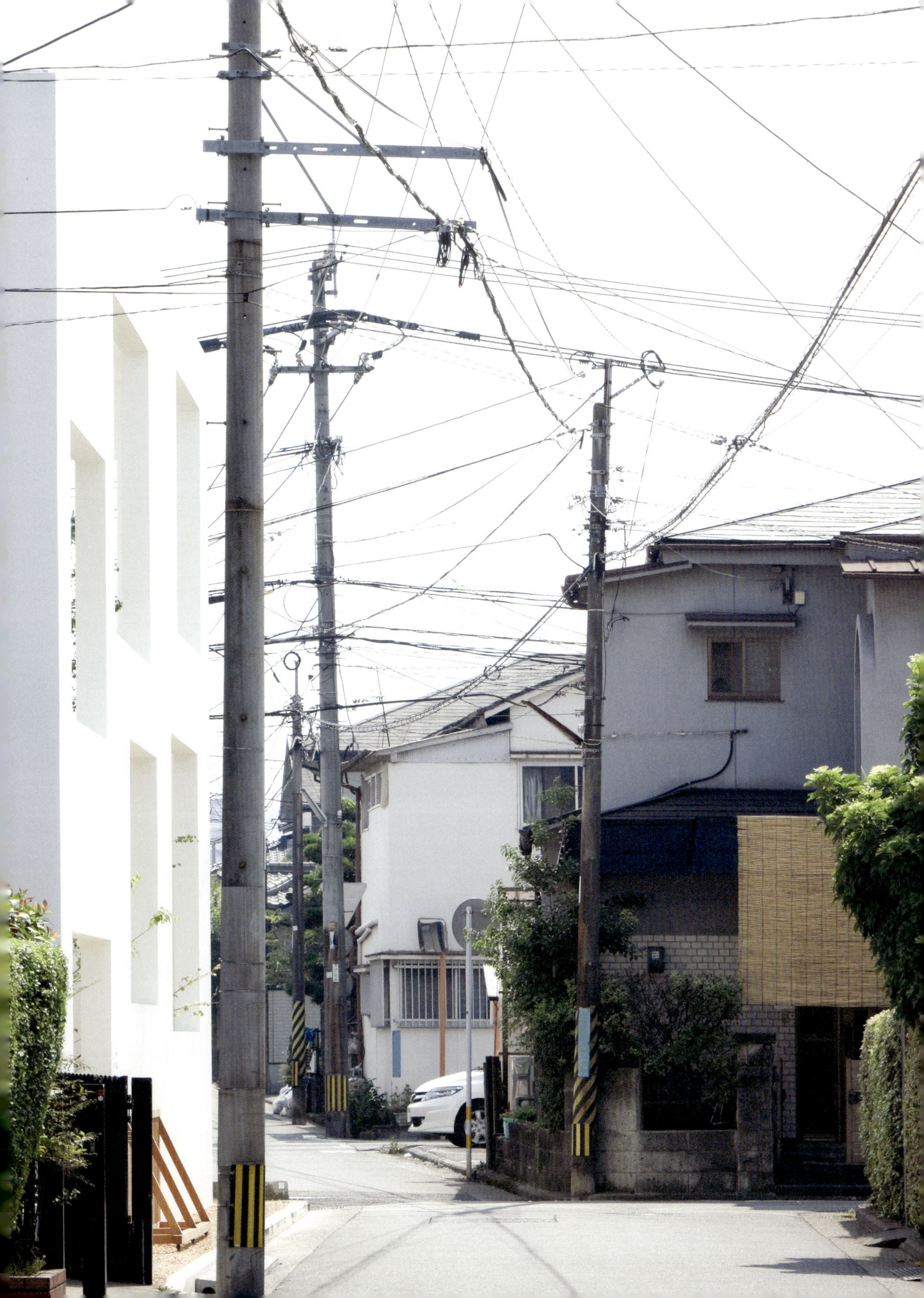

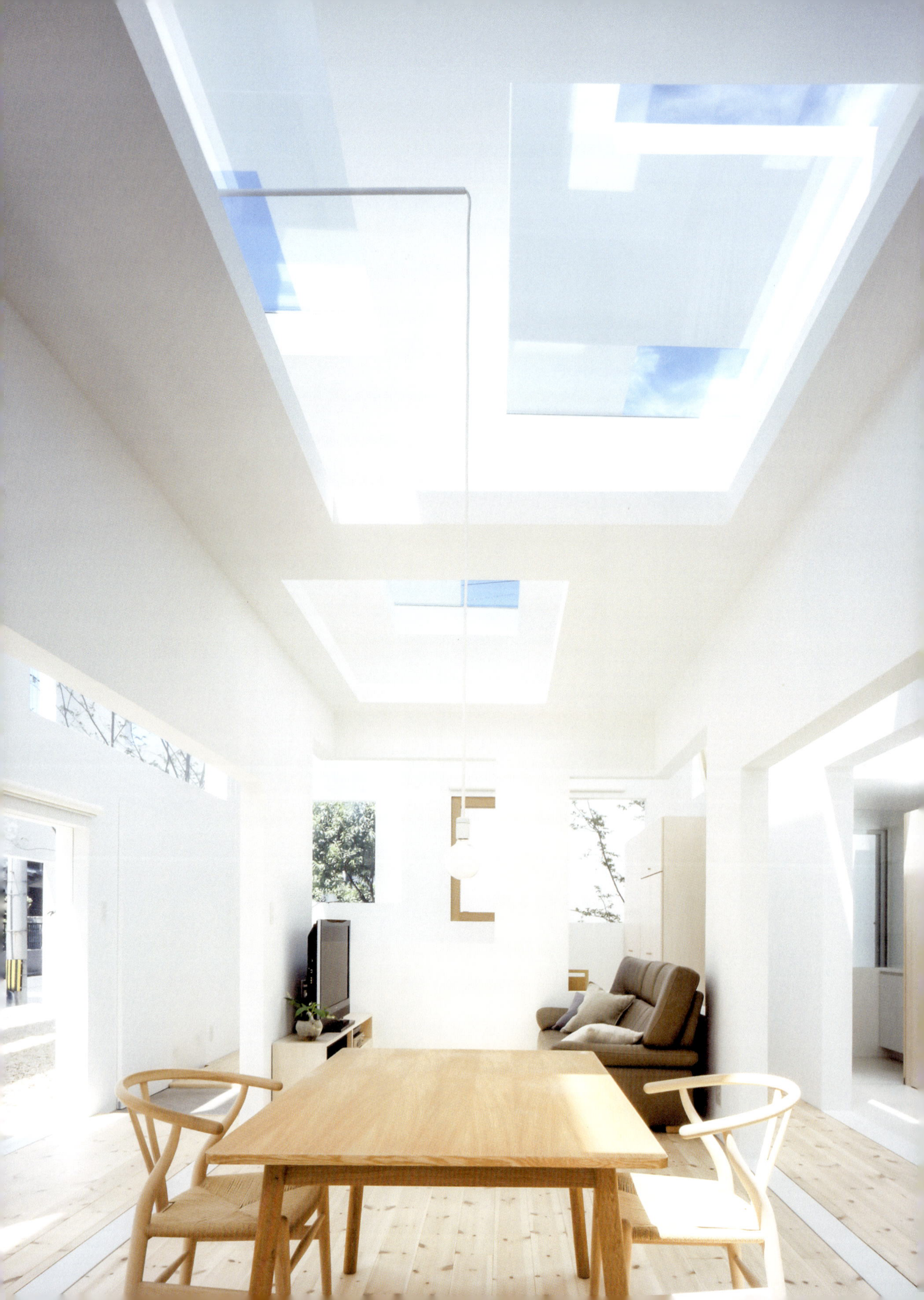

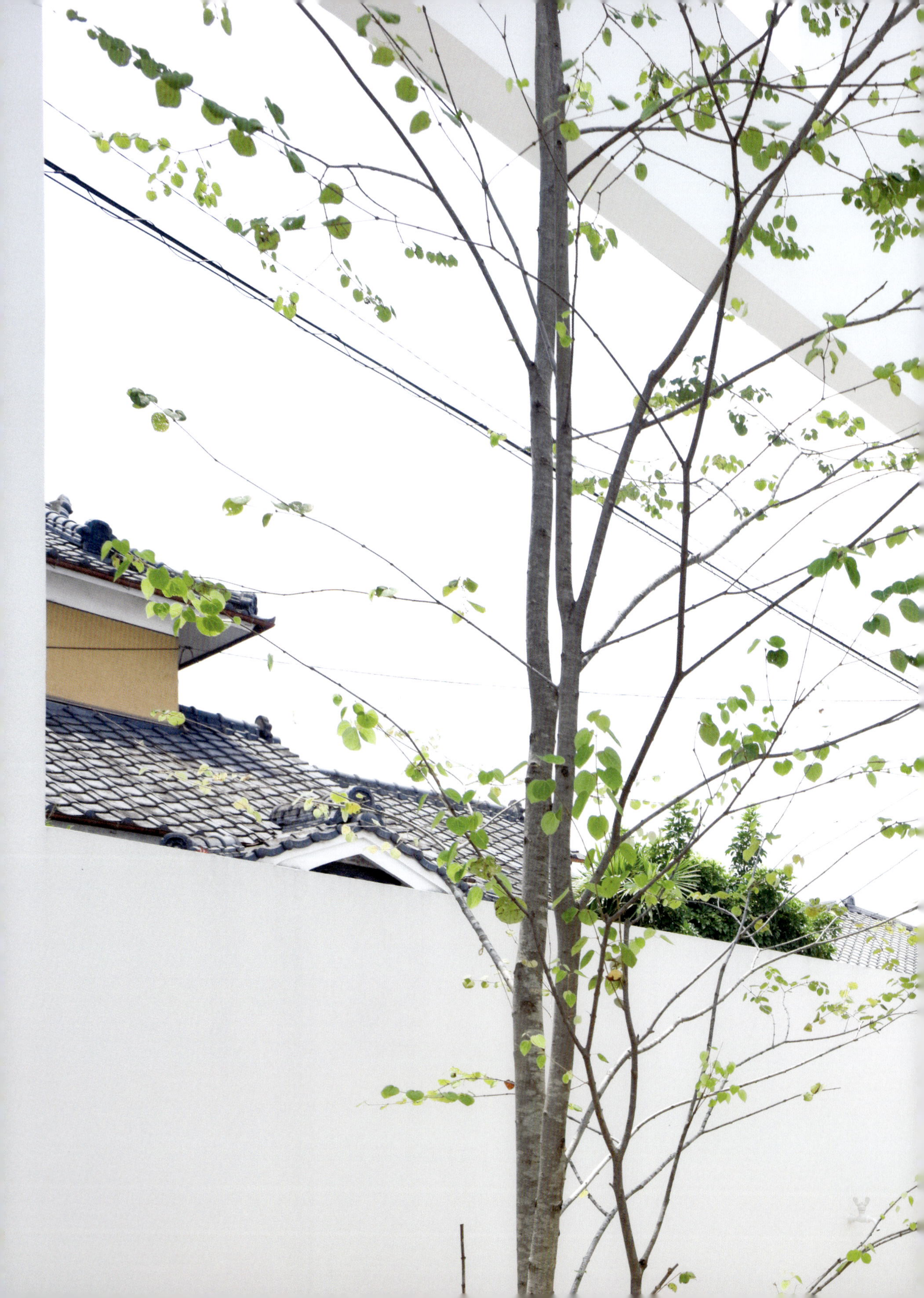

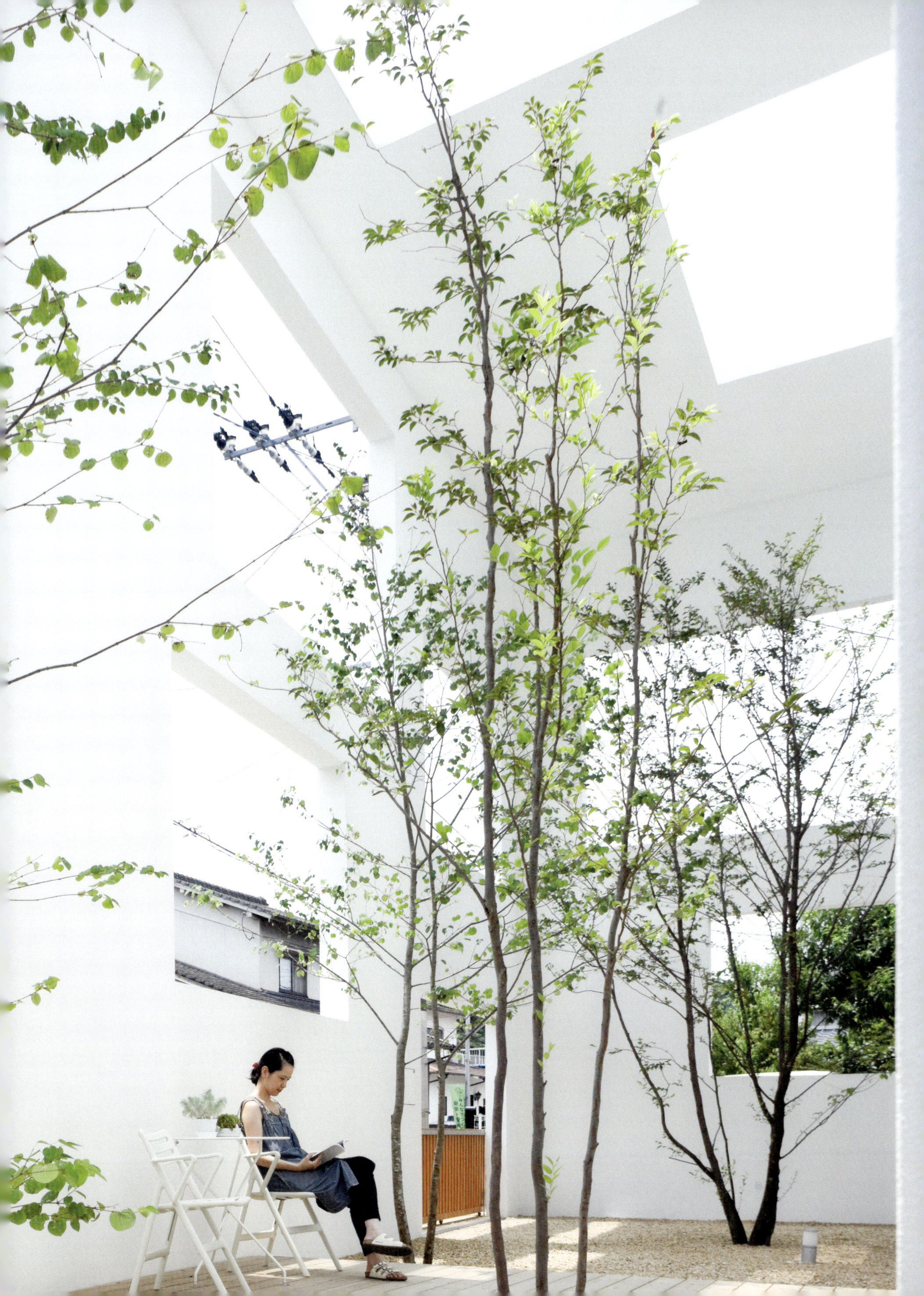

house/trees in Basel
BASEL, SWITZERLAND 2008

Hybrid of tree and architecture
When nature grow from and become part of architecture,
walls become the ground

A small installation designed for an art fair in Basel. Here I felt charged to think about new ways in which natural elements meet or converge with architecture (which is essentially man-made). It felt logical to address the quintessential proposition of architecture in its purest form, since the mode of installation allows liberation from the usual limitations inherent in the design of a building. Plants typically grow from and are rooted to Mother Earth. If architecture is able to traverse the boundary between nature and artificiality, nature will grow from and become part of architecture; walls and other elements are an extension of the Earth and thus terrain for the plants. Such a semi-architectural/semi-natural condition was expressed in the form of a conceptual model using transparent acrylic sheets. Also, as is evident in the design of the *House before House* project that was in progress at the same time, we were experimenting with various approaches to reveal new ways of interweaving nature and the man-made. Treating architectural elements as extensions of the earth is an intriguing concept, and a design inheriting the same idea can be seen in the *Omotesando Branches*, completed in 2014.

バーゼル・アートフェアのためにデザインされた小さなインスタレーション。ここでは自然物と人工的な建築物が、いままでにない形で融合するあり方を考えた。インスタレーションという、ある意味で制限のない状況の中では、より建築の根源に遡る問いを立てることが意味をもつと考えたのだ。植物は普通地面に植わっている。地球に植わっているとも言える。もし建築が、人工物と自然物の境界を越えていくとするなら、建築から文字通り直接植物が生えているという可能性はないだろうか？　壁が地球の、そして地面の延長であり、その地面的な壁から樹木が生えていく。そのような半建築／半自然の有り様を透明なアクリル壁を使ってつくり上げたコンセプチュアルなモデルである。設計が進行していた「House before House」から発展する形で、自然と人工のより先鋭的な融合を試行錯誤していた。この地球の延長としての建築という考え方は面白いと思う。2014年に竣工した「Omotesando Branches」もこの思考が異なる形で育ったものである。

028 house/trees in Basel

BASEL, SWITZERLAND
2008

→ Related Projects
008 030 031 048 088

Final Wooden House

KUMAMOTO, JAPAN 2008

Matter / Space
Object / Void
Figure / Ground

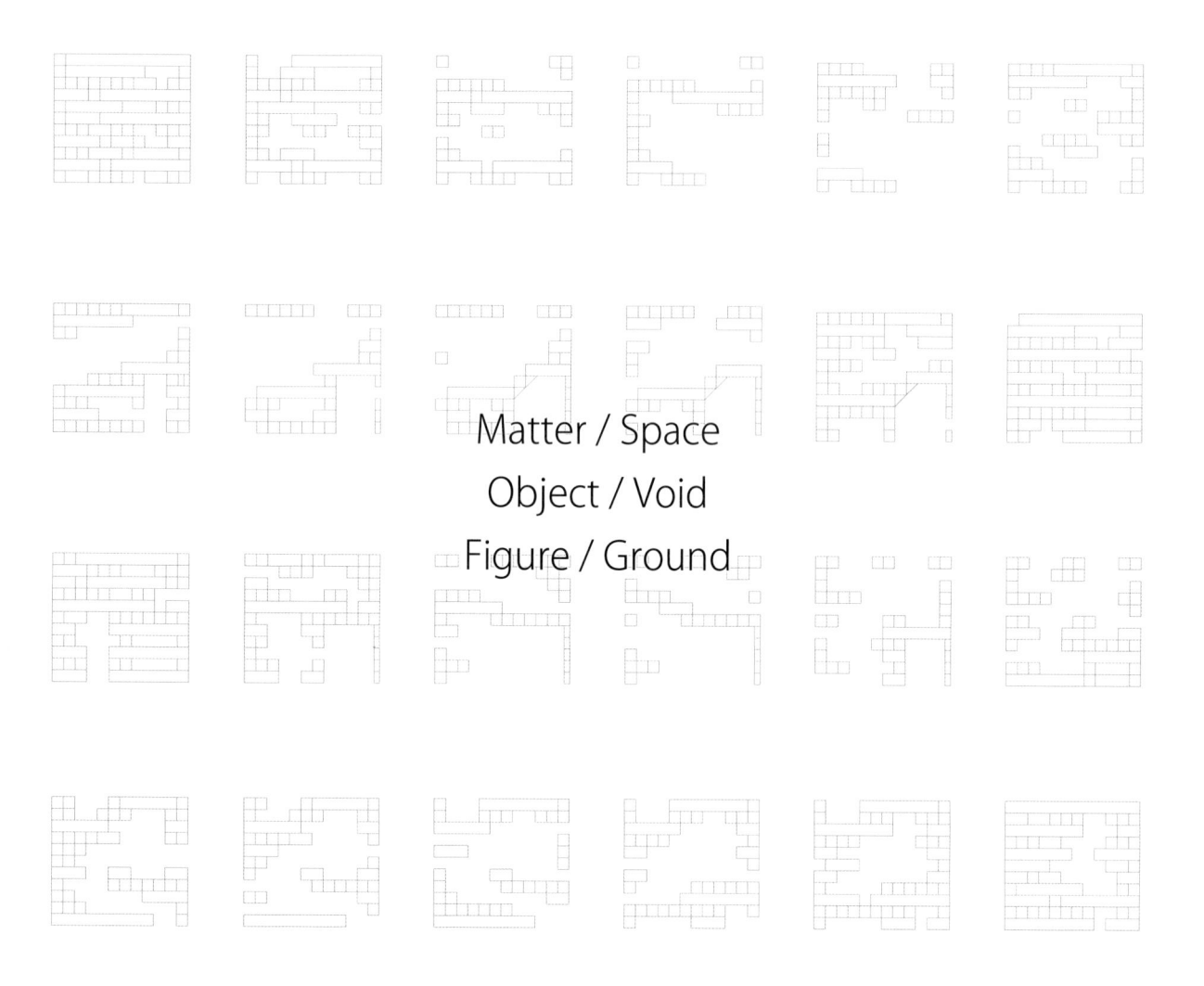

The existence of this small bungalow touches upon the antecedent being of matter. The structure, composed of stacked 350x350 timber blocks, is akin to an inversion of matter and space, almost identical to stacking volumes of air, or a void. Much in the same way, the notion of floor, wall and ceiling become increasingly ambiguous, and the various elements that compose architecture such as windows, insulation, structural frame, and kitchen furniture defy static definitions and reciprocate as the user interacts with the matter in space. It is as if the indeterminacy of quantum mechanics theory has taken form, where the classification of space diminishes into the nebulous vortex moments after the instance it is defined. This is a most contemporary yet primitive bungalow, traversing notions of matter/space, function/body, and substance/transition.

この小さな小屋は、モノの在り様の原型に触れる存在だ。350mm 角の木材を積み上げてつくられる構造体は、見方を変えれば同じ大きさの空気の塊を積み上げて場所をつくっているとも言える。モノと空間の間が常に入れ替わっている。そしてまた床と壁と天井の意味が常に揺らぎ入れ替わり、そればかりか窓や断熱や構造体やキッチンや椅子やテーブルなど建築におけるあらゆるものの意味が、常に居住者の身体との関係においてその瞬間瞬間に定義されまた意味を失っていく。ここでは量子力学的な不確定性が形を伴って現れているとさえ言えるかもしれない。観察者によるある瞬間の切り取りによってすべては一瞬だけ確定されるが、次の瞬間にはまた揺らぎの渦の中に消えていく。モノと空間、機能と身体、意味と揺らぎを横断していく新しい原初の小屋。

029

Final Wooden House
"1st Prize" in Wooden House Competition in Kumamoto

くまもとアートポリス設計競技 2005：次世代モクイへ 1等受賞

KUMAMOTO, JAPAN
2008

→ Related Projects
007 017 064 077 079

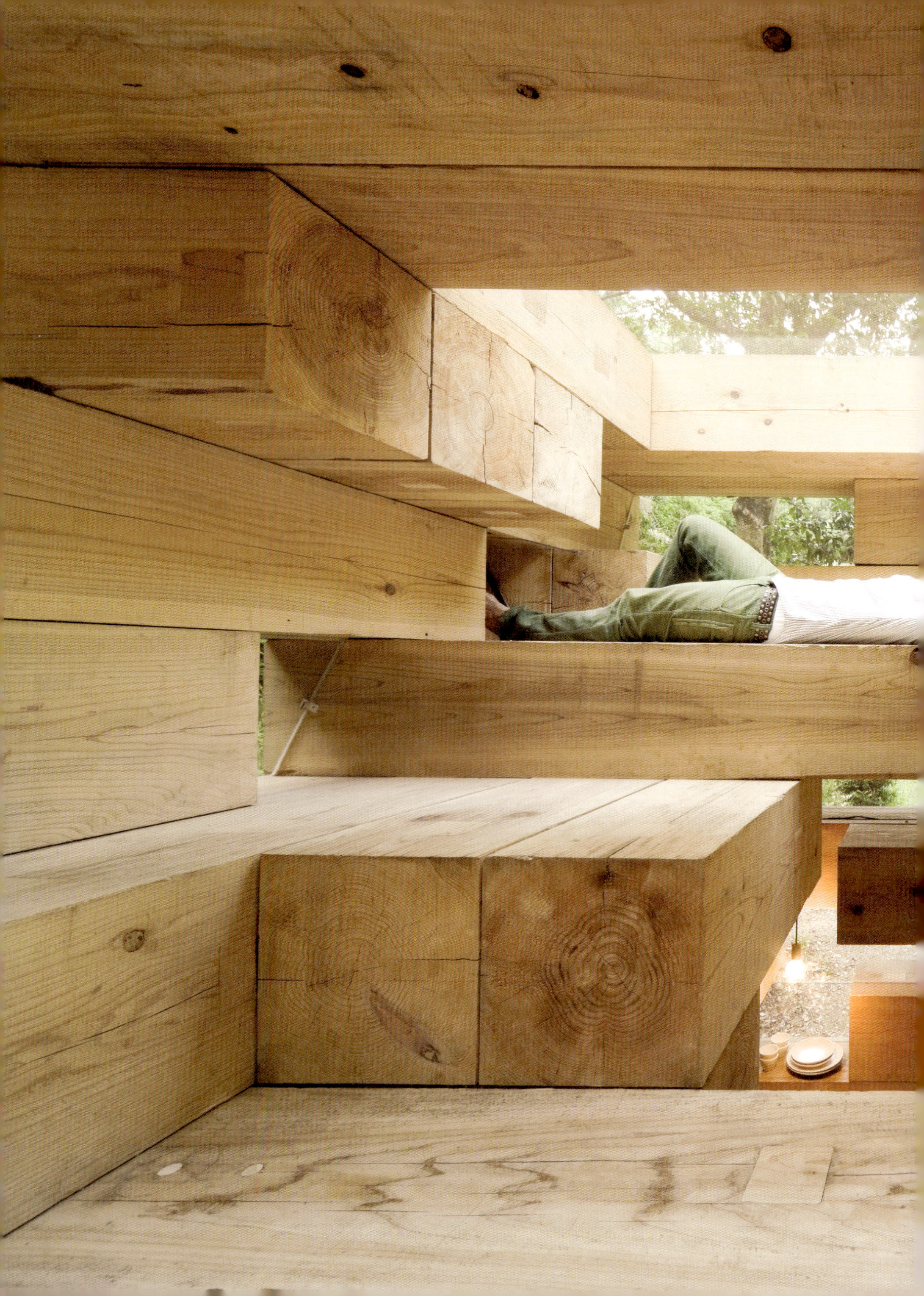

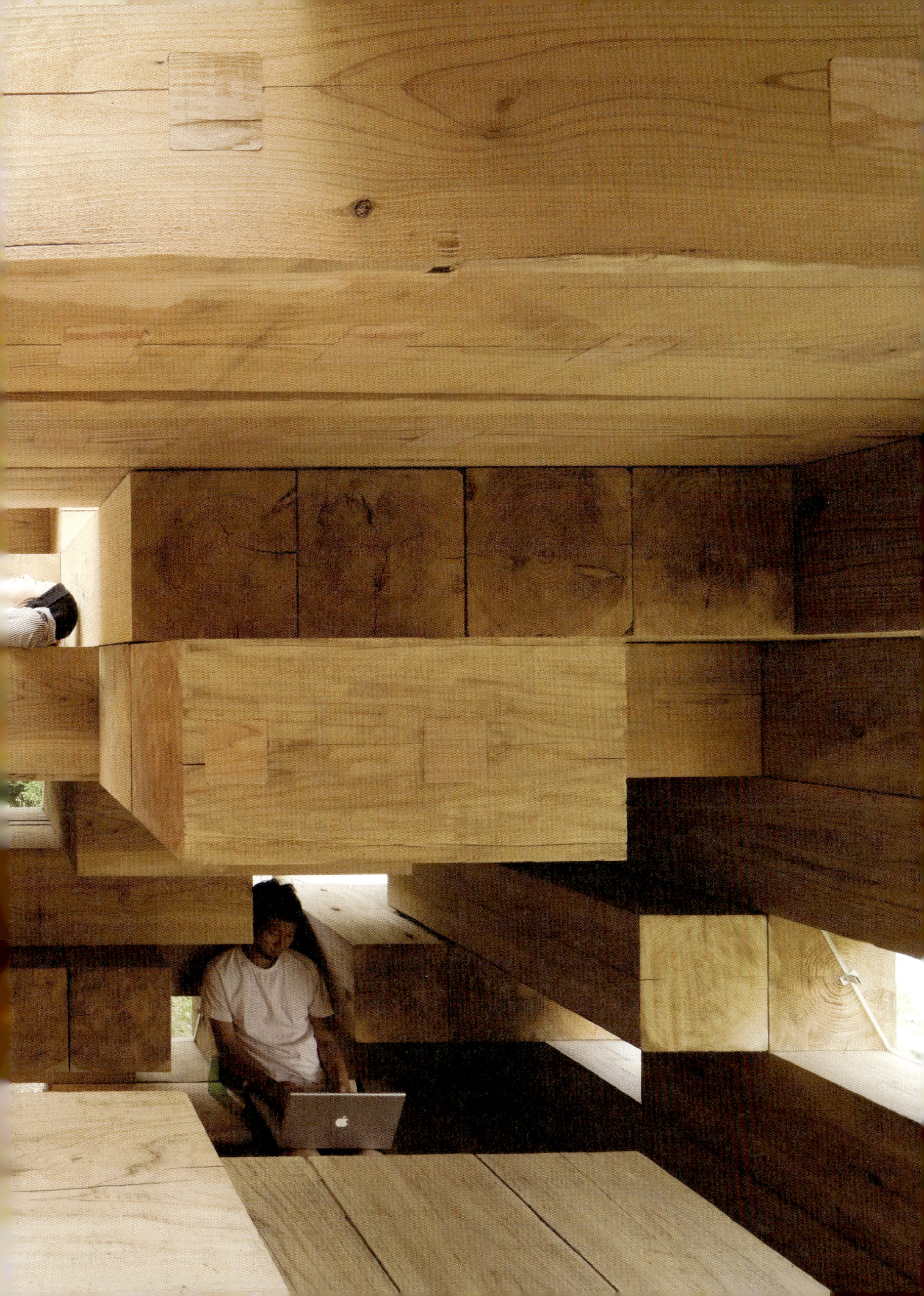

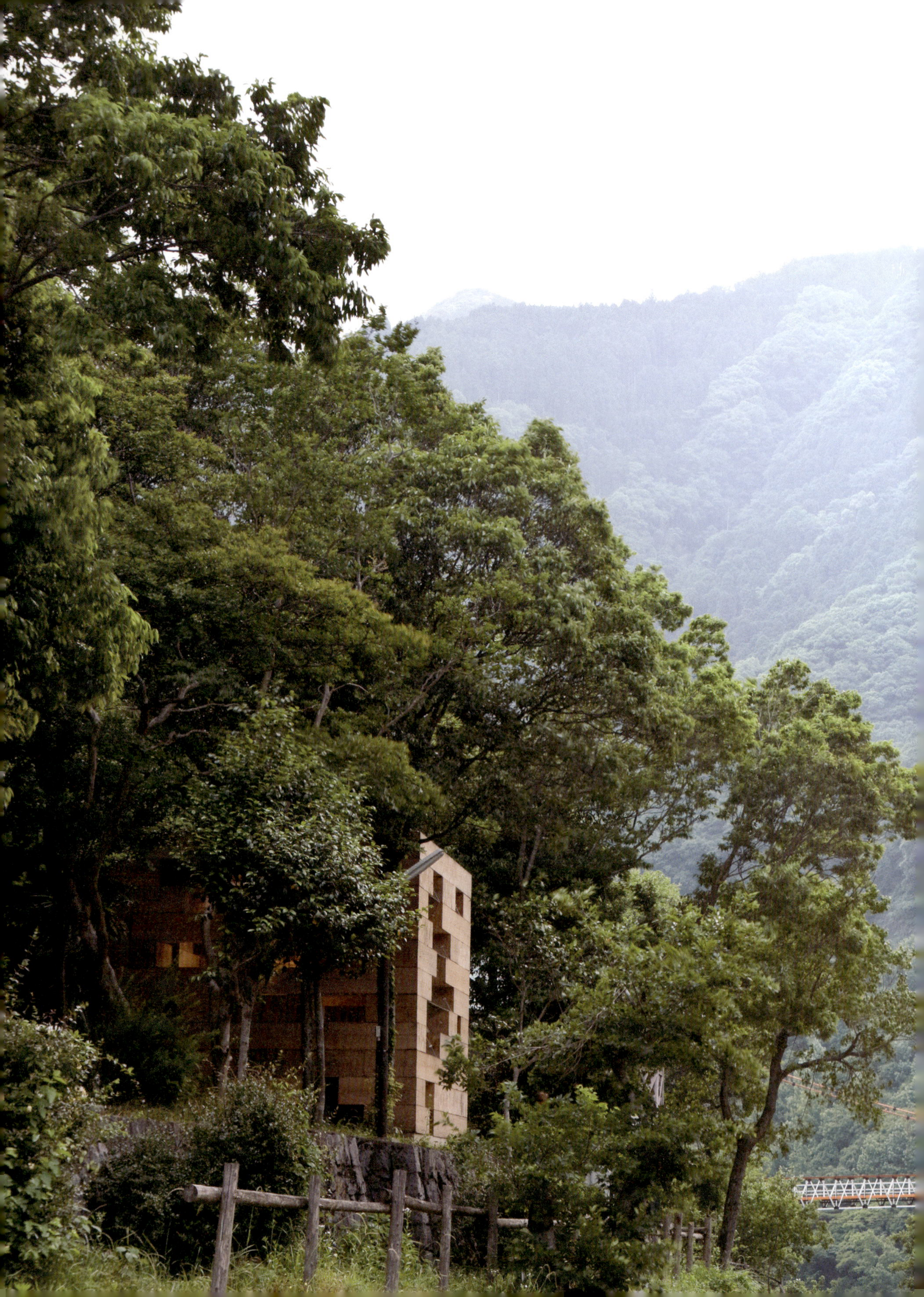

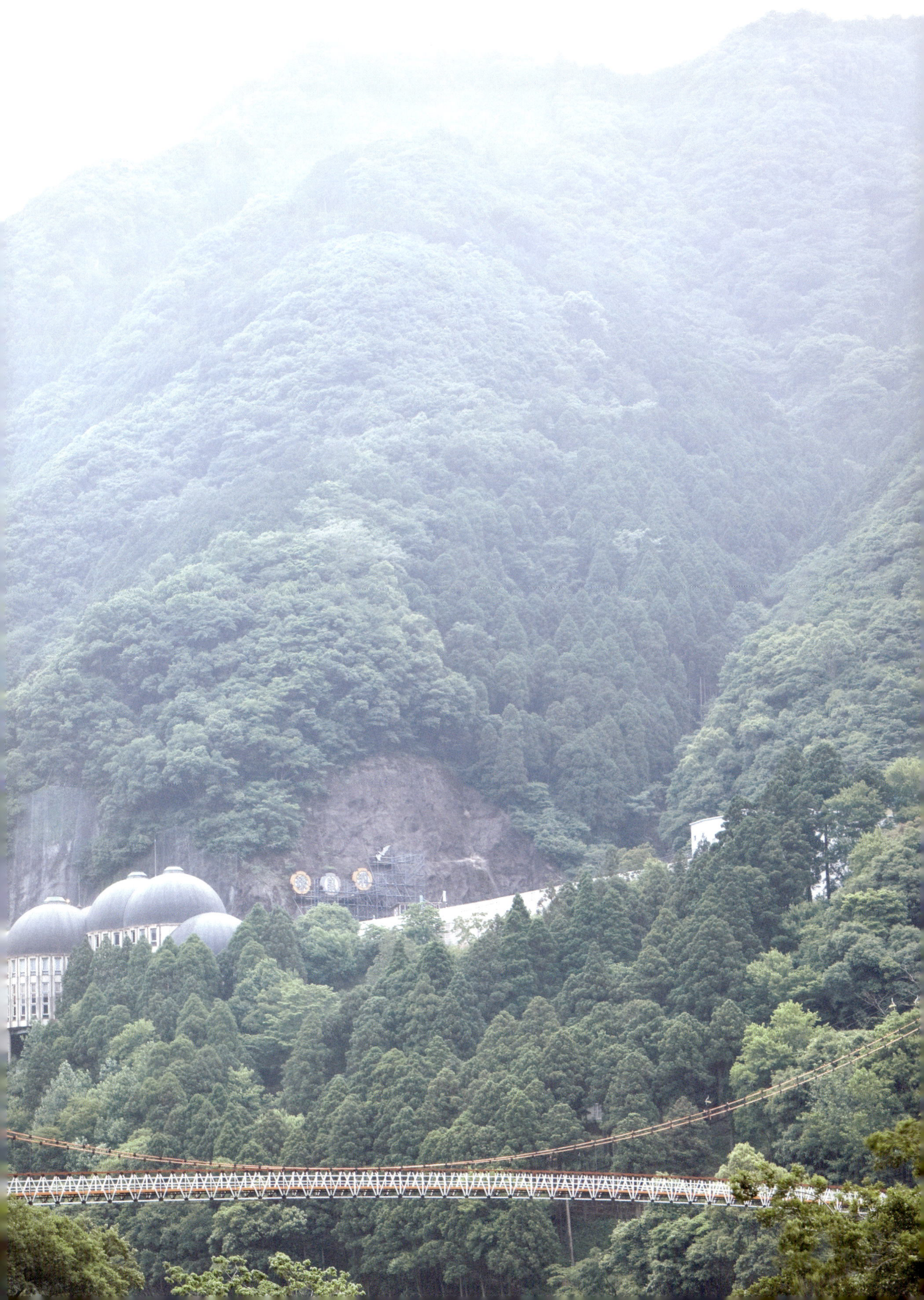

House before House
TOCHIGI, JAPAN 2008

Forest as Architecture / City as Forest / Architecture as City

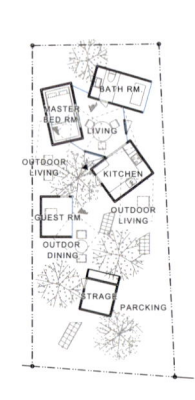

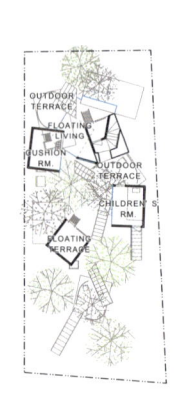

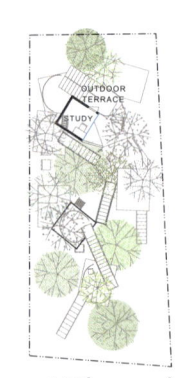

PLAN 0 5m

I consider architecture, forest and city as akin to one another. Qualities inherent in each are synergistically linked and lead to an ideal image of living, being artificial yet natural, simple yet multifaceted, diverse yet palpable, and having the openness to embrace others yet bearing the intimacy to shelter the unique. In this experimental house, I sought to reformulate various elements by taking them apart, and infusing the essences of city, forest and architecture as entities. Houses are segmented down to small rooms, forest into trees, and the city as volumes and staircases. Each fragment, all loosely relating to one another, all conspire to form an embryonic condition in creating this place. The idea of "fragmenting and re-assembling," initially conceived in the *Network by Walk* project, over a decade later evolved into an unexpected form– opening up new conceptions and fostering the development of various future projects.

建築と森と街は似ている、と考えてみる。それぞれの意味が連鎖して、ひとつの理想の生活空間像にたどり着く。それは人工的でありながら自然的で、単純でありながら複雑で、多様でありながら理解可能であり、他者を受け入れる許容力をもちながら特別なひとりを守ってくれる親密さをもつ。この小さな実験住宅においては、要素を細分化して混ぜ合わせることで森と街と建築を溶け合わせることを試みた。家は小部屋に分節され、森は小さな木々に、そして街はボリュームと階段へと分節されていった。それらの断片が相互に関係をもちながら寄り集まってこの場所はできあがった。10年以上前に構想した「Network by Walk」で生まれた＜分節して混ぜ合わせる＞というアイデアが思いもよらないかたちで建築化したことで、思考は開放され、その後のさまざまなプロジェクトへと展開していく。

030 | House before House | TOCHIGI, JAPAN 2008 | → Related Projects 008 018 028 040 088

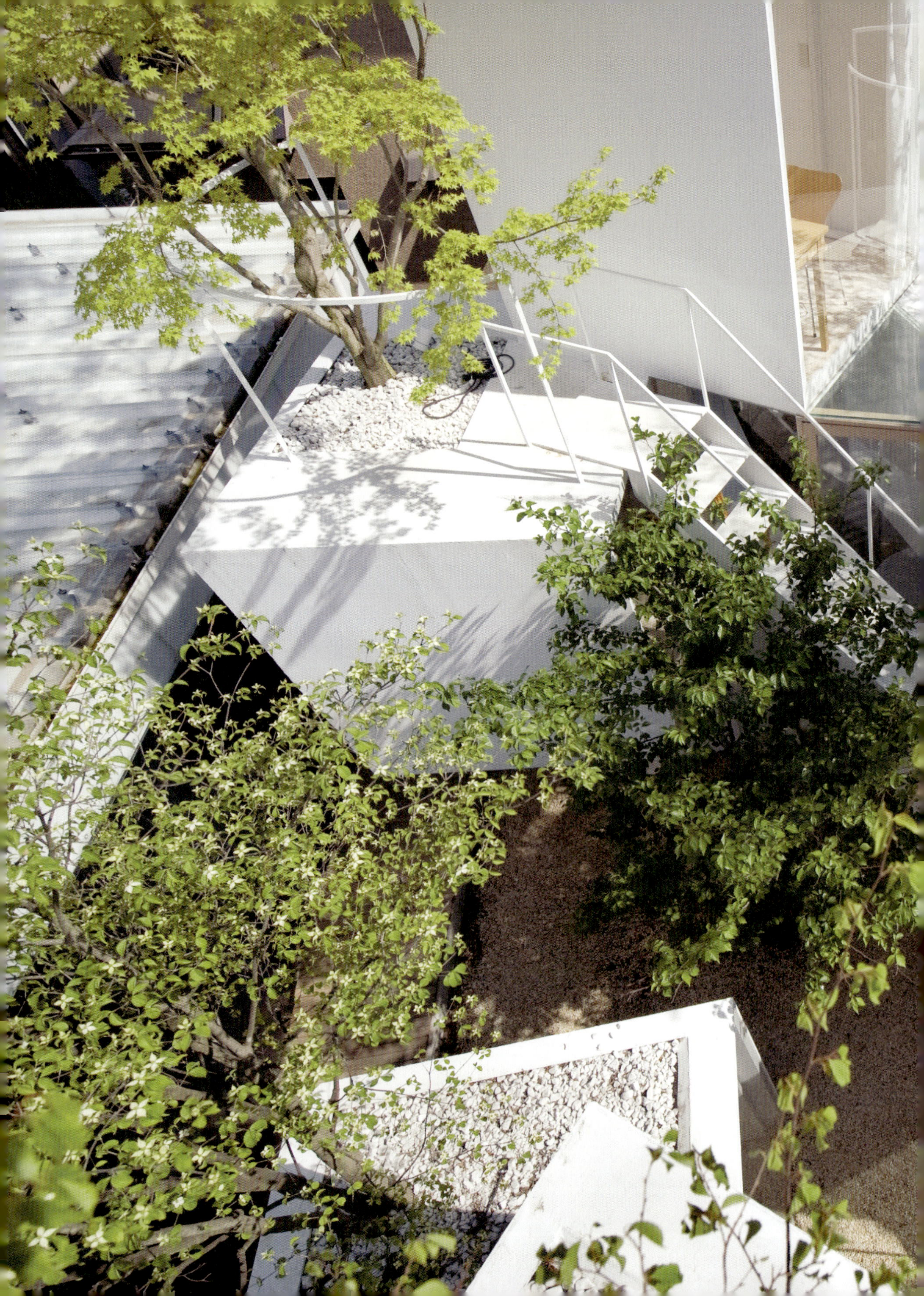

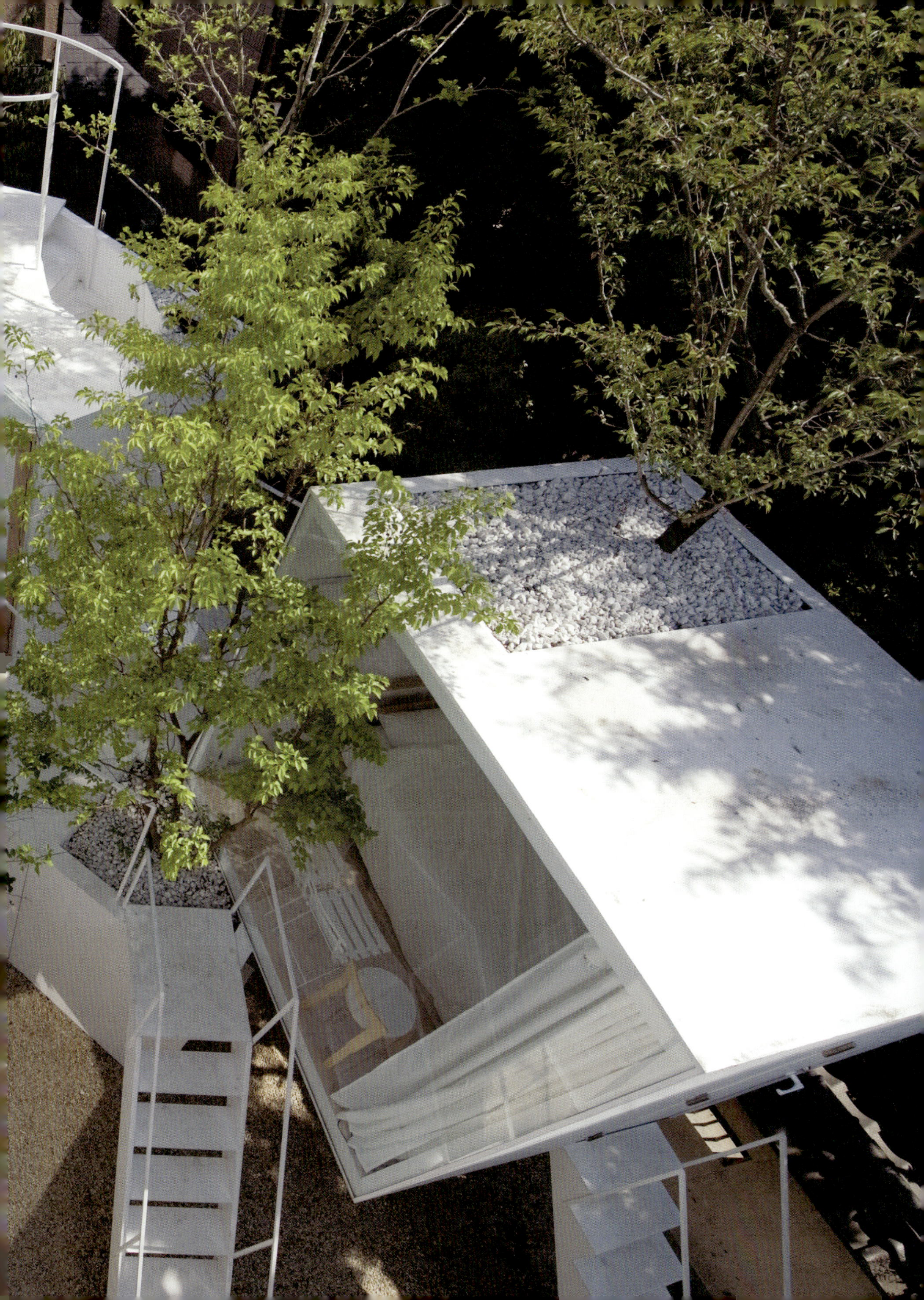

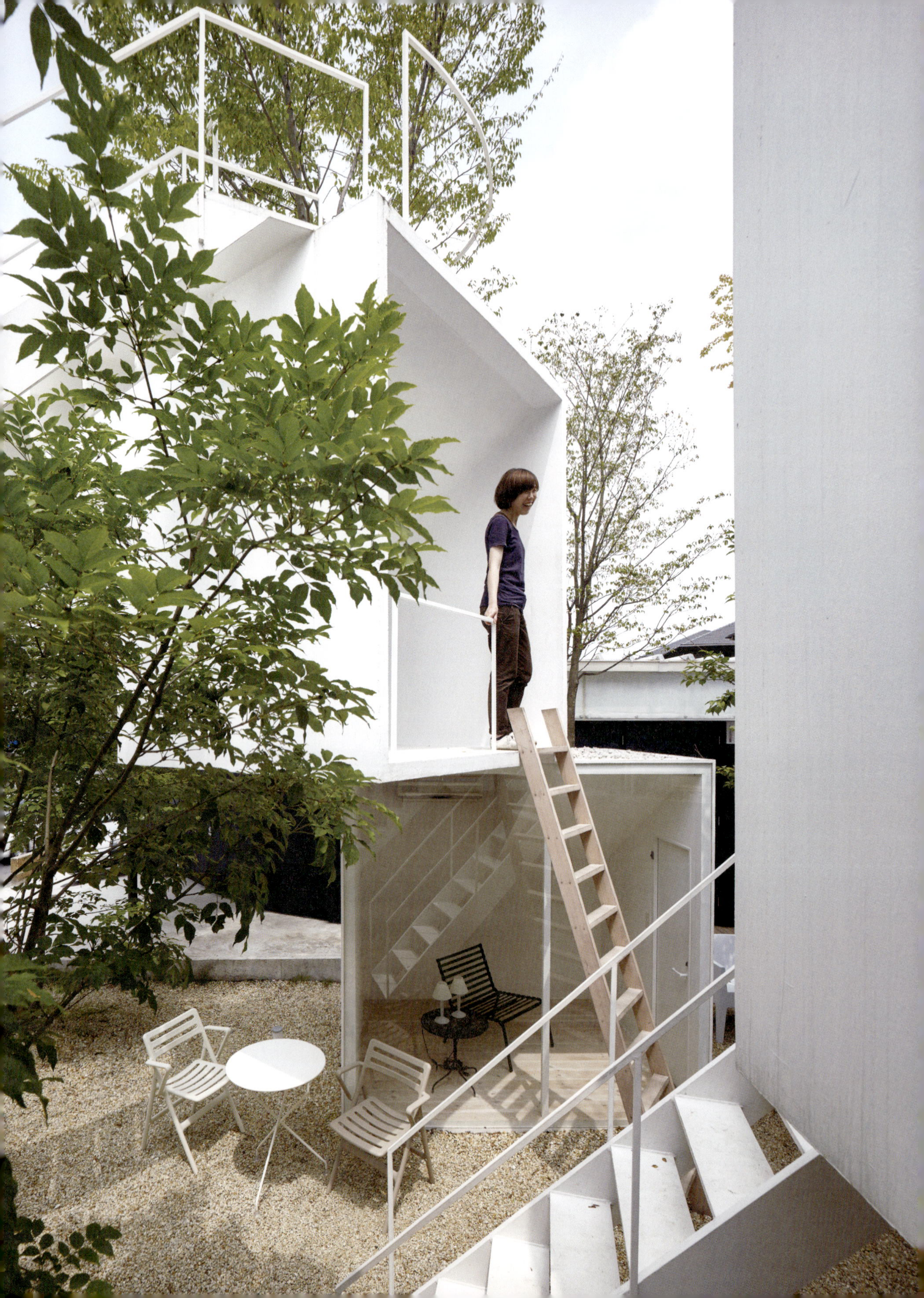

DETAIL SECTION

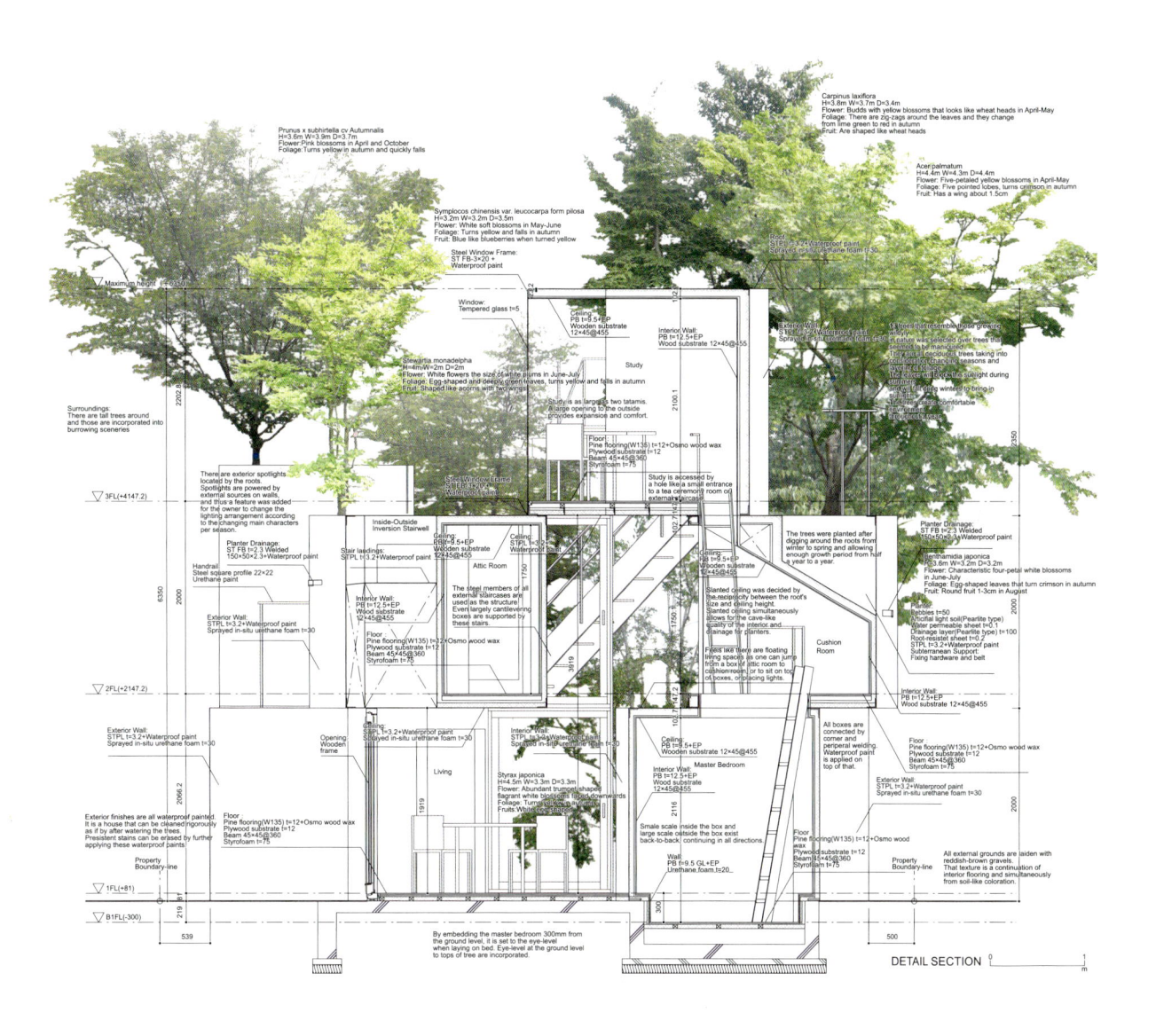

Benetton Building

TEHERAN, IRAN 2009

Interiorized exterior / Exteriorized interior

DETAIL SECTION

Needless to say, our living environment is composed of a mixture of the natural and manmade. Diversity is born from variegated resolutions of the aforementioned mixture. This project seeks to experimentally abstract this relationship of nature and the artificial, and remix them both in a new order. Each glass box houses a tree of the same size, with these boxes stacked to make up an architectural volume. The interiors of the boxes are habitable spaces in which users work and live under or around the trees. Sunlight delicately passes through the boxes through a glass ceiling and floor, to engender a volumetric artificial forest. Inverting interiority and exteriority, and artificially re-orchestrating the natural order: in this way, this project signifies the new relationship between nature and man.

私たちの生活環境をつくり出すものは、人工物と自然物の混合体である。それらがどのような解像度でどのように混ざり合うのかによって、僕たちの生活環境の多様性が生まれてくる。このプロジェクトは、そんな自然と建築の関係を実験的に解体し再混合するものである。ガラスの箱の中に、その箱にちょうど合うサイズの木が植わっている。その樹木入りのガラス箱を無数に積み上げて、建築物をつくる。ガラスの箱の内部は居住空間であり、人びとは樹木の下や周りで働き、生活する。床や天井もガラスであり、日差しが柔らかく通り抜ける立体的で人工的な森が形づくられる。内部と外部を反転し、自然物である森を人工的に再構築すること。自然と人工の新しい関係を象徴するプロジェクトである。

031

Benetton Building

Benetton Building

TEHERAN, IRAN
2009

→ Related Projects
004 030 043 049 062 088

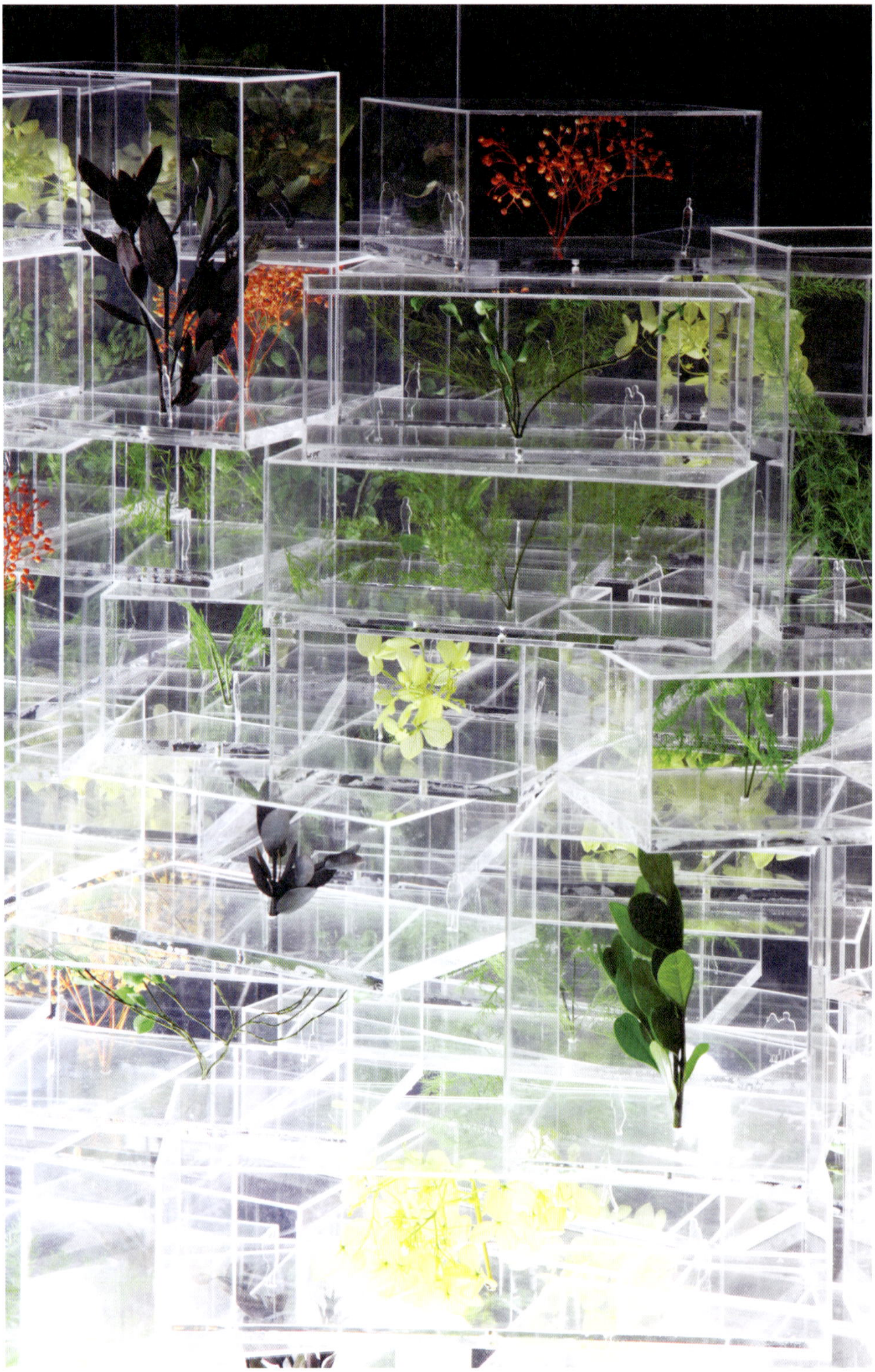

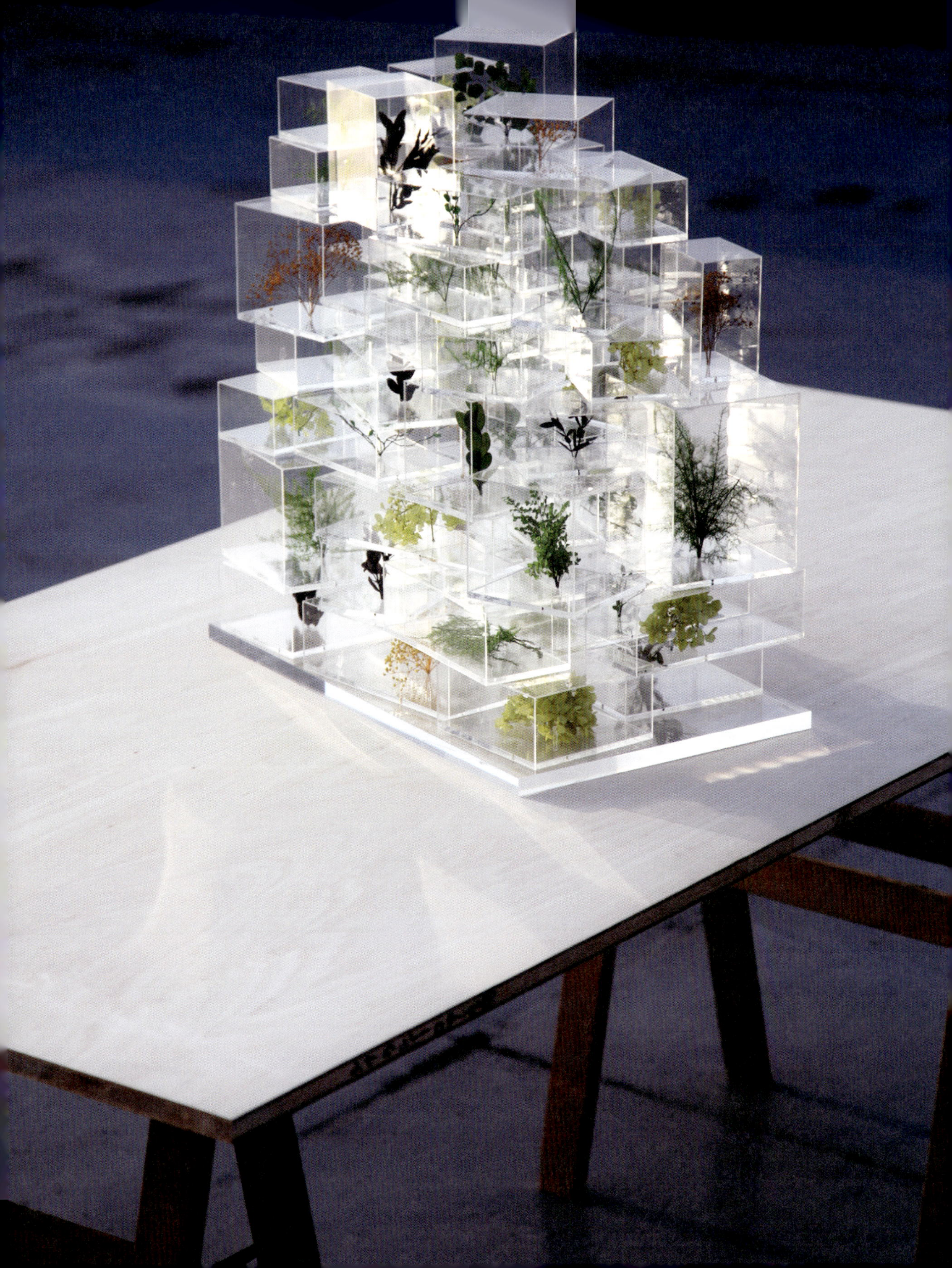

Sumida Hokusai Museum

TOKYO, JAPAN 2009

When the ground transforms into a wall,
concept of floors will change

SECTION

The idea of connecting a building to the surrounding city or square is an appealing one. This would free the structure from being a simple body and redefine it in terms of various fluctuating experiences. As I was required to deal with the square from the front in this competition, I came up with the idea of integrating the square, functioning as a front garden, and the building with a slope. By making it possible to access the slope from any of the building's four floors, I thought I could create a closer connection between the building and the ground. In the *Peak-Oslo National Museum* competition, which was held at almost the same time, I also tried to create a three-dimensional link between the city and the museum. Later, in *House K* I realized this on a residential scale, but this architectural format holds a special charm not only for houses but also for more public buildings.

建築を周辺の都市や広場に連続させるという考えは、やはり魅力的だ。それは建築を単体の物体という存在から解き放ち、体験の多様な抑揚の揺らぎの中で再定義する。このコンペでは、正面に広場を取ることが求められていたことから、前庭としての広場と建築を斜面で一体化することを考えた。4層からなる建物のどの階にもこの斜面を上ってアクセスできることで、建物と地面との関係がより緊密な連続性をもつのではないかと考えたのである。同時期に行っていた「Peak-Oslo National Museum」でも、やはり街と美術館の立体的な連続性を試みている。後に「House K」において住宅スケールで実現したが、住宅にとどまらず、より公共的な建築において魅力を発揮する建築形式に違いない。

032 | Sumida Hokusai Museum | 墨田区北斎会館 | TOKYO, JAPAN 2009 | → Related Projects 024 034 041 042 067 080

City as Architecture, Architecture as Mountain, Mountain as City

TOKYO, JAPAN 2009

Architecture as mountain / Mountain as city

City   Mountain

This was a unique and visionary project in which the future of Tokyo was considered through a series of workshops with architects (Toyo Ito, Akihisa Hirata) and structural engineer Jun Sato. The common starting point and aim was to visualize the next-generation high-density city while retaining the attributes of Tokyo, and we eventually designed a gigantic mountain-like architecture/city, with a large void in the central atrium creating what may be described as an urban-interior micro-climate. Between the aggregation of small dwelling scales and the grand urban space, diverse types of habitable city-spaces are dispersed to add to the gradation of varying scales. Also taking some formal hints from the design of *House OM*, which we were working on at the time, it was refreshing to witness the moment when a residential-scale concept flourished into an entity on an enormous urban scale. Although very different in execution, and unintentionally, I feel that this project bears some resemblance to *Taiwan Tower* and some of the later *Souk Mirage/Particles of Light*. It is worth noting that the series of workshops held for this particular project was repeated far more intensely in the collaboration for the 2012 Venice Architecture Biennale.

建築家の伊東豊雄さん、平田晃久さん、構造家の佐藤淳さんとワークショップを重ねながら東京の未来を考えるプロジェクト。東京の街の特徴を引き継ぎながらも新しい高密度都市を構想できないか、という出発点から、最終的には、巨大な山のような建築／都市が生まれた。中央には半外部的な巨大な吹き抜けを持ち、都市内自然環境を作りだしている。小さなスケールの集積と巨大な都市空間の間にグラデーションを描くようにさまざまな都市居住空間が点在する。当時設計を進めていた個人住宅「House OM」の形式にもヒントをえて、個人住宅が一気に都市スケールへと拡張した。図らずも後の「台湾タワー」や「Souk Mirage/Particles of Light」に繋がる萌芽を見ることができる。またこのワークショップ形式は、2012年のヴェネチアビエンナーレにおいてより濃密に実現することとなった。

033 | City as Architecture, Architecture as Mountain, Mountain as City | 建築のような都市、都市のような山、山のような建築 | TOKYO, JAPAN 2009 | → Related Projects **016 025 042 045**

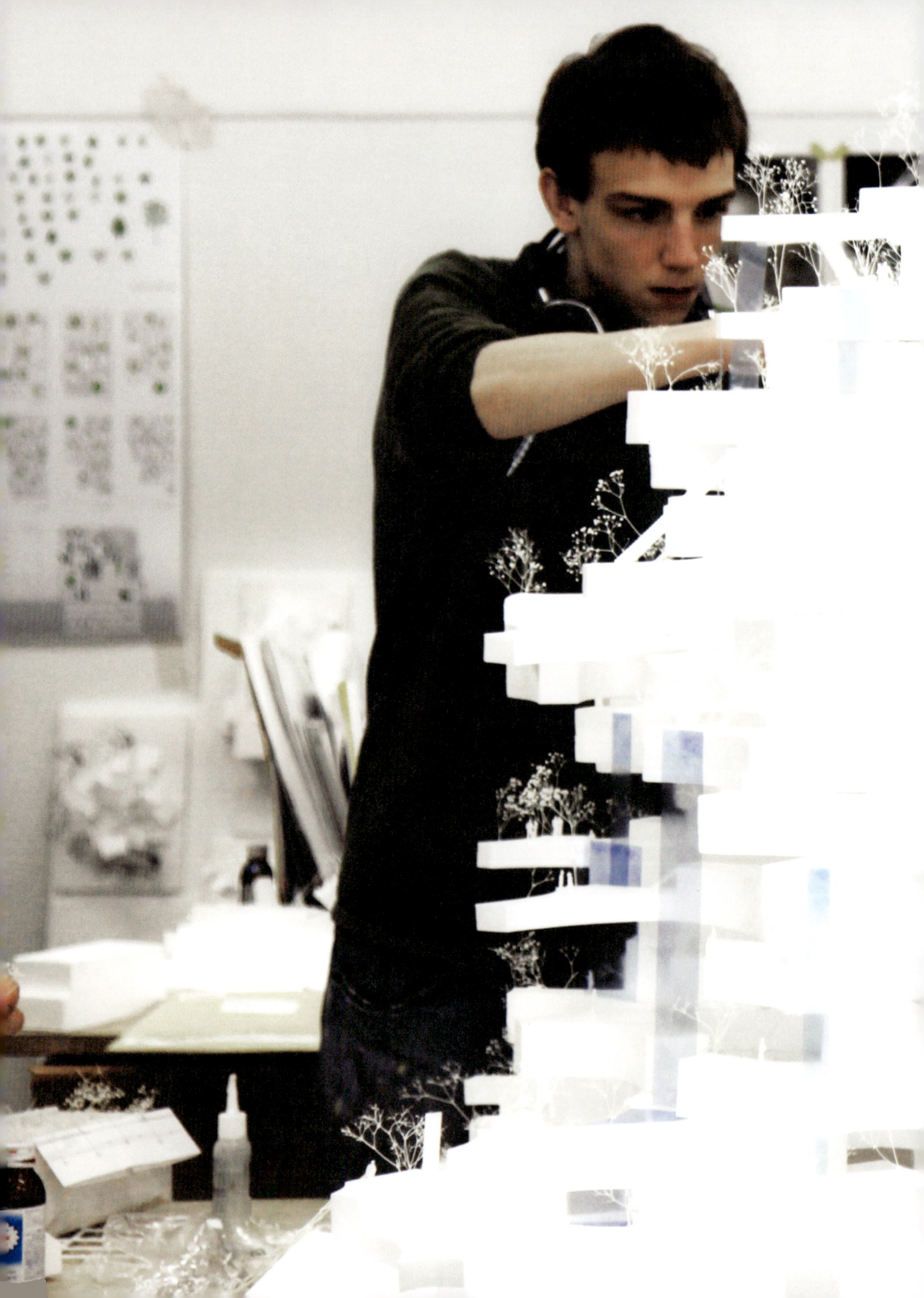

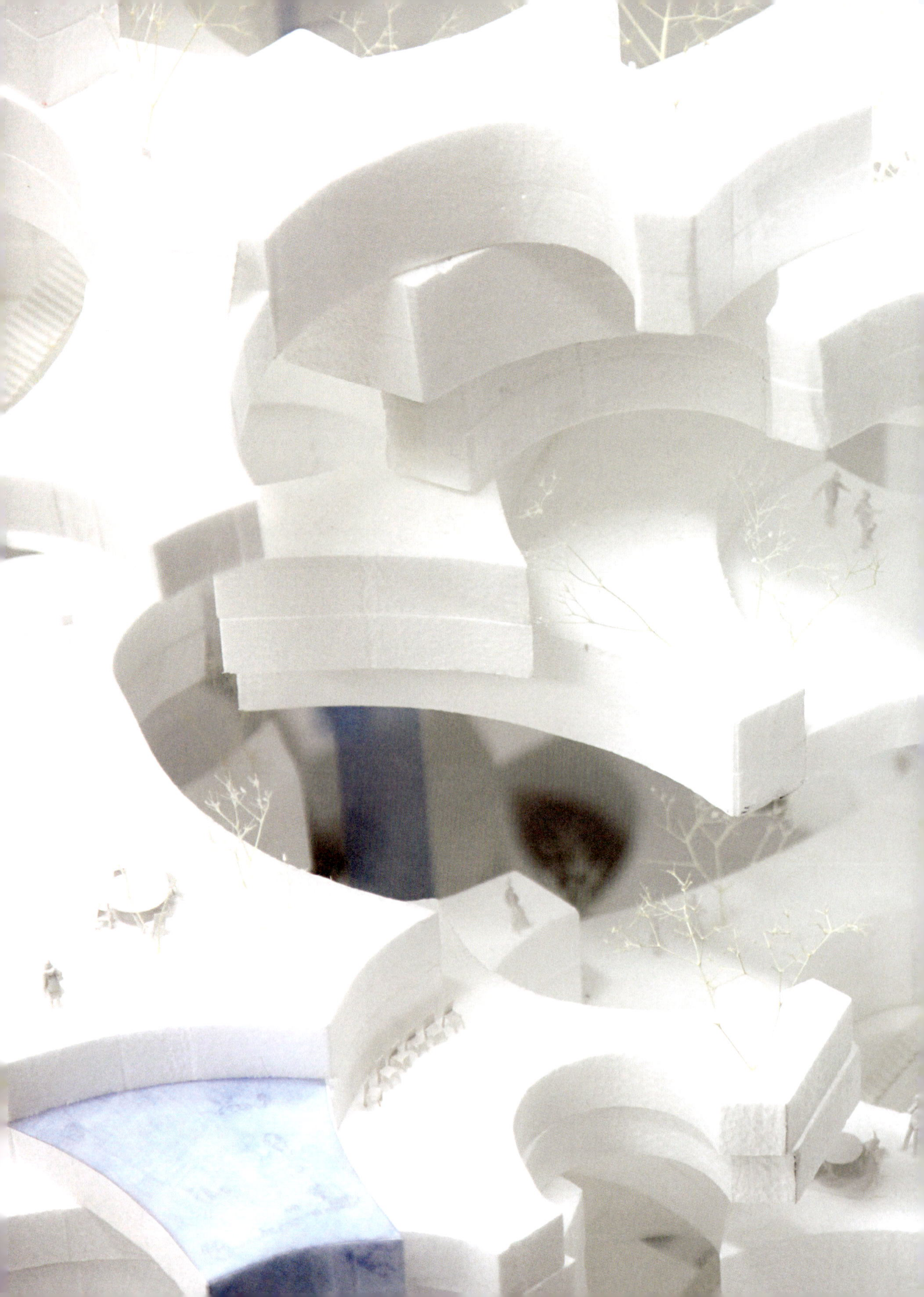

Peak-Oslo National Museum

OSLO, NORWAY 2009

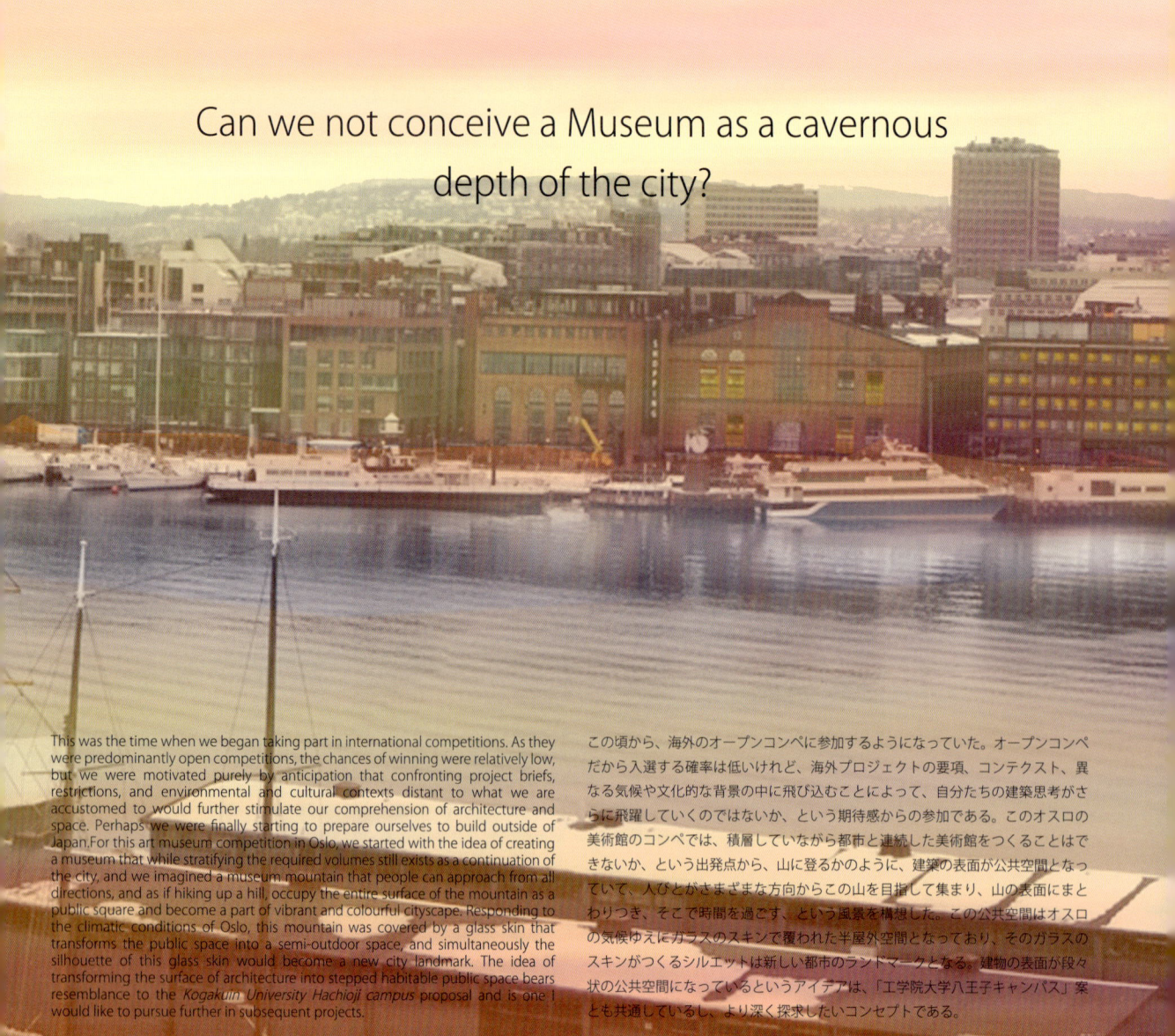

Can we not conceive a Museum as a cavernous depth of the city?

This was the time when we began taking part in international competitions. As they were predominantly open competitions, the chances of winning were relatively low, but we were motivated purely by anticipation that confronting project briefs, restrictions, and environmental and cultural contexts distant to what we are accustomed to would further stimulate our comprehension of architecture and space. Perhaps we were finally starting to prepare ourselves to build outside of Japan. For this art museum competition in Oslo, we started with the idea of creating a museum that while stratifying the required volumes still exists as a continuation of the city, and we imagined a museum mountain that people can approach from all directions, and as if hiking up a hill, occupy the entire surface of the mountain as a public square and become a part of vibrant and colourful cityscape. Responding to the climatic conditions of Oslo, this mountain was covered by a glass skin that transforms the public space into a semi-outdoor space, and simultaneously the silhouette of this glass skin would become a new city landmark. The idea of transforming the surface of architecture into stepped habitable public space bears resemblance to the *Kogakuin University Hachioji campus* proposal and is one I would like to pursue further in subsequent projects.

この頃から、海外のオープンコンペに参加するようになっていた。オープンコンペだから入選する確率は低いけれど、海外プロジェクトの要項、コンテクスト、異なる気候や文化的な背景の中に飛び込むことによって、自分たちの建築思考がさらに飛躍していくのではないか、という期待感からの参加である。このオスロの美術館のコンペでは、積層していながら都市と連続した美術館をつくることはできないか、という出発点から、山に登るかのように、建築の表面が公共空間となっていて、人びとがさまざまな方向からこの山を目指して集まり、山の表面にまとわりつき、そこで時間を過ごす、という風景を構想した。この公共空間はオスロの気候ゆえにガラスのスキンで覆われた半屋外空間となっており、そのガラスのスキンがつくるシルエットは新しい都市のランドマークとなる。建物の表面が段々状の公共空間になっているというアイデアは、「工学院大学八王子キャンパス」案とも共通しているし、より深く探求したいコンセプトである。

034 Peak-Oslo National Museum | OSLO, NORWAY 2009 | Related Projects 007 032 033 042 061 079

City in Continuum

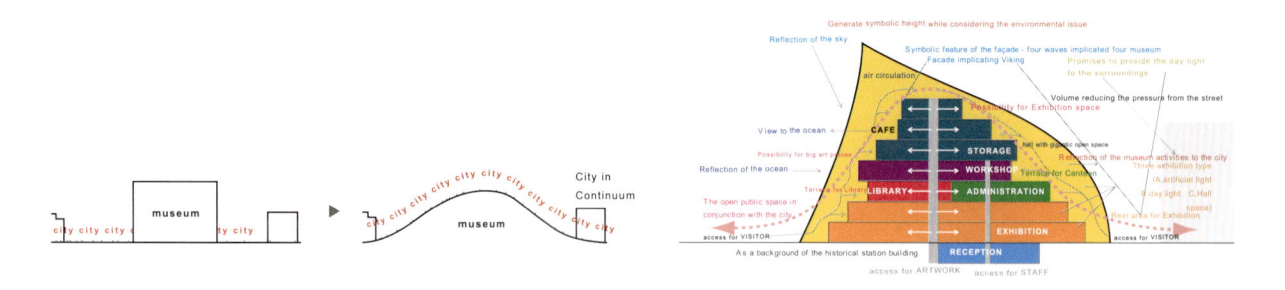

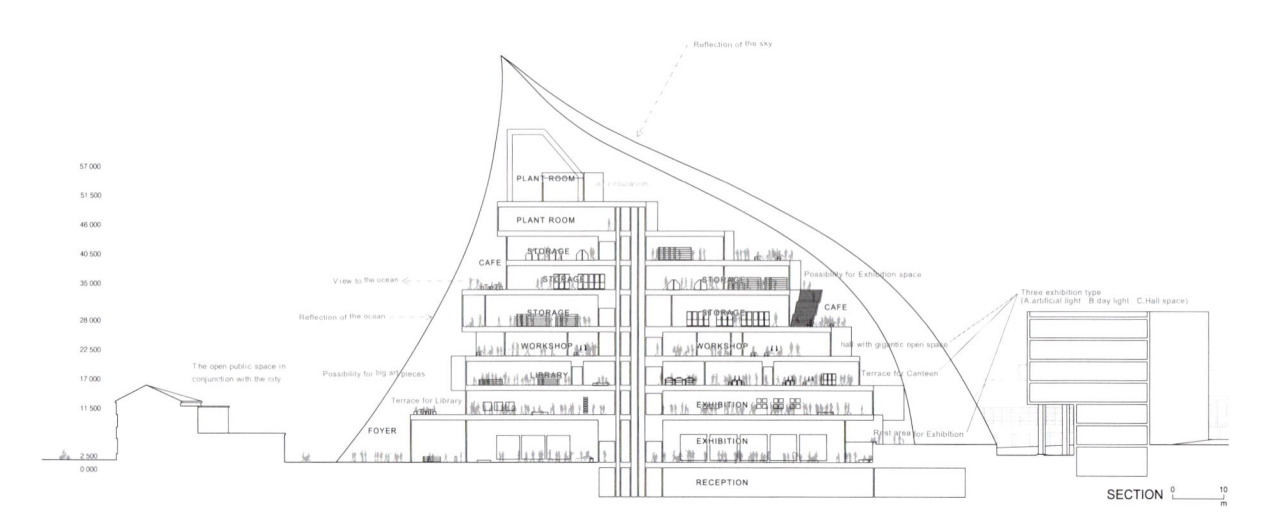

SECTION

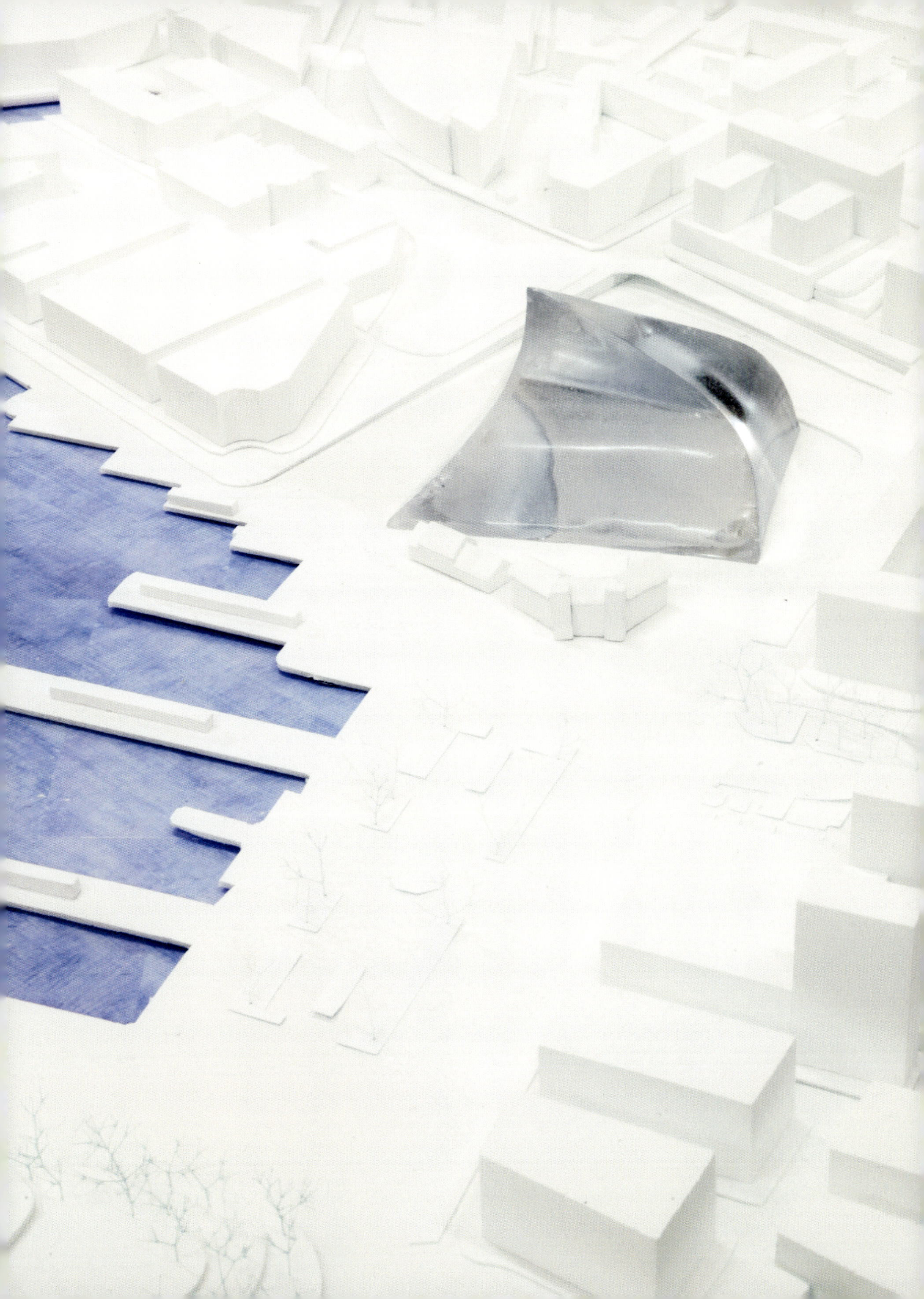

House as water way
2009

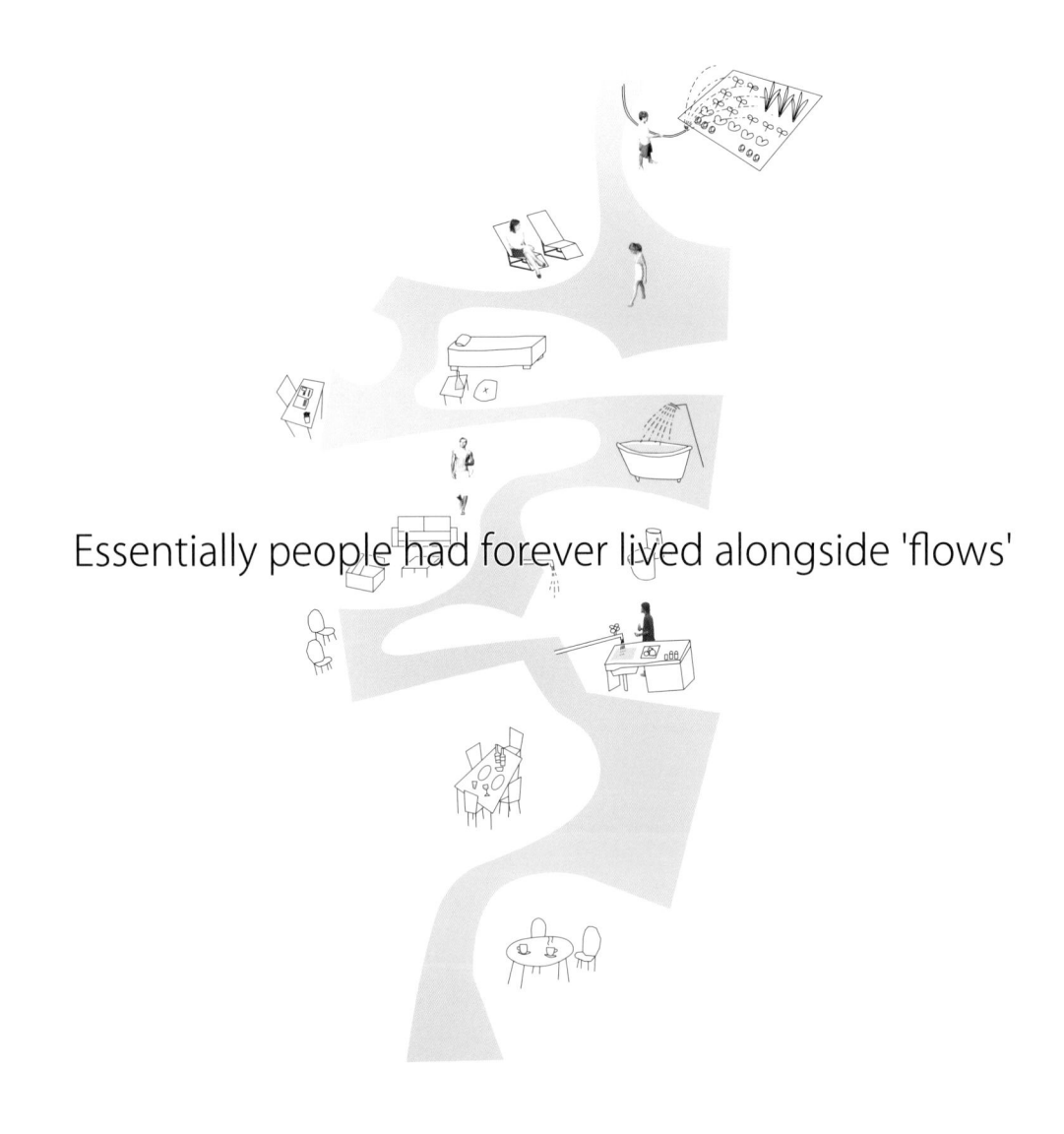

Essentially people had forever lived alongside 'flows'

This house is based on the theme of the bathroom. I traced this concept back to its source and thought about what it means to live with water. Civilization was born next to a river and our lives are inseparable from water. However, since the modern era, water has been strictly controlled and concealed, causing it to disappear from our daily lives. Based on the hypothesis that it might be possible to once again live with water, I proposed a house with a small river running through it. At different points, the river would become a puddle or a fall, conveying a variety of aquatic expressions. By dividing the water into functions – water for drinking would be upstream, water for washing clothes and cooking midstream, and water for toilets and showers downstream – one could segregate its flow. The floor has an undulating shape to guide the flow of water, and these undulations would also create diverse places for living. Rather than trying to control water artificially, by entwining water, imbued with a richness rooted in uncertainty that is akin to nature itself, with daily life, one could definitely create a living space that would be both primitive and futuristic. Someday I would like for realize this idea.

浴室がテーマの住宅。そこで浴室から遡って、水とともに生きる生活とは？　という根源を問うことにした。文明は河の側に生まれ、僕たちの生活も水とともにある。その一方で、近代以降、水は厳密に管理され、隠蔽され、生活の場から姿を消してしまった。そこで僕たちは、未来においては、ふたたび水とともに生きる暮らしがあり得るのではないか、という仮説のもとに、家の中を小さな川が流れるような住宅を提案した。川はときに水たまりとなり、また滝となって、さまざまな水の表情をつくり出す。飲み水は上流で、洗濯や料理は中流で、そしてトイレやシャワーは下流で、という機能と水の流れの棲み分けが生まれる。床は水の流れを導くかのように起伏をもち、その起伏が生活のための多様な居場所をつくり出す。人工的にコントロールされた水ではなく、自然そのものであるような不確定性ゆえの豊かさをもった水と生活が絡み合うことで、原初的で未来的な生活空間が生まれるに違いない。いつか実現したいアイデアである。

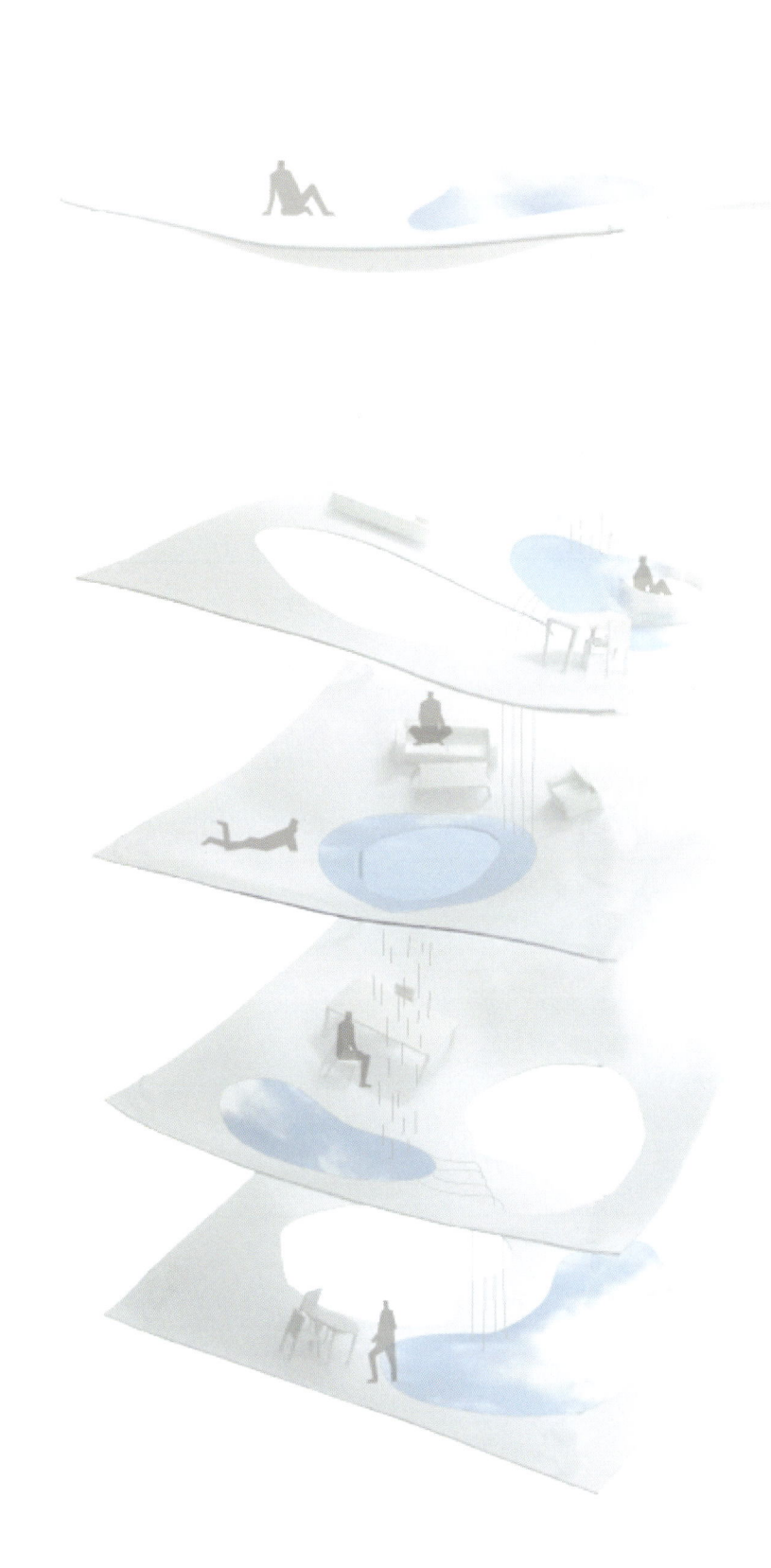

035 | House as water way | House as water way | 2009 | → Related Projects 023 074 080 090

House H

TOKYO, JAPAN 2009

What lies beyond the beyond / New dimension of stairs

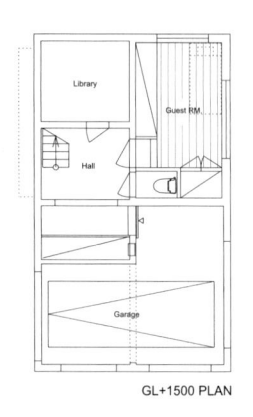

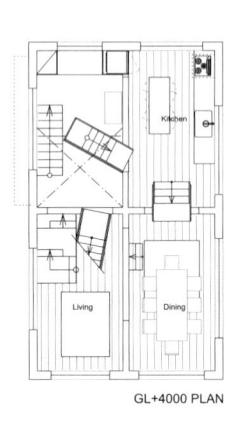

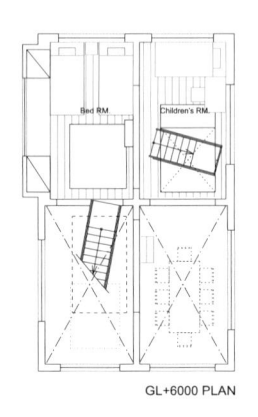

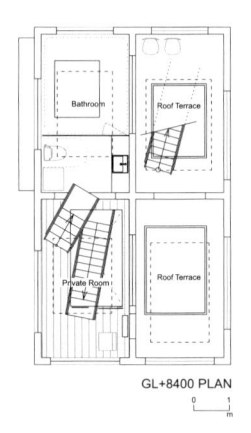

A residential project for a family of three. Coincidentally commencing at the same time as House NA, it was the first residential commission of three storeys or more. When simply stacking the rooms requested by the client, I found the three-storey volume became awfully segmented internally into small compartments. Considering the daughter was still very young, it felt out of line to let her and the family to live in space(s) either far or separate from each other. So I decided to open large apertures in the faces of the stacked rooms. The segmented compartments, while maintaining the outline of each room, became a single three-storey interconnected room. Being a single "room" yet with infinite corners/recesses allowing spaces to be connected and separated at the same time, in a sense it inherited the spatial conceptions from the T house and House O projects in a three-dimensional modulation of space. Moreover, numerous staircases suspended throughout the space render form to the network of circulation and movements within. Looking at House NA's slab-oriented scheme, it is also intriguing for me to note that the two collateral projects applying a synonymous concept unfold in very distinct physical forms.

3人家族のための住宅。ほぼ同時に設計がスタートした「House NA」と並んで、初めて3層以上に積層する住宅の依頼であった。ご要望の部屋を積み重ねていくと、3層でしかもかなり細かく分節されてしまうことがわかった。娘さんがまだ小さかったことを考えても、家の中に別々の場所がたくさんできて家族が離ればなれになってしまうのは寂しい気がした。そこで積み上げた部屋のすべての壁と床に大きな開口を開けていって、無数の部屋でありながらすべてが繋がりあった3層吹き抜けのワンルーム、とでも言えるような空間が生まれた。ひとつの空間でありながら無数の隅っこがあり、繋がりながら離れている、という意味で、それ以前の「T house」や「House O」で試みたことの3次元的な展開となった。またここでは階段を無数に配置することで、3次元的に広がりのある空間の中を縦横無尽に移動するかのようなネットワーク的な動線をつくり出している。「House NA」のスラブ的な展開に対して、同じコンセプトでありながら壁と開口という異なる方法で展開しているのも面白い。

036

House H

TOKYO, JAPAN
2009

Related Projects
004 027 055 078 085

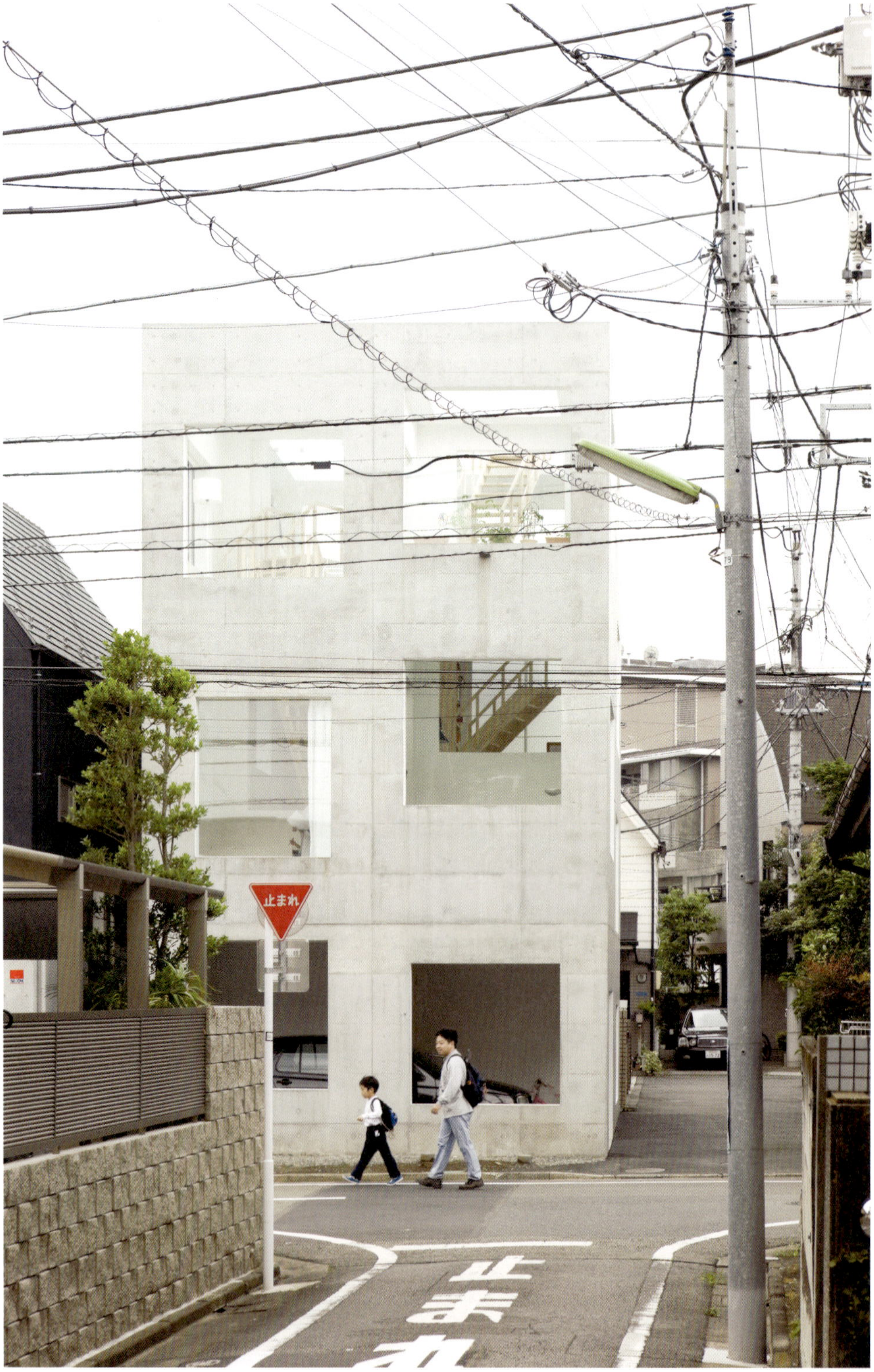
止まれ
止まれ

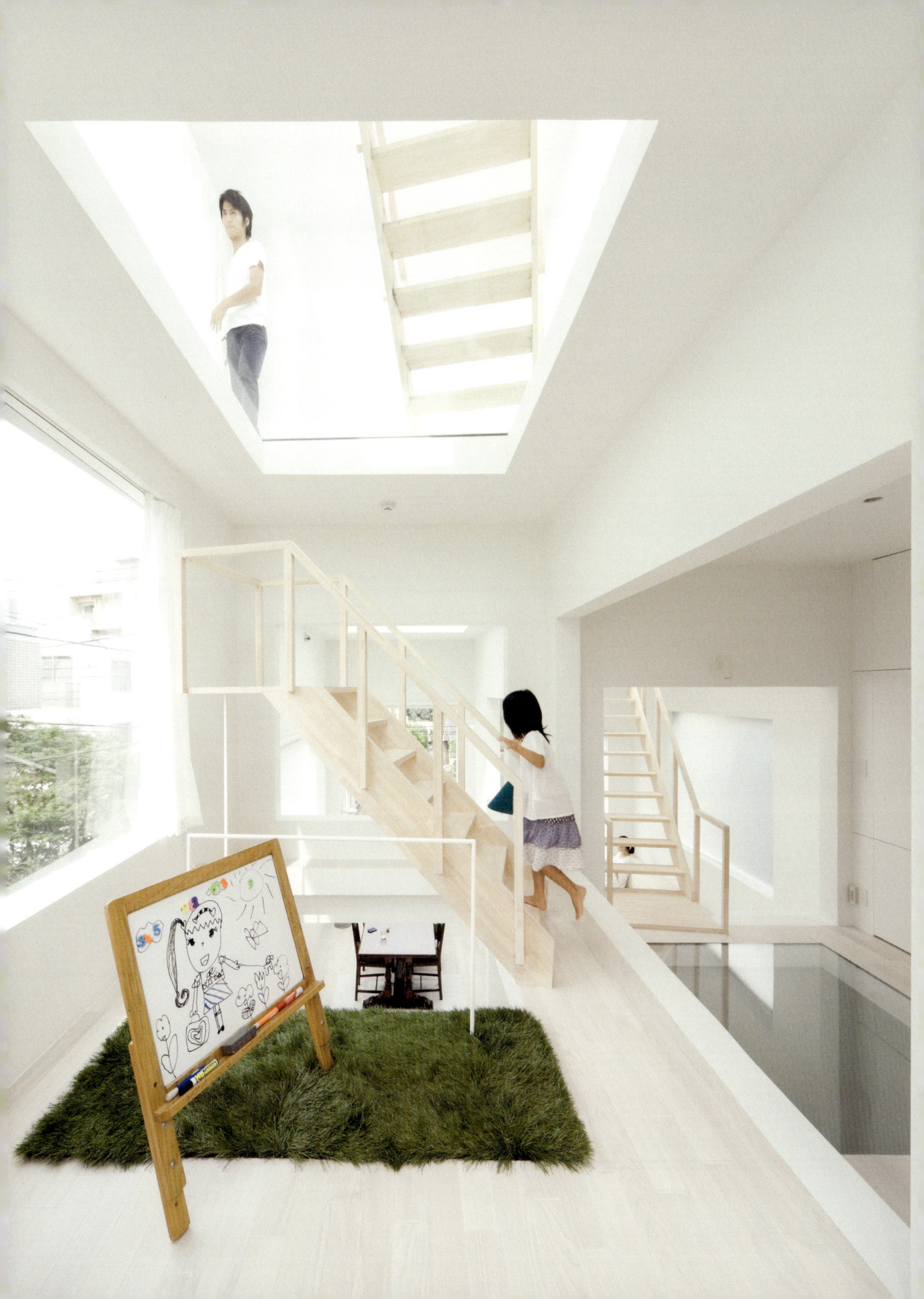

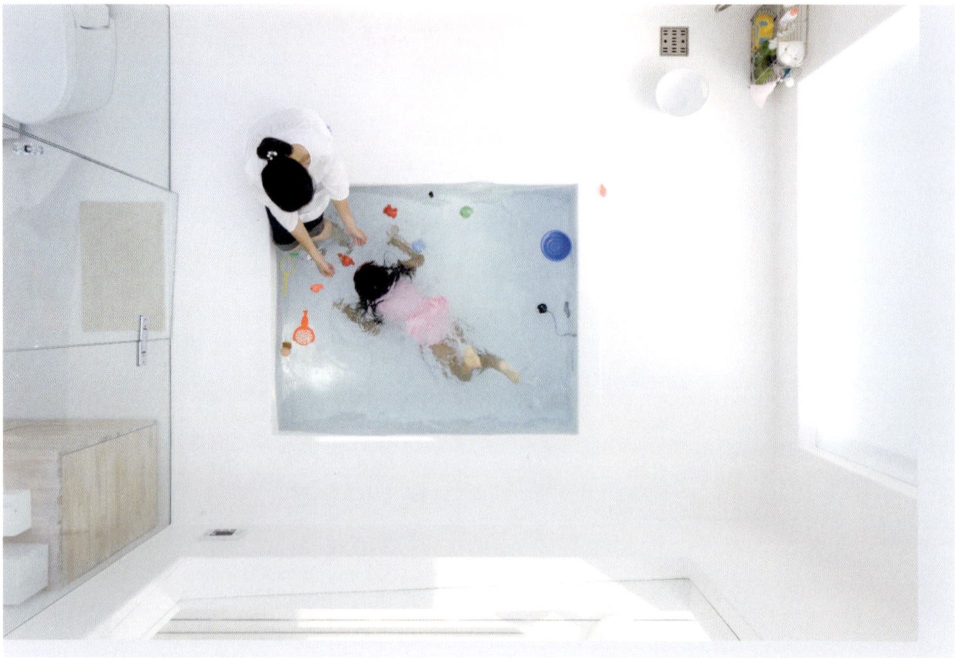

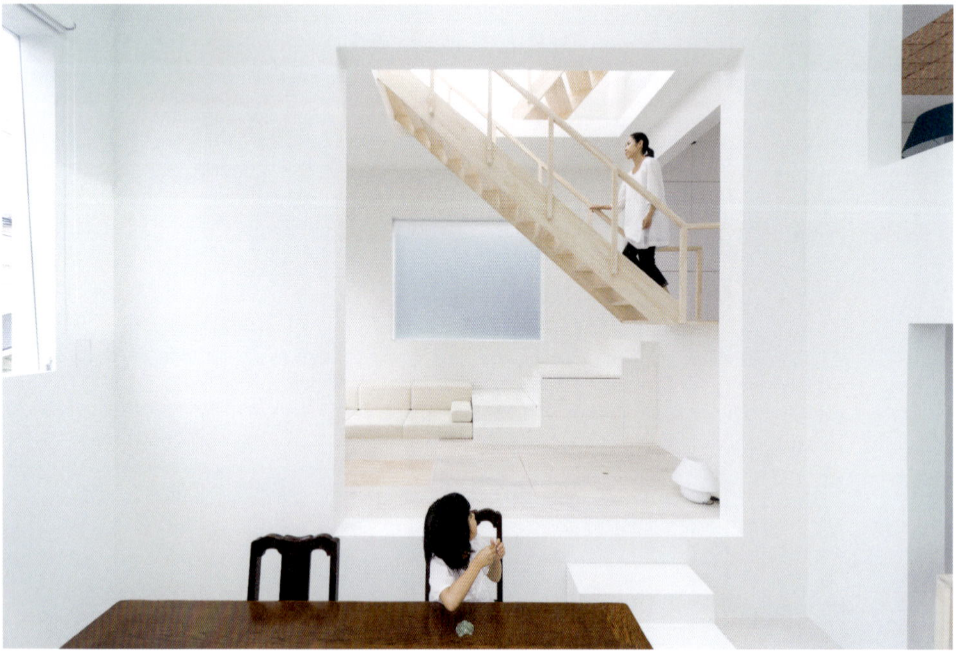

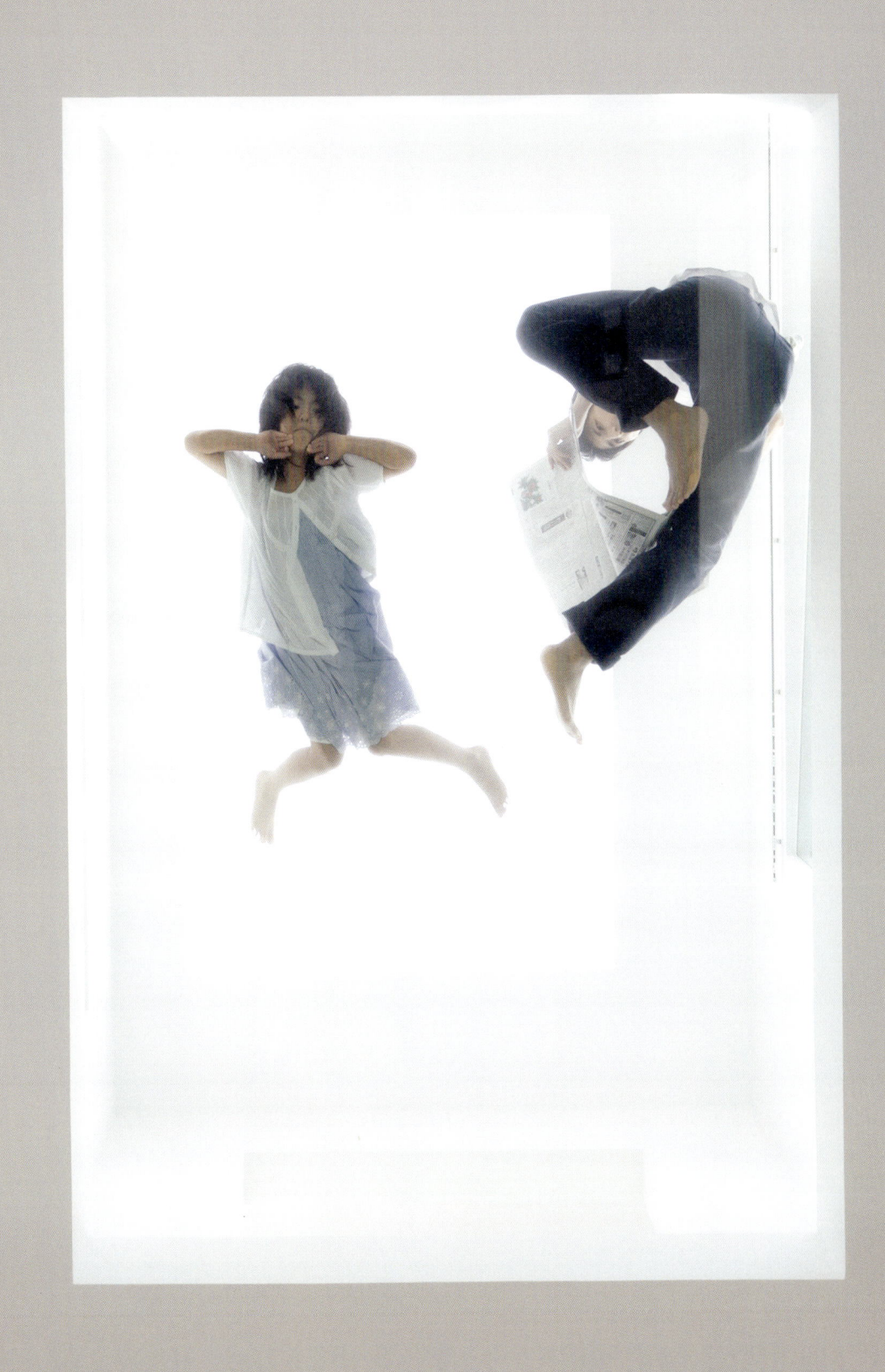

Art Museum in China

CHINA 2009

Is architecture a cave with exterior?

Is architecture a cave with exteriors? A cave is in essence a singular space, yet connects to and subsumes countless individual places, all uniquely diverse. If manifested as a spatial entity, it would be a complex agglomeration of diverse entities unified as a single whole. This co-existence of singularity and multiplicity, simplicity and complexity infers conditions for contemporary public spaces and urban spaces. The masterplan was made by the Chinese architects MAD and was designed as a project in which architects of the same generation from all over the world were invited to take part. BIG, JDS, MASS Studies, and Michel Rojkind all contributed spectacular designs, but unfortunately the project reached an impasse.

建築とは外観をもった洞窟なのだろうか？ 洞窟はひと繋がりの空間でありながら無数の異なる場所を内包する。その洞窟が外観をもつとき、それはまたひとつの存在でありながら無数の枝が複雑に絡み合った無数の存在の集合のようでもある。この単一性と複数性の両立する在り方、単純さと複雑さの同居する存在は、現代における公共空間や都市空間の在り方を示唆しているに違いない。マスタープランを中国の MAD が行い、世界各国から同世代の建築家が招待されたプロジェクトのひとつとして計画したものである。BIG や JDS、MASS studies やミシェル・ロイキンドなどが参加する華やかな計画だったが、残念ながら頓挫してしまった。

037

Art Museum in China

Art Museum in China

CHINA
2009

→ Related Projects
014 020 056 088 095 107

122 | 123

Another Island

KAGAWA, JAPAN 2009

Perhaps the most fundamental form of architecture is, to design the site itself

An island about 40 meters in diameter that is made of many FRP(fiberglass reinforced plastic) ships that are no longer in use.

Installation projects continually provide us with opportunities that allow us to rethink the threshold between architecture and art. Even if the object is intended for exhibition outdoors and devoid of specific architectural functions, it is pertinent for me to capture the installation from an architectural point of view for the reason that it allows me to question and to ponder the underlying principles of architecture. For this project, rather than selecting an island for the installation site from the diverse range of islands that occupy the Setouchi Inland Sea, I questioned whether it may be possible to make an island itself––analogous to creating the premise of the site itself. As opposed to conventional architectural planning in which the site is a prefixed condition and equal to the code of the project itself, I inquired into what it means to conceive the site itself. Simultaneously, I envisaged this new island as concocting a dialogue with the sublime Setouchi island scenery, bearing the potentiality for something much bigger. Furthermore, this is a mobile island. With the prospect that this island would engender a new addition to the network of the islands, I sought to introduce a new perspective to the scenery of Setouchi.

インスタレーションのプロジェクトはいつも、建築とアートの境界を考えるきっかけを与えてくれる。屋外に設置されるものだとしても、特定の機能をもたないインスタレーションを建築的な視点で捉えることは、自分が何をもって建築の大本と考えるかという大きな問いである。このプロジェクトでは、無数の島々が点在する瀬戸内の地で、どこかの島を選んでそこに建てるのではなく、そもそも敷地の前提となる＜島そのもの＞をつくることができないだろうか、と考えた。普段の建築の設計では敷地を与えられて建築を構想するのに対して、その地面そのもの、敷地そのものを構想すること。同時に、ひとつの島をつくり出すことによって、無数の島々が織りなす瀬戸内の風景全体を視野に入れた広大な提案ともなり得るかもしれない。さらにこの島は移動する島である。島々を繋ぐネットワークを生み出すという意味で、瀬戸内の風景に新しい視点を生み出すことができればと考えた。実現はしなかったが、その根源性ゆえに自分にとってとても重要なプロジェクトである。

038 | Another Island | もう一つの島 | KAGAWA, JAPAN 2009 | Related Projects 010 018 053 105

1000m² House - ORDOS 100

ORDOS, CHINA 2009

Ruins are not the end of architecture, but its origin

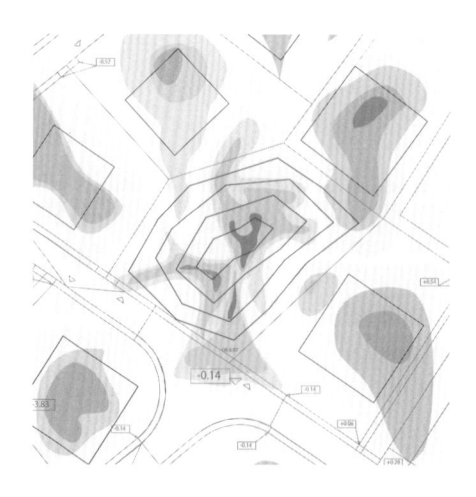

This fantastic project called for 100 architects from all over the world to design houses in the middle of the desert in Inner Mongolia. Perhaps because the desert site was essentially devoid of material context, I designed a living environment as a nested territory, which is gently protected from the surroundings. Like a ruin that has existed there since ancient times, the bricks walls, containing openings, create a landscape that predates the distinction between house, garden, and the city, and here and there in the layered walls, you find a living room or interior space. These ruins mark the beginning of something new.

内モンゴルの砂漠に、世界各地から集まった100人の建築家が住宅を設計するという奇想天外なプロジェクト。コンテクストがまったくないと言っていい砂漠の敷地ゆえに、家というよりも、周囲から緩やかに守られていく領域の入れ子として住環境を設計した。開口が開いたレンガ造の壁は、まるで昔からそこに存在した廃墟のように、家と庭と街とが分かれる以前のランドスケープをつくり出し、その壁の重なりのそこかしこに、内部空間としての居室が発見されていった。はじまりとしての廃墟。

1000m² House -ORDOS 100

1000m² House -ORDOS 100

ORDOS, CHINA
2009

→ Related Projects
001 021 027 044 106

Gunma Agricultural Technology Center

GUNMA, JAPAN 2009

The field ridge paths may become the architecture itself
Designing the entire order of the site

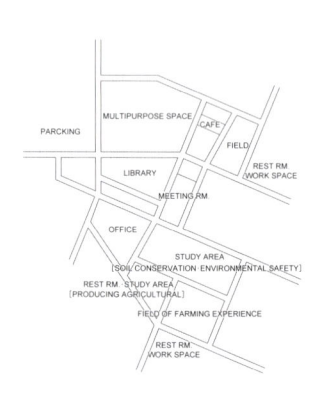

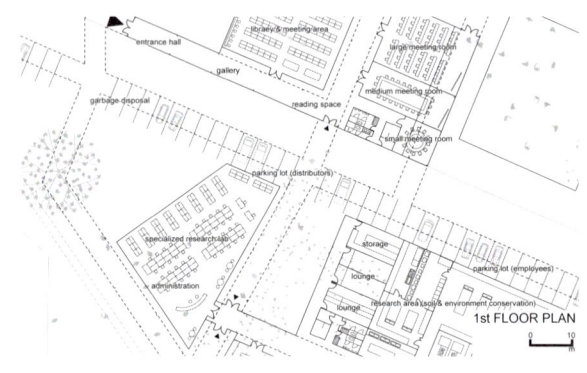

When planning an Agricultural Technology centre on an open field site, it instinctively seems the project must incorporate the surrounding agricultural land beyond the border of the building itself. Under this premise, I sought to build an eave-like roof that traces and drapes over the field ridge pathways that branch out across the fields, and naturally ties together the building, fields, courtyards and vehicular loading areas all under one roof. The lineage of a network-like roof, which began from the *Kumamoto Station Plaza* and *House as Cloud*, has, over the course of time and continued dialogues, evolved into a proposition both architectural and landscape-like that subsumes and loosely connects diverse spaces together. From around this time, it feels as though there has been an increase in projects where we see the surroundings' context or situations gradually metamorphosing into architecture. Perhaps being exposed to diversely variegated contexts through international competition allowed us to open up and engage in a deeper dialogue with the context. It is almost like the subconscious stream of architectural thoughts is enlivened through new encounters with various site conditions, climates, and cultures.

畑が広がる敷地に農業技術センターを計画する。その活動は建築そのものだけではなく、周囲の耕作地をも含み込んだものになるはずだ。そうだとすれば、周囲に広がるあぜ道のネットワークをそのまま庇状の屋根として建ち上げて、建築も農地も搬入エリアもコートヤードもその屋根の連なりの中に自然と融合されるような建築の在り方がふさわしいのではないか、と考えた。「House as Cloud」や「熊本駅前広場」から始まる屋根のネットワークの系譜は、さまざまな場所を取り込みつつ緩やかに繋がる建築／ランドスケープの提案だ。この頃から、周囲の敷地や状況が徐々にメタモルフォーズしながら建築になっていくような提案が増えてきている気がする。海外のコンペを行うようになって、建築自体の形式性だけではなく、より周囲のコンテクストとのコミュニケーションを楽しむようになったからかもしれない。建築的思考の根底を流れる思考が、さまざまな敷地や気候、文化的な背景に出合ってさまざまに開花する。

040

Gunma Agricultural Technology Center

群馬県農業技術センター

GUNMA, JAPAN
2009

→ Related Projects
001 024 046 061 089 105

Taipei Pop Music Center
TAIPEI, TAIWAN 2009

Could the flow of people itself be architecture?

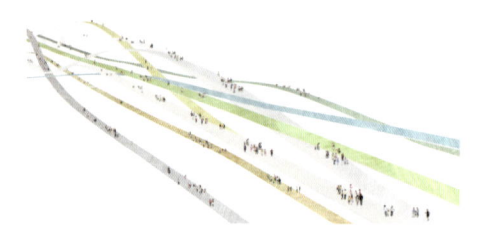

This competition site occupied a remarkably grand and elongated outline. Thus in the end, the proposal became one that spanned beyond a mere proposal for a building, one that proposed imparting form to the urban flow of people–simultaneously infrastructural and part of a greater landscape. As far as competence as a competition brief goes, I dare say that the proposal even came close to winning, but in any case the scheme is a memorable one personally, as this unusually bold architectural proposal constituting infinite entwined paths inspired by the immensity of the scale proved to be a seed that eventually led to the winning proposals for the *Beton Hala Waterfront Center* and the *Taiwan Tower*. Upon reflection, this concept of many paths collectively crafting the loci may have inherited genes from the *Kumamoto Station Plaza*. In a way, perhaps what constitutes a city in my understanding is, as this proposal indicates, the various modulations of flow–and its degrees of interaction inherent in the infinite paths.

このコンペの敷地はとても長大であった。それゆえ、最終的には建築というよりも都市的な人の流れにそのまま形を与えたインフラ的でしかもランドスケープ的な提案となった。コンペの応募案としてはまったくもって良い出来ではなかったが、この都市的なスケールに触発されて、無数の路が絡み合う不思議な建築が生まれてきて、それが数年後に「Beton Hala Waterfront Center」や、「台湾タワー」へと繋がっていくのだと思うと、不思議な感じがする。路が集まって場が生まれる、というこのコンセプトは、遡ると「熊本駅前広場」のコンペ案から遺伝子を受け継いでいるかもしれない。僕の都市の理解は、ある部分でこの案が示している無数のパスが繋がり離れてつくり出す＜流れ＞そのもの、なのかもしれない。

041 | Taipei Pop Music Center

Taipei Pop Music Center
TAIPEI, TAIWAN
2009

→ Related Projects
024 040 052 058 060 063

Kogakuin University Hachioji campus

TOKYO, JAPAN 2009

A place where people flow through like a waterfall
Simultaneously being a place where people sit,
gather and spend their time

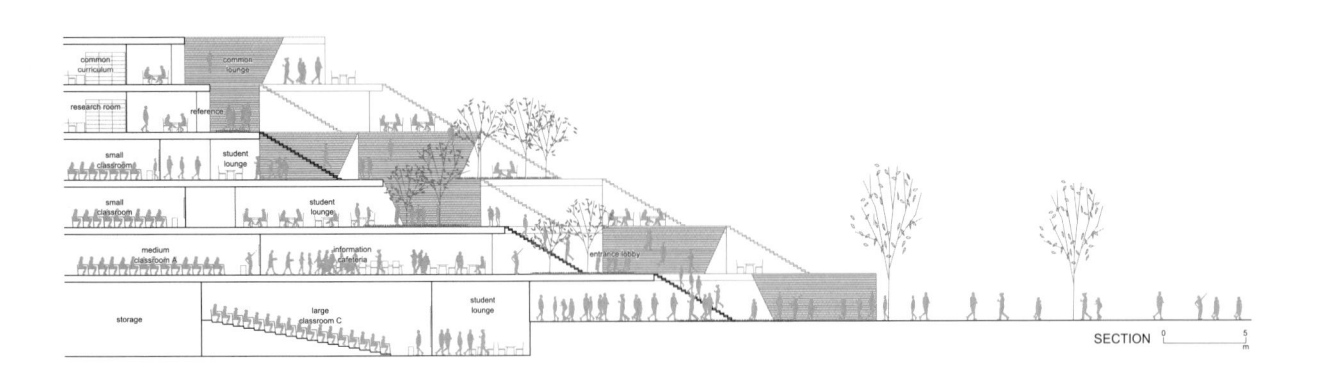

SECTION

Rather than a mere assembly of buildings, a university campus should be a place that embraces diverse activities of students and be a source of stimulus to prompt subsequent actions. In this project, I pictured students spilling out after class and populating the staircase like a waterfall. Architecture takes form as a stepped staircase-shaped plaza, where people can gather, loiter, and discover pockets of space for themselves, relating with one another in many different ways. At times the staircase acts as eaves, making the spaces below a hub where rich interactions occur. Several years after the Primitive Future House project, here we discover that the concept of defining spatial qualities through a series of steps with which the body interacts has evolved in the form of a grand staircase. Interactions with the steps are uniquely varied due to the degree of scales, yet the grand staircase extending over six storeys pronounces a place with an immense sense of solidarity and coexistence, a place charged with richness through evolution. Staircases are indeed captivating, and many possibilities exist: from a simple functional type to a staircase that traverses the notion of dimension and appears before us as a plane. This exploration of staircases is extended later in the *Taiwan Cafe* project, with a staircase exemplifying access as a network.

大学のキャンパスというのは、建築というよりも、学生たちのさまざまな活動を受け止め、刺激し、引き起こすための＜場＞のようなものではないだろうか？　ここでは、授業時間が終わると同時に大勢の学生たちが教室から溢れ出し、滝のようにこの階段に流れ出す様を想像した。建築がそのまま段々状の広場であり、そこかしこで人びとがとどまり、集まり、ひとりの時間を楽しみ、関係し合っている。階段はときに庇となり、その下にもまた豊かな場所が生まれる。初期の「Primitive Future House」以来の、段々が生み出すさまざまな場所性への追求が、とてもストレートな大階段となって現れた。個々の段の小ささゆえの個人的家具的なスケールと、6層にわたる巨大な階段のみがもつ巨大な一体感が同居する豊かな場所である。階段は面白い。単体の階段から面としての階段、そして後に出てくる「Taiwan Cafe」のようなネットワークとしての階段まで、さまざまな可能性が広がると思う。

042

Kogakuin University Hachioji campus
工学院大学八王子キャンパス

TOKYO, JAPAN
2009

→ Related Projects
007 055 058 078 105

Tokyo Apartment

TOKYO, JAPAN 2010

Stacked architecture becomes a city, three-dimensional paths become architecture

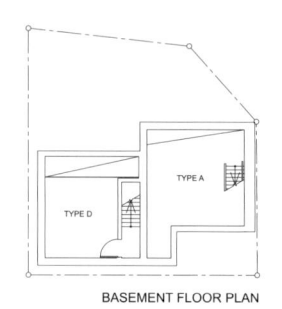

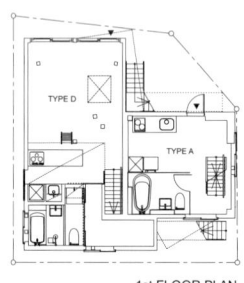

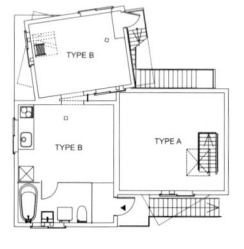

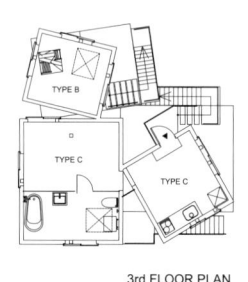

BASEMENT FLOOR PLAN

1st FLOOR PLAN

2nd FLOOR PLAN

3rd FLOOR PLAN

Tokyo is a city in which houses, small alleyways, streets, and the city are intricately connected in a mass, to create a complex yet pleasant living environment. In this project, rather than treating it as a single apartment building, I sought to create a place like an embodiment of Tokyo where architecture, the street, and the city are infused in close relativity to one another. Housing units are stacked and streets intertwined in multiple layers, appearing before us as an enigmatic mass describable neither as mixture of house and streets, nor as a small city converged together. If we were to manifest what lies dormant between architecture, street and the city, perhaps it would be something like this: strangely primordial yet eccentric in its appearance, fundamentally disseminating the essence of Tokyo, yet taking a form that has never existed in Tokyo. I cannot but herald the possibility of aspiring to something that is innately architecture, yet an architecture that has never before existed.

東京という街は、建築と路と都市が混ざり合って、ある複雑でありながら快適な人間のための生活環境をつくり出している。このプロジェクトでは、単体の建築として集合住宅をつくるのではなく、建築と路と都市が混ざり合ったような、東京そのもののような場所をつくることができないかと考えた。住居は即物的に積み上がり街路は立体化して絡みつき、小さな街とも家とも路の塊とも言えない不思議な存在が現れてきた。路と街と家の間に横たわる未知なる領域に形を与えると、例えばこんな姿をとるのではないだろうか？ それは根源的でありながら突飛であり、もっとも東京的でありながらかつて存在しなかった東京である。その方法の先に、もっとも建築的でありながら、かつて一度も存在しなかった建築の可能性を感じることはできないだろうか？

043 | Tokyo Apartment | TOKYO, JAPAN 2010 | → Related Projects 013 035 058 078 080 090

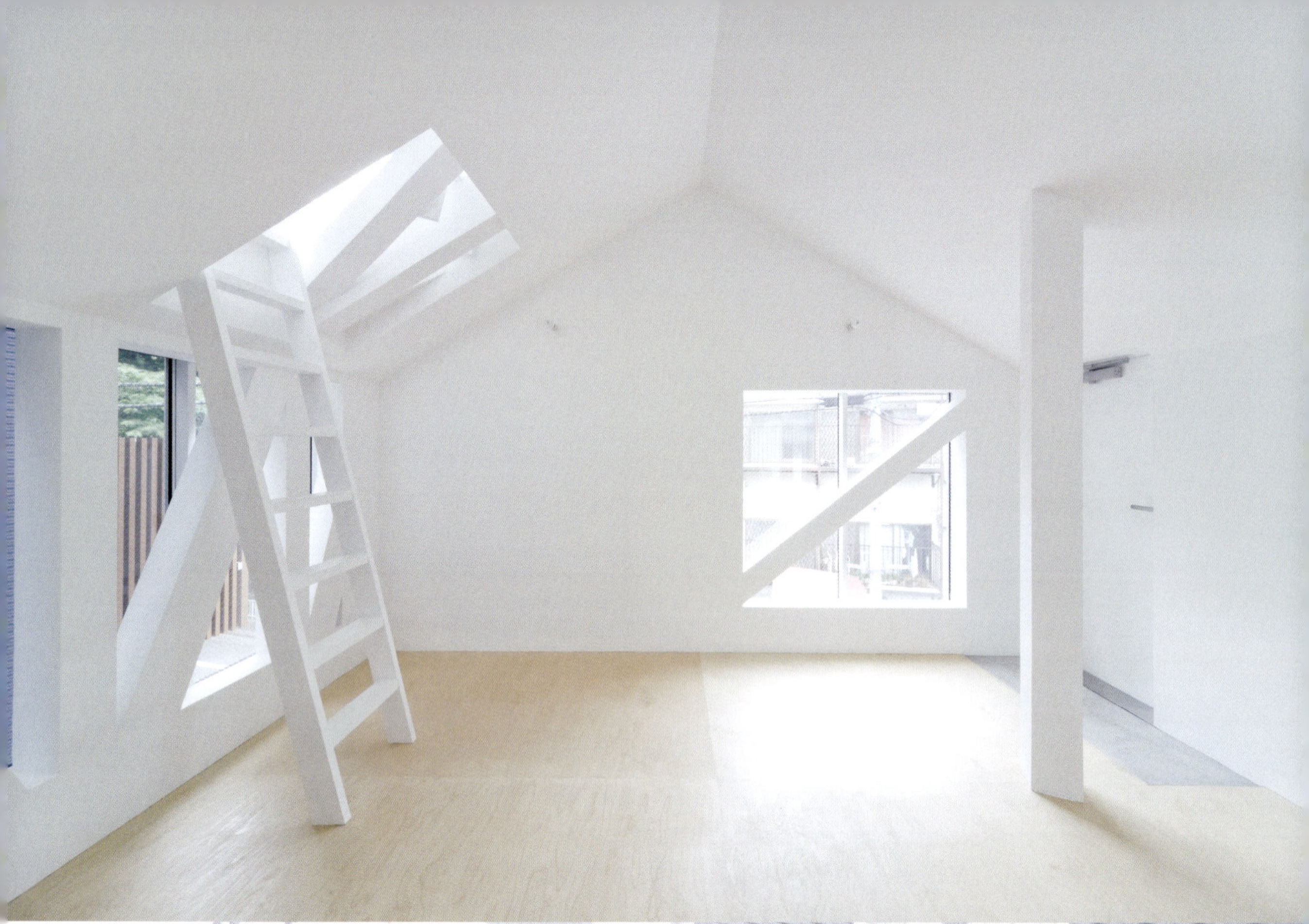

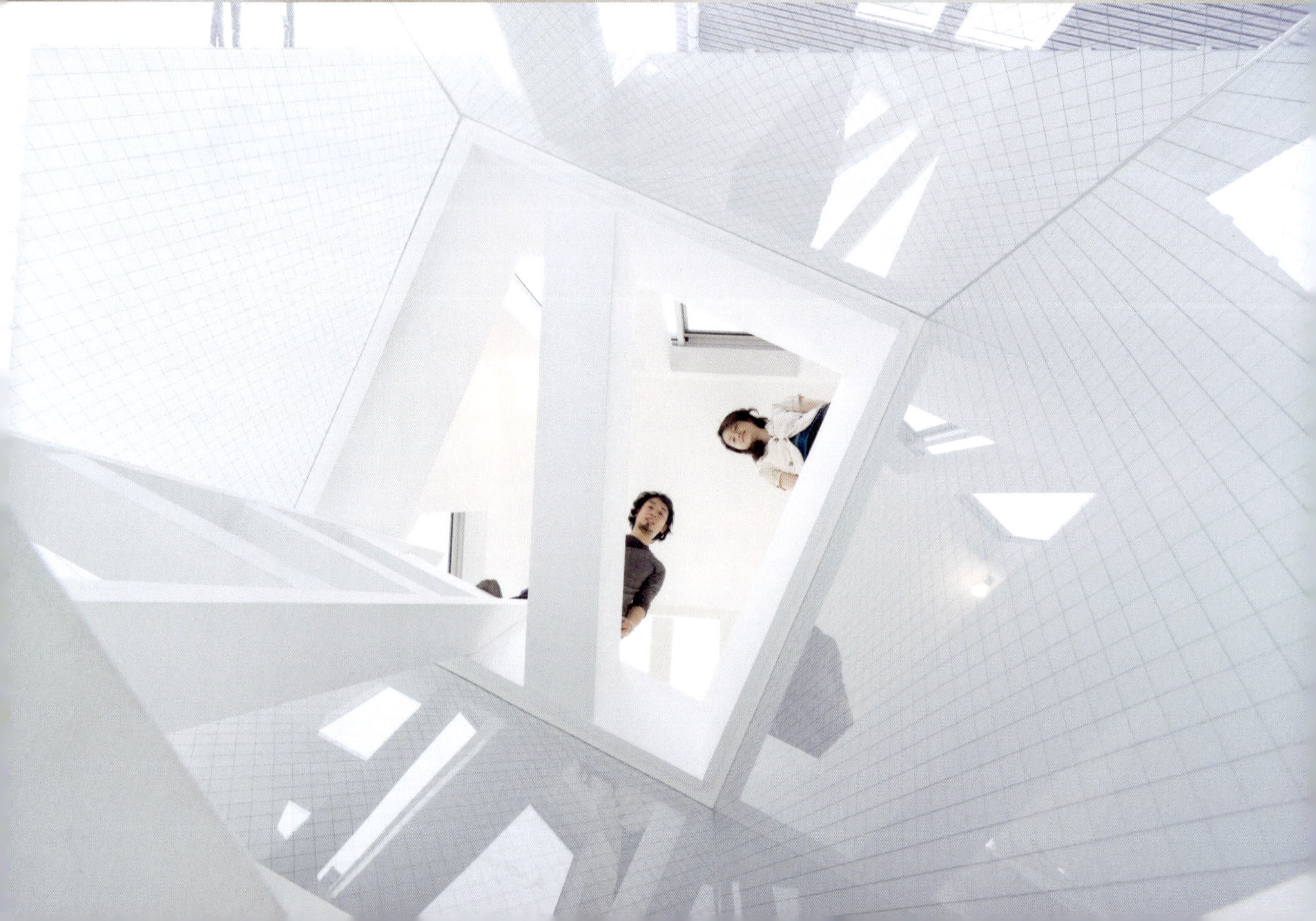

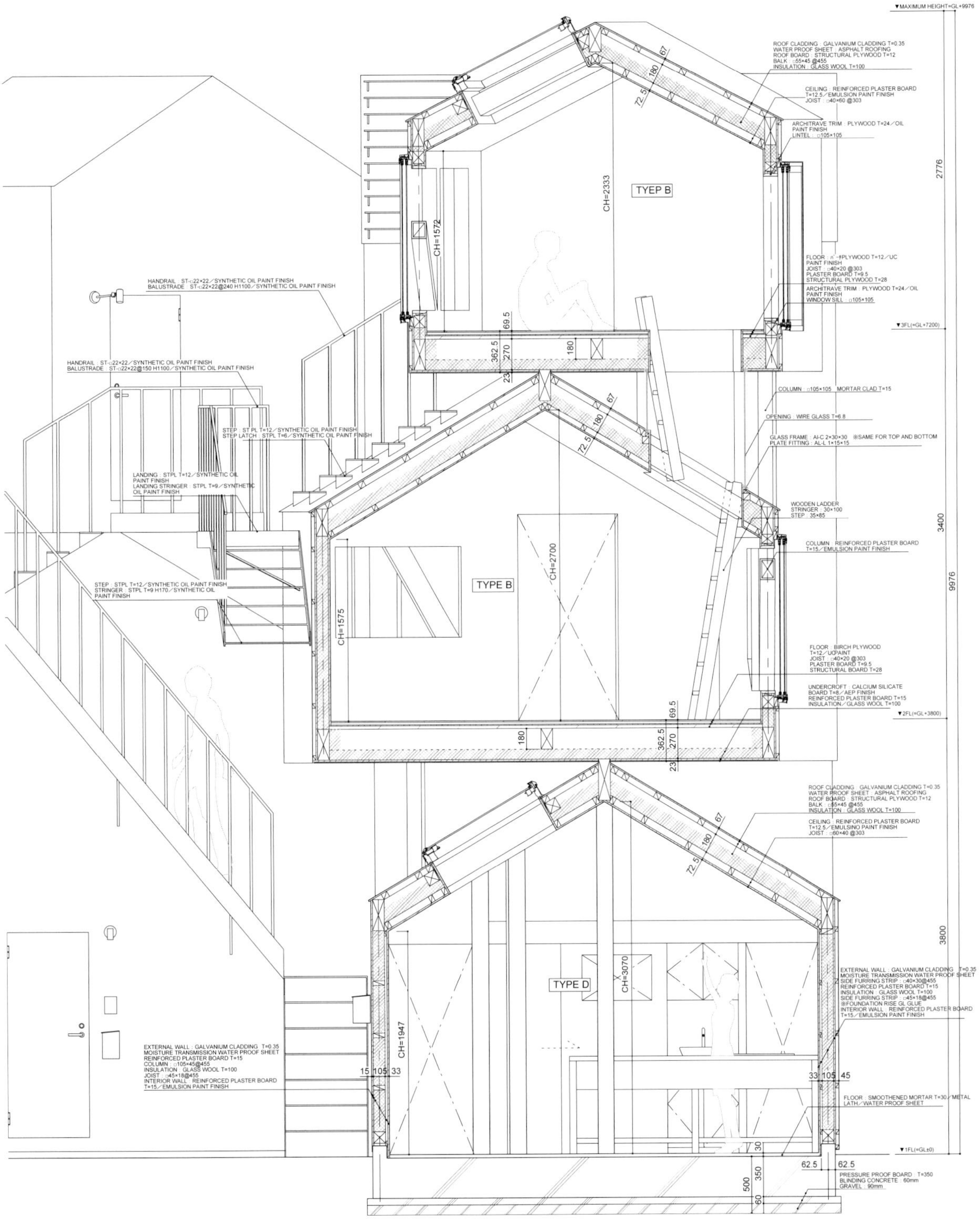

Musashino Art University Museum & Library
TOKYO, JAPAN 2010

Searchability / Strollability
A place like a forest inspiring one to meander endlessly

I think a library is a place akin to a forest. People drift through the space in both intentional and fortuitous wanderings, eventually discovering things beyond their comprehension. On the one hand, there is the notion of searchability, a systematic form allowing one to search and find the book intended, and on the other hand there is strollability, meandering through space following where one's senses lead, stimulated by thoughts and ideas that eventually lead one to unexpected discoveries. A library is a place where these two apparent contradictions are allowed to coexist. Searchability desires for systematic order, and strollability desires for a multifarious order like a forest. This is a contradistinction between nature and artificiality, order and chaos, triviality and immensity, simplicity and complexity. Considered in this light, a library is in itself an analogy of architecture, and perhaps of the constructed spatial world. Could this be what Borges implied in his literature?

図書館とは、森のような場所ではないだろうか？ 人はそこをさまよいながら、目的と無目的の間で、自分を超えた何かに出合う。目当ての本を見つけるという検索性に対して、何というわけでもなくさまよい歩く中で生まれてくるアイデアや未知の本との出合いへと繋がる散策性。この対極的なふたつの性格をあわせもつ場所が図書館である。検索性は整然とした秩序を求め、散策性は複雑な森のような秩序を求める。それは人工と自然の対比でもあり、秩序と乱雑さの、小さな場所と大きな場所の、そして単純さと複雑さの対比でもある。そう考えると、図書館とはそのまま建築の原型であり、そしておそらく、世界の原型でもあるだろう。それこそはボルヘスが示唆したことではなかっただろうか？

044

Musashino Art University Museum & Library

武蔵野美術大学美術館・図書館

TOKYO, JAPAN
2010

→ Related Projects
001 003 005 021 027 051

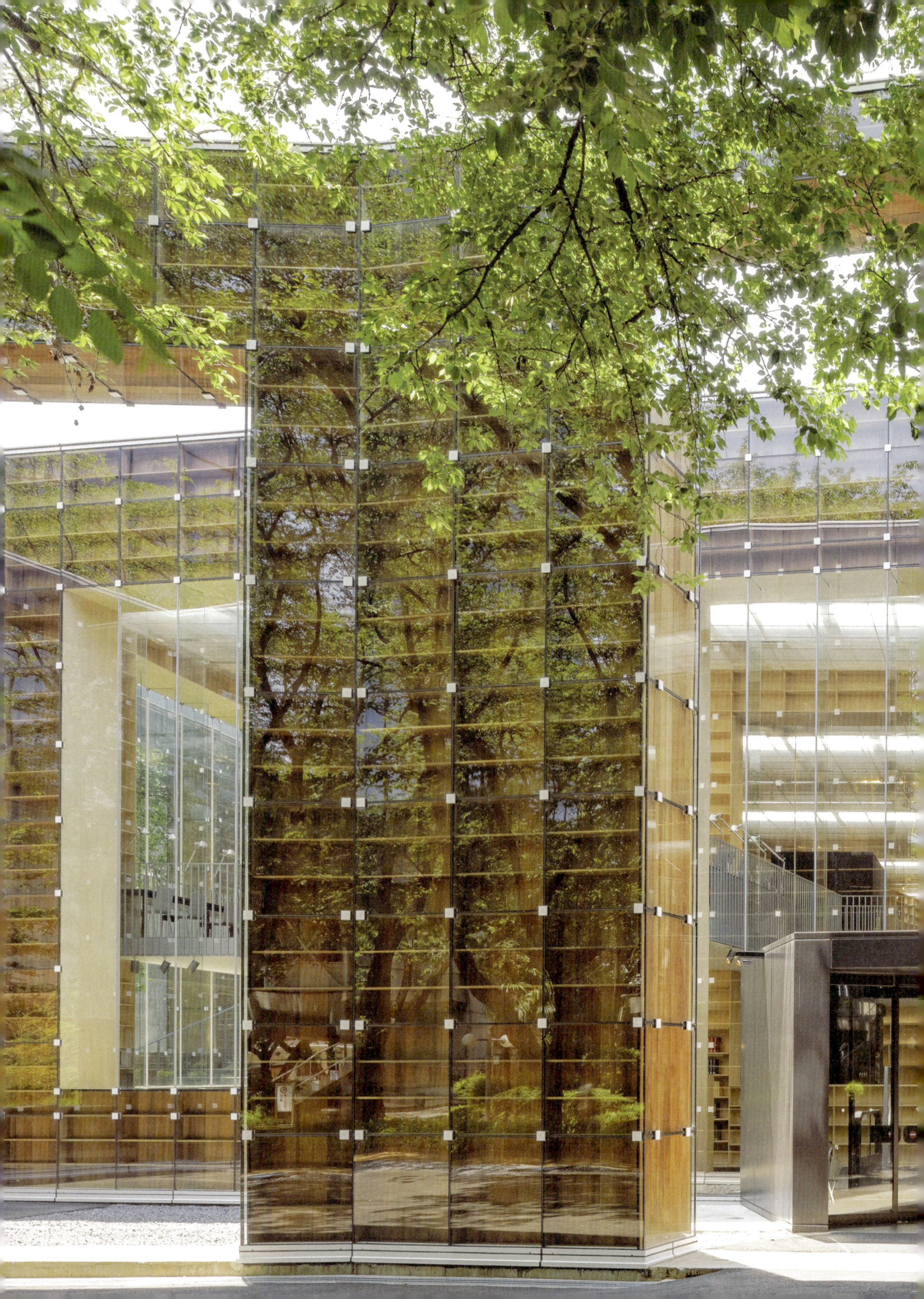

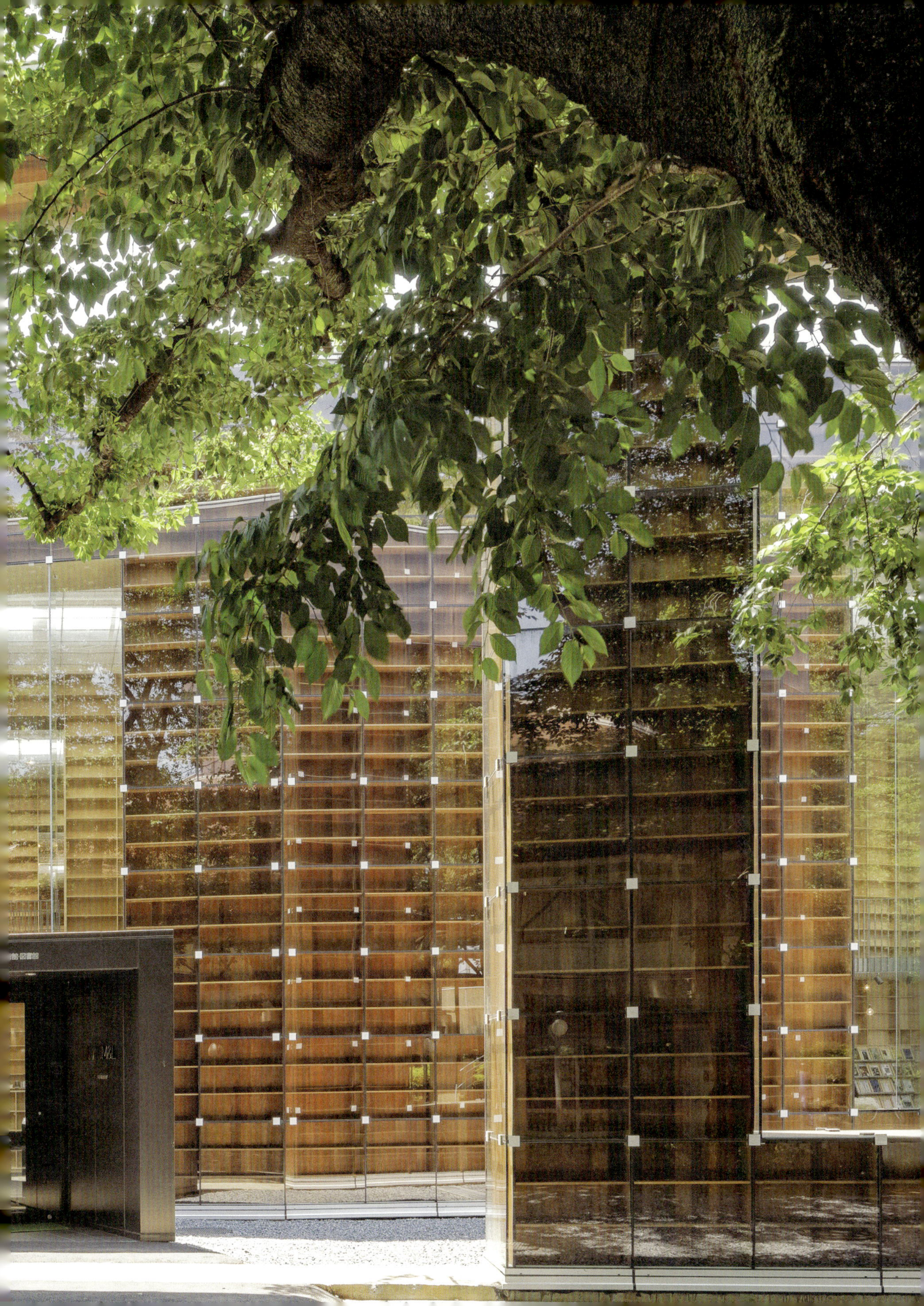

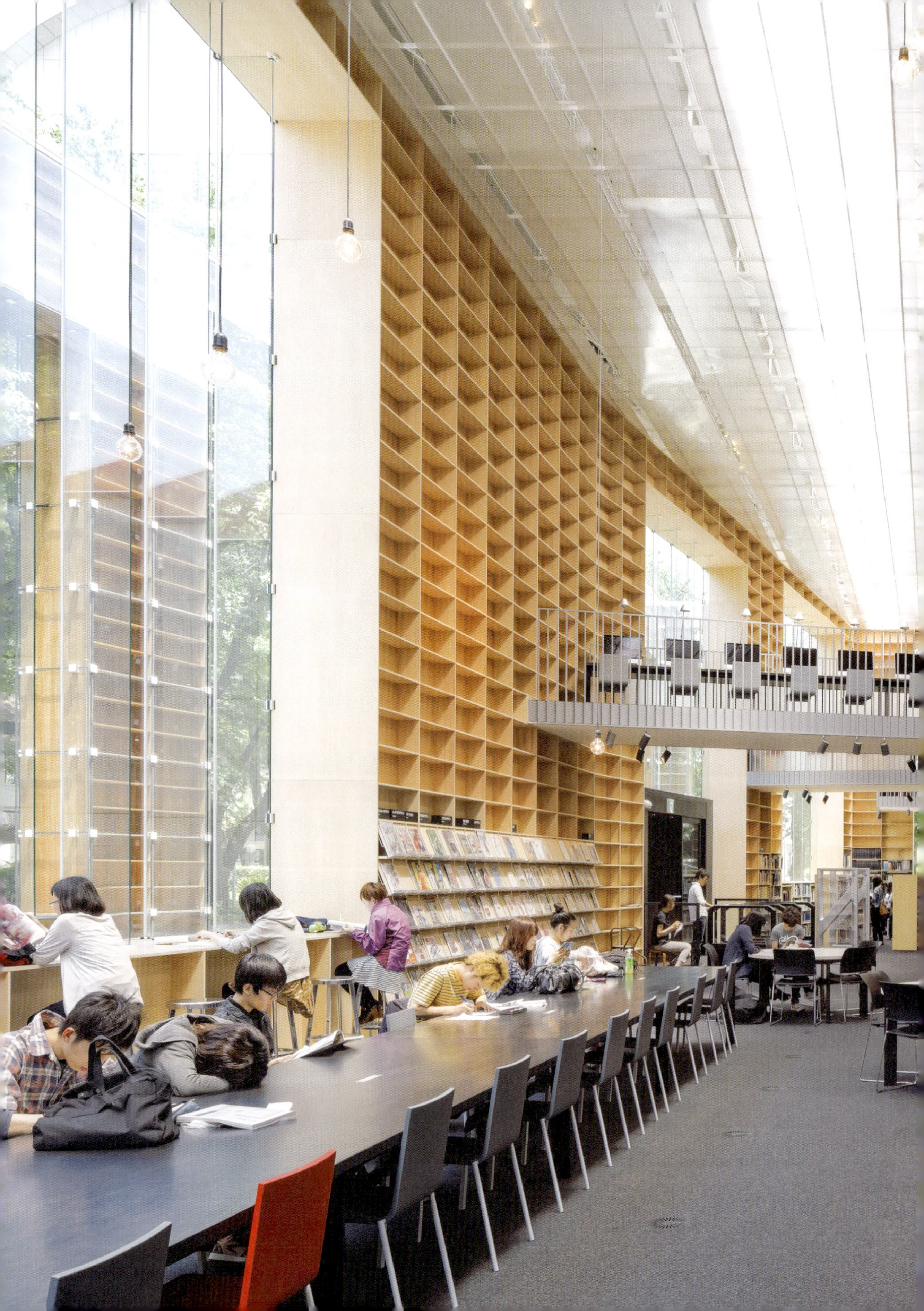

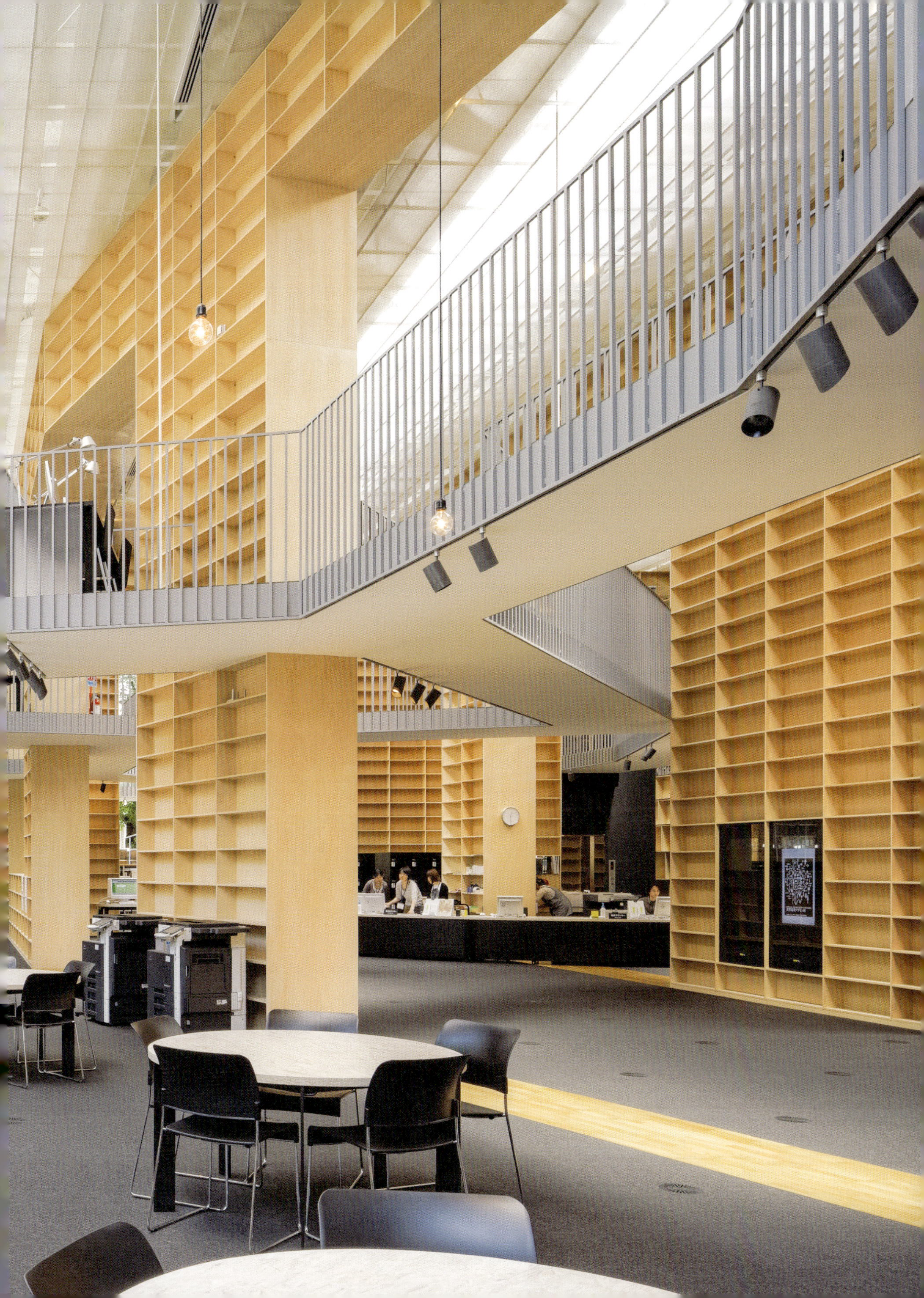

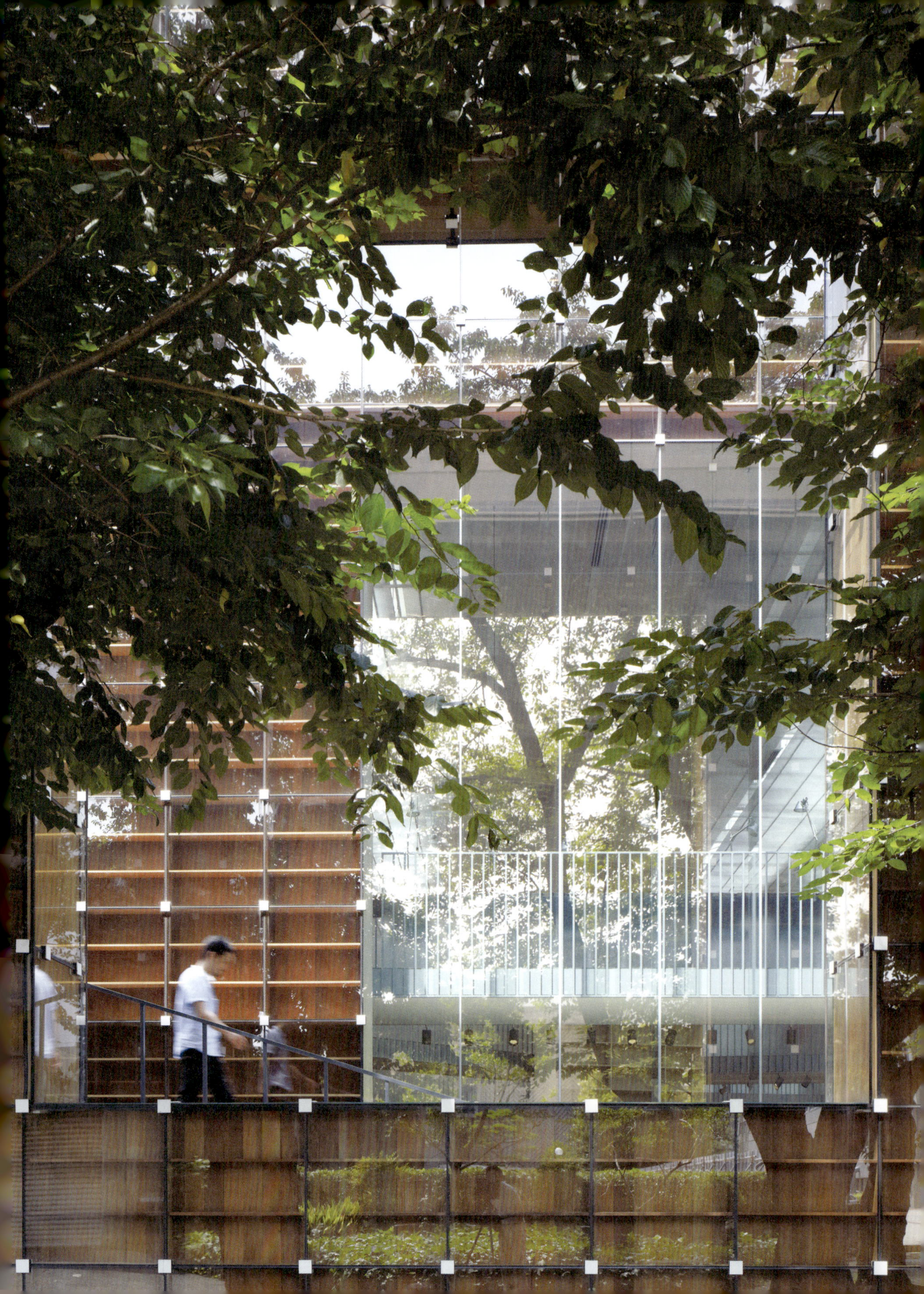

1st FLOOR PLAN

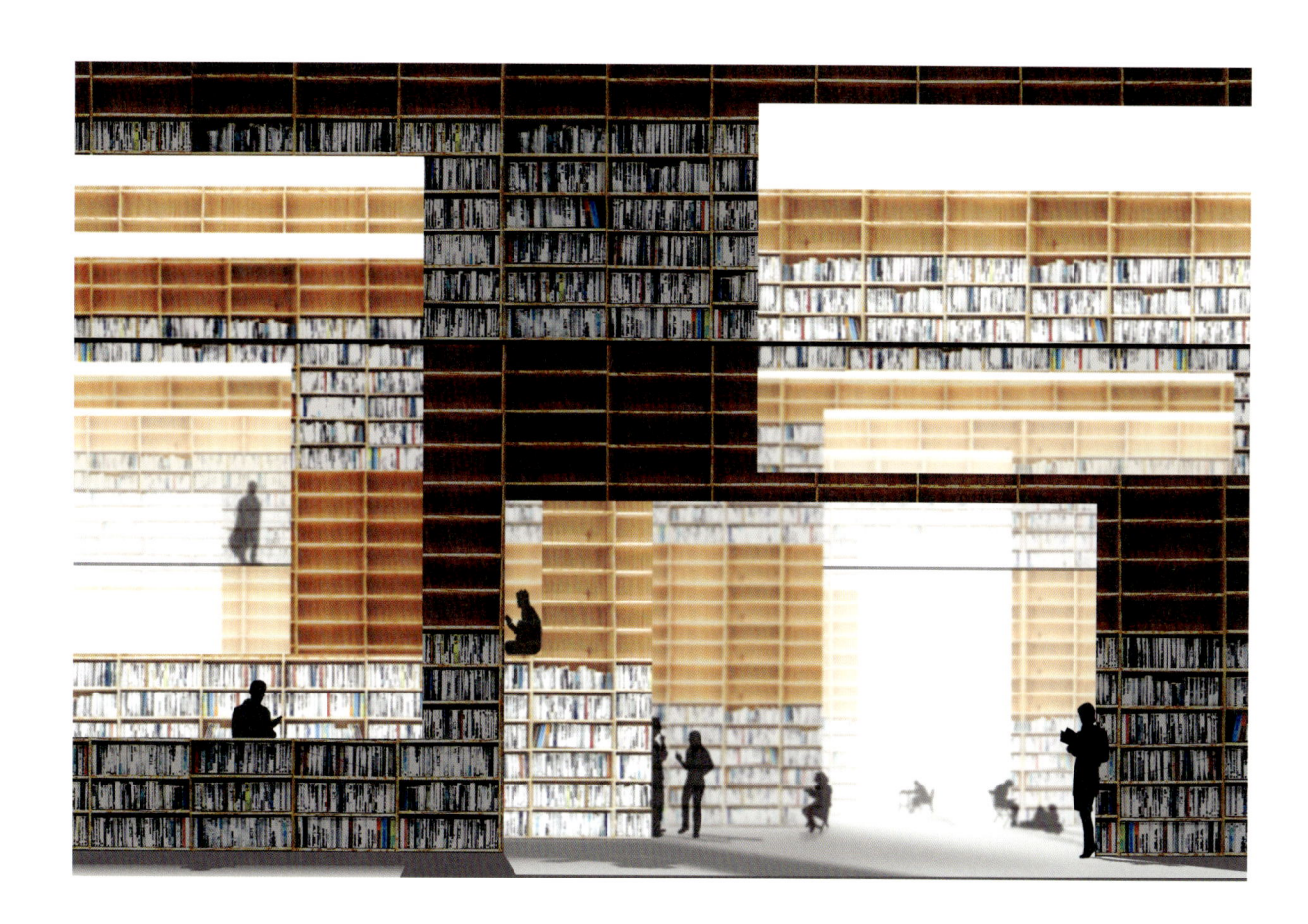

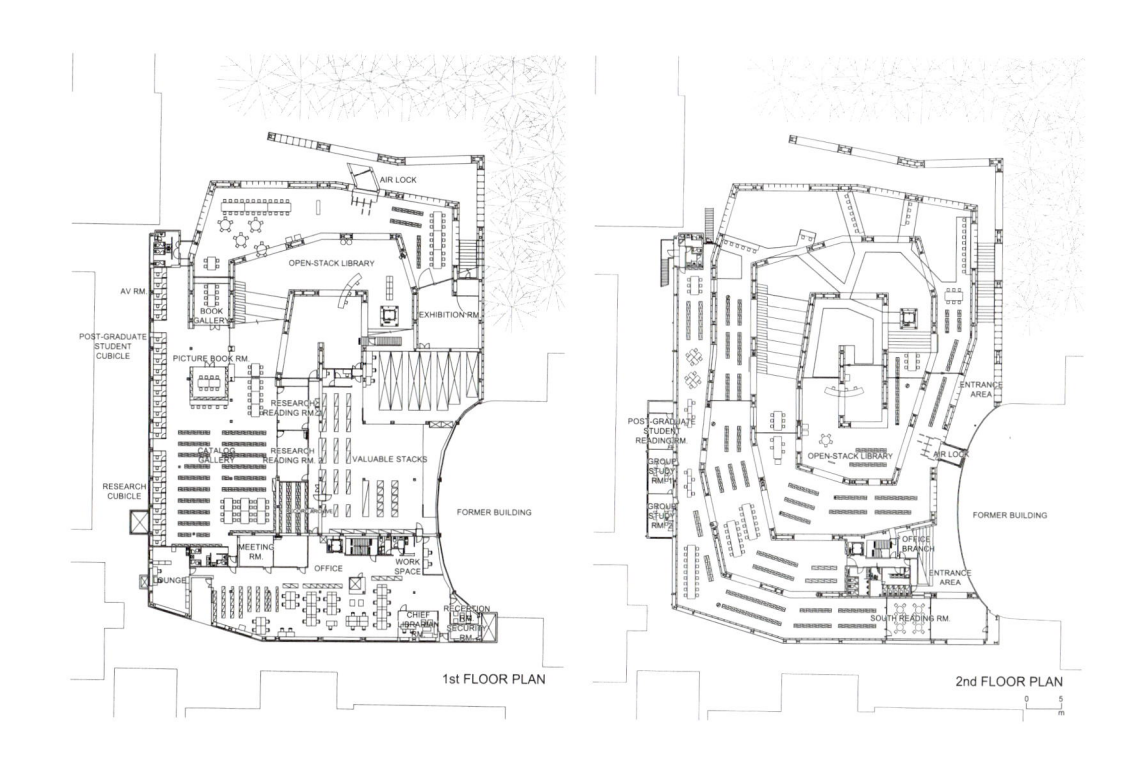

2nd FLOOR PLAN

House OM
KANAGAWA, JAPAN 2010

Interior sculpturing the exterior, and exterior sculpturing the interior

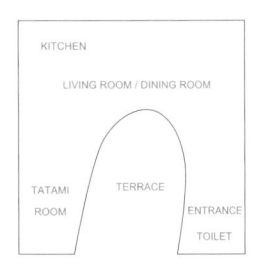

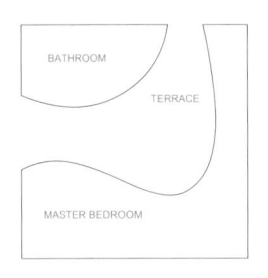

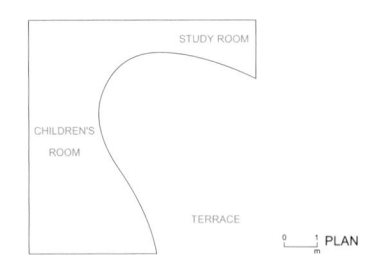

A house for a young couple: the project kicked off with a simple brief for "a house with a courtyard." Architecturally, I believe a courtyard is a very primordial place, in the sense that it is a space where indoor mixes with outdoor–not like a threshold, but a place where rich spatial exchanges occur. In this project, exterior courtyard and interior space shape one another equally–the house is made manifest through the interdependency of interior and exterior, neither being subordinate to the other. From any of the levels, one is able to access the three-dimensional courtyard stacked over three storeys, and gain access to the living quarters again on any level. Within such a configuration, interior and exterior are harmoniously interwoven. As developed in the *City as Architecture, Architecture as Mountain, Mountain as City* project, I believe this method or architectural modulation is one that has the potential to expand beyond residential scale and to be applied to something much bigger: apartment complexes, urban facilities, and so on. Also, this was my first realized project with curvilinear surfaces.

夫婦ふたりのための住宅。中庭のある家を、というご要望からプロジェクトがスタートした。中庭とは、内部と外部が交流する場所であるという意味において、建築的にとても根源的な場所だ。ここでは、中庭が室内をつくり、室内が中庭をつくる。内外の相互依存的な住宅である。内部と外部、どちらが主であるというのでもない、どちらもがどちらをも相互に規定し合っている。3層にわたって積層された立体的な中庭／住居のどの階からも中庭に出て、また別のフロアから住居内に入ることができる。こうして内部と外部が編み込まれたような建築がつくられる。「City as Architecture, Architecture as Mountain, Mountain as City」プロジェクトで展開したように、住宅スケールを超えて集合住宅や都市施設へと展開していく可能性を秘めた建築形式なのではないかと期待している。また初めて曲線を試みたプロジェクトでもあった。

045 | House OM | House OM | KANAGAWA, JAPAN 2010 | → Related Projects 022 025 033 073 095

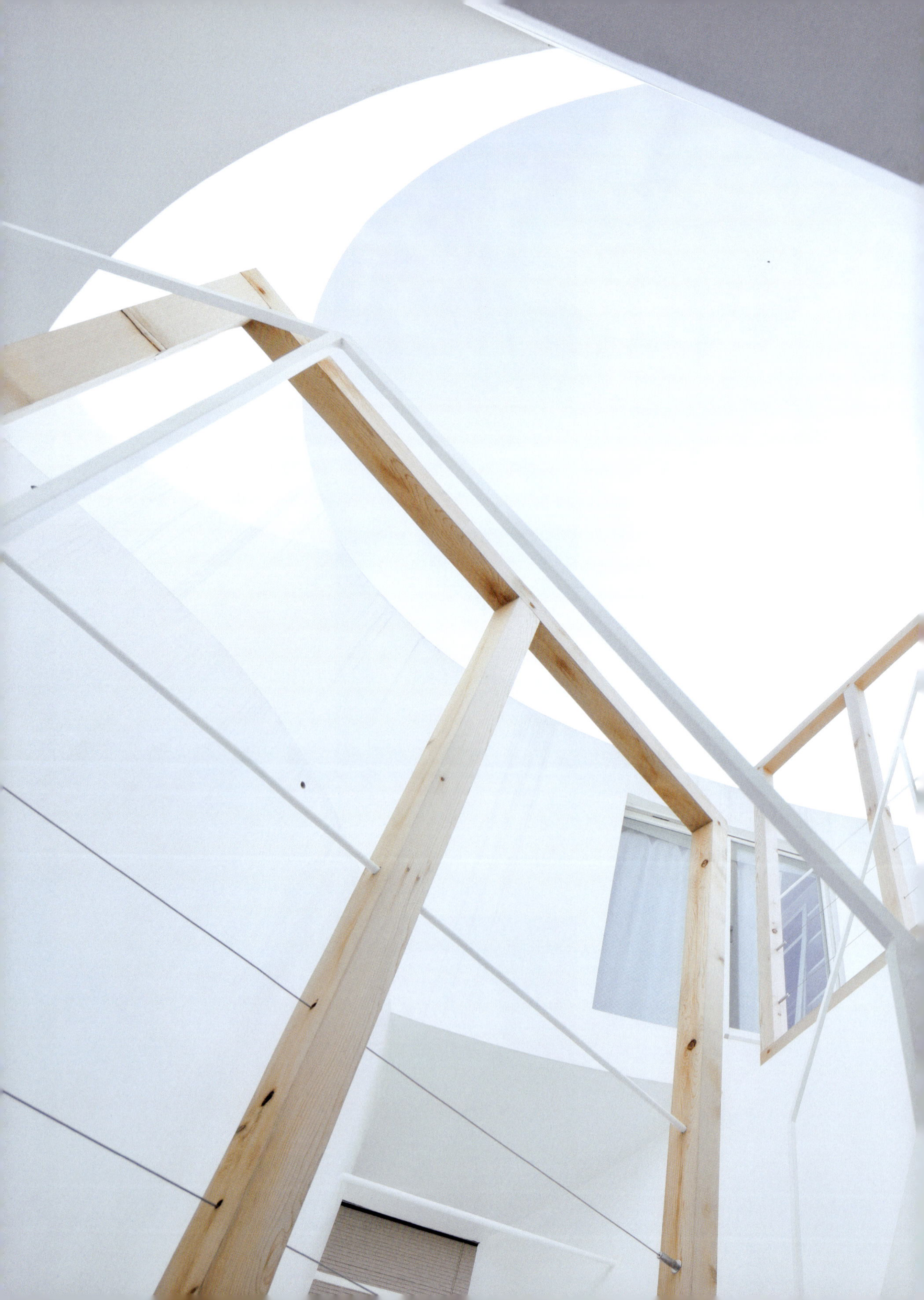

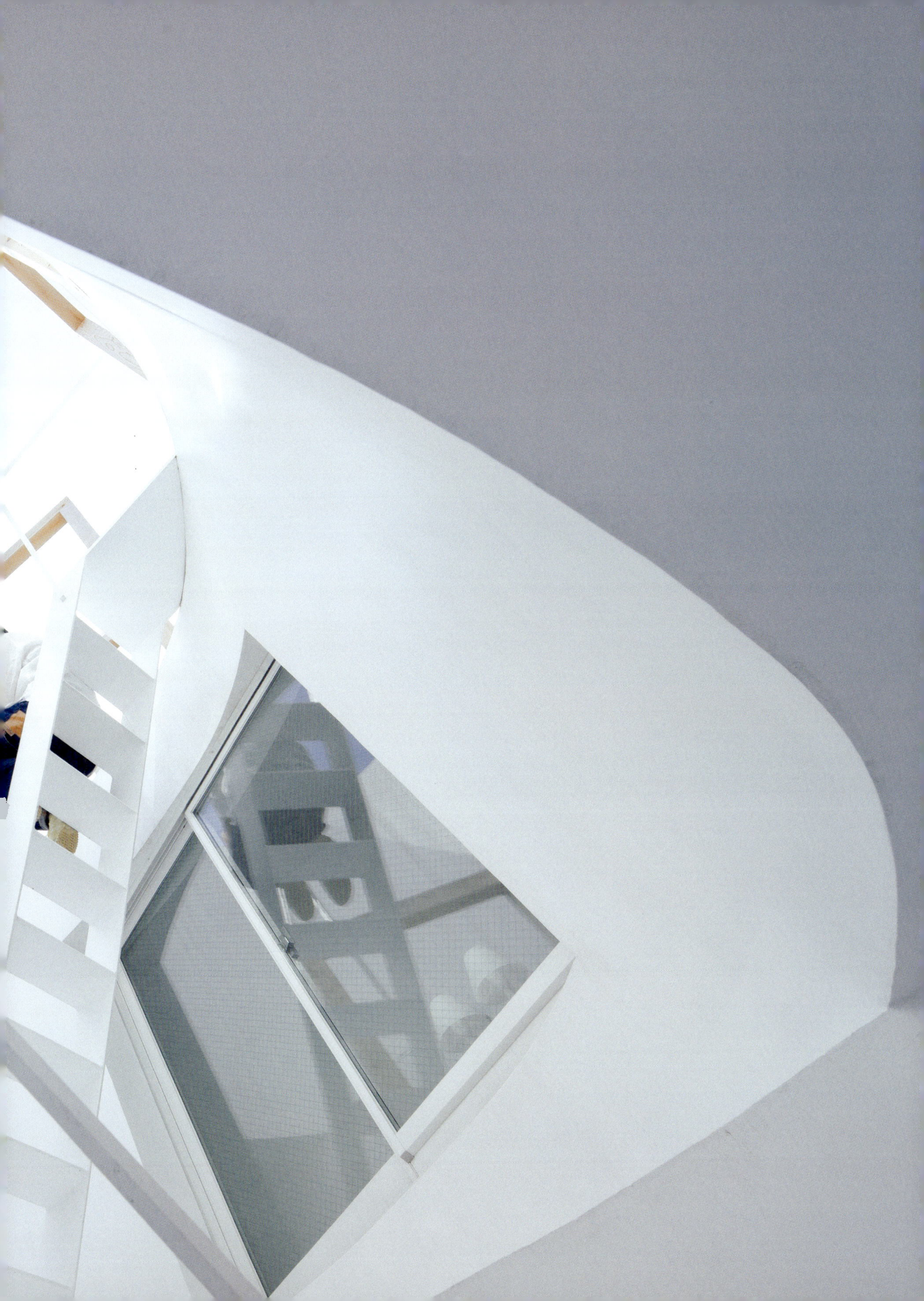

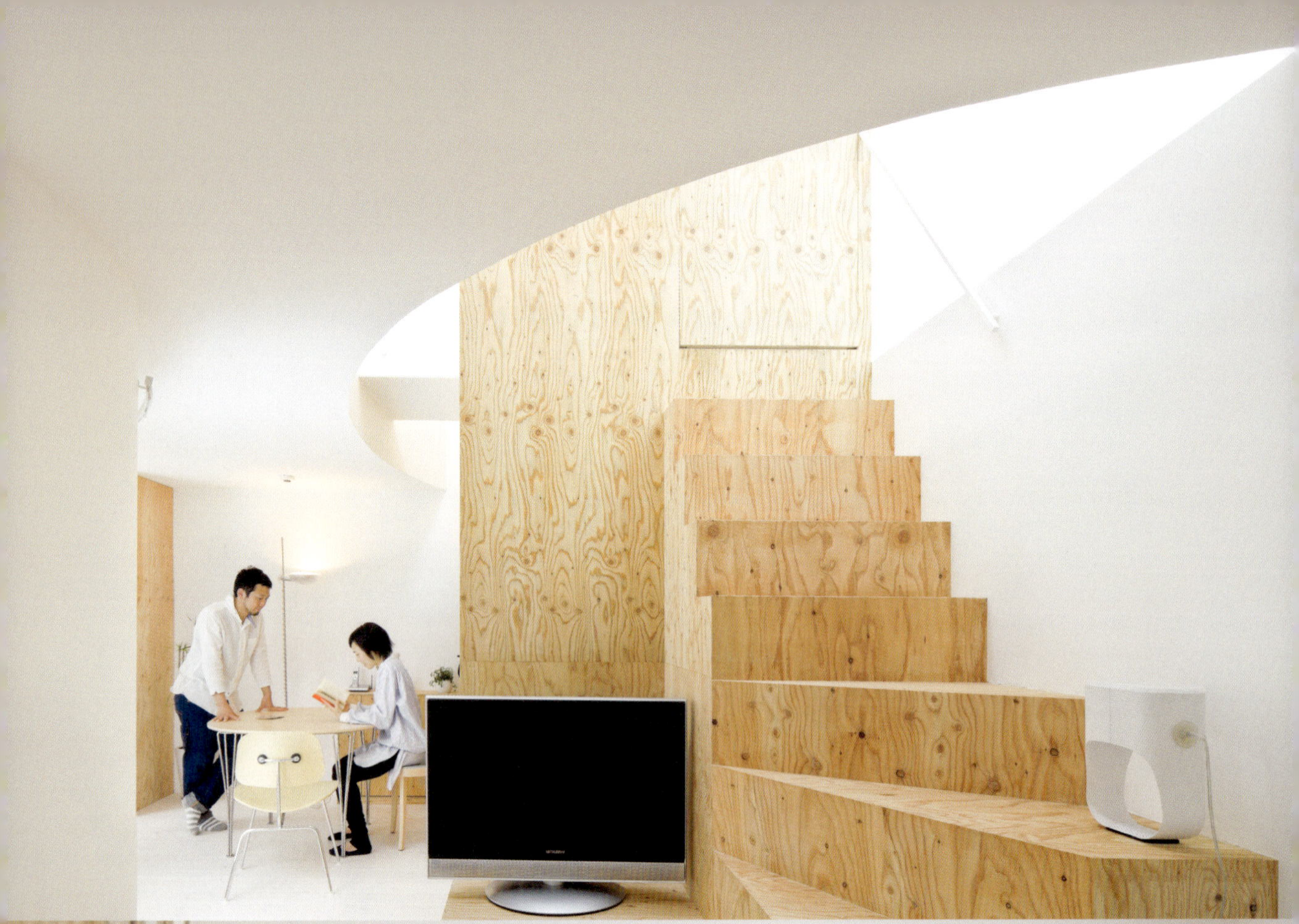

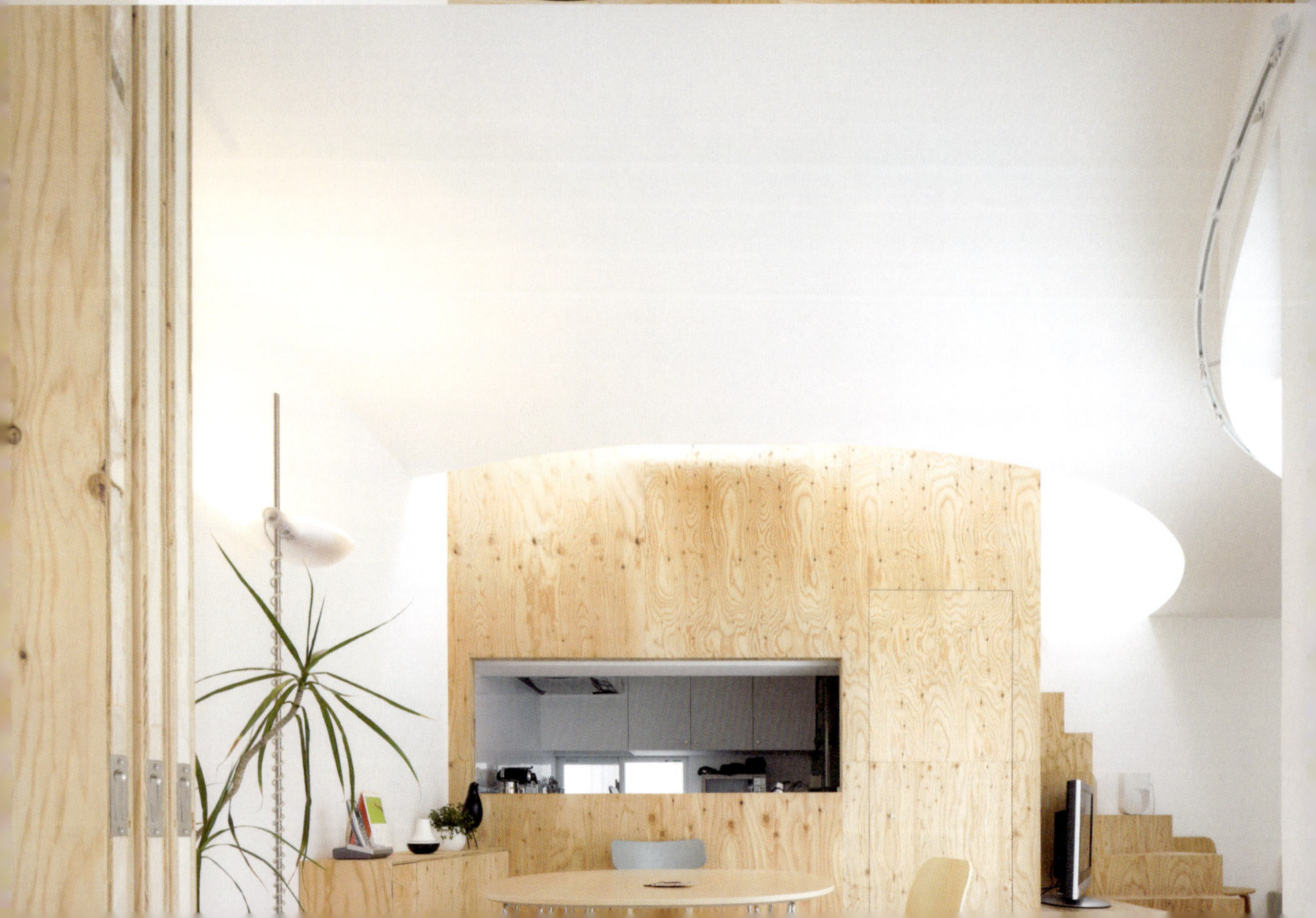

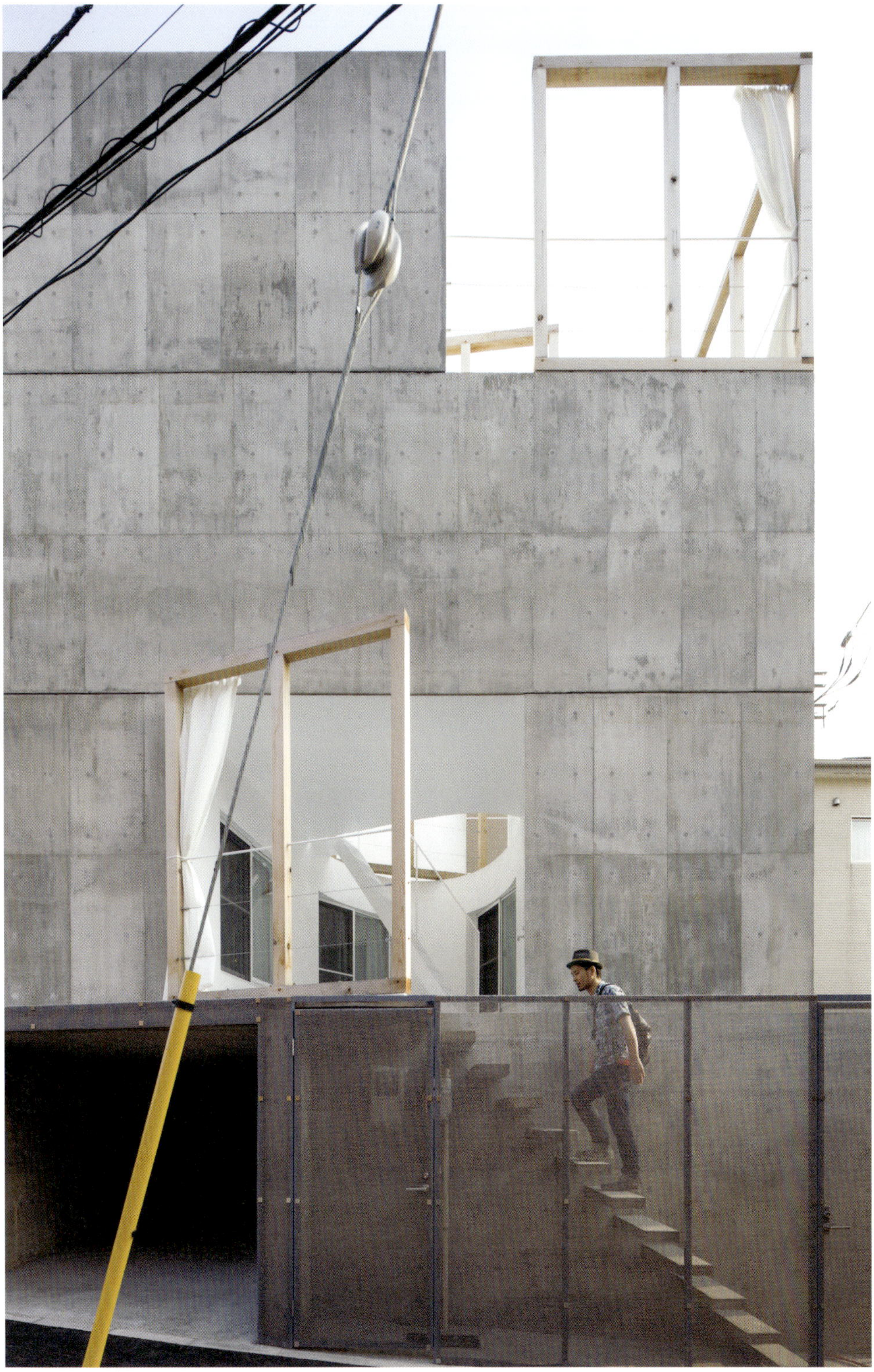

House as Cloud

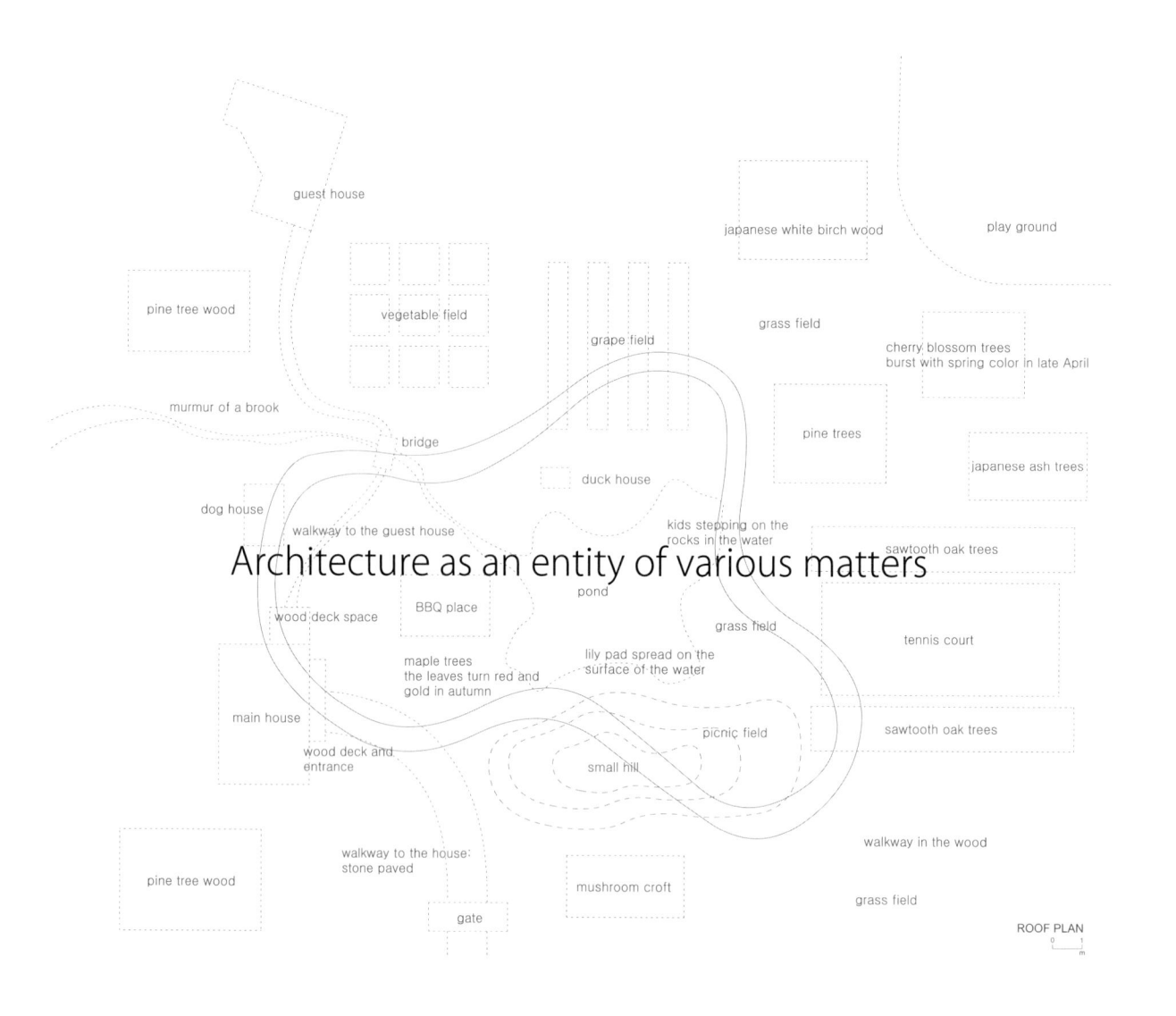

HOKKAIDO, JAPAN 2010

Architecture as an entity of various matters

ROOF PLAN

Rather than designing the building as an object, to subsume building(s) and all their surroundings as a whole, into diverse and variegated living places for people. Instead of delineating building, landscape and city as distinct disciplines, I am both intrigued and inspired by new values and spatial qualities generated from the synthesis of places; building, garden, city, street, furniture, room, eaves, terrace, and so on. This small project was for an extension to the house where I grew up in Hokkaido. The house sits on a site richly endowed with nature, and shows that over the course of time we have exercised our lives in a variety of places surrounding the house–from small ponds, bushes, vegetable patches, a tennis-court, and a dog kennel to an abandoned shiitake mushroom field. I envisaged a single roof that brings together this disparate yet characteristic set of places and redefines the whole as territory for living. From this point onwards, exploration into architecture in which the roof acts as a landscape device began appearing in a diverse lineage of works. It could be said that this pivotal project reiterated the essence of the urban idea from the *Taipei Pop Music Center* and *Kumamoto Station Plaza* proposals into an architectural condition.

物体としての建物ではなく、むしろ建物とその周囲に広がる＜人間が住むためのさまざまな場＞のようなものが全体をつくり出すこと。建物と庭、建物と街などと分けるのではなく、建物から庭、街、路、家具、部屋、軒下、テラスなど、さまざまな場所が溶け合い新しい価値と空間性を生み出すことができれば、とても面白いだろう。この小さな計画は、僕の育った実家の住宅を増築する試みである。実家は北海道の自然豊かな場所にあり、家本体の周りに美しい庭や池、菜園やテニスコート、犬小屋や放置された椎茸畑など、いろいろな場所が点在している。それらの特徴的な場所をひと繋がりの屋根で縫い上げるように繋げていくことで、全体を人間が住むための領域として再構築する。これ以降、ランドスケープ的な屋根による建築の系譜が現れてさまざまに展開していく、その最初の試みであると同時に、「Taipei Pop Music Center」や「熊本駅前広場」で試みた都市的なアイデアを建築的に展開したものとも言える。

046 — House as Cloud

HOKKAIDO, JAPAN
2010

Related Projects
024 025 061 105

Cloud Bridge
MARIBOR, SLOVENIA 2010

Fusing structure, experience and the scenery into a single form

Designing a bridge is a very attractive assignment, which fuses structure, form, experience, scenery, with simple and pure methods. The thin concrete slabs attain structural strength by undulating in an appropriate manner, and through this series of rises and falls create a rich experience of the landscape that was previously lacking in bridges. The slightly fluctuating ribbon-like form of the bridge is imbued both with a sense of modesty, which avoids obstructing the view of the historically significant bridge as a backdrop, and a distinct identity as a symbol of technology from a new age.

橋のデザインというのは、構造と形と体験と景観とがシンプルで純粋な方法によって融合する、とても魅力的な課題だ。ここでは、薄いコンクリートスラブが適切にうねることによって構造的な強度を発揮し、その起伏をもった形状がいままでの橋にはない豊かなランドスケープの体験をつくり出すことを考えた。さらにかすかに揺らいだ帯のような橋の姿は、背後に控える歴史遺産の橋への景観を妨げない控えめさと、それでいて新しい時代のテクノロジーの象徴としてのアイデンティティをあわせもつ。

047 | Cloud Bridge

MARIBOR, SLOVENIA
2010

Inside Outside Tree

LONDON, UNITED KINGDOM 2010

Point / Line / Surface / Space

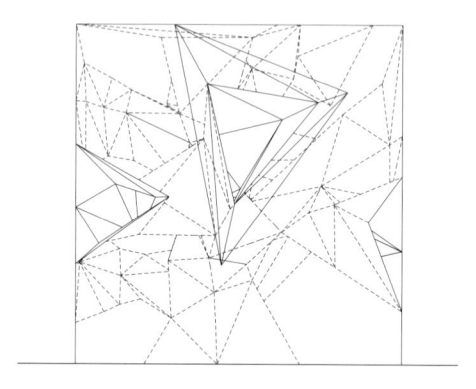

This installation was shown at the Victoria and Albert Museum in London. Installations are difficult. My inability to conceive of a space without concrete functions and a surrounding environment lies in the fact that I'm a dyed-in-the-wool architect. Here I explored an experimental space from the perspective of material, structure, and construction. My first idea was to make transparent trees and a transparent forest. In the cube-shaped space, I reduced the complex dendritic space as a void. All of the surfaces were made of acrylic-resin polyhedrons, giving rise to a space filled with infinite reflections and permeations. The overall structure was acrylic and planar, and the intricate combination of surfaces worked together structurally. I used plastic-resin cable ties to join the acrylic boards together. This idea was the result of considering numerous aspects such as workability, a degree of flexibility that would allow for combinations using many different angles, and cost; however the countless "dots" that rose up in three dimensions inside the transparent structure visualized the geometry of the space in a different dimension. It was as if myriad flowers were blooming on the trees.

ロンドンのヴィクトリア＆アルバート博物館で展示されたインスタレーション。インスタレーションというのは難しい。具体的な機能や周辺環境がないままに空間を構想することができないのは、僕が根っからの建築家だからだろう。ここでは、素材と構造と構法という視点から、実験的な空間を模索した。透明な樹木、透明な森、というのが最初のアイデアだった。キューブ状の空間の中に、ヴォイドとして複雑な樹状の空間を削り込んでいく。すべての面はアクリル樹脂の多面体でつくられ、無数の反射と透過によって満たされた空間が生まれる。全体の構造はアクリルによる面構造であり、複雑な面の組み合わせが構造的に機能する。アクリル板同士の結合には樹脂製の結束バンドを用いた。施工性やさまざまな角度の結合に対応する柔軟性、コストなどを検討する中で生まれたアイデアだったが、透明な構造の中に立体的に浮かぶ無数の＜点＞は、この空間の幾何学を別の次元で可視化する。それはあたかも樹木に咲いた無数の花のようでもあった。

048

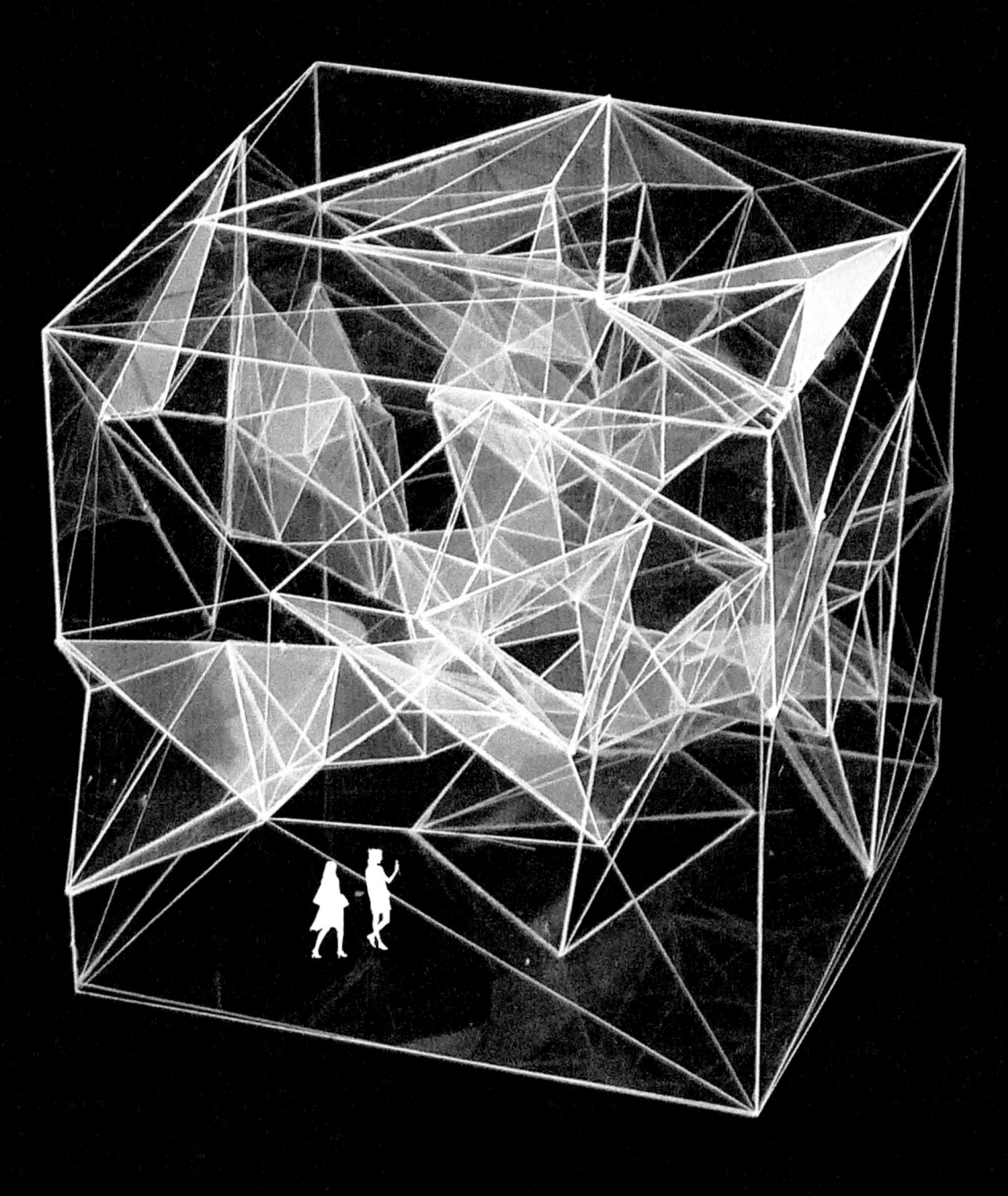

Inside Outside Tree

LONDON, UNITED KINGDOM
2010

→ Related Projects
008 022 028 099

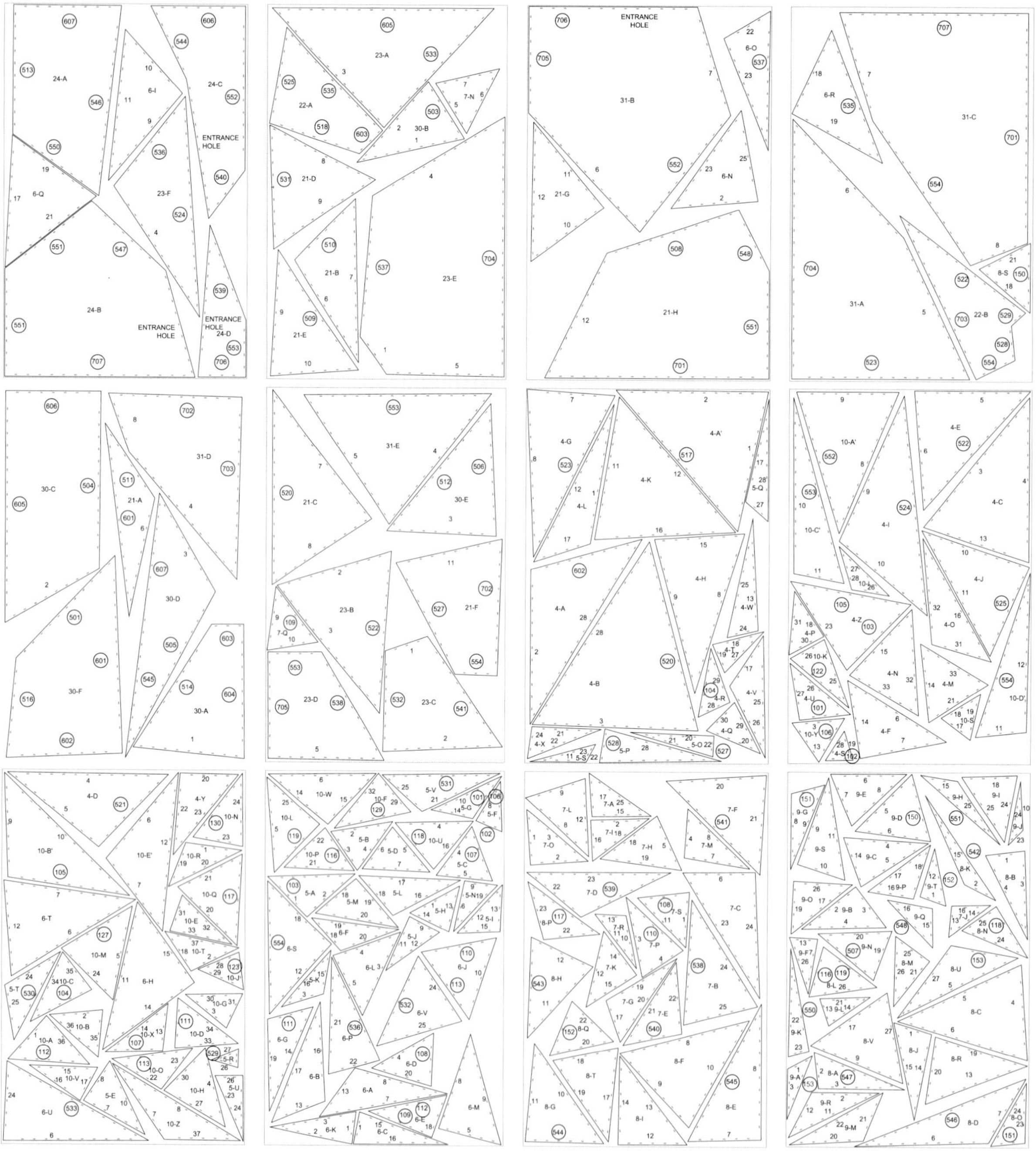

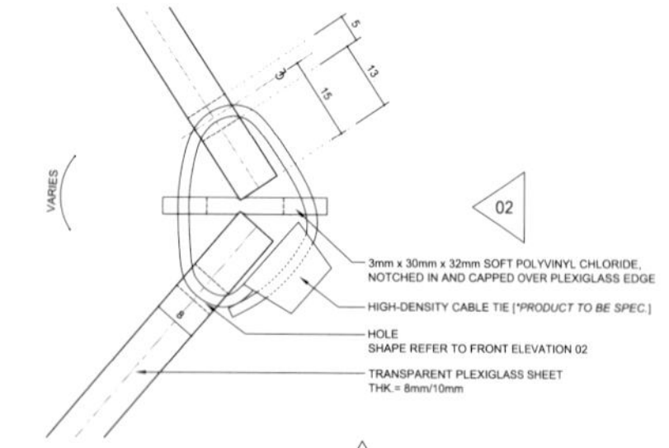

01 TYPICAL CONNECTION SECTION DETAIL 03

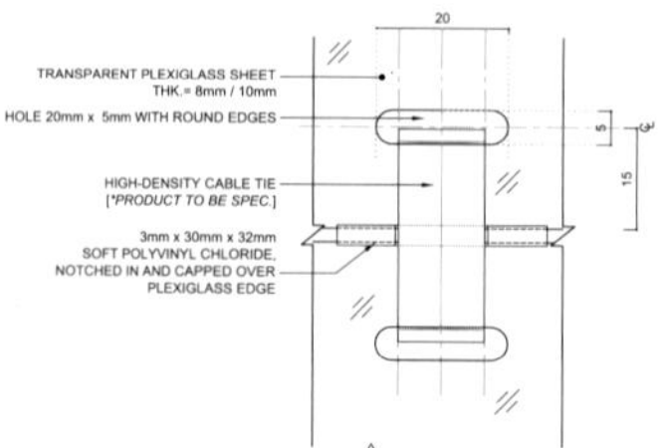

02 TYPICAL CONNECTION ELE. DETAIL 03

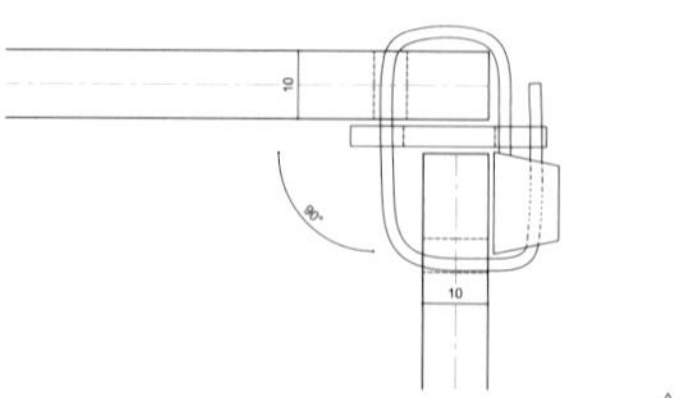

04 TYPICAL CONNECTION SECTION DETAIL WALL TO ROOF 03

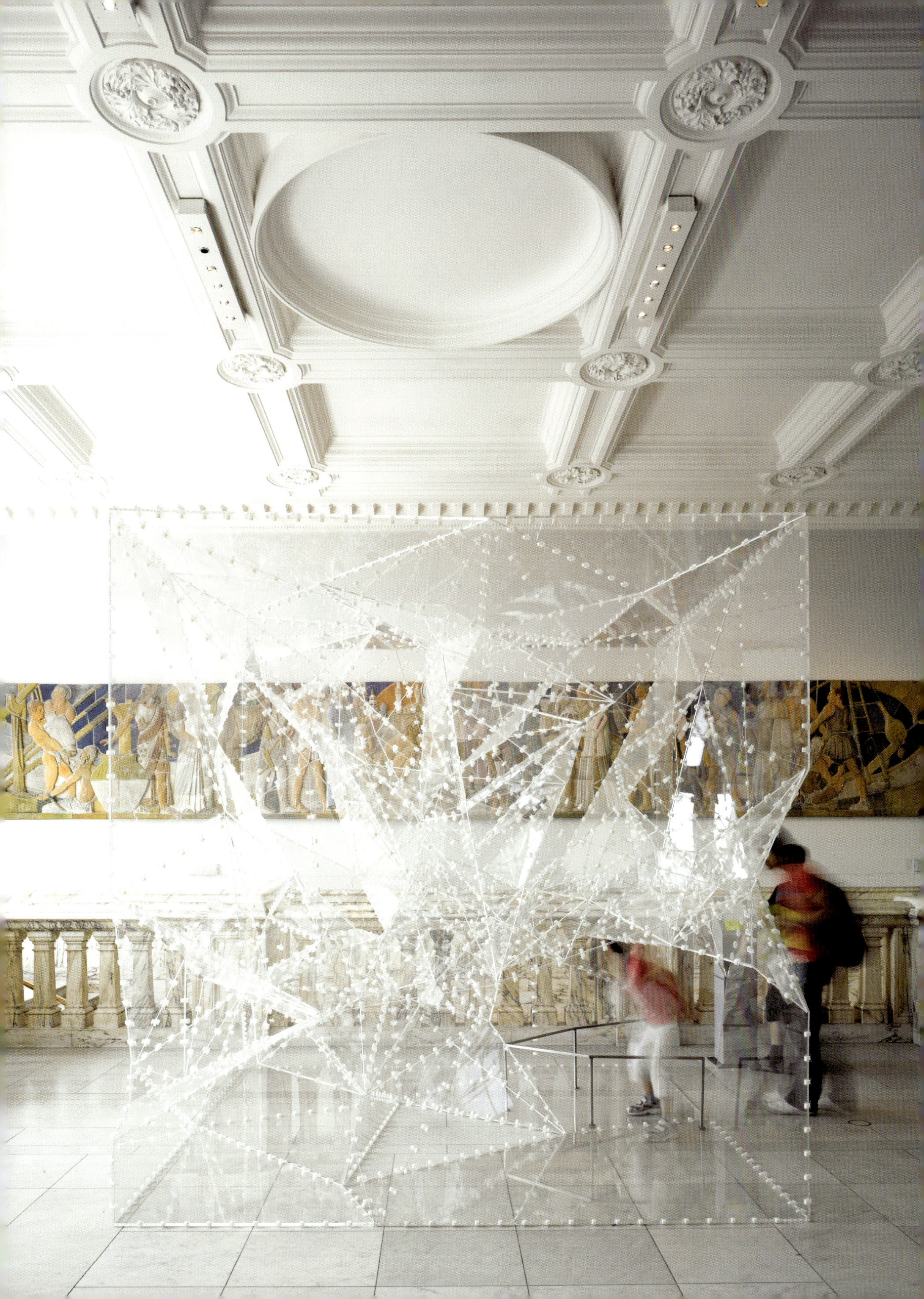

House B

HANOVER, GERMANY 2010

Tower of light / Architectural tree

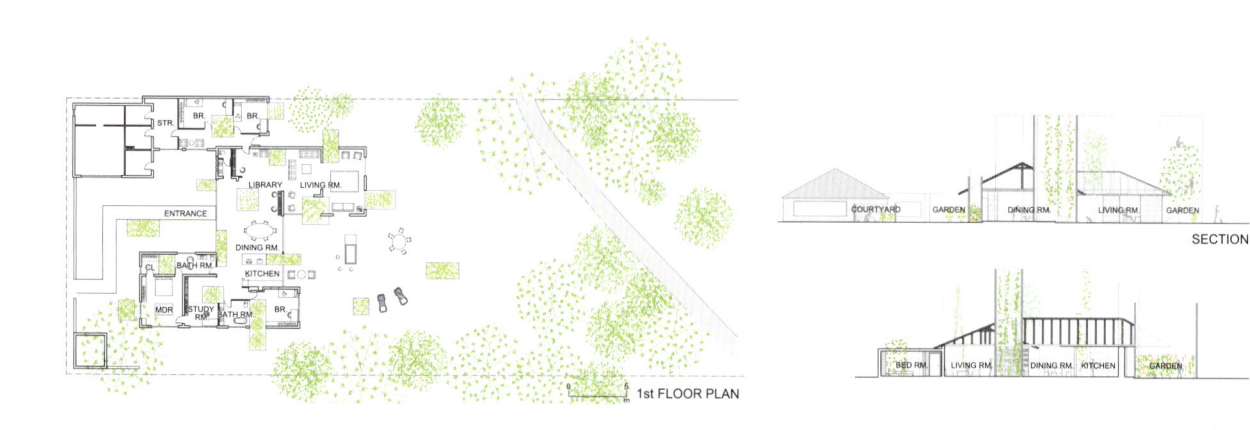

1st FLOOR PLAN

SECTION

I received a request to renovate this house from a family in Hannover, Germany. Contrary to the beautiful site surrounded by an abundance of nature, the existing single-story building was overly "architectural." I envisioned a situation in which vegetation and trees would not only exist outside in the garden but would form a grove inside. I came up with this proposal in which an inner courtyard of countless glass towers would penetrate the house. In addition to bringing light and greenery inside, the inner courtyard imbues the entire site with a density made up of the tree-shaped natural elements and the forest of artificial elements.

ドイツ、ハノーバーの家族から依頼された住宅のリノベーション。豊かな自然に囲まれた美しい敷地に対し、既存の平屋の建物はあまりにも＜建築＞だった。そこで周囲の自然や樹木が庭だけではなく家の中にも林立するさまをイメージして、無数のタワー状のガラスの中庭を既存建物に貫入させることを提案した。これらの中庭は室内に光と緑を取り入れるとともに、敷地全体に樹状の自然物と人工物の林立する密度感をつくり出す。

049

House B

House B

HANOVER, GERMANY
2010

→ Related Projects
008 031 050 062

Vertical Forest
LONDON, UNITED KINGDOM 2010

Making architecture is, equal to layering the natural environment

This was an international competition to design a landmark tower on an intersection in the city center to coincide with the inauguration of the London 2012 Olympics. I find that designing a landmark is challenging. If the sole purpose of the object is simply to be seen, I find it very difficult to expand on my creative thinking as an architect. It is only when the object becomes a field activated by, and providing opportunities for, a variety of people experiencing and unfolding their various behaviors, that I can start to exercise my thinking as an architect. In this project I proposed a stratified vertical garden in the center of London. Visitors travel on a lift to the uppermost garden, and enjoy a stroll down through the gardens. The three-dimensional/vertical garden scheme was inspired by the countless exquisite gardens throughout London. Over the past decade I have sought various ways to conceptualize natural or forest-like architecture, and although this proposal was a rather explicit one, it is definitely one that strongly influenced the development of later projects such as *Taiwan Tower* and *L'Arbre Blanc*.

ロンドンオリンピックに合わせて行われた、市内の交差点に建つランドマークのコンペ。最終審査選考まで残った案。ランドマークというのは難しい。それが単に見るためのオブジェクトである場合、建築家としての僕の思考は広がらない。そこに人間が入ることができたり上ることができたりという体験が伴うときに、初めて思考が動き出す。ここではロンドンのど真ん中に積層した空中庭園を提案した。人は最上階の庭園まで上ることができ、そこから階段を伝って散歩を楽しむ。これはロンドンに無数にある公園にインスピレーションを得た立体公園である。樹木的、森的な建築ということは、この10年来ずっと模索してきた。このプロジェクトはどちらかというとかなり直接的な表現となったが、後のモンペリエの集合住宅「L'Arbre Blanc」や「台湾タワー」などへと繋がる構想である。

050 | Vertical Forest | Vertical Forest | LONDON, UNITED KINGDOM 2010 | → Related Projects 030 031 033 063 085

UNIQLO Shinsaibashi
OSAKA, JAPAN 2010

Beyond the beyond

This was a project for the Osaka flagship store of the international brand Uniqlo. This was my first design for this type of commercial retail facility, but instead seeing it as a way of presenting style, I saw it as a way of providing a variety of experiences that are all thoroughly connected to the merchandise. This created a very architectural theme similar to the *Musashino Art University Museum & Library*. I covered the entire surface of the walls that faces the long slender void with merchandise, and by covering all of the shelf boards, ceiling, and the small holes in the slabs with a mirror finish, I imbued the site with multiple layers of spatial depth. The sense of here and there, and a place beyond the beyond created an architectural experience.

世界的なブランド・ユニクロの大阪旗艦店。このような商業施設をデザインするのは初めてであったが、それがスタイルの提示ではなく＜どこまでも連なる商品とそこをさまざまに巡る体験＞であると考えると「武蔵野美術大学美術館・図書館」にも連なるとても建築的なテーマだと思えた。ここでは細長い吹き抜けに面して向かい合う壁全面をひたすら商品の棚とし、さらに棚板や天井面、スラブの小口をすべて鏡面仕上げとすることで、幾重にも写り込む空間の奥行きをつくり上げた。こちらとあちら、向こうの向こうの向こう、という感覚が、建築的な体験をつくり出す。

051

UNIQLO Shinsaibashi

UNIQLO 心斎橋店

OSAKA, JAPAN
2010

→ Related Projects
044 055 077 086

Nube Arena

MURCIA, SPAIN 2010

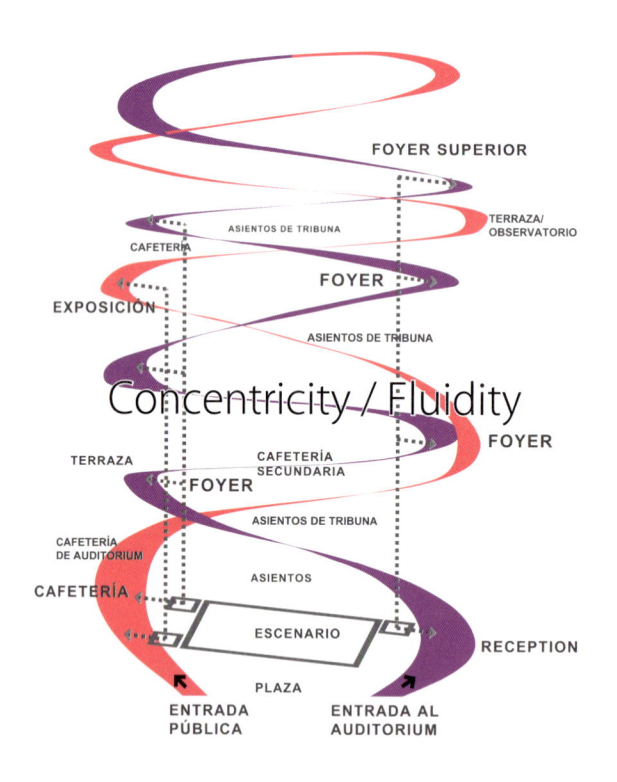

I was awarded second prize for this competition proposal for an 800-seat concert hall in Murcia, Spain. I searched for a new typology for a music hall. The rising slope, made of a double helix, encloses a central void, forming the structure of the three-dimensional theatre. By positioning a fly tower in the center, half of the cylinder serves as an indoor theatre, and the other half an outdoor venue. Both parts could also be combined depending on the occasion. The slope functions as an entrance, which continues on from the city, a foyer, and part of the tiered seating section as well as an exhibition space and gallery in the upper part. The space combines a sense of completion and openness, and concentration and diffusion. This idea for a spiral-shaped path generated by the function of a music/theatre hall, was later developed into an urban plaza space in the *Beton Hala Waterfront Center*.

スペインのラス・トレス・デ・コティージャスの街に800席のコンサートホールを設計するコンペの2等案。音楽ホールの新しいタイポロジーを模索した。2重螺旋で上昇するスロープが中央のヴォイドを取り巻き、立体的な劇場の構造をつくり出す。中央にフライタワーを配置することで、円筒の半分は屋内の劇場、もう一方は屋外劇場となり、ときにふたつを融合して使うこともできる。スロープは都市から連続するエントランスであり、ホワイエであり、また積層する客席の一部でもあり、また上部では展望スペースやギャラリーでもある。完結性と開放性、求心性と拡散性をあわせもった空間。劇場というプログラムから発想したこの螺旋状のパスのアイデアは、後の「Beton Hala Waterfront Center」において都市的な広場空間として発展的に継承されていく。

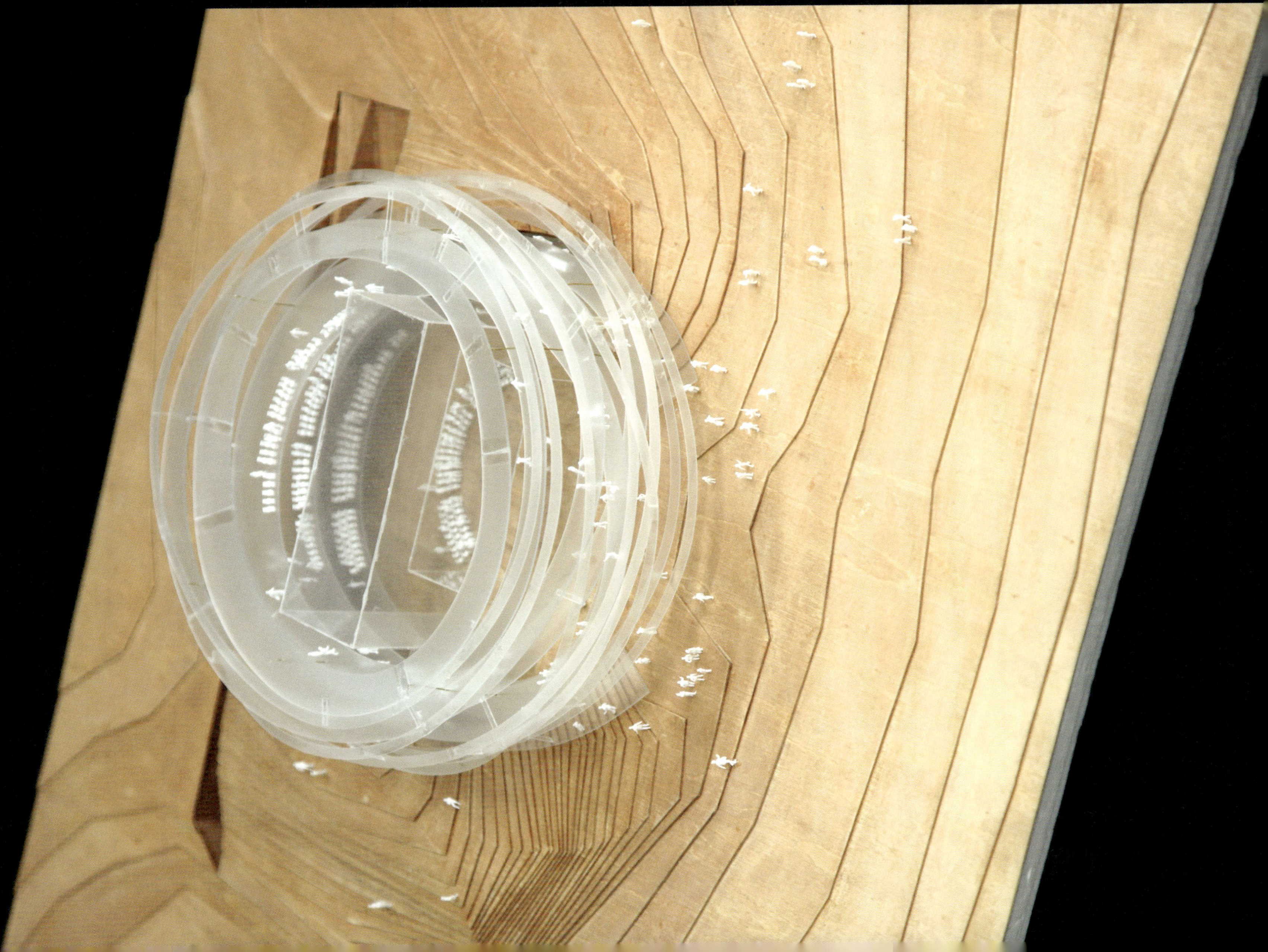

Kultur Projekte Berlin
BERLIN, GERMANY 2011

A light-filled cave made up of air

I was fortunate enough to have the opportunity to partake in a by-invitation competition to design a temporary mobile art-museum facility in the center of Berlin. Captivated by the term "mobile art-museum," I was inspired to propose a visionary scheme in which countless balloons collectively constitute a grand roof—which, when required, will float and be transported up into the sky. The gaps between the myriad large spheres create a unique spatial continuum that is neither completely transparent nor completely segmented. I find it imperative to frequently think outside the box and dwell upon visionary forms of what architecture could become. Furthermore, the process of expanding one's imaginative faculties is a very enjoyable one.

ベルリンの中心部に仮設の移動美術館をつくるプロジェクトの招待コンペに参加した。移動美術館という言葉からのインスタレーションで、無数のバルーンが寄り集まってひとつの大きな屋根を形成し、移動時にはその屋根全体が浮上し空中を移動していくという、空想的な提案を行った。無数の球体の隙間に生まれる空間が、繋がりながら分節された魅力的なシークエンスをつくり出す。ときにはこのような空想的な建築を考えることで、自分たちの想像力の範囲を拡張するのはとても楽しい作業だ。

053

Kultur Projekte Berlin

Kultur Projekte Berlin

BERLIN, GERMANY
2011

→ Related Projects
006 038 054 057

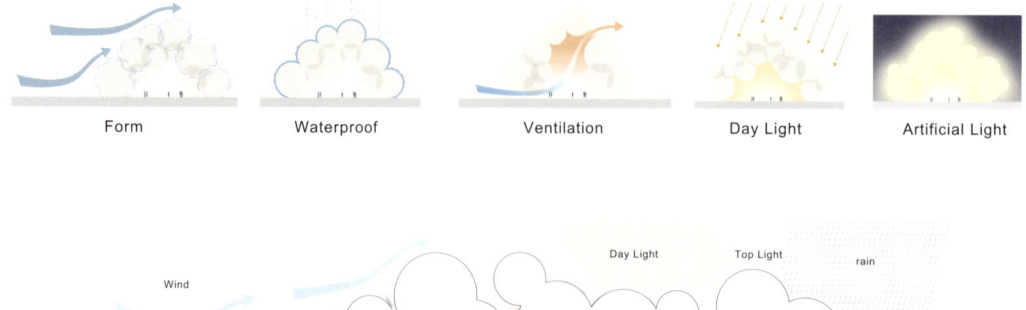

| Form | Waterproof | Ventilation | Day Light | Artificial Light |

Wind
reflected light from the river
Ventilation
Day Light
Top Light
rain
Waterproof membrane
Interior space protected by clouds
Exterior Exhibition
Exhibition
Lounge
Cafe
Helium + Air
Curtain dividing interior and exterior space

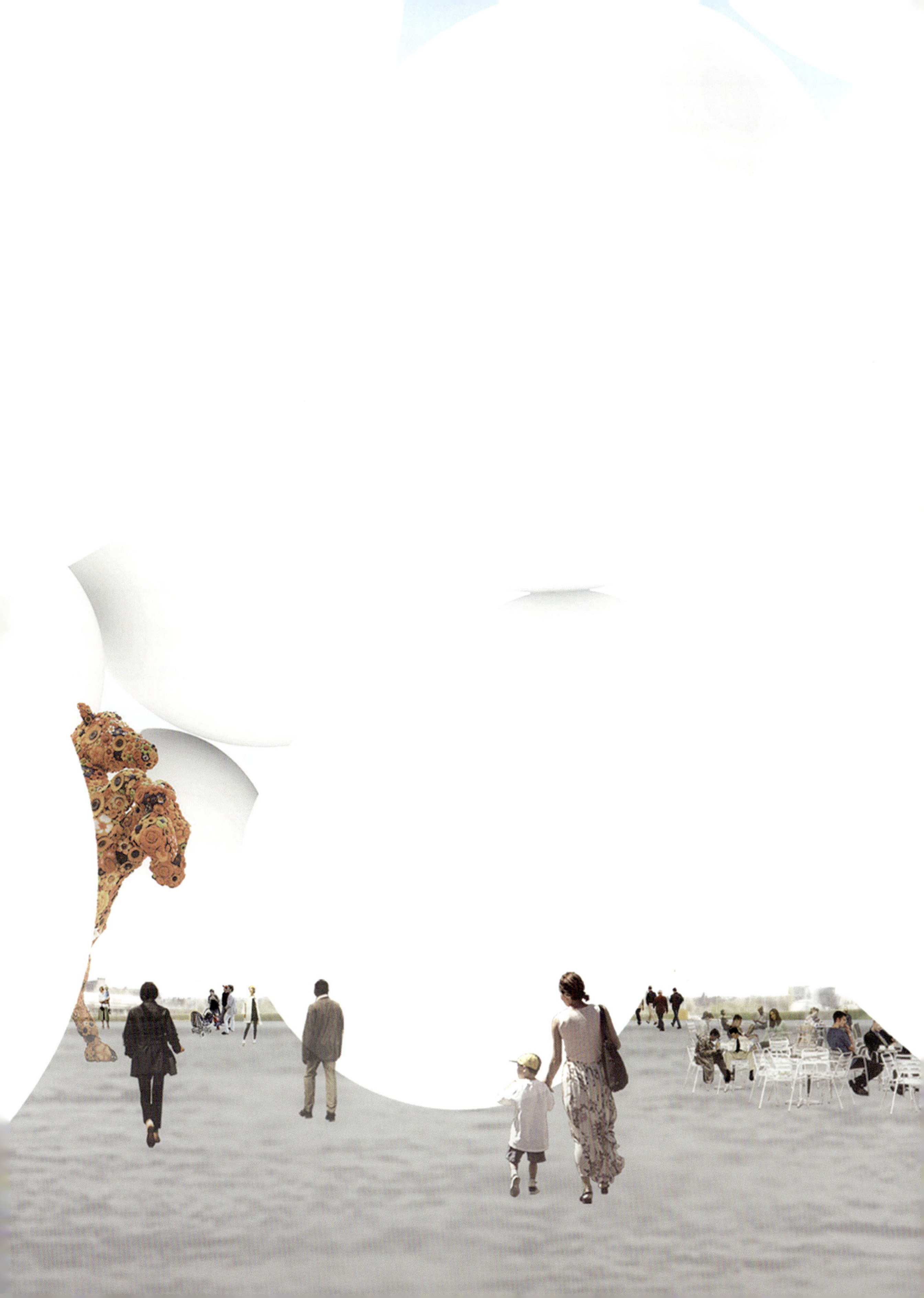

LA Small House

LOS ANGELES, USA 2011

Simultaneously a wall, an opening, furniture, architecture, space and void

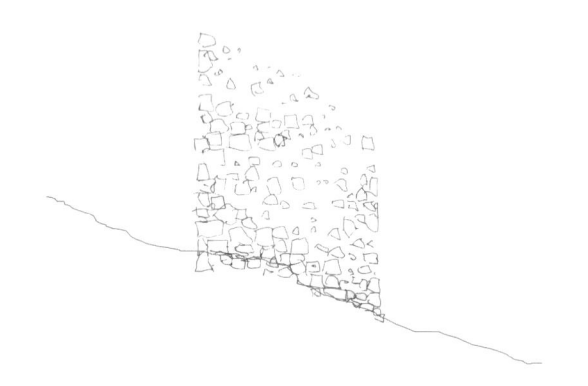

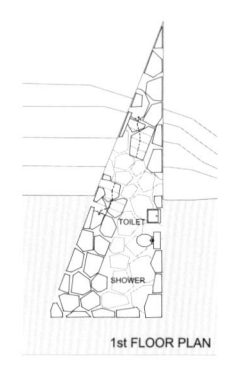

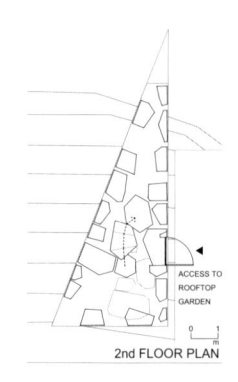

1st FLOOR PLAN

2nd FLOOR PLAN

What lies between a wall and a window? Or between a wall and furniture? And eventually between matter and space? In this proposal for a small guesthouse, I envisioned redefining architecture as the chiaroscuro of various densities of stones. Stone has long been a novel element of architecture. When its density rises it becomes a wall, and when its density falls it offers up an opening. Stone elements are combined to form furniture and platforms to stand upon, opening up into another space beyond. The rich spatial intonation formed by the distribution of such stone elements and their gaps enables people's activities, belongings, and diverse matter to exist. Such a place sees a new organic bond between people, living elements, activities, and architecture. I can say that the basic image of this project is rooted in an astounding encounter with the layout of diverse objects during my visit to Sir John Soane's Museum, and afterwards progressed through the *Network by Walk* project, later evolving into *Serpentine Gallery Pavilion 2013* back in London.

壁と窓の間とは何だろうか？ また壁と家具の間とは？ モノと空間の間とはなんだろうか？ この小さなゲストハウスの計画案では、建築を浮遊する岩の粗密でつくられる場の抑揚として再定義しようと試みている。岩とは建築の新しい粒子であり、それは密度をもつと壁に近づき、粗になれば窓に近づく。いくつかの岩が組み合わさって家具や床となり、その隙間を上っていくと別の空間が開ける。岩という粒子の分布によってつくられたこの緩やかな場は、その隙間に、人間の身体や住み手の所持品などさまざまなモノを取り込む許容力をもち、それら生活の断片と結合することで建築と生活と身体が融合した有機的な場所をつくり出す。このプロジェクトの原イメージはジョン・ソーンの自邸の、さまざまなモノが溢れかえった光景を見たときの衝撃からきている。それは最初期の「Network by Walk」プロジェクトとも繋がり、また「Serpentine Gallery Pavilion 2013」へと進化していく。

054

LA Small House

LOS ANGELES, USA
2011

→ Related Projects
007 010 018 029 077 081

House NA

TOKYO, JAPAN 2011

Density created by an infinite collection of small matters, linking body, architecture and the city

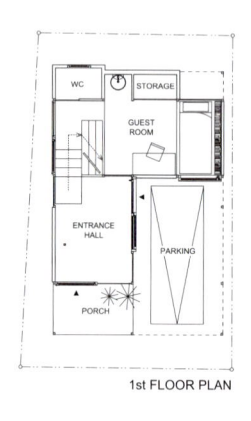

1st FLOOR PLAN

2nd FLOOR PLAN

3rd FLOOR PLAN

Whenever I design a house, I reflect on what an archetypal living place might be. For example, is it a place that exists between a state of openness and closure that gently surrounds various objects connected to our daily lives? Is it like a search for a comfortable place while moving from one branch to another in an artificially created forest? In a place where transparency and opacity live side-by-side, is it possible to freely choose a scale that ranges from something approaching the size of your own body to an endless expanse? Here, by stratifying countless furniture-scale floors in space on a small site in Tokyo, I created a kind of artificial thicket. At the same time, the work resembles the way in which the city of Tokyo itself was made – i.e., many small-scale objects are assembled in various ways. This forms an intersection between the human body, architecture, and the city. It is a primitive form of house.

住宅を設計する時にはいつも、住むための場所の原型とはどのようなものだろうかと考える。それは例えば、生活にまつわる無数のモノたちに緩やかに囲まれた、開かれていることと閉じられていることとの間のような場所ではないだろうか？それは例えば、人工物でできた林の中で、枝から枝へと動き回りながら自分の心地よい居場所を見つけることではないだろうか？　透明性と不透明性の同居する場所で、身体に近いスケールからどこまでも広がっていくスケールまでの間を自由に選び取ることではないだろうか？　この住宅は、東京の小さな敷地の中で、家具スケールの無数の床を立体的に積層することで、そのような人工的な茂みをつくり出している。それは同時に、小さなスケールのモノたちがさまざまに寄り集まってできている東京の街そのもののつくられ方にも似ている。人間の身体と建築と都市とを横断していく。住むための場所の原初的な姿である。

055 | House NA | House NA | TOKYO, JAPAN 2011 | → Related Projects 007 016 064 068 076 077

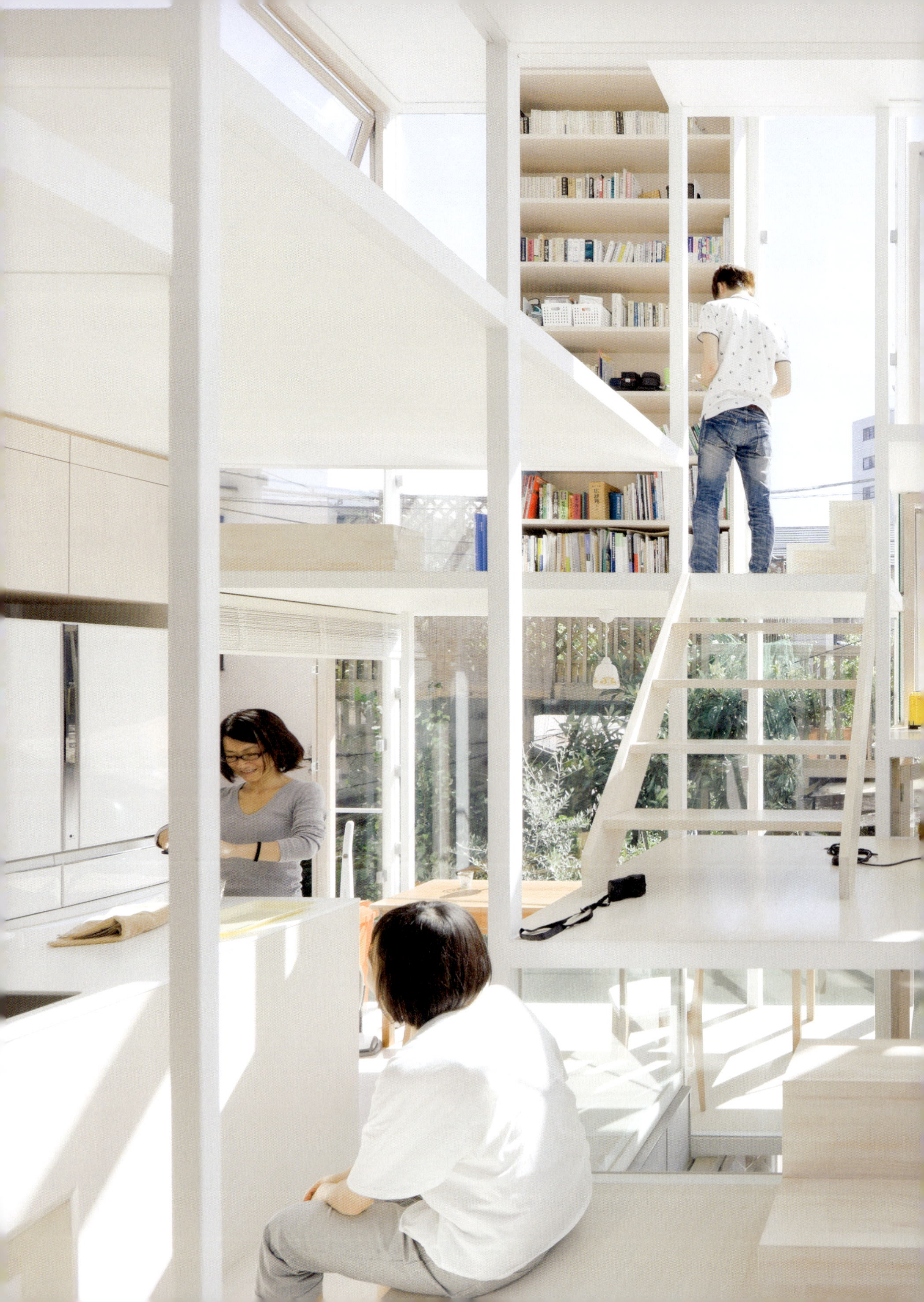

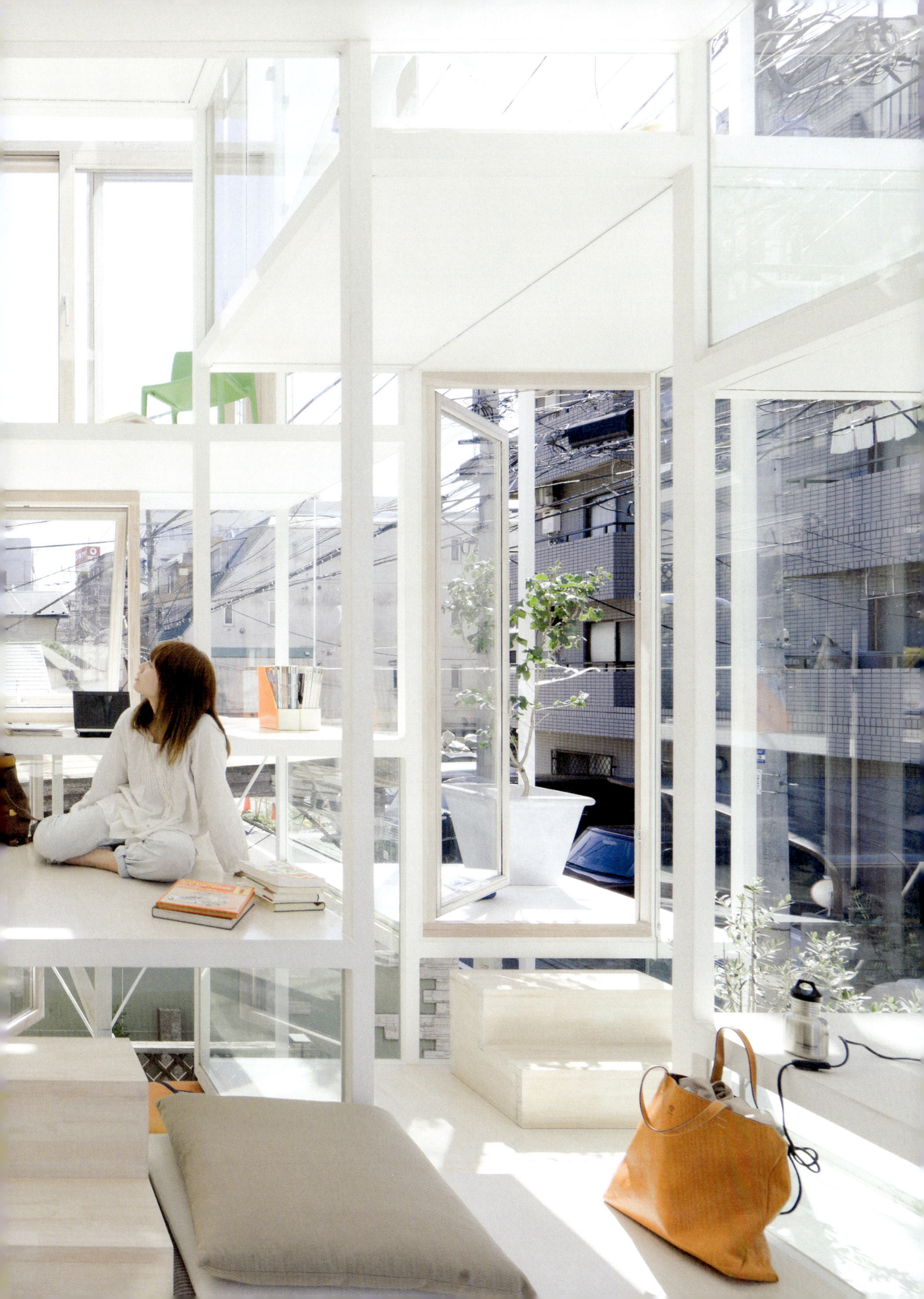

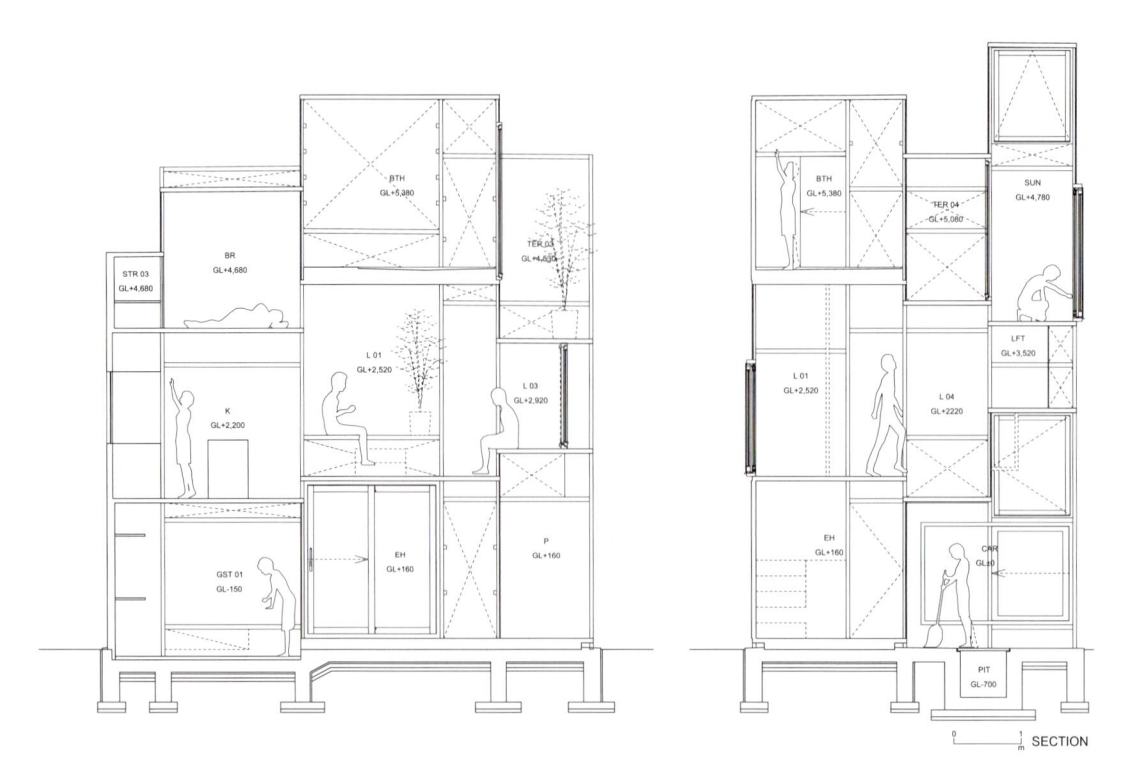

SECTION

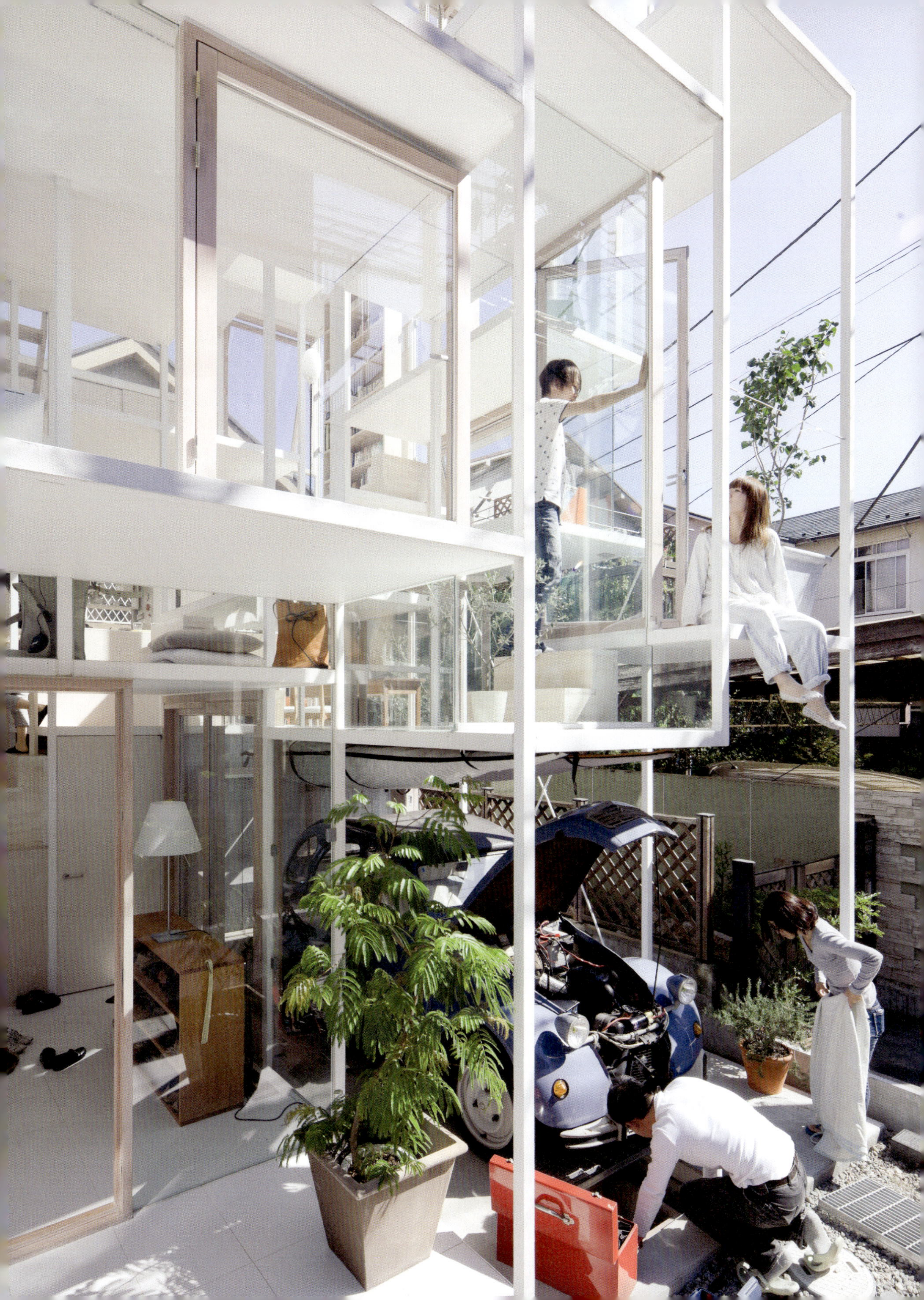

Tree Skyscraper
HUMLEBAEK, DENMARK 2011

Skyscraper is the new landscape

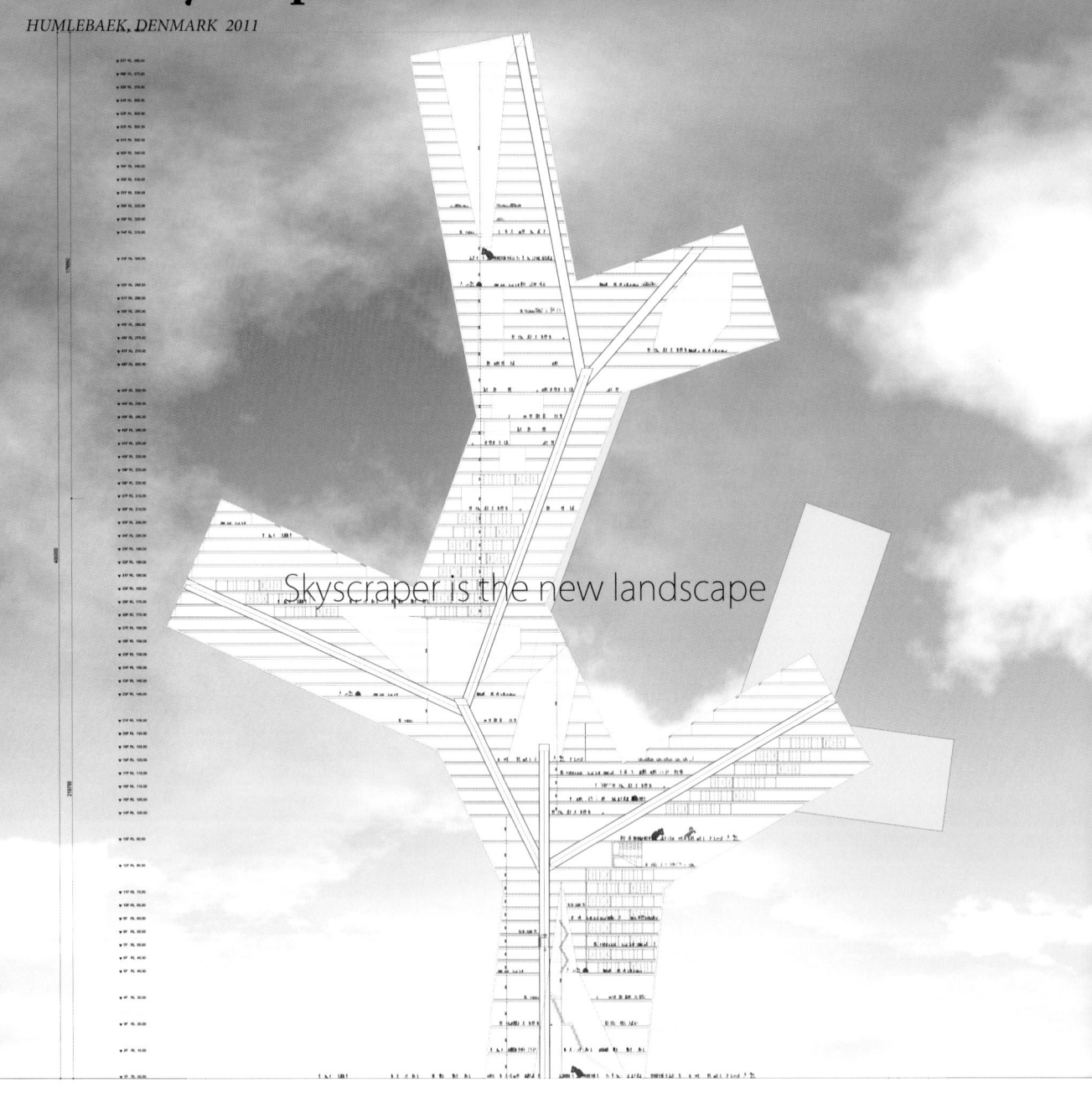

This project is one of the new works I showed at the Louisiana Museum of Modern Art in Denmark. It was the first time I had produced a design for a super-high-rise building. I visited the Louisiana in preparation for the show, and the theme of merging architecture and landscape naturally occurred to me. I was deeply impressed by the museum's beautiful fusion of natural terrain and built structure, and I decided to focus on new kinds of relationships between the two. A high-rise building is an accumulation of stories, but they are discontinuous (not linked), whereas the natural landscape is one continuous, connected entity. To my mind, this meant that a new fusion of architecture and landscape could fall in the middle ground between continuous and discontinuous. The many diagonally branching-off floors of this super-high-rise structure feature stepped terraces. The building as a whole extends diagonally, and the outdoor terraces are something halfway between terrain and architecture, between discontinuous and continuous. This extravagant design was also an enjoyable chance for me to shatter my own conceptions of high-rise buildings.

このプロジェクトは、デンマークのルイジアナ美術館での展覧会に参加した時に、新作として発表したもののひとつである。超高層のプランをつくるのは、初めてだった。ルイジアナ美術館での展覧会ということで、現地を訪れ、自然と心に浮かんだテーマは、建築とランドスケープの間、ということだった。ルイジアナ美術館が地形と建築の豊かな融合を実現していることに心を打たれ、その先に、新しい地形／建築を考えることを目指した。床が積層した高層ビルを考える時、それは非連続の重なりである。一方で自然の地形は連続体だ。ならば建築とランドスケープの新しい融合とは、この連続と非連続の間に起こるのではないかと考えた。この枝分かれした超高層は、斜めに張り出したいくつもの枝状の各階に段々の屋外テラスをもっている。ビルが斜めに延びることによって段上の屋外テラスが、半地形／半建築として非連続の連続体をつくり出すことができるのではないだろうか。同時にこの突拍子もないビルの形自体が、自分の高層ビルの概念を乗り超えていく楽しさもあった。

056

Tree Skyscraper

HUMLEBAEK, DENMARK
2011

→ Related Projects
020 037 048 088 107

Louisiana Cloud

HUMLEBAEK, DENMARK 2011

Architecture is segmentation, landscape is continuation
Possibility lies in between them

Like *Tree Skyscraper*, this is a concept developed for the exhibition at the Louisiana Museum of Modern Art, exploring new combinations of architecture and landscape, and inspired by the museum itself. While *Tree Skyscraper* featured branching terraces on each floor, this is a more dispersed model, a "floating" structure with countless islands connected by countless bridges, and an investigation of new modes of segmentation and continuity. The basis for this idea goes back to *House before House*, but here is expanded beyond the scale of architecture to that of urban terrain. This composition is also related to that of *House NA*, completed that same year, and its concept underlies a range of experiments with continuity and discontinuity on scales ranging from furniture up to urban planning. Later, in the proposal for the *Media Forest -Axel Springer Campus*, it was developed into something more befitting to realistic programs.

「Tree Skyscraper」と同じく、ルイジアナ美術館での展示のために制作したコンセプトモデル。ルイジアナ美術館からインスピレーションを得て、地形／建築の新しい形を模索した。段々のテラスと枝分かれした形が特徴の「Tree Skyscraper」に対して、ここでは、離散的、立体的に浮遊するいくつもの島を無数のブリッジが連結するという方法で、分節性と連続性の新しい形を模索した。このアイデアの原型は「House before House」にまで遡るが、それを都市スケールにまで拡張することで建築のスケールを離れた地形的な展開にできないかと考えた。同時にその構成はこの年に竣工した「House NA」とも繋がるものであり、家具スケールから都市スケールまでを横断する連続／非連続のさまざまな試みの起点となっている。後の「Media Forest -Axel Springer Campus」ではより現実のプログラムに即した展開を見せている。

057

Louisiana Cloud

HUMLEBAEK, DENMARK
2011

→ Related Projects
003 018 054 055 081

Layered Plaza
2011

A place where various people can gather in various ways
and do various things

I was asked to design a facade for a building that abutted an urban square, but rather than to simply create a plane, I thought I could make a facade that would be a place or a kind of fusion between the building and the square. You might say a square is a place where a variety of people gather in a variety of ways to do a variety of things. It is a tolerant place, and at the same time it is a place that is filled with countless opportunities and inspiration. It is also a place where many different senses of distance and scale overlap. Normal squares are planes, but through a network of many staircases, I thought I could create a multilayered activity space. Staircases produce vertical movement and a number of level differences, and the steps also provide places to sit down. Through these staircases, the gently covered ground space seems to exist in the shadow of a tree or inside a nest. And though it is an urban space, I anticipated that it would create a new experience that was half-inside and half-architectural. If an urban square is a place where people gather, a three-dimensional place where people communicate is certain to imbue the urban square with new potential.

都市広場に面した建物のファサードデザインの依頼を受け、面としてのファサードにとどまらない、場所をつくるファサード、あるいは建築と都市広場の融合するような何かをつくることはできないかと考えた。広場とは、さまざまな人がさまざまな集まり方でさまざまなことをすることができる場である、と言えるのではないだろうか。それは許容性の場であり、同時に無数のきっかけに満ちた、インスピレーションの場でもある。さまざまな距離感とスケール感が重なり合う場である。通常の都市広場とは、ひとつの面であるが、無数の階段のネットワークによって、重層的な活動空間を生み出すことを考えた。階段は上下移動といくつものレベル差を生み出し、またその段々は腰掛ける場ともなる。これらの階段によって緩やかに覆われた地上空間は、木陰のような、あるいは巣の中のような場所となり、都市空間でありながら、半内部、半建築のような、新しい体験をもたらすのではないかと期待している。人が集まる場所が都市広場だとするなら、立体的に人がコミュニケーションをとるこの場所は、新しい都市広場の可能性を切り拓くに違いない。

058 Layered Plaza

Garden Gallery
COLOGNE, GERMANY 2011

An eternal ruin

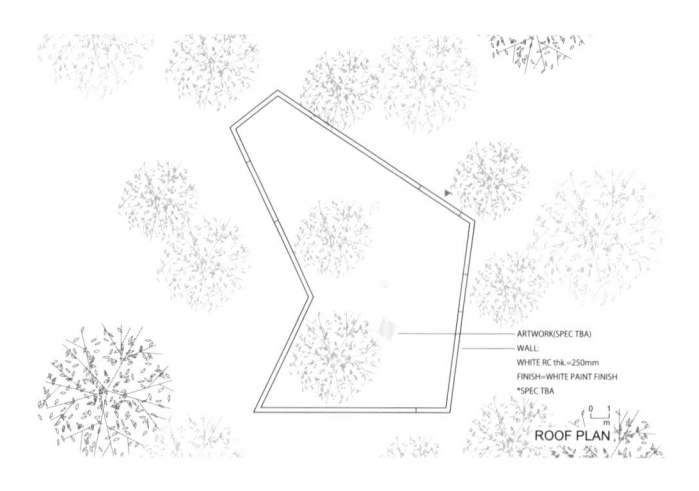

ARTWORK(SPEC TBA)
WALL:
WHITE RC thk.=250mm
FINISH=WHITE PAINT FINISH
*SPEC TBA

ROOF PLAN

This is a pavilion serving as a gallery in a sculpture garden in Cologne, Germany. The seven-meter-high wall, with three apertures and one entrance/exit, encircles an irregularly shaped area, and there is no roof and no floor, with the grass of the ground inside left as is. In this sense it echoes the beauty of ruins, where only walls remain and grass has grown up inside. However, here, as the structure is a ruin from the moment it was conceived, it will forever exist in this unique way. It could also be said that the frame for the scenery itself is the architecture. Or, that the encircled interior is actually the exterior, while at the same time that sense of encirclement is what actually lies at the very root of architectural space, what gives architecture its reason for existence: the separation of interior and exterior. The scene shifts as people walk around the outside and the area inside this wall/building, and the experience of the structure changes depending on the time of day and the season. This illustrates the fact that architecture does not consist simply of structures or spaces, but of a wide range of transient phenomena presented to our awareness as we experience these structures and spaces.

ケルン市内の屋外彫刻公園の中につくられた展示スペースとしてのパヴィリオン。3つの開口とひとつの入り口が開いた高さ7ｍの壁が不定形の領域を囲いとった場所であり、屋根もなく、また地面も緑の草地がそのままむき出しになった建物である。ここは、例えば壁だけが残って内部に草が生い茂った美しい廃墟のような場所だと言えるかもしれない。それは生まれた時から廃墟であり、それゆえにいつまでも新しい廃墟である。またこの場所は、周囲の風景を切り取る窓枠そのものが建築なのだと言えるのかもしれない。あるいはまた囲まれた内部がしかし外部であり、それでもその囲まれた感覚は建築空間の最初の兆しのようなものであるゆえに、内外の間に建築が生まれるきっかけだと言えるかもしれない。そしてこの壁＝建物は、その周りや内部を歩き回るにつれて情景が刻々と変化し、時間や季節によって体験が変化していくゆえに、建築とは、モノや空間そのものを指すのではなく、そこにまつわり生起するさまざまな事柄が認識の俎上に浮かんでは消えていくさまを指しているのではないか、とも思えるのである。

059 | Garden Gallery

COLOGNE, GERMANY
2011

→ Related Projects
014 027 044 066 106

sacai Minamiaoyama
TOKYO, JAPAN 2011

Small labyrinth / synthesis of disparate materials and textures

This was a design for the world-renowned brand sacai's first street-level store. It called for the renovation of an existing building located behind Omotesando. When I visited the site with the sacai's designer Chitose Abe, she said, "it feels very Tokyo." I had the same feeling. A variety of different things exist side-by-side on Tokyo's back roads; they are filled with a sense of diversity and surprise. These are also characteristics of sacai's designs – both make use of a combination of different materials and textures. I dealt with the existing concrete walls by leaving one bare in the adjoining room, painting another one white, and removing unnecessary slabs and displaying the demolished section. This made it possible to carefully combine a variety of textures that were inherent to the building. The finished was imbued with surprise and a wondrous harmony that connected one place to another and also a place that you could endlessly walk around like a small maze. This work has parallels with the *Musashino Art University Museum & Library* and my early work *T house*. I had the sense that I had expanded upon my sense of possibility for the city of Tokyo.

今や世界的に評価の高いブランドとなったsacaiの初めての路面店。表参道の奥にある既存建物の改修である。この場所を一緒に訪れた時、sacaiのデザイナー阿部千登勢さんは＜東京を感じる＞と言った。そこに僕は共感した。東京の裏道の、さまざまな異なるものが共存することで、多様性と意外性が生み出される場所。それはまたsacaiのデザインの特色のひとつでもある、異なる素材や質感の組み合わせということとも共鳴した。そこで既存のコンクリート壁にガラス面を合わせたり、隣接する部屋を一方はコンクリートむき出しで、もう一方は真っ白に塗装したり、また不要なスラブを撤去してその撤去後を荒い破損断面として見せるなど、既存建物に内在するさまざまな質感を丁寧に組み合わせていった。できあがった場所は、ある場所からある場所へと、意外性と不思議な調和をもって連続していく空間となり、いつまでも歩き回ることができる小さな迷宮のような場所になった。それは「武蔵野美術大学美術館・図書館」とも通じるところがあり、また初期の「T house」のようでもある。東京という街の可能性が、自分の中でまたひとつ拡張した気がした。

060

sacai Minamiaoyama

sacai 南青山店

TOKYO, JAPAN
2011

→ Related Projects
004 015 044 051 072

Beton Hala Waterfront Center

BELGRADE, SERBIA 2011

World is made up of flows
- Cadences of flow create diverse places

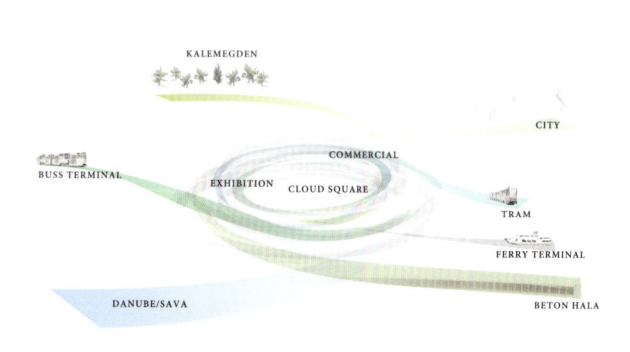

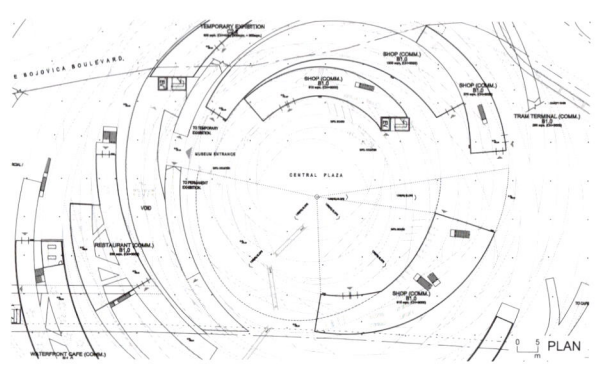

Surrounded by Belgrade's historical town, a cultural heritage-listed castle and the Sava river, and as a vital center to the city's infrastructure, the site needed to become a new hub for transportation and a new city center. Urban public spaces are architecture, and also city squares, extensions of roads, and park-like places. But above all, aren't they a physical manifestation of the flow of people? In analyzing the various flows of traffic and people that converge on the site, I came up with the idea of turning the flow of people itself into architecture. While equipped with a very concentrated core, it would contain a diversity that creates flows in various directions. As a place founded on the ambiguity between concentration and diffusion, it seemed that that would convey the dynamism of the city. When cut into sections, the form, a collection of countless sloping bands, created a geometrical variant of the level differences seen in *House NA*. That made it a very important project in terms of capturing a focus that spanned everything from furniture scale to architecture, the city, and the landscape. The flow of people creates roads, layers of roads create a building, and a building also creates flows of people.

ベオグラード旧市街と文化遺産である城跡、そして交通の起点となるサヴァ河に囲まれた敷地に求められたのは、さまざまな交通の結節点であり、同時に都市の新しい中心であった。都市的な公共空間とは、建築でありながら同時に都市広場であり、路の延長でもあり、公園のような場所でもある。しかし何よりそれは、人の流れそのものの形象化ではないだろうか？　この敷地に集まるさまざまな交通の流れや人の流れを分析している中で、そのような人の流れそのものを建築にするというアイデアが生まれた。それはとても求心的な中心をもちながら、同時にさまざまな方向への流れを生み出す多様性をあわせもつ。求心性と拡散性との両義性の場所であり、それこそが都市のダイナミズムではないだろうか？　無数のスロープの帯が集まるこの形状は、断面で切ると「House NA」のような段差の幾何学の発展形であることがわかる。それゆえ家具的なスケールから建築、都市、そしてランドスケープまでを横断する視点を獲得したとても重要なプロジェクトだ。人の流れが路をつくり、路の積層が建築となり、建築が人の流れをつくり出す。

061

Beton Hala Waterfront Center
International Competition for Waterfront Center First Prize
ベトンハラウォーターフロントセンター 国際設計競技 等佳賞

BELGRADE, SERBIA
2011

→ Related Projects
006 024 041 052 058

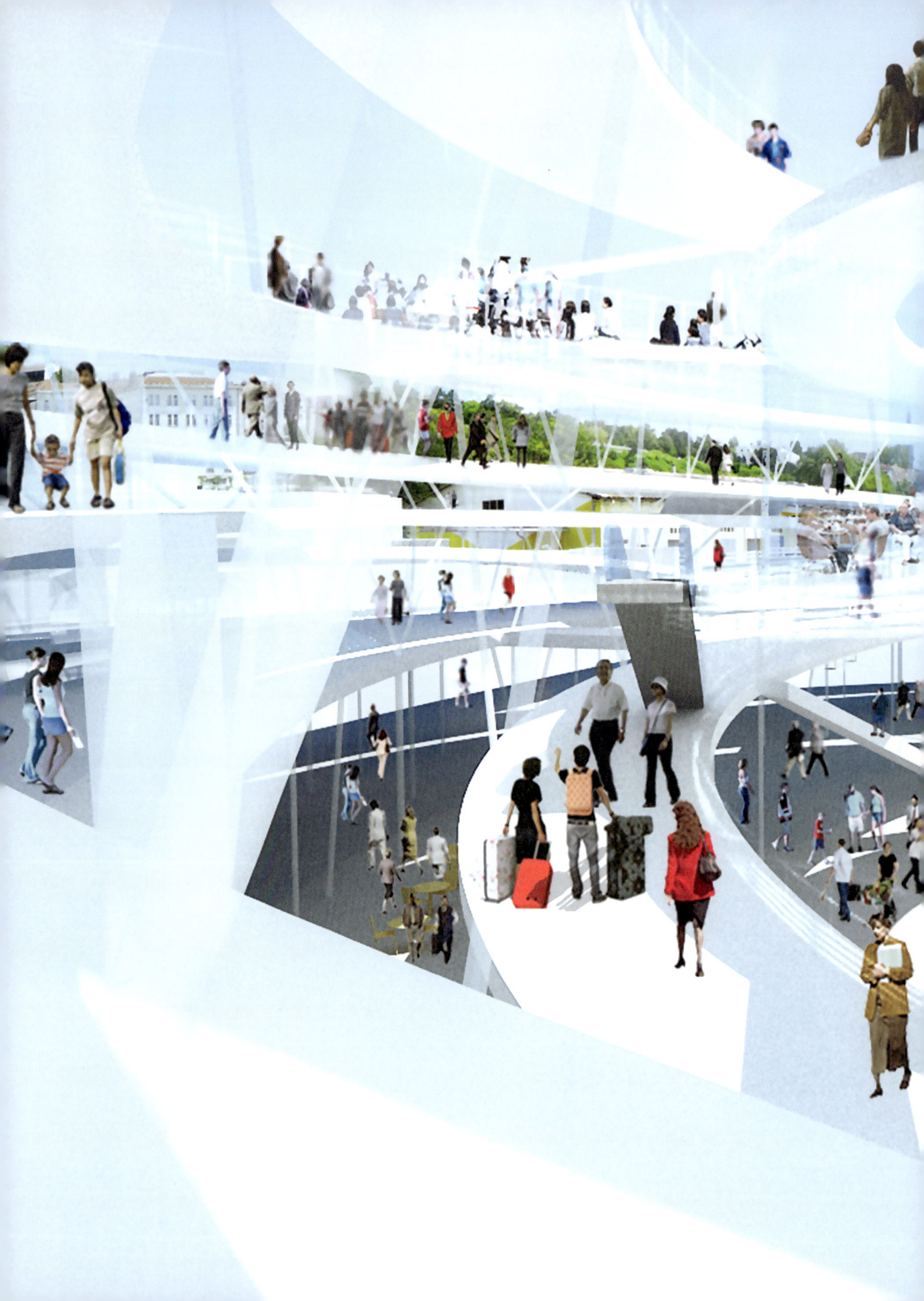

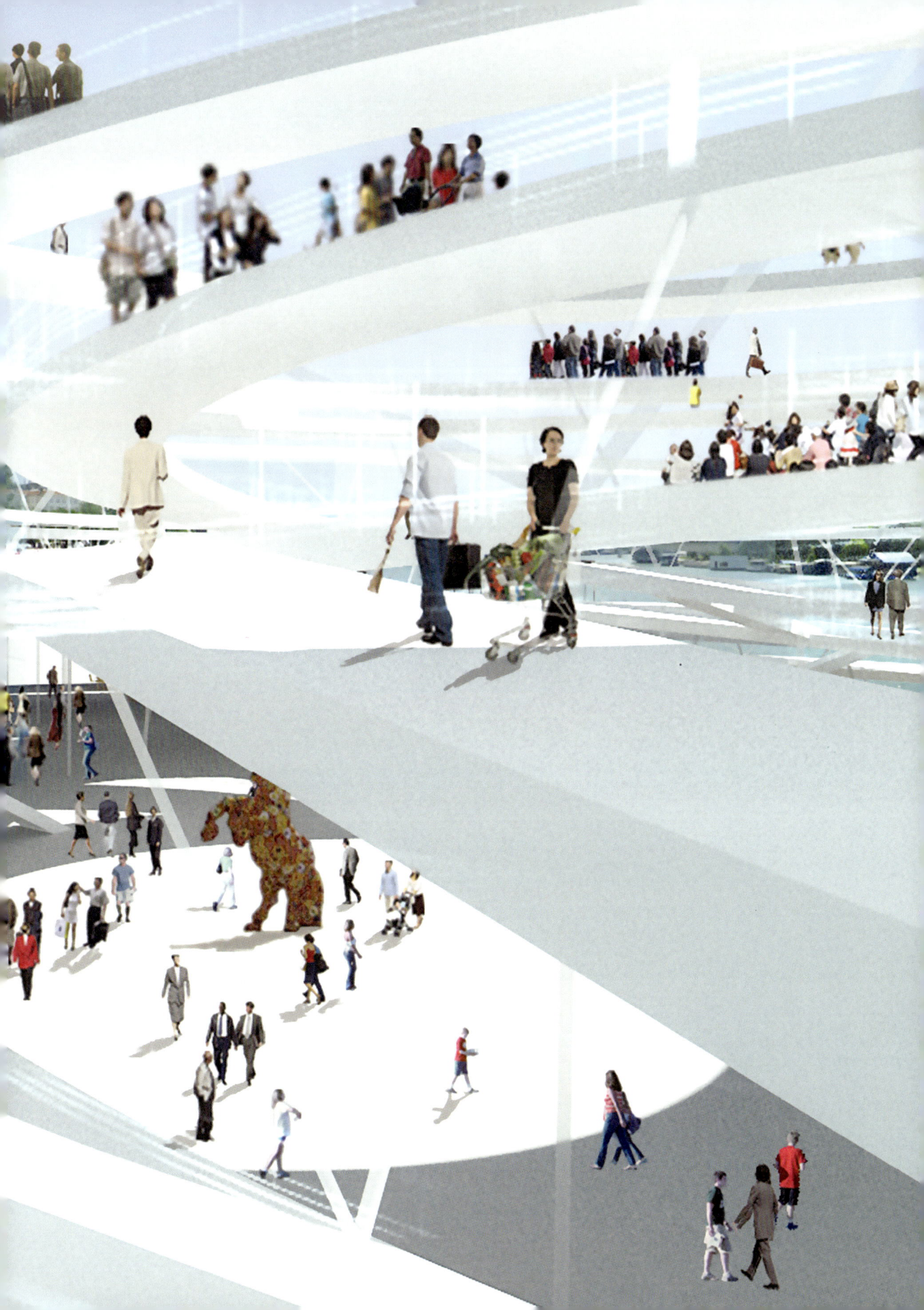

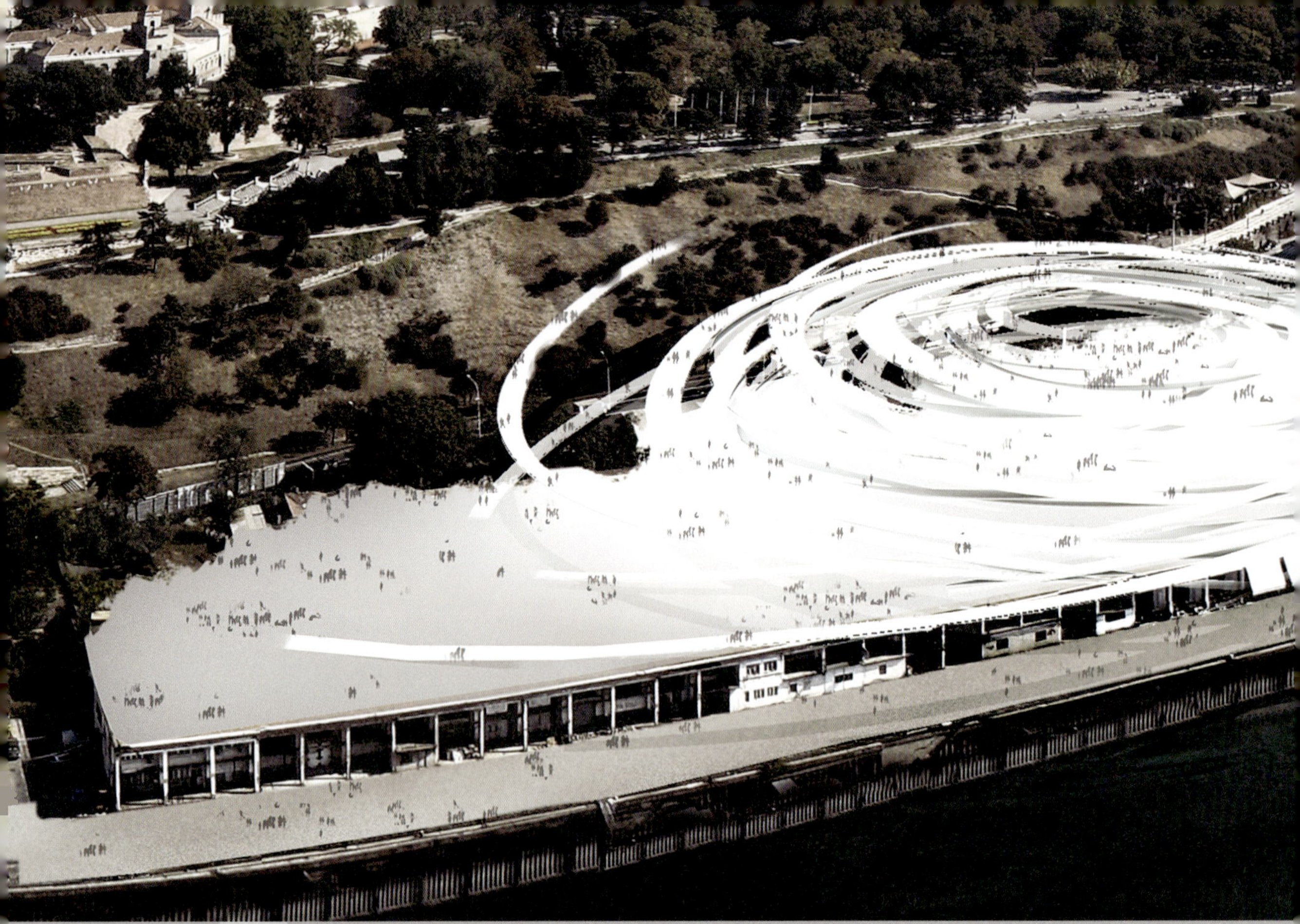

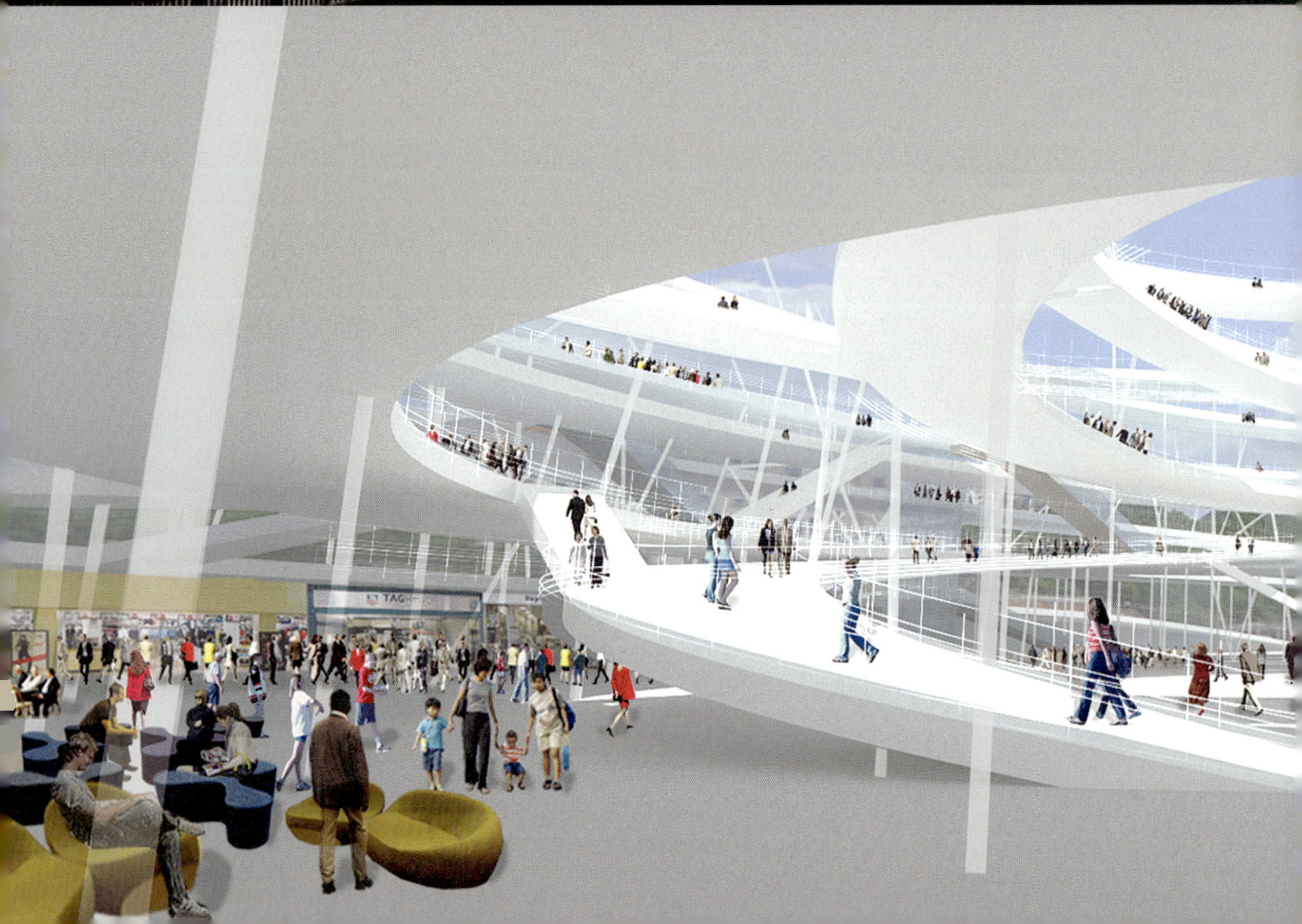

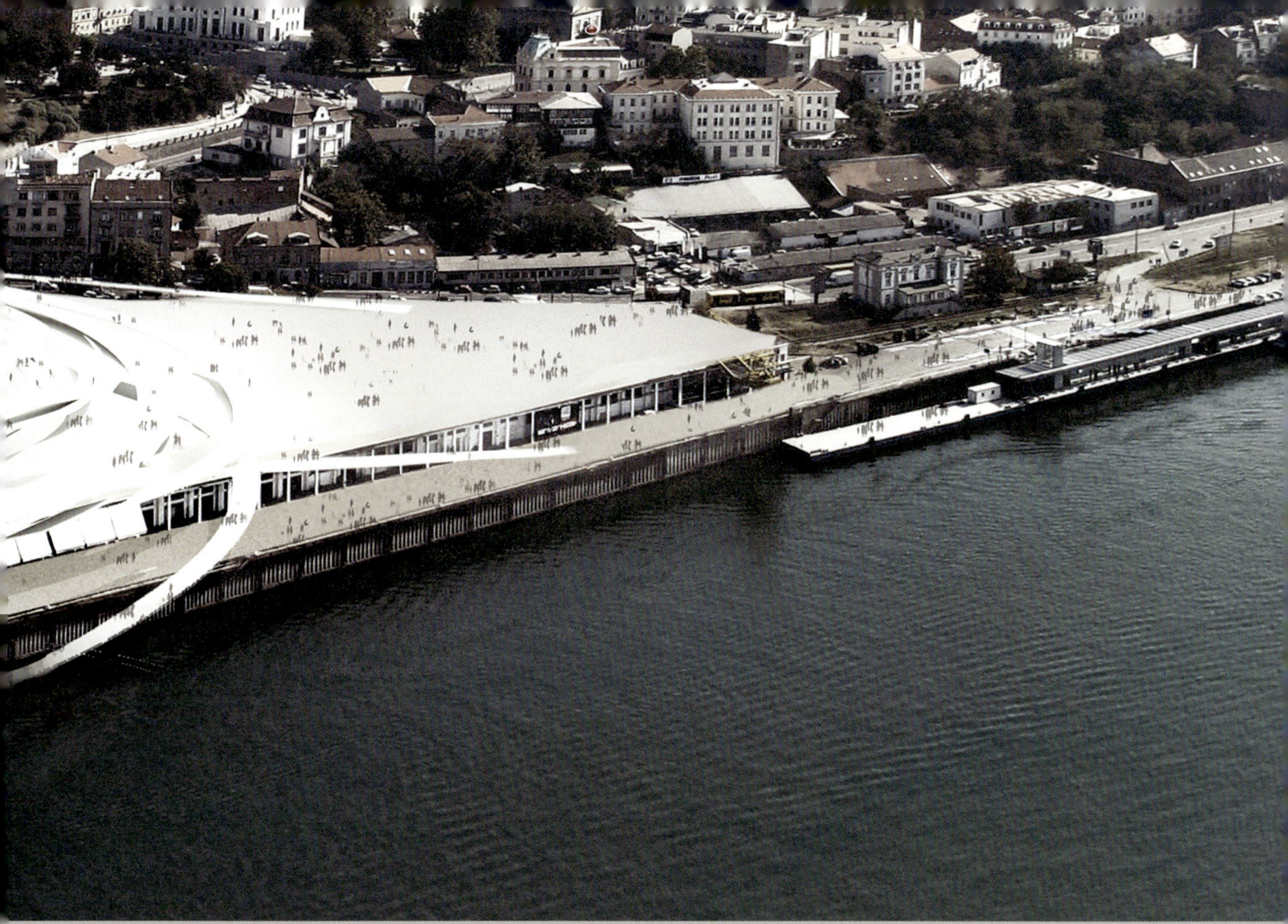

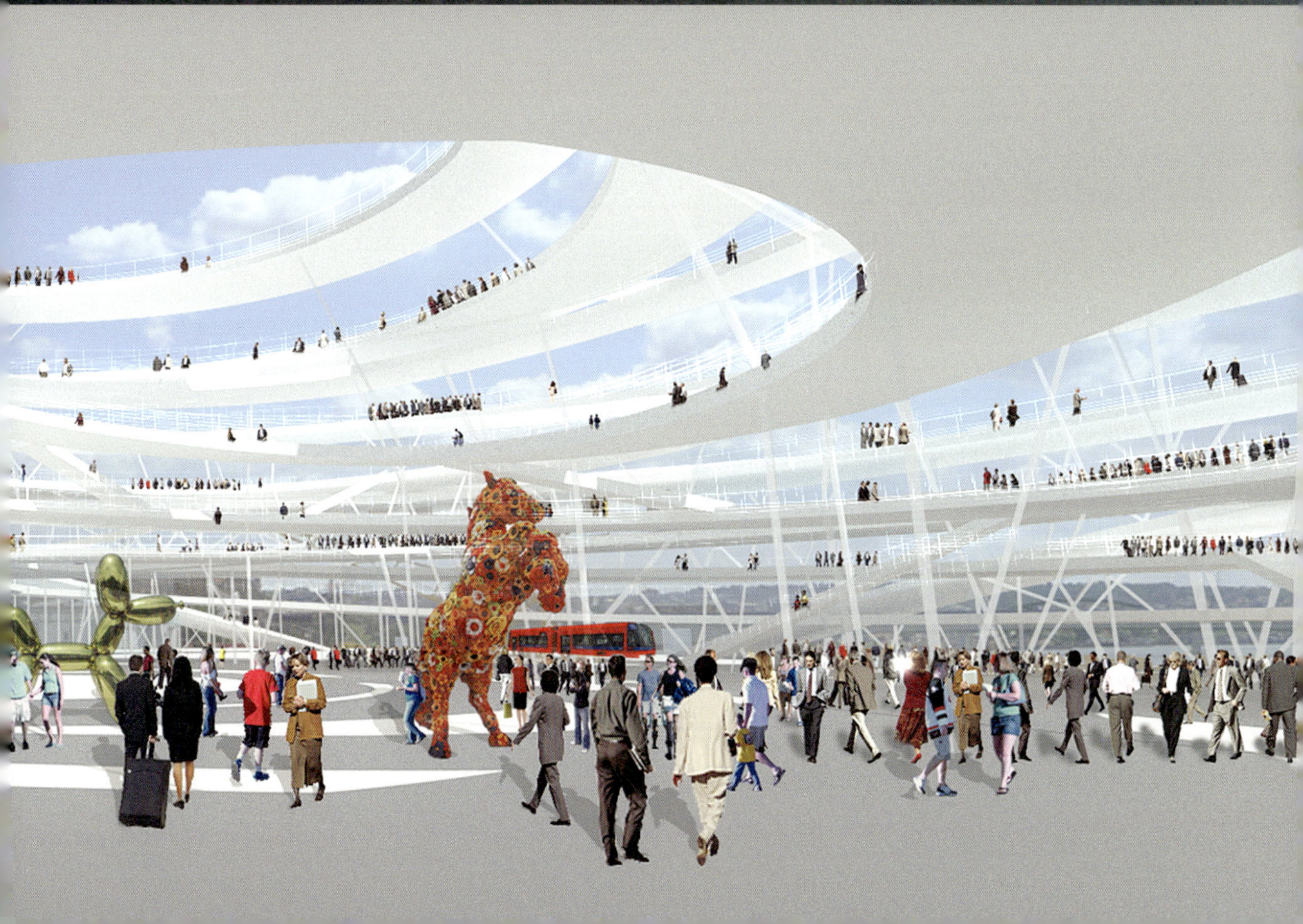

Jyoshutomioka Station
GUNMA, JAPAN 2011

Insert forest into the city

This small train station would fall not so much into the category of architecture but rather function as a temporary place of rest in the city, an essential part of the inhabitants' daily lifestyles as well as the "face" or symbol of the city. It would also be the face of a well-known tourist region and thus make many appearances in the media, and would be not only directly experienced, but also indirectly examined in other modes as well. What should such a simple and at the same time complex and multifaceted structure look like? This proposal was for a small forest to act as the station. When the train arrives, passengers disembark to find themselves in sun-dappled forest shade, as if they have suddenly stepped into another world. The station will be a focal point in an otherwise nondescript landscape. In general, a train station is not solely a functional structure where people get on and off trains, it is also a meaningful place where they naturally spend their day-to-day lives. This station as forest would be truly unique and give the community a new, rebranded media identity. Although the proposal did not win the competition, I would still like to put this idea into practice at a small train station at some point.

この小さな駅は、建築というよりもむしろ都市の中の居場所であり、同時に街の顔であり、象徴でありながら日常生活のよりどころである。またこの駅は、有名な観光地の顔でもあり、それゆえにその存在はメディアを通して拡散され、実体験とは別の解像度で理解され得る。そのような、とても単純でありながらとても多様で複雑な存在を受け止める駅の姿とはどのようなものだろうか？　ここでは＜小さな森＞そのものが駅である、という提案をした。電車が駅に着くと、人は木陰の森の中に降り立つ。突然別世界へと足を踏み入れたかのように。その駅は周囲の捉えどころのない風景の中での特異点となる。駅は単に電車に乗るための機能的な場所ではなく、人びとが日々の生活で無意識に立ち寄る場所となる。また森そのものであるこの駅は、唯一無二の存在としてメディアの中でこの街の新しいアイデンティティとなる。コンペには敗れたが、いつかどこかの小さな駅で実現したいアイデアだ。

062

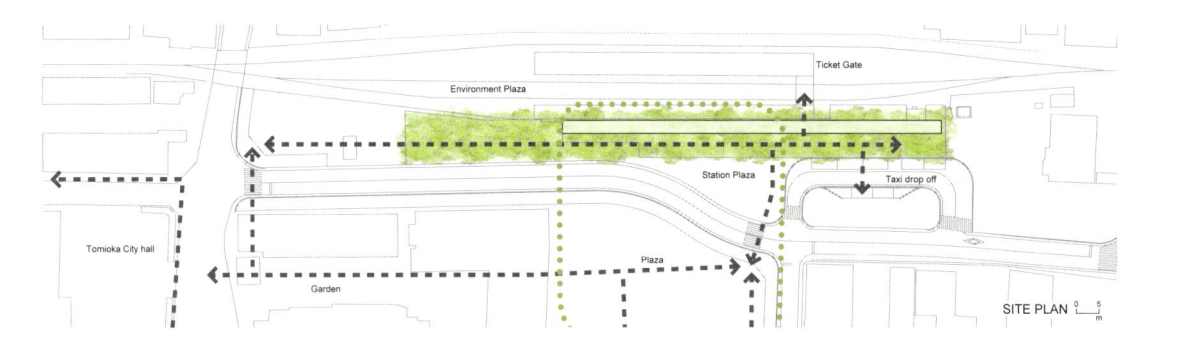

Environment Plaza | Ticket Gate
Station Plaza | Taxi drop off
Tomioka City hall | Plaza
Garden

SITE PLAN 0 5 m

Jyoshutomioka Station

上州富岡駅舎

GUNMA JAPAN
2011

→ Related Projects
008 030 031 065 103

Taiwan Tower
TAICHUNG, TAIWAN 2011

Architecture of emptiness
Emptiness is implied space

Eiffel Tower

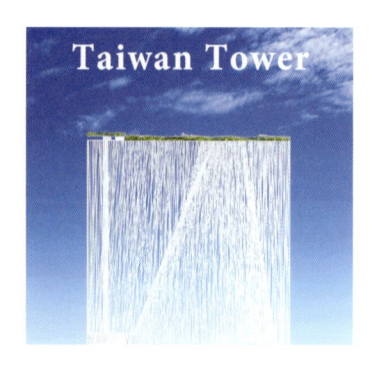

Taiwan Tower

This was the winning entry in an international design competition for a 300-meter tower that would be the symbolic face of Taichung, the third largest city in Taiwan. It would be part of a major redevelopment project on a large former airport site. A tower could be categorized as one of the oldest typologies in architecture. History has seen a wide array of innovative towers over the centuries, each reflecting the spirit of the age: obelisks, five-storied pagodas, "tower cities," church steeples, the Eiffel Tower, and skyscrapers of all shapes, in a diverse range of materials, structures, and geometries. This project embodies the very question of what a tower of the coming era should be. I believe towers will become not masses but fields. Not icons to be seen from a distance, but spaces wherein people gravitate to and assemble within. This tower would be an enormous public space with a 300-meter ceiling, and take on endlessly changing aspects in the manner of clouds or mist – a space resembling a bamboo grove or forest, and one where fiction cohabits side by side with the real.

台湾第3の都市である台中市のアイデンティティとなる高さ300mのタワーを設計する国際コンペの1等案。空港跡地の広大な開発の中のひとつとして計画された。タワーというのは、建築の最も古いタイポロジーのひとつではないだろうか？ それゆえ、いつの時代にもその時代の新しいタワーを生み出してきた。オベリスクや五重塔、塔状の都市や教会の尖塔、エッフェル塔、そしてさまざまなスカイスクレーパーまで、素材や構造、形状など実にさまざまである。このプロジェクトは、これからの時代の塔とはどのようなものなのか、という問いそのものである。これからの塔は、物体ではなく領域のようなものではないだろうか？ あるいはそれは、見るためのアイコンではなく、そこに集まるための場所としてのタワーだろうか？ 天井高さ300mの巨大な広場空間を足元にたたえ、雲か霞のように刻々と表情が変化するような存在。巨大な竹林か森のような場所。虚であることと実であることが同居する場所。

063

Taiwan Tower — International Competition for Taiwan Tower, First Prize

台湾タワー 台湾タワー国際設計競技 等奨賞

TAICHUNG, TAIWAN — 2011

Related Projects: 007 023 041 083 092 107

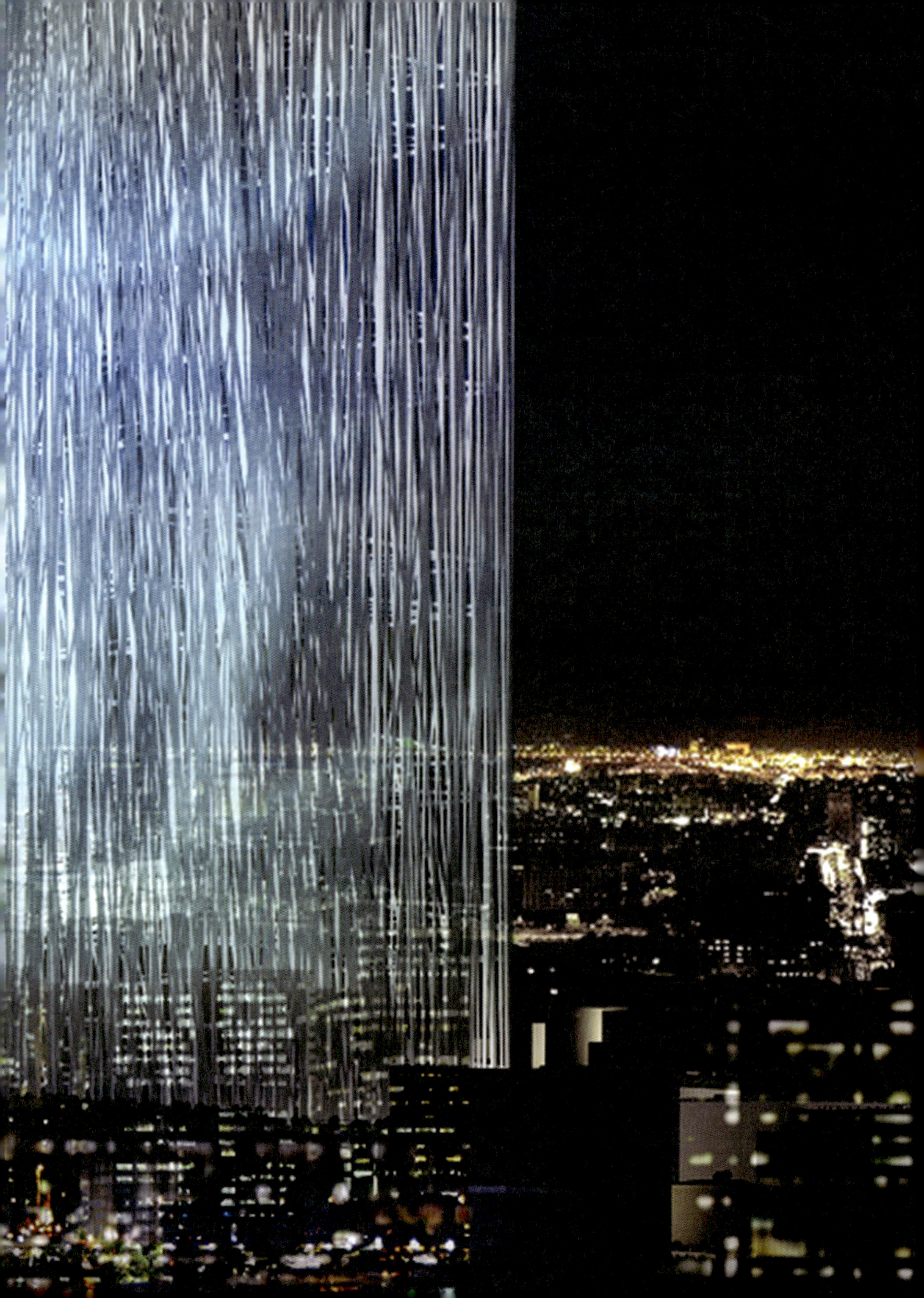

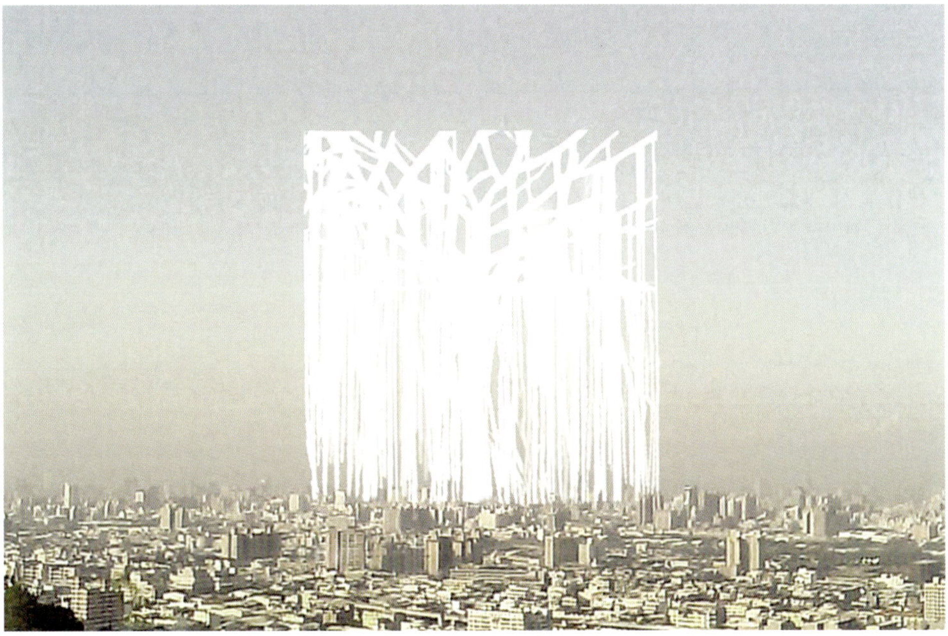

Geometric Forest -SOLO Houses Project

CRETAS, SPAIN 2011

Regular nature / Irregular artificiality

This design is for a vacation house in gorgeous natural surroundings in central Spain. Visiting the site, where the sunlight is very strong, I naturally felt a strong need to block it and simultaneously provide a moderate sense of enclosure. At the same time I had the image of humans being like birds building nests amid this vast natural landscape. That inspired this lattice-like structure of natural timbers of irregular shape and length. The grid is the ultimate imposition of order by humankind, but here it is made of irregular pieces of wood in an attempt to combine the appealing aspects of the natural and the artificial. The density of the wood permits an appropriately controlled amount of light, the wind can blow through the structure, and people inside the building can climb upward, all of which makes the structure simultaneously like a tree and like a treehouse. The lattice, or three-dimensional grid framework, is one of the oldest structures we know, and here it is made new by something even older, namely raw wood in its natural state. These thoughts about the grid were later developed in other projects including *Serpentine Gallery Pavilion 2013, No Dog, No Life -ARCHITECTURE FOR DOG*, and the *Souk Mirage/Particles of Light*.

スペイン中部の美しい自然に囲まれた敷地に別荘を設計する。日差しが強い敷地を訪れて、自然と、この場所では日差しを遮り、適度な囲まれ感をつくり出すものこそが必要だ、と感じた。同時に、この広大な自然の中で、人間が巣をつくって住む光景が思い浮かんだ。そうしてこの不定形な木材を組み合わせた格子状の構造が生まれた。グリッドは究極の人工的な構築物だが、それがイレギュラーな形の木材によってつくられることで、自然と人工の魅力的な融合が生まれる。材の密度によって適度にコントロールされた光が差し込み、風が抜け、またこの格子の中を人が上がって行けることから、構造体全体が樹木でありツリーハウスのようでもある。最も古い形式のひとつであろうグリッド格子を、それ以上に古い生の木材によって新しく生まれ変わらせる。ここでのグリッドの気づきが、「Serpentine Gallery Pavilion 2013」や「No Dog, No Life -ARCHITECTURE FOR DOG」、「Souk Mirage/Particles of Light」などへと展開していくこととなった。

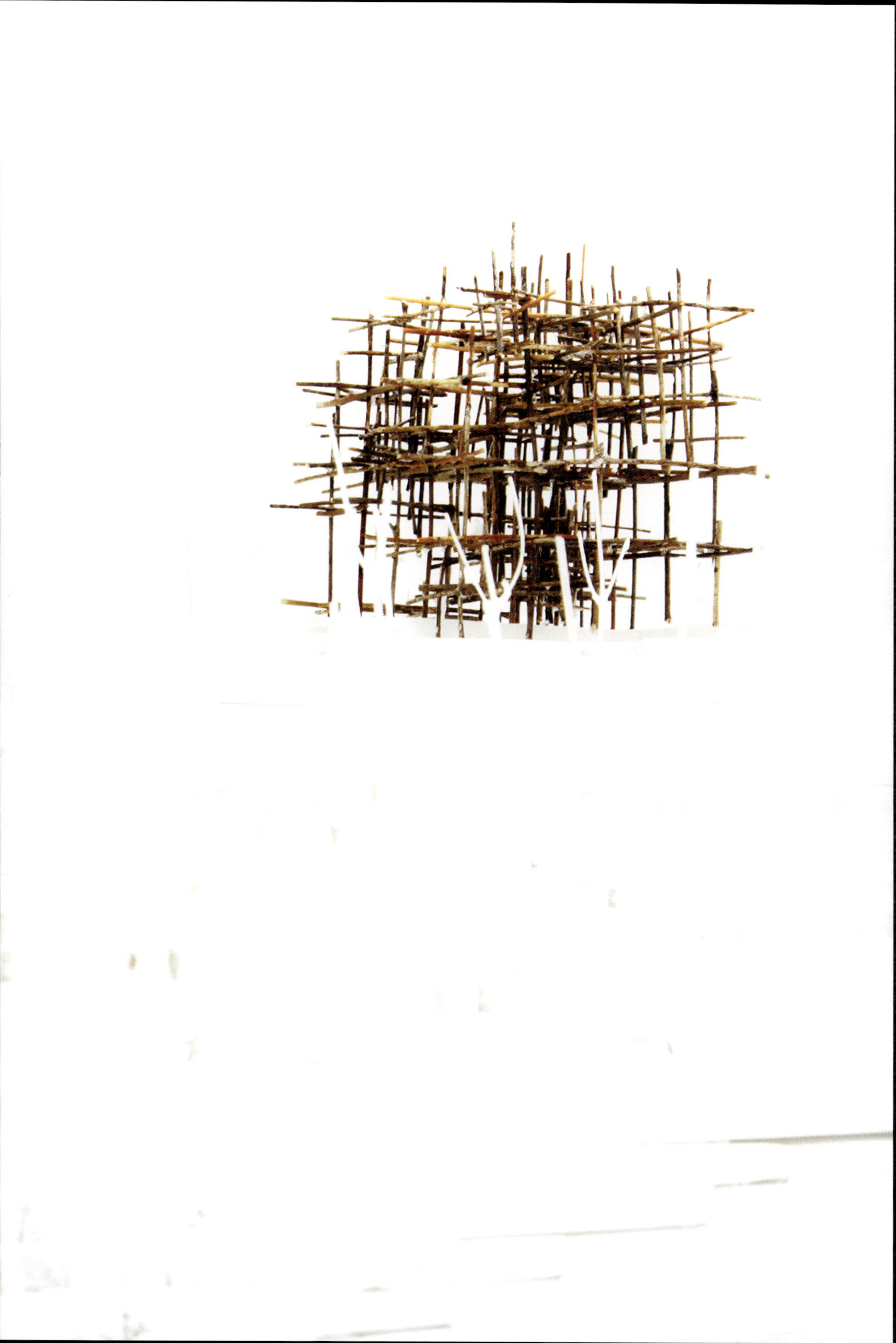

Geometric Forest -SOLO Houses Project

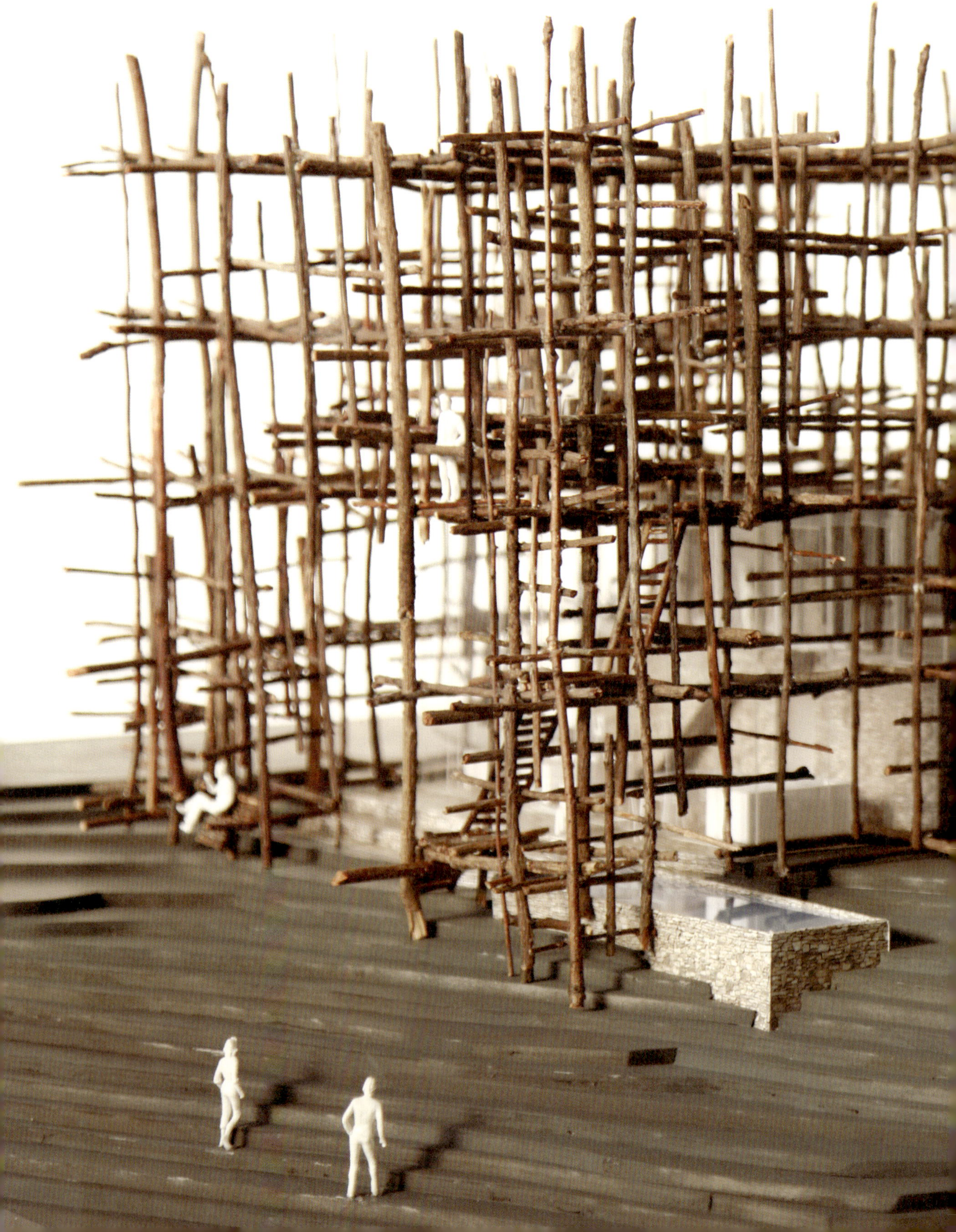

2nd FLOOR PLAN

1st FLOOR PLAN

FOREST OF SILENCE
ZEMST, BELGIUM 2011

When the light itself becomes a roof, forest transforms into architecture

This proposal was submitted to a closed competition for a crematorium in Zemst, Belgium. The grounds are surrounded by woods, and landscaped so that the experience of the scenery is coordinated with the sequence of the crematorium. This scenery is subsumed into the architecture by covering the main area of the premises with delicate louvered surfaces. This creates an exterior yet at the same time partially interior space, and nature is incorporated into architecture. The cloudlike louvers form a translucent roof, penetrated by trees, with greenery and water spreading out beneath them. Nature with a roof over it, or a building with the outdoors inside it: this concept connects to that of the *Garden Gallery*, and to later projects like the *Serpentine Gallery Pavilion 2013*, a *TAINAN MUSEUM OF FINE ARTS*, and a *São Paulo House - Louver Cloud*.

ベルギーのゼムストの街に葬祭場を設計する指名コンペ提出案。敷地全体を森で取り囲み、葬祭場のシークエンスをランドスケープの体験とともにデザインした。そのランドスケープを建築化するにあたり、敷地の主要部分を繊細なルーバーの面によって覆っている。外部でありながら半内部的な場所をつくり出し、自然全体を建築化する試みである。ルーバーは雲のような半透明な屋根であり、木々が貫き、その下には緑と水が広がる。屋根が架かった自然、あるいは外部を内包した建築である。「Garden Gallery」にも通じるコンセプトであり、後に生まれる「Serpentine Gallery Pavilion 2013」や「TAINAN MUSEUM OF FINE ARTS」、「São Paulo House - Louver Cloud」などへと繋がっていく。

065

FOREST OF SILENCE

ZEMST, BELGIUM
2011

1st FLOOR PLAN

STROOIWEIDE

BACK OFFICE
OVENRUIMTE
AULARUIMTE 1
HORECA
CATERING
AULARUIMTE 2
INFO

INGANG PERSONEEL

SYMBOLISCHE BOOM
BIJ ENTREE OVENGEBOUW

WATER ALS ZICHT BIJ VERLATEN AULA
EN SYMBOLISCHE GRENS TUSSEN DE OVEN
RUIMTE EN PLECHTIGHEDEN

INGANG BEGRAFENIS-
ONDERNEMER
EN PERSONEEL

SCHEIDING VERSCHILLENDE
FAMILIES BIJ AANVANG CEREMONIE

INGANG CREMATORIUM
VOOR BEZOEKERS

LADEN EN LOSSEN
RESTAURANT

165 PARKEERPLAATSEN
BEZOEKERS

UITGANG
PAD TERUG NAAR DE PARKEERPLAATSEN

INGANG BEZOEKERS,
GASTEN EN FAMILIE

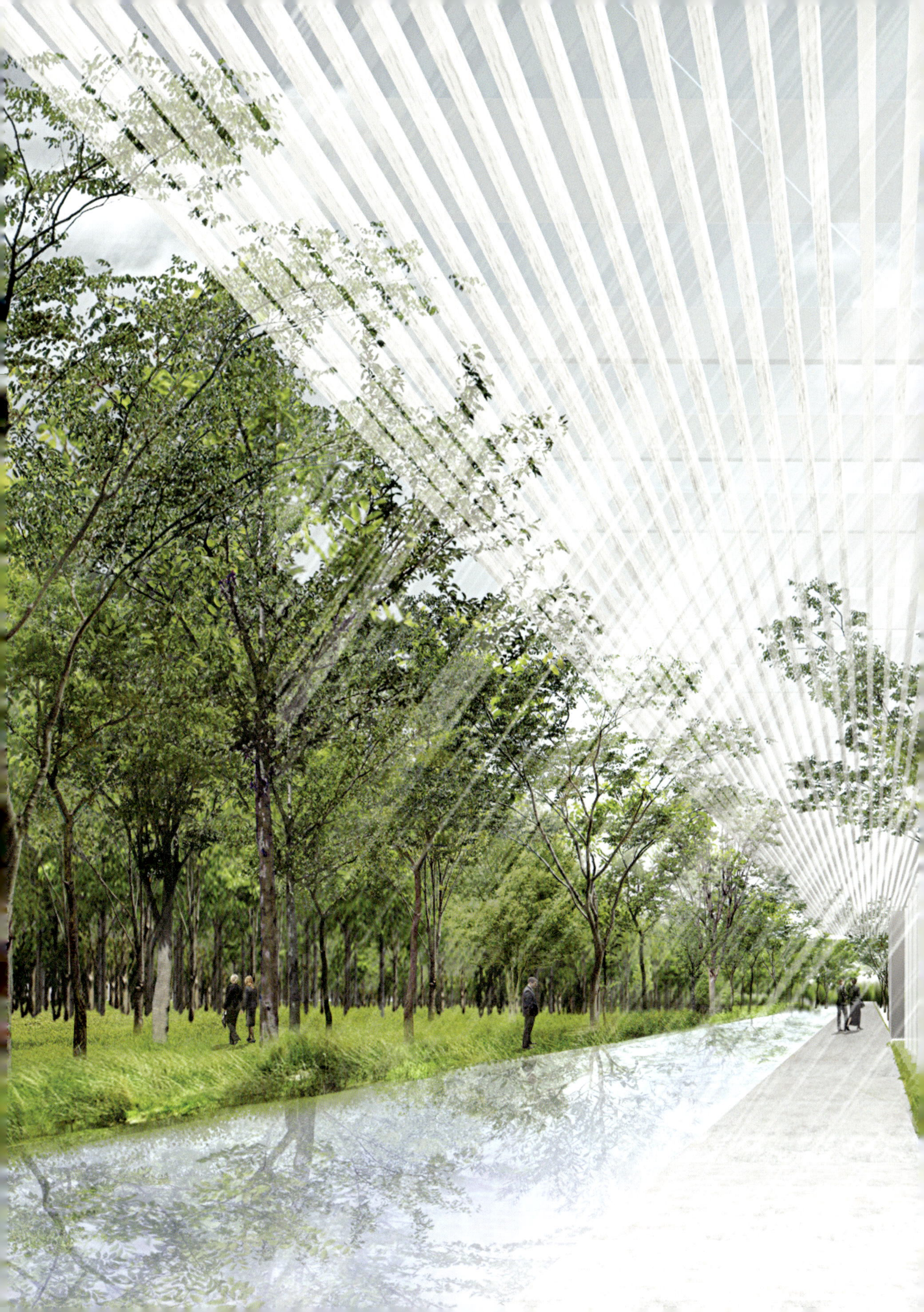

Toilet in Nature
CHIBA, JAPAN 2012

The most private / the most public

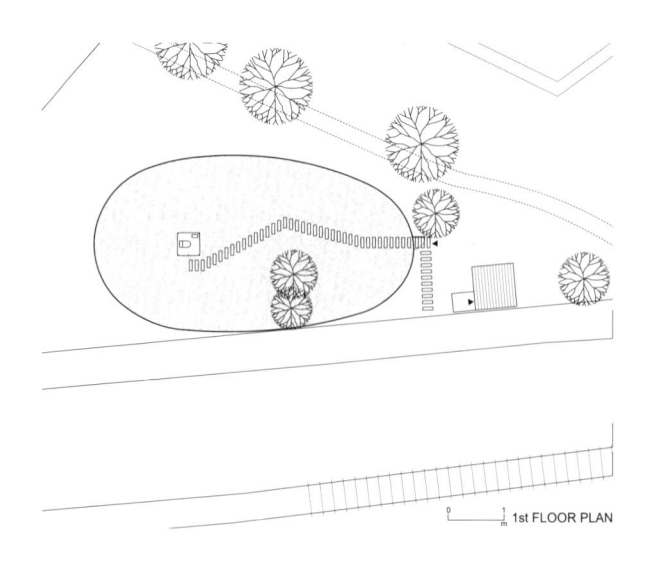

1st FLOOR PLAN

I designed a small public restroom to be built amid the lovely pastoral scenery of Ichihara, Chiba Prefecture. Public restrooms are one of the archetypal categories of architecture. They are by nature public and at the same time private spaces. Being in such beautiful surroundings, leads to a contradiction of wanting to open up to these surroundings while also ensuring that it is closed off to provide privacy. Indeed these two themes, opening up and closing off, are primal currents running through architecture. Here, due to the smallness of the built object, the relationship between the building and the natural environment is directly and spatially experienced. Approximately two-meter-high walls are built around the entire building site, encircling an exterior garden. This garden in turn surrounds a glass box that is the restroom. Nature and architecture, interior and exterior, and private and public are gradually reconciled to one another, and the resulting restroom feels very open while at the same time being closely protected from the outside world.

千葉県市原市の美しい田園風景の中に、小さな公衆トイレを設計した。公衆トイレというのは、建築的にとても原型的な建物だ。それは公共 (public) でありながら、同時にとてもプライベートな場所である。また今回のように美しい風景の中では周囲に対して開きたいという思いと、しかし絶対的に閉じていなくてはならないという矛盾。開くことと閉じることという建築の根源的なテーマに触れている。さらに極小の建築ということで周囲の自然と建築の関係がそのまま空間体験となる。敷地いっぱいの大きさで高さ 2 m ほどの壁を巡らせ、守られた外部の庭をつくり出す。その庭の中にガラスの箱としてのトイレを設置する。自然と建築、内部と外部、プライベートとパブリックの間が少しずつ溶け合って、とても開放的で、それでいてとても守られたトイレが生まれた。

066

Toilet in Nature

CHIBA, JAPAN
2012

→ Related Projects
001 026 027 059 106

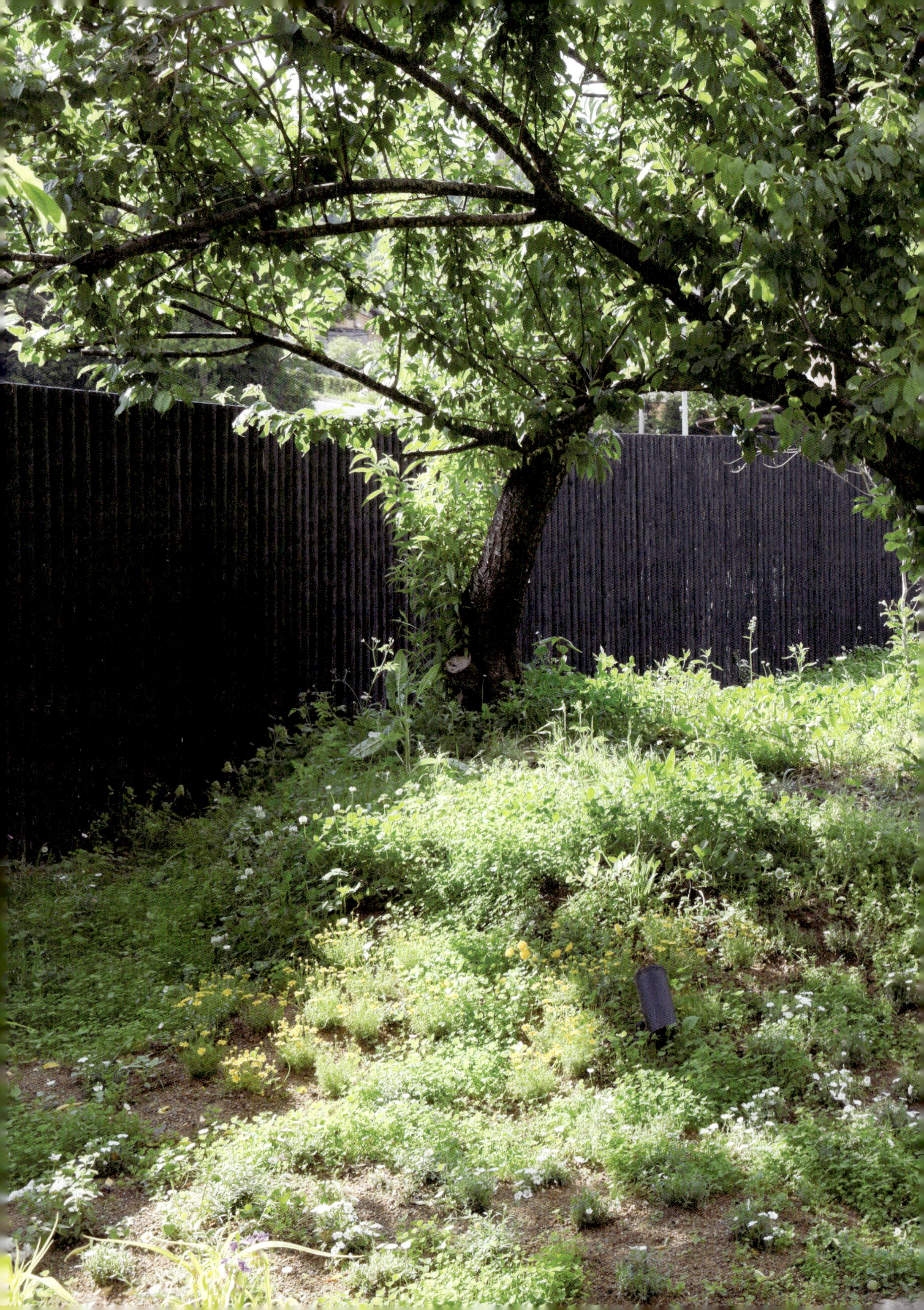

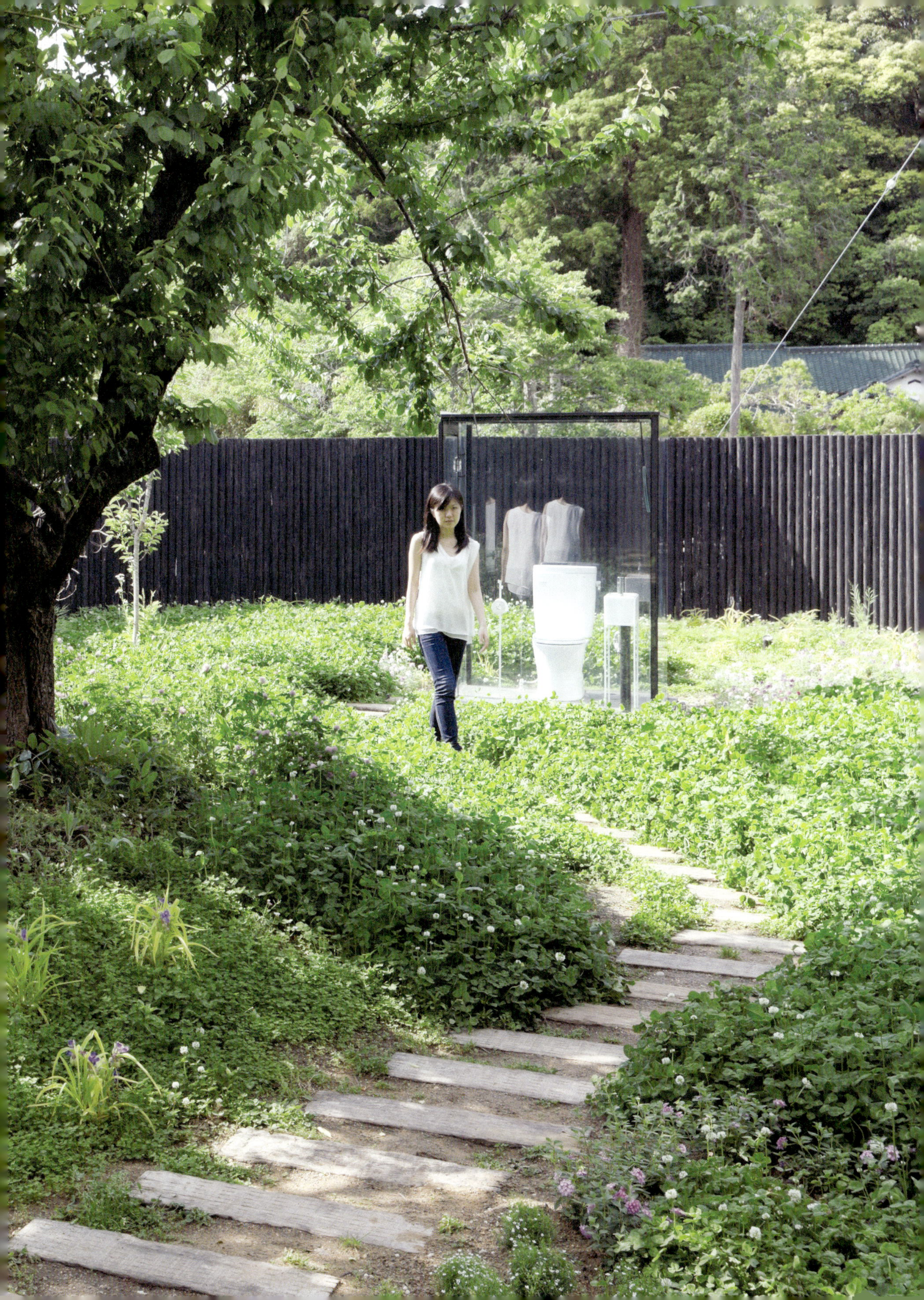

House K

HYOGO, JAPAN 2012

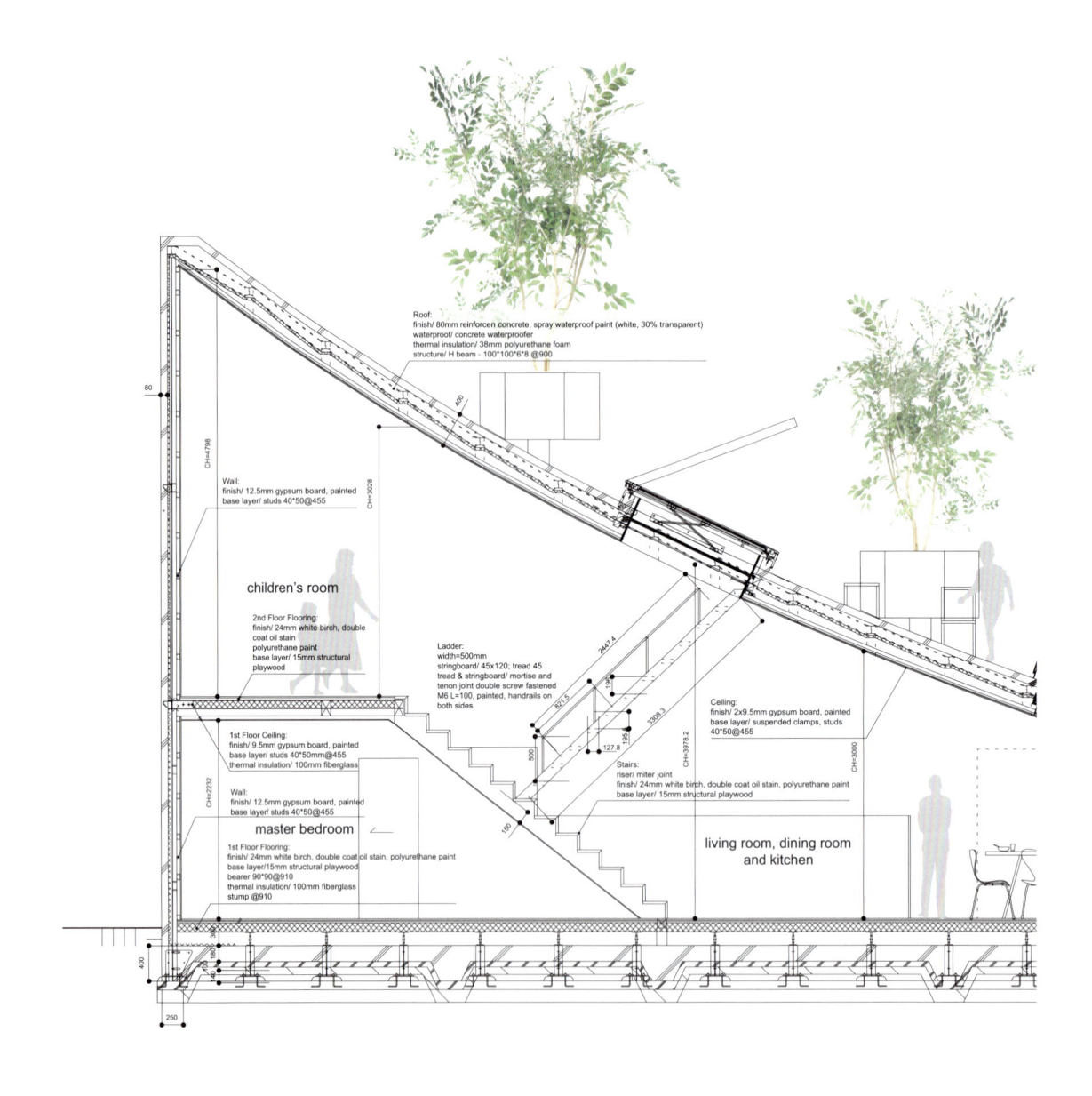

I am interested in the relationship created by the continuous gradations from ground to architecture, and from the city to the house. In these intermediate zones, the lines between architecture, community, and landscape are blurred, and propound potentiality to a new category of place. This house, for a family of four, is on a compact urban site with houses all around the premise and a narrow belt of woods on the western side, so it is only open to the sky above. A roof (roof garden) slopes from the ground up to its highest point in a gradually curving diagonal, reconfiguring the normal relationship between garden, house, and city. The house under this roof is all one expansive room but with different floor heights in different areas, and large skylights that let in soft natural light. And on the sloping roof garden there is furniture, a gazebo-like outbuilding, and trees in planters. The house can be entered from the highest of the skylights, and the overall structure features circulation between interior and exterior, the height differentials inside echoing the slope of the roof. This design was inspired in part by Louis Kahn and Isamu Noguchi's playground.

地面から建築まで、そして都市から住宅までが連続的に繋がるような関係に興味がある。そこでは建築と街とランドスケープの境界が溶け合って新しい場が生まれる予感がする。4人家族のためのこの住宅は、敷地の周囲を隣家に囲まれて、西側に狭く広がる林と、真上の空に開けた敷地に建つ。そこで地面から緩やかな斜面で斜めに伸び上がる大屋根＝屋上庭園によって、庭と家と街の関係を再構築することとした。屋根の下に広がる住居は段差をもった伸びやかなワンルームで、屋根に空いた開口から柔らかく光が差す。斜面状の庭には家具や東屋、そして樹木が設置されて立体的な外部の部屋となっている。庭を上りきった先の窓から家の中に入ることもできて、内部の段差と外部の斜面を巡って、内外を行き来する循環が生まれる。ルイス・カーンとイサム・ノグチによるプレイ・グラウンドの計画案にも影響を受けている。

To stand on, the roof is a ground, and looking up, the ceiling is a sky

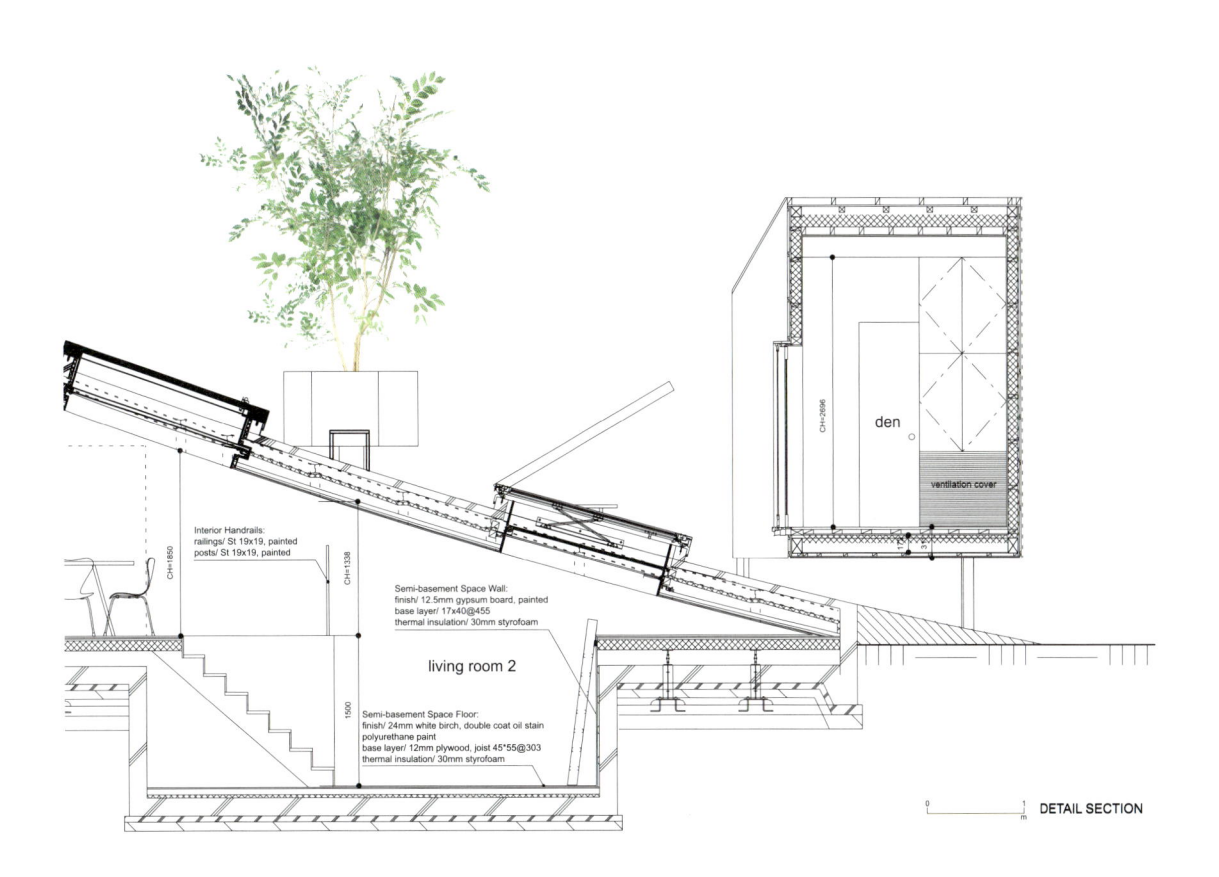

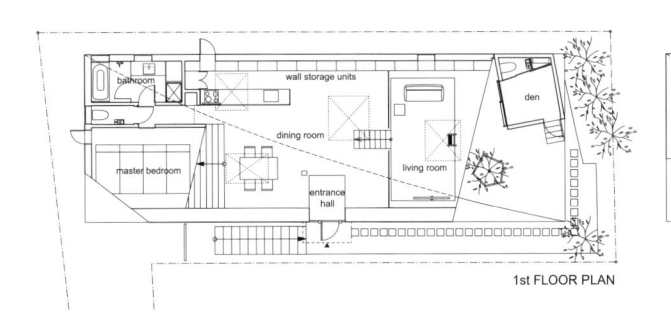

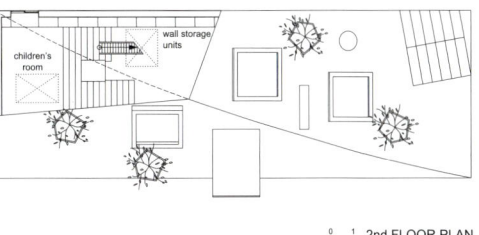

DETAIL SECTION

1st FLOOR PLAN

2nd FLOOR PLAN

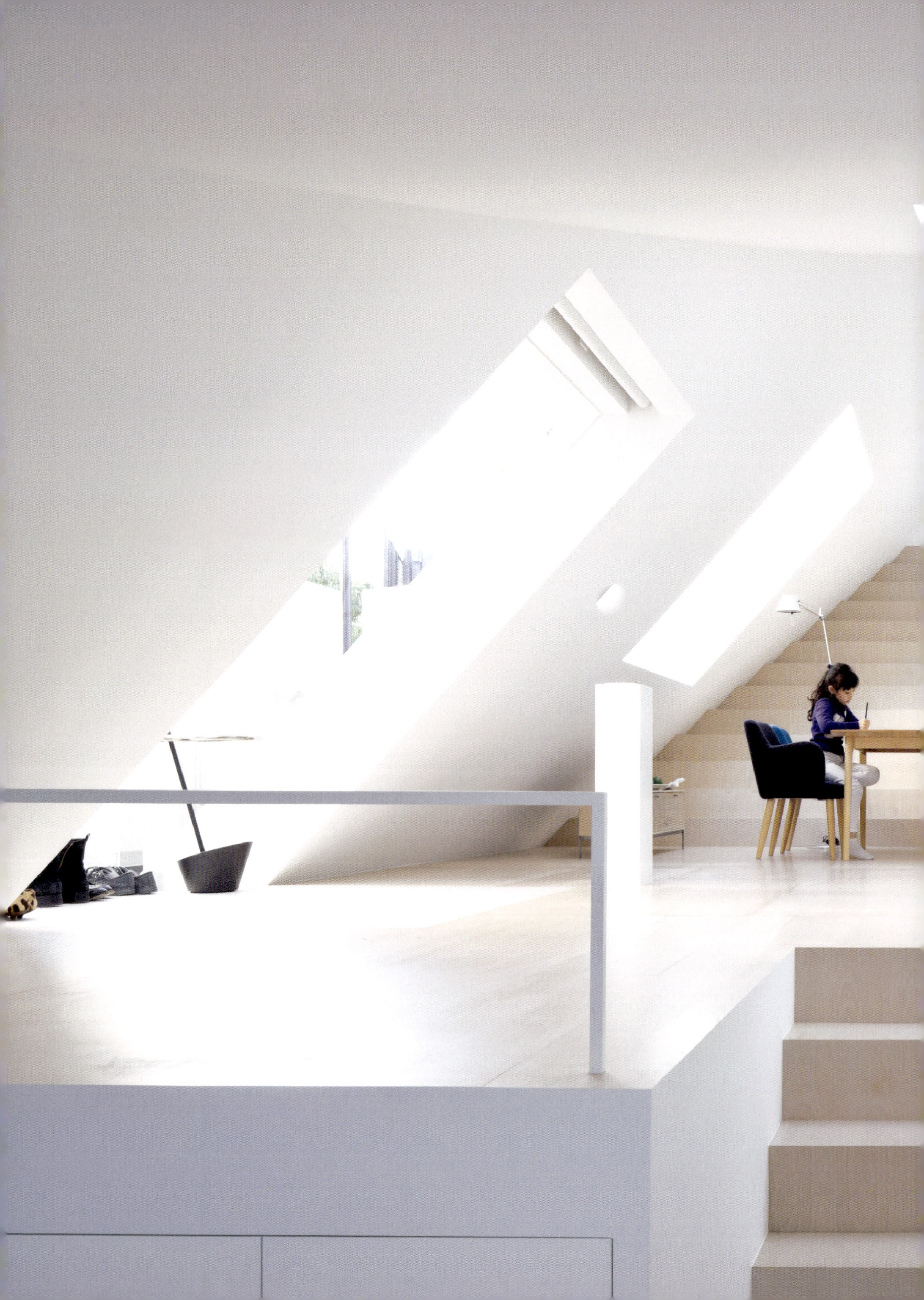

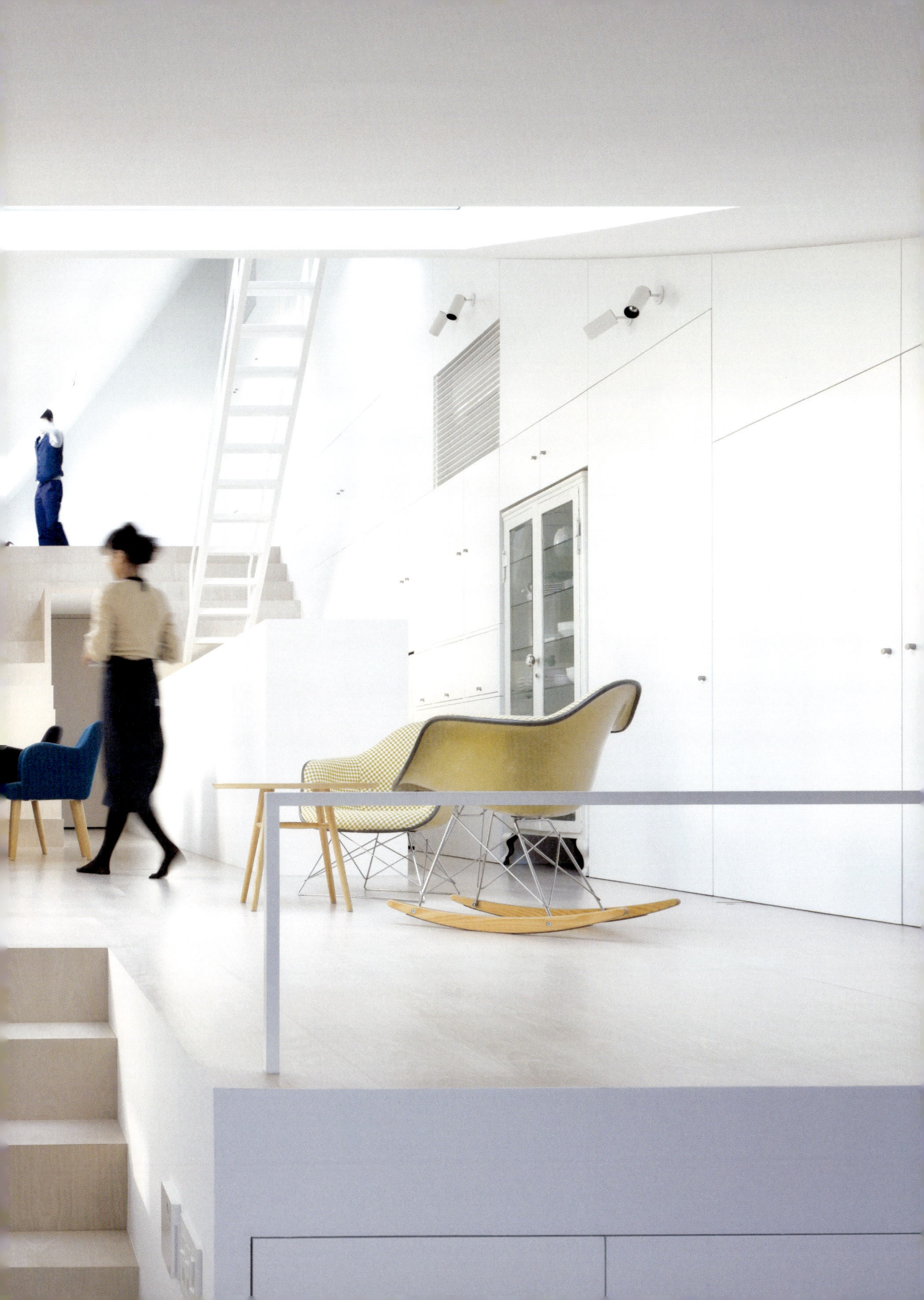

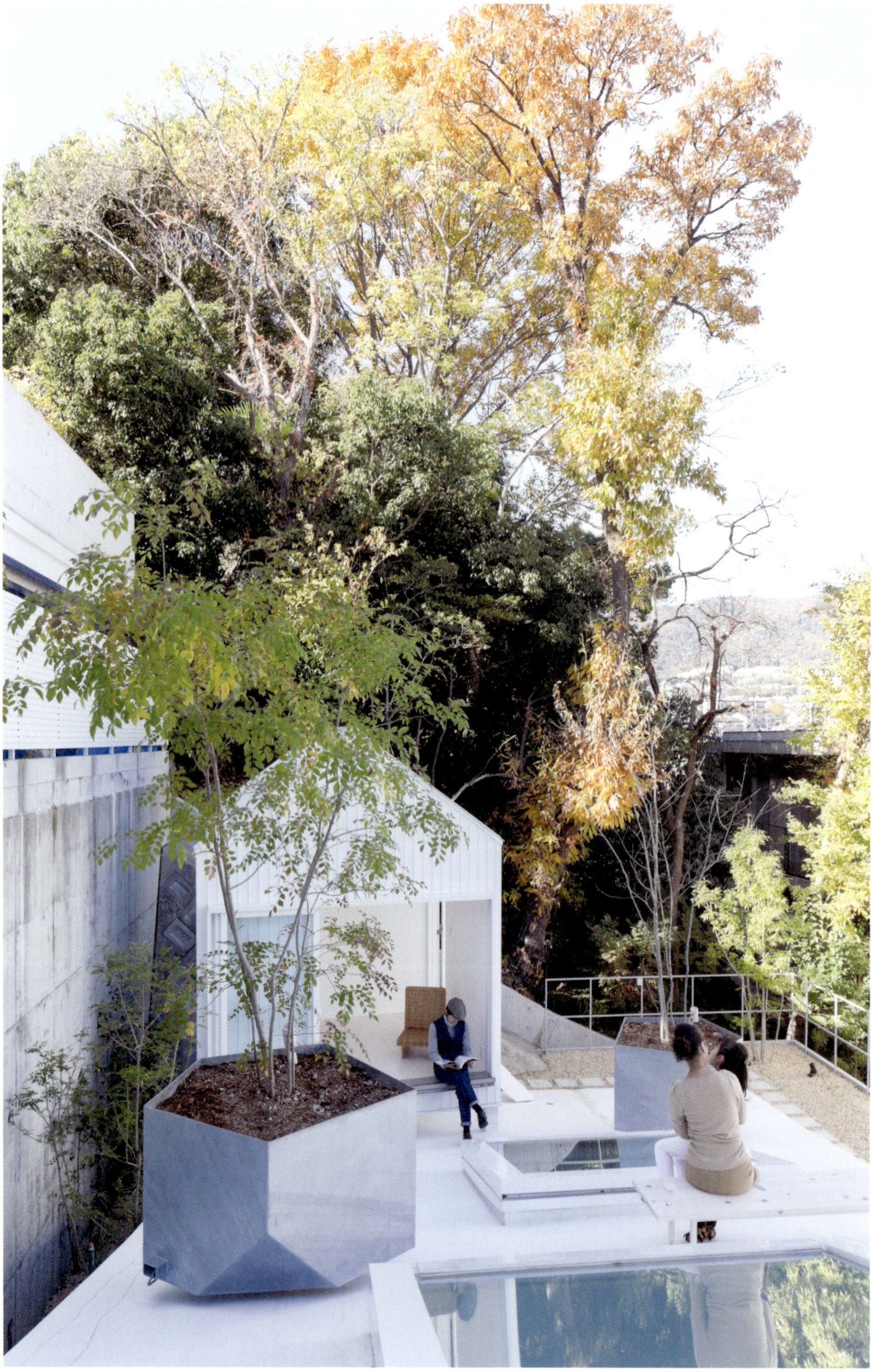

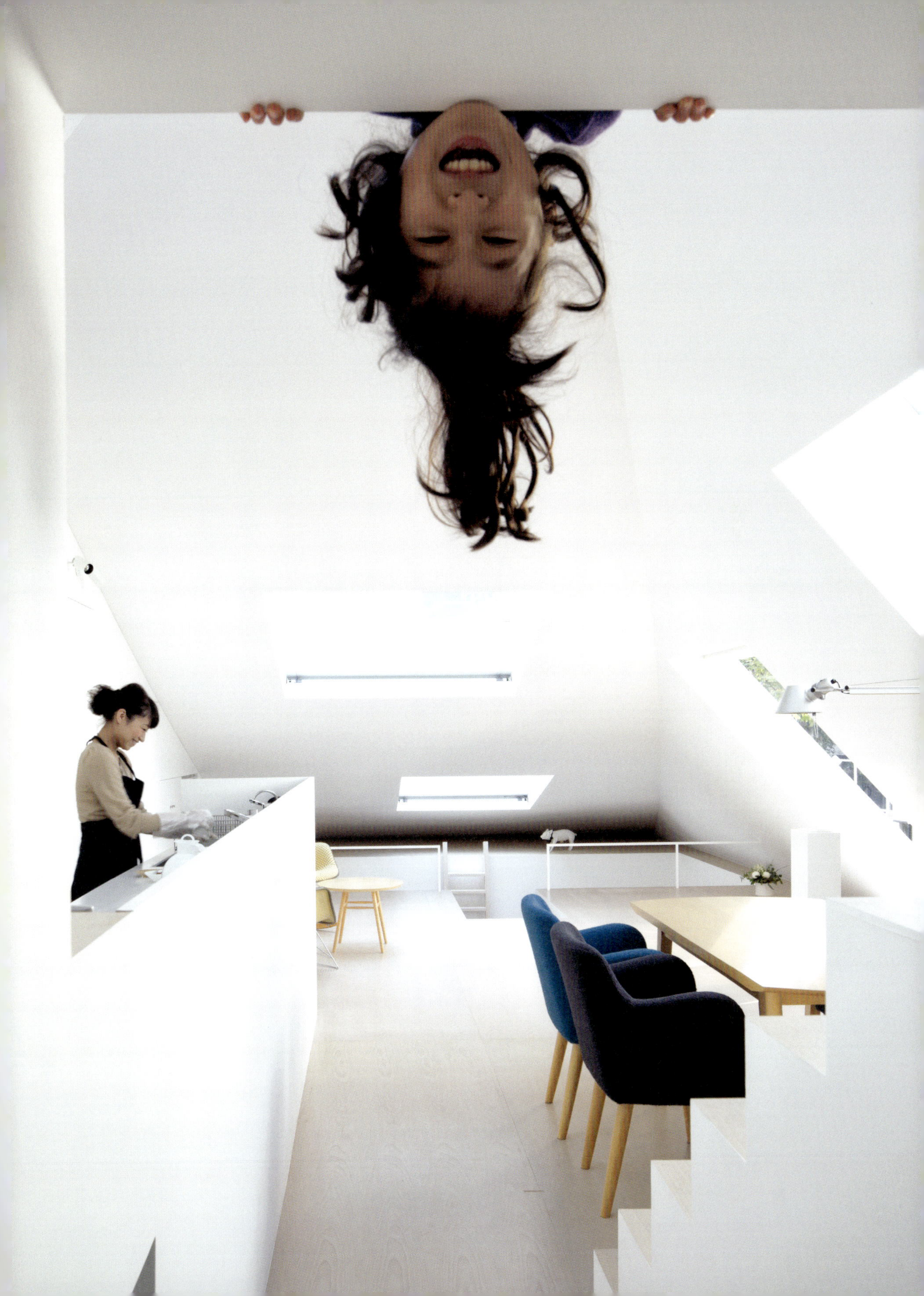

Home-for-All in Rikuzentakata

IWATE, JAPAN 2012

Architecture bridging the past, present and future

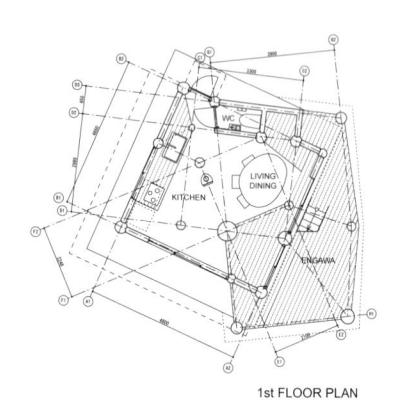

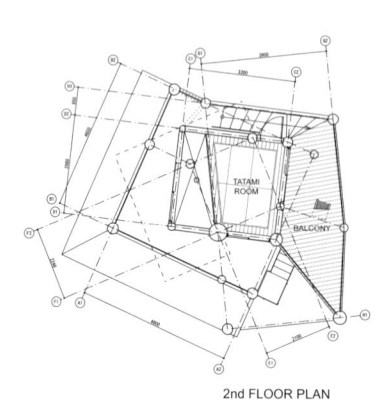

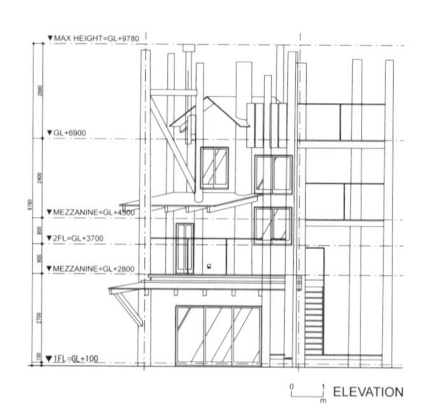

1st FLOOR PLAN

2nd FLOOR PLAN

ELEVATION

Home for All is a plan for a community center to be built at the foot of a hill in Rikuzentakata, which was devastated by the Tohoku earthquake and tsunami of March 11, 2011. Toyo Ito reached out to me and two other architects of the same generation, Kumiko Inui and Akihisa Hirata, and along with photographer Naoya Hatakeyama we formed a five-person design team. We were five designers with distinct styles that occasionally clashed at the start, making for slow progress at first. However, as we engaged with the site the local residents had selected, its significance, and the residents' day-to-day thoughts and feelings, we discovered that architectural design came together simply by delicately capturing the emerging ideas fostered through discussion and giving them form. We were recreating the primitive community of humankind, and starting to gain sight of the primal role that architecture plays in that community. Architecture is a common thread connecting past, present, and future, connecting people and facilitating communication through place. I feel this building touches on the very essence of architecture, being an independent entity – belonging to nothing – and at the same time, something that could only be built on this particular site.

2011年3月11日の東日本大震災で被災した陸前高田の丘の足元に、地域のためのスペースをつくる計画。伊東豊雄さんの呼びかけに応答して、僕と同じ世代の乾久美子さん、平田晃久さんとチームを組み、さらに写真家の畠山直哉さんを加えた5人の共同設計でつくり上げた。5人の個性がぶつかりあうチームでの設計であったことから、当初、設計は難航した。しかし地元の方の選んだ敷地、その場所の意味、地元の方の日常や思いに触れるうちに、そこから自然と湧き上がるさまざまなものを丁寧にすくい上げ、形を与えて積み上げていく作業が、そのまま建築を生み出すことだと気づかされることとなった。原始共同体が再生し、その中で建築が果たす原初的な役割が見え始めた。建築は、過去と現在と未来を繋げるものである。人とコミュニケーションの場所を繋げるものである。この建物は、何にも属さないような、それでいてこの場所でしか立ち上がらなかったであろう、建築というものの本質に触れている。

068

Home-for-All in Rikuzentakata
The Golden Lion for Best National Participation to the Japan Pavilion at the 13th International Architecture Exhibition - La Biennale di Venezia

陸前高田みんなの家
第13回ヴェネチアビエンナーレ国際建築展金獅子賞受賞

IWATE, JAPAN
2012

→ Related Projects
025
055
064
091
092

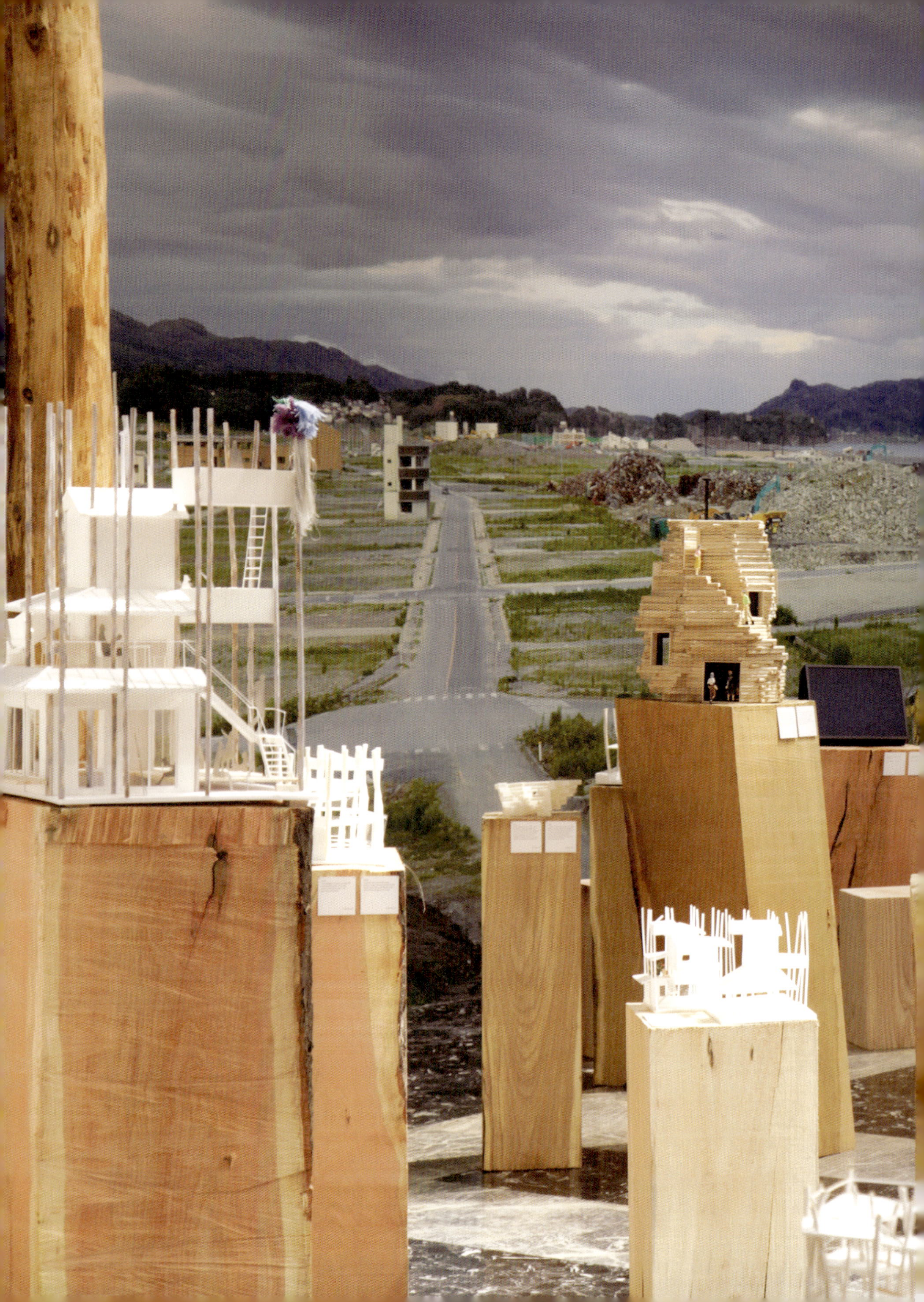

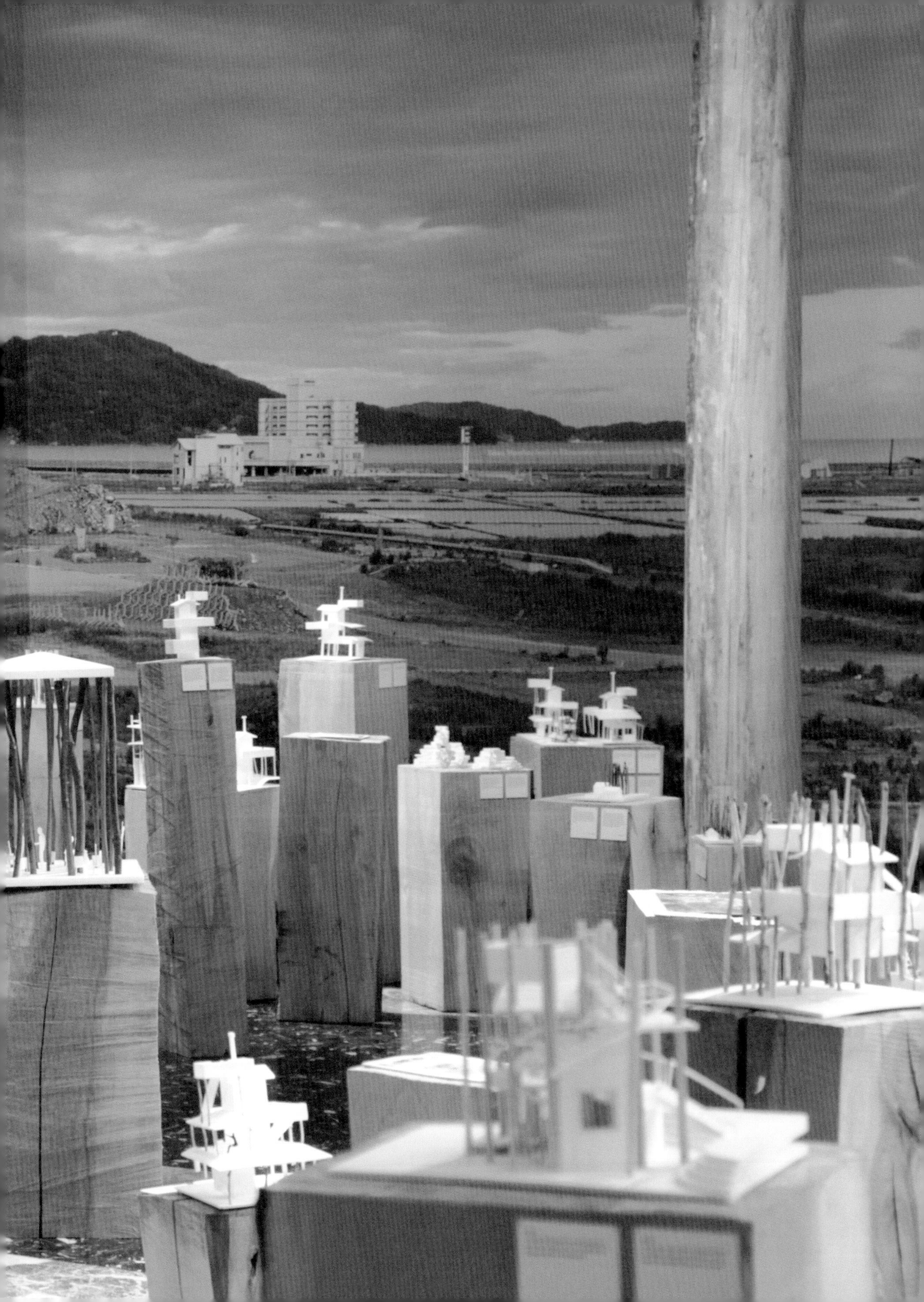

No Dog, No Life - ARCHITECTURE FOR DOGS
TOKYO, JAPAN 2012

Architecture is the distribution of all matters associated to life

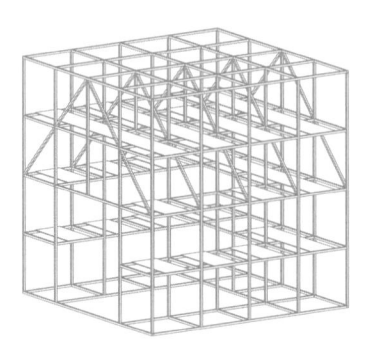

The small building arose from a request from designer Kenya Hara, to create architecture for dogs. I thought this meant making not just simply a place for dogs to occupy, but one for dogs and humans to communicate. When I considered architecture for both, the biggest difference between the two was the scale, so I elected to create a frame at a scale that was a common denominator between dogs and humans. This lattice frame can act as a shelf, as a cave to be entered, and as a site for communication revolving around the canine and human belongings placed inside it. The positioning of these objects, as a result of this communication, gives each house/shelf its unique character. The elements of the home are in constant flux, and this generates further opportunities for communication, offering hints for living together, interacting proactively, and heightening the density and quality of communication.

デザイナーの原研哉さんからの、犬のための建築を構想してほしい、という依頼から生まれた小さな建築。単なる犬のための場所ではなく、犬と人間のコミュニケーションのための場所をつくることを考えた。犬と人間の両方のための建築を考えた時に、一番大きな違いはスケールである。そこでここでは、犬と人間の両方に意味のある公約数的なスケールに基づき、場所の枠組みをつくり出した。このグリッドのフレームは、棚でもあり、潜り込める洞穴でもあり、そこに置かれる双方の所有物を巡ってコミュニケーションが生まれる場所でもある。コミュニケーションの結果としてのモノの配置そのものが、家を形づくると言ってもよい。その家の様相は常に変化し、その変化が更なるコミュニケーションを生む。住むためのかすかな手がかり、行為が始まるための最初の密度をつくり出す試み。

069

No Dog, No Life -ARCHITECTURE FOR DOGS

No Dog, No Life -ARCHITECTURE FOR DOGS

TOKYO, JAPAN
2012

→ Related Projects
007 044 051 077 092 100

Smallest/Largest Art Museum

AIX-EN-PROVENCE, FRANCE 2012 -

Relationship of scenery,

art and the body is constantly under transformation

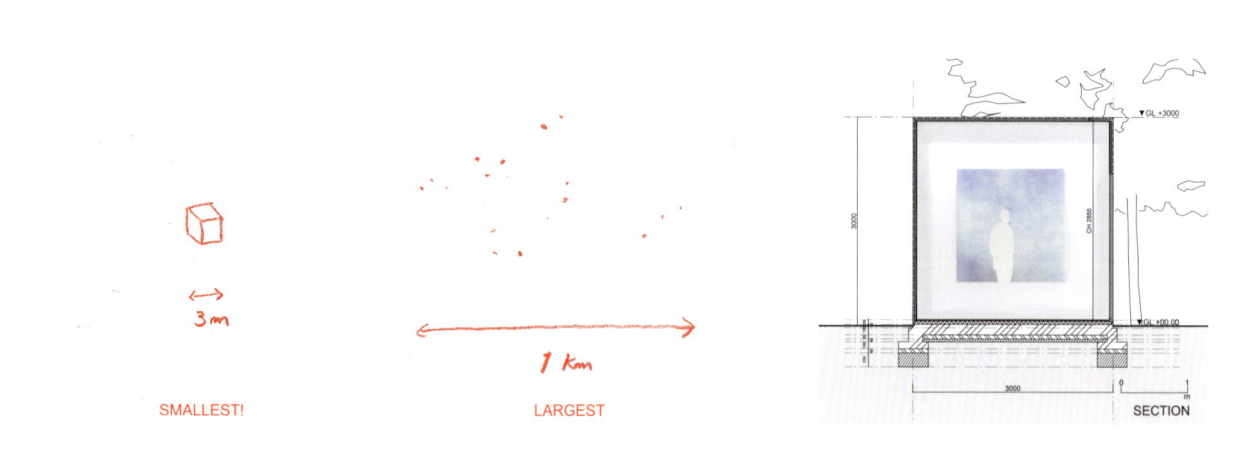

3 m

SMALLEST!

1 km

LARGEST

SECTION

On the outskirts of Aix-en-Provence in southern France there is a winery called Château de Lacoste. This is a proposal for an art museum on a site, where large number of artists and architects have planned a variety of art projects. Was it possible for the entirety of the winery site to constitute one vast museum? The elements making up this museum are small, three-meter-cubed boxes. One face of each box is entirely glass, enabling viewers to see works of art placed inside them. The rest of the exterior face is given a mirrored finish, making the box blend invisibly into the landscape so that the viewer's attention goes only to the work of art. Each box is a micro-gallery, and they are scattered all over the site. Strolling through the beautiful natural scenery of southern France, visitors experience the outdoor museum as if the artwork is placed right in the landscape, and the museum experience itself is changed and reconfigured in various ways via the relationships among landscape, art, and viewer. In principle, these cubes could be scattered over as wide an area as one wishes, and the boxes could have a wide range of sizes. Each one would be the world's smallest museum, while the entire museum would be the world's largest.

南仏エクス・アン・プロヴァンスの郊外に、シャトー・ラ・コストというワイナリーがある。さまざまな芸術家や建築家がアート作品を計画しているその敷地に美術館を設計するものである。この敷地全体を美術館と捉えることはできないだろうか？3mキューブの小さな箱が、この美術館の要素である。その箱の1面は全面ガラスであり、内部に展示される作品を外からも見ることができる。箱の外装は鏡面仕上げとなっていて、風景の中ではこの箱そのものは不可視であり、ただ内部にある作品のみが見えてくる。この極小の展示室のキューブが、敷地内に点々と散在する。美しい南仏の自然の中を歩きながら、来館者はいくつもの作品が風景の中に点在するかのように感じるであろう。風景と作品と自分の立ち位置の関係性によって、美術館体験の構造が刻々と変化し再構築される。概念的には、この箱はどこまでも広く点在していくことが可能であろう。箱の大きさもさまざまに変化し得るだろう。その時、もっとも小さくて、もっとも大きな美術館が姿を現すのである。

070

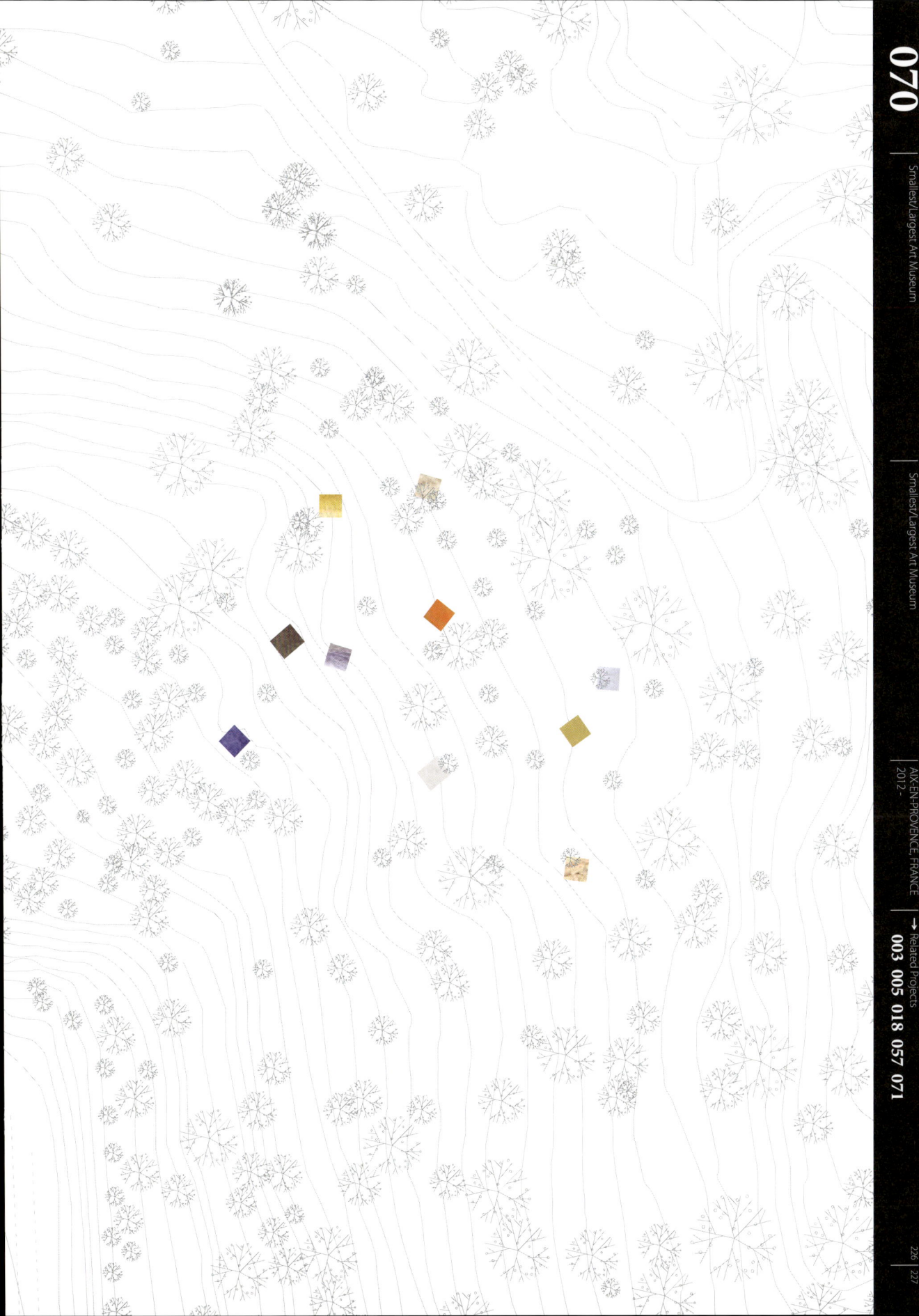

Smallest/Largest Art Museum

AIX-EN-PROVENCE, FRANCE
2012 –

→ Related Projects
003 005 018 057 071

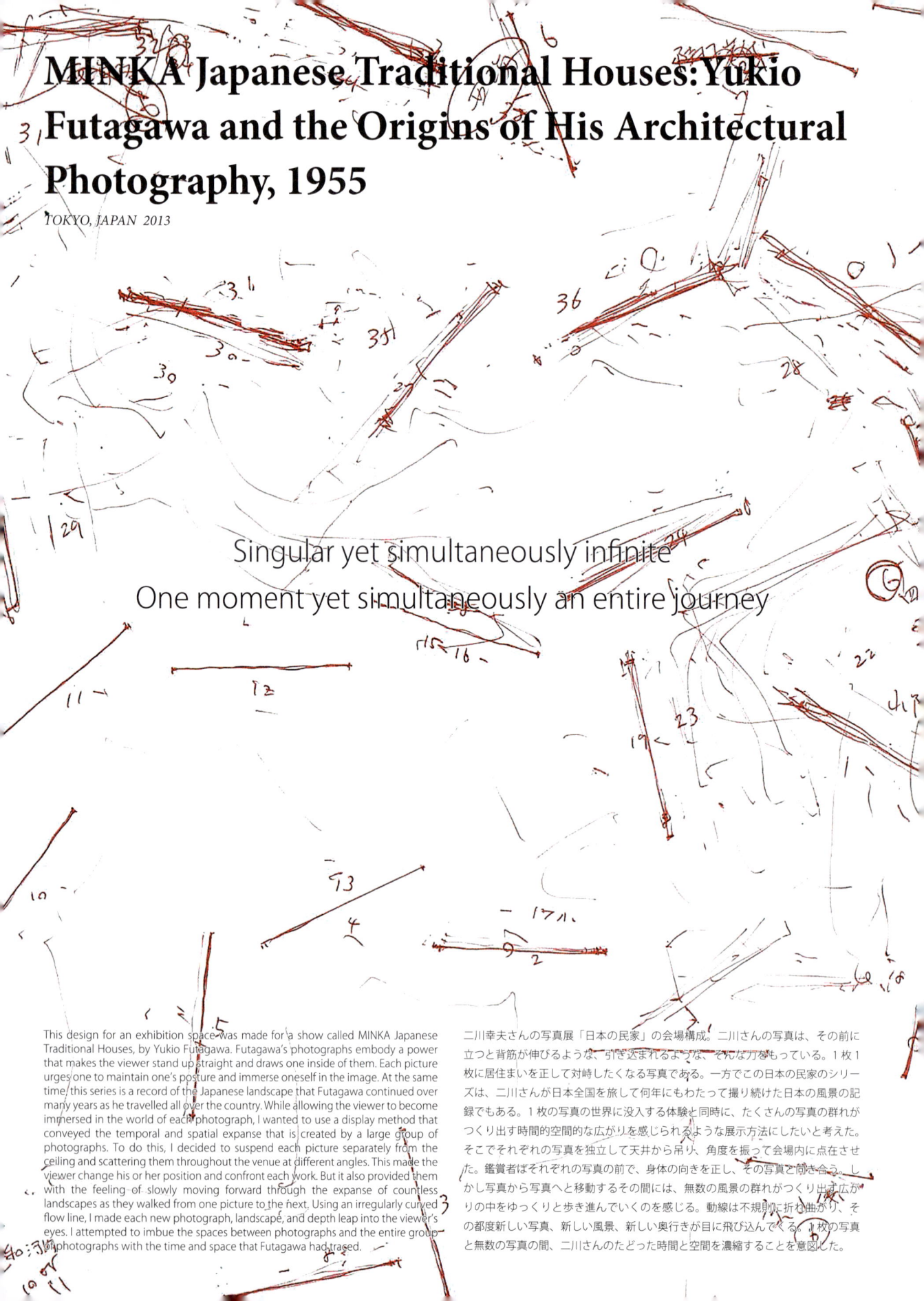

MINKA Japanese Traditional Houses: Yukio Futagawa and the Origins of His Architectural Photography, 1955

TOKYO, JAPAN 2013

Singular yet simultaneously infinite
One moment yet simultaneously an entire journey

This design for an exhibition space was made for a show called MINKA Japanese Traditional Houses, by Yukio Futagawa. Futagawa's photographs embody a power that makes the viewer stand up straight and draws one inside of them. Each picture urges one to maintain one's posture and immerse oneself in the image. At the same time, this series is a record of the Japanese landscape that Futagawa continued over many years as he travelled all over the country. While allowing the viewer to become immersed in the world of each photograph, I wanted to use a display method that conveyed the temporal and spatial expanse that is created by a large group of photographs. To do this, I decided to suspend each picture separately from the ceiling and scattering them throughout the venue at different angles. This made the viewer change his or her position and confront each work. But it also provided them with the feeling of slowly moving forward through the expanse of countless landscapes as they walked from one picture to the next. Using an irregularly curved flow line, I made each new photograph, landscape, and depth leap into the viewer's eyes. I attempted to imbue the spaces between photographs and the entire group of photographs with the time and space that Futagawa had traced.

二川幸夫さんの写真展「日本の民家」の会場構成。二川さんの写真は、その前に立つと背筋が伸びるような、引き込まれるような、そんな力をもっている。1枚1枚に居住まいを正して対峙したくなる写真である。一方でこの日本の民家のシリーズは、二川さんが日本全国を旅して何年にもわたって撮り続けた日本の風景の記録でもある。1枚の写真の世界に没入する体験と同時に、たくさんの写真の群れがつくり出す時間的空間的な広がりを感じられるような展示方法にしたいと考えた。そこでそれぞれの写真を独立して天井から吊り、角度を振って会場内に点在させた。鑑賞者はそれぞれの写真の前で、身体の向きを正し、その写真と向き合う。しかし写真から写真へと移動するその間には、無数の風景の群れがつくり出す広がりの中をゆっくりと歩き進んでいくのを感じる。動線は不規則に折れ曲がり、その都度新しい写真、新しい風景、新しい奥行きが目に飛び込んでくる。1枚の写真と無数の写真の間、二川さんのたどった時間と空間を濃縮することを意図した。

MINKA Japanese Traditional Houses:Yukio Futagawa and the Origins of His Architectural Photography, 1955

日本の民家 一九五五年 二川幸夫・建築写真の原点

TOKYO, JAPAN
2013

→ Related Projects
003 **005** **018** **040** **070**

Mirrored Gardens - Vitamin Creative Space
GUANGZHOU, CHINA 2013 -

Architecture emerge within the seam of time and place

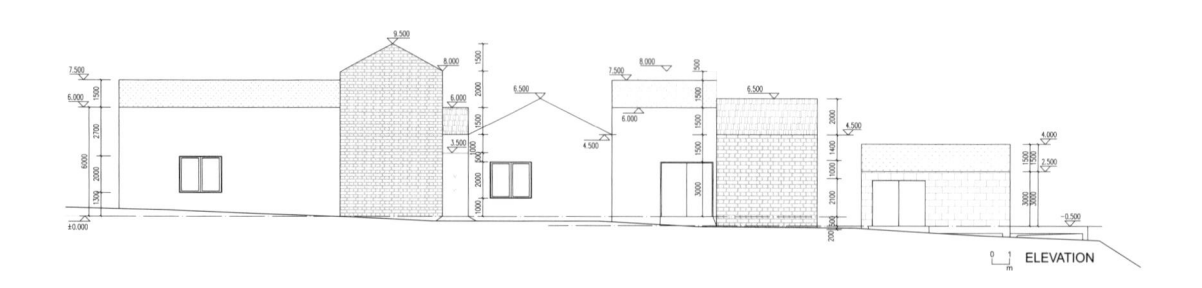

This design is for a gallery on the outskirts of Guangzhou, China, one branch of the China-based international art gallery Vitamin Creative Space. I visited the site prior to starting the design, and in conversations with the client, already a friend of mine, it was determined that as a starting point the design should have affinity to the village surrounding the grounds, should employ materials that represent the area, and should explore agricultural themes. The result resembles a conglomeration of many houses of different sizes with gabled roofs, with narrow alleys between them, and has modalities of both architecture and urban design. The individual buildings show variations, with several different types of bricks, oyster shell, and grass or thatched roofs employed. Perhaps because the conceptualization of the design and its actual building progressed gradually, in parallel, it has a relaxed aura as if it had grown up naturally, and inherits the legacy of the gabled structures of *Tokyo Apartment*.

中国に拠点を置くインターナショナルなアートギャラリーであるVitamin Creative spaceのために、広州の郊外にデザインしたギャラリー。設計を始めるにあたって現地を訪れ、以前から友人であった施主と話をする中で、敷地周辺の集落のような場所とすること、このエリアに特徴的な素材を用いること、さらに農業的な在り方を模索することが出発点となった。建物はいくつもの大きさの異なる切妻屋根の家々が集合した形をとっている。これらの家々は内部で連続しており、また間に細い路地が通るなど、建築と街の間の様相をもつ。それぞれの建物には何種類かの異なるレンガ、牡蠣殻、草屋根や藁屋根などで変化がつけられている。さらに設計と施工自体が、徐々に構想され、施工されるというかたちをとったために、ある種の自然発生的なおおらかさをもつことができたのではないかと思う。「Tokyo Apartment」などの切妻の系譜の先に、とてもリラックスした建物ができあがった。

072

Mirrored Gardens –Vitamin Creative Space

GUANGZHOU, CHINA
2013–

Related Projects
013 015 019 043 060 090

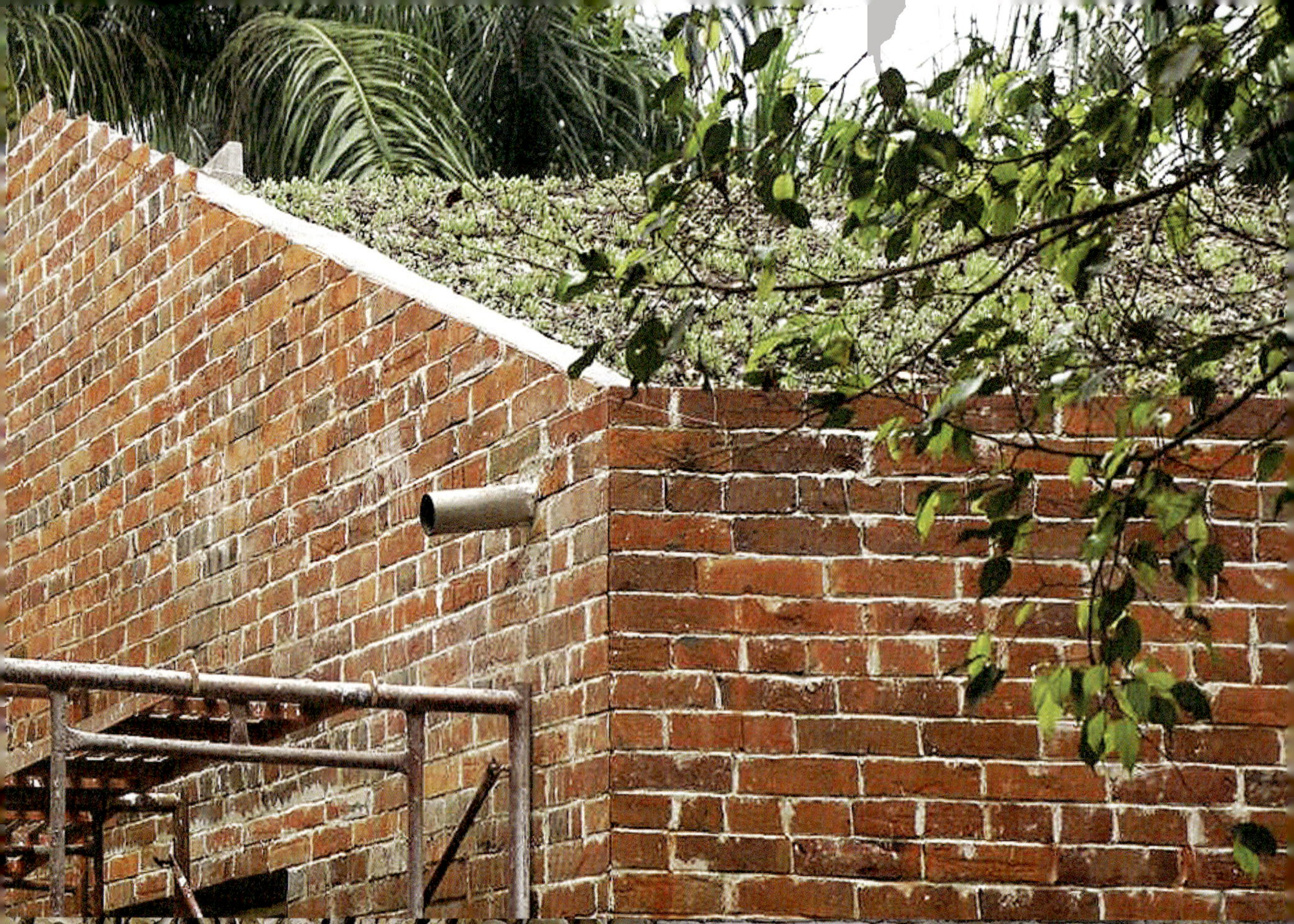
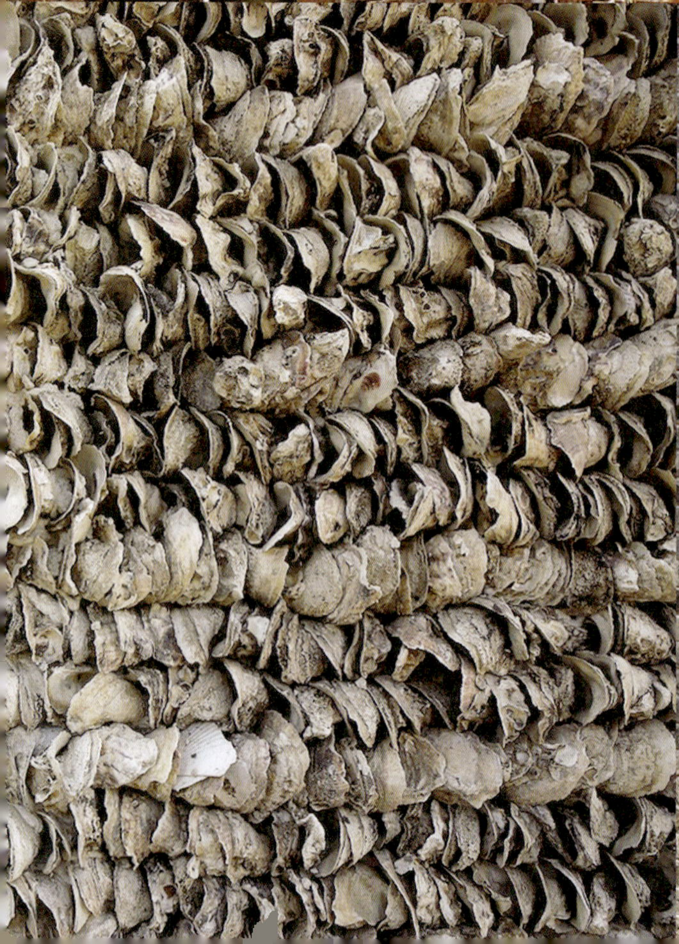
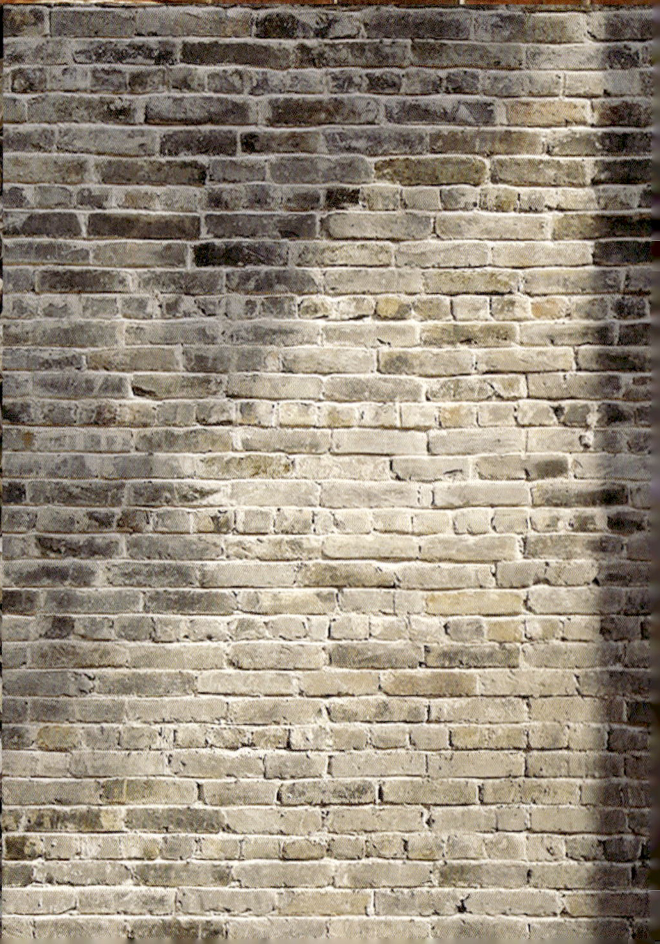

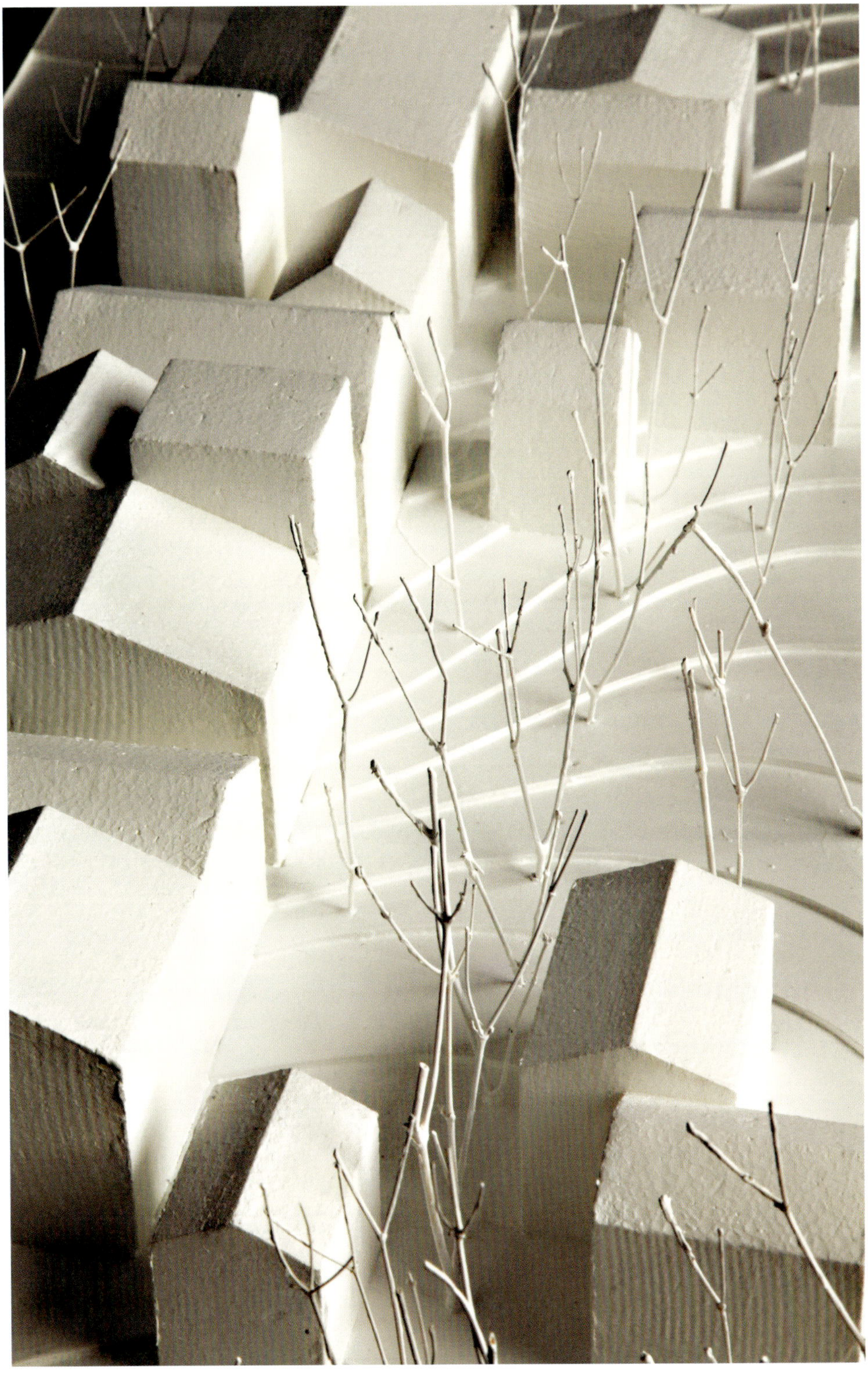

Energy Forest

ROME, ITALY 2013

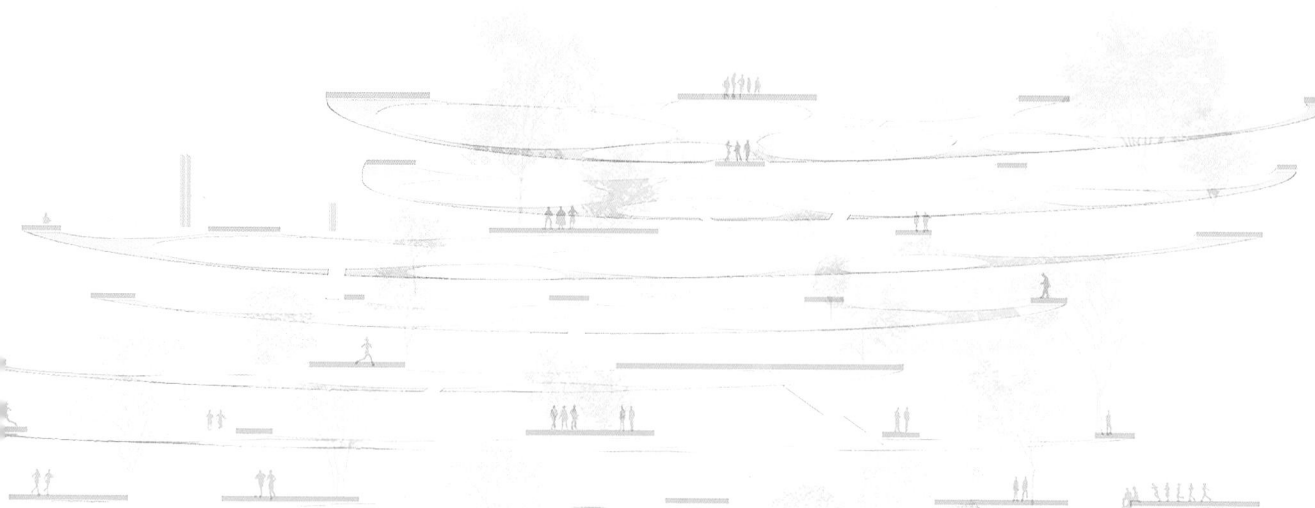

The field for communication of the future is an architectural forest

This is my image of a future city created for an exhibition at the MAXXI Museum in Rome. The plan hinged on mobility and the type of the city that would emerge as a result. I envisioned a future in which personal vehicles are flying through the sky. If personal planes were flying back and forth like birds, wouldn't that lead to places that were like huge trees where these artificial birds could gather and perch? These huge architectural trees, made of multilayered slabs filled with holes, would be a new communication platform for people. Numerous slab-shaped trees would sprout up, creating a forest-like place with a fusion of natural and artificial elements. In *Catalunya House*, I expanded this thought experiment based on a three-dimensional forest to a giant scale.

ローマの美術館 MAXXI での展覧会のために構想された未来の都市像。未来のモビリティとそこから発想される都市の在り方を求められた。ここではパーソナルな乗り物が空を飛び回っている未来を想像した。鳥のようにパーソナルエアプレインが行き来する未来、それら人工的な鳥たちが集まる止まり木のような巨大な樹木のような場所が生まれてくるのではないだろうか？ それは幾重にも積層した穴だらけのスラブによってつくられる建築的な巨樹であり、人びとの新しいコミュニケーションのプラットフォームである。スラブ上には無数の樹木が植えられ、自然と人工の融合した森的な場所となる。「Catalunya House」において構想していた立体的な森を、巨大スケールにまで拡張した思考実験である。

073 | Energy Forest

ROME, ITALY
2013

→ Related Projects
007 023 057 074 104

Catalunya House
CALDES DE MALAVELLA, SPAIN 2013

A new type of forest where trees are floating in space

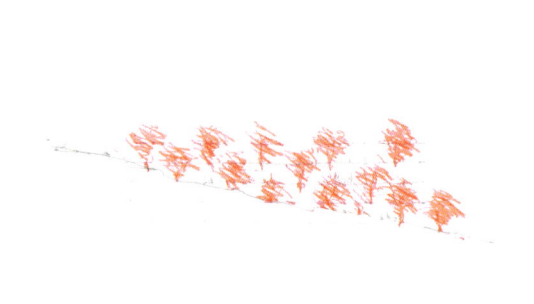

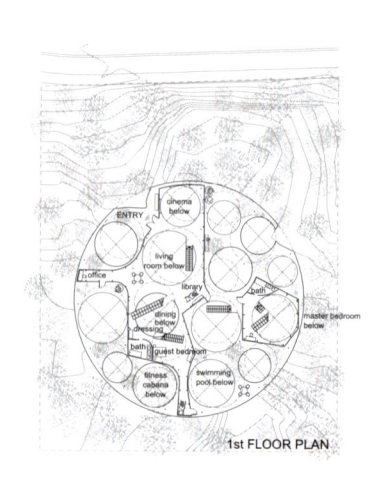

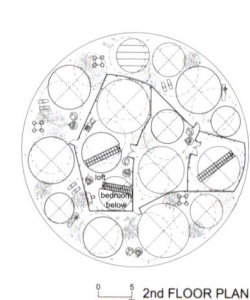

1st FLOOR PLAN

2nd FLOOR PLAN

This project was a design for a villa on a lot with an abundance of nature in Catalonia, Spain. On the gently sloping site surrounded by a forest, I decided to create a three-dimensional forest out of the building and trees. By layering round slabs filled with countless round openings, I created an atrium that was both staggered and connected in a complex manner. Then I placed the trees among the slabs as if they were piercing the foyer. This made it seem as if all of the trees were floating and surrounding the living space in three dimensions, gently restricting the limits of the house. Most of the slab area was an outside terrace and due to the mild climate, formed a variety of living spaces that were moderately protected from sunlight. This format, which I had explored in the *Energy Forest*, enabled me to develop various scales and programs.

スペイン、カタルーニャの自然豊かな敷地に別荘を計画するプロジェクト。周辺を森に囲まれた緩やかな斜面の敷地に対して、建築と樹木による立体的な森を構築することを考えた。無数の円形の開口が開いた円形スラブを積層させ、複雑にズレながら連続する吹き抜け空間を生み出す。その吹き抜けを貫通するように、スラブに樹木を配置していく。それはあたかも、無数の樹木が浮遊しながら居住空間を立体的に取り囲み、家の領域を緩やかに規定するかのようだ。大部分のスラブエリアは屋外テラスであり、温暖な気候ゆえに、適度に日差しから守られたさまざまな生活空間となる。「Energy Forest」で展開したように、異なるスケール、異なるプログラムに展開することが可能な形式である。

074

Catalunya House

CALDES DE MALAVELLA
SPAIN 2013

→ Related Projects
007 008 030 073 095 104

Setonomori Houses

HIROSHIMA, JAPAN 2013

Where mountain, village and paths merge

1st FLOOR PLAN

In the mountains near the Seto Inland Sea, I designed a housing complex with 26 units. In the surrounding area, there are rows of old houses with gabled roofs and attractive stepped alleys between them, forming an expansive cityscape. In this new design, I sought to combine the houses and alleys in a way that the surrounding cityscape seemed to expand into nature. On the other hand, since the rich mountain greenery is one of the area's strongest features, I planted over 100 trees between the houses and by covering the surface of the house-shaped volume with mirrored stainless steel. This reflected the surrounding greenery and created a landscape in which the architecture and the trees blend into one. The mirrored walls also reflect different changes in the colour of the sky, such as the orange of twilight, the pink of dusk, and white on blue.

瀬戸内海にほど近い山間に、26戸の集合住宅を計画する。周辺には古くからある切妻屋根の民家が軒を連ね、その間を魅力的な階段状の路地が結び合わせる街並が広がっている。そこでこの新しい計画も、あたかも周辺の街並が自然に広がったかのように、家と路地を組み合わせていくこととした。一方で、この豊かな山の緑もまたこの場所の大きな特徴であったことから、家々の間に合計100本以上の樹木を植樹し、また家型のボリュームの表面を鏡面ステンレスで覆うことで、周辺の緑を映し込み、建築と樹木が溶け合う風景をつくり出した。この鏡面の壁面はまた、さまざまに変化する空の色をも映し込み、夕方にはオレンジ色に、朝焼けにはピンク色に、水色に白にと表情を変化させる。

075

Setonomori Houses

せとの森住宅

HIROSHIMA, JAPAN
2013

→ Related Projects
013 018 043 070 073

Connecticut Pool House

CONNECTICUT, USA 2013

Being both a roof, a window, terrace, stair, wall and scenery

I designed this small second house in a beautiful natural area in the American state of Connecticut. Since the house is in a natural setting, the trees naturally block the sight line from the outside, so I tried to create a structure that was as open as possible but still cut out the sunlight. As there was also a plan to create outdoor living spaces such as a pool, field, and terrace, I made a level difference in relation to the ground, so that the roof of the building could be used as an extension of the outdoor living spaces. The stepped roof blocks the sunlight while enhancing the view of the sky, and as with House K, it encourages internal and external spatial movement. I set out to imbue the form of the overall building, which resembles a tent and a tree, with a feeling of lightness along with a sense of security and openness, as if you were living in the shade of a tree.

アメリカ、コネチカット州の美しい自然の中に、小さなセカンドハウスを計画する。周辺からの視線を気にする必要のない自然のただ中の家であることから、できるだけ開放的に、しかし不要な日差しは遮るような構造を考えた。周囲にはプールや畑やテラスなどの屋外での生活の場所がつくられる予定なので、建物の屋根面も外部の生活空間の延長として使うことができるように、地上から連続する段差をつくり上げた。段々状の屋根面は、日差しを遮りながら空への視線を豊かに生み出すものであり、また「House K」と同じく、内外の空間的な連動をつくり出す。テントのような建物全体の形は、同時に樹木のようでもあり、軽やかさとともに、木陰で生活するような安心感と開放感を意図している。

076 Connecticut Pool House

CONNECTICUT, USA
2013

→ Related Projects
012 055 079 105

1st FLOOR PLAN

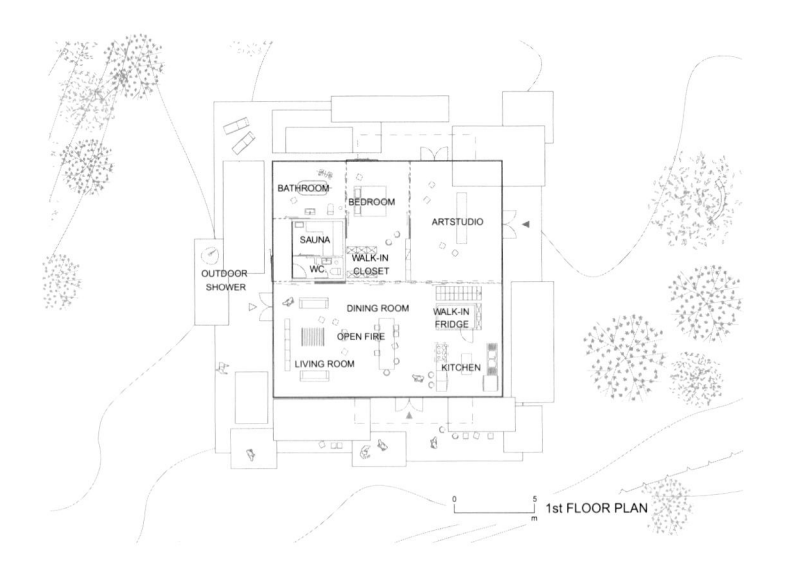

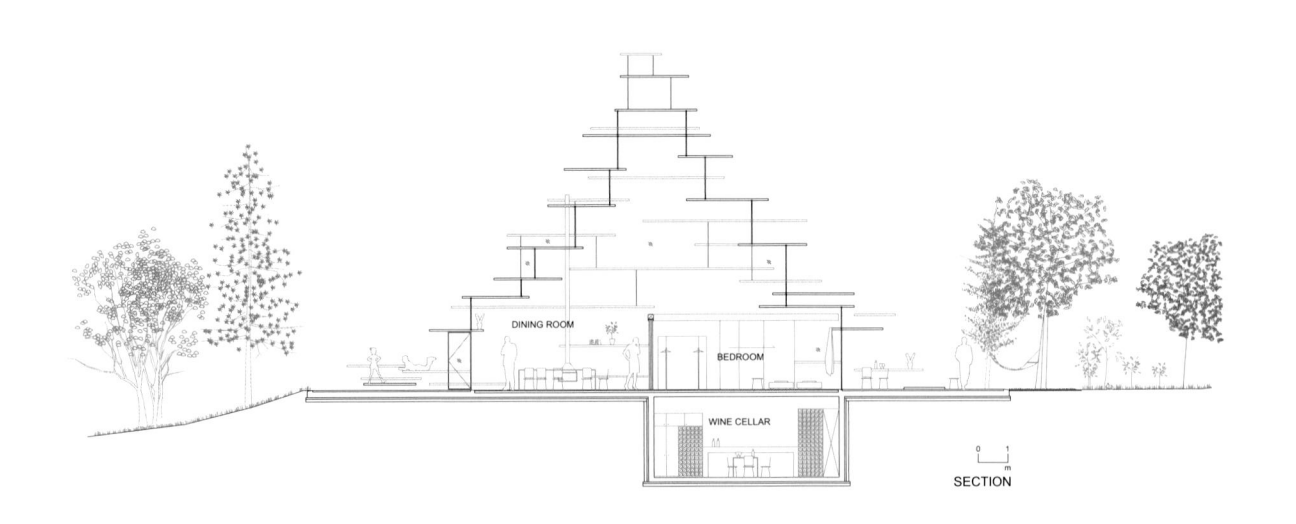

SECTION

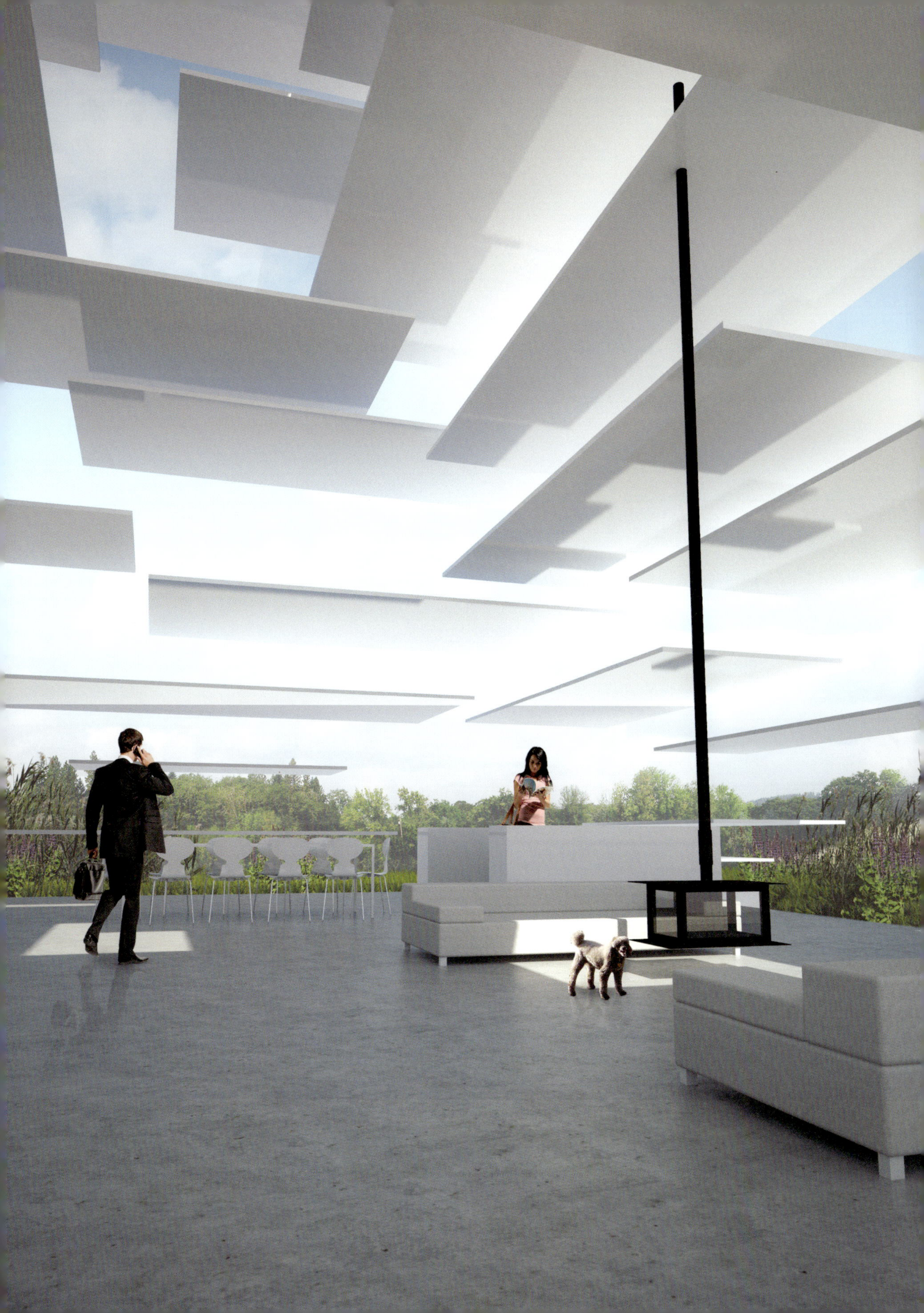

Serpentine Gallery Pavilion 2013

LONDON, UNITED KINGDOM 2013

Nature / Artificiality / Simplicity / Complexity / Interior / Exterior
Furniture / Architecture / Wall / Roof / Joinery/ Window
-All synthesize into an amorphous locus

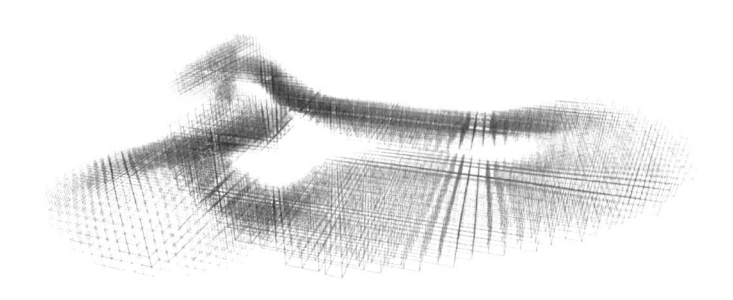

In many different ways, this project is a culmination of the essence of my architecture. The structure, made of a grid lattice of two-centimetre square steel pipes, is a proposal for a place transcending the natural and artificial. The interior and exterior subtly trade places with each other, the transparent and opaque qualities are constantly changing due to the layered structure. The 40-centimeter grid functions as a bench and also at times as a staircase, creating a variety of places where people can relax. Formed out of an artificial order of straight lines and 90 degrees, the building is also imbued with a diversity that includes a cloud-like softness and indeterminate forms. There is a striking harmony between simplicity and complexity, and the structure, light, experience, and function all blend together into a single form. It is a rediscovery of all the basics of architecture, including nature, artifice, simplicity, complexity, interior, exterior, furniture, walls, roofs, shelves, windows, structure, and light. This work is certain to be an archetype for new architecture in the contemporary age.

このプロジェクトは、さまざまな意味において藤本建築のエッセンスが凝縮されたものとなっている。2cm角のスチールパイプのグリッド格子によってつくられたこの構造は、自然と人工の間を切り拓く場の提案である。内部と外部は曖昧に入れ替わり、透明性と不透明性は構造の重なり具合によって常に変化する。40cmの格子はベンチとして機能し、またときに階段となり、人びとが滞在するためのさまざまな居場所をつくり出す。直線と90度という人工的な秩序でつくられていながら、それは雲のような柔らかさと不確定な形のもつ多様さをあわせもつ。単純さと複雑さの見事な調和があり、構造と光と体験と機能が溶け合ってひとつの形式となる。自然、人工、内部、外部、家具、壁、屋根、棚、窓、構造、光、そのほか、建築にまつわるすべてを原初に立ち返って再発明する。現代における、新しい建築の原型となるであろう。

077

Serpentine Gallery Pavilion 2013

LONDON, UNITED KINGDOM
2013

Serpentine Gallery Pavilion 2013

→ Related Projects
001 007 055 064 069 078

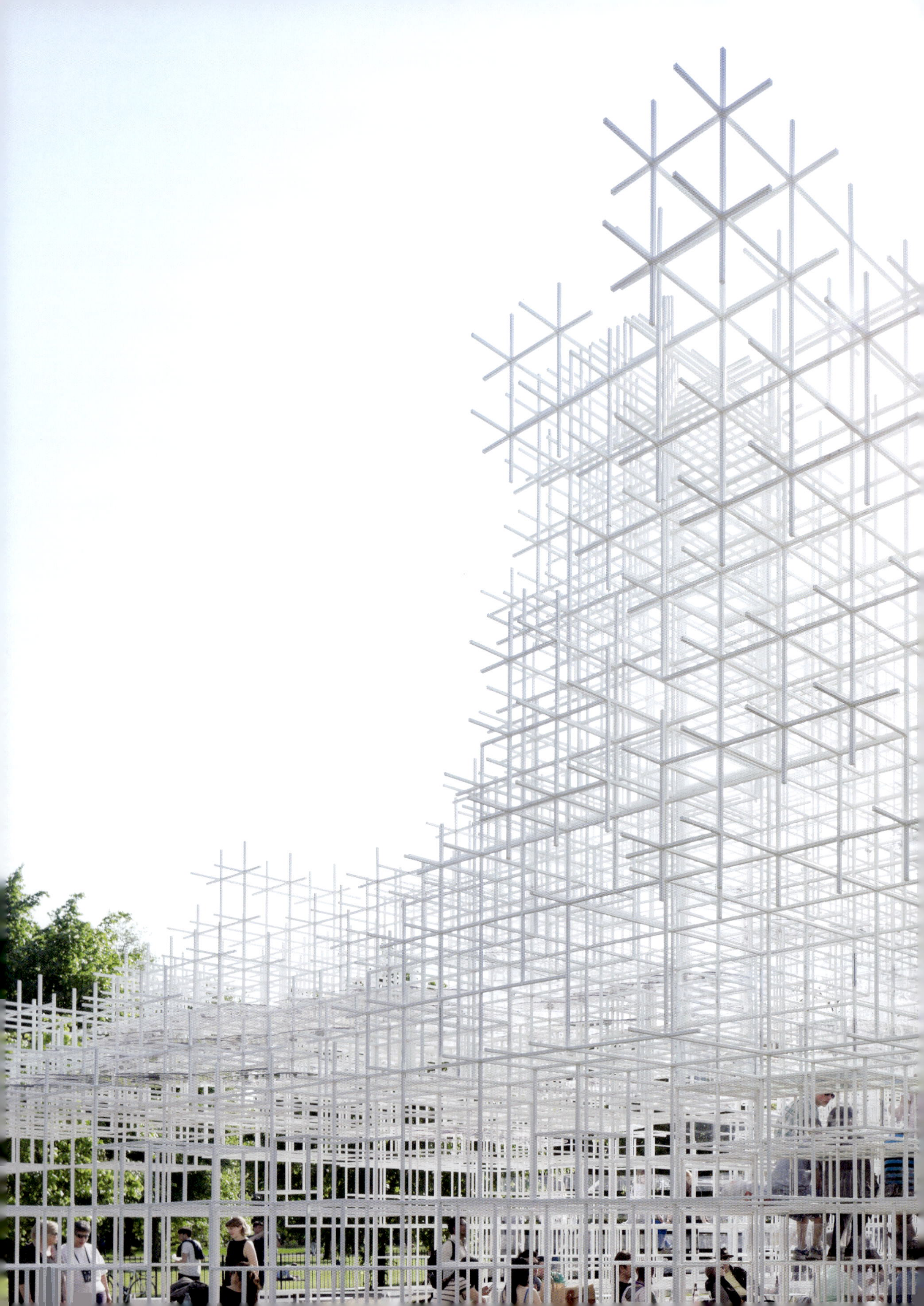

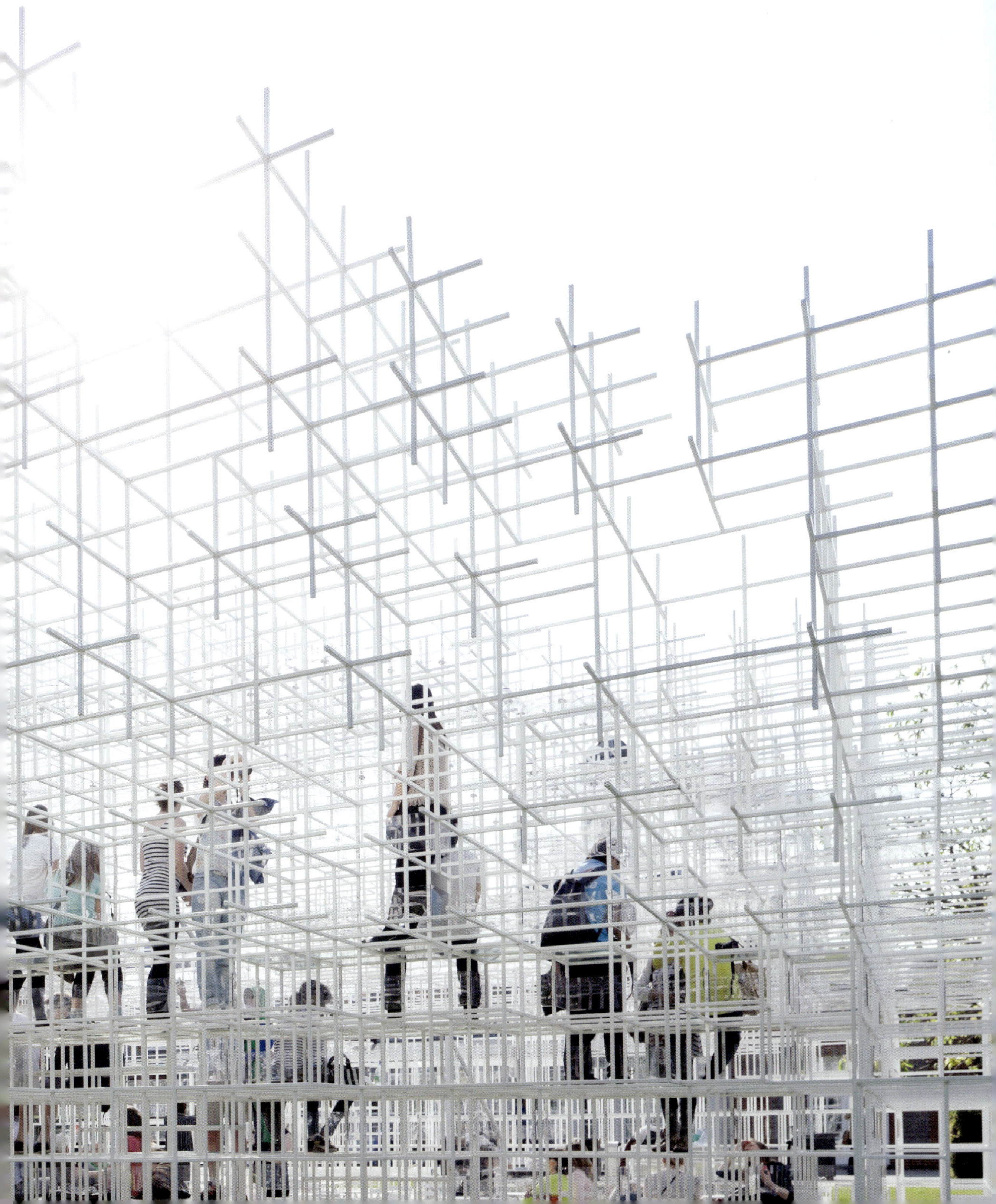

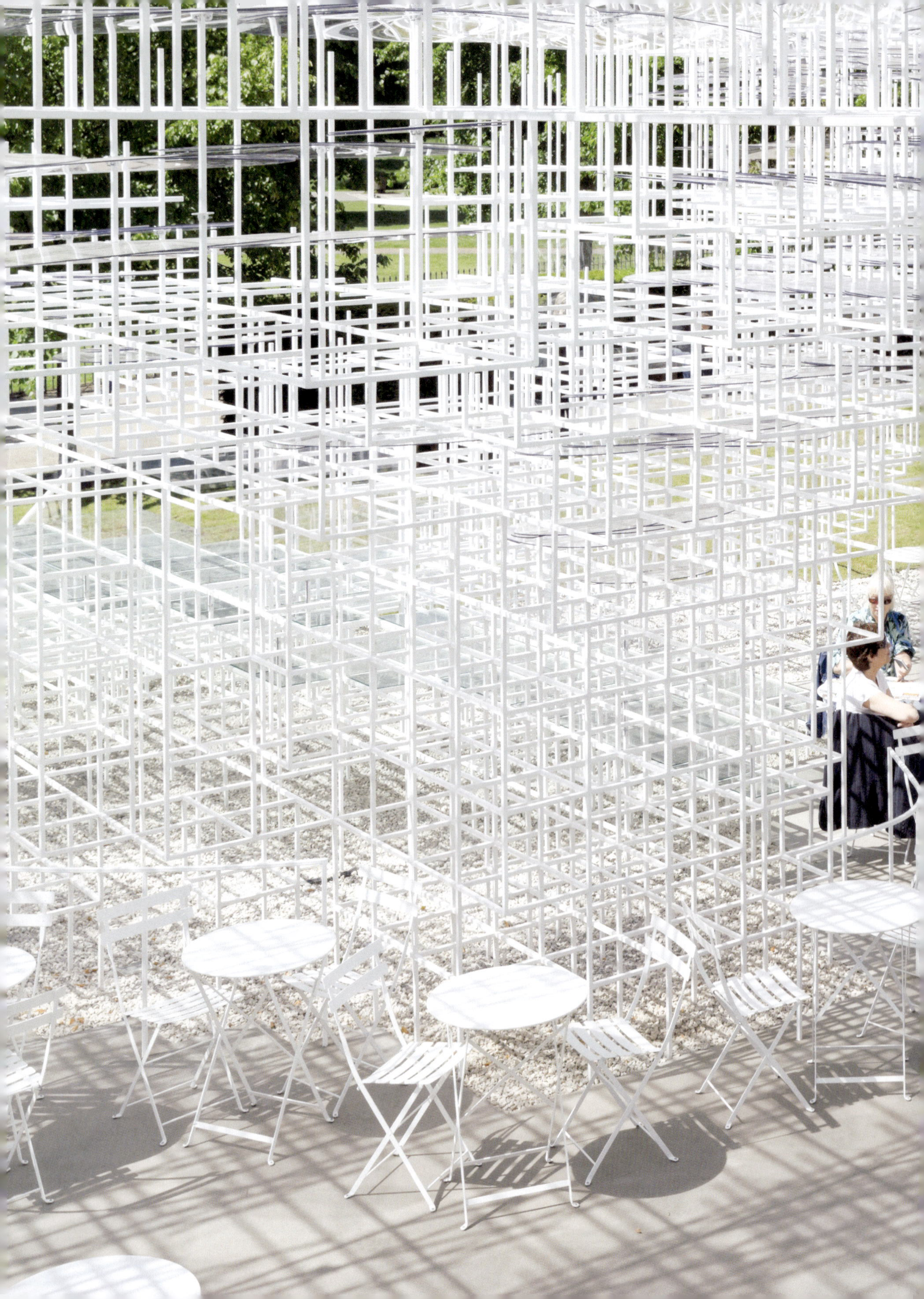

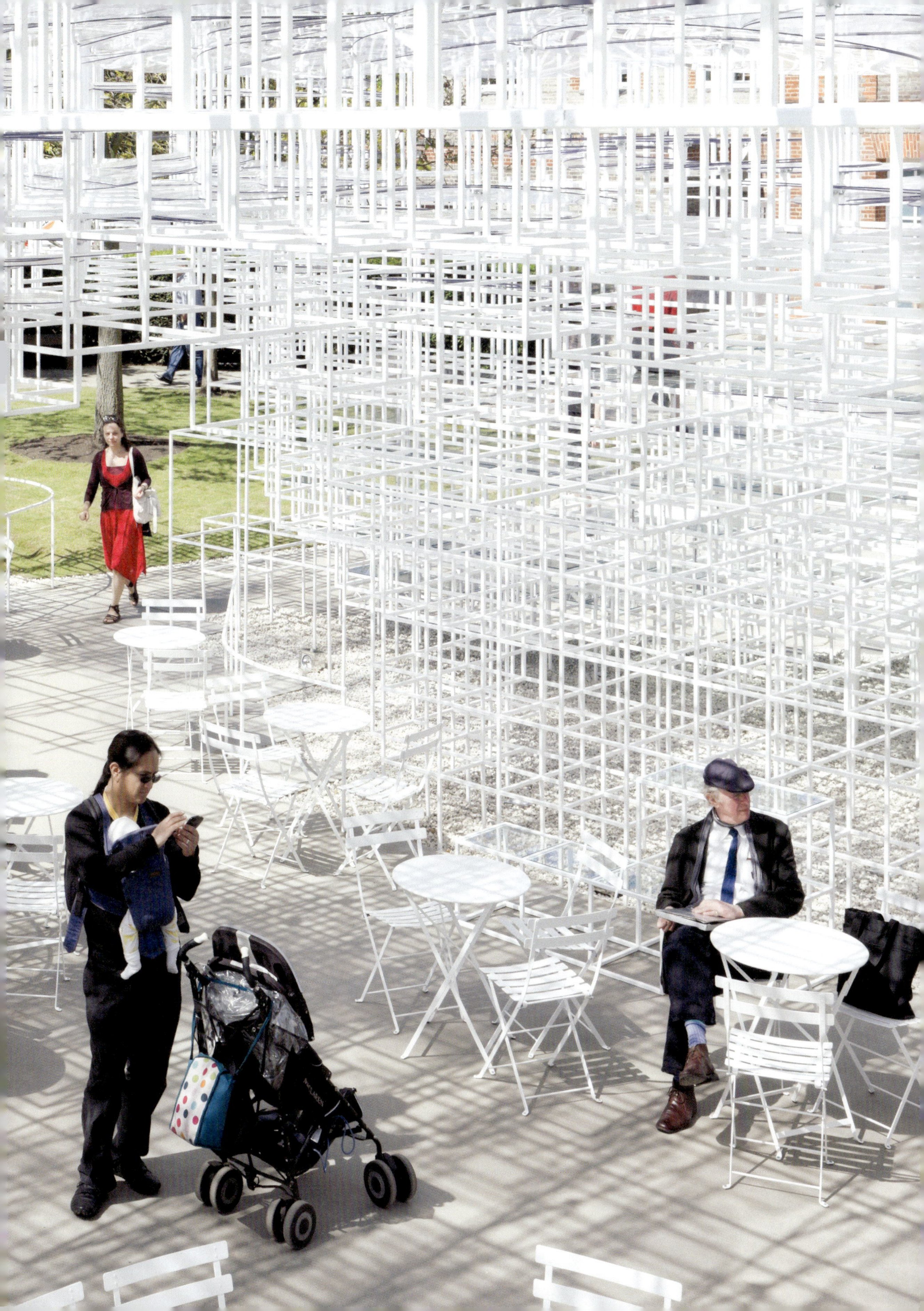

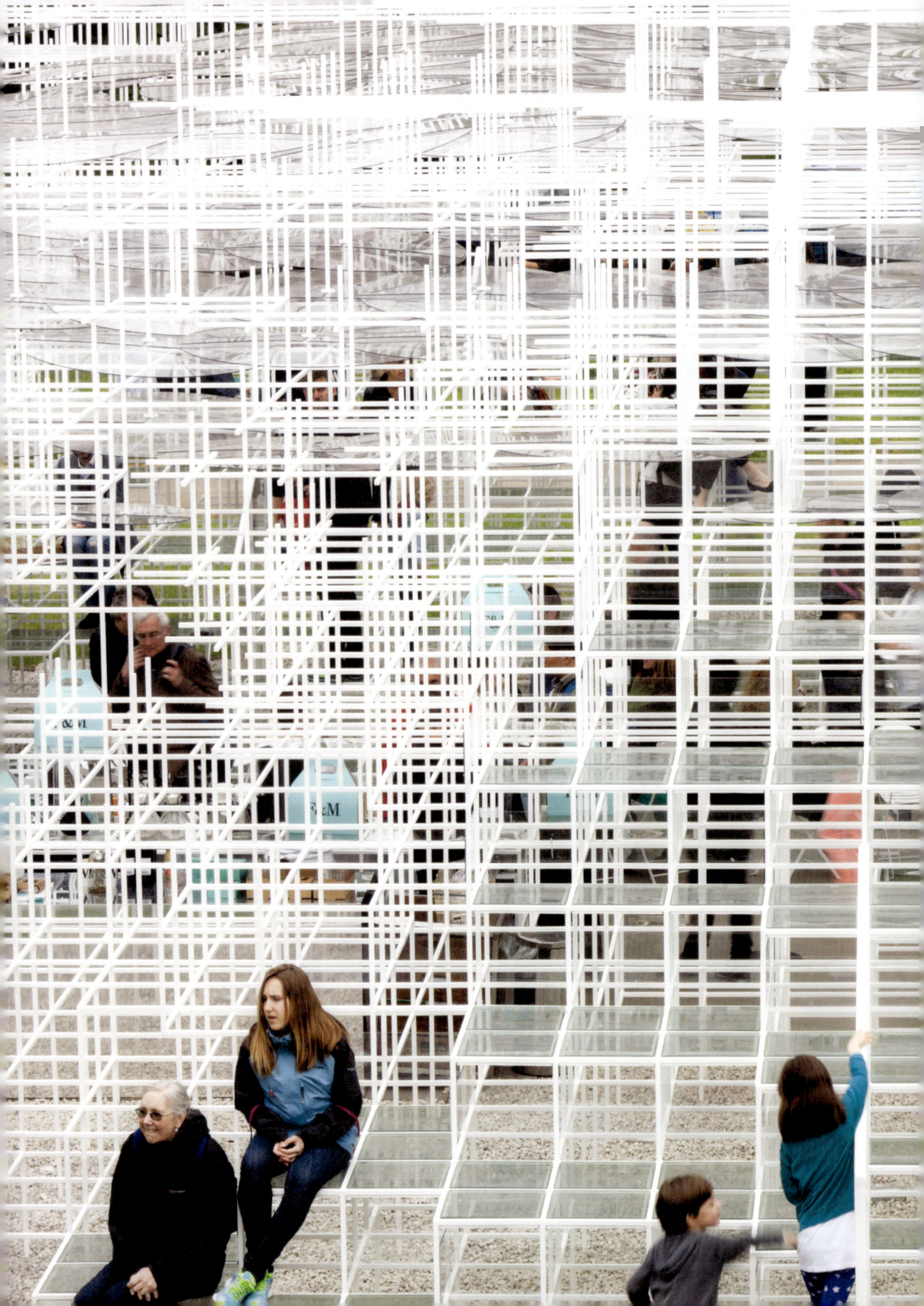

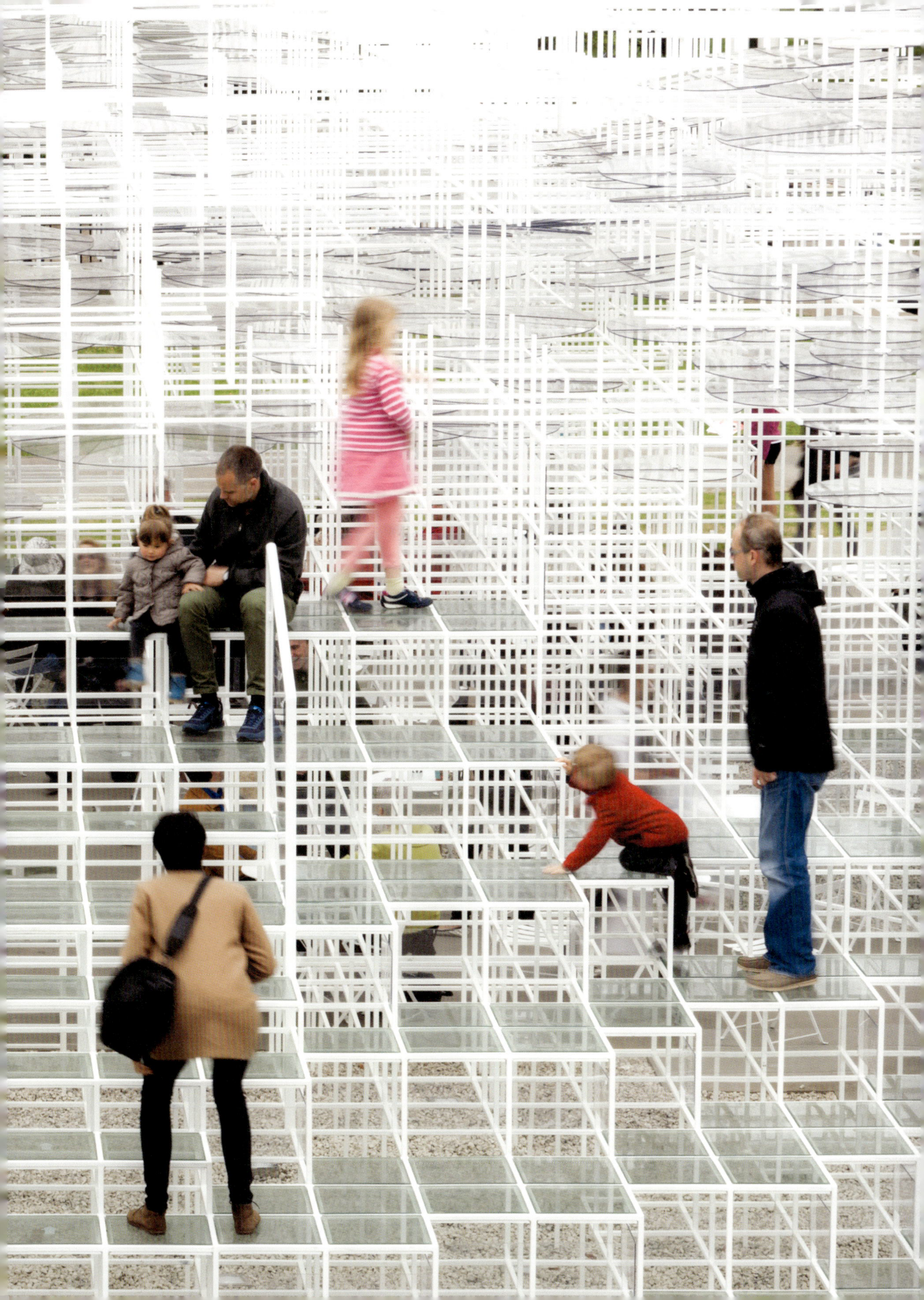

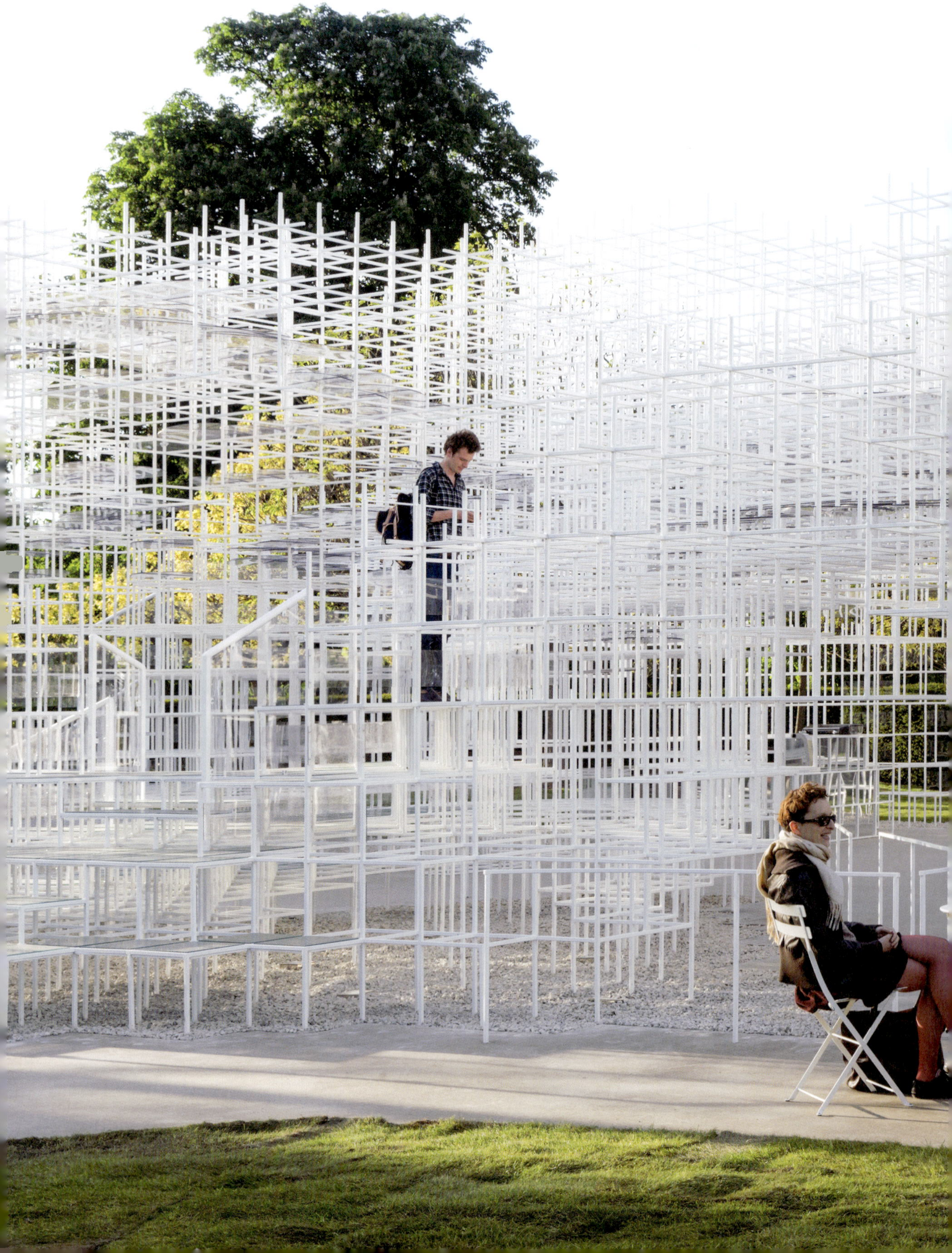

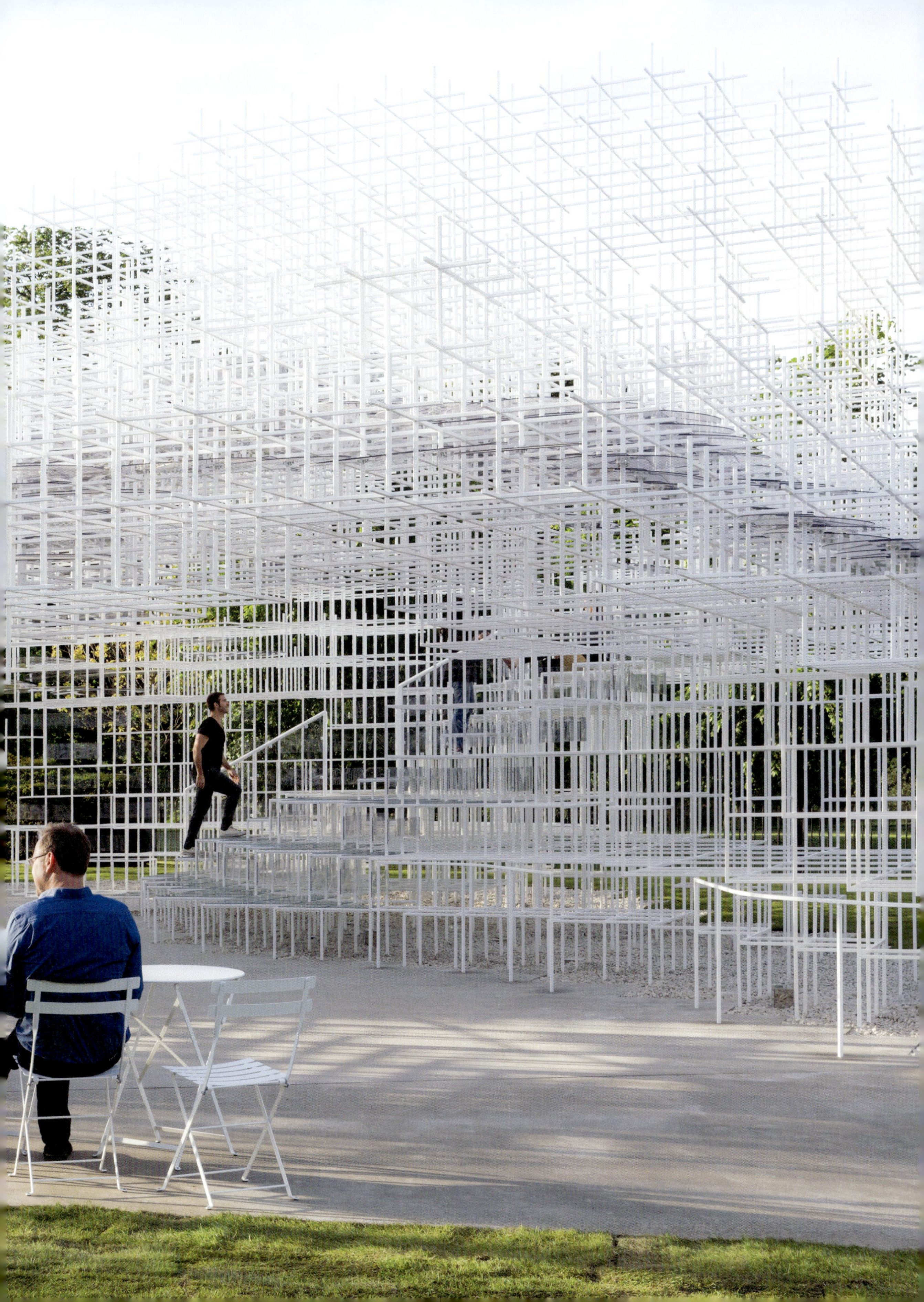

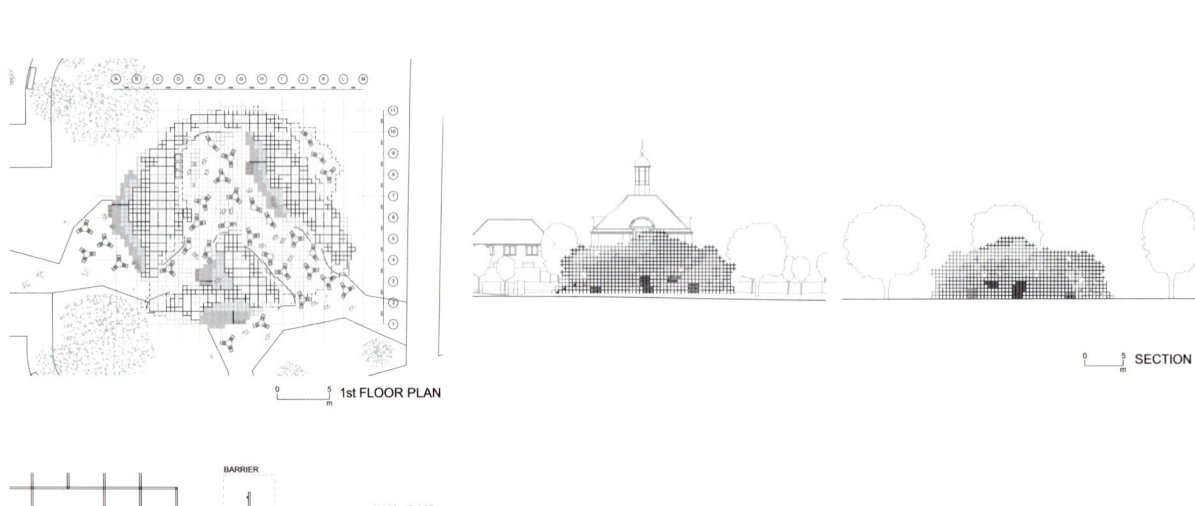

1st FLOOR PLAN

SECTION

BARRIER
GLASS FLOOR
non-slip tempered double layered glass
BARRIER : STEEL MESH
MOVABLE CUSHION
HANDRAIL : STEEL PIPE
STAINLESS STEEL
BARRIER STAINLESS STEEL BAR
BARRIER STEEL MESH
STRUCTURE : STEEL TUBE
CONCRETE SLAB
FINISH LEVEL
UPLIGHTER
GRAVEL
FREE DRAINAGE GRANULAR MATERIAL
BARRIER

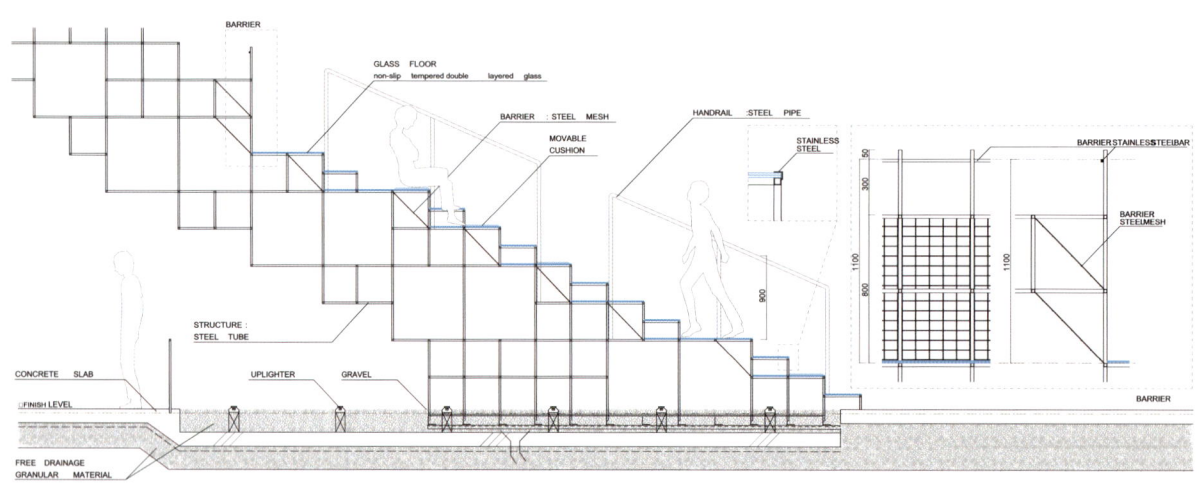

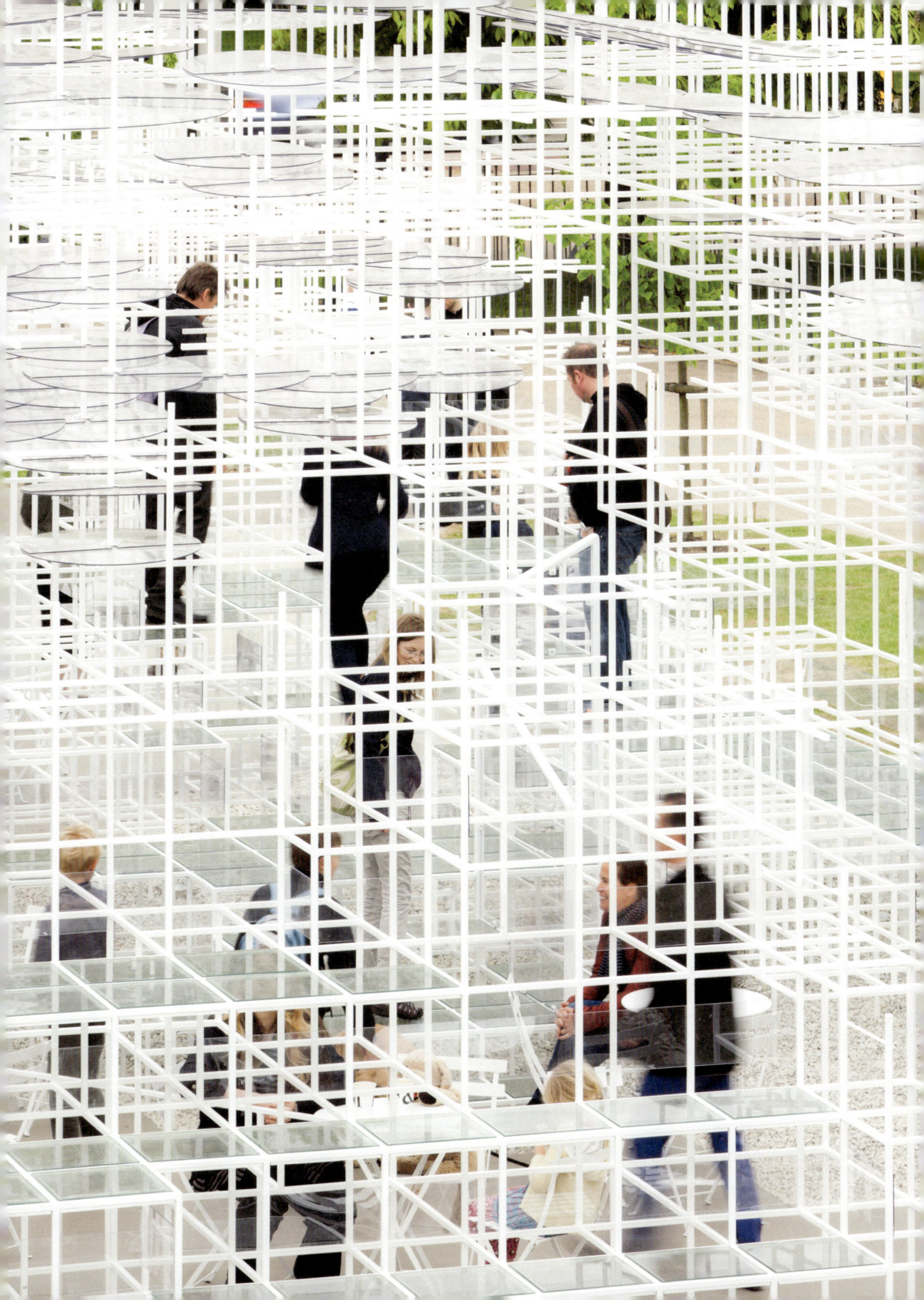

Taiwan Cafe
TAINAN, TAIWAN 2013

Stairs / Furniture / Paths / City / Architecture

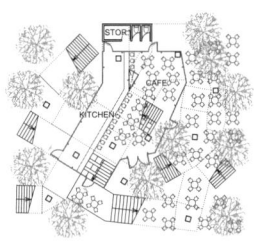

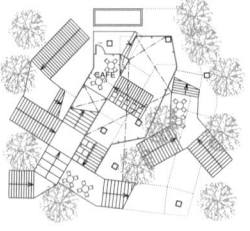

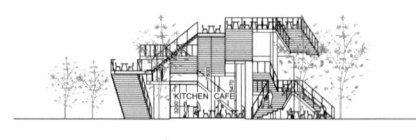

1st FLOOR PLAN

2nd FLOOR PLAN

SECTION

As I mentioned in the entry for the *JJ99 Youth Hostel*, the back streets of Tainan are filled with attractive qualities. When I was asked to design a cafe in the city, I thought I'd like to create something that was not simply a building but was also an attractive alley. At heart, a cafe is both a building and an urban space. If I could create a place that made the alley three-dimensional and architectural, I was sure that it would be an extremely rich building and urban space. And since it was a cafe, I thought I could create a place where various people could sit and enjoy drinking tea by making a three-dimensional alley out of stairs. Each tread of the staircase functions as furniture, a path, and allows people to enjoy drinking tea on a platform floating in the air. By stacking up trees in this network of stairs, I created a kind of tree house, which blocked out sunlight and led up to the tree canopy. This prototype enables people to walk around endlessly like Escher's staircase.

「JJ99 Youth Hostel」のプロジェクトでも説明したように、台南の街は、その裏道に魅力が溢れている。台南の市街地にカフェを計画したいという依頼を受けた時に、それは単なる建築であるだけではなく、台南の魅力的な路地そのものをつくり出すものになりはしないだろうかと考えた。そもそもカフェという場所は、建築であると同時に都市空間でもある。そして路地を立体化して建築化した場所をつくることができれば、それはとても豊かな建築＝都市空間になるに違いない。さらにカフェゆえに人びとがいろいろな所に腰掛けてお茶を楽しむことができないだろうかと空想し、立体的路地を階段でつくり上げることとした。階段の段は家具にもなり、路にもなり、空中に浮かぶプラットフォームでお茶を楽しむこともできる。この階段のネットワークに樹木を重ね合わせ、日差しを遮るとともに樹冠へと上がっていくツリーハウス的な体験をも生み出している。それはエッシャーの階段のような無限に巡り歩くことができる原型性を獲得した。

078

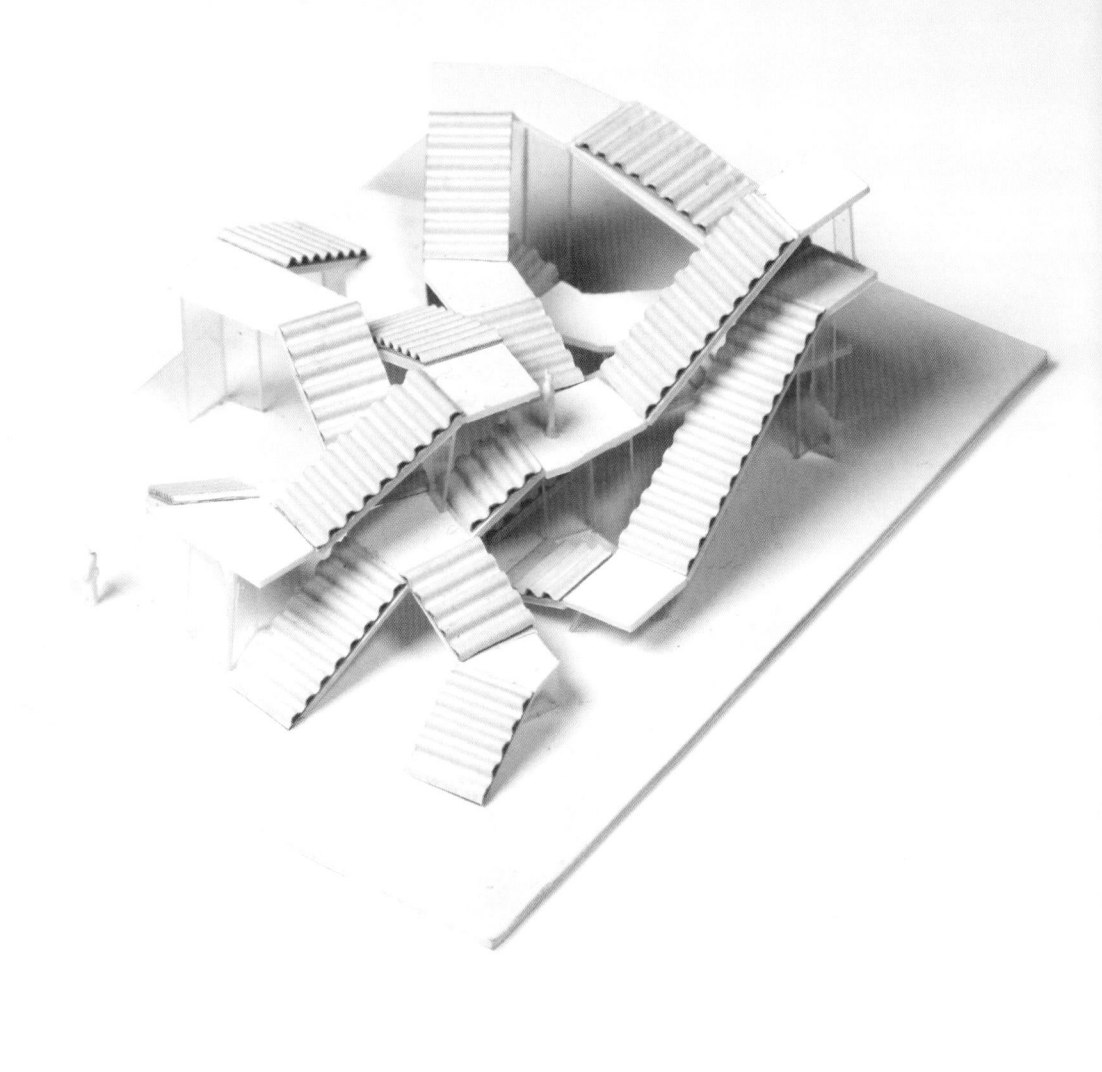

Taiwan Cafe

TAINAN, TAIWAN
2013

→ Related Projects
003 010 024 041 042 061

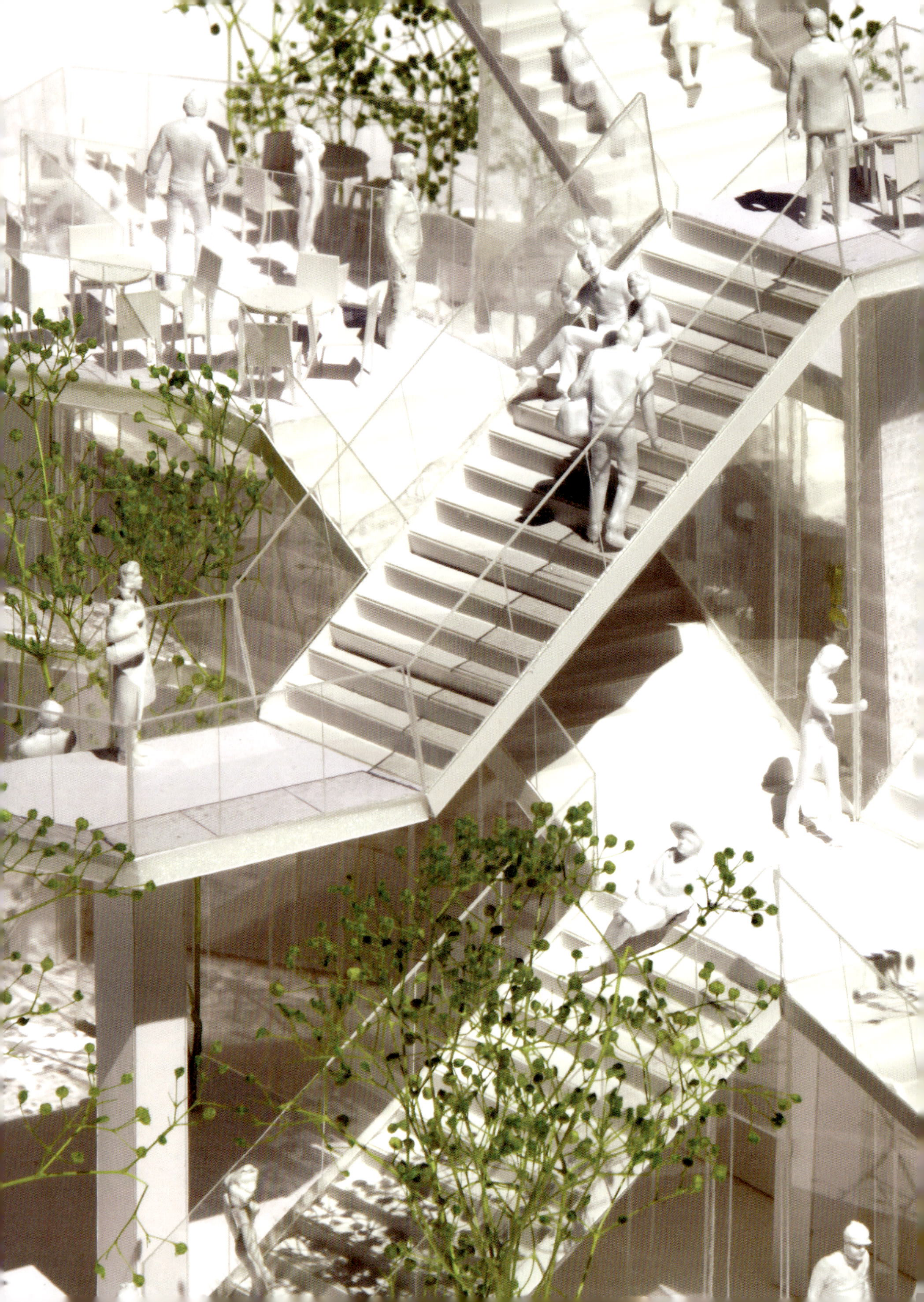

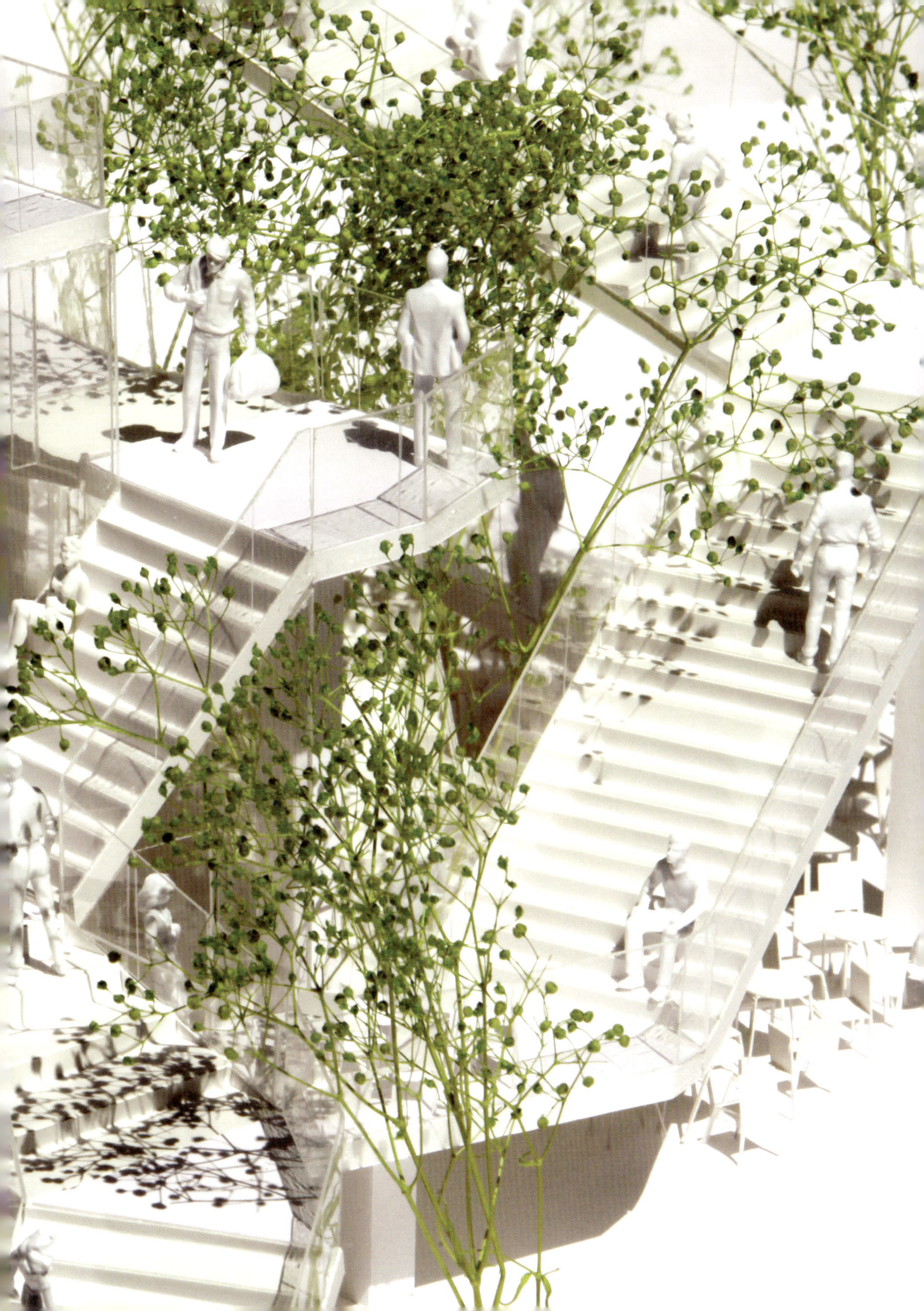

Souk Mirage/Particles of Light
2013

Everything is made of particles of light

SECTION

This project was a design for a huge 1 km-long shopping area in a Middle Eastern city. This was my first project to design in the Middle East. Because of this, I anticipated that the huge sense of scale, and the climatic and cultural context would provide me with an endless source of imagination and allow me to develop in new directions. To protect against the Middle Eastern sunlight, I devised a building that would be covered with countless small grids. Not only would it be covered with them, but the layers of various grids would form the entire building. In this work, I expanded the grid concept from the *Serpentine Gallery Pavilion 2013* and achieved a scale that was far beyond my expectations. As a landmark, the tower would contain a void space, providing natural ventilation and doubling as a huge foyer in the shopping area. The light that penetrated the grids would be broken down into particles that would pour down into the foyer. The grids that formed the structure also created an arch, and the layers of grids enveloped the entire building as a simple yet complex filter. Though the work shares the same basic concept as the *Serpentine Gallery Pavilion 2013*, its appearance is enormously different. In fact, the disparity between the two conveys the power of the concept.

中東の都市に、長さ1kmにわたる巨大なショッピングエリアを計画するプロジェクト。中東でのプロジェクトはこれが初めてであった。それゆえ、その巨大なスケール感、気候や文化的な背景が、僕たちの想像を超えたインスピレーションを生み出し、新しい方向性を切り拓くことを期待した。中東の日差しに対応するために、建物を無数の小さな格子で覆うことを考えた。さらに覆うだけではなく、さまざまな格子の積層によって建物全体がつくられる。それは「Serpentine Gallery Pavilion 2013」のグリッドが拡張して、予想を超えたスケールを獲得する瞬間であった。ランドマークとしてのタワーは自然換気のためのヴォイド空間を内包し、それがショッピングエリアの巨大な吹き抜けへと変化する。無数の格子を透過する光は、光の粒子となって吹き抜けに降り注ぐ。構造体である格子はアーチの形を与えられ、その格子のレイヤーはシンプルかつ複雑な光のフィルターとなって建物全体を包み込む。「Serpentine Gallery Pavilion 2013」とこのプロジェクトは、そのコンセプトを共有しながら、とてつもなくかけ離れた建ち現れ方をしている。そのギャップこそが、コンセプトの強度を物語っている。

079

Souk Mirage/Particles of Light

2013

→ Related Projects
007 017 034 077 099 107

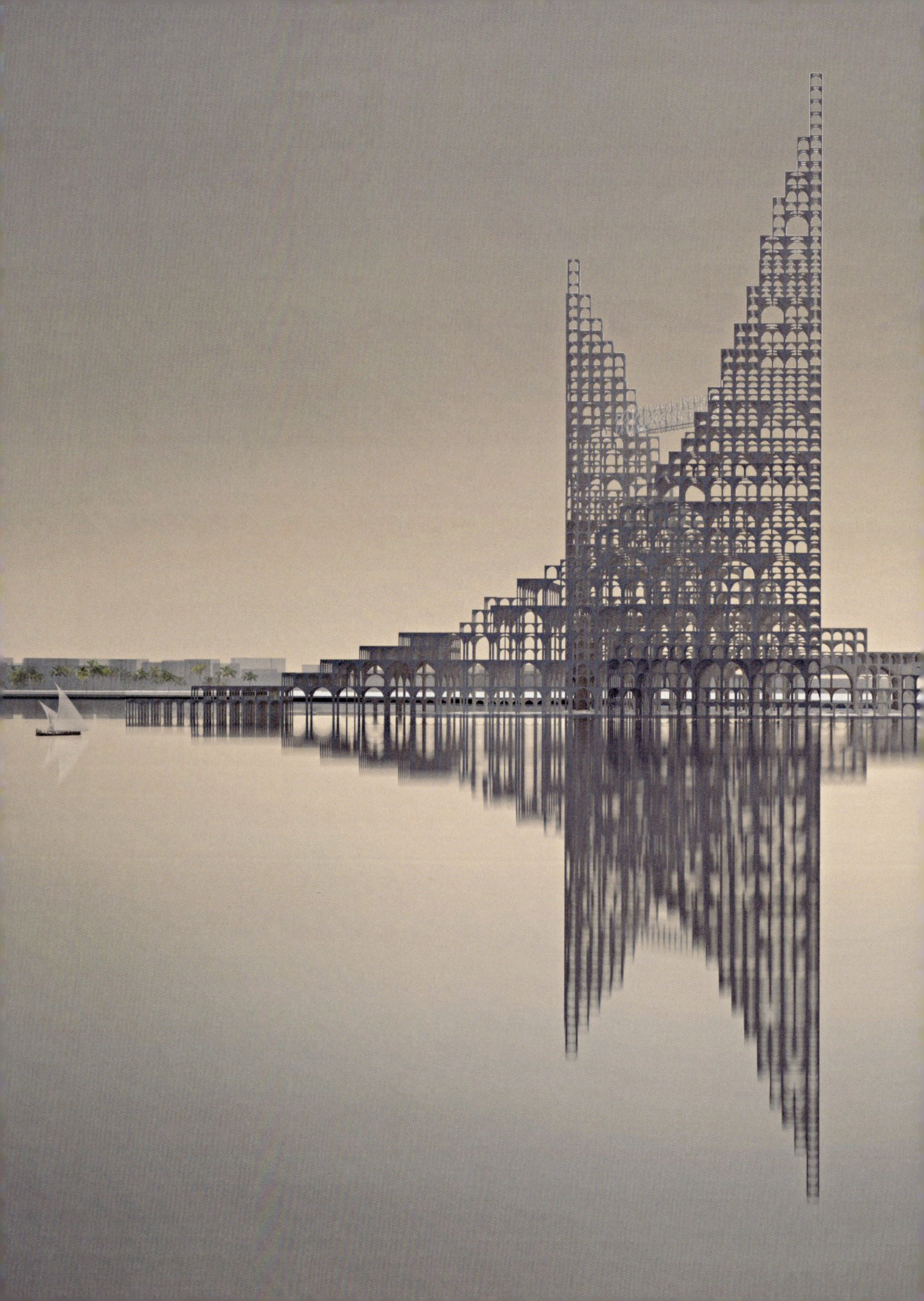

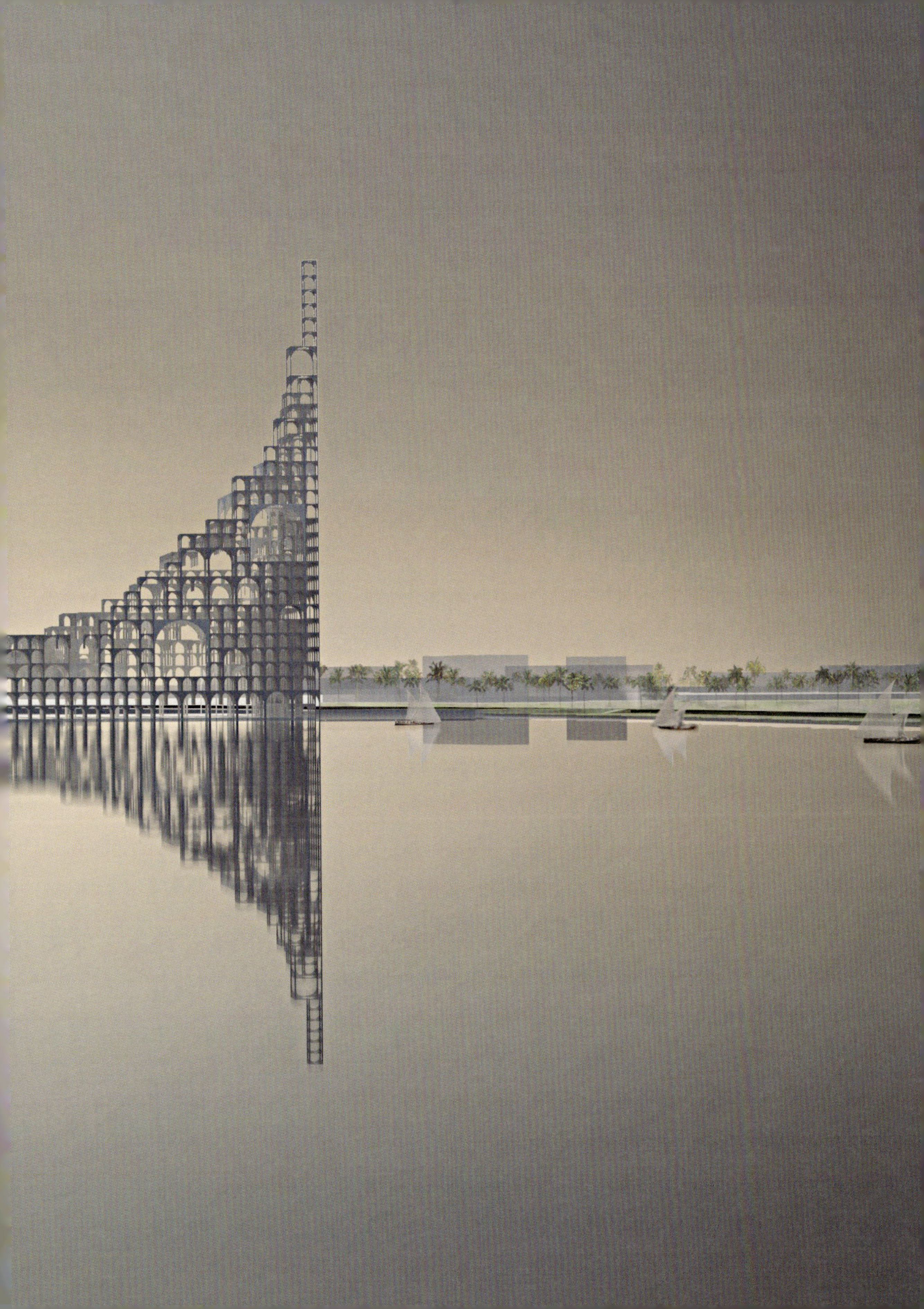

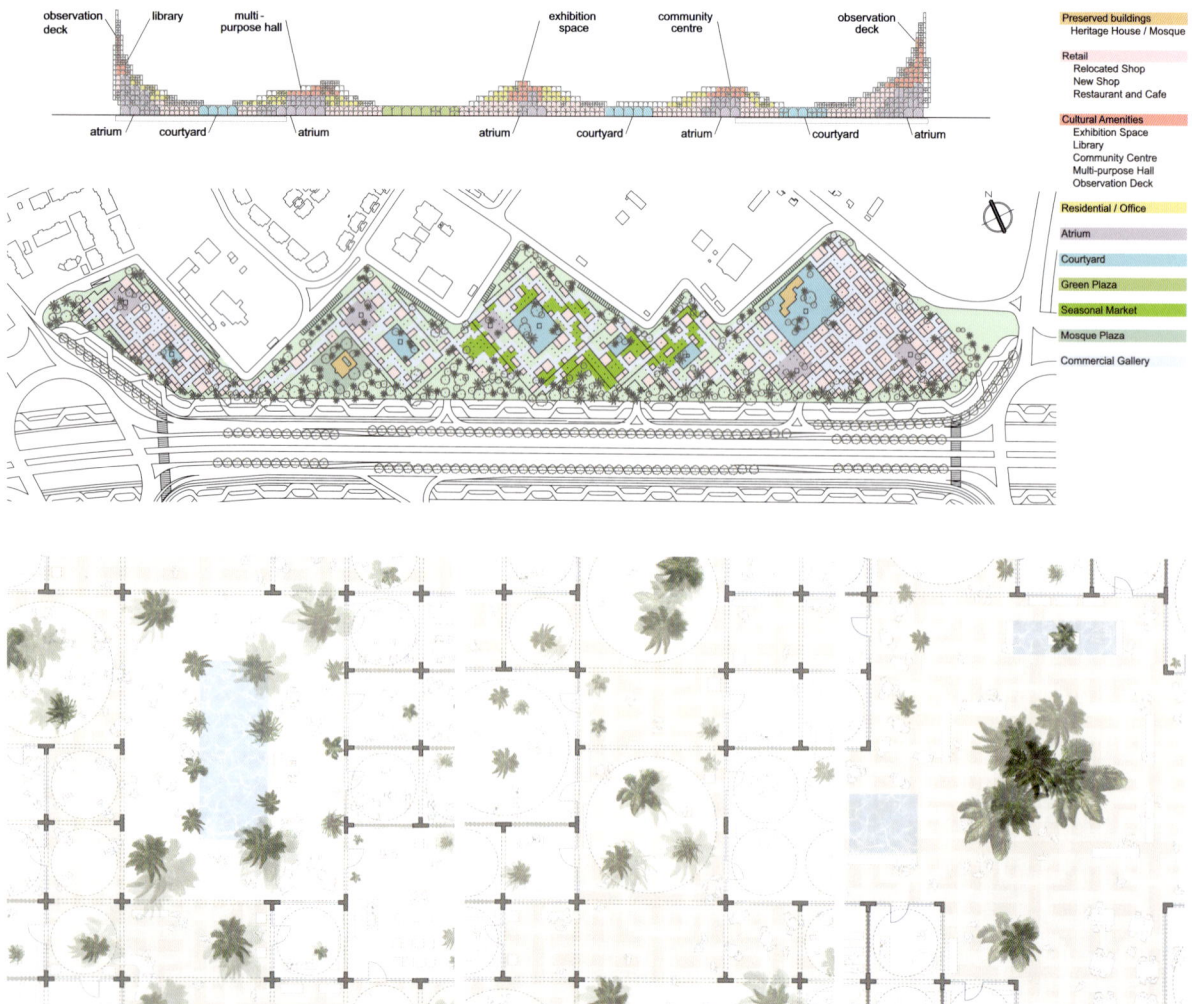

observation deck · library · multi-purpose hall · exhibition space · community centre · observation deck
atrium · courtyard · atrium · atrium · courtyard · atrium · courtyard · atrium

Preserved buildings
Heritage House / Mosque

Retail
Relocated Shop
New Shop
Restaurant and Cafe

Cultural Amenities
Exhibition Space
Library
Community Centre
Multi-purpose Hall
Observation Deck

Residential / Office

Atrium

Courtyard

Green Plaza

Seasonal Market

Mosque Plaza

Commercial Gallery

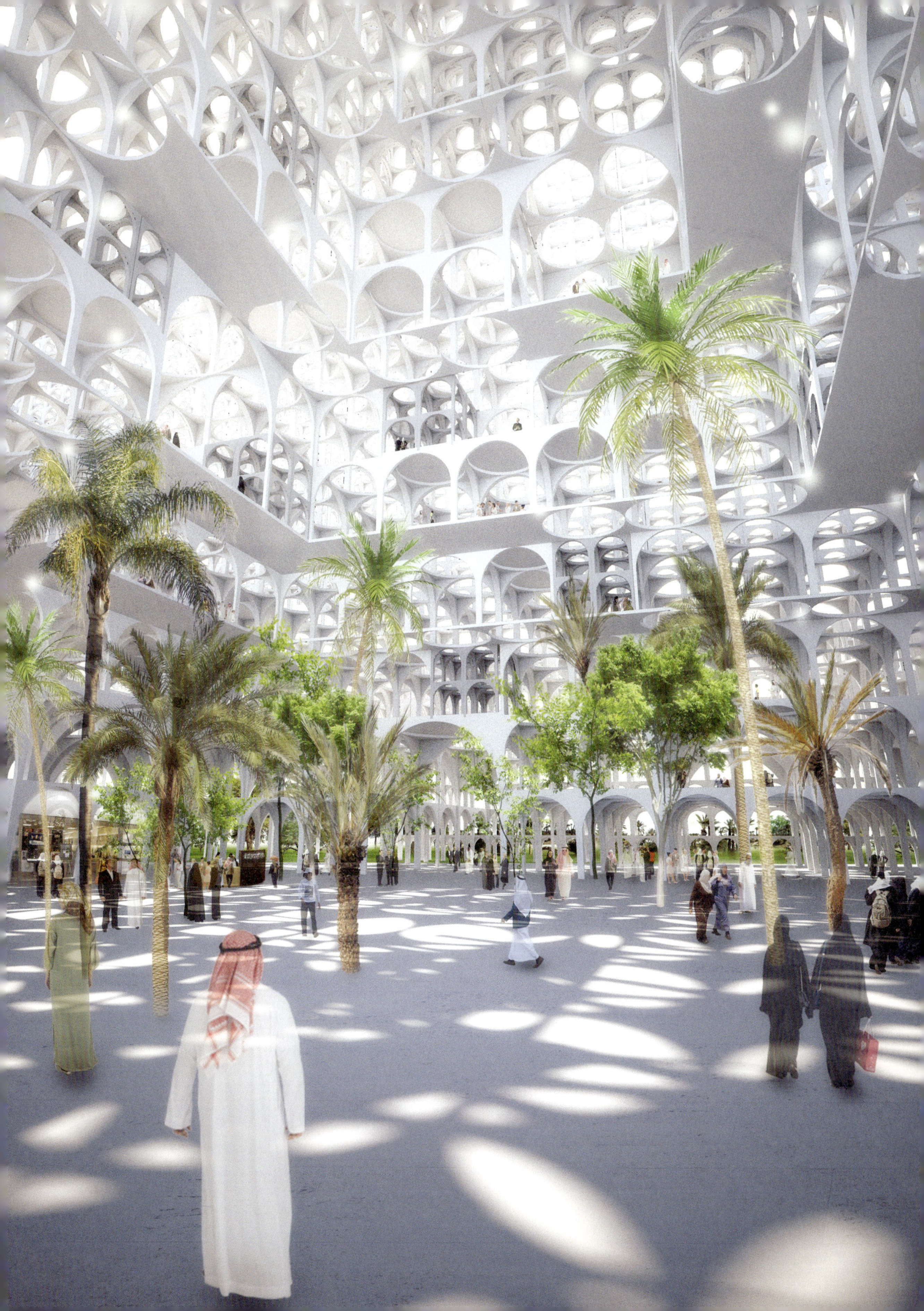

Kunsthalle Bielefeld Annex

BIELEFELD, GERMANY 2013

When landscape is stratified, it becomes architecture

In the small German city of Bielefeld is a museum designed by Philip Johnson. I had an exhibition there in 2012, and out of that grew a proposal for a new wing of the museum. The museum is situated in a large park in the city center, and the building itself is preserved as historical heritage preventing any extension to be directly added. Therefore, I sought to architecturally renovate the park rather than adding to the building itself. Stratifying a series of slopes which rise up from the park atop one another, creating a kind of architectural landform. Trees are planted on this landform/structure, generating a new typology that merges park and building. Inside, it houses galleries and other functions, and an access leading directly from the lobby out onto the sloping outdoor terrace. Accumulating landforms to create architecture: this approach, with sloping surfaces and height differentials used to merge architecture and terrain, interior and exterior, was used in various other projects in diverse environments, including *House K* and the *Taiwan Cafe*.

ドイツの小都市ビーレフェルドに、フィリップ・ジョンソンが設計した美術館がある。2012年にそこで展覧会をした縁で、美術館の増築計画のコンセプトを提案した。美術館は市の中心に広がる大きな公園の中に建ち、建物自体は歴史遺産として直接的な増築が禁止されていた。ここでは、建物を増築するのではなく、＜公園を建築的に増築する＞と考えることにした。公園から連続して上昇する斜面が積層して、立体的な地形がつくられる。この地形的なボリュームには樹木が植わり、公園と建築が融合した新しいタイポロジーとなるであろう。展示室などの諸機能はボリュームの中に収まり、ロビーからは直接斜面の外部テラスへと出ることができる。地形を積層して建築をつくる。斜面や段差を用いて建築と地形と内部と外部を溶け合わせるこの方法は、「House K」や「Taiwan Cafe」のような異なるプログラム、異なる周辺環境によってさまざまに展開していくこととなる。

080

Kunsthalle Bielefeld Annex

BIELEFELD, GERMANY
2013

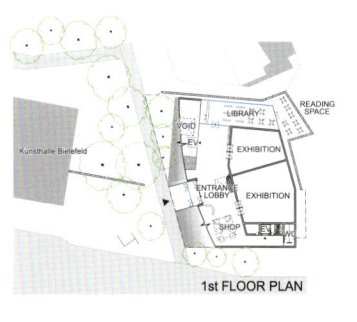

1st FLOOR PLAN · 2nd FLOOR PLAN · SECTION

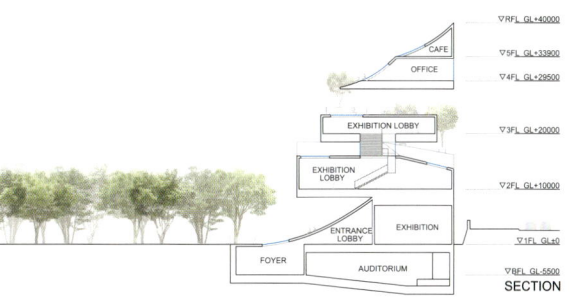

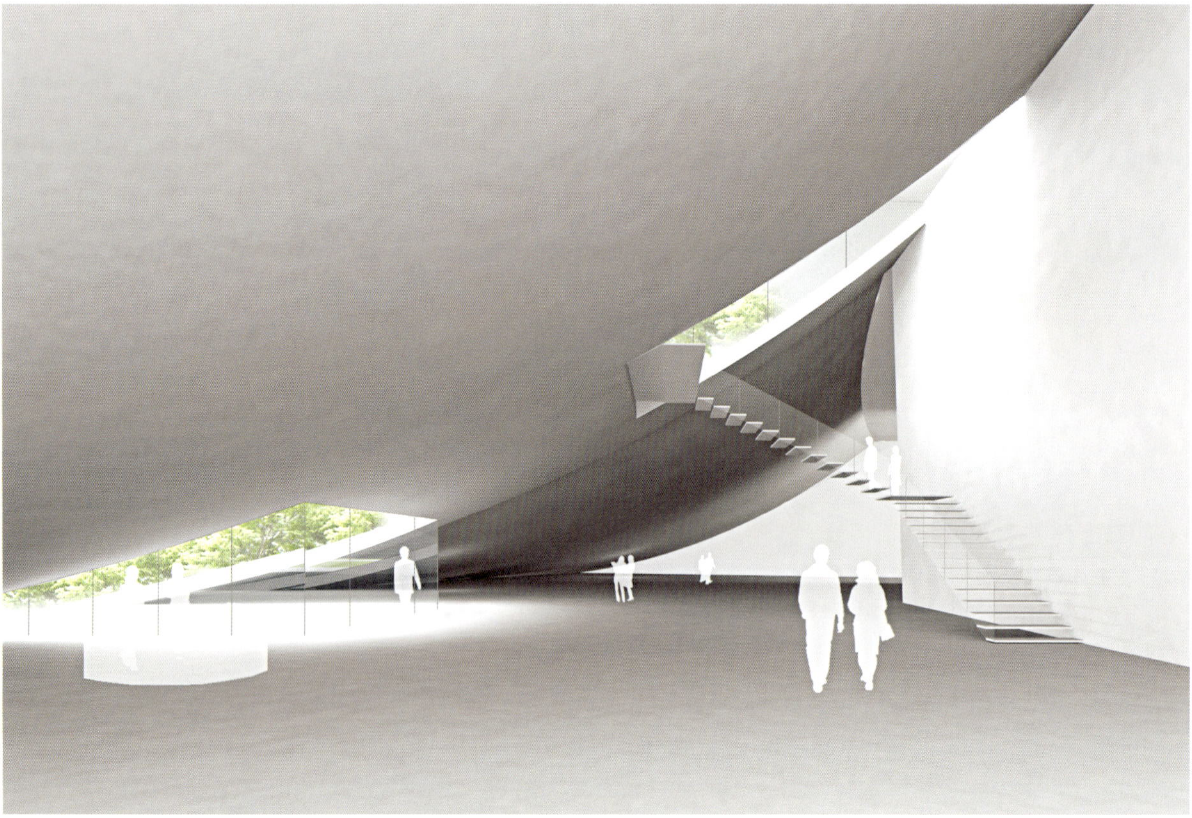

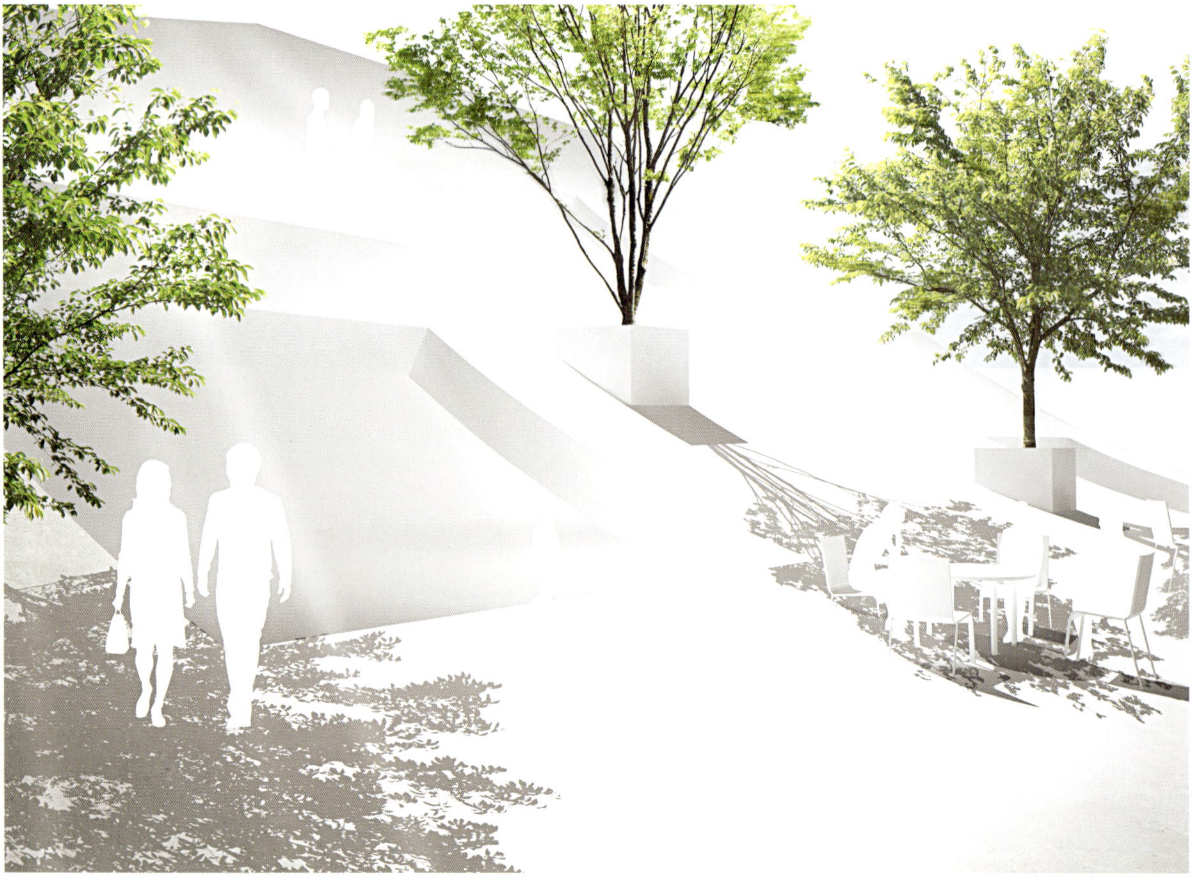

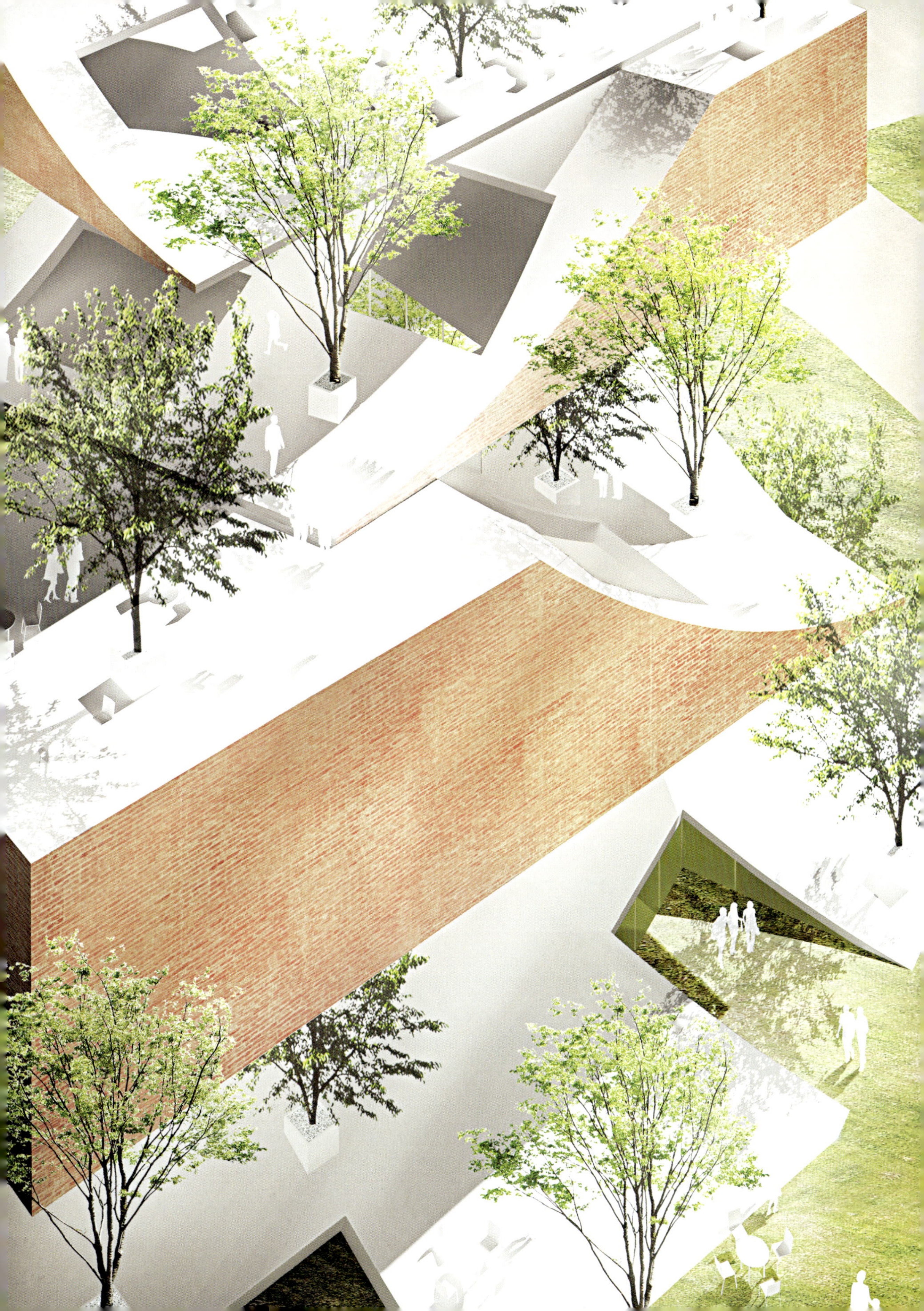

Media Forest - Axel Springer Campus
BERLIN, GERMANY 2013

RELATION/NETWORK

Individual and collective come together through diverse scales in a network-like relationship

The competition proposal for an office space that would foster a new style of work for a German media company. Our response for the new style of work for the new age was a forest-like place. In such a place, a variety of individuals and groups – one person, a few people, a middle-sized group, and a group of many people – would be able to coexist while engaging in a wide range of relationships with each other. Floating volumes, referred to as "islands," are linked to one another in a three-dimensional network. A forest of trees sprouts up from the top of the island, and by using bridges to connect different places, the floating forest functions as a three-dimensional network. People could discover places with a scale that was suitable for their activities there and work as they communicated with others working around them. Inside the island volume, there are a variety of rooms, including huge multipurpose space with a four-storey foyer, a space made up of several floors similar to a regular office space, and an interior space that is minutely segmented. The ground plane is open to the city and this new forest-like building would function as part of a public space. Its outward appearance would also resemble a three-dimensional forest, creating a new landscape within the city.

ドイツのメディア企業が、新しいワークスタイルのオフィス空間を求めたコンペへの応募案。新しい時代のワークスタイルとは？　僕たちは、それは森のような場所だと考えた。そこではひとりと、数人と、中くらいのグループと、大勢のグループなど、さまざまな個や集団が、互いにさまざまな関係をもちながら、共存し合える場所である。浮遊するアイランドと呼ばれるボリュームが、ネットワーク状に立体的に接続する。アイランドの上は樹木の茂る森であり、ブリッジで連結することで、浮遊する森は立体的なネットワークとなる。人びとはその森の中で、自分の活動に合ったスケールの場所を見い出し、周囲の活動とコミュニケーションを取りながら働くことになる。アイランドのボリューム内には、4層吹き抜けの巨大な多目的スペースから、通常のオフィスに近い複数の床が積層した空間、細かな部屋に分節された内部空間まで、さまざまな部屋が用意されている。地上は都市に開かれ、この新しい森的な建築が公共空間の一部となる。外観もまさに立体的な森という姿で、都市の新しい風景をつくり出す。

081

Media Forest - Axel Springer Campus

BERLIN, GERMANY
2013

→ Related Projects
003 011 018 030 054 098

ZONING

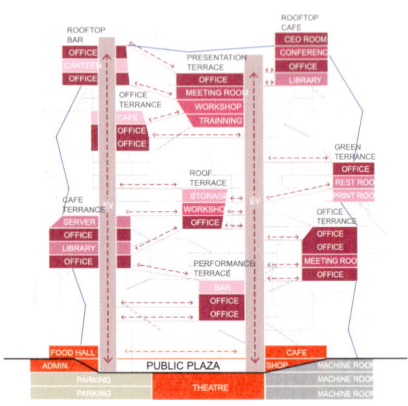

SPACIOUS FLOOR AREA / SIZE OPTIONS

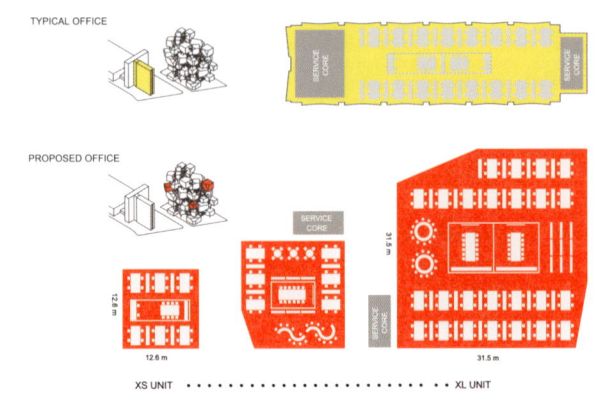

TYPICAL OFFICE

PROPOSED OFFICE

XS UNIT .... XL UNIT

FLEXIBLE ARRANGEMENT

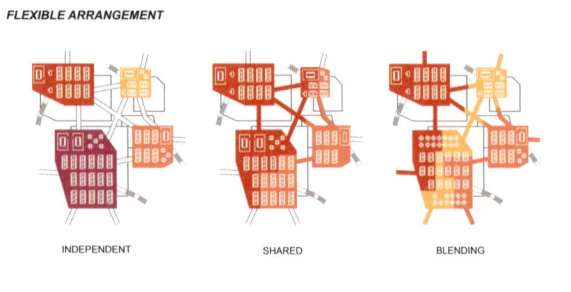

INDEPENDENT   SHARED   BLENDING

LIGHTING + SOLAR PANEL

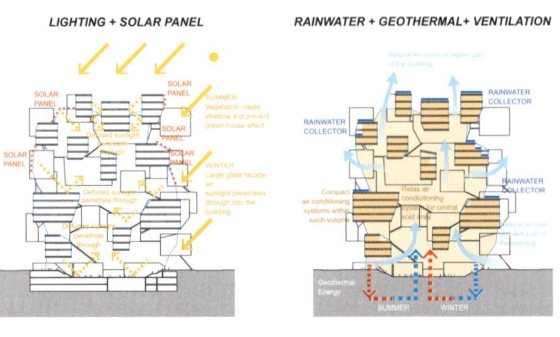

RAINWATER + GEOTHERMAL + VENTILATION

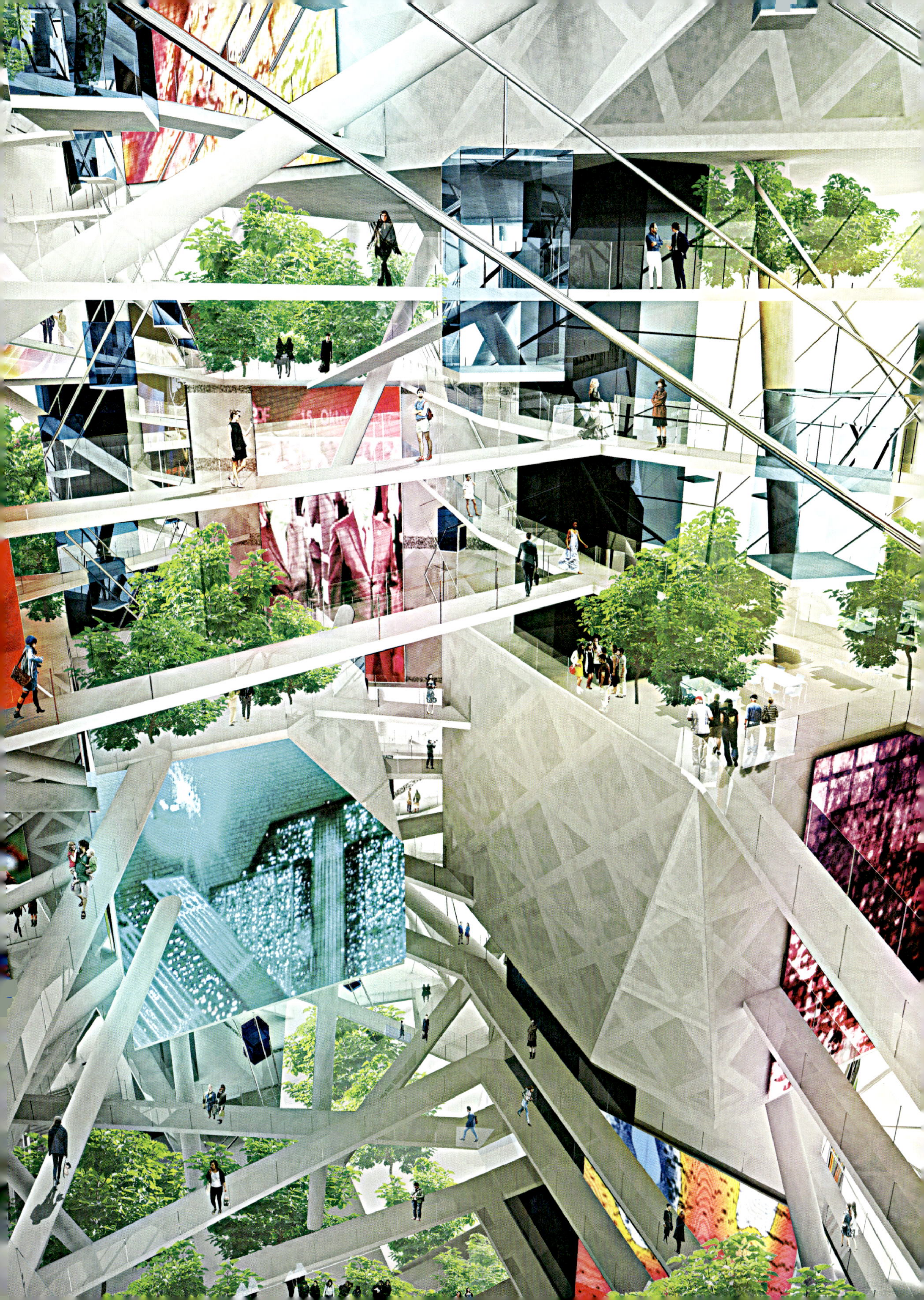

| INDIVIDUAL | GROUP | GATHERING | CROWD |

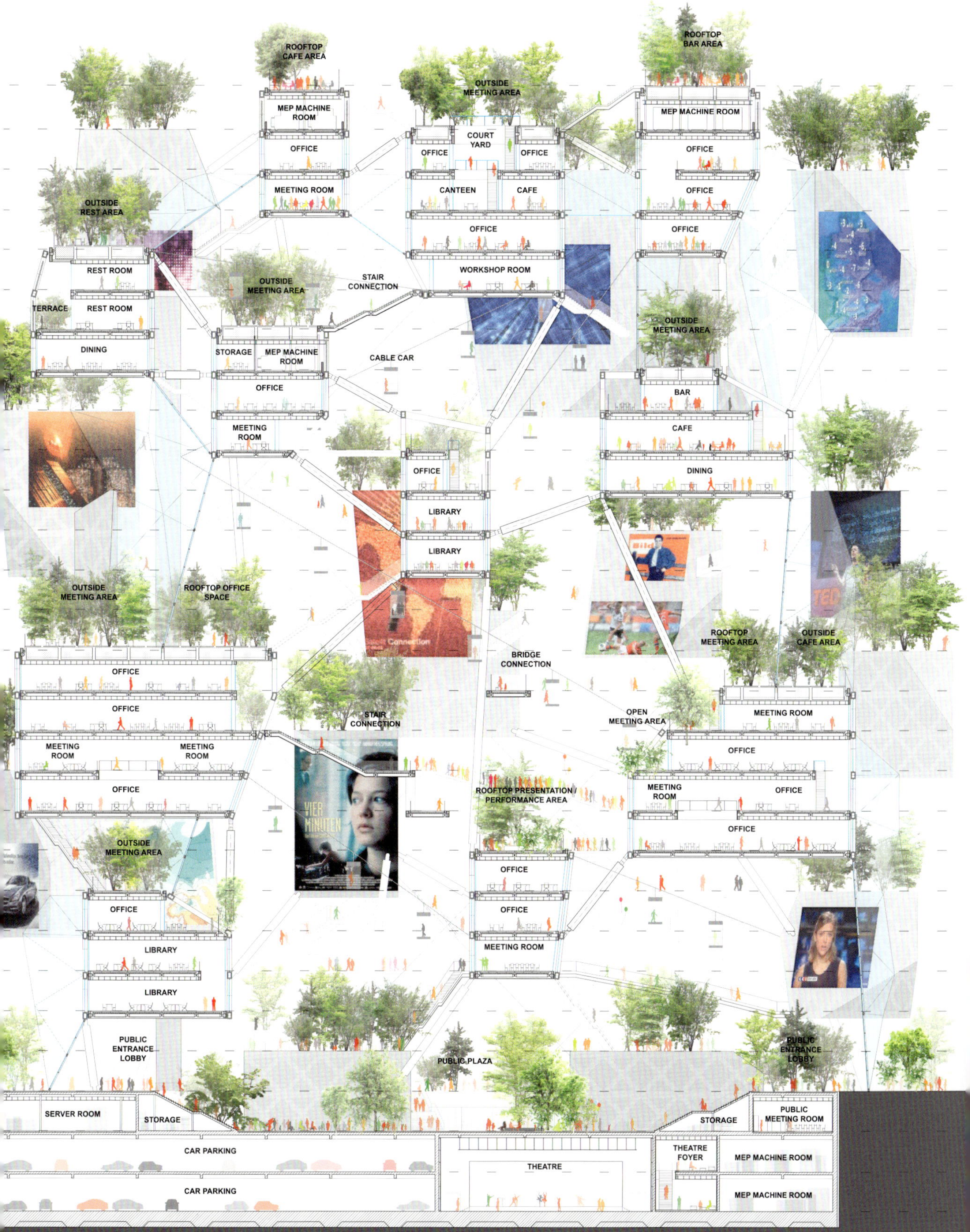
ROOFTOP CAFE AREA
MEP MACHINE ROOM
OFFICE
MEETING ROOM
OUTSIDE MEETING AREA
COURT YARD
OFFICE
OFFICE
CANTEEN
CAFE
OFFICE
WORKSHOP ROOM
ROOFTOP BAR AREA
MEP MACHINE ROOM
OFFICE
OFFICE
OFFICE
OUTSIDE REST AREA
REST ROOM
TERRACE
REST ROOM
DINING
OUTSIDE MEETING AREA
STAIR CONNECTION
STORAGE
MEP MACHINE ROOM
OFFICE
MEETING ROOM
CABLE CAR
OUTSIDE MEETING AREA
BAR
CAFE
DINING
OFFICE
LIBRARY
LIBRARY
OUTSIDE MEETING AREA
ROOFTOP OFFICE SPACE
BRIDGE CONNECTION
ROOFTOP MEETING AREA
OUTSIDE CAFE AREA
OFFICE
OFFICE
MEETING ROOM
MEETING ROOM
OFFICE
STAIR CONNECTION
OPEN MEETING AREA
MEETING ROOM
OFFICE
MEETING ROOM
OFFICE
OFFICE
VIER MINUTEN
ROOFTOP PRESENTATION / PERFORMANCE AREA
OUTSIDE MEETING AREA
OFFICE
LIBRARY
LIBRARY
OFFICE
OFFICE
MEETING ROOM
PUBLIC ENTRANCE LOBBY
PUBLIC PLAZA
PUBLIC ENTRANCE LOBBY
SERVER ROOM
STORAGE
STORAGE
PUBLIC MEETING ROOM
CAR PARKING
CAR PARKING
THEATRE
THEATRE FOYER
MEP MACHINE ROOM
MEP MACHINE ROOM

Museum in the Forest
TAOYUAN, TAIWAN 2013 -

Architecture and forest are not disparate things, they are connected in gradation

A design for a small museum located in the middle of a forest in Taiwan. The building has very simple functions, and primarily consists of a single gallery and a multi-purpose space used for lectures and so forth. Imagine a person walking through a forest and realizing they are gradually being enveloped by white fog, until finally they are completely surrounded by the white walls of the gallery. Could I design a building that would effectively reflect this gradation over time? Here, the experience of the forest and that of the white cube-style gallery are connected using gradually shifting degrees of transparency. While the 100-meter-long structure occupies part of the forest, it blends halfway into its surroundings. The materials used for floors, louvers and curtains, and the way the space twists and turns, create a sense of architectural gradation.

台湾の森の中に、小さな美術館を設計するプロジェクト。ワンルームの展示スペースとレクチャーなどに使える多目的なスペースがメインの、とてもシンプルな機能である。森の中を歩いていて、気がついたら自分の周囲が徐々に白い森に包まれてきて、最終的に白い壁で囲まれた展示空間の中に身を置いている。そんなグラデーションそのもののような建築をつくることはできないだろうか？　森の体験と、ホワイトキューブとしての展示室の体験が、緩やかに変化していく透明度の中で繋ぎ合わされる。森の中に長さ100mにわたって存在しながら、その半分は森と溶け合っている。ルーバーやカーテン、床の素材、また空間の曲がり具合や幅の変化によって、建築的なグラデーションをつくり出す。

082 | Museum in the Forest | Museum in the Forest | TAOYUAN, TAIWAN 2013– | → Related Projects 001 002 027 054 104

ENTRANCE
ENTRANCE HALL
TICKET COUNTER

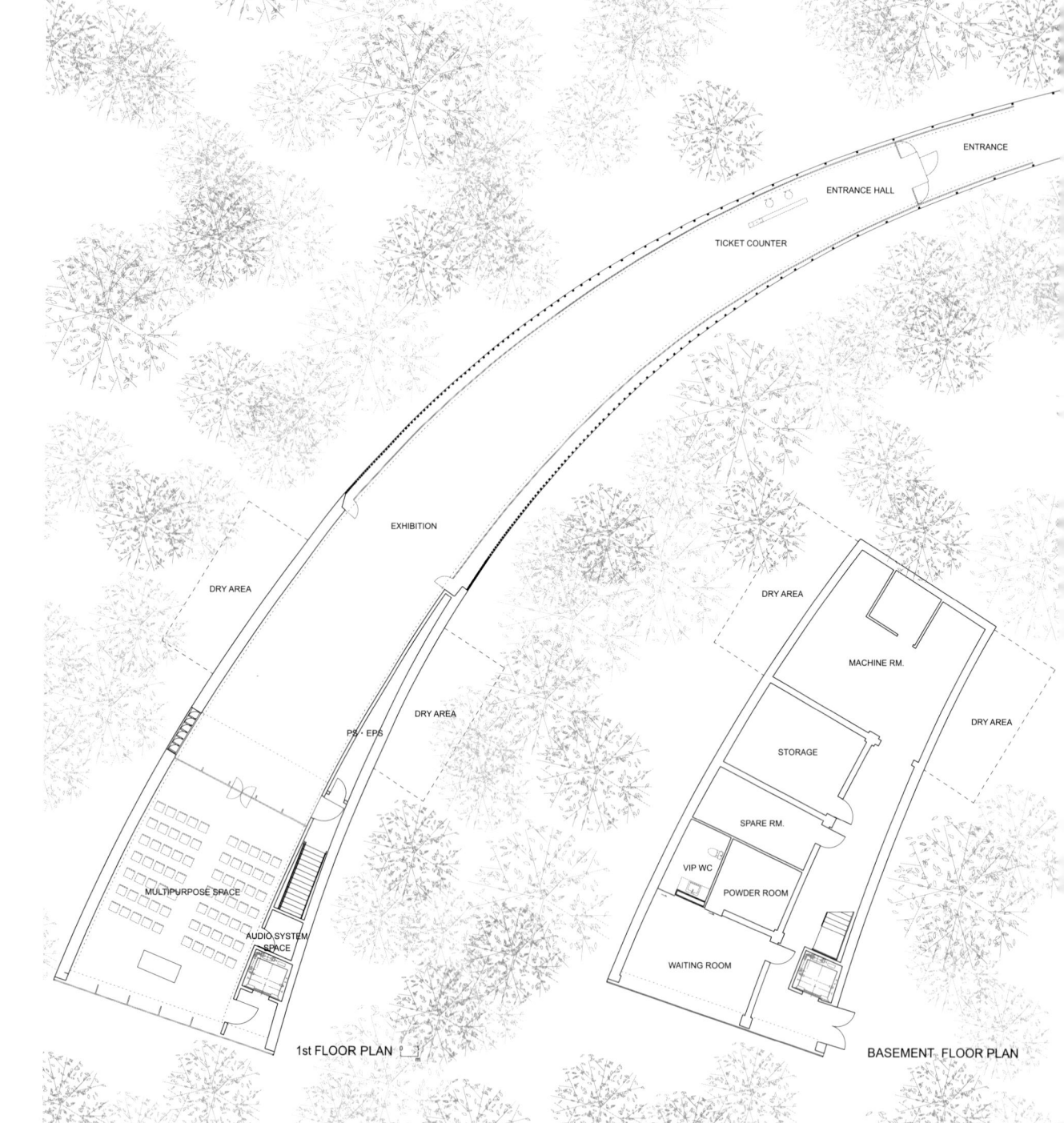

EXHIBITION

DRY AREA

DRY AREA

DRY AREA

MACHINE RM.

STORAGE

DRY AREA

PS · EPS

SPARE RM.

VIP WC
POWDER ROOM

MULTIPURPOSE SPACE

AUDIO SYSTEM SPACE

WAITING ROOM

1st FLOOR PLAN

BASEMENT FLOOR PLAN

CANOPY STRAGE BENCH

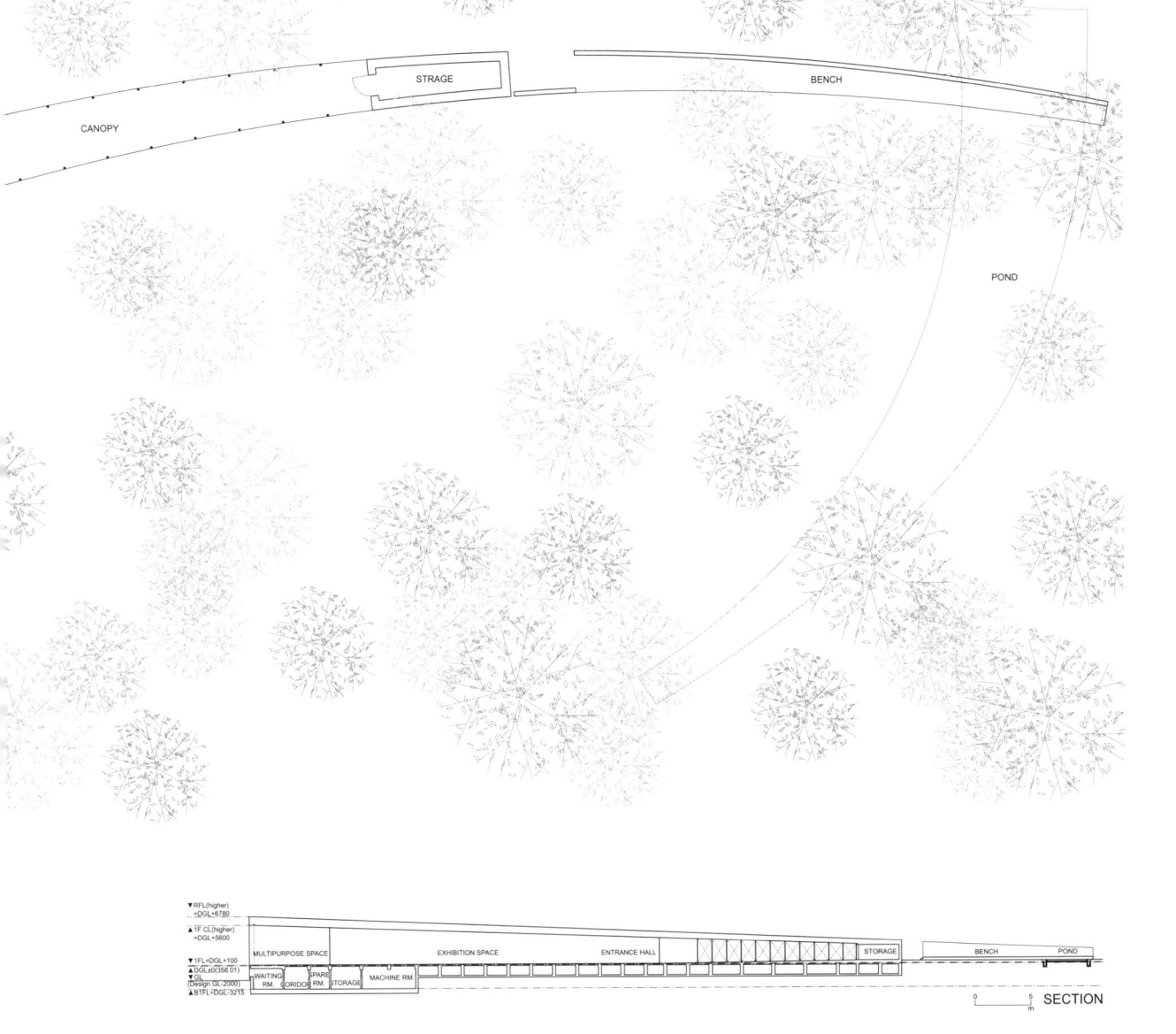

POND

SECTION

Salford Sphere
MANCHESTER, UNITED KINGDOM 2013

Bridge is neither a line nor a surface, it is a space

This is my proposal for a competition to design a bridge as a landmark in the city of Manchester. To make it a landmark, I wanted something with the height of the road, but the river was quite a bit lower than the road. If I was going to go to trouble of designing a bridge, I wanted to create a new riverfront space by making something that led down to the river and didn't simply span it. This inspired an idea for a spherical truss structure that would expand not only in terms of height but also in a downward direction. The translucent spherical truss would serve as a landmark with a strong presence and new form. The experience of crossing the bridge would also create a floating sensation as a person passed through the spherical space, and the spiral passageway would provide a wide range of experiences, allowing people to approach the river, and climb to the top of the sphere and look out at the surrounding area. This is an idea that I would really like to realize.

マンチェスターの街に、ランドマークとなるような橋をデザインするコンペへの応募案。ランドマークとなるには路レベルからの高さが欲しいが、川面は路よりもかなり低い所を流れている。せっかく橋をつくるのであれば、たんに川を渡るのではなく、川面近くまで降りていくことで新しい水辺空間をつくることができないかと考えた。そこで、高さ方向にも、また下方向にも広がりをもつ構造体として、この球体のトラス構造のアイデアが生まれた。半透明のトラスの球体は、その強い存在感で新しい形のランドマークとなる。橋を渡る体験は、この球体の空間の中を通過していく浮遊感に満ちたものとなり、また螺旋状の通路によって、川面近くまで降りていったり、球の上部まで上がって周囲を展望したりという多様な体験をつくり出す。ぜひ実現したいアイデアである。

Steel Cable to suspend the Box Girder Bridge from the Sphere

Box Girder Bridge

Handrail: Glass

Slide bearing

Structure of the Entrance Platform

Amakusa City Hall
KUMAMOTO, JAPAN 2013

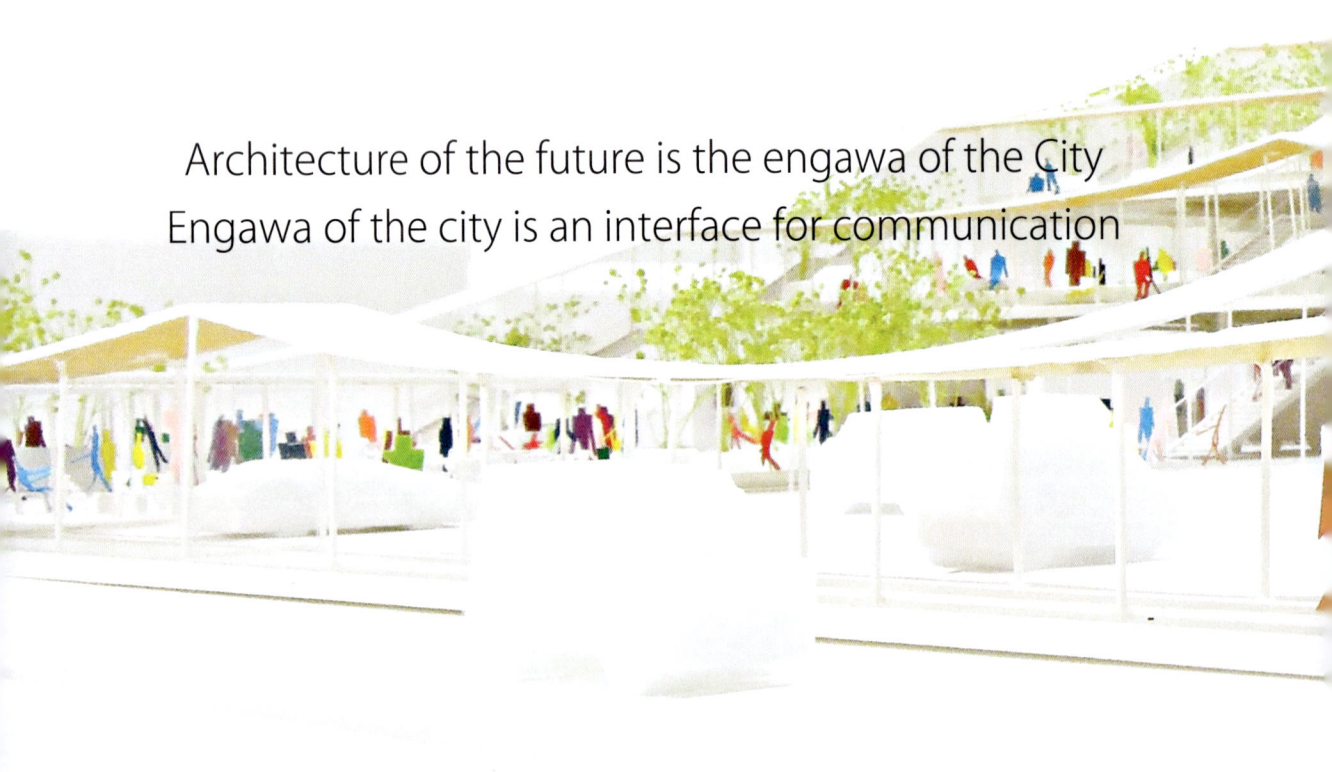

Architecture of the future is the engawa of the City
Engawa of the city is an interface for communication

In recent years, city halls have increasingly become huge office buildings, which, it seems to me, weakens the connection and bond with the citizens and their everyday lives. In this work, I proposed a network made of an engawa-like (traditional Japanese veranda) space under the eaves as a means of connecting a huge working space and people's lives. This space, beginning at the main street, includes bus stop and car pick-up/drop-off areas as a roofed space with a human scale, and also invites people to the entrance. The entrance area and the surrounding public office space provide a frontage that can be used as a private place where people enjoy coming even when they don't have any business at city hall. It also functions as a three-dimensional path that runs all around the building and a buffer zone that connects the huge city hall with a human scale. This network of engawa, which gives the building a gently undulating appearance, is segmented into suitable scales to harmonize with the surrounding cityscape. In this era, in which the gap between the city, a place for people, and buildings grows increasingly larger, this type of architecture / city, made out of interim spaces, is sure to grow more valid.

市庁舎という場所は、近年ますます巨大なオフィスビルと化してきて、人びとの日常生活の場所との繋がりが薄れてきているのではないだろうか？　ここでは、巨大な執務空間と人びとの生活を繋ぐものとして、縁側的な軒下空間のネットワークを提案した。大通りから始まるこの縁側空間は、人間的なスケールの屋根下空間としてバス停や車止めなどを内包しながら、人びとをエントランスへと導く。エントランス周辺やその周りの役所空間にも、用がなくても気軽に立ち寄れるような、都市の中のプライベートな居場所としての軒先を提供する。それは建物全体を巡り歩く立体化された路でもあり、巨大な市役所と人間スケールの間を繋ぎ合わせる緩衝帯でもある。建物の外観は緩やかに波打つこの縁側のネットワークによって、適度なスケールに分節され、周辺の街並へと調和する。人間のための場所としての街と巨大建築のギャップがますます大きくなっていくこれからの時代に、このような＜間の空間＞によってつくられる建築／都市が有効となるであろう。

084

Amakusa City Hall

天草本庁舎

KUMAMOTO, JAPAN
2013

→ Related Projects
003 024 040 061 089 105

SECTION

- People wait for buses under the sogawa roofs
- The plaza connects to the cityscape
- Trees here provide natural shade
- Retractable awnings provide shelter from wind and rainwater
- A 4-story building design that does not intimidate the surroundings
- View over the ocean from the assembly lobby
- Clear 4-story program layout

BUS STOP | PLAZA | CITY'S PLAZA | FUNCTION: CITIZENS' EXCHANGE | FUNCTION: RECEPTION | FUNCTION: RECEPTION | GARDEN | SHELTER | LOBBY FOR PUBLIC ATTENDANCE | ASSEMBLY RM. | LOBBY
OFFICE | OFFICE | EMERGENCY CONTROL CENTER
OFFICE | MEETING RM.
OFFICE | MEETING RM.

0 10 m

Ginza Building

TOKYO, JAPAN 2013

Vertical alley-garden

ELEVATION

This is a design for an extremely long, slender building of the kind that is unique to Tokyo, in the heart of that city. Although the interior is inevitably occupied by a single room and a core, by positioning the legally-required egress stairs near the front facade, I sought to create a balcony-like space that would allow each tenant to expand their territory. The facade is created out of an irregularly undulating and rising staircase, and the landing and various things related to everyday life gradually seep out there. Because the staircase is connected vertically, it becomes a three-dimensional, engawa-like place for communication. This high-rise building, with a height of 30 meters, clearly creates an attractive place made up of different layers of life. The idea that the staircase used to access your apartment also being a part of your territory explored initially in the *Tokyo Apartment* project is unique to Tokyo. Here, I have expanded further on this idea. The form is completely different, but there are parallels between this work and the semi-outdoor area I later created as a living space in the *L'Arbre Blanc* apartment complex.

東京都心に、東京特有のとても細長いビルを計画する。内部プランは必然的にワンルームとコアで占められてしまうが、必要とされる避難階段のひとつを建物正面にもってくることで、各テナントが自分たちの領域を拡張できるバルコニー空間を生み出すことを考えた。建物正面が不規則にうねりながら上昇する階段でつくられ、その踊り場や段々には生活にまつわるさまざまなモノたちがにじみ出てくる。階段は上下で連続するゆえに、そこは立体的な縁側のようなコミュニケーションの場所ともなる。高さ30mにもなる高層建築が、生活の積層でつくられているような魅力的な場所ができあがるに違いない。「Tokyo Apartment」の時に、アクセスする階段も住人の敷地の一部であると考えることがとても東京的だと思われたが、ここではその考えをさらに拡張している。形はまったく異なるが、後の「L'Arbre Blanc」にも通じる、生活空間としての半外部空間の提案である。

085 | Ginza Building

Ginza Building

TOKYO, JAPAN
2013

→ Related Projects
003 043 055 068 086

284 285

JJ99 Youth Hostel
TAINAN, TAIWAN 2013 -

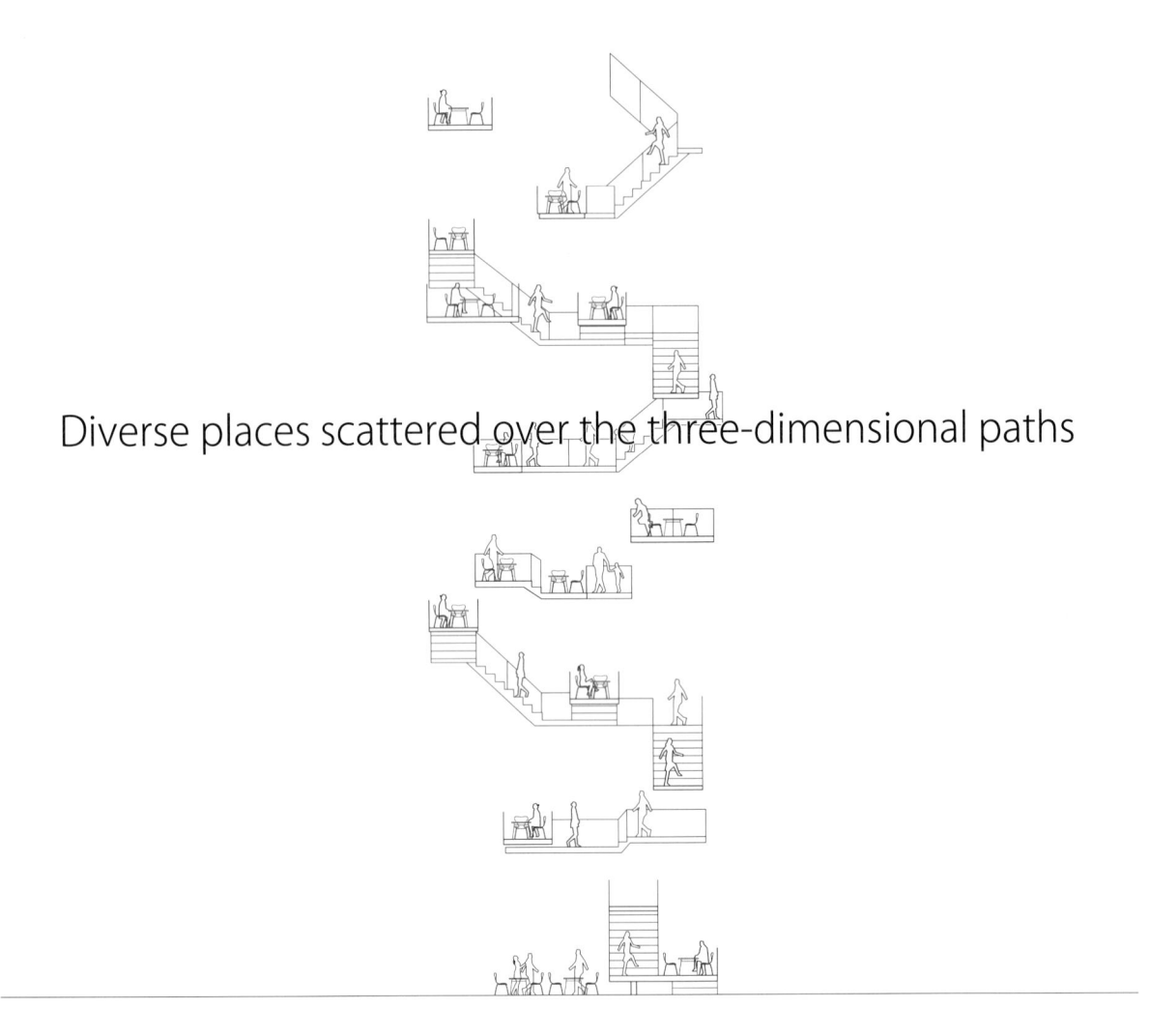

Diverse places scattered over the three-dimensional paths

In this project, a seven-story building in central Tainan is to be renovated as a hotel. One very appealing thing about Tainan is its narrow back streets and alleyways, with charming shops and cafes scattered among the narrow, twisting labyrinthine streets. This proposal aimed to create an innovative urban space by incorporating this kind of back-street environment into the spatial design of the entire building façade, which faces onto a larger road. For this, all the floors would be removed from the front section of the existing building, creating a large atrium with a ceiling seven stories high. This atrium would contain a multi-leveled network of "alleys" involving stairs and platforms, which would incorporate café tables, part of the hotel lounge, and special balcony sections. I believe this design could create a new and vital space in the zone between interior and exterior, and between street and building.

台南の中心部にある7階建てのビルを、ホテルにリノベーションするプロジェクト。台南の街は、裏道空間が魅力的である。細く曲がりくねった裏路地に、雰囲気のよいお店やカフェが点在している。このホテルプロジェクトでは、路に面したビルの正面全体に、そのような路地空間を立体的に展開することで新しい都市空間をつくり出すことを提案した。既存ビルの正面部分の床をすべて抜いて、高さ7層分にもわたる巨大な吹き抜け空間をつくる。その吹き抜けに、階段とプラットフォームでつくられた立体路地が縦横無尽に展開する。それはカフェのテーブル席でもあり、ホテルのラウンジの一部でもあり、また特別なバルコニーでもある。内部と外部、路と建築、その間に新しい場所の価値をつくり出すことができればと考えている。

086

JJ99 Youth Hostel

TAINAN, TAIWAN
2013–

Related Projects
003 007 036 055 078

Taipei Apartment
TAIPEI, TAIWAN 2013 -

Architecture of the future maybe enveloped in an artificial feather-like tuft

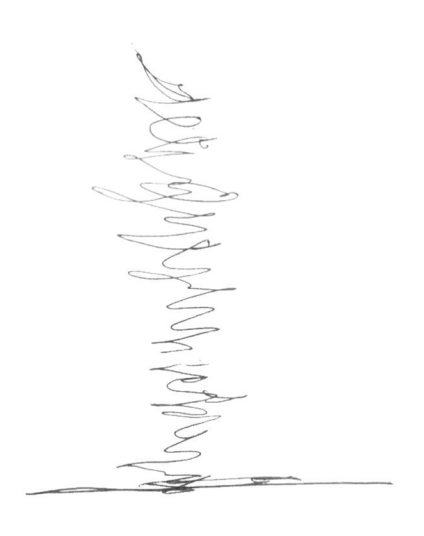

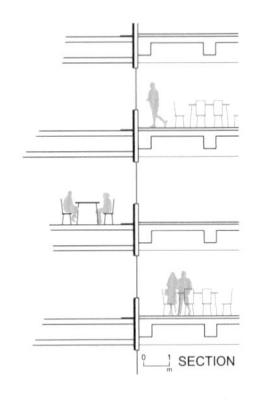

This high-rise apartment building was a plan for Taipei. In light of the Taiwan's climate, with lots of strong sunlight, I created eaves using louvers on each floor. Using so many louvers made the building look as if it was covered with soft feathers or like an irregular form enveloped in clouds. The louvers also function as an extension of the floor inside, forming a balcony. They also obstruct the external sight line and provides an expansive view of the city from the inside. The design of the exterior alone created a fusion between the state of the building in the city and my proposal for a living environment that could deal with the climate and the need for privacy.

台北に計画中の高層マンション。日差しが強い台湾の気候を考慮して、各階にルーバーによる庇を設置した。無数のルーバーによって、外観は柔らかい羽毛に覆われたような、あるいは雲に包まれたような不定形の姿をとる。このルーバーはまた、内部からは延長した床面となり、バルコニーを形成する。ルーバーによって周囲からの視線を遮り、室内からは水平に広がる広大なビューを獲得する。アパートの外装部分のみのデザインだが、都市の中の建築の在り方と、気候やプライバシーに対応した居住環境の提案を融合させることができた。

087

Taipei Apartment

Taipei Apartment

TAIPEI, TAIWAN
2013-

→ Related Projects
007 023 065 077 091 097

Omotesando Branches
TOKYO, JAPAN 2013 -

Architecture / Forest – City is an architectural forest

The back alleys of Omotesando around the site form a rich urban space in which the small buildings unique to Tokyo blend together with small trees and plants. Taking inspiration from this scenery, I envisioned a building that would create a new fusion of nature and architecture. It makes use of a conventional rigid concrete frame. The frame corresponds to the surrounding environment, fluctuates according to the demands of the interior, and then begins to branch off. Trees are positioned at the ends of the concrete frame. This makes it seem as if natural trees are sprouting out of a huge artificial tree, and the building itself seems to be part of the earth or a three-dimensional extension of the ground. The living spaces are surrounded by greenery, blocking out the sunlight and ensuring a stable environment. At the same time, the building's outward appearance harmonizes with the surrounding area through a fusion of artificial and natural elements. Through its simplicity and openness, this format, a hybrid of grid frame and trees, can be expanded from the small scale of a house to that of an enormous high-rise. Though primordial, this is a proposal for a new form of architecture.

敷地周辺の表参道の裏路地には、東京特有の小さな建物が小さな植栽と混ざり合って豊かな都市空間をつくり出している。その情景からインスピレーションを得て、自然と建築が新しい形で融合する建築を構想した。建物の骨格は、いわゆる普通のラーメン構造のコンクリートフレームでできている。そのフレームが、周辺環境への応答や内部の要請によって揺らぎ、枝分かれし始める。そのコンクリートのフレームの先端に、樹木を配置した。それはあたかも、人工的な巨樹の端部から自然の樹木が芽吹き始めたかのようでもあり、建築そのものが地球の一部、あるいは地面の立体化であるかのようでもある。居住空間は緑に囲まれ、日差しが遮られた安定した環境を獲得し、また都市に対する外観は人工物と自然物の混合によって周辺環境と調和する。グリッドフレームと樹木のハイブリッドというこの形式は、そのシンプルさと許容力によって、住宅スケールから高層建築の巨大さに至るまで、拡張可能であろう。根源的でありながら新しい建築の姿の提案である。

088

Omotesando Branches

TOKYO, JAPAN
2013 -

→ Related Projects
008 028 031 049 056 107

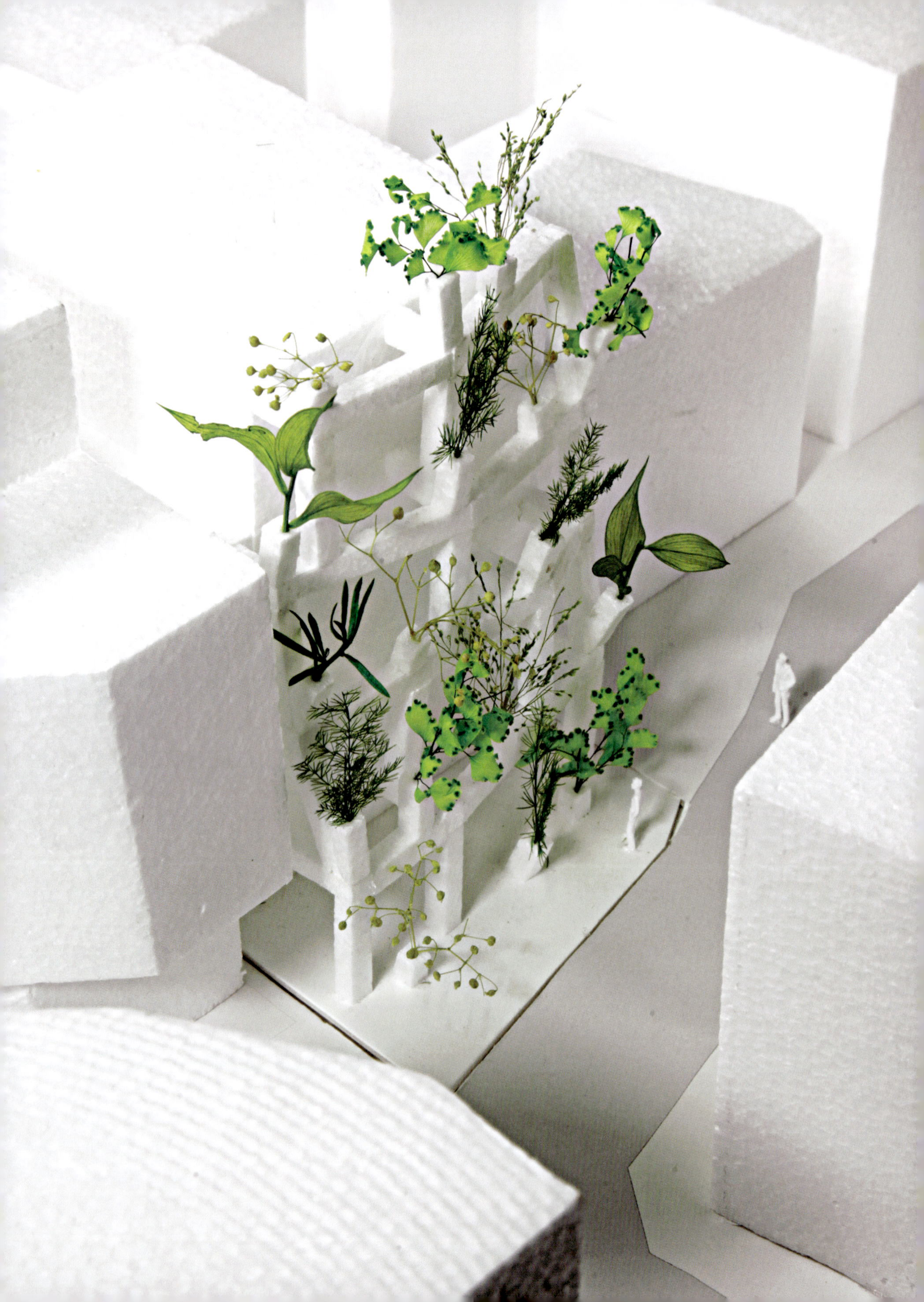

DETAIL SECTION

living room, dining room, and kitchen

Flat Roof: polyurethane waterproofing

Skylight: see additional drawings for details
Skylight protrusion: reinforced concrete, 25mm sprayed polyurethane foam, 9.5mm gypsum board, painted

Slanted Roof: polyurethane waterproofing

Gutter: polyurethane waterproofing

Ceiling: hallow-core slabs, 71mm sprayed polyurethane foam, light-weight steel structure, 9.5mm gypsum board, painted

Floor (directly over slab):
base layer: ceremic-based self-leveling cement, 12mm structural plywood
finish: 15mm veneer laminate flooring
*leave space for electric outlets in floor

Beams: reinforced concrete fair faced, waterproofing paint
Rise around Sash: polyurethane waterproofing, bent steel plate (see additional drawings for details)

reinforced concrete planter: see additional drawings

Reinforced Concrete Beams (500x500) waterproofing paint

Ceiling: hallow-core slabs, light-weight steel structure, 9.5mm gypsum board, painted

office

balcony

Parapet Cap: 3mm stainless flat bar beveled
Parapet: 12mm+2mm double tempered glass
Parapet frames (sides): slots in concrete with sealant
parapet frames (bottom): welt galvanized steel, rubber packs, sealant

Floor (directly over slab):
base layer: ceremic-based self-leveling cement, 12mm structural plywood
finish: 15mm veneer laminate flooring
*leave space for electric outlets in floor

Aluminum Sash: see additional drawings for details

handrail = 1:100

galvanized steel grating (bearing angles: steel 50*50)

auto-watering system fitting adjudsted individually

Ceiling: hallow-core slabs, light-weight steel structure, 9.5mm gypsum board, painted

Insulation: 25mm sprayed polyurethane foam (300mm from the corner)

large meeting room

Floor (directly over slab):
base layer: ceremic-based self-leveling cement, 12mm structural plywood
finish: 15mm veneer laminate flooring
*leave space for electric outlets in floor

Aluminum Sash: see additional drawings for details

Beams: reinforced concrete fair faced, waterproofing paint
Rise around Sash: polyurethane waterproofing, bent steel plate (see additional drawings for details)

reinforced concrete planter: see additional drawings

Ceiling: fair faced concrete

retail space for lease

Floor: concrete (screed and float)

Fixed and Double Doors: stainless

penetrating waterproofing application

gutter cover: galvanized steel, fixed, openings around 6mm

exterior/ outdoor area:
1. 100mm colored concrete paving C-30 grade
2. foudation for outdoor equipment: 150mm concrete (screed and float)
3. 20mm gravel along the long side

reinforced concrete planter: see additionaldrawings

Foundation:
60mm stone, 50mm concrete (leveled), 200mm concrete foundatioin slabs

Fuke Nursery School
SHIGA, JAPAN 2013 -

Covering a roof over an in-between space, the space becomes the engawa of the city

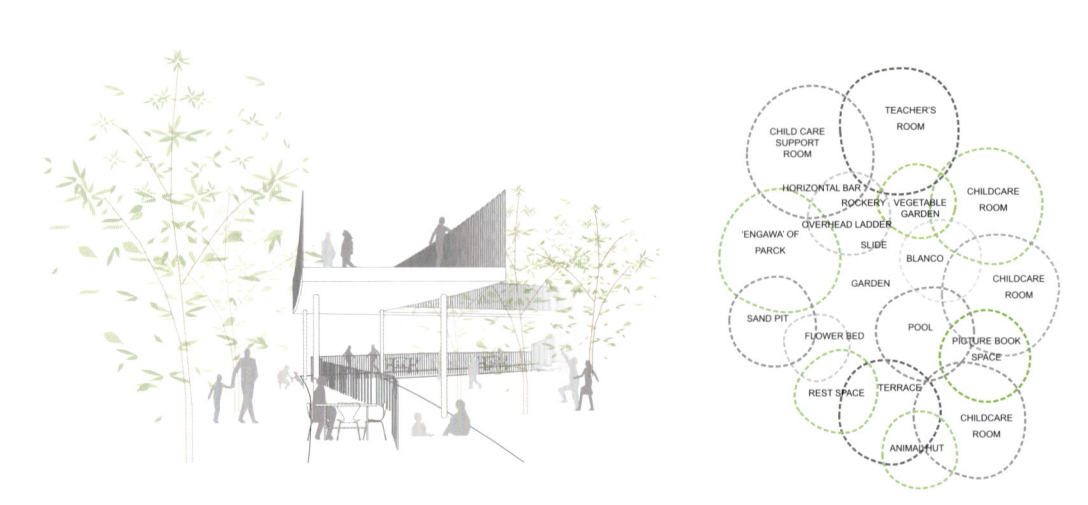

This was a design for a nursery school and a park in the city of Moriyama, Shiga. Though nursery schools tend to be closed, by making a plan that integrated the school with the adjacent park, it was possible to create a new place and relationship between the school and the local society. The open road-like space, covered with a roof, might be called an "urban engawa". The space runs between the nursery school and park. The roof is part of the school's rooftop deck, making a condensed space surrounded by the garden. At the same time, the roofed "urban engawa" functions as a place for local residents to stop and spend some time. And because the space is directly connected to the school's garden, it also naturally becomes a place for communication between the children and local residents. I thought that my proposal for the engawa, a part of the park that is protected from the sun and a place that people pass in the course of everyday life, would create a modest yet new type of urban space. The concept fostered in the *Gunma Agricultural Technology Center* and the *Amakusa City Hall* proposals is now moving towards realization after being selected as the winning proposal.

滋賀県守山市の市街地に、保育園と公園を計画するプロジェクト。通常閉鎖的になりがちな保育園だが、ここでは隣接する公園と一体的に計画することで、保育園と地域社会の間に新しい場所と関係をつくり出す。それは街の縁側と呼べるような、屋根のかかったオープンな路的空間である。その屋根面は保育園の屋上デッキの一部であり、園庭を取り囲んで集約的な空間をつくり出す。その一方で＜街の縁側＞の屋根下は、地域の住民が立ち寄り、腰掛けて時間を過ごす場所となる。それは保育園の園庭に直接面している場所ゆえに、子供たちと地域住民の自然なコミュニケーションの場所ともなる。日差しから守られた公園の一部であり、また日常生活で通りかかる場所でもあるこの縁側は、さりげないけれども都市の新しい場所の在り方の提案になるのではないかと考えている。「群馬県農業技術センター」コンペ案や「天草本庁舎」で試みていたことが、このコンペで１等に選ばれたことで実現へと向かっている。

089 | Fuke Nursery School | Fuke Nursery School Competition First Prize | 守山市浮気保育園 | 守山市浮気保育園設計競技 1等受賞 | SHIGA, JAPAN 2013- | →Related Projects 024 040 061 084

House in Guangzhou

GUANGZHOU, CHINA 2013

When a roof is stratified, roofs are no longer roofs
They become floors, landscape and stairs

I designed this house on the top of a hill in a nature-rich area in the suburbs of Guangzhou, China. Due to the strong sunlight in the area, the roof and space under the eaves were the most important features. I thought I could create a house by stacking up a series of layers beneath the eaves. The roof, which recalls a traditional building with its gentle curves, is made of multiple layers that are both staggered and overlapping. By creating a level difference in the top of the roof, it provides people with a comfortable space. Under the eaves, the exterior and interior blend together, and the layers of the three-dimensional roof create a variety of places to dwell, like different layers in the branches of a tree. Though the roof is layered, the house is an architectural tree or a forest. The lineage of the layered design can be traced back to *Tokyo Apartment* and the *Kunsthalle Bielefeld Annex* plan, and connects traditional architecture with nature.

中国、広州の郊外の自然豊かな丘の上に住宅を設計する。日差しの強い広州の中では、何より屋根と軒下空間が求められる。そこで軒下を積層させることで住宅をつくることはできないかと考えた。緩やかに反った伝統的な建築を思わせる屋根が幾重にもズレながら重なり合う。屋根の上面には段差を設けて、居場所として機能するように設えた。軒下空間で内部と外部が溶け合い、立体的な屋根の積層がまるで樹木の中の枝の積層のようにさまざまな居場所をつくり出す。これは屋根の積層であると同時に、建築的な樹木であり、また森でもある。「Tokyo Apartment」や「Kunsthalle Bielefeld Annex」に見られる積層の系譜が、伝統建築と自然とを繋ぎ合わせていく。

090

House in Guangzhou

GUANGZHOU, CHINA
2013

→ Related Projects
007 019 032 067 080

L'Arbre Blanc

MONTPELLIER, FRANCE 2014 -

Architecture of "many, many, many"
Diverse lifestyles itself is the architecture

TYPICAL FLOOR PLAN

I designed this apartment complex, consisting of about 110 units, in Montpellier in the south of France. In this city with a Mediterranean climate, it is warm enough to eat outside even in the winter, so the local residents spend a lot of time on their balconies and outdoor terraces. The new typology I proposed in this plan, calling for an over 50-meter-high building, was inspired by this type of climate and lifestyle. The idea is extremely simple. Countless, huge balconies extend from the 17-floor apartment building. The structure is linked to a riverside greenbelt, and through the process of controlling the visibility from surrounding buildings, the built volume naturally became an organic form. The hundreds of balconies combine with the curved form of the structure, giving the overall building a distinctive appearance, like a huge tree. In a sense, combining an apartment building with balconies is a very common and conventional technique, but by contrasting the climate, lot, and balconies, it is possible to invent a new, contemporary architectural form. The various lives that spill out onto the balconies create the form of the building, and in the truest sense, defining the regional identity.

南フランス、モンペリエに計画中の約110戸の集合住宅。地中海気候のこの街では、冬でも屋外でランチを食べられるほどに温暖であり、地元の人びとはバルコニーや屋外のカフェテラスで長い時間を過ごす。高さ50m超の高層集合住宅を計画するにあたって、そのようなこの場所ならではの気候とライフスタイルからインスピレーションを得た新しいタイポロジーを提案したいと考えた。アイデアはとてもシンプルである。17階建てのマンションから無数の巨大なバルコニーが張り出す。川沿いのグリーンベルトを連続させ、周辺の建物からの視線をできるだけ確保することを考慮すると、建物のボリュームは有機的な形となった。数百のバルコニーとこの曲線的な形状が相まって、建物全体の姿は巨大な樹木のような、特徴あるものとなった。集合住宅とバルコニーという組み合わせはある意味ではありふれたとても古典的な手法だが、気候と敷地とバルコニーの比重によって、現代的で新しい建築形式として再発明されたと言える。そしてこのバルコニーに滲み出すさまざまな生活そのものが、この建物の姿をつくり出し、真の意味での地域のアイデンティティとなるであろう。

091

L'Arbre Blanc
Invited International Competition for the Second Folly of Montpellier First Prize

L'Arbre Blanc
モンペリエ国際設計競技 | 最優秀賞

MONTPELLIER, FRANCE
2014-

→ Related Projects
007 027 055 077 091

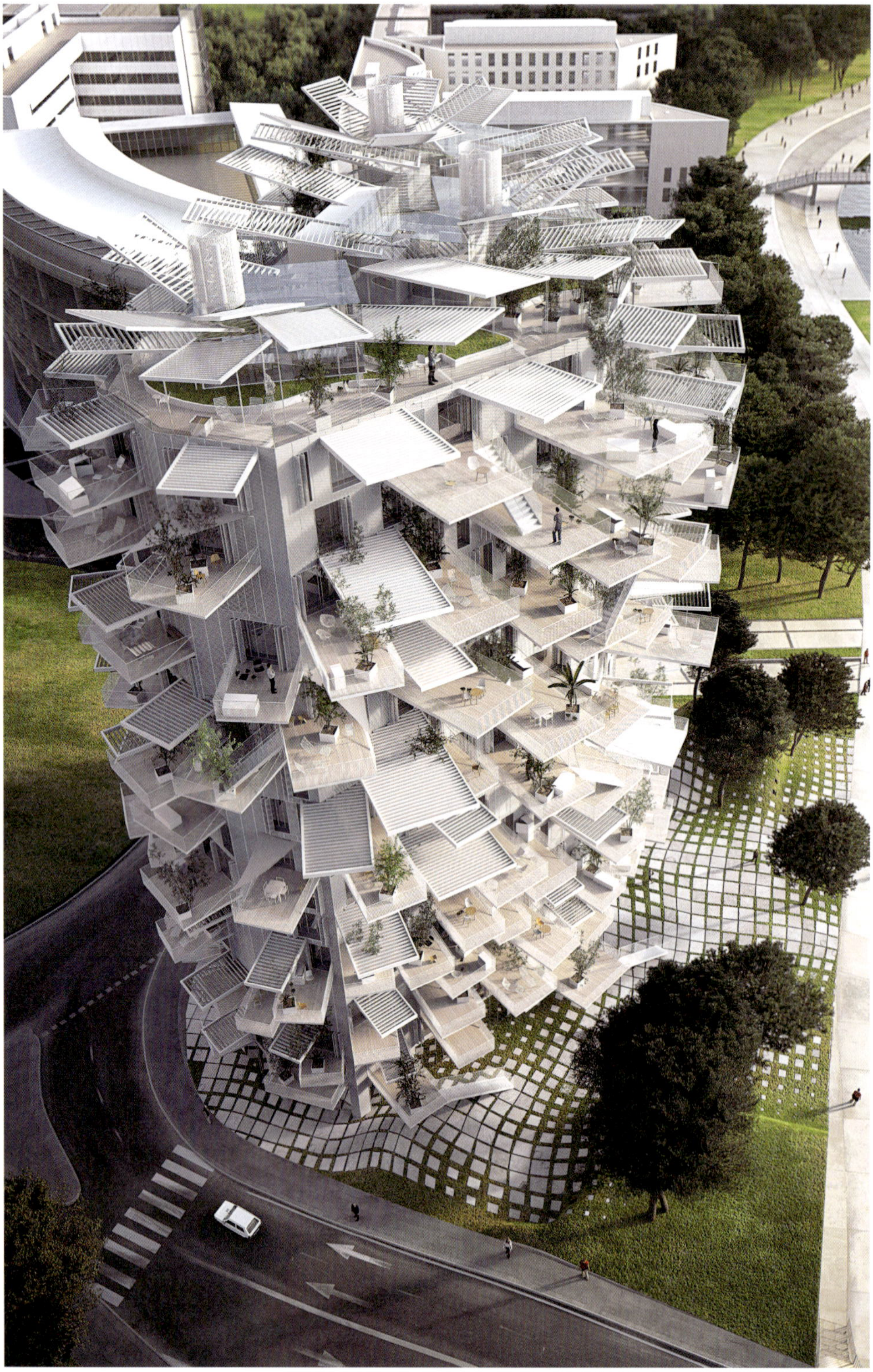

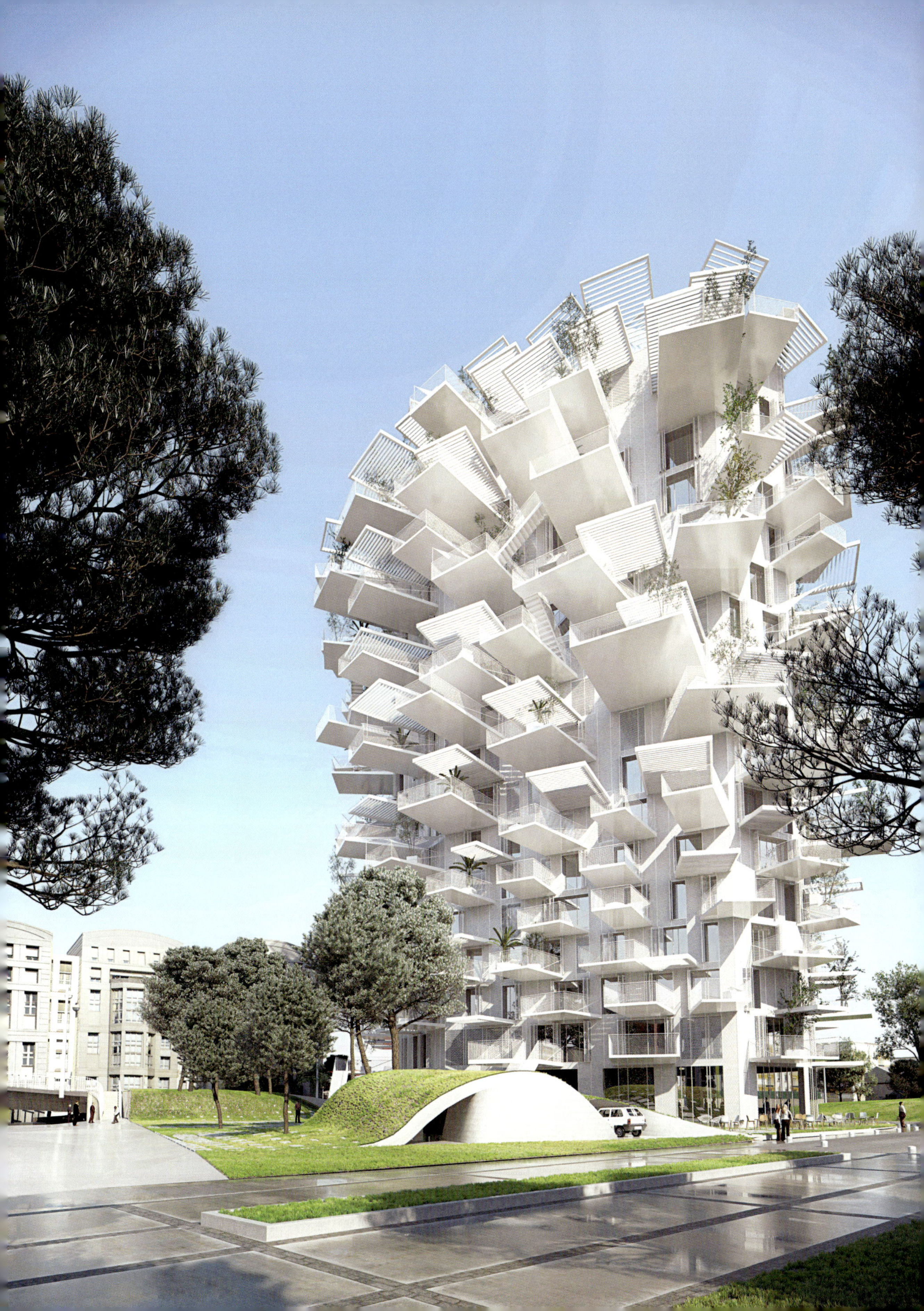

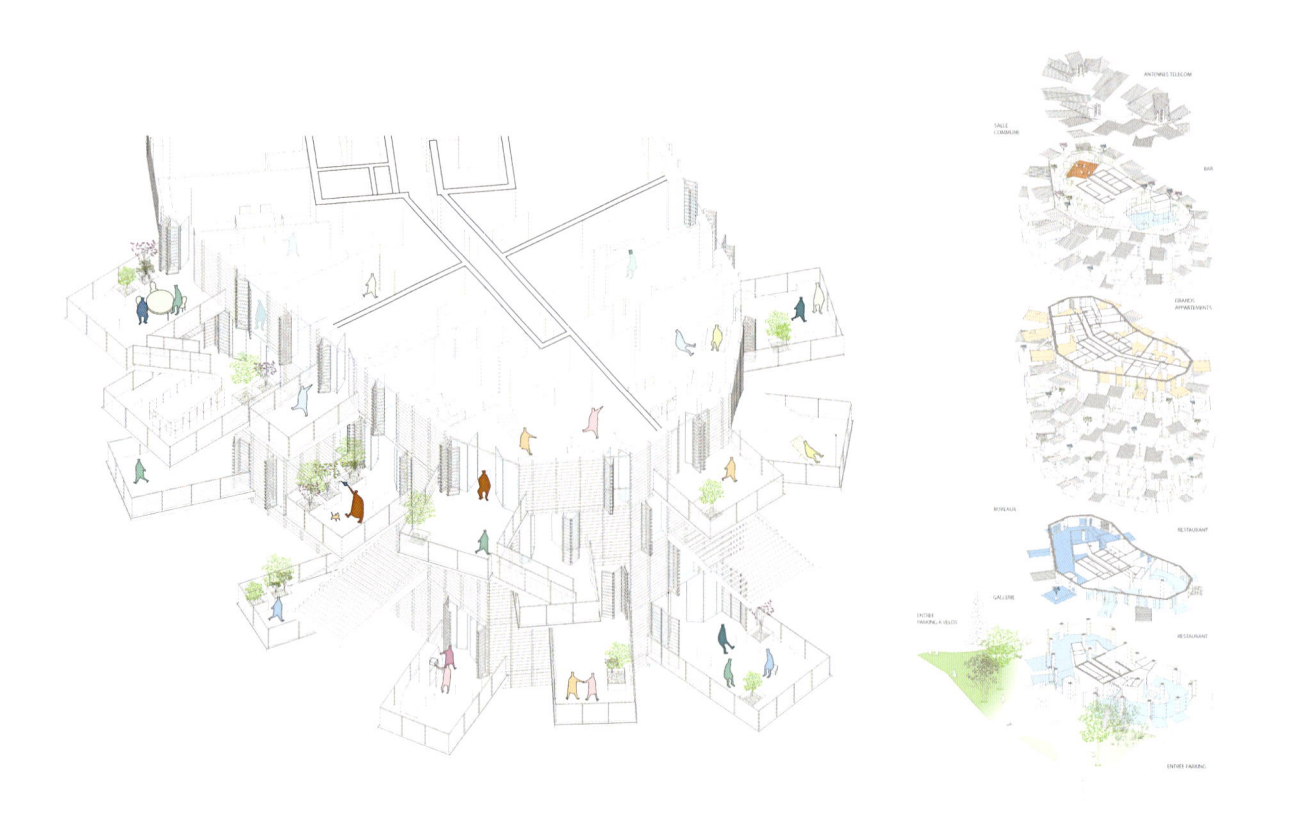

Bibliothèque Interuniversitaire de Montpellier

Place Christophe Colomb

Avenue du Pont Juvenal
Rue Thétis
Avenue de la Pompignane
Rue Costebelle
Rue Pierre bon
Avenue du Pirée
Le Lez
Allée du Capitaine Dreyfus
Rue Vendémiaire
Avenue de Mer Raymond

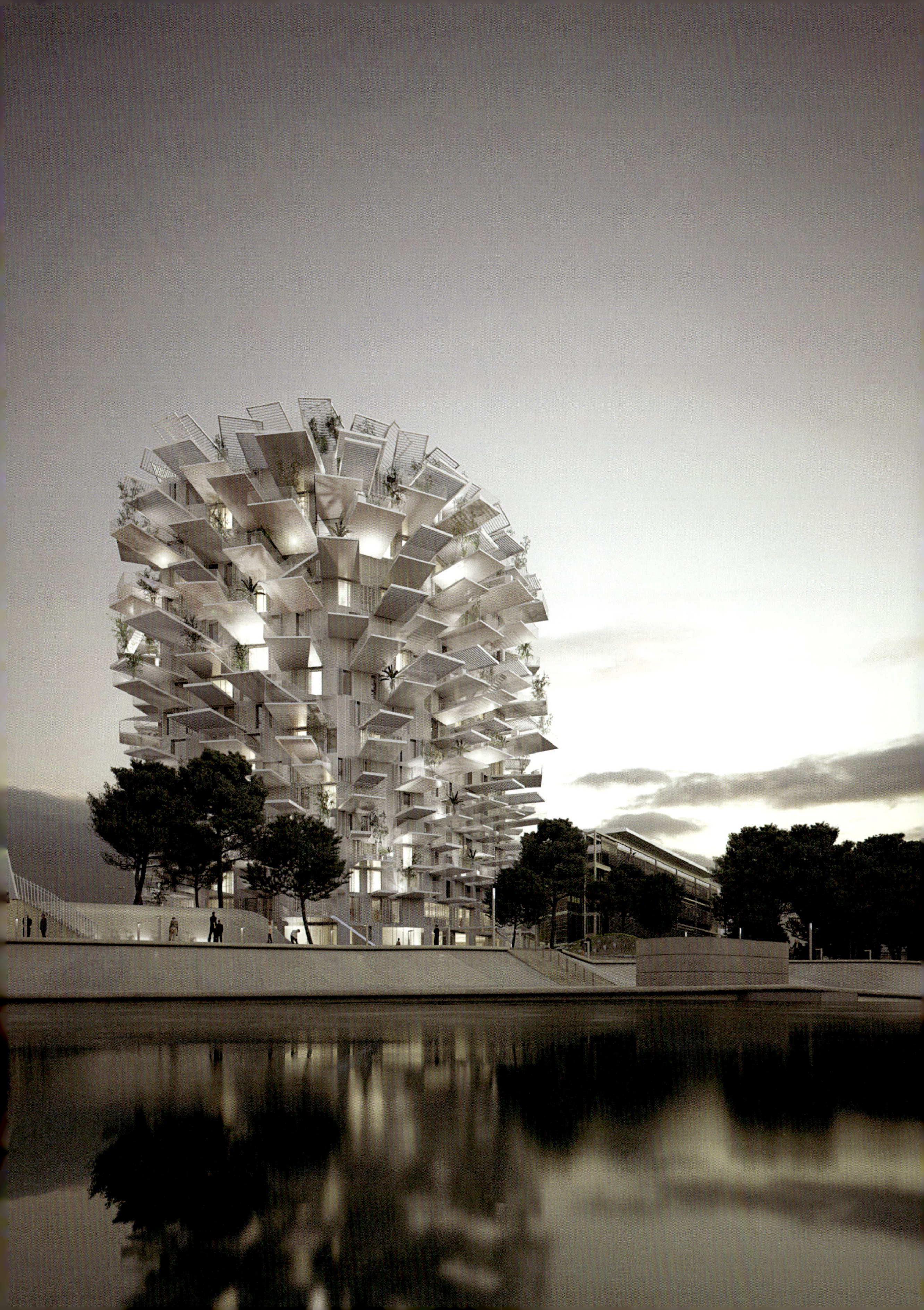

bus stop in Krumbach
KRUMBACH, AUSTRIA 2014

Density of air itself makes the architecture, becomes a place and a landmark

This is a bus stop in Krumbach, a small village in Austria. The landscape, with a scattering of houses and mountains, and more mountains off in the distance is truly beautiful. After visiting the area, I thought the bus stop should be visible from distance acting as a landmark, and at the same time, should function like an observation deck, providing a commanding view of the surroundings. Consisting of a bristle of white columns, from a distance the bus stop appears like a white blur on the mountain. Within this landscape, surrounded by nature, it will create a uniquely soft but firm presence. On the other hand, when you approach the stop, you find that the columns are equipped with footboards and a staircase-like form, and you realize that they lead up to an observation deck. You can gaze far off in the distance as you wait for your bus. Or you can think about where you're headed. The important point is that though the bus stop itself is small, it deals with a sense of very large distance. In this village, a bus stop is a private place but also a place for social interaction, and a place to think about an invisible place some time away, giving the work an extremely rich architectural meaning.

オーストリアの小さな村、クルンバッハのバス停。点在する家々と丘の風景、そして遠くに望む山々という風景はとても美しい。その場所を訪れて、このバス停は、遠くからも見えるランドマークであり、同時に、この場所から周囲を見渡す展望台のような場所でもあるのではないかと感じた。無数の白い柱が林立することで、それは遠景からは丘を背景に見える白い〈にしみ〉のように見えるであろう。自然に囲まれた風景の中で、柔らかく、しかし確固たる存在感をもつはずだ。一方で近づいていくと、その無数の柱には階段状の踏み板がついていて、これが上っていける展望台ということが分かる。上に上って遠くを眺めながらバスを待つ、あるいは自分の向かう先へと思いを馳せる。小さいけれども、とても大きな距離を扱うことが重要であった。この村では、バス停とは、個人的な場所でありながら社会的な交流の場所でもあり、この先の時間とまだ見ぬ場所へと思いを馳せる場所でもある。とても豊かな建築的意味をもつのだ。

092

bus stop in Krumbach

KRUMBACH, AUSTRIA
2014

→ Related Projects
007 048 055 063 077 101

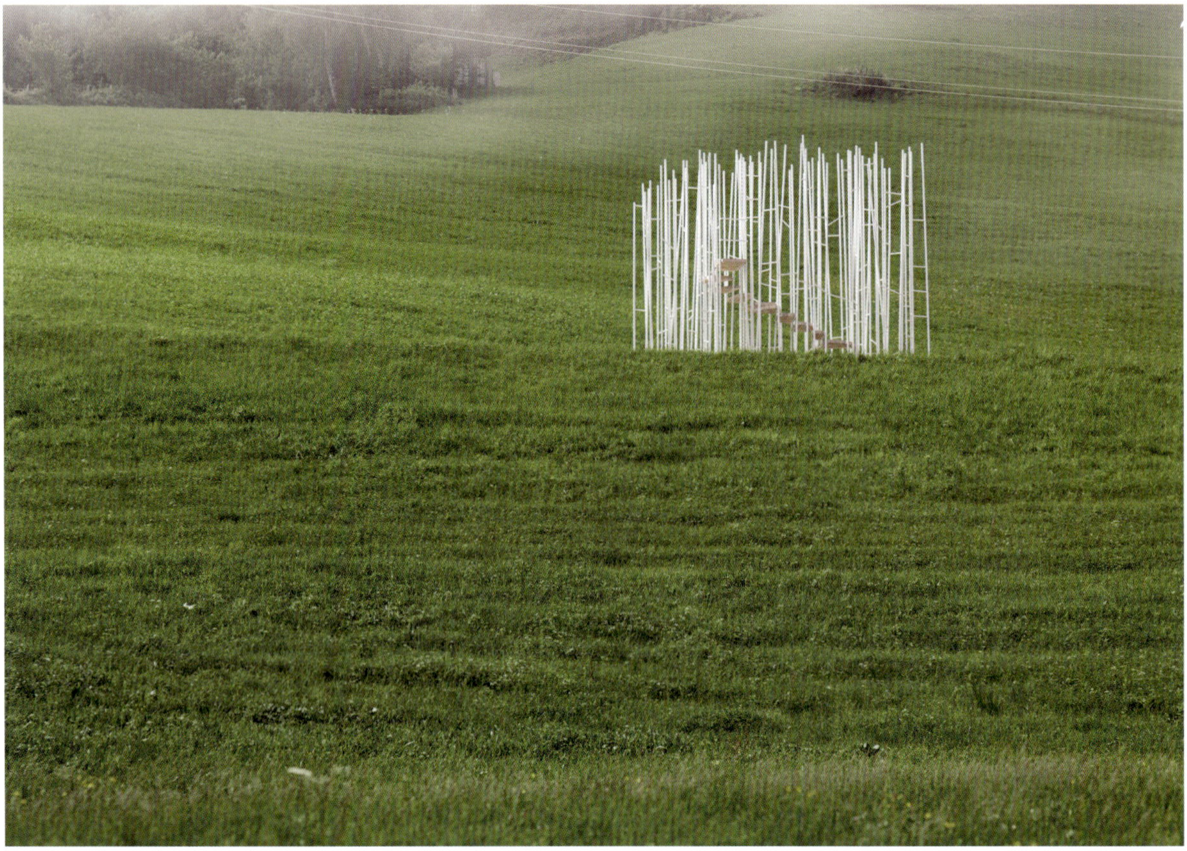

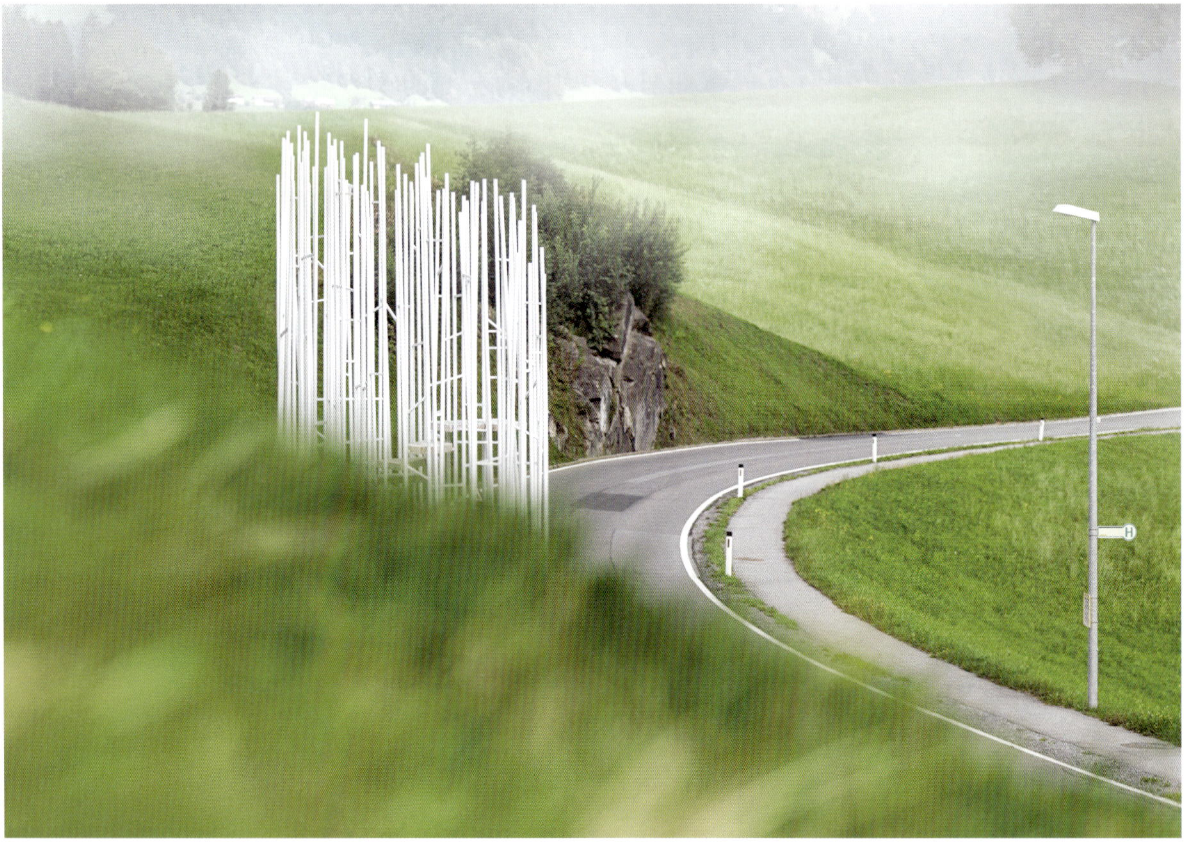
H

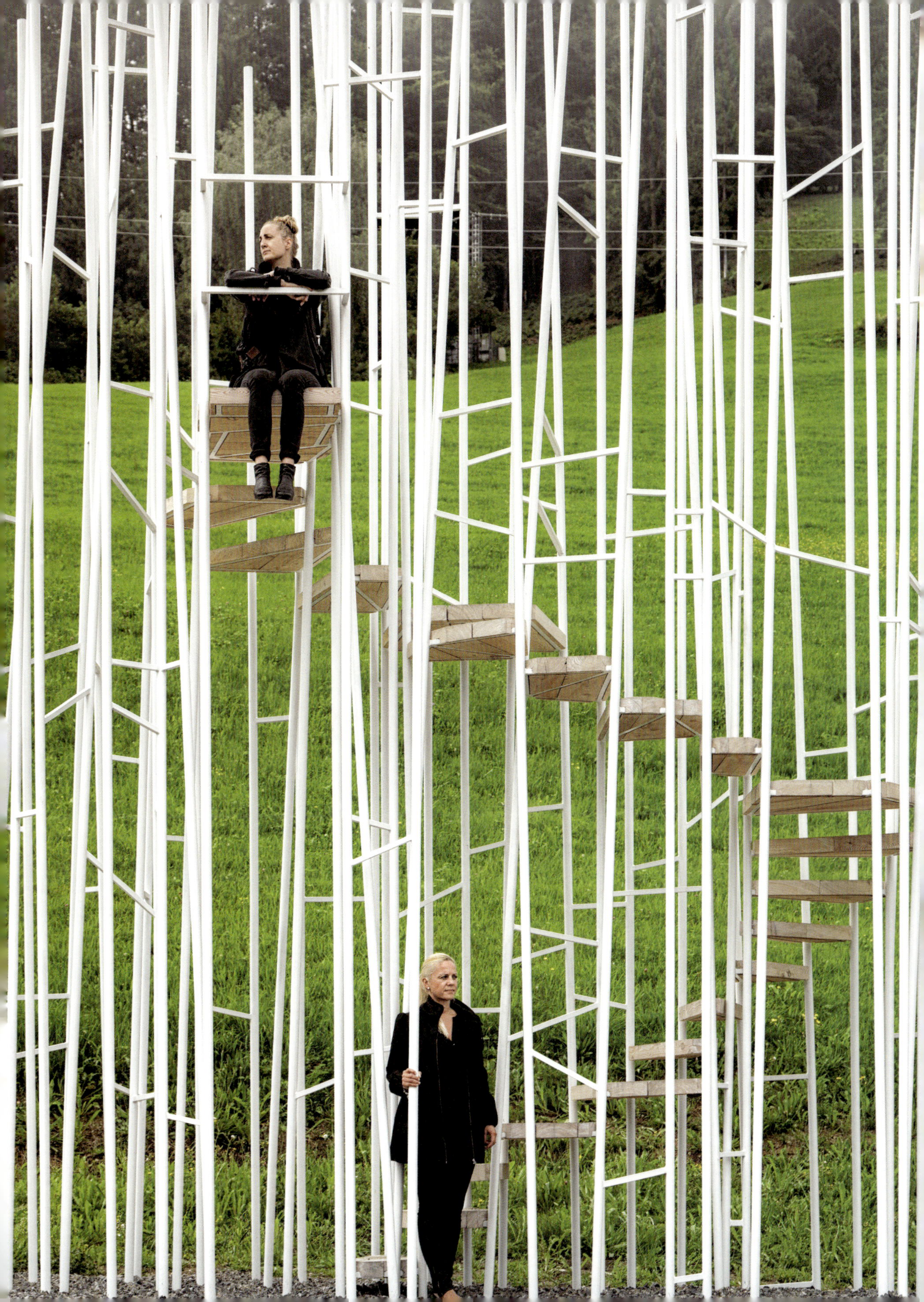

Naoshima Pavilion

KAGAWA, JAPAN 2014 -

Architecture of the future may become
a geometric cloud-like place

On the port side of Naoshima, renowned as an island of art and architecture, I designed a small public space where a variety of people, including local residents and tourists, can relax. I anticipate that it would function as a community space and a new landmark. The town of Naoshima consists of 27 islands. We decided to create one more, the 28th island. The space is softly enveloped in a white metal mesh structure. Outside, it resembles an irregular stone, floating like an island on the ground. Inside, the space also has an irregular topography, allowing people to find a place where they feel comfortable and sit down. The interior space, cloaked in the translucent mesh, creates the sensation of a soft white spatial membrane, only allowing the wind, sounds, and smells of the port in. It is a kind of an inverted island and a new form of space that is different from rigid architectural spaces made with conventional floors, walls, and ceilings. While our sense of vision is diminished, our sense of hearing, touch, and smell are enhanced, allowing us to experience the place with all of our senses. Though small, this is an ambitious work designed to provide a new architectural experience.

アートと建築の島として名高い直島の港の側に、地元の人びとから観光客まで、さまざまな人が立ち寄ることのできる小さな公共空間を設計する。コミュニティスペースであると同時に、新しいランドマークとしても期待されている。直島町は27の島からなる。そこで僕たちは、もうひとつの島、28番目の島をつくろうと考えた。空間は白い金属のメッシュ構造によって柔らかく包まれた場所である。その外形は不定形の岩のような姿をしていて、地上に浮いた島のようである。内部はやはり不定形な地形状の場所であり、そこに人は自分の居場所を見つけて腰掛ける。半透明の白いメッシュに覆われた内部空間は、白い柔らかな空間的な膜に包まれた感覚で、ただ港の風や音、匂いだけが感じられる。それは反転した島である。従来の床壁天井でつくられた確固たる建築空間とは異なる新しい領域のつくられ方である。視覚が弱められ、聴覚、触覚、嗅覚が引き立つことで、全感覚的な場所の体験を可能にする。小さいながらも、新しい建築的な経験にチャレンジした意欲作である。

093 | Naoshima Pavilion | 直島パヴィリオン | KAGAWA, JAPAN | 2014– | → Related Projects 009 025 038 077 083 099

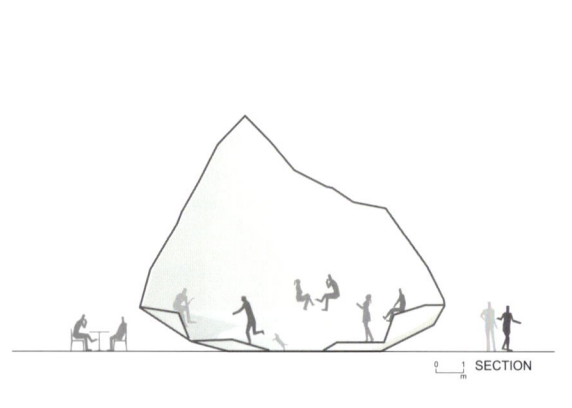

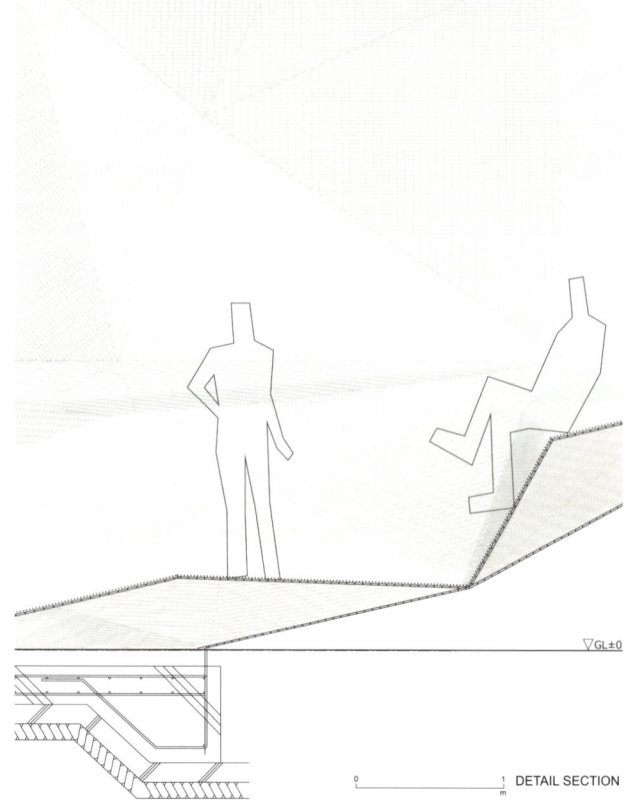

SECTION

DETAIL SECTION

TAINAN MUSEUM OF FINE ARTS
TAINAN, TAIWAN 2014

Under the volume of light, various activities are engendered

This competition proposal was for a project to plan a contemporary art museum in the city of Tainan. Planned in the heart of the city, with abundance of strong sunlight and lots of rain, I imagined that by placing a large roof on top, I could create a place that was both a museum and a new public space. Covered with louvers, the light roof can be used to moderately control the amount of sunlight. Beneath the roof is a scattering of galleries, which are open to the city, and event spaces, making it possible for visitors to enjoy walking through the same kind of alley spaces that are unique to Tainan. The louver-covered roof, also seen in the Belgian crematorium project, is employed here as a methodology of making the building dissolve into the natural environment, and this is in turn also related to the project for Budapest. Because the louvers can encompass a diverse range of programs, some of which must be closed, this format ensures flexibility. Along with the urban engawa, the concept of a large urban roof provides a key to creating a fusion between architecture and the city.

台南の市街地に現代美術の美術館を計画する設計競技応募案。日差しが強く雨の多い台南の街の中心部に、大きな屋根を架けることで、美術館でありながら街の新しい公共空間であるような場所を構想した。この大屋根はルーバーで覆われており、適度に日差しがコントロールされた明るい屋根である。屋根下には都市に開いた展示室やイベントスペースが点在し、台南に特有の路地空間のように巡り歩く楽しさをつくり出している。ルーバーによる大屋根は、ベルギーの葬祭場でも試みた、いわば自然環境の中に建築が溶け込んでいく方法論でもあり、ブダペストの計画へと連続していく。ルーバーで覆われたボリュームはさまざまな＜閉じなくてはならないプログラム＞を内包するもので、この形式の柔軟性を確保している。都市の大屋根という考え方は、都市の縁側とともに、建築／都市の融合を試みる手がかりになるであろう。

094

TAINAN MUSEUM OF FINE ARTS

TAINAN MUSEUM OF FINE ARTS

TAINAN, TAIWAN
2014

→ Related Projects
024 034 065 102 104

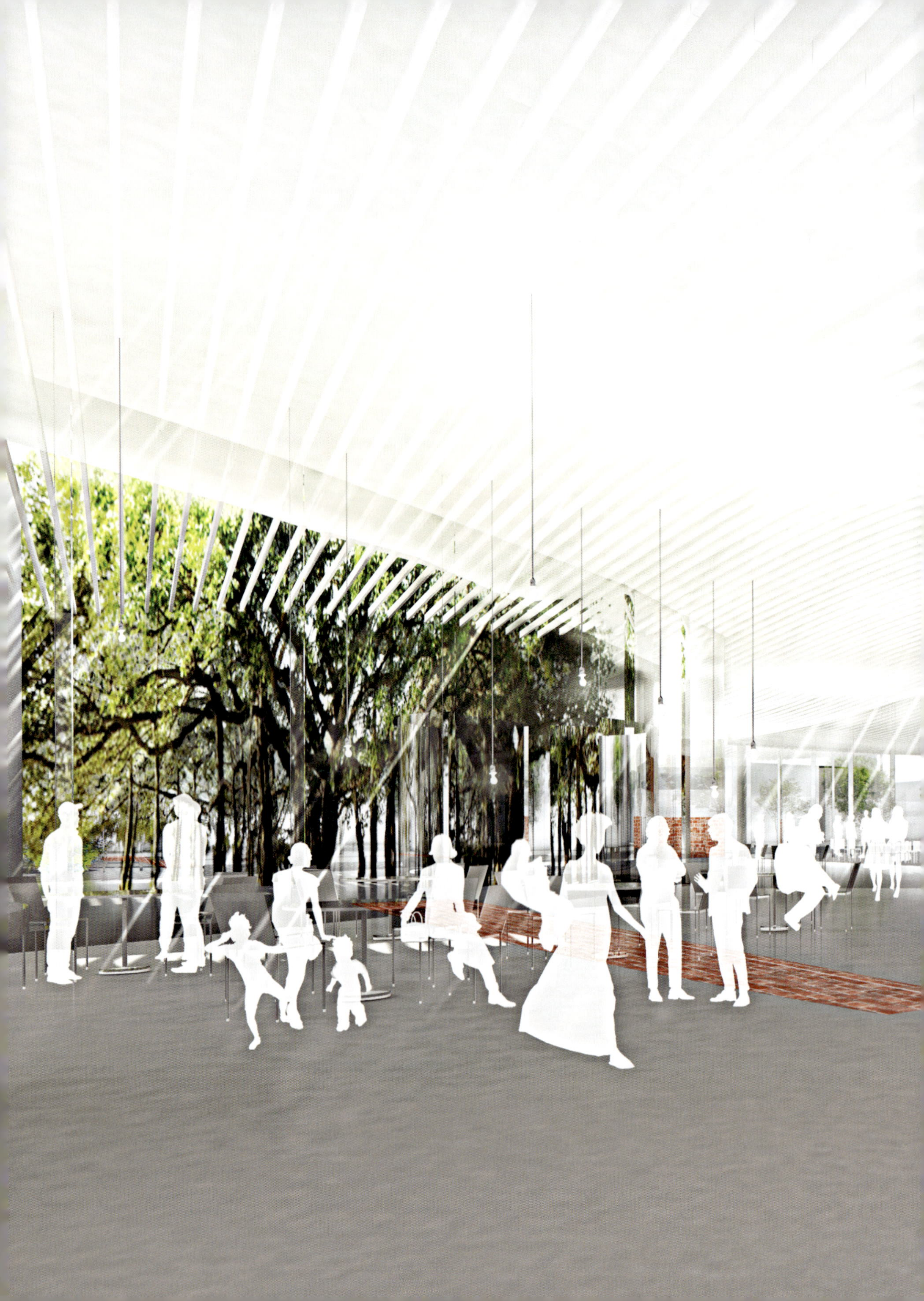

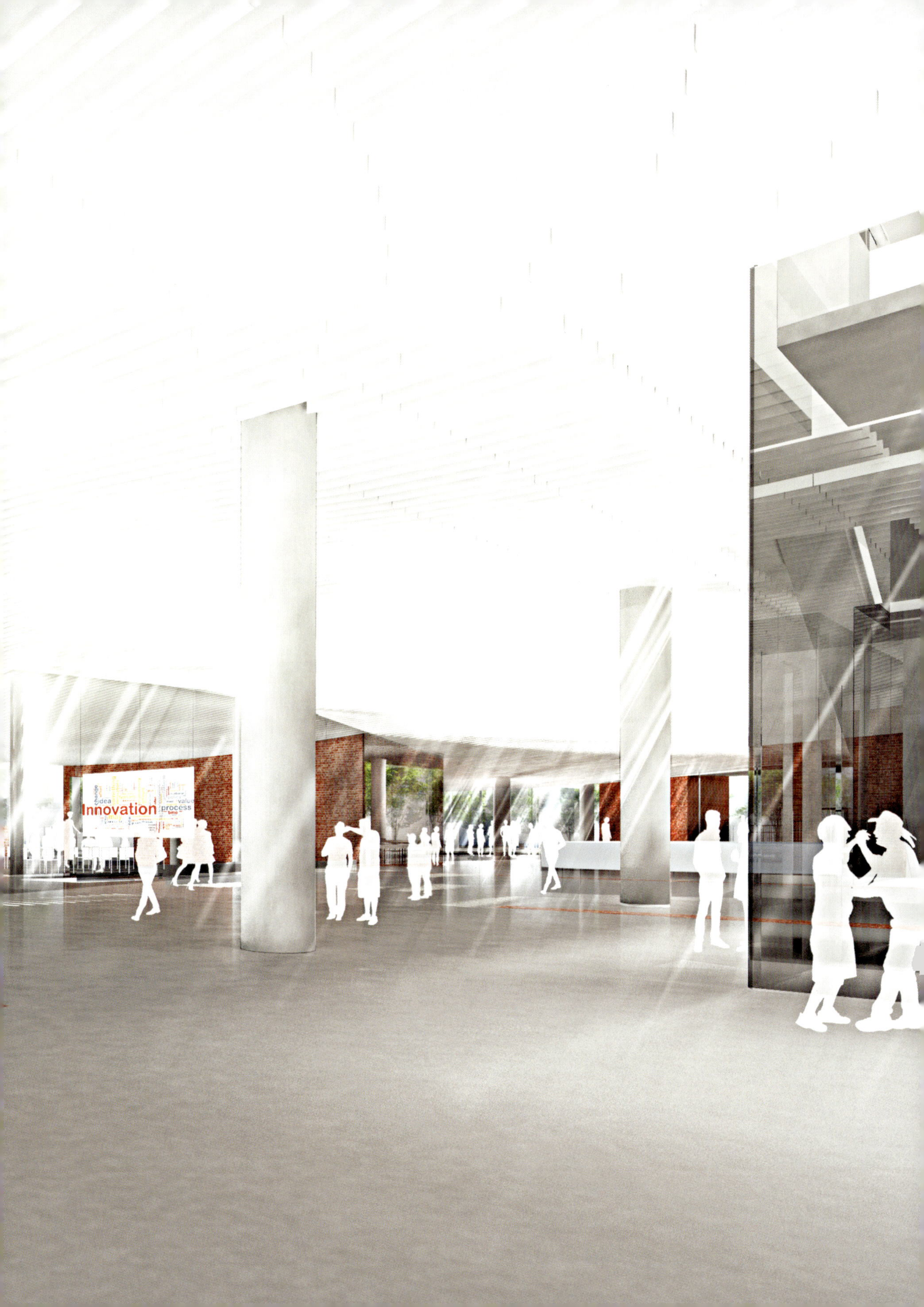
change
idea
Innovation
process
time

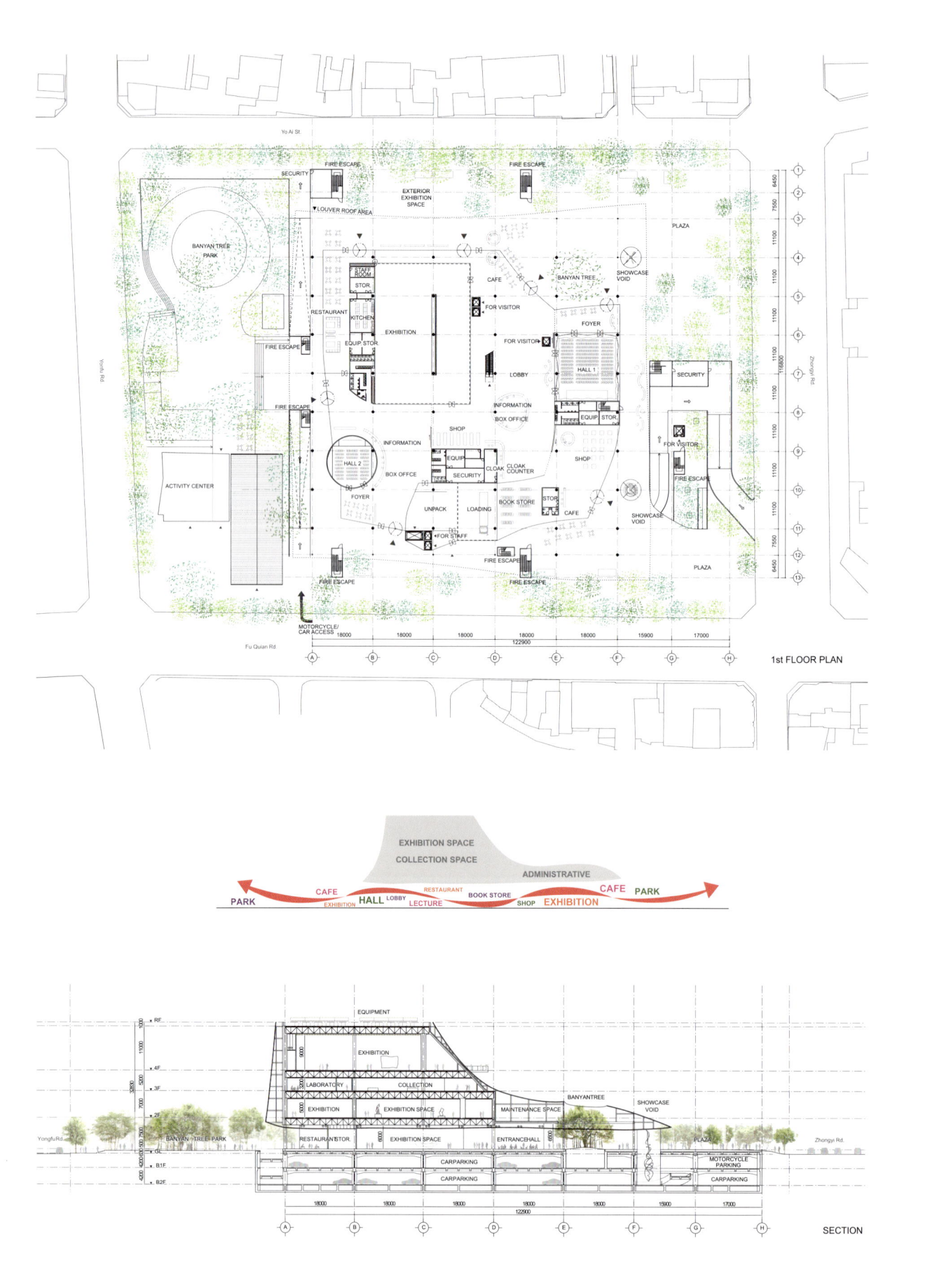

1st FLOOR PLAN

SECTION

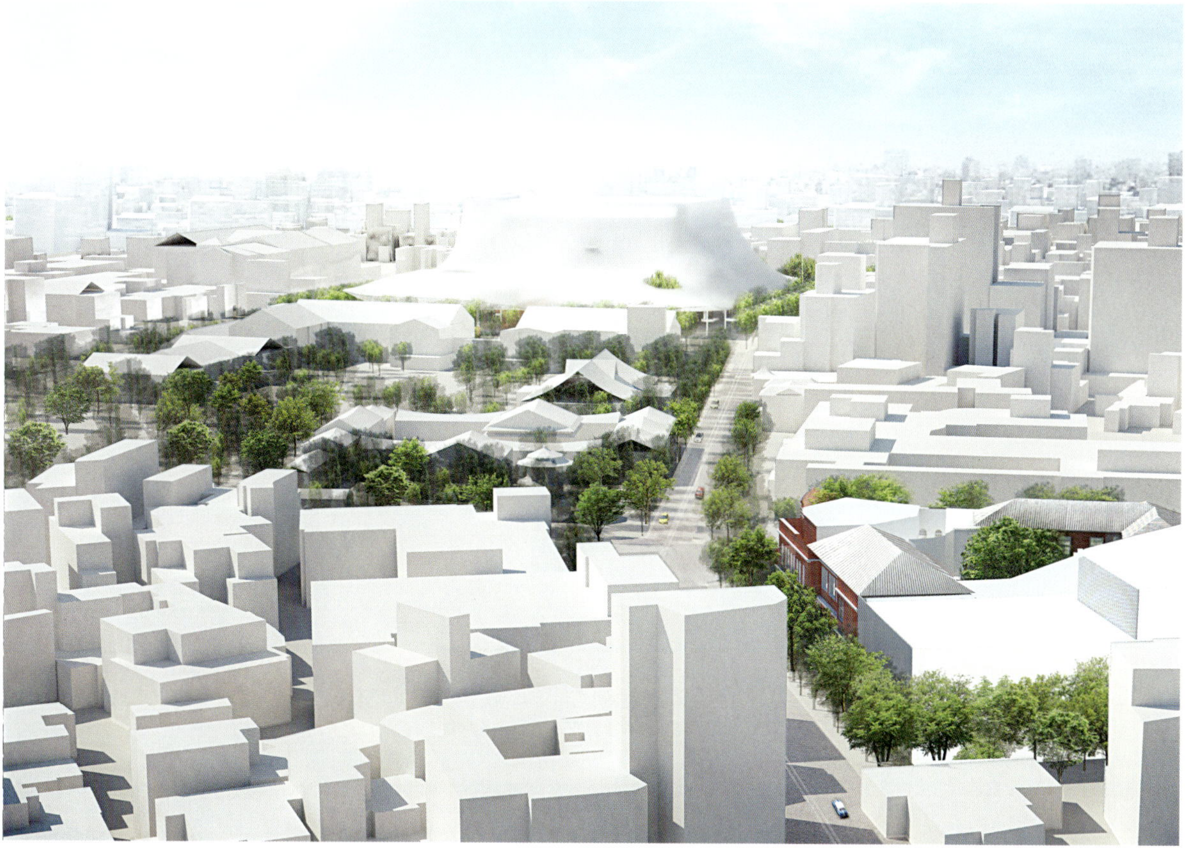

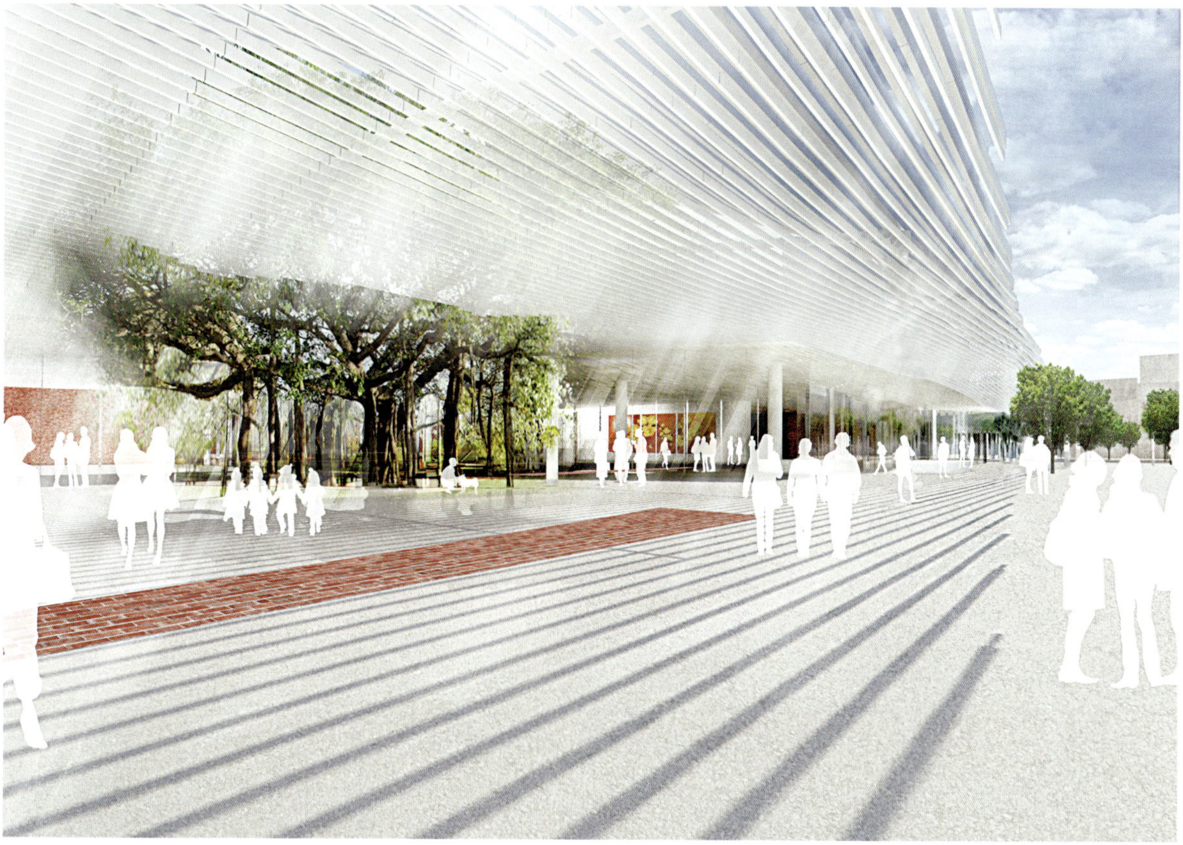

São Paulo House - Branch
SÃO PAULO, BRAZIL 2014 -

When a forest is stratified,

is it architecture or a private space by urban infrastructure?

This house was designed for a vast forest in the centre of São Paulo. In response to the conditions of the site, where a large number of splendid trees still stood, I created a multilayered house of an irregular volume that arose out of a need to avoid the trees. I placed the bedrooms in this volume, and the aboveground floor, covered by the multilayered volume, functions as the living space that covers over both the interior and exterior. By placing trees of about the same size as the existing trees to the ends of the branch-like volume, I realized a three-dimensional, architectural forest space. In order to create a uniquely São Paulo living space in which the interior blends together with the exterior, I proposed a gentle covering formed by the tree-shaped volume. Like the *Omotesando Branches*, this plan calls for a three-dimensional fusion between architecture and trees.

サンパウロ市内に残る広大な森の中に計画中の住宅。立派な既存樹木が多く残る敷地に対して、それらの樹木を避けることで必然的に生まれる不定形なボリュームを積層して住居としている。ボリュームの中には寝室が入り、積層ボリュームに覆われた地上階が、内部と外部にまたがるリビング空間である。枝状のボリュームの端部には既存樹と同じくらいの大きさの樹木を配置することで、立体的で建築的な森空間を実現している。サンパウロ特有の、内部と外部が溶け合うような生活空間を実現するために、樹状のボリュームによる緩やかな覆いを提案した。「Omotesando Branches」にも繋がる、建築と樹木との立体的な融合である。

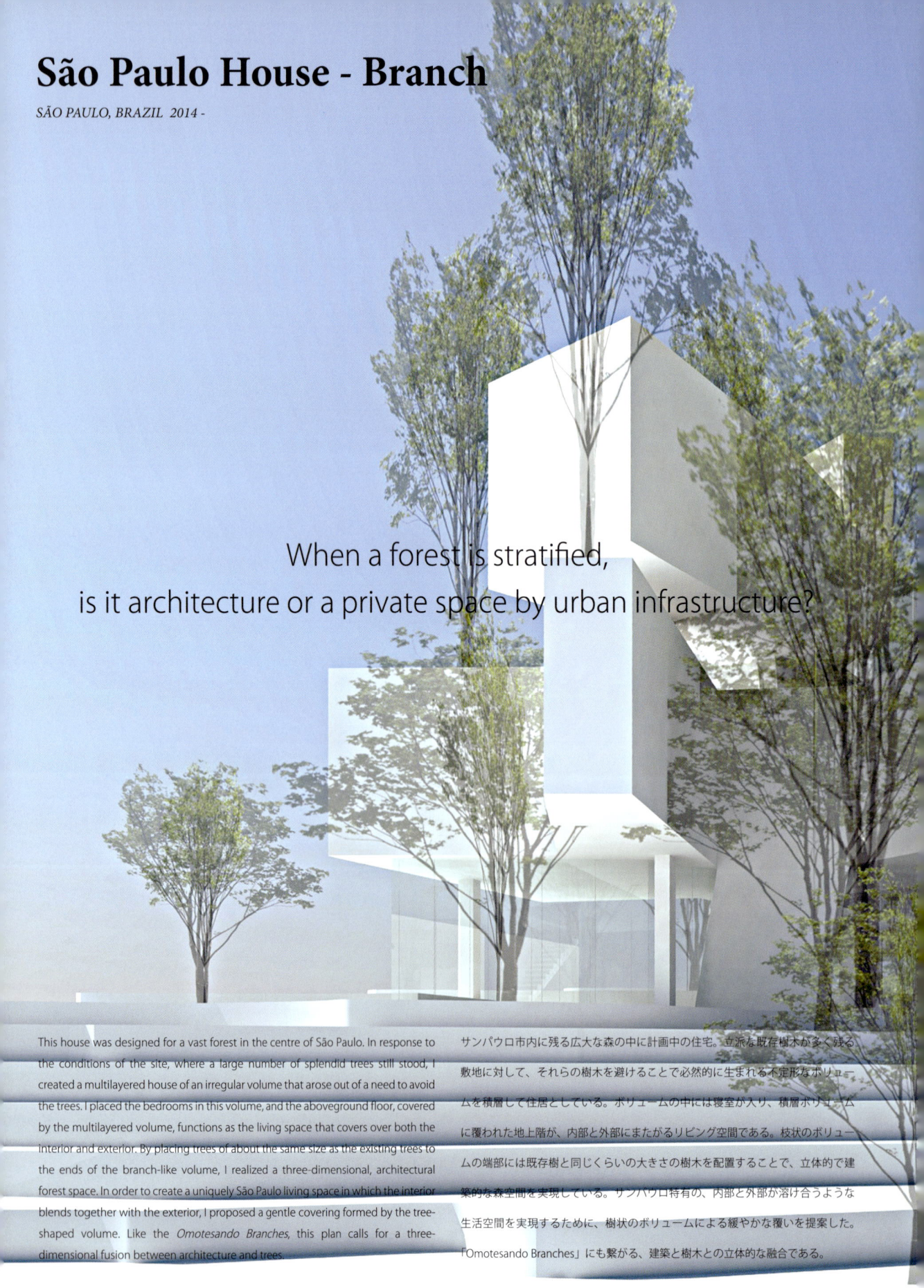

095

São Paulo House - Branch

SÃO PAULO, BRAZIL
2014-

→ Related Projects
008 020 030 088 107

1st FLOOR PLAN | 2nd FLOOR PLAN | 3rd FLOOR PLAN

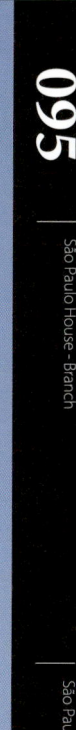

São Paulo House - Cave
SÃO PAULO, BRAZIL 2014 -

A cave covered in stone is a place where openness and security coexist

Another proposal for the same project site described in *São Paulo House - Branch*. The idea was to enclose the entire site, including the existing trees, to create a living space. To do this, I devised a method of forming a gentle enclosure out of several lumps of rock, making it seem as if you are inside a cave instead of conventional walls and roof. The bedrooms and bathroom are located within the rock-shaped volume, and both the interior and the exterior of the living area extend through this large cave-like space. This idea arose almost at the same time as I was working on the house in Chile. On the exterior, the rocks have a sharp, chopped-off appearance, with light seeping into between the cracks in the stones. As water is an important element of living spaces in São Paulo, I envisioned a waterfall cascading down from the roof and forming a link with the basin on ground level. I would like to explore the potentiality inherent in this type of stone-like architecture further.

「São Paulo House - Branch」と同じ敷地に提案している別案。既存の樹木を含めた敷地全体を取り囲んで、居住空間にしてしまおうというアイデア。その際、いわゆる建築的な壁や屋根ではなくまるで洞窟の中にいるかのようないくつもの岩の塊によって緩やかに取り囲まれている方法をとった。寝室や浴室は岩状のボリュームの中に配置し、リビングエリアは内部も外部もともにこの洞窟的な大空間の中に広がる。チリの住宅とほぼ同時進行で生まれたアイデア。外観は岩をシャープに切り落としたような姿をとり、岩と岩の隙間から光が漏れる。サンパウロでは水が生活空間の重要な要素となるため、ここでは屋根の上から滝を落とし、地上レベルの水盤と連続させた。この岩的な建築の可能性をもう少し推し進めてみたいと思っている。

São Paulo House - Cave

SÃO PAULO, BRAZIL
2014-

→ Related Projects
001 017 029 054 093 098

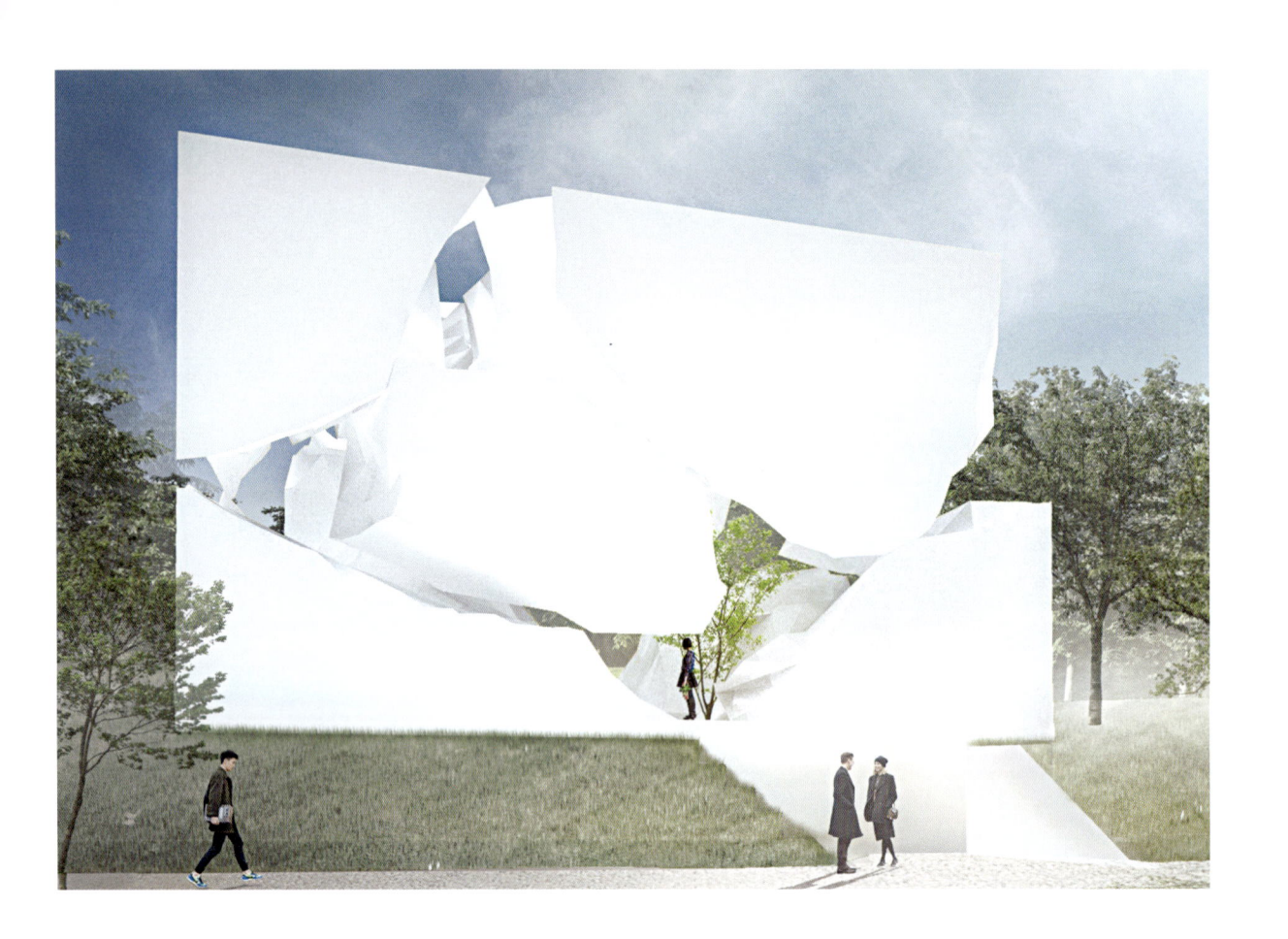

BASEMENT FLOOR PLAN   1st FLOOR PLAN   2nd FLOOR PLAN

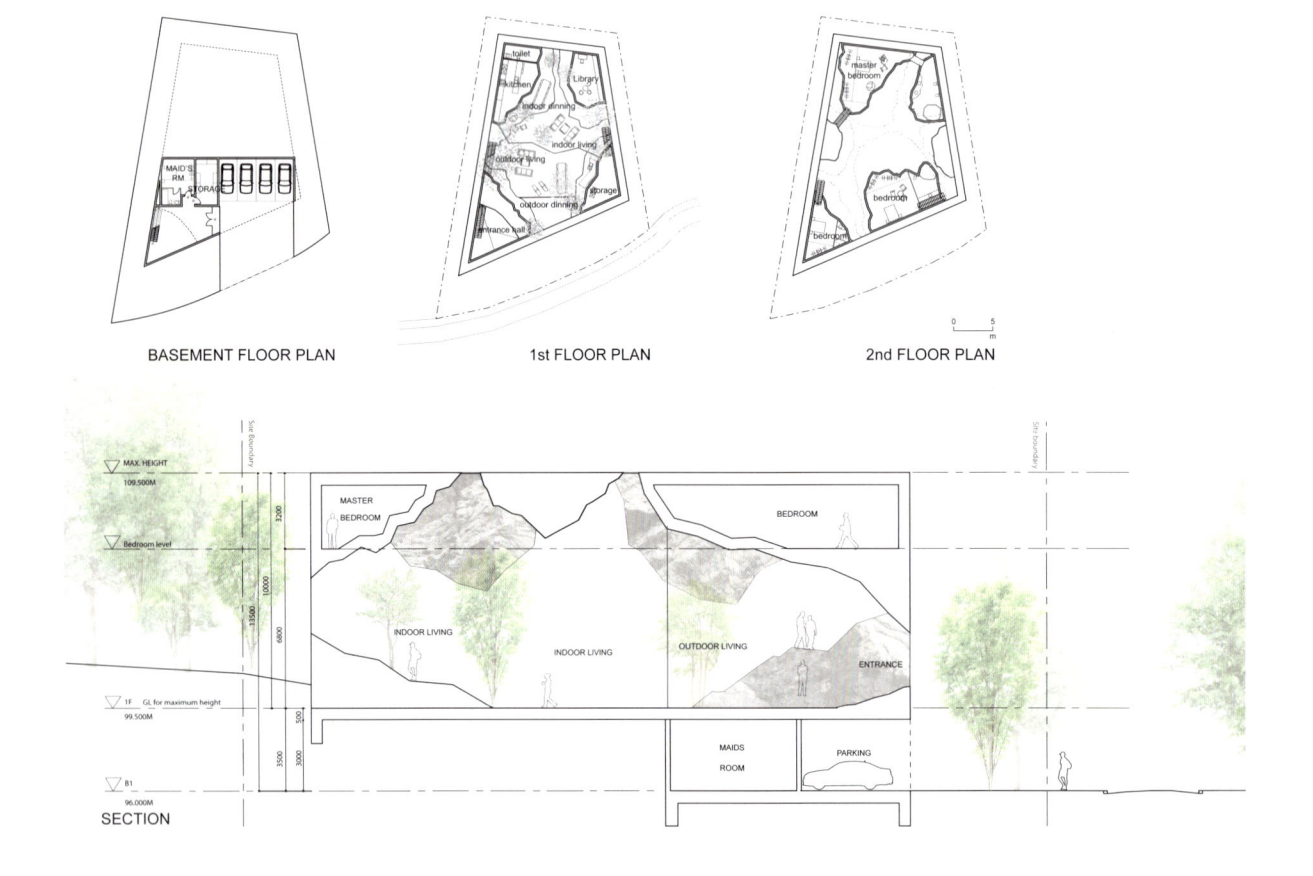

SECTION

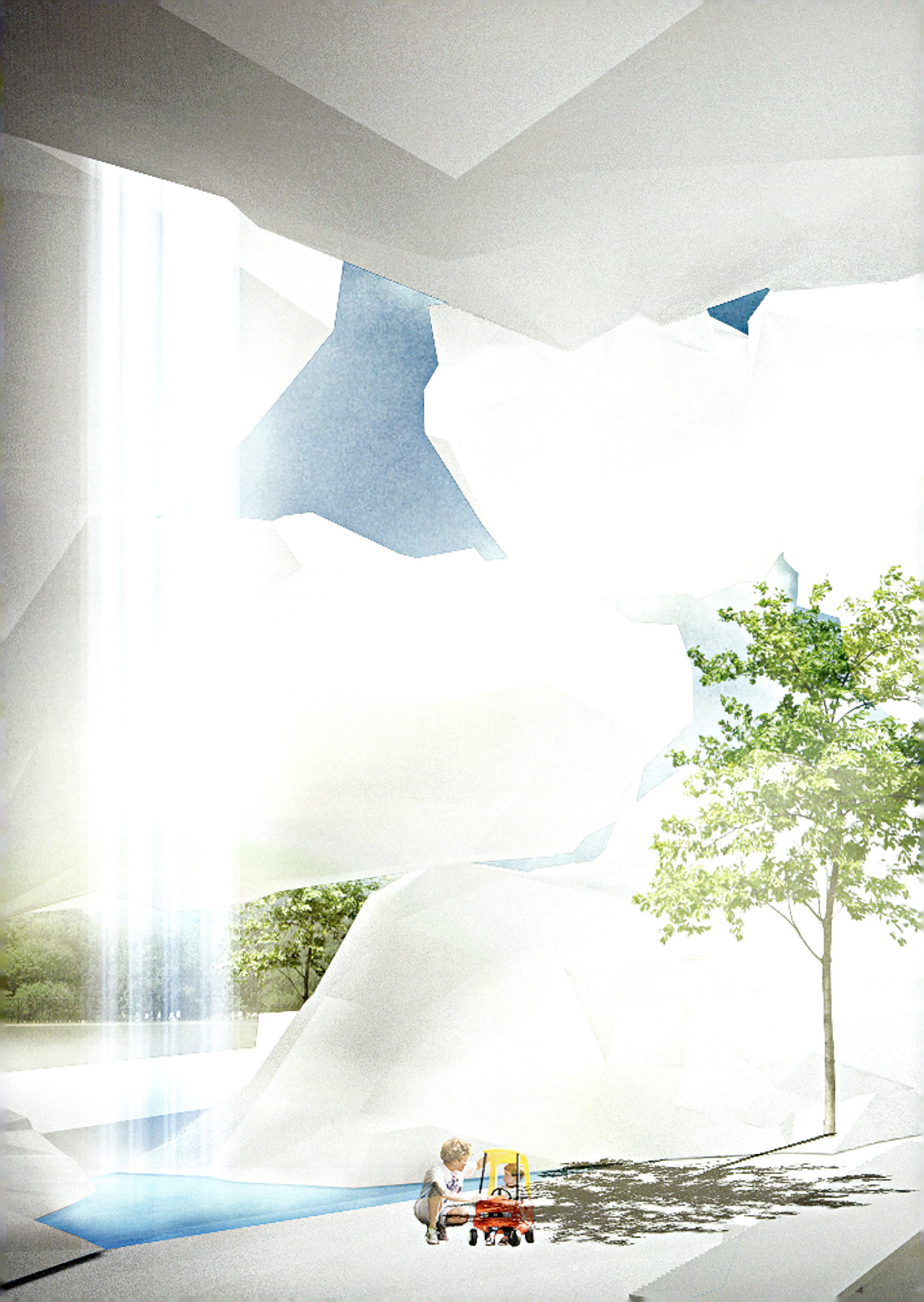

São Paulo House - Louver Cloud

SÃO PAULO, BRAZIL 2014 -

Forest itself is already a rich living environment
One needs only to draw light to it

An alternative scheme for the residential project in São Paulo. Not only with this project, it is common for several different schemes to be developed in parallel. This is especially true of São Paulo because we were exposed to a new climate, culture, lifestyle and technical planning procedures. We found ourselves making many new discoveries and hence having many new ideas. Such ideas, even if they are not chosen for this project, will become seeds for future projects, blossoming under new programs and climatic conditions. This scheme is an attempt to capture the forest-filled site as a semi-outdoor/semi-indoor space for living using a delicate roof formed by a series of louvres. The space in which the interior and exterior are seamlessly connected will be a place that distinctly matches the context of São Paulo. The space above the louvres is also expected to become a majestic roof-top terrace creating a sensation of standing above the clouds. This is an example of generating pleasant spaces that respond to the rich and diverse tropical climate. Closely linked to the *TAINAN MUSEUM OF FINE ARTS* project, this work is part of the lineage of my other amorphous louvre projects.

同じく、サンパウロの住宅の別案。このサンパウロの住宅に限らず、住宅の計画ではしばしば複数案が平行して進む。とくにサンパウロの場合には、初めての気候、文化、ライフスタイルでの設計作業だけに、さまざまな気づきや発見が連なった。こうして試みたいくつものアイデアは、たとえ最終的に採用されなかったとしても、別のプロジェクトの種となるはずで、異なるプログラムや気候条件によって、また異なるかたちで芽を出すはずである。このルーバー案は、敷地である森全体を、ルーバーのかすかな屋根によって、半屋外／半内部の居住空間として捉える試みである。内外が連続するサンパウロならではの場所となるに違いない。またルーバーの上は雲の上にいるかのような屋上テラスとなる予定。「TAINAN MUSEUM OF FINE ARTS」とも繋がりがある、波打つルーバーの系譜である。

097 | São Paulo House – Louver Cloud | SÃO PAULO, BRAZIL 2014– | → Related Projects 024 041 065 094 104

Stacked Rock House
LOS VILOS, CHILE 2014 -

Inside-out cave

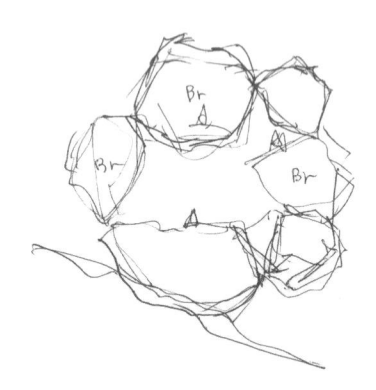

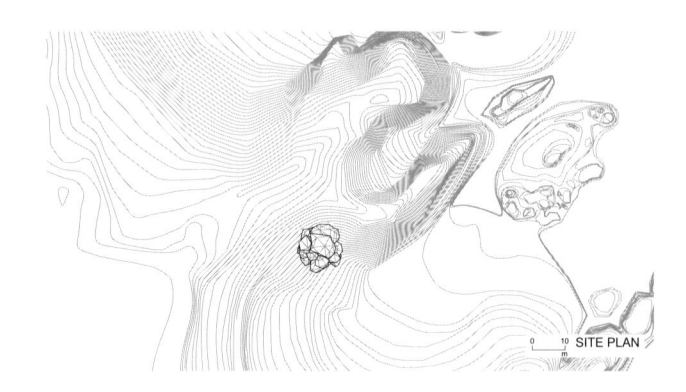

SITE PLAN

I designed this villa in a marvellous landscape abutting the Pacific Ocean, about a three-hour drive from Santiago, Chile. What kind of architecture is possible in this type of natural environment? Having no restrictions gave me the idea that I'd like to make something like an architectural archetype. In a way, this house is a place where people began to live after finding an open space between a pile of huge rocks. The rocks are piled up in an almost unnaturally spherical form, they are part of nature and also exemplify the antithesis of natural objects. The interior is a complex, three-dimensional space that expands between the indeterminate form of the rocks. People can move from place to place via a staircase that stretches through the space. The bedrooms and bathroom are enclosed in the rocks to ensure privacy. This format is a very strong yet flexible artificial cave. It allows people to discover various uses and comfortable spots in various places, constantly encouraging interactions between space and body. In that sense, the house is similar to the antithetical form of the *Serpentine Gallery Pavilion 2013.*

チリのサンチアゴから車で3時間ほどの、太平洋に面した素晴らしい風景の中に別荘を計画する。このような自然の中で、どのような建築が可能なのだろうか？何の制約もないからこそ、建築の原型に迫る何かをつくりたいという思いにかられた。この家は、言ってみれば、巨大な岩が積み上がったその間に空間を見つけ出し、人びとが住み始める、という場所である。その外観は不自然なほどに球状に積み上げられた岩であり、それは自然の一部であると同時に、自然物の対極でもある。内部空間は不定形な岩の間に広がる3次元的な複雑な空間であり、その中を伸びていく階段によってさまざまな場所へと移動できる。寝室や浴室は岩の内部に収められており、住宅的なプライバシーの確保が実現する。この形式は、とても強く、しかし柔軟な、人工的な洞窟である。それゆえ人はさまざまな場所にさまざまな使い方や居場所を発見し、常に空間と身体のインタラクションを繰り返す。その意味において、対極の姿をもつ「Serpentine Gallery Pavilion 2013」と繋がるものがあるのである。

098 | Stacked Rock House

Stacked Rock House

LOS VILOS, CHILE
2014–

→ Related Projects
010 029 053 081 096

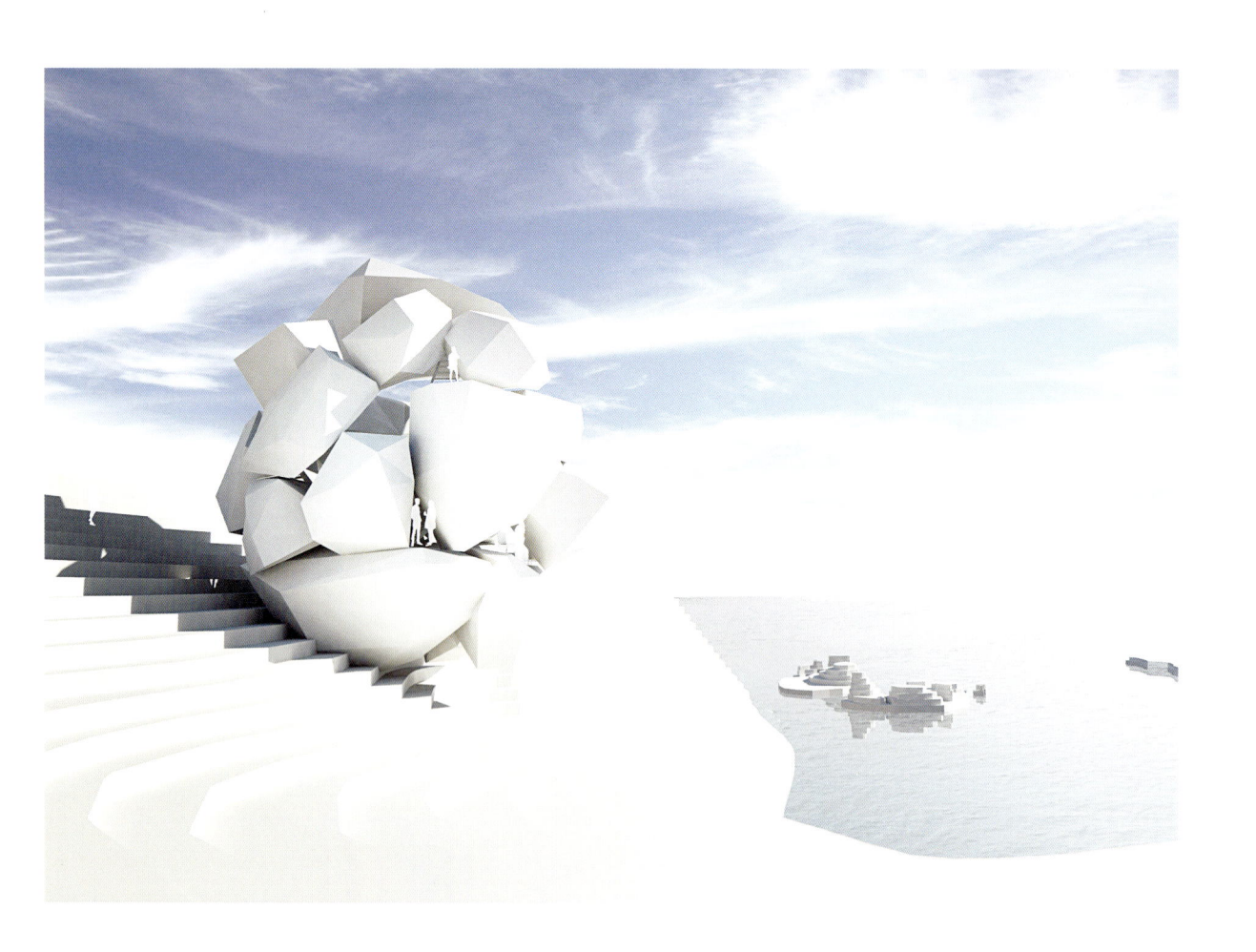

| 1st FLOOR PLAN | 2nd FLOOR PLAN | SECTION |

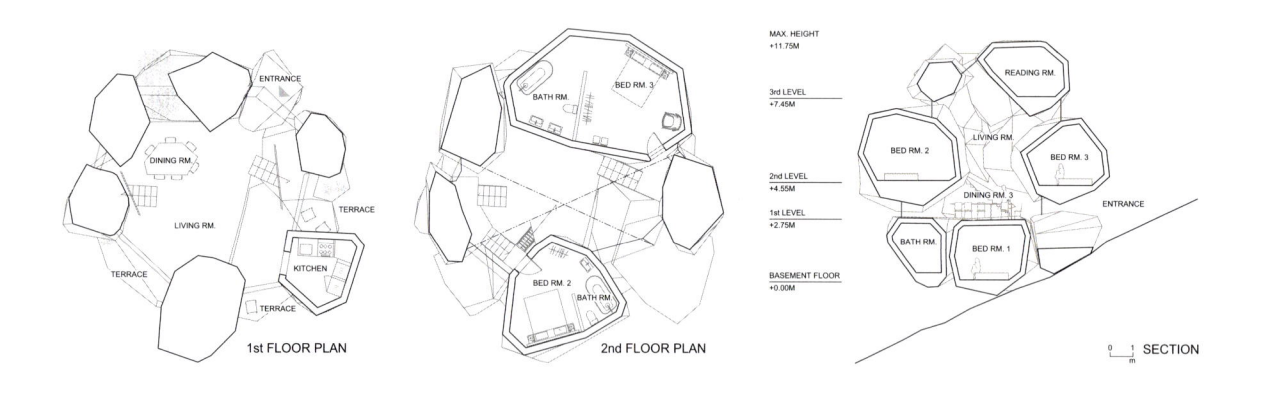

1st FLOOR PLAN labels: ENTRANCE, DINING RM., LIVING RM., KITCHEN, TERRACE

2nd FLOOR PLAN labels: BATH RM., BED RM. 3, BED RM. 2, BATH RM.

SECTION labels:
MAX. HEIGHT +11.75M
3rd LEVEL +7.45M
2nd LEVEL +4.55M
1st LEVEL +2.75M
BASEMENT FLOOR +0.00M

READING RM., LIVING RM., BED RM. 2, BED RM. 3, DINING RM., ENTRANCE, BATH RM., BED RM. 1

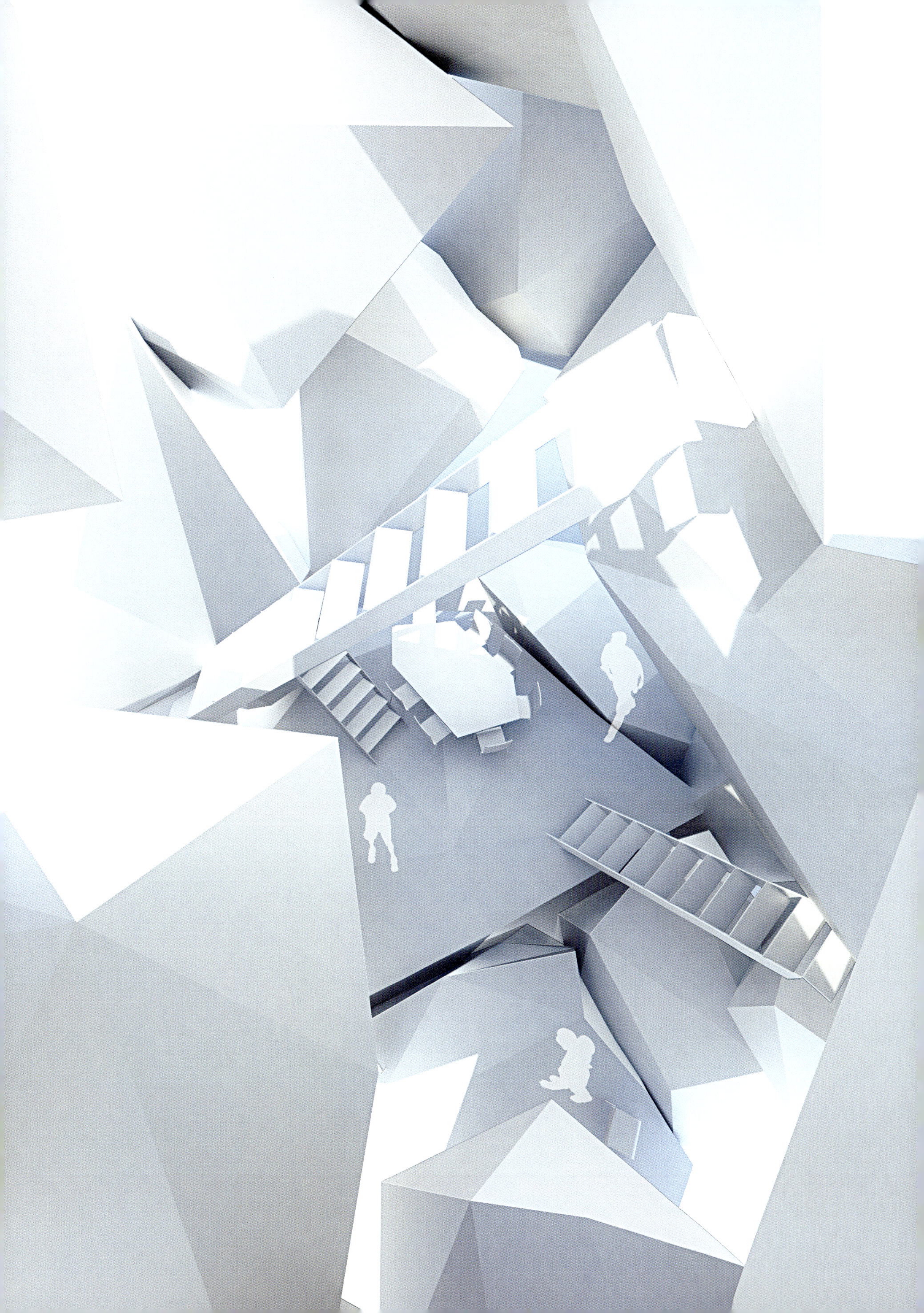

Many Small Cubes -Small Nomad House

PARIS, FRANCE 2014

The nest for people of the future is made of chasms and depth

This installation was produced for a limited two-month project in Jardin des Tuileries, the park in front of the Louvre Museum. I envisioned it as a concept model for a residential space of the future. In conceptual terms, I see an architectural or residential space as a group of diverse matters delicately covering a particular place imbued with depth. There are no walls in the conventional sense; there is only a space and countless gaps and depth. The textural differences in the things that are collected here give rise to a place that is both open and protected. There are a variety of architectural elements needed to produce this kind of place, but in this project I used a cube covered with aluminum panels to create a place where geometric and organic qualities live side-by-side with sharpness and flexibility. Several other cubes take the form of pods, creating a fusion with trees and plants. In this work, I set out to realize a fundamentally ambiguous state of architecture and nature. This is a purely conceptual work, but I believe that it presages a new direction in architecture of the future.

パリ、ルーブル美術館の前に広がるチュイルリー公園に2か月限定で制作したインスタレーション。未来の居住空間のコンセプトモデルとして構想した。コンセプチュアルな意味で僕が考える建築空間、居住空間とは、いくつものさまざまなものたちが、奥行きをもって柔らかくある場所を包み込んでいる状態である。そこには従来の意味での壁はなく、ただ空間と無数のものの隙間と奥行きがある。また寄り集まったものたちの粗密の変化によって、開かれた場所、守られた場所がつくられる。そのような場所をつくり出す建築的な要素はさまざまであるが、このプロジェクトではアルミパネルで覆われたキューブを用いることで、幾何学性と有機性、シャープさと柔らかさの同居する場所とした。さらにいくつかのキューブはポッド状となっており、樹木や植栽が融合する。建築と自然という、根源的な両義性を実現しようとした。これは純粋なコンセプトワークであったが、この先の建築のひとつの方向を予感するものと期待したい。

099

Many Small Cubes - Small Nomad House

PARIS, FRANCE
2014

→ Related Projects
007 011 030 054 077 091

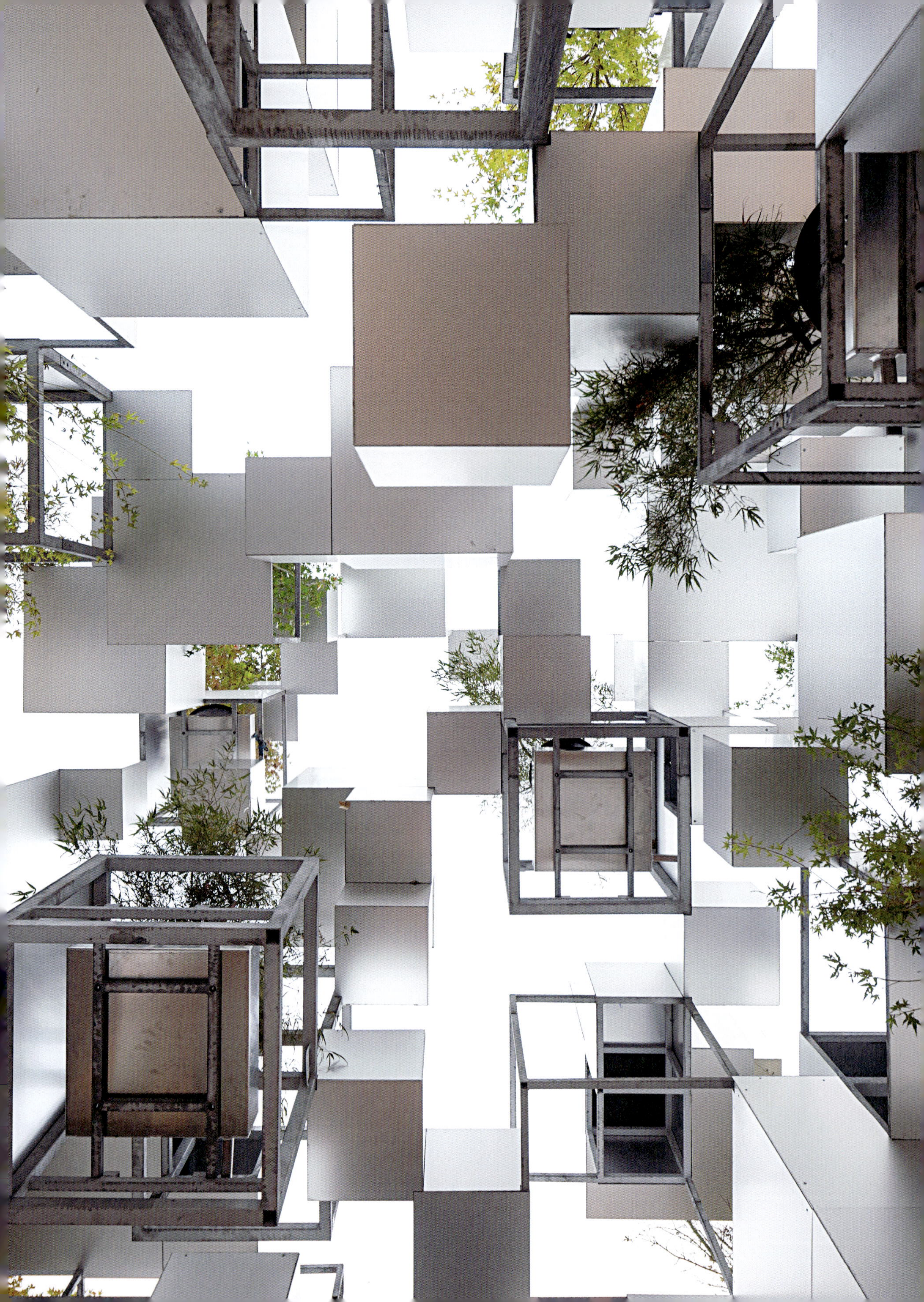

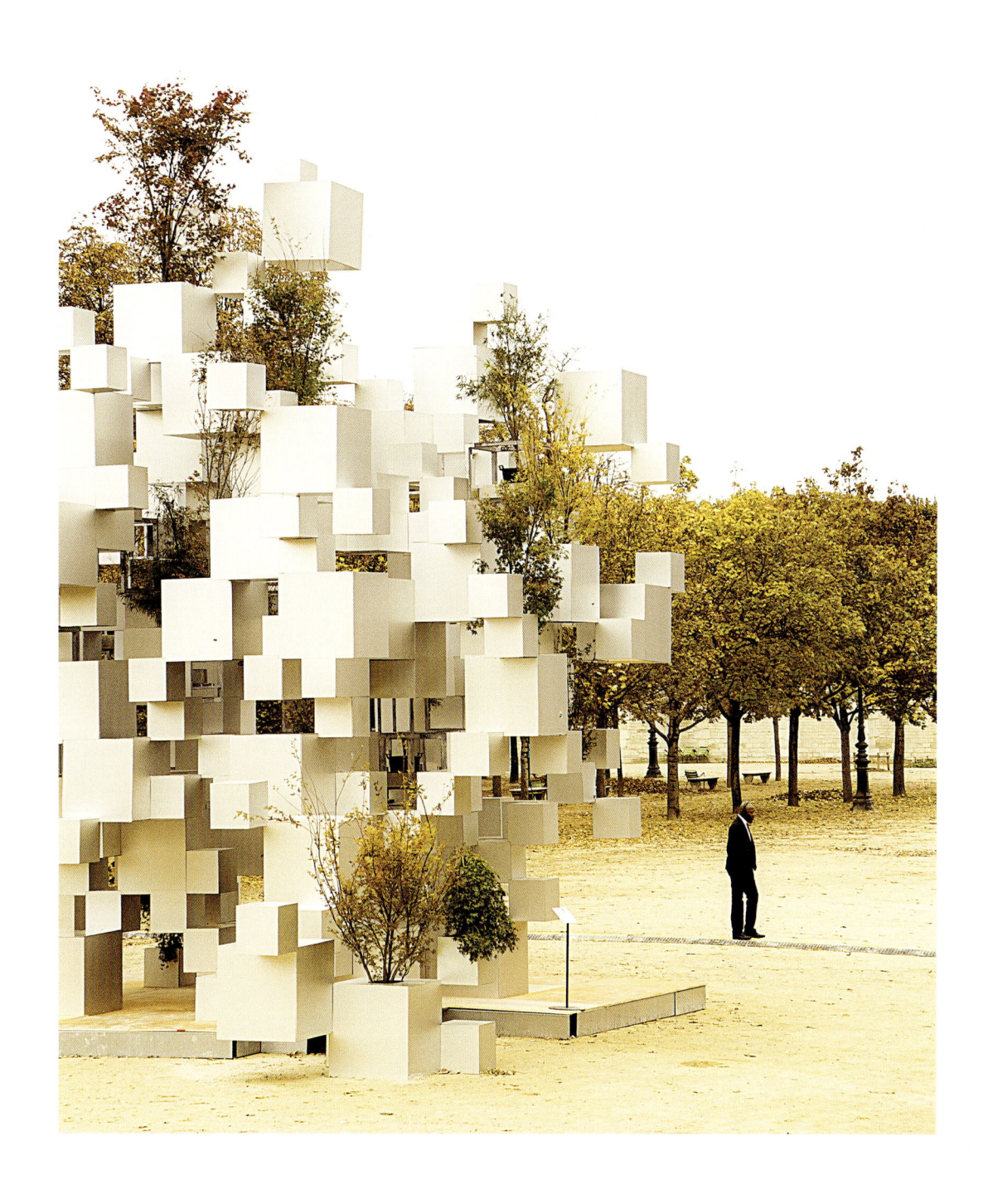

House of sliding doors
HYOGO, JAPAN 2014 -

A house is a place where diverse matters are delicately interwoven

This house was designed for a family of four in a residential area of Hyogo Prefecture. Since the site was surrounded on three sides by other houses, and directly abutted the road, I conceived of a house that was protected from outside but seemingly expansive inside. Like my plan for the *Musashino Art University Museum & Library*, I wondered if the expansive space could be a place where transparency and opacity existed side-by-side, and a place that was partially concealed and partially visible. I used layers of ordinary fusuma (sliding paper doors) and sliding doors to create this sense of ambiguity. These doors make it possible to subdivide the large space according to application or situation, and they are also extremely practical in the sense that they affect the heating and cooling, and allow for changes in private and public aspects of the house. Using the doors in such a complete way imbues the traditional Japanese house with a new sense of values for the future.

兵庫県の住宅地に建つ4人家族のための住宅。三方を隣家に囲まれて前面は直接道路に面しているため、外部には守られていて、内部で広がりの感じられる住宅を構想した。広がりがある空間とは、例えば「武蔵野美術大学美術館・図書館」のように半ば隠され、半ば見通せるような、透明性と不透明性が共存する場ではないだろうか？　ここではそのような両義性を、いわゆる普通の襖＝引き戸の積層を使ってつくり上げている。これらの引き戸は、大きな空間を用途や状況に応じて細分化することが可能で、冷暖房効率や家の中のプライベートとパブリックの柔軟な変化に対応することができるという意味で、とても実用的でもある。ここまで引戸を徹底することで、日本の伝統家屋は未来に向けて新しい価値をもち始めるであろう。

100

House of sliding doors

HYOGO, JAPAN
2014-

→ Related Projects
004 015 044 055 091

SECTION

1st FLOOR PLAN

The Miami Design District Palm Courtyard
MIAMI, USA 2014

Between city and architecture / Between inside and outside / Between sunshine and rain

SECTION

A commercial facility located in the corner of the Miami Design District, this two-story building will be home to over 17 retail tenants. Initially the commission was a facade design project, but after visiting the site and experiencing the rich climatic variance of Miami, I sought to create a corridor-like space that protects visitors. At the same time, I wanted to manifest a form that was open to the fresh rain and sunlight, rather than making a simple facade. The space is made up of four different tones of glass in the form of vertical louvres, which recall crystallized rays of light or the solidified motion of raindrops. The design ultimately became a facade, a place for people to gather, and a grand 13-meter tall public atrium. In recent years, I have inserted unique in-between (or ma) spaces with both traditional and novel values, creating places that exist between architecture and the city that become sites for stimulating experiments.

マイアミのデザインディストリクトの再開発の一角に完成した商業施設。2階建ての建物に17のテナントが入る。当初はファサードデザインのプロジェクトだったが、現地を訪れ、マイアミの日差しと雨に感銘を受けたことで、単なるファサードではなく、日差しと雨から人びとを守りながら、同時にその美しい日差しと鮮烈な雨に形を与えたような、そんなコリドーをつくることができないかと考えた。4種類の色ガラスルーバーを組み合わせ、結晶化した日差しのような、あるいは物質化した雨のような、空間をつくり上げた。それはファサードでありながら、人びとを受け入れる場であり、高さ13mにもなる巨大な都市空間でもある。建築と都市の間に、古典的でありながら新しい価値をもつ＜間＞の空間をつくることは、近年僕の中でますます面白い課題になってきている。

101 The Miami Design District Palm Courtyard

MIAMI, USA
2014

→ Related Projects
006 027 039 082 094

OPEN ART MUSEUM - HELSINKI GUGGENHEIM MUSEUM

HELSINKI, FINLAND 2014

Disassembling the system of Museum and infusing it into the city

This is a competition proposal for a new Guggenheim Museum in Helsinki. In the past, museums were in a sense introduced to different cities as complete packages. People didn't need to give much thought to how the system worked, and enjoyed the show on a superficial level. What should you strive for in order to transcend the closed package of the museum and create something that truly permeates the local area and invigorates the place? In this plan, all of the functions and elements of the museum are scattered and open. Everything from the galleries to the preparation room, the office, the machine room, and all of the other back-of-the-house areas are contained in glass boxes and are dispersed across the site. People not only look at the displays, but all of the museum-related activities, including various operations, the preparation process, the loading and packaging of works, and meetings, as part of the local area. Local shops, cafes, and performances are also drawn to the area, and combine with the museum. The entire entity, both interior and exterior, is gently covered with an undulating glass roof. This conceptual proposal was intended to be a reinterpretation of the museum.

ヘルシンキに計画されたグッゲンハイム美術館の設計競技応募案。従来の美術館は、美術館という完成されたパッケージをさまざまな都市にもち込むものであったと言える。人びとはそのシステムがどう動いているのかは気にせず、表面に見えてくるショーを楽しめばよかった。しかし、もし本当の意味で地域に浸透していき、その場所を活性化させる美術館を考えるなら、そのような閉じたパッケージとしての美術館を超えた何かを模索するべきなのではないだろうか？ ここでは、美術館のあらゆる機能、あらゆる要素がばらばらにされ、開かれる。展示室はもちろん、準備室、オフィス、機械室、すべての裏方のエリアまでが、ガラスの箱に収められて敷地とその周辺に散在する。人は展示物だけではなく、それが運営されている情景、準備中の過程、搬入や梱包、ミーティングの様子など、美術館にまつわるあらゆる活動を地元の街の一部として見聞きする。さらに地域の店舗やカフェ、パフォーミングなどがそのエリアに引き寄せられ、混ざり合っていく。その全体を、内外を問わず波打つガラス屋根が柔らかく覆う。美術館を再解釈するためのコンセプチュアルな提案である。

102 | OPEN ART MUSEUM –HELSINKI GUGGENHEIM MUSEUM | OPEN ART MUSEUM –HELSINKI GUGGENHEIM MUSEUM | HELSINKI, FINLAND 2014 | → Related Projects **003 005 040 070 094 104**

Tähititornin vuori Park

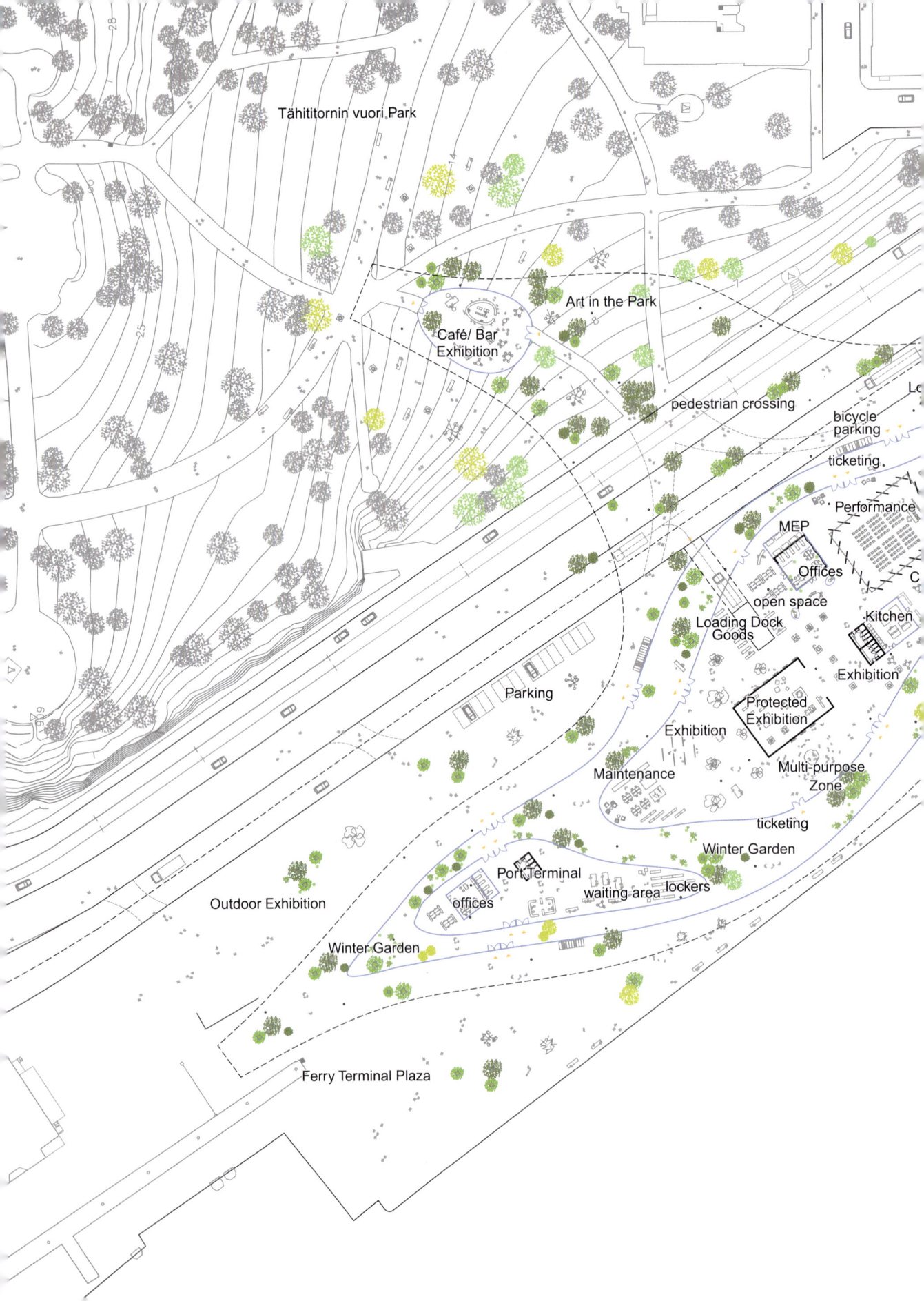

Art in the Park

Café/ Bar
Exhibition

pedestrian crossing

bicycle parking

ticketing

Performance

MEP

Offices

open space

Loading Dock Goods

Kitchen

Exhibition

Parking

Protected Exhibition

Exhibition

Multi-purpose Zone

Maintenance

ticketing

Winter Garden

Port Terminal

offices

waiting area

lockers

Outdoor Exhibition

Winter Garden

Ferry Terminal Plaza

Tramway Station

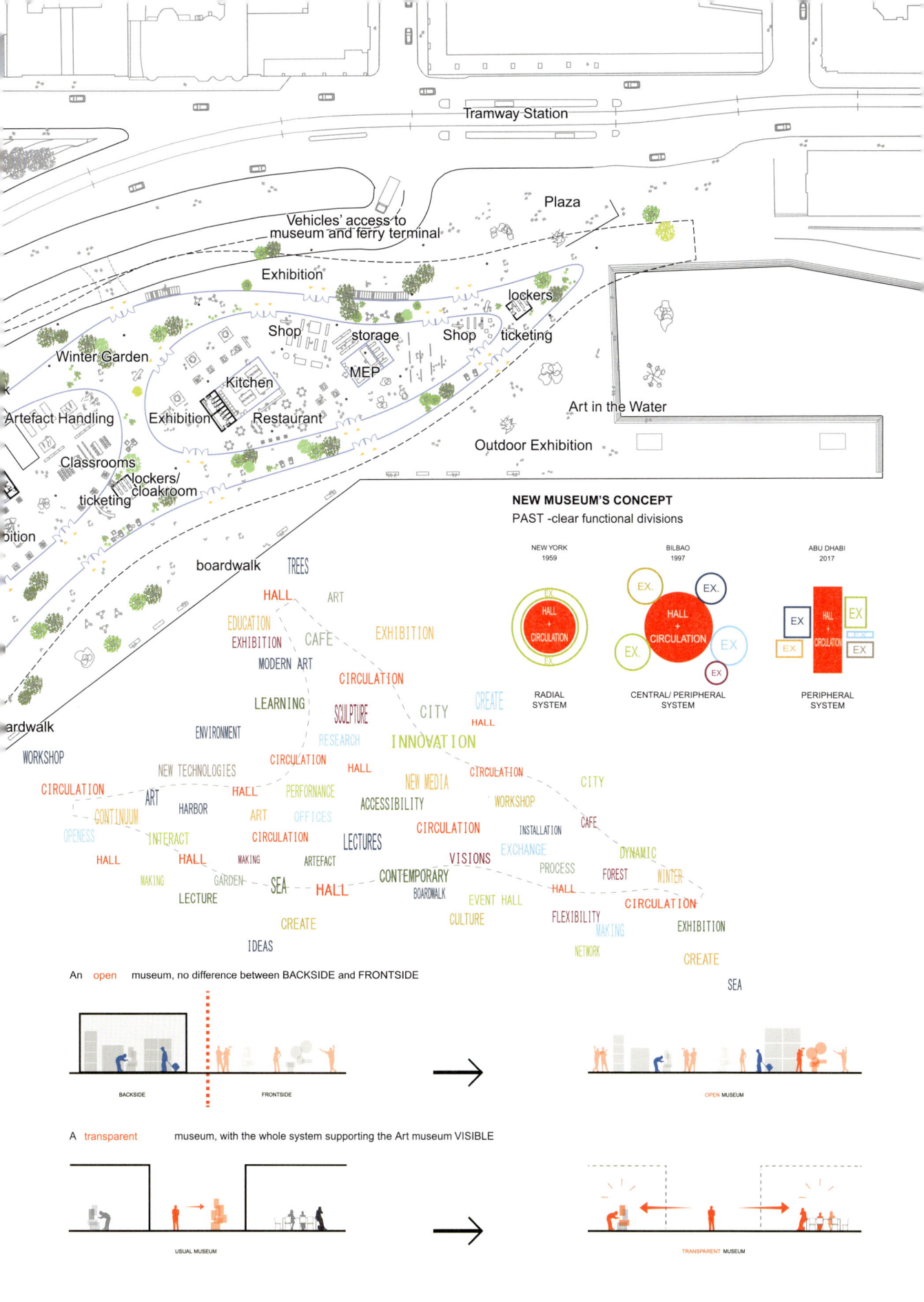

Vehicles' access to museum and ferry terminal

Plaza

Exhibition
lockers
Shop   storage   Shop   ticketing
Winter Garden   MEP
Kitchen
Artefact Handling   Exhibition   Restaurant
Art in the Water
Classrooms
lockers/cloakroom
ticketing
Outdoor Exhibition

boardwalk   TREES

NEW MUSEUM'S CONCEPT
PAST - clear functional divisions

NEW YORK 1959	BILBAO 1997	ABU DHABI 2017
RADIAL SYSTEM	CENTRAL/ PERIPHERAL SYSTEM	PERIPHERAL SYSTEM

HALL   ART
EDUCATION   CAFE   EXHIBITION
EXHIBITION   MODERN ART   CIRCULATION
LEARNING   SCULPTURE   CITY   CREATE
ENVIRONMENT   RESEARCH   INNOVATION   HALL
WORKSHOP   NEW TECHNOLOGIES   CIRCULATION   HALL   CIRCULATION   CITY
CIRCULATION   ART   HALL   PERFORMANCE   NEW MEDIA   WORKSHOP   CAFE
CONTINUUM   HARBOR   ACCESSIBILITY   INSTALLATION
OPENESS   INTERACT   ART   OFFICES   CIRCULATION   DYNAMIC
HALL   HALL   CIRCULATION   LECTURES   EXCHANGE   FOREST   WINTER
MAKING   ARTEFACT   VISIONS   PROCESS
MAKING   GARDEN   CONTEMPORARY   HALL   CIRCULATION
LECTURE   SEA   HALL   BOARDWALK   EVENT HALL   EXHIBITION
CREATE   CULTURE   FLEXIBILITY   CREATE
IDEAS   MAKING
NETWORK

SEA

An **open** museum, no difference between BACKSIDE and FRONTSIDE

BACKSIDE | FRONTSIDE → OPEN MUSEUM

A **transparent** museum, with the whole system supporting the Art museum VISIBLE

USUAL MUSEUM → TRANSPARENT MUSEUM

Beijing Cultural and Art Center
BEIJING, CHINA 2014 -

Forest in the air

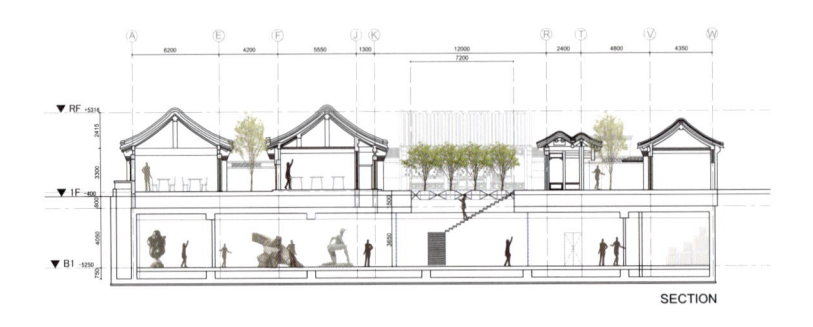

SECTION

In an area of Beijing where there are still many hutong alleyways, this was a plan to renovate a traditional Siheyuan residence into a complex building housing an art museum and commercial facilities. For the most part, since the above-ground structures were historically protected, I made a proposal for an inner courtyard that would provide access to an underground exhibition space. I created an opening for the entire courtyard, and a skylight for the underground space. Twelve trees float above this huge void. From ground level, it looks as if the trees are bristling up from the transparent glass floor, and then when you go underground through the foyer, you realize that they are floating there along with a pod. The underground courtyard is a light-court in which the floating trees act to moderately control the amount of light coming in, and also provides the vital function of circulation leading to the galleries. By replacing the ground-plane with transparent glass, the trees, which would normally be supported by the ground, become floating elements. While incorporating the fresh natural setting of a traditional Siheyuan garden, the transparent ground invites people into the underground galleries. This courtyard forms a link between the past, present, and future.

北京の市内、古い胡同(フートン)が多く残るエリアで、四合院を改装して美術館と商業施設の複合建物とする計画。地上部分の建物はほとんど手をつけることができず、地下に配置される展示空間へのアクセスのために四合院の中庭を新しく提案することになった。中庭全体に開口を開けて、地下空間への天窓とする。巨大な穴に、12本の樹木が浮遊する。地上レベルからは透明なガラス床から樹木が林立しているように見え、吹き抜けを伝って地下に降りていくと、それらの樹木がポッドとともに浮遊しているのが分かる。地下の中庭は樹木によって適度に日差しを遮られた光庭であり、展示室へと向かう主導線でもある。地面レベルが透明ガラスに置き換えられ、それゆえに普段地面に支えられているはずの樹木たちが浮き上がるのだ。伝統的な四合院の庭にさわやかな自然をもち込むと同時に、透明な地面が地下の展示室へと人を誘う。伝統と現代、そして未来を繋げる中庭である。

103 | Beijing Cultural and Art Center | First Prize
北京ギャラリー・改修プロポーザル｜等奖賞

BEIJING, CHINA
2014-

→ Related Projects
008 030 050 057 088

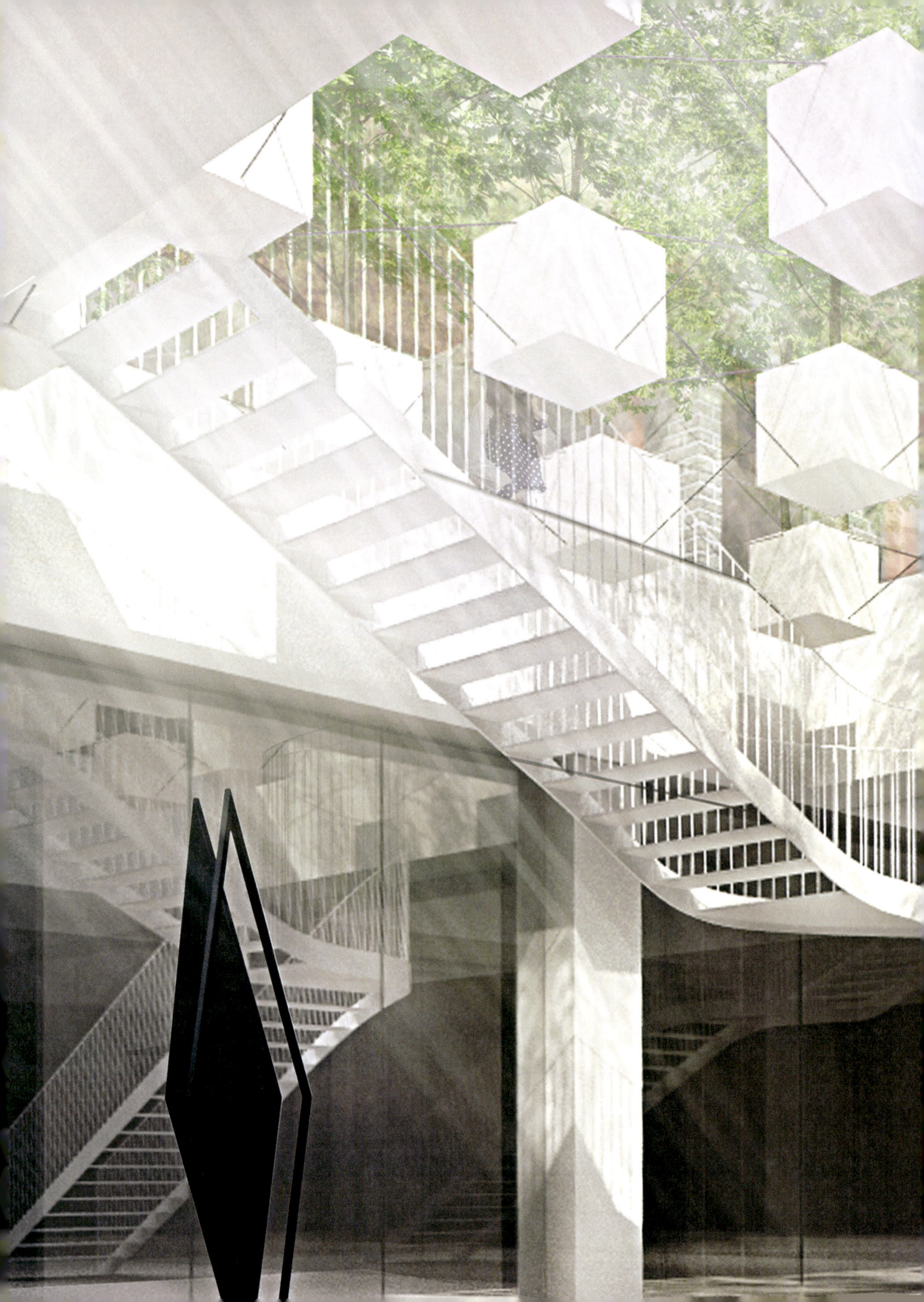

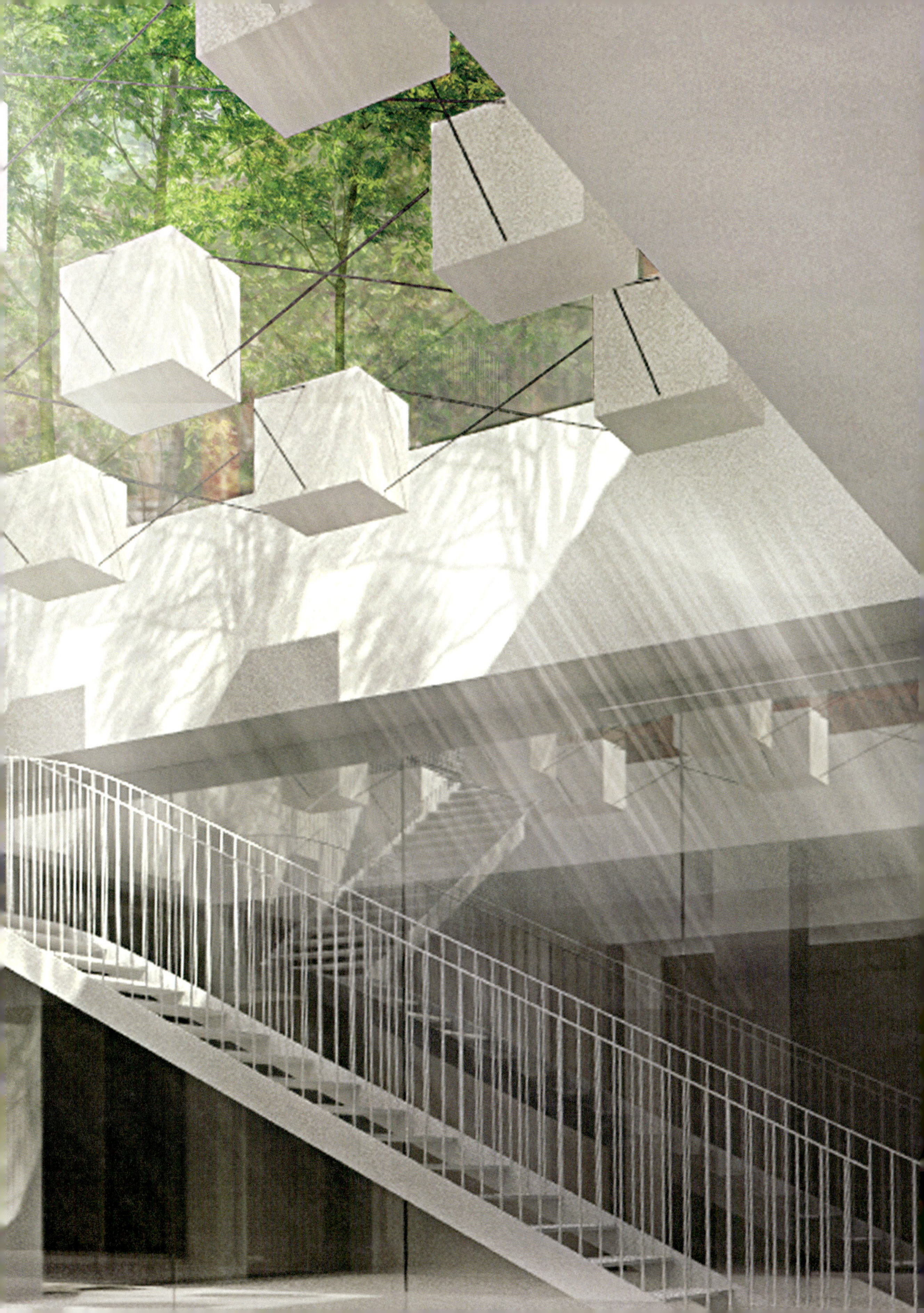

Forest of Music
BUDAPEST, HUNGARY 2014 -

The forest takes form of a roof with a gradation
A Music hall in the woods

The winning proposal, selected in a competition to design the House of Music, a combination of music museum and hall, is located in an expansive park in the centre of the Hungarian capital of Budapest. As the site was situated in a forest inside the park, I envisioned an archetypal landscape of someone performing music among the trees. I created a space that was open to the surrounding forest, but was also protected from the weather. I covered the space with a large roof to create an architectural forest that occupied the entire site. The roof is filled with numerous skylights, allowing light to seep in like sunbeams streaming through the trees below. this covered in glass is a music hall, an outdoor performance area, and other elements. I placed the large volume of the exhibit space underground, and an office, practice rooms, and other small rooms inside the roof. As the building is surrounded by trees, its exterior is almost completely invisible. If you were walking through the forest, you would gradually notice that the trees changed into a large architectural roof. You suddenly find yourself in front of a concert hall in the middle of the architectural forest. The gradual change from nature to building gives rise to a new architectural experience.

ハンガリーの首都ブダペストの中心に広がる公園の中に、音楽博物館と音楽ホールの複合した"House of Music"を設計するコンペでの1等案。敷地が公園内の森の中であったことから、森の木々の中で音楽を演奏する原型的な情景が頭に浮かんだ。そこで敷地全体を建築的な森としての大屋根で覆い、天候から守られながら周囲の森に開かれた場所をつくり出した。大屋根には無数の天窓が開いて木漏れ日のように光が落ちてくる。そのしてガラスに囲まれた音楽ホールや屋外のアンフィシアターなどが展開する。大きなボリュームである展示スペースは地下に配置し、またオフィスや練習室などの小部屋は屋根の中に収めた。屋根は音響的な効果を考慮して不規則にうねっている。木々に囲まれているため、この建物は外観がほとんど見えない。ただし、森の中を歩いているうちに、徐々にその木々が建築的な大屋根に移り変わっていて、気がつけば建築的な森の中の音楽堂にたどり着いている。その自然から建築へのグラデーションが、新しい建築体験を生み出すであろう。

104

Forest of Music
Liget Budapest House of Hungarian Music First Prize

BUDAPEST, HUNGARY
2014-

→ Related Projects
014 044 065 074 082 094

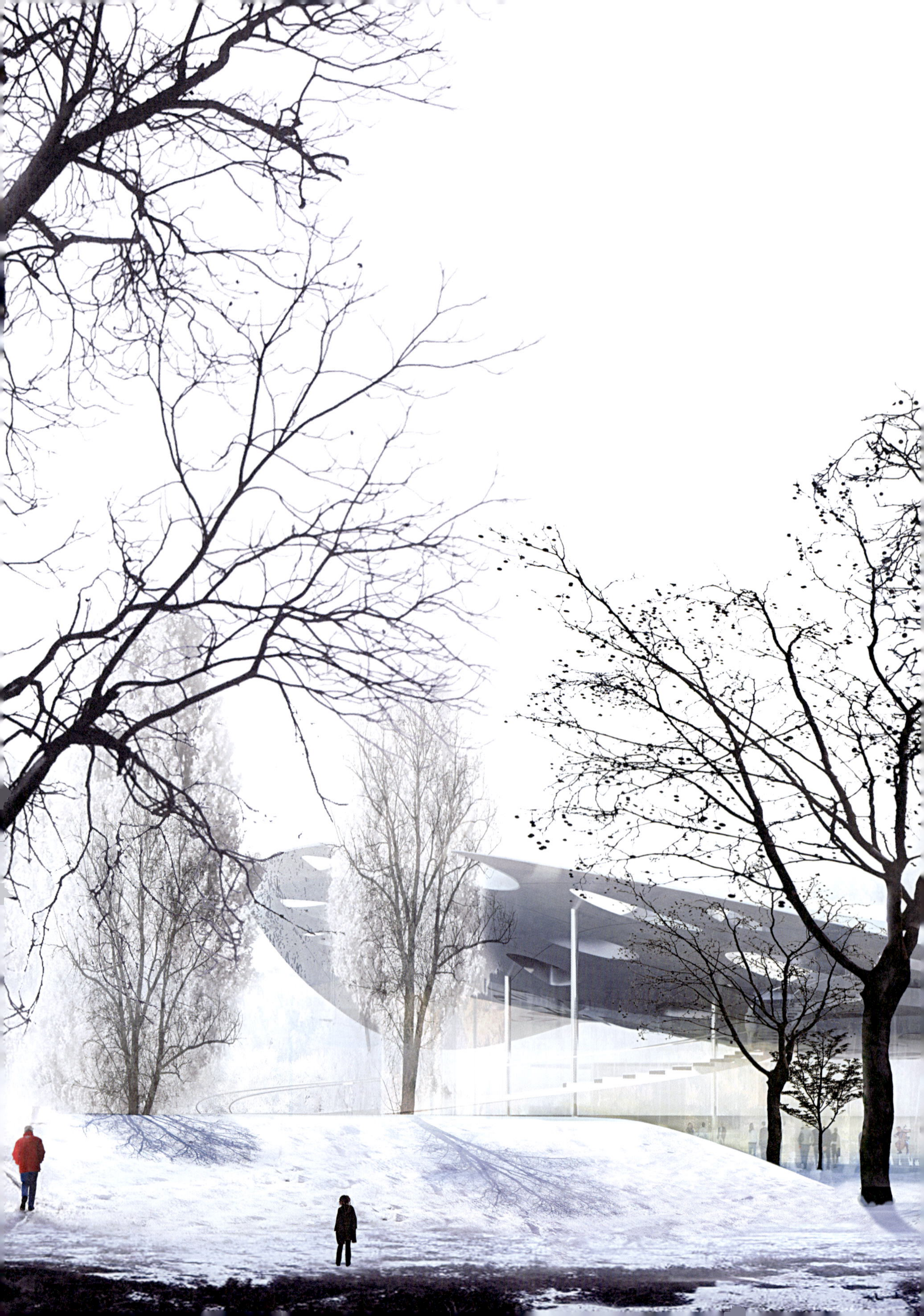

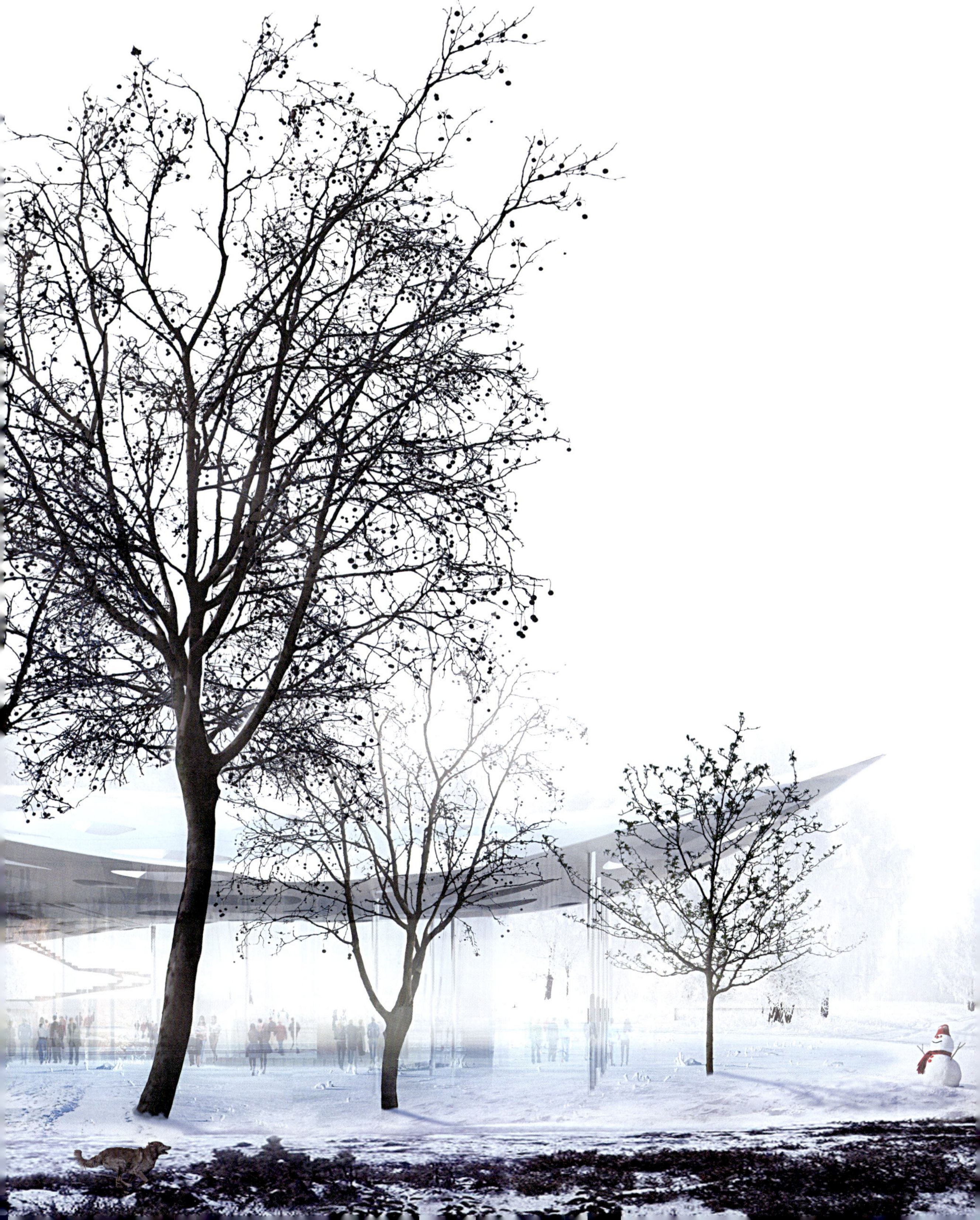

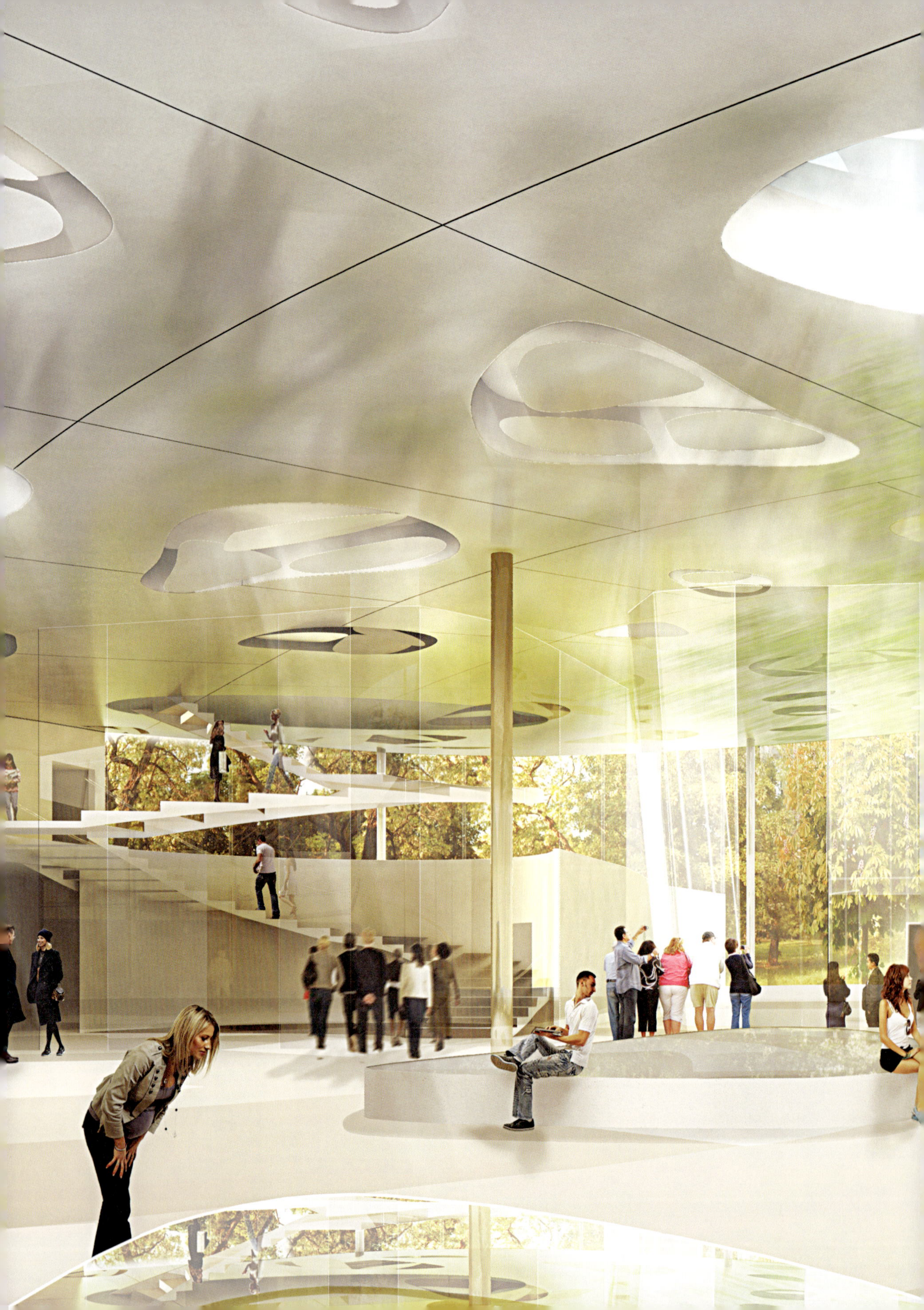

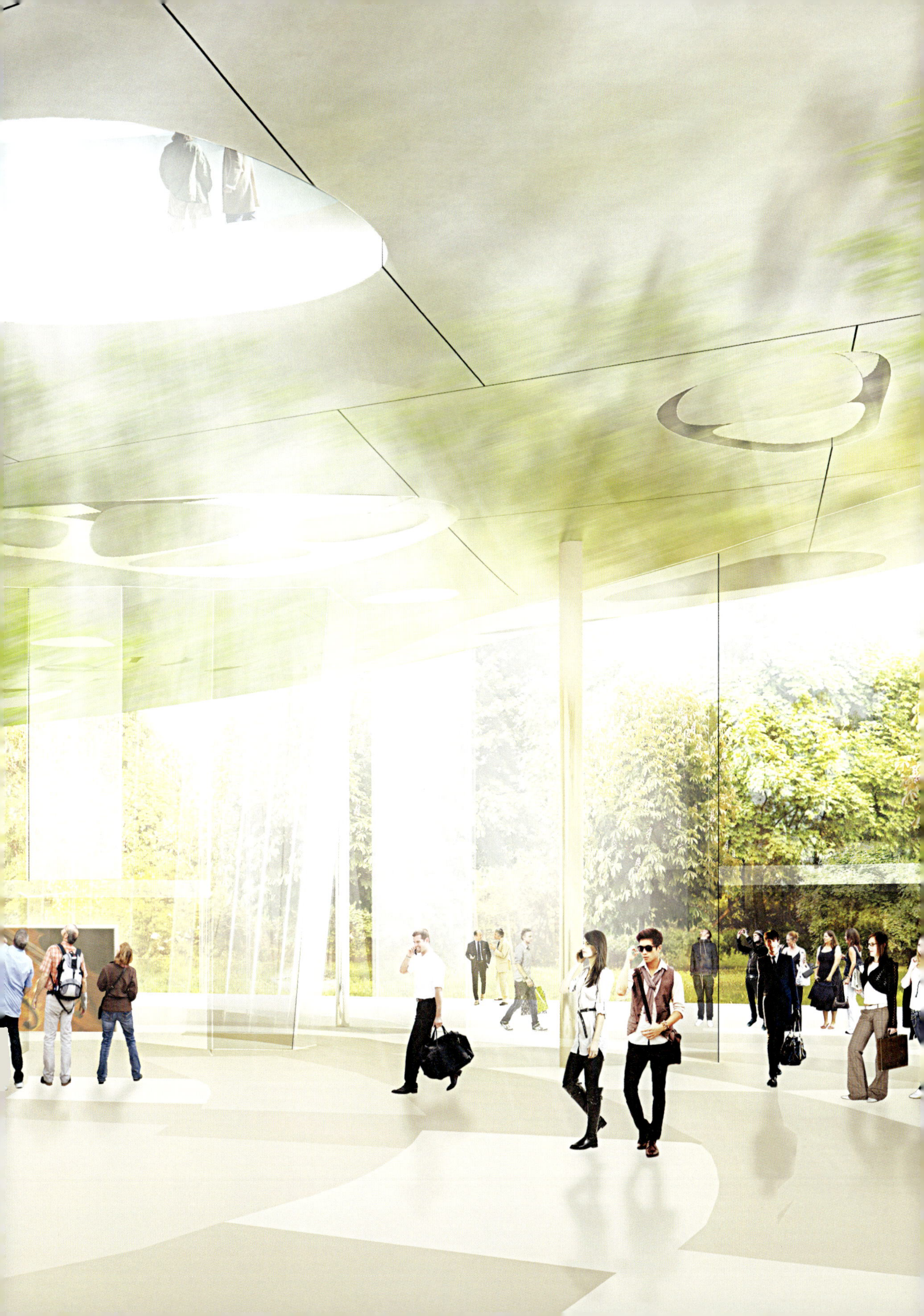

1st FLOOR PLAN

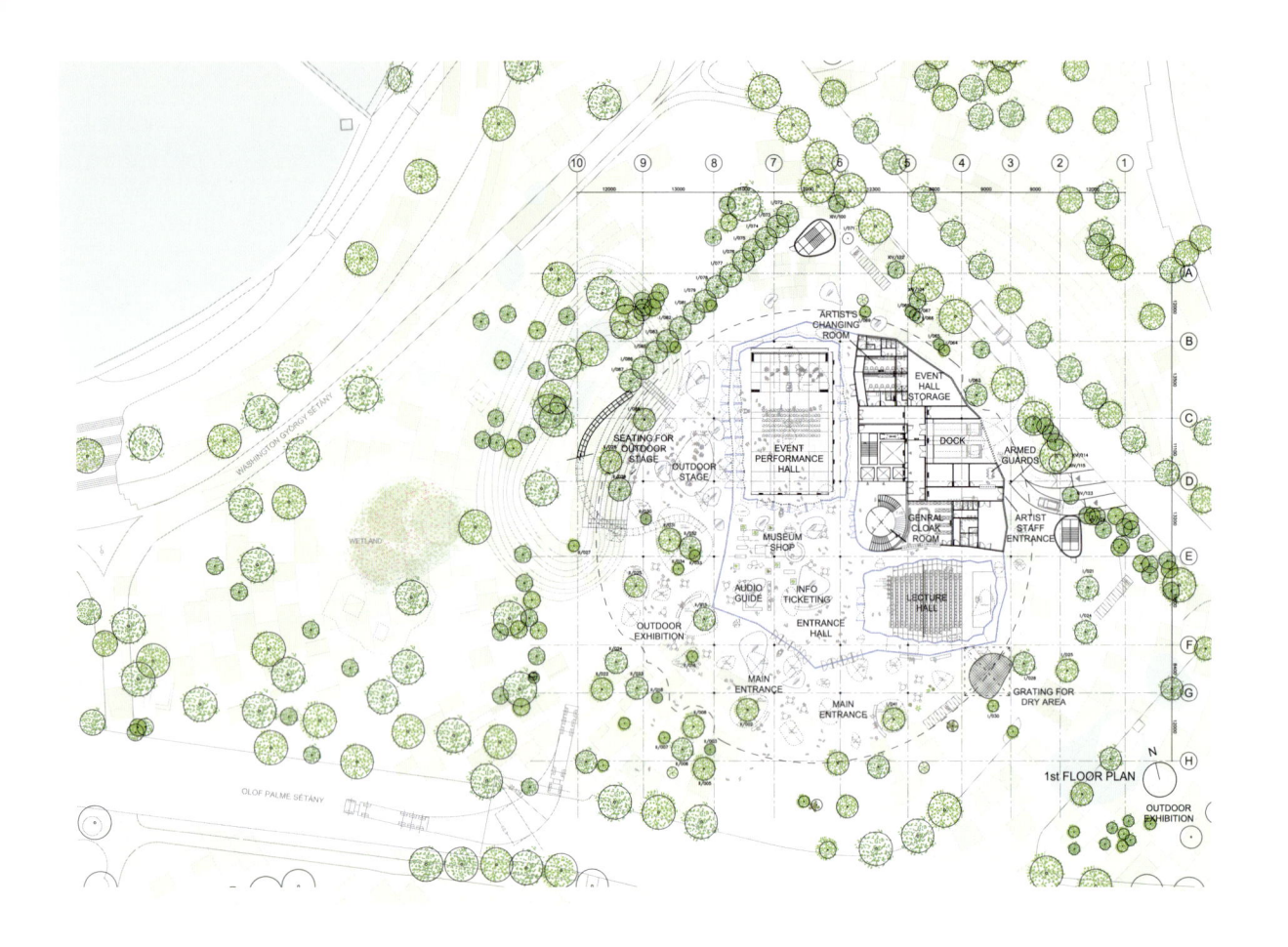

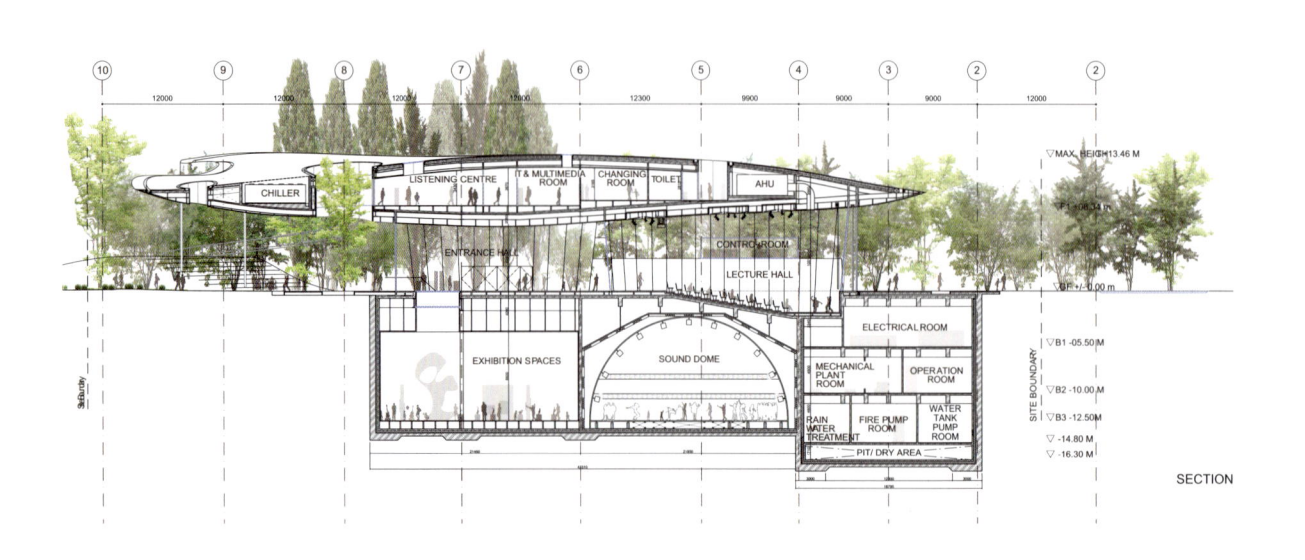

SECTION

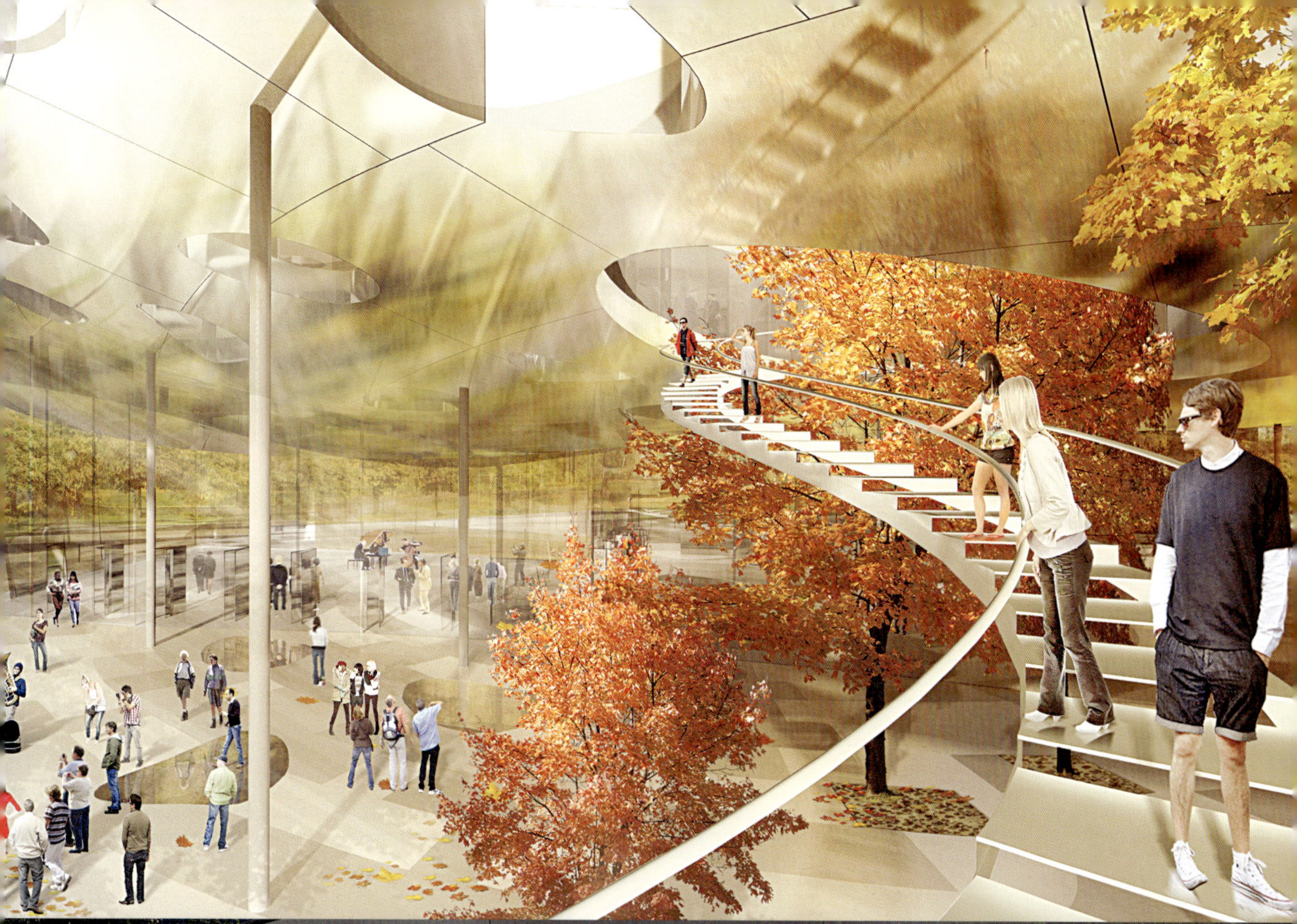

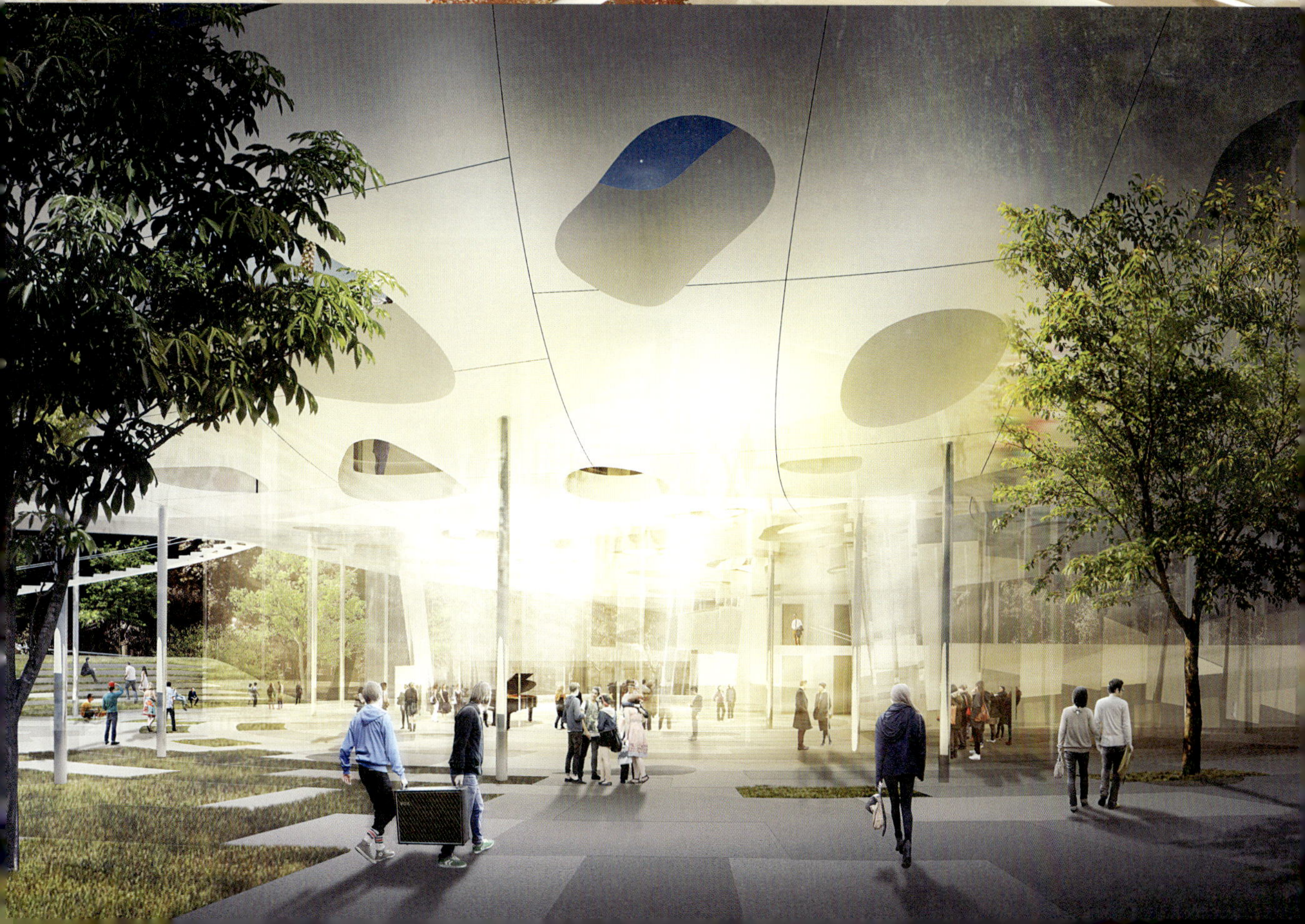

Art Museum in Shiga

SHIGA, JAPAN 2014

A gentle roof connects various matters in one
Architecture is born not through creating space but by inheriting
the qualities of the place

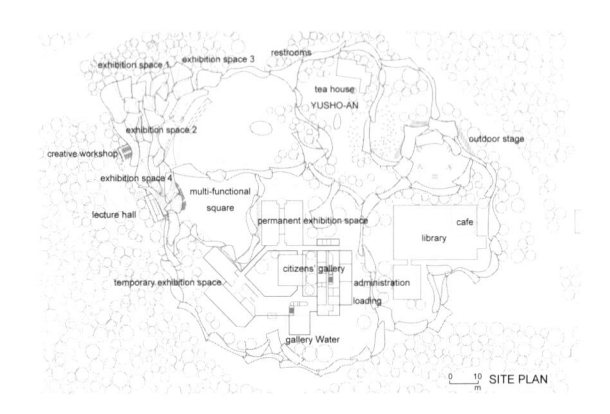

This was a proposal I made for a competition to expand the prefectural art museum in Shiga. I set out to create a new image of the museum based on a network of roofs that would gently enfold not only the existing museum but also the adjacent library and surrounding park. I envisaged the museum as a total entity transcending the divisions such as pre-existing and newly built, and interior and exterior. Irregular pieces of roof are composed in series of layers, which in some cases cover narrow walkways, in other case integrate outside exhibit spaces, and also serve as a canopy for the existing building and form a new passageway. Through the overlapping aspect of the roof, which recalls a terraced rice field, the new contemporary art area gives rise to an architectural space. Seen from the inside, the ceiling and the sky melt together as if they are lightly covered with clouds, and the building's gently raised hill-like appearance makes it stand out from the surrounding landscape while at the same time harmonizing with it. This work is part of the same lineage of works as the *House as Cloud* project described in *House as Cloud*, and with the urban engawa space explored in *Amakusa City Hall* and *Bus stop in Krumbach*. This concept of unification will surely become an important direction in architecture of the future.

滋賀県の県立美術館を増築する設計競技の応募案。既存の美術館だけではなく、隣接する図書館やその周囲を取り巻く公園など、既存／新築、内部／外部の区別を超えた全体を美術館エリアと捉え、それらを緩やかに取りまとめる屋根のネットワークによって新たな美術館像をつくり上げようとした。屋根は不定形の分節した屋根が次々と重なり合い、時に細い散策路を覆い、時にまとまりのある屋外展示空間となり、また既存建物のキャノピーとなったり新たな通路を生み出したりする。そして新設する現代美術エリアは、これらの屋根が棚田のように重なり合うことで建築的な空間をつくり出す。それは内部から見ると軽やかに雲に覆われたように天井と空が溶け合い、緩やかに盛り上がった丘のような姿によって周囲の風景の中で際立ちながら調和する。「House as Cloud」の住宅プロジェクトや街の縁側を試みた「天草本庁舎」や「bus stop in Krumbach」から繋がる系譜。この統合する、という考え方は、これからの建築の大きな方向性のひとつとなるに違いない。

105 | Art Museum in Shiga | 滋賀県立近代美術館 | SHIGA, JAPAN 2014 | → Related Projects 003 024 040 046 076 102

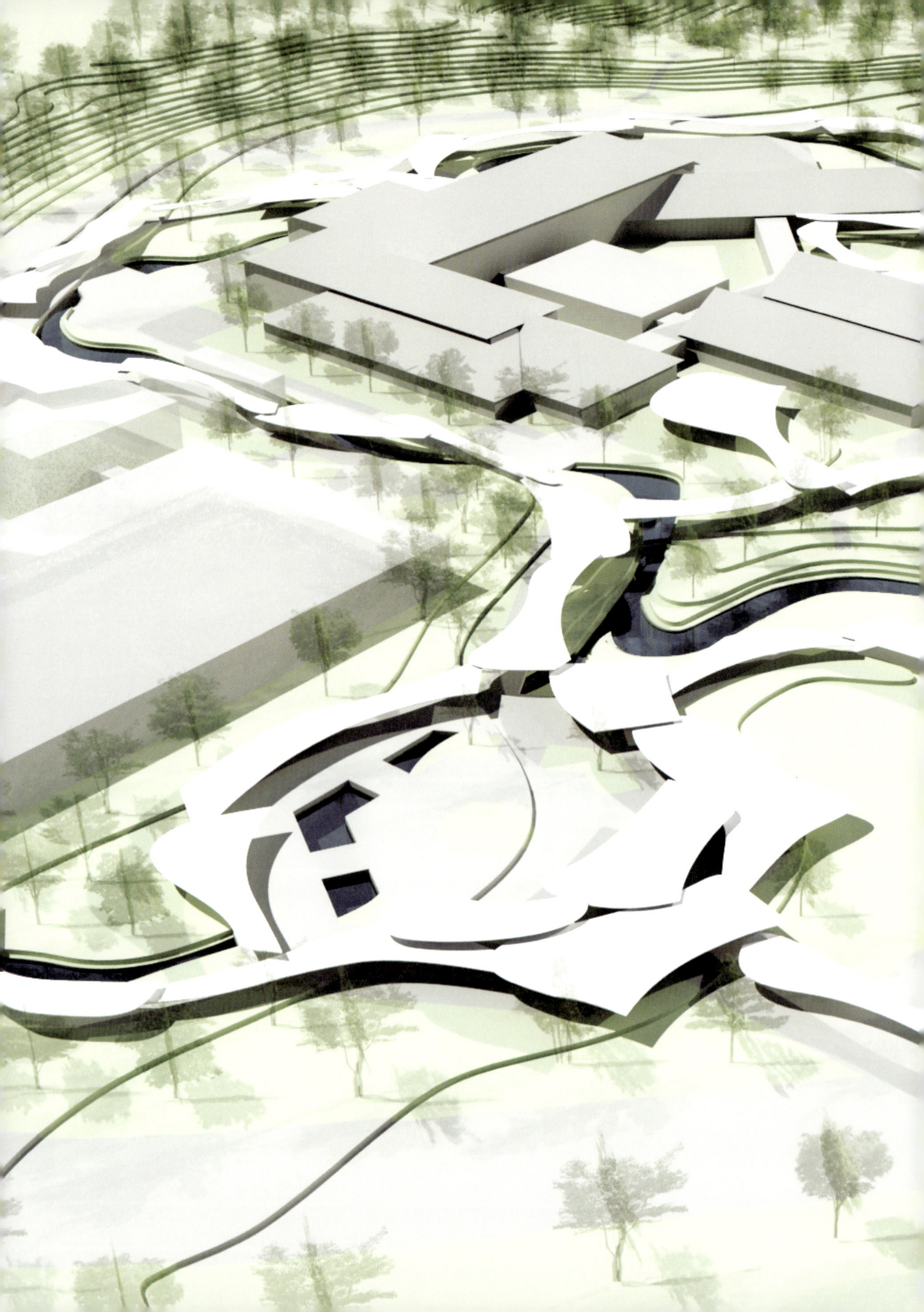

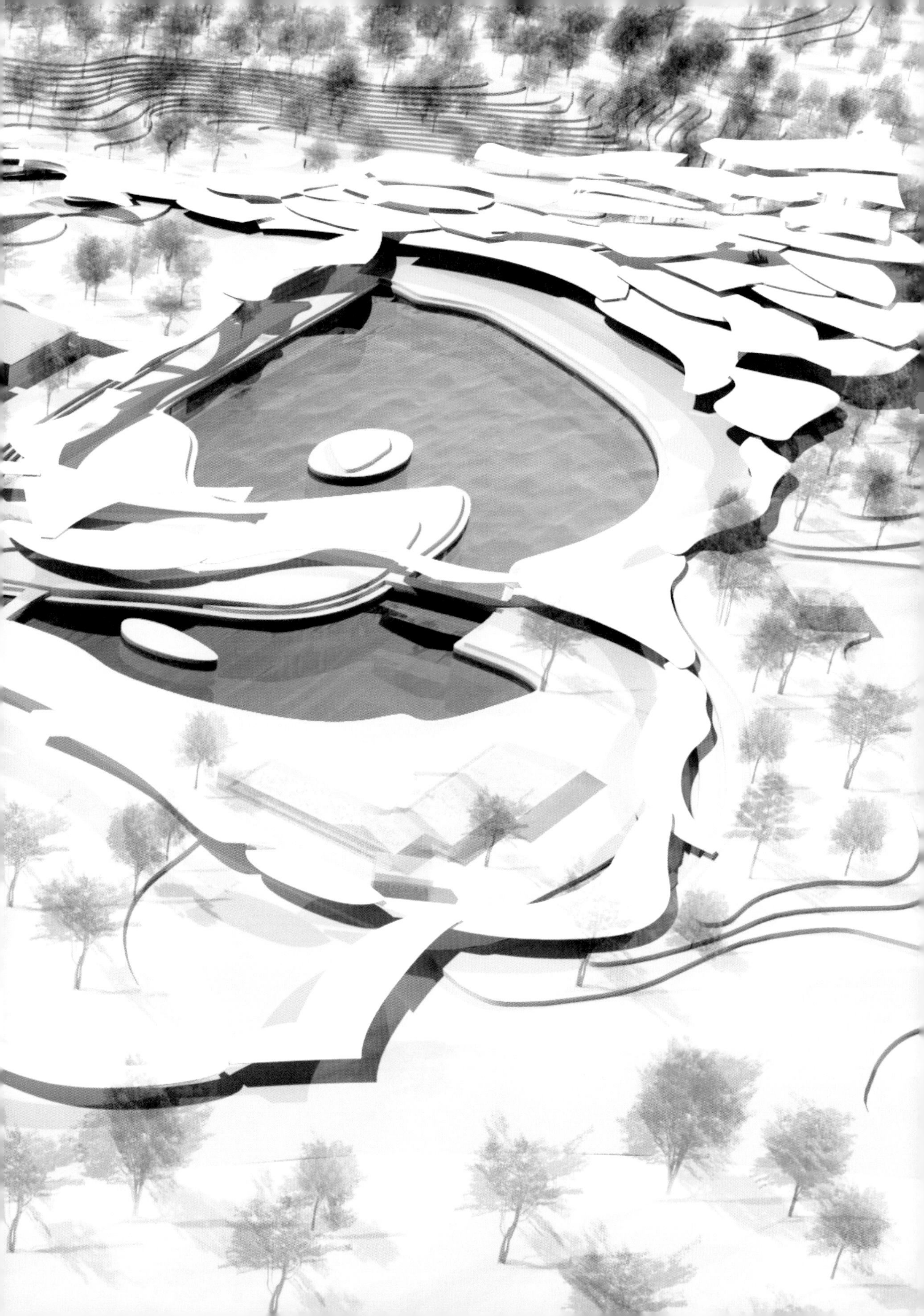

House I

CHIBA, JAPAN 2014 -

Modulation of terrain is, another form of architecture

On an expansive lot in the suburbs of Kisarazu, I designed this complex building made up of a house, an animal protection facility, and a work space. Though each function called for a different spatial form, because the client will be using all of them in an integrated way, each function was arranged to have its own garden. And in response to the need for open places indoors and in the garden but also some degree of protection from the surroundings, I positioned a landscape-type wall and hill around the architectural volume to control the sightline. By incorporating the architecture into the landscape, the entire lot is accented by the undulations, producing variety of features such as an open place, a protected place, an enclosed place, a situation in which things come in and out of view. Unlike *House K* and the *Kunsthalle Bielefeld Annex*, this was an attempt to discover a new relationship between landscape and architecture.

木更津の郊外、広がりのある敷地の中に、住居と動物保護施設、そして作業スペースを複合した建物を計画している。各機能にはそれぞれ異なった空間形式が求められるが、そのすべてを施主が一体的に運用することから、全体をコンパクトにひとつのボリュームにまとめ、それぞれの機能がそれぞれの庭をもつように配置した。さらに周辺から適度に守られながら、しかし室内や庭からは開放的な場所であってほしいという要望に対応するため、建築ボリュームの周囲にランドスケープ的な壁と丘を配置して、視線をコントロールしている。このランドスケープは建築部分をも含み込んで、敷地全体が波打つ場の抑揚となり、その抑揚の中に、開けた場所、守られた場所、囲まれた場所、見え隠れする関係など、さまざまな特徴が生まれてくる。「House K」や「Kunsthalle Bielefeld Annex」とはまた異なる、ランドスケープと建築の新しい関係の模索。

ENTRANCE
GARDEN

GARDEN

GARDEN

風向　南南西

Skyscraper/Forest

2015 -

Here architecture becomes a lattice-structural augmentation of the earth

Because of its flexibility, the tree hybrid and tree-shaped structural frame that emerged from the *Omotesando Branches* contains the potential for various developments. In transforming it into a high-rise building, the frame is not merely a structure but contains functions related to the shaft and circulation. As the structural frame itself is very simple, the position, frequency, and density of the tree that is grafted onto it can be designed in many different ways. If Le Corbusier's domino system was an archetype based solely on artificial materials, the archetype of the future might be an even simpler architectural form – a new hybrid form that is fused with a tree, the antithesis of architecture.

「Omotesando Branches」から生まれた樹状の構造フレームと樹木のハイブリッドは、その柔軟性ゆえにいろいろな展開が可能であろう。それが高層建築に変化していった時には、フレームは単なる構造だけではなく、設備シャフトやサーキュレーションも含み込んだ機能をもち得るだろう。構造フレーム自体はとてもシンプルなものなので、そこに接ぎ木される樹木の配置や頻度、密度感などをさまざまに設計していくことができる。ル・コルビュジエのドミノシステムが、人工材料のみによる原型性だったとするなら、これからの時代の原型は、ドミノよりもさらに純化した建築フレームと、建築の対極である樹木の融合した新しいハイブリッド状態なのかもしれない。

107

Skyscraper/Forest

Skyscraper/Forest

2015-

→ Related Projects
008 028 031 063 087 088

Sou Fujimoto Chronology

1995

I had graduated from university the previous spring, but was in a state of indecision about how to proceed with life. As I watched my friends get hired by famous architectural firms or go to study overseas, I myself lacked the confidence to take even the first step. Just after the New Year, I returned to my parents' home in Hokkaido. Away from the hustle and bustle of Tokyo, I intended to take the opportunity to think deeply about what had originally driven me to leave home with the intention of becoming an architect. I needed some time to explore, in my own way, what future directions architecture might take.

Toyo Ito's competition proposal for the Sendai Mediatheque, released around this time, made a tremendous impact on me and became a sort of starting point. Another thing that contributed to my development was Ilya Prigogine's Order Out of Chaos (Japanese translation 1987, Misuzu Shobo), which I happened to read during all the free time I had on my hands. The simple yet complex new image of order depicted in the book continues to inform my architectural design to this day. During my senior year of university I had traveled to France, Spain, and Italy, but the one-month trip I took to Turkey and Greece during this year following graduation was truly unforgettable.

It was during this year that I started work on my first small project, something I designed for my parents.

1996

Seidai Hospital Annex, a small building I had been designing since the previous year for my parents' hospital, was completed. While I was still more or less clueless about what I wanted to do as an architect, in any case it was a major event for a building to be finished.

However, for me life in Hokkaido was all too comfortable. Worried that I was going to slip into a slow-paced, relaxing lifestyle where nothing got done, I made up my mind to return to Tokyo. The experience of studying architecture in the capital, returning to Hokkaido for a time, and then living in Tokyo again, was highly significant for my development, as it caused me to reexamine the urban and rural extremes that these two places represent from an architectural perspective.

Afterward, I realized that placing the natural and artificial environments of Hokkaido and Tokyo respectively on equal footing, and seeking to fuse them, formed the basis of my approach to architecture.

It was during this year that I first met Akihisa Hirata, who had been hired at Toyo Ito & Associates, Architects. We went on to have many an intense discussion over drinks. These discussions with a trusted friend were a valuable way for me to explore ideas and deepen my understanding, as I worked alone on architectural designs.

1997

Around this time, I began having talks with the Hokkaido-based psychologist Dr. Ogino, whom my father had introduced me to late the previous year. Dr. Ogino later went on to commission a variety of projects, including the *Residential treatment center for emotionally disturbed children*. Our discussions of the future directions medical facilities ought to take inspired many thoughts about the future of living environments in general and the relationship of the individual and society. Looking back on the early days of my career, starting off with my father's hospital annex and continuing by exploring the nature of psychiatric facilities was a very valuable, if coincidental, course of events. Psychiatric facilities are both residences and entire communities. Considering their design meant thinking about architecture from both of these angles, and opened my eyes to the diversity of human living environments that lies between the two. The fundamental question of how human beings can live in comfort underlies it all. Weighing this question on both small scale and large, with a wide range of schemes progressing simultaneously, later became key to my design process.

1998

I get a strange sensation when I look back on my life around this time. In a way it seems like several years went by in a single day, and in another it seems like every day lasted years.

After reading Prigogine, my interests turned to areas like complex systems and affordance theory, and I took various approaches to the exploration of architecture featuring a relaxed order formed by the relations of its parts. My daily life, though, didn't seem like that of a man on the road to becoming a full-fledged architect: sleeping late in the mornings, aimlessly wandering the streets of my neighborhood, Nishi-Shinjuku, kneading over ideas. Those were some good times, though.

1999

Because of the lifestyle I have described above, I can't remember clearly how I spent this year. My ideas, which were slowly and gradually taking shape over a long period of time, seem in retrospect like sudden leaps of inspiration. At this time construction was underway on an expansion of my family's hospital in Hokkaido, which had begun the preceding year, and I was back and forth between Hokkaido and Tokyo. Around the end of that year I was working out my proposal for the *Art Museum in Aomori* design competition, which would be a decisive turning point in my architectural career. At the time, of course, I had no idea what this project would come to mean, and I felt like I was wandering in a dark labyrinth with no exit. It was at this time that I began thinking about the forest in relation to architecture. This was simply because the museum site was surrounded by forest, but from this time onward, the forest would come to be an important metaphor for me.

2000

My proposal for the the *Art Museum in Aomori* design competition, which I had been working on since the end of 1999, ended up coming in second place, which was a landmark event for me. This was less because it came in second place than because of who I got to know during the public screening of proposals: Toyo Ito and Terunobu Fujimori, two men who would shape my destiny. Until then, it was as if I was feeling around at the bottom of a deep sea, and all was murky, including the question of whether my architectural ideas had any merit whatsoever. Ito's understanding and approval, however, pulled me up from the depths and into the light, where I could see the way forward. Since then I have benefited in so many ways from my acquaintance with him, and am deeply in his debt. After this I made up my mind to get a real workspace, rather than working in my small studio apartment, and established my own office. This is not to say that I had any jobs yet, but things started getting a little livelier as I prepared for the SD Review exhibition, which I had been accepted into for the first time in three years. Another crucial event from this time: Ryuji Fujimura, who at the time was still a student at Tokyo Institute of Technology, did an internship for me, and later that winter I hired my first paid employee.

2001

My ideas were starting to gather steam thanks to the Aomori competition experience and bringing new people on board at the office. Still, there were few if any actual jobs coming in. It was around this time that I started work on *Primitive Future House*, a pivotal project that connects with what I am doing even today. For several years I had been exploring ways of combining furniture/interiors, architecture, and landscape, and after entering proposals in a few idea competitions and project competitions, I had finally arrived at a clear architectural approach. In a way it was my own response to Ito Toyo's Sendai Mediatheque, which had made such an impact on me five years before.

The fact that it took five years to come up with a response illustrates the extent to which I was feeling my way in the dark. This project and several ensuing models were based on Ludwig Mies van der Rohe's Farnsworth House, and it is evident that I was trying to arrive at a new architectural paradigm that could succeed Mies van der Rohe. It was a critical and fundamental step that connected to later works such as the Serpentine Gallery Pavilion.This was also the year when I first submitted a text detailing my ideas to an architectural journal. It was a very short text, entitled "The Architecture of Parts," describing ideas about a new type of order based on local networks, which drew inspiration from Prigogine and the theory of complex systems. In 2011 I also began my first part-time instructorship at Tokyo University of Science, having been invited to teach by Kazuhiro Kojima. Teaching was a new form of communication that I found gave me new ideas and invigorated me. It was also an opportunity to establish relationships with a lot of other architects through review panels and so forth.

2002

After the Aomori competition, I entered a large number of project competitions. One that particularly (and painfully) stands out in my memory is the *Oura Town Hall* (Gunma Prefecture) design competition, in which I made it to the final stage only to be severely criticized and roundly defeated. This experience, however, led to my winning first place in the *Annaka Environmental Art Forum* competition the following year.

My *Oura Town Hall* proposal was the first attempt at combining architecture with trees, a methodology that I went on to apply repeatedly in projects such as *House N*, *House Before House*, and *Omotesando Branches*. I have vivid memories of several buildings completed around this time being sharply criticized by my friend Akihisa Hirata. The concept and the finished project didn't match, the practical approaches betrayed lack of maturity, I wasn't building the ideas I had come up with. It was rough stuff, but I had to admit he was right. These shortcomings reflected the fact that I had never worked for someone else's firm. From this time onward I was occupied with the problem of how to overcome these shortcomings and create full-fledged, genuine architecture.

2003

I remember this year particularly vividly. First of all, it was the first time a proposal of mine came in first place in a project competition. This competition was for a multi-purpose plaza known as the Environment Art Forum. Building on the lessons I learned from my loss in the *Oura Town Hall* competition, also in Gunma, the previous year, I made the most thorough of preparations, and I believe this helped me to achieve better results this time around.Right around the same time I submitted to an architectural journal, for the first time, a text containing the phrase "primitive future." This started as the title of a text I had been asked to write, and was a phrase I began using without a clear idea of what it meant. From this time onward, however, it became a touchstone that I kept coming back to in a variety of situations, and its meaning seemed to keep expanding in scope. This course of events somehow naturally led me to stop submitting designs to the SD Review exhibition, as I had done in 1995, 1997, and for four consecutive years beginning in 2000, submitting a total of seven works in all.

2004

This is another year that I can't clearly remember. Probably I was wholly absorbed in the design and at the construction site of my first residential project, *T house*. The plan for the building was in itself ambitious, and the process entailed redefining everything from structure and finish to the presentation of windows and electrical wiring. At this time I was grappling with the architectural issues that Akihisa Hirata had pointed out critically before. This was also the year I delivered a lecture overseas for the first time. I recall frantically scrawling the text on the plane on my way to deliver the lecture in Kuala Lumpur.

2005

My first residential project, *T house*, was completed. It was an ambitious project that explored an essential issue, that of being simultaneously divided and connected. I made a point of thinking everything through thoroughly, from the basic structure down to the smallest details, something I was able to do thanks to the flexible open-mindedness of the client. Toyo Ito and Terunobu Fujimori still say that this *T house* is the best thing I've done. It's a comment that makes me feel simultaneously happy and dismayed. In the winter of this year my design took first place in the *Final Wooden House* competition. The head of the selection committee was Ito-san. Five years after the Aomori competition, I felt like I was finally able to give something back to him. In December, my design *Dormitory in Date* won a commendation in the AR Emerging Architecture Awards hosted by the London-based journal The Architectural Review, and I visited London for the first time. When I went to the award ceremony, I found that one of the first-prize winners was Taira Nishizawa, then a part-time instructor at the university I had graduated from. Once again I was simultaneously happy and dismayed, and I swore I would come back to London again some day to collect the grand prize. At the time I had no idea this would come true the very next year.

2006

This year the *Residential treatment center for emotionally disturbed children* was completed, and I feel it was the culmination of a series of medical facilities I had designed in Hokkaido. It went on to win the grand prize at the Architectural Review awards, which I had come away from with mixed feelings after collecting a less prestigious prize the previous year, and as a result requests to deliver lectures overseas gradually started to come in. At the time I was still writing speeches beforehand and reading them off the paper, a naive and artless style compared to what I've been doing recently, but it was very encouraging that there were attendees who took an interest nonetheless.

It was also this year that I started to work out the concepts for *House N* and *Tokyo Apartment*. At the time I had nothing yet but rough models, but I had the strong sense that these would be crucial projects, and I intentionally submitted the proposals to a journal in unfinished form.

2007

In spring I was asked to produce a proposal for the *Musashino Art University Museum & Library*, which was approved, and I was selected as architect. Now that I think of it, I prepared all of the materials for this proposal by myself, from concept to text, from illustrations to diagrams. It was an ideas competition, all concept and vision and no blueprints, the work of preparing the proposal lasted right up until the day it was submitted, and I felt compelled to complete the whole thing by myself, my brain and the submitted materials connected by a direct link. I am deeply grateful to this client for selecting me despite my lack of experience at that time with anything at this scale. I also recall the Tokyo Gas "Sumika Project," which began in the spring of this year. In this project, Toyo Ito, Terunobu Fujimori, Taira Nishizawa, and myself each designed a small residence or pavilion. While we designed things separately, we held discussions together, and I gained a palpable sense of how our design approaches differed from one another's.

2008

The year 2008 began with preparations for the publication of Primitive Future (INAX, 2008), my first collection of works to be released in April of that year. I have many memories of this book, which I labored over until I was satisfied with composition and layout, pondering how to express my architectural ideas in images and text. This was also the year that *House N* and *Final Wooden House* were completed, two projects that were very important to me personally and in terms of how my work was viewed internationally. *Final Wooden House* won the top prize in the Private House category at the World Architecture Festival, and around this time the number of invitations to lecture overseas skyrocketed. Another memorable event this year was my office's moving to a new location, in Kagurazaka, where it remains today.

This year I also had the unforgettable experience of participating in Ordos 100, a fascinating project in which 100 architects gathered in the desert of inner Mongolia and each created a house. It was quite surreal to be one of a huge group of architects staying at a Holiday Inn in the middle of the desert, and the experience of meeting architects from around the world is one I'll always treasure. It was in the middle of the desert site where we were working that I first met the photographer Iwan Baan, and I have to say the site somehow suited Iwan.

2009

A big event for me this year was the construction of the *Musashino Art University Museum & Library*.

Another was the Spanish publisher GG's decision to release a collection of my work in its 2G Series. Primitive Future, which I had released the previous year, was really more of a concept book, but this time I intended to publish a genuine collection of works. Also, at the end of that year I heard from another Spanish publisher, El Croquis, that they wanted to do a collection as well. El Croquis's series of collections of architects' works was one I had admired since my student days, and I was overjoyed and also a bit terrified to receive this offer.

2010

Starting around this year, things really got busy, and in retrospect, every year I had so much going on I'm amazed I managed to do it all. In spring of 2010 the *Musashino Art University Museum & Library* was completed, and looking back on it this was a building that I really struggled with, but at the same time I felt like I could see the way forward as I watched an architectural project of this scale take shape, compounding body-sized sense of scale, spatial concepts, and complex functions.

This was the first building of mine photographed by Yukio Futagawa.

I was unable to be there for the photo shoot, but I was happy to hear that Futagawa was very impressed with it. Right around this time I was invited by Hitoshi Abe to teach as a part-time instructor at UCLA, and began my first overseas teaching job.

Another unforgettable experience this year was my honeymoon trip to Morocco. In summer was my first exhibition, at the Watari Museum of Contemporary Art, and my first time taking part in the Venice Biennale, thanks to an invitation from Kazuyo Sejima. Then in autumn, the El Croquis book came out.

2011

The massive earthquake and tsunami that occurred this year is something I'll never forget. After the disaster I wasn't sure how I ought to move forward as an architect, but I just lost myself in my work, and as a result I secured first place in two international design competitions.

I made many trips to Belgrade, the capital of Serbia, for the competition there, an urban plaza and mixed cultural and commercial facility called *Beton Hala Waterfront Center*.

Toward the end of the year I won first place in the *Taiwan Tower* competition to design a 300-meter tower in Taichung, Taiwan. Both were extremely large-scale projects, and I believe I was able to win the competitions due to the experience entering major overseas competitions I had been amassing over the preceding several years. After this I started getting more orders for projects in Taiwan. In May I took part in an exhibition at the Louisiana Museum of Modern Art in Denmark.

I was bowled over by the beautiful melding of landscape and architecture at this museum, and afterwards I made more conscious attempts to blend architecture with nature or landscape in my own designs. However, even with all of this going on, I was unable to shake the sense of powerlessness I felt in the aftermath of the quake and tsunami. Then, I was asked by Toyo Ito to participate along with him in the Venice Biennale. I was deeply moved by Ito's passionate determination to present a disaster-zone project to the world, and provoke thought about what architecture can do to shape the future, and joined a team that also included Kumiko Inui, Akihisa Hirata, and the photographer Naoya Hatakeyama to work over the course of a year on a project for the devastated city of Rikuzentakata.

2012

I met with the team, sometimes as often as once a wekk, to discuss the Rikuzentakata project, in progress since the year before.Through this process, I believe I came to grasp the inevitable course of architecture's emergence from the primal collective (before the individual and the group were divided) as a means of connecting people and people; people and things; people and places; people and history and the future. I felt as if I had discovered the fundamental wellspring of architecture.

Then in August, our work at the Japan Pavilion of the Venice Biennale International Architecture Exhibition won the top Golden Lion award. Our project, the *Home-for-All in Rikuzentakata*, was completed in early winter. My first overseas solo exhibition, at a museum in the small German city of Bielefeld, was held in spring of this year. With all of this going on I was traveling frequently overseas.

In November, a letter arrived from the Serpentine Galleries in London asking me to do something that had been a dream of mine for over 10 years: to design a *Serpentine Gallery Pavilion 2013* for their ongoing pavilion series.Six months of unparalleled intensity, simultaneously grueling and thrilling, were about to begin.

2013

The *Serpentine Gallery Pavilion 2013*, I believed, ought to incorporate everything: what I had done thus far, what I was thinking about at the time, and my presentiments for the future. I trembled when I was asked, during the first meeting about the project in London, to "design a present-day answer to Mies van der Rohe's Barcelona Pavilion." This was to be a process that entailed not only considerable introspection but also thought about the relation of architecture to the world's primordial roots and to the future. Soon after the new year the Serpentine co-director Julia Peyton-Jones visited my office, I presented the proposal, and she gave me the go-ahead on the spot. Afterwards Julia-san and I went on to have any number of fights, but these served to strengthen the project, tempering it as a fire does steel. Today, I feel we are as close as family. After this there were near-daily telephone conferences between Tokyo and London, with engineers and construction supervisors sitting in, and the design moved ahead with breathtaking speed. Dialogues with Serpentine's other co-director, Hans Ulrich Obrist, helped sharply bring out the essence of the proposal. I won't soon forget the opening week, a rare week of continuous sunshine in London, which made the pavilion glow under the early-summer sun like it was made of light. Many visitors came and enjoyed the space in their own chosen manner. I am sure this project stands as the greatest single turning point in my career thus far. There was one other major event this year. In January was the opening of the architectural photographer Yukio Futagawa's Minka: Traditional Japanese Houses exhibition, for which I had been preparing the layout since the year before. I vividly remember Futagawa's response when I made my first presentation of the layout proposal, a loud and clear "Sounds great!" that rang out practically before I had finished with my explanation. It was decided then and there. Futagawa's reminiscences about the photos, which he told me about during the preparations, were lively and vivid as if they had happened yesterday. Just before the opening he and I walked around the venue to check on things, and I listened to him speak this time in a hushed murmur. The day of the opening, he looked delighted, and I was overjoyed to see this. Just two short months later, in March, I heard the news that he had left us.

2014

In spring I won a design competition for an apartment building in Montpelier, in the beautiful south of France. In connection with this I visited Paris several times, and in summer I went to Brazil for the first time, visiting Brasilia, Rio de Janeiro, and São Paolo. Brazilian architecture, including that of Niemayer, was a fresh new inspiration for me. With wins in closed and open competitions in Beijing and Budapest respectively, I am excited about the new experiences and challenges that await in 2015.

藤本壮介年表

1995

前年の春に大学を卒業したが、今後の身の振り方について決めあぐねていた。著名な設計事務所に就職したり、海外に留学する友人たちを見ながら、しかし自分に自信がもてず1歩を踏み出すことができずにいた。1995年の年明け、実家の北海道に戻る。東京の喧嘩から離れて、将来自分が建築家としてひとり立ちした時にその思考の核となるようなものについて、この機会にひとりでゆっくりと考えたいという思いもあった。これからの建築の在り方について、自分なりの思索の時間が必要だった。そのころに発表された、伊東豊雄さんのせんだいメディアテークのコンペ案は大きな衝撃であり、当時の僕にとってのひとつの出発点となった。また、あり余るほどの時間の中でたまたま読んだ、イリヤ・プリゴジンの『混沌からの秩序』(邦訳、1987年、みすず書房)は啓示であった。そこに描かれていた、単純で複雑な新しい秩序のイメージは、今に至るまで僕の建築を支えている。大学4年の時に、フランス、スペイン、イタリアを旅したが、この年には、トルコとギリシャを1か月かけて旅したことも忘れがたい。親のための小さなプロジェクトが始まったのもこの年だった。

1996

前年から設計を進めていた親の病院のための小さな建物、「聖台病院作業療法棟」が竣工した。
何もわからない中で、ともかくもひとつ建物を完成させたことは重要な出来事だった。しかし北海道の環境は僕には快適すぎた。このまま穏やかな生活が続くことに不安を覚えて、東京に戻ることを決意した。建築を学んだ後に一度北海道に戻り、そして再び東京で住み始めたことは、その両極端を建築的な視点で再構築せざるを得ないという意味で、とても重要な転機だった。以後、北海道の自然と東京の人工環境の等価性や融合が、気がつかない内に自分の建築のバックグラウンドとなっていった。伊東事務所に入社が決まっていた平田晃久さんに初めて出会ったのもこの年だった。以後よく飲みながら議論するようになる。ひとりで設計作業をしていた僕にとって、信頼できる友人との議論によって思考を深めるという経験はとても貴重なものであった。

1997

前年末に父の紹介で出会い、後の「児童心理治療施設」に至るさまざまなプロジェクトの施主となってくれた北海道の精神科医、荻野先生との対話が始まったのがこの頃だった。これからの医療施設の在り方を話し合うことは、僕にとっては、これからの居住環境や個と社会の在り方について大きな示唆を与えてくれた。父の病院から始まり、キャリアの初期を、精神医療施設をめぐる思考でスタートしたことは、今思うと、偶然とはいえとても貴重なことだった。精神医療施設とは、家であり同時に街である。それは建築を、家と街の両端から同時に思考することであり、その間に広がる＜人間の居住環境＞の多様性に開くことであった。そこには人がいかに快適に過ごすことができるか、という根源的な問いがあった。小さなスケールから大きなスケールまで、そして多様なプログラムを同時並行で進めていく今の僕の設計の方法に繋がるものである。

1998

この頃の生活は、思い返してみても不思議な感覚だ。数年間が1日のようでもあり、また1日が数年間にも感じられる。プリゴジンの影響から、さらに複雑系やアフォーダンス理論などへと興味が広がり、部分が関係することによる緩やかな秩序のような建築をさまざまに模索していた。しかし日々の生活は、朝遅くに起き、当時住んでいた西新宿の裏路地をあてもなくぶらぶら歩き回ってアイデアを練る、という感じで、どう考えても建築家へと繋がる路には思えなかった。しかしそれはそれで楽しい日々だったのだ。

1999

そんな毎日を送っていたので、この年に何をやっていたのか、正確には思い出せない。
長い時間をかけて少しずつ考えを進めて徐々に形になっていったアイデアが、今振り返るとある瞬間のインスピレーションのようにも感じられる。前年から始まっていた、実家の病院の増築プロジェクトが現場に入っていたので、北海道と東京を行き来していた。年末、その後の僕の建築家人生に決定的な大きな出来事となる「青森県立美術館」コンペの構想を練っていた。
しかし当時は、当然ながらそのプロジェクトがもつ意味を知る由もなく、出口の見えない闇の中をさまよっているような気分だった。
この時初めて＜森＞というものを建築と対置して思考した。敷地が森に囲まれていたからだが、以後、森は僕にとって重要なメタファーとなる。

2000

前年末から準備して、結果的に2等に選ばれた「青森県立美術館」の設計コンペは、とても大きな出来事だった。2等だったことよりも、公開審査の会場で、初めて伊東豊雄さんと藤森照信さんと出会ったことは、運命的なものだった。それまで、言ってみれば深い海の底で、自分の建築的な思考が意

味をもつのかさえ分からないままにひたすらわが路を模索していた僕は、伊東さんからの評価によって、深い海から浮上し、日の当たる場所にようやく立つことができた気がした。以後、伊東さんにはさまざまな重要な場面でお世話になることになった。そのこともあって、それまで6畳ワンルームの自宅が仕事場でもあったのだが、ちゃんとした事務所スペースを借りるべきではないか、と考えて事務所を設立した。勿論仕事があったわけではないが、3年ぶりに入選したSDレビューの準備などで、にわかに事務所は活気づいた。その時に初めてオープンデスクに来てくれたのがまだ東工大の学生だった藤村龍至君だったのも思い出深い。そして冬には、最初のスタッフを雇うことになる。

2001

青森のコンペとスタッフが加わったことで、僕の建築的思考は勢いづいていた。といっても具体的な仕事はほとんどなかったのだが。そんな中で、今の活動にまで繋がる重要なプロジェクト「Primitive Future House」が生まれた。数年前から家具的なものと建築、そしてランドスケープを混ぜ合わせる方法を模索していて、いくつかのアイデアコンペや実施コンペを経て、ようやく建築形式として明確に現れてきたのだ。それは同時に、5年前に衝撃を受けた伊東さんのメディアテークへの僕なりの応答だった。応答に5年もかかっていたことが、なによりもその暗中模索ぶりを表している。このプロジェクトの最初のいくつかのモデルは、ミースの「ファンズワース邸」をベースにつくっていて、ミースに代わる新しい建築の在り方を見出したい、という思いが感じられる。
サーペンタインにまで繋がる、とても根源的な、重要な一歩だった。またこの年、自分の建築思考を初めて建築雑誌に寄稿した。とても短い文章だったが、＜部分の建築＞というタイトルで、プリゴジンや複雑系の理論にインスパイアされた、ローカルなネットワークによる新しい秩序の在り方を記述したものだった。
小嶋一浩さんに誘っていただき、初めての非常勤講師というものを東京理科大学で始めたのもこの年だった。教えるというコミュニケーションによって思考が広がる感覚が新鮮だった。
また講評会などを通して多くの建築家と交流が始まるきっかけともなった。

2002

青森のコンペ以降、いくつもの実施コンペにチャレンジした。なかでもこの年行われた群馬県「邑楽町役場」設計コンペは、最終審査に臨みながらそこで徹底的に批判されて惨敗するという悔しい思いをした。その経験が、翌年の「安中環境アートフォーラム」コンペ1等獲得へと繋がっていく。
この邑楽町コンペ案は、建築と樹木を組み合わせ

た初めての試みだった。「House N」や「House Before House」、「Omotesando Branches」など、以後のひとつの方法論となる樹木と建築の融合が始まった。この頃竣工したいくつかの建物を、友人の平田さんに、かなり辛辣に批判されたことをよく覚えている。
コンセプトと実現したものが整合していない、実現の方法が未熟で、コンセプトを建築化できていない、というものだった。悔しかった。しかし本当にその通りだと思った。
僕がどこの設計事務所でも働いていなかったゆえに抜け落ちていた部分だ。以後、いかにこの批判を克服して、本当の意味での建築をつくることができるかが大きな課題となった。

2003

この年は記憶に残っている。たぶん、初めて実施コンペで1等を獲ったことがまず大きかった。
群馬県安中でアートフォーラムという多目的広場のような建築をつくるコンペだった。前年に惨敗した同じ群馬の「邑楽町役場」コンペからの教訓を生かして、徹底的に準備をした結果の1等だっただけに、一段上のレベルに行けた気がした。それと前後して、初めて＜Primitive Future＞という言葉を使った原稿を建築雑誌に寄稿したのもこの年だった。最初は、依頼された原稿のタイトルとして、漠然と使い始めた言葉だったが、以後、いろいろな場面でこの言葉に立ち戻り、その意味はますます大きくなっていった。そのような流れから、95年、97年、そして2000年から4年連続、計7作品を出品したSDレビュー展の応募を、この年で最後にしようという決断が自然と起こった。

2004

この年、何をやっていたのかあまり思い出せない。たぶん、初めての住宅作品となる「T house」の設計と現場に没頭していたからだろう。この建物はプランも野心的だったが、構造や仕上げの考え方、窓納まりや電気の線の見せ方など、建築のすべてを自分たちで再定義していくような作業であった。以前に平田さんから批判されていた＜建築をつくるということ＞と真っ向から向き合っていた時期だった。海外で初めてレクチャーをしたのもこの年だった。クアラルンプールでのレクチャーのために、機内で必死に手書き原稿を書いたことを思い出す。

2005

初めての住宅である「T house」が竣工した。離れていながら繋がっている、という建築の本質的な問いを形にした野心作だ。しかも基本構想からディテールに至るまで、徹底的に突き詰めていった。施主の寛容がそれを可能にしてくれた。

いまだに伊東さん藤森さんは、この「T house」が僕の作品の中で1番良いという。それはちょっと悔しいが、でも嬉しい言葉だ。
この年の冬に、「Final Wooden House」のコンペで1等に選ばれた。審査委員長は伊東さんだった。青森のコンペから5年ようやく伊東さんに恩返しができた。
12月、ロンドンの『The Architectural Review』誌のアワードで、「伊達の援護寮」が優秀賞に選ばれて、初めてロンドンを訪れた。
表彰会場に行ってみると、1等は、当時同じ大学で非常勤講師をしていた西沢大良さんだった。嬉しかったが、悔しかった。いつかグランプリを獲りたいと誓ってロンドンを去った。翌年それがかなうとはまだ知らなかったが。

2006

「児童心理治療施設」が竣工した。
一連の北海道の医療施設シリーズの集大成だ。前年悔しい思いをしたARアワードの大賞に選ばれたことで、少しずつ海外での講演会の依頼が入り始めた。まだこの頃は、原稿を書いて、それを読むというスタイルだった。
今行っているレクチャーに比べればとても稚拙なものだったと思うが、それでも興味をもってくれる人がいることが大きな励みになった。「House N」と「Tokyo Apartment」の構想が生まれたのもこの年だ。まだざっとした模型しかできていなかったが、これらが重要なプロジェクトになることが強く感じられたので、あえて未完成の状態で雑誌に発表したのだった。

2007

春に「武蔵野美術大学美術館・図書館」の指名プロポーザルで設計者に選出された。
今思い出してみると、このプロポーザルの提出資料は、コンセプトからテキスト、画像およびダイアグラムまで、すべてを僕ひとりでつくったのだった。設計図を描いてはいけないコンセプトとビジョンのみのコンペだったこともあり、また作業が本当に提出当日のぎりぎりまでかかってしまったこともあり、自分の脳内と提出書類を直結させてひとりでつくり切るしかなかったのだ。
この規模の建築経験がなかった僕を選んでくれた施主に感謝したい。
また春から始まったTokyo Gasの「Sumikaプロジェクト」も思い出される。伊東豊雄さん、藤森照信さん、西沢大良さんと僕とで、それぞれがひとつずつ小さな住宅やパヴィリオンを設計するプロジェクト。
個別に設計しながら、打ち合わせは皆一緒に行うことで、それぞれの設計の仕方の違いや個性がリアルに感じられた。

2008

この年は、4月に出版された初めての作品集『原初的な未来の建築』(2008年、INAX出版)の出版準備で幕を開けた。自分の建築思考をイメージとテキストでどう表現するのか、構成からレイアウトに至るまで自分の納得するまでつくり込んだ思い出深い本である。また、「House N」と「Final Wooden House」という、自分にとっても、そして世界的な評価という意味でもとても重要なプロジェクトが竣工した年でもあった。11月にバルセロナで行われたワールドアーキテクチャーフェスティバルで「Final Wooden House」が住宅部門の最優秀賞に選ばれたこともあり、海外でのレクチャーへの招待が激増していった。また現事務所である神楽坂のスペースに移転したのもこの年である。「オルドス100」という不思議なプロジェクトに参加したことも忘れがたい。内モンゴルの砂漠に100人の建築家が集まり、別荘をつくるプロジェクト。砂漠の真ん中のホリデイ・インに、大勢の建築家が集合しているさまは奇妙だった。このとき世界中の建築家に出会えたことは貴重な財産だ。写真家のイワン・バーンさんと最初に会ったのは、この敷地の砂漠の真ん中だった。いかにもイワンさんらしい気がする。

2009

2009年は「武蔵野美術大学美術館・図書館」の現場がやはり大きかった。スペインの出版社GGから2Gシリーズの作品集を出してもらえることになったことも大きかった。前年に出た『原初的な未来の建築』がどちらかというとコンセプトブック的な本であったのに対し、これはまさに本格的な作品集だった。さらにこの年の年末、同じくスペインのエル・クロッキース (EL Croquis) から作品集を出したいという連絡があった。エルクロは学生時代から憧れていた作品集のシリーズだったので、なんだか恐ろしいような嬉しさを感じたのを覚えている。

2010

この年あたりから、本当に毎年いろいろなことがあって、思い出してみてもよくやっていたなと思う。春に「武蔵野美術大学美術館・図書館」が竣工した。今思い返してもとても苦労した建物だったが、この規模の建築を、身体スケールと空間のコンセプト、そして複雑な機能を複合させて実現できたことで、目の前が開けた気がした。二川幸夫さんが初めて撮影してくれた建物だった。僕自身は撮影に同行できなかったが、二川さんがとても喜んでくださっていたと聞いた。嬉しかった。前後して、阿部仁史さんに呼んでいただいて、初めて海外で教えることとなったUCLAでの非常勤講師が始まった。新婚旅行でモロッコを訪れたこともとても大きな忘れぬ体験だった。夏には僕の初めての展覧会が、ワタリウム美術館で始まった。そして妹島和世さんに誘って頂き、初めてのヴェネチアビエンナーレに参加。秋にはエル・クロッキースが出版された。

2011

大震災があったこの年は忘れがたい。震災のあとも建築家としてどうしていいのか分からず、ただひたすらに設計に打ち込んでいた。結果として、この年にはふたつの国際コンペで1等に選ばれた。春から夏にかけて、セルビアの首都ベオグラードで行われた「ベトンハラウォーターフロントセンター」という都市広場と文化商業の複合施設のコンペでは、何度も現地に足を運んだ。秋から冬にかけては、台湾の台中市に高さ300mのタワーを建てる「台湾タワー」コンペで勝利した。どちらもかなり大きな規模のものだが、数年前からチャレンジして少しずつ蓄積を重ねてきた海外大規模コンペの経験が開花したものだった。以後台湾でのプロジェクトが入るようになる。5月にはデンマークのルイジアナ美術館での展覧会に参加。美術館のランドスケープと建築の見事な融合に感銘を受け、これ以降、自然と建築、ランドスケープと建築が溶け合うさまを、より意識するようになっていった。しかしこれらの活動の背後では、震災後の世界で、自分は何もできないのではないか、という無力感が消えなかった。そんな時、伊東豊雄さんから、ヴェネチアビエンナーレで協働しないかというお誘いを受けた。被災地でのプロジェクトを世界に問うことで、この先の建築の思考をしたい、という伊東さんの熱い思いに突き動かされ、乾久美子さん、平田晃久さん、写真家の畠山直哉さんとのチームによる、1年にわたる＜陸前高田のプロジェクト＞が始まった。

2012

前年から続く＜陸前高田のプロジェクト＞は、時に週1回のペースなど、かなり頻繁に打ち合わせが続いていた。このプロセスを通して、僕は、個と共同体が分かれる以前の、未分化の原始共同体から、建築が、場として、つまり人と人、人ともの、人と場所、人と歴史と未来に繋がる場として、必然的に建ち現れるさまを実感した気がする。建築というものの根源に出会えた気がした。そして8月のヴェネチアビエンナーレで僕たち日本館は、金獅子賞を受賞した。冬の初めには、陸前高田の地に＜みんなの家＞ができあがった。ドイツの小都市ビーレフェルドの美術館で、海外での初めての展覧会が始まったのもこの年の春だった。相変わらず国内外を移動する中で、11月、サーペンタインギャラリーからの手紙が届いた。10年以上前から、いつかはやってみたいと夢に見ていたサーペンタインギャラリーパヴィリオンの設計依頼だった。過酷で、でもとてもエキサイティングで、2度と味わうことができないであろう濃密な6か月がスタートした。

2013

「Serpentine Gallery Pavilion 2013」のプロジェクトは、僕たちが、今までやってきたこと、現在考えていること、そして未来に向けての予感のすべてを含み込んだ何かになるべきだった。ロンドンで行われた最初の打ち合わせで＜現代のバルセロナパヴィリオンをつくってください＞と言われた時には震えた。それは自分を見つめる作業であるだけでなく、建築と世界の根源と未来を思考することだった。年明け早々、サーペンタインのダイレクターのジュリアさんが事務所に来て、案をプレゼン、その場で即OKが出た。ジュリアさんとは本当になんども大げんかしたが、それが案を鍛え上げてくれた。今では親子のように思ってくれていると思う。いや姉弟というべきだろうか。そこからは毎日のようにロンドン－東京の電話会議が行われ、エンジニアと施工者も交えてとてつもないスピード感で設計が進んでいった。もうひとりのディレクター、ハンス・ウルリッヒさんがとの対話によって案の本質が鋭くあぶり出された。オープニングの1週間は、忘れがたい。ロンドンには珍しく、1週間晴れっぱなしで、その初夏の光の下、パヴィリオンは光そのもののようであった。多くの人びとが訪れ、思い思いに時間を過ごしていた。このプロジェクトは、たしかに自分のキャリアの中の最大のターニングポイントとなるであろう。もうひとつ、この年にはとても大きな出来事があった。前年から準備をしていた二川幸夫さんの＜日本の民家＞の展覧会が1月に始まった。二川さんに最初に案をプレゼンした時のことは忘れがたい。僕の説明が終わるか終わらないかの内に＜これは良いね＞という大きな声が部屋に響き渡って、それで即決だった。準備の際に二川さんが話してくれた当時の思い出話はとてもリアルで生き生きとしていた。オープニングの直前に会場にチェックに来られた二川さんとふたりで会場内を歩き回ったことも思い出される。小声でささやくように話されるすべての言葉に耳を傾けた。オープニングの日、二川さんは本当に嬉しそうにしておられた。それが何よりも嬉しかった。そして間もない3月に、二川さんが他界されたのを知った。

2014

春に、南フランスの美しい街、モンペリエで集合住宅を設計するコンペに勝利。それもあって、パリに何度も足を運んだ。夏には初めてブラジルを訪れた。ブラジリア、リオ、サンパウロを回り、ニーマイヤーをはじめとするブラジル建築は僕にとって新しいインスピレーションだった。北京での指名コンペとブダペストのオープンコンペに勝利して2015年へと踏み出していく。

Data on Works
作品データ

Number of Work/ 作品番号
Name of Work
作品名
1   Location / 所在地
2   Design period / 設計期間
3   Construction period ／ 施工期間
4   Principal use ／ 主要用途
5   Joint design ／ 共同設計
6   Structure / 構造
7   Scale ／ 規模
8   Structural engineer ／ 構造設計
9   Facility engineer ／ 設備設計
10 Contructor ／ 施工
11 Site area ／ 敷地面積
12 Building area ／ 建築面積
13 Total floor area ／ 延床面積

001 House of Gradation
2   1995.02-1995.04
4   Private House / 専用住宅

002 Seidai Hospital Occupational Therapy Ward
聖台病院作業療法棟
1   Hokkaido, Japan / 北海道、日本
2   1995.04-1996.03
3   1996.04-1996.08
4   Medical Facility / 医療施設
6   Reinforced Concrete
    /鉄筋コンクリート造
7   2 stories / 地上 2 階
8   Ishiguro Architects / 石黒設計事務所
10 TOSEI KENSETU,.co.ltd / 東成建設
11 28,267.55㎡
12 168.51㎡
13 181.23㎡

003 Network by Walk
1   Tokyo, Japan / 東京都、日本
2   1997.05-1997.07
4   Private House / 専用住宅

004 Seidai Hospital Annex
聖台病院新病棟
1   Hokkaido, Japan / 北海道、日本
2   1998.02 -1999.01
3   1999.02-1999.06
4   Medical Facility / 医療施設
6   Masonry structure / ブロック造
7   1 storey / 地上 1 階
8   Ishiguro Architects / 石黒設計事務所
9   Office Saito / オフィスサイトー
10 TOSEI KENSETU,.co.ltd / 東成建設
11 28,845.55㎡
12 426.42㎡
13 426.42㎡

005 Art Museum in Aomori
青森県立美術館
1   Aomori, Japan / 青森県、日本
2   1999.10-2000.03
4   Museum / 美術館
6   Steel Frame / 鉄骨造
7   2 stories / 地上 2 階
11 129536.37㎡
12 6907.47㎡
13 10868.03㎡

006 Day-care Center
1   Hokkaido, Japan / 北海道、日本
2   2000.06 – 2000.09
4   Medical Facility
    / 医療施設
6   Steel Frame / 鉄骨造
7   2 stories / 地上 2 階
8   Jun Sato Structural Engineers
    / 佐藤淳構造設計事務所
11 34,217㎡
12 204.8㎡
13 274.5㎡

007 Primitive Future House
2   2001.06 – 2001.09
4   Private House / 専用住宅
6   Steel Frame / 鉄骨造
8   Jun Sato Structural Engineers
    / 佐藤淳構造設計事務所

008 Oura Town Hall
邑楽町役場
1   Gunma, Japan / 群馬県、日本
2   2000.01 – 2002.03
4   town hall / 役場
6   Steel Frame / 鉄骨造
7   2stories / 地上 2 階
8   Jun Sato Structural Engineers
    / 佐藤淳構造設計事務所
11 23,000㎡
12 7965㎡
13 11,019.72㎡

009 Glass Cloud
1   Tokyo, Japan / 東京都 , 日本
2   2002.06 – 2002.09
4   Private House / 専用住宅
7   Steel Frame / 鉄骨造
8   3 stories / 地上 3 階
9   ARUP
12 83.90㎡
13 50.12㎡
14 122.20㎡

010 Hana Café
2   2002.06 – 2002.09
4   Cafe / カフェ
6   ポリカーボネート成型
    /Polycarbonate Resin

011 Shijima Lodge
しじま山荘
1   Nagano, Japan / 長野県、日本
2   2000.10-2002.08
3   2002.08-2002.11
4   Lodging facility / 宿泊施設
6   Timber frame、reinforced concrete
    / 木造、鉄筋コンクリート造
7   1 basement、1 storey
    / 地下 1 階、地上 1 階
8   Jun Sato Structural Engineers
    / 佐藤淳構造設計事務所
11 1388.26㎡
12 62.12㎡
13 117.59㎡

012 House N (Preliminary version)
1   Oita, Japan / 大分県、日本
2   2003.06-2003.09
4   Private House / 専用住宅
6   Timber frame / 木造
7   2 stories / 地上 2 階
8   Jun Sato Structural Engineers
    / 佐藤淳構造設計事務所
11 223.54㎡
12 97.65㎡（増築部分 25.65㎡）
13 139.65㎡（増築部分 25.65㎡）

013 Dormitory in Date
伊達の援護寮
1   Hokkaido, Japan / 北海道、日本
2   2001.12-2003.09
3   2003.09-2003.12
4   Medical Facility / 医療施設
6   Steel Frame / 鉄骨造
7   2 stories / 地上 2 階
8   Jun Sato Structural Engineers
    / 佐藤淳構造設計事務所
10 HIRAGUCHI KENSETU,.co.ltd / 平口建設
11 5,402.34㎡
12 405.54㎡
13 567.00㎡

014 Annaka Environmental Art Forum
安中環境アートフォーラム
1   Gunma, Japan / 群馬県、日本
2   2003.08-2004.08
4   Hall / 多目的ホール
6   Steel Frame / 鉄骨造
7   1 storey / 地上 1 階
8   Jun Sato Structural Engineers
    / 佐藤淳構造設計事務所
11 29159.023㎡
12 7091.56㎡
13 7091.56㎡

015 T house
1   Gunma, Japan / 群馬県、日本
2   2003.01-2004.06
3   2004.06-2005.02
4   Private House / 専用住宅
6   Timber frame / 木造
7   1 storey/ 地上 1 階
8   Jun Sato Structural Engineers
    / 佐藤淳構造設計事務所
10 Yasumatsu Takken Co., Ltd / 安松託建
11 144.47㎡
12 90.82㎡
13 90.82㎡

016 Atelier in Hokkaido
1   Hokkaido, Japan / 北海道、日本
2   2005.01-2005.06
4   Atelier+ Private House / アトリエ兼住宅
6   Timber frame / 木造
7   1 basement, 3 stories / 地下 1 階、地上 3 階
8   Jun Sato Structural Engineers
    / 佐藤淳構造設計事務所
11 28,267.55㎡
12 61.56㎡
13 126.79㎡

017 House in Hayama
1   Kanagawa, Japan / 神奈川県、日本
2   2005.11-2006.04
4   Private House / 専用住宅
6   Reinforced Concrete / 鉄筋コンクリート造
7   1 basement, 2 stories / 地下 1 階、地上 2 階
8   Jun Sato Structural Engineers
    / 佐藤淳構造設計事務所
11 468.60㎡
12 247.00㎡
13 561.00㎡

018 Residential treatment center for emotionally disturbed children
児童心理治療施設
1   Hokkaido, Japan / 北海道、日本
2   2004.07-2005.07
3   2005.07-2006.05
4   Medical Facility / 医療施設
6   Reinforced Concrete / 鉄筋コンクリート造
7   2 stories / 地上 2 階
8   Jun Sato Structural Engineers
    / 佐藤淳構造設計事務所

9　SIRIUS LIGHTIG OFFICE (lighting Design)
　　シリウスライティングオフィス（照明）
10　SHIMIZU CORPORATION / 清水建設
11　14,590.00㎡
12　1,604.62㎡
13　2,536.49㎡

019　7/2 House
1　Hokkaido, Japan / 北海道、日本
2　2004.07-2005.07
3　2005.07-2006.05
4　Medical Facility / 医療施設
6　Timber frame / 木造
7　1 storey/ 地上 1 階
8　Jun Sato Structural Engineers
　　/ 佐藤淳構造設計事務所
10　SHIMIZU CORPORATION、Asamizu Corporation
　　/ 清水建設、浅水建設
11　14,590.00㎡
12　102.06㎡
13　102.06㎡

020　House O
1　Chiba, Japan / 千葉県、日本
2　2006.01-2006.06
3　2006.07-2007.05
4　Private House / 専用住宅
6　Reinforced Concrete
　　/ 鉄筋コンクリート造
7　1 storey / 地上 1 階
8　Jun Sato Structural Engineers
　　/ 佐藤淳構造設計事務所
9　SIRIUS LIGHTIG OFFICE (lighting Design)
　　シリウスライティングオフィス（照明）
10　artweb-house / アートウェブハウス
11　656.46㎡
12　127.97㎡
13　127.97㎡

021　Spiral House
1　Tokyo, Japan / 東京都、日本
2　2007.04-2007.08
4　Private House / 専用住宅
6　Reinforced Concrete / 鉄筋コンクリート造
7　1 storey / 地上 1 階
11　93㎡
12　90㎡
13　90㎡

022　House Inside-Out Tree
2　2007.09-2009.03
4　Private House / 専用住宅

023　Dubai Skyscraper
1　Dubai, UAE
　　/ ドバイ、アラブ首長国連邦
2　2007.11-2008.01
4　Observation Tower / 展望台
6　Steel Frame / 鉄骨造
7　1 basement ,2 stories / 地上 2 階、地下 1 階
8　Jun Sato Structural Engineers
　　/ 佐藤淳構造設計事務所
12　866.96㎡
13　7,125㎡

024　Kumamoto station plaza
　　熊本駅前広場
1　Kumamoto, Japan
　　/ 熊本県、日本
2　2008.01-2008.03
4　Plaza / 駅前広場
6　Steel Frame / 鉄骨造
7　1 storey / 地上 1 階
8　Jun Sato Structural Engineers
　　/ 佐藤淳構造設計事務所
11　5,700㎡
12　2500㎡

025　Empty House
2　2007.09-2009.03
4　Private House / 専用住宅

026　House/Garden
1　Tochigi, Japan / 栃木県、日本
2　2007.11-2009.09
4　Private House / 専用住宅
6　Reinforced Concrete / 鉄筋コンクリート造
7　2 stories / 地上 2 階
8　Jun Sato Structural Engineers
　　/ 佐藤淳構造設計事務所
11　405.12㎡
12　63.86㎡
13　83.05㎡

027　House N
1　Oita, Japan / 大分県、日本
2　2006.10-2007.03
3　2007.09-2008.06
4　Private House
　　/ 専用住宅
6　Reinforced Concrete
　　/ 鉄筋コンクリート造
7　1 storey / 地上 1 階
8　Jun Sato Structural Engineers
　　/ 佐藤淳構造設計事務所
9　SIRIUS LIGHTIG OFFICE (lighting Design)
　　シリウスライティングオフィス（照明）
10　Saiki Kensetsu Co., Ltd / 佐伯建設
11　236.57㎡
12　150.57㎡
13　85.51㎡

028　house/trees in Basel
1　Basel, Switzerland
　　/ バーゼル、スイス
2　2008.01-2008.05
3　2008.05-2008.06
4　Pavilion / パヴィリオン
6　Acrylic / アクリル
7　1 storey / 地上 1 階
8　Jun Sato Structural Engineers
　　/ 佐藤淳構造設計事務所
12　12.5㎡
13　12.5㎡

029　Final Wooden House
1　Kumamoto, Japan
　　/ 熊本県、日本
2　2005.11-2006.12
3　2007.12-2008.07
4　Lodging facility
　　/ 宿泊施設
6　Timber frame / 木造
7　1 storey+Mezzanine
　　/ 地上 1 階+ロフト
8　Jun Sato Structural Engineers
　　/ 佐藤淳構造設計事務所
9　SIRIUS LIGHTIG OFFICE (lighting Design)
　　シリウスライティングオフィス（照明）
10　Tanakagumi
　　/ 田中組
12　15.13㎡
13　22.63㎡

030　House before House
1　Tochigi, Japan
　　/ 栃木県、日本
2　2007.04-2008.08
3　2008.06-2008.11
4　Private House
　　/ 専用住宅
6　Steel Frame / 鉄骨造
7　3 stories / 地上 3 階
8　Jun Sato Structural Engineers
　　/ 佐藤淳構造設計事務所

9　SIRIUS LIGHTIG OFFICE (lighting Design)
　　/ シリウスライティングオフィス（照明）
10　AGA Construction Co., Ltd
　　/ アガ設計工業
11　163.43㎡
12　59.48㎡
13　61.31㎡

031　Benetton Building
1　Teheran, Iran / テヘラン、イラン
2　2009.01-2009.03
4　Office / 事務所
6　Steel Frame
　　/ 鉄骨造
7　7 stories / 地上 7 階
8　Jun Sato Structural Engineers
　　/ 佐藤淳構造設計事務所
11　750㎡
12　700㎡
13　7,125㎡

032　Sumida Hokusai Museum
　　墨田区北斎会館
1　Tokyo, Japan / 東京都、日本
2　2009.01-2009.03
4　Museum / 美術館
6　Reinforced Concrete / 鉄筋コンクリート造
7　4 stories, 1 basement / 地上 4 階、地下 1 階
8　Jun Sato Structural Engineers
　　/ 佐藤淳構造設計事務所
11　72.28㎡
12　50.52㎡
13　124.87㎡

033　City as Architecture, Architecture as Mountain, Mountain as City
　　建築のような都市、都市のような山、山のような建築
1　Tokyo, Japan / 東京都、日本
2　2008.06-2009.06
4　Mixed-use complex / 複合施設
6　Steel Frame / 鉄骨造
7　25 basements ,25 stories
　　地下 25 階、地上 25 階
8　Jun Sato Structural Engineers
　　/ 佐藤淳構造設計事務所
11　17,500㎡
12　15,000㎡
13　91,779㎡

034　Peak-Oslo National Museum
1　Oslo, Norway / オスロ、ノルウェー
2　2009.03-2009.06
4　Museum / 美術館
6　Steel Frame / 鉄骨造
7　1 basement,7 stories / 地下 1 階、地上 7 階
8　Jun Sato Structural Engineers
　　/ 佐藤淳構造設計事務所
11　34,500㎡
12　12,500㎡
13　54,000㎡

035　House as water way
2　2008.02-2008.08
4　Private House / 専用住宅
6　Steel Frame / 鉄骨造
7　5 stories / 地上 5 階
12　100㎡
13　500㎡

036　House H
1　Tokyo, Japan / 東京都、日本
2　2006.12-2008.04
3　2008.04-2009.07
4　Private House / 専用住宅
6　Reinforced Concrete
　　/ 鉄筋コンクリート造

7   3 stories / 地上 3 階
8   Jun Sato Structural Engineers
    / 佐藤淳構造設計事務所
9   SIRIUS LIGHTIG OFFICE (lighting Design)
    シリウスライティングオフィス（照明）
10 Heisei Construction Co., Ltd
    / 平成建設
11 72.28㎡
12 50.52㎡
13 124.87㎡

037 Art Museum in China
1   China / 中国
2   2008.05-2009.07
4   Museum / 美術館
6   Reinforced Concrete
    / 鉄筋コンクリート造
7   3 story / 地上 3 階
12 4638㎡
13 6000㎡

038 Another Island
    もう一つの島
1   Kagawa, Japan / 香川県、日本
2   2009.06-2009.08
4   Installation / インスタレーション

039 1000㎡ House -ORDOS 100
1   Ordos, China / オルドス、中国
2   2008.06-2009.08
4   Private House / 専用住宅
6   Reinforced Concrete
    / 鉄筋コンクリート造
7   1 basement、2 story
    / 地下 1 階、地上 2 階
8   Jun Sato Structural Engineers
    / 佐藤淳構造設計事務所
11 1000㎡
12 600㎡
13 1000㎡

040 Gunma Agricultural Technology Center
    群馬県農業技術センター
1   Gunma, Japan / 群馬県、日本
2   2009.07-2009.09
4   Research Institute / 研究所
6   Steel Frame, Reinforced Concrete
    / 鉄骨造、鉄筋コンクリート造
7   1 storey / 地上 1 階
11 14,835.83㎡
12 2,396.28㎡
13 2,396.28㎡

041 Taipei Pop Music Center
1   Taipei, Taiwan / 台北、台湾
2   2009.08-2009.10
4   Mixed-use complex / 複合施設
6   Steel Frame / 鉄骨造
7   1 basement, 6 stories
    / 地下 1 階、地上 6 階
11 76,500㎡
12 60,000㎡
13 40,000㎡

042 Kogakuin University Hachioji campus
    工学院大学八王子キャンパス
1   Tokyo, Japan / 東京都、日本
2   2009.10-2009.12
4   University Building / 大学施設
6   Steel Frame / 鉄骨造
7   1 basement, 6 stories
    / 地下 1 階、地上 6 階
8   ARUP
9   ARUP
11 220,000㎡
12 3,686㎡
13 8,395㎡

043 Tokyo Apartment
1   Tokyo, Japan / 東京都、日本
2   2006.03-2009.05
3   2009.05-2010.03
4   Collective Housing / 長屋
6   Timber frame / 木造
7   1 basement, 3 stories / 地下 1 階、地上 3 階
8   Jun Sato Structural Engineers
    / 佐藤淳構造設計事務所
10 UBM
11 83.14㎡
12 58.19㎡
13 180.70㎡

044 Musashino Art University
    Museum & Library
    武蔵野美術大学美術館・図書館
1   Tokyo, Japan/ 東京都、日本
2   2007.04-2009.02
3   2009.03-2010.03
4   大学図書館 /University Library
6   Steel Frame, Reinforced Concrete
    / 鉄骨造、鉄筋コンクリート造
7   1 basement, 2 stories / 地下 1 階、地上 2 階
8   Jun Sato Structural Engineers
    / 佐藤淳構造設計事務所
9   KANKYO-ENGINEERING, SIRIUS LIGHTIG OFFICE
    (lighting Design), Taku Satoh Design
    Office(Sign,Furniture) / 環境エンジニアリング
    シリウスライティングオフィス（照明）、佐藤卓
    デザイン事務所（家具・サイン）
10 TAISEI CORPORATION / 大成建設
11 111,691㎡
12 2,883㎡
13 6,419㎡

045 House OM
1   Kanagawa, Japan / 神奈川県、日本
2   2007.09-2009.03
3   2009.03-2010.03
4   Private House / 専用住宅
6   Reinforced Concrete / 鉄筋コンクリート造
7   3 stories / 地上 3 階
8   Jun Sato Structural Engineers
    / 佐藤淳構造設計事務所
10 UBM
11 72.72㎡
12 43.60㎡
13 97.07㎡

046 House as Cloud
1   Hokkaido, Japan / 北海道、日本
2   2008.09-2009.02
4   Private House / 専用住宅
6   Steel Frame / 鉄骨造
7   1 storey / 地上 1 階
11 28,267.55㎡
12 330.04㎡
13 66.58㎡

047 Cloud Bridge
1   Maribor, Slovenia / マリボル、スロベニア
2   2010.01-2010.03
4   Bridge / 橋
6   Steel Frame / 鉄骨造
7   1 storey / 地上 1 階
8   Jun Sato Structural Engineers
    / 佐藤淳構造設計事務所
12 1,574.5㎡
13 1,574.5㎡

048 Inside Outside Tree
1   London, United Kingdom / ロンドン、イギリス
2   2009.09-2010.03
3   2010.03-2010.04
4   Installation / インスタレーション
6   Acrylic / アクリル

7   1 storey / 地上 1 階
8   Jun Sato Structural Engineers
    / 佐藤淳構造設計事務所
12 9㎡
13 9㎡

049 House B
1   Hanover, Germany / ハノーファー、ドイツ
2   2008.03-2009.03
3   2009.03-2010.05
4   Private House Renovation
    / 専用住宅 改修
7   2 stories / 地上 2 階
8   ARUP
9   ARUP
11 1,300㎡
12 446.28㎡
13 376.11㎡

050 Vertical Forest
1   London, United Kingdom / ロンドン、イギリス
2   2010.05-2010.07
4   Tower / タワー
6   Reinforced Concrete / 鉄筋コンクリート造
7   12 stories / 地上 12 階
8   Jun Sato Structural Engineers
    / 佐藤淳構造設計事務所
10 400㎡
11 55㎡
12 370㎡

051 UNIQLO Shinsaibashi
    UNIQLO 心斎橋店
1   Osaka,Japan / 大阪府、日本
2   2009.03-2008.08
3   2009.09-2010.09
4   Shop / 物販店舗
6   Reinforced Concrete, Steel Frame
    / 鉄筋コンクリート造、鉄骨造
7   1 basement,4 stories
    / 地下 1 階、地上 4 階
8   NIKKEN SEKKEI LTD
    OBAYASHI CORPORATION
    / 日建設計、大林組
9   NIKKEN SEKKEI LTD
    OBAYASHI CORPORATION
    SIRIUS LIGHTIG OFFICE (lighting Design)
    / 日建設計、大林組
    シリウスライティングオフィス（照明）
10 OBAYASHI CORPORATION
    / 大林組
11 1,190.37㎡
12 995.95㎡
13 4,631.13㎡

052 Nube Arena
1   Murcia, Spain / ムルシア、スペイン
2   2010.06-2010.08
4   Theatre / 劇場
6   Gras Arquitectos
6   Steel Frame / 鉄骨造
7   2 basements, 4 stories
    / 地下 2 階、地上 4 階
8   ARUP
9   ARUP
11 3,600㎡
12 1,256㎡
13 5,344㎡

053 Kultur Projekte Berlin
1   Berlin, Germany / ベルリン、ドイツ
2   2010.11-2011.01
4   Exhibition Space / 展覧会会場
6   Balloon / バルーン
7   1 storey / 地上 1 階
12 2,500㎡
13 2,500㎡

054 LA Small House
1. Los Angeles, USA
   / ロサンゼルス、USA
2. 2009.08-2010.02
4. Summer House / 別荘
6. Steel Frame+Stone / 鉄骨造、石
7. 2 stories / 地上 2 階
8. ARUP
12. 13.8㎡
13. 13㎡

055 House NA
1. Tokyo, Japan / 東京都、日本
2. 2007.02-2009.12
3. 2010.01-2011.04
4. Private House / 専用住宅
6. Steel Frame / 鉄骨造
7. 3 stories / 地上 3 階
8. Jun Sato Structural Engineers
   / 佐藤淳構造設計事務所
10. Heisei Construction Co., Ltd / 平成建設
11. 53.77㎡
12. 32.33㎡
13. 84.91㎡

056 Tree Skyscraper
1. Humlebaek, Denmark / フムルベック、デンマーク
2. 2011.01-2011.05

057 Louisiana Cloud
1. Humlebaek, Denmark / フムルベック、デンマーク
2. 2011.01-2011.05

058 Layered Plaza
2. 2012.05 –2014.12
4. Pubric Plaza / 都市広場
6. Steel Frame, Reinforced Concrete
   / 鉄骨造、鉄筋コンクリート造

059 Garden Gallery
1. Cologne, Germany / ケルン、ドイツ
2. 2010.06 – 2011.01
3. 2011.02 – 2011.05
4. Pavilion / パヴィリオン
6. Reinforced Concrete
   / 鉄筋コンクリート造
7. 1 storey / 地上 1 階
11. 34,300㎡
12. 140㎡
13. 140㎡

060 sacai Minamiaoyama
sacai 南青山店
1. Tokyo, Japan / 東京都、日本
2. 2011.05-2011.08
3. 2011.08 -2011.09
4. Shop / 物販店舗
5. Daisuke Gemma Office
   / 源馬大輔事務所
6. Reinforced Concrete
   / 鉄筋コンクリート造
7. 3 story / 地上 3 階
10. F.H.C.
13. 405.85㎡

061 Beton Hala Waterfront Center
1. Belgrade, Serbia / ベオグラード、セルビア
2. 2011.03-2011.10
4. Mixed-use complex / 複合施設
5. AAA
6. Steel Frame / 鉄骨造
7. 4 stories / 地上 4 階
8. ARUP
9. ARUP
11. 92,300㎡
12. 22,194㎡
13. 34,741㎡

062 Jyoshutomioka Station
上州富岡駅舎
1. Gunma, Japan / 群馬県、日本
2. 2011.04-2011.06
4. Station,Plaza / 駅舎、駅前広場
6. Steel Frame / 鉄骨造
7. 1 storey / 地上 1 階
8. ARUP
9. ARUP
11. 1,311.81㎡
12. 750㎡
13. 750㎡

063 Taiwan Tower
台湾タワー
1. Taichung, Taiwan / 台中、台湾
2. 2011.11-
4. Observation Tower, Museum
   / 展望台、美術館
5. Fei&Cheng Associates / 宗邁建築師事務所
6. Steel Frame, Reinforced Concrete
   / 鉄骨造、鉄筋コンクリート造
7. 2 basements, 13 stories / 地下 2 階、地上 13 階
8. ARUP
   SUPERTECH CONSULTANTS INTERNATIONAL
   / ARUP、超偉工程顧問有限公司
9. ARUP
   HENG KAI ENGINEERING CONSULTANTS INC.
   SIRIUS LIGHTIG OFFICE (lighting Design)
   UNOLAI DESIGN(lighting Design)
   dA VISION DESIGN （LANDSCAPE）
   / ARUP、恆凱工程顧問有限公司、シリウスライティングオフィス（照明）
   十津照明設計有限公司（照明）
   達觀規劃設計顧問有限公司（ランドスケープ）
11. 43,398㎡
12. 10,000㎡
13. 46,600㎡

064 Geometric Forest -SOLO Houses Project
1. Cretas, Spain / クレタス、スペイン
2. 2011.10-
4. Guest House / ゲストハウス
6. Timber frame, Reinforced Concrete
   / 木造、鉄筋コンクリート造
7. 1 basement, 2 stories / 地下 1 階、地上 2 階
12. 196㎡
13. 222㎡

065 FOREST OF SILENCE
1. Zemst, Belgium / ゼムスト、ベルギー
2. 2011.10-2011.12
4. Crematorium / 葬祭場
5. VDDR Architecten
6. Steel Frame / 鉄骨造
7. 1 storey / 地上 1 階
8. B.A.S. bvba
9. RCR-studiebureau、Daidalos Peutz
11. 29,401㎡
12. 9,461㎡
13. 2,905㎡

066 Toilet in Nature
1. Chiba, Japan / 千葉県、日本
2. 2011.08-2011.12
3. 2012.01-2012.03
4. Public toilet / 公衆トイレ
6. Steel Frame, Timber frame / 鉄骨造、木造
7. 1 storey / 地上 1 階
8. Jun Sato Structural Engineers
   / 佐藤淳構造設計事務所
9. Archi Build Co.,ltd
   / 株式会社アーキビルド
10. Sakuma juken / 佐久間住研
11. 643.56㎡
12. 209.48㎡
13. 209.48㎡

067 House K
1. Hyogo, Japan / 兵庫県、日本
2. 2010.07-2011.06
3. 2011.07-2012.07
4. Private House / 専用住宅
6. Steel Frame / 鉄骨造
7. 2 stories / 地上 2 階
8. Jun Sato Structural Engineers
   / 佐藤淳構造設計事務所
9. SIRIUS LIGHTIG OFFICE (lighting Design)
   / シリウスライティングオフィス（照明）
10. TOKUOKA KOUMUTEN Co.,Ltd.
    / 徳岡工務店
11. 310.24㎡
12. 118.23㎡
13. 118.23㎡

068 Home-for-All in Rikuzentakata
陸前高田みんなの家
1. Iwate, Japan / 岩手県、日本
2. 2011.10-2012.05
3. 2012.05-2012.11
4. Gatherring Place / 集会場
5. Toyo Ito&Associates Architects
   office of kumiko inui
   akihisa hirata architecture office
   伊東豊雄建築設計事務所
   乾久美子建築設計事務所
   平田晃久建築設計事務所
6. Timber frame / 木造
7. 2 stories / 地上 2 階
8. Jun Sato Structural Engineers
   / 佐藤淳構造設計事務所
10. SHELTER CO,LTD.
    / 株式会社シェルター
11. 901.71㎡
12. 30.18㎡
13. 29.96㎡

069 No Dog, No Life
-ARCHITECTURE FOR DOG
1. Tokyo, Japan / 東京都、日本
2. 2012.02-2012.08
4. Dog House / 犬小屋
5. Kenya Hara/ 原研哉
6. Timber frame / 木造
7. 1 storey/ 地上 1 階
12. 0.64㎡
13. 0.64㎡

070 Smallest/Largest Art Museum
1. Aix-en-Provence, France
   / エクサンプロヴァンス、フランス
2. 2009.11-
4. Gallery / ギャラリー
6. Timber frame / 木造
7. 1 storey / 地上 1 階
8. Jun Sato Structural Engineers
   / 佐藤淳構造設計事務所
12. 55㎡
13. 370㎡

071 MINKA Japanese Traditional Houses:
Yukio Futagawa and the Origins of His
Architectural Photography, 1955
日本の民家 一九五五年
二川幸夫・建築写真の原点
1. Tokyo, Japan / 東京都、日本
2. 2012.09-2012.12
3. 2012.12-2013.01
4. Exhibition / 展覧会
7. 1 storey / 地上 1 階
8. Jun Sato Structural Engineers
   / 佐藤淳構造設計事務所
10. Shokado co.,ltd.
    / 株式会社 商華堂
13. 269.67㎡

072 Mirrored Gardens -Vitamin Creative Space
1. Guangzhou, China
   / 広州、中国
2. 2011.11-2013.08
3. 2013.8-
4. Art Gallery
   / アートギャラリー
6. Reinforced Concrete
   / 鉄筋コンクリート造
7. 1 storey / 地上 1 階
11. 2,500㎡
12. 550㎡
13. 550㎡

073 Energy Forest
1. Rome, Italy
   / ローマ、イタリア
2. 2012.07-2013.01
3. 2013.01-2013.02
4. Exhibition
   / 展覧会
6. Polycarbonate,Wire
   / ポリカーボネート、ワイヤー

074 Catalunya House
1. Caldes de Malavella, Spain
   カルデス・デ・マラベーリャ、スペイン
2. 2012.08-2013.03
4. Private House / 専用住宅
6. Steel Frame, Reinforced Concrete
   鉄骨造、鉄筋コンクリート造
7. 3 stories / 地上 3 階
11. 2,414㎡
12. 939㎡
13. 400㎡

075 Setonomori Houses
せとの森住宅
1. Hiroshima, Japan / 広島県、日本
2. 2012.07-2012.10
3. 2012.10-2013.04
4. Collective Housing / 集合住宅
6. Timber frame / 木造
7. 2 stories / 地上 2 階
8. Jun Sato Structural Engineers
   / 佐藤淳構造設計事務所
9. EOS plus
10. KOSEI CORPORATION / 広成建設岡山支店
11. 5,468.61㎡
12. 916.11㎡
13. 1,832.22㎡

076 Connecticut Pool House
1. Connecticut, USA / コネチカット、USA
2. 2012.10-2013.05
4. Pool House / プールハウス
6. Steel Frame / 鉄骨造
7. 1 basement, 1 story
   / 地下 1 階、地上 1 階
11. 1,500㎡
12. 531.5㎡
13. 728.8㎡

077 Serpentine Gallery Pavilion 2013
1. London, United Kingdom / ロンドン、イギリス
2. 2012.11-2013.04
3. 2013.04-2013.06
4. Pavilion / パヴィリオン
6. Steel Frame / 鉄骨造
7. 1 storey / 地上 1 階
8. AECOM
9. AECOM
10. Stage One
11. 540㎡
12. 357㎡
13. 357㎡

078 Taiwan Cafe
1. Tainan, Taiwan / 台南、台湾
2. 2013.03-
4. Cafe / カフェ
6. Steel Frame / 鉄骨造
7. 2 stories
   / 地上 2 階
8. RGB STRUCTURE
11. 598.5㎡
12. 309.51㎡
13. 121.30㎡

079 Souk Mirage/Particles of Light
2. 2013.02-2013.07
4. Mixed-use complex
   / 複合施設
6. Reinforced Concrete
   / 鉄筋コンクリート造
11. 130,000㎡
12. 64,400㎡
13. 83,000㎡

080 Kunsthalle Bielefeld Annex
1. Bielefeld, Germany
   / ビーレフェルト、ドイツ
2. 2013.06-2013.08
4. Museum / 美術館
6. Steel Frame, Reinforced Concrete
   / 鉄骨造、鉄筋コンクリート造
7. 1 basement, 5 stories
   / 地下 1 階、地上 5 階
11. 1,883㎡
12. 1,534㎡
13. 4,537㎡

081 Media Forest -Axel Springer Campus
1. Berlin, Germany
   / ベルリン、ドイツ
2. 2013.06-2013.08
4. Mixed-use complex
   / 複合施設
6. Steel Frame, Reinforced Concrete
   / 鉄骨造、鉄筋コンクリート造
7. 2 basements, 23 stories
   / 地下 2 階、地上 23 階
11. 9260㎡
12. 5542㎡
13. 84095㎡

082 Museum in the Forest
1. Taoyuan, Taiwan / 桃園、台湾
2. 2012.10-
4. Museum / 美術館
6. Steel Frame, Reinforced Concrete
   / 鉄骨造、鉄筋コンクリート造
7. 1 basement, 1 storey
   / 地下 1 階、地上 1 階
8. Tomita Structural Design
   / 冨田構造設計事務所
9. SIRIUS LIGHTIG OFFICE (lighting Design)
   Yoko Ando Design(Fabric)
   / シリウスライティングオフィス（照明）
   安東陽子デザイン（ファブリック）
11. 46,578㎡
12. 531.5㎡
13. 728.8㎡

083 Salford Sphere
1. Manchester, United Kingdom
   / マンチェスター、イギリス
2. 2013.07-2013.09
4. Bridge / 橋
6. Steel Frame
   / 鉄骨造
8. ARUP
12. 1256.63㎡
13. 276.68㎡

084 Amakusa City Hall
天草本庁舎
1. Kumamoto, Japan / 熊本県、日本
2. 2013.06-2013.08
4. City Hall / 市庁舎
6. Steel Frame, Reinforced Concrete
   / 鉄骨造、鉄筋コンクリート造
7. 4 stories / 地上 4 階
8. ARUP
9. P.T.Morimura & Associates,LTD / 森村設計
11. 11,000㎡
12. 5,350㎡
13. 16,000㎡

085 Ginza Building
1. Tokyo, Japan / 東京都、日本
2. 2012.11-2013.10
4. House, Office / 住宅、事務所
6. Steel Frame / 鉄骨造
7. 14 stories / 地上 14 階
8. Jun Sato Structural Engineers
   / 佐藤淳構造設計事務所
9. EOS plus
11. 57.35㎡
12. 48.64㎡
13. 474.46㎡

086 JJ99 Youth Hostel
1. Tainan, Taiwan / 台南、台湾
2. 2012.10-
4. Hotel / ホテル
5. JIA-JIA Hotel Group / 佳佳旅住文創股份有限公司
6. Steel Frame, Reinforced Concrete
   鉄骨造、鉄筋コンクリート造
7. 1 basement, 8 stories / 地下 1 階、地上 8 階
11. 517.5㎡
12. 400㎡
13. 2,612㎡

087 Taipei Apartment
1. Taipei, Taiwan / 台北、台湾
2. 2013.11-
4. Collective Housing / 集合住宅
6. Reinforced Concrete / 鉄筋コンクリート造
7. 4 basements, 24 stories, 2 penthouse / 地下 5 階
   地上 14 階、塔屋 2 階
9. SIRIUS LIGHTIG OFFICE(lighting Design)
   / シリウスライティングオフィス（照明）
11. 1,517㎡
12. 550㎡
13. 10,080㎡

088 Omotesando Branches
1. Tokyo, Japan / 東京都、日本
2. 2013.07-2014.04
3. 2014.04-2014.12
4. House, Office, Shop
   / 住宅、事務所、店舗
6. Reinforced Concrete
   / 鉄筋コンクリート造
7. 4 stories / 地上 4 階
8. ARUP
9. EOS plus, P.T.Morimura & Associates,LTD
   / EOS plus、森村設計
10. Shin co.,ltd. / 株式会社 辰
11. 162.08㎡
12. 115.71㎡
13. 357㎡

089 Fuke Nursery School
守山市浮気保育園
1. Shiga, Japan / 滋賀県、日本
2. 2013.08-2014.03
3. 2014.03-
4. Nursery School / 保育園
6. Steel Frame / 鉄骨造
7. 2 stories / 地上 2 階

- 8　ARUP
- 9　EOS plus
- 10　TSUJIMASA Co.,Ltd. / 株式会社辻正
- 11　2,277.47㎡
- 12　920.42㎡
- 13　1,394㎡

090　House in Guangzhou
- 1　Guangzhou, China / 広州、中国
- 2　2013.10-2014.02
- 4　Private House / 専用住宅
- 6　Reinforced Concrete
　　/ 鉄筋コンクリート造
- 7　2 stories / 地上 2 階
- 12　209.37㎡
- 13　144.05㎡

091　L'Arbre Blanc
- 1　Montpellier, France / モンペリエ、フランス
- 2　2014.01-
- 4　Collective Housing / 集合住宅
- 5　NICOLAS LAISNÉ ASSOCIÉS
　　+ MANAL RACHDI OXO ARCHITECTS
- 6　Reinforced Concrete / 鉄筋コンクリート造
- 7　3 basements, 17 stories / 地下 3 階、地上 17 階
- 8　ANDRE VERDIER
- 9　FRANK BOUTTÉ CONSULTANTS
- 11　2,534㎡
- 12　786㎡
- 13　10,225㎡

092　bus stop in Krumbach
- 1　Krumbach, Austria / クルムバハ、オーストリア
- 2　2013.06-2014.04
- 3　2014.04-2014.05
- 4　Bus Stop / バス停
- 6　Steel Frame / 鉄骨造
- 7　2 stories / 地上 2 階
- 8　ARUP、gbd、Dornbirn
- 10　Schwarzenberg Haller Bau、Sulzberg
- 11　21㎡
- 12　8㎡
- 13　5㎡

093　Naoshima Pavilion
　　直島パヴィリオン
- 1　Kagawa, Japan / 香川県、日本
- 2　2014.03-
- 4　Pavilion / パヴィリオン
- 6　Steel Frame / 鉄骨造
- 7　1 storey / 地上 1 階
- 8　Jun Sato Structural Engineers
　　/ 佐藤淳構造設計事務所
- 10　Amron Corporation / 株式会社アムロン
- 11　386.89㎡
- 12　64㎡

094　TAINAN MUSEUM OF FINE ARTS
- 1　Tainan, Taiwan / 台南、台湾
- 2　2014.07-2014.09
- 4　Museum / 美術館
- 6　Steel Frame, Reinforced Concrete
　　/ 鉄骨造、鉄筋コンクリート造
- 7　2 basements, 4 stories
　　/ 地下 2 階、地上 4 階
- 8　S.T.YEH Architects / 葉世宗建築師事務所
- 9　TAI-JHOU Construction co.,
　　S.T.YEH Architects
　　SIRIUS LIGHTIG OFFICE(lighting Design)
　　DDAI & Tsai Pei Huan studio(Interior Design)
　　/ 泰洲營造有限公司、
　　葉世宗建築師事務所
　　シリウスライティングオフィス（照明）
　　曠日蔡佩烜室内裝修工作室（インテリア）
- 11　24,490.82㎡
- 12　6,335㎡
- 13　20,130㎡

095　São Paulo House - Branch
- 1　São Paulo, Brazil
　　/ サンパウロ、ブラジル
- 2　2014.03-
- 4　Private House / 専用住宅
- 7　1 basement, 3 stories
　　/ 地下 1 階、地上 3 階
- 11　774㎡
- 12　277㎡
- 13　521㎡

096　São Paulo House - Cave
- 1　São Paulo, Brazil
　　/ サンパウロ、ブラジル
- 2　2014.03-
- 4　Private House / 専用住宅
- 7　1 basement, 3 stories
　　/ 地下 1 階、地上 3 階
- 11　774㎡
- 12　324㎡
- 13　486㎡

097　São Paulo House - Louver Cloud
- 1　São Paulo, Brazil
　　/ サンパウロ、ブラジル
- 2　2014.03-
- 4　Private House / 専用住宅
- 7　1 basement, 3 stories
　　/ 地下 1 階、地上 3 階
- 11　774㎡
- 12　386㎡
- 13　376㎡

098　Stacked Rock House
- 1　Los Vilos, Chile
　　/ ロス・ビロス、チリ
- 2　2012.08-
- 4　Private House / 専用住宅
- 6　Reinforced Concrete
　　/ 鉄筋コンクリート造
- 7　2 stories / 地上 2 階
- 11　4,400㎡
- 12　140㎡
- 13　235㎡

099　Many Small Cubes -Small Nomad House
- 1　Paris, France / パリ、フランス
- 2　2014.02 -2014.09
- 3　2014.09- 2014.10
- 4　Pavilion / パヴィリオン
- 7　Steel Frame / 鉄骨造
- 8　1 story / 地上 1 階
- 10　Deliconstruct
- 13　35㎡
- 14　35㎡

100　House of sliding doors
- 1　Hyogo, Japan / 兵庫県、日本
- 2　2014.09 -
- 4　Private House / 専用住宅
- 6　Timber frame / 木造
- 7　2 stories / 地上 2 階
- 11　100.94㎡
- 12　54.99㎡
- 13　85.45㎡

101　The Miami Design District Palm Courtyard
- 1　Miami, USA / マイアミ、USA
- 2　2012.05 -2013.11
- 3　2013.11 -2014.11
- 4　Commercial Building / 商業施設
- 6　Steel Frame/ 鉄骨造
- 7　2 stories / 地上 2 階
- 10　Coastal Construction
- 12　586㎡
- 13　586㎡

102　OPEN ART MUSEUM -HELSINKI GUGGENHEIM MUSEUM
- 1　Helsinki, Finland / ヘルシンキ、フィンランド
- 2　2014.06-2014.08
- 4　Museum / 美術館
- 6　Steel Frame / 鉄骨造
- 7　1 storey / 地上 1 階
- 11　18,688㎡
- 12　15,375㎡
- 13　15,375㎡

103　Beijing Cultural and Art Center
- 1　Beijing, China / 北京、中国
- 2　2014.07-2014.09
- 4　Gallery / ギャラリー
- 6　Steel Frame, Reinforced Concrete
　　/ 鉄骨造、鉄筋コンクリート造
- 7　1 basement, 1 storey
　　/ 地下 1 階、地上 1 階
- 8　Tongji Architectural Design Co.,Ltd.
- 9　Tongji Architectural Design Co.,Ltd.
- 11　900㎡
- 12　755㎡
- 13　1,750㎡

104　Forest of Music
- 1　Budapest, Hungary
　　ブダペスト、ハンガリー
- 2　2014.03-2014.11
- 4　Music Hall / 音楽ホール
- 6　Steel Frame, Reinforced Concrete
　　鉄骨造、鉄筋コンクリート造
- 7　2 basements, 2 stories
　　地下 2 階、地上 2 階
- 8　ARUP
- 9　ARUP,NAGATA ACOUSTICS
　　/ARUP、永田音響
- 11　7,711㎡
- 12　2,253㎡
- 13　9,220㎡

105　Art Museum in Shiga
　　滋賀県立近代美術館
- 1　Shiga, Japan / 滋賀県、日本
- 2　2014.11 –2014.12
- 4　Museum / 美術館
- 6　Steel Frame, Reinforced Concrete
　　/ 鉄骨造、鉄筋コンクリート造
- 7　3 stories / 地上 3 階
- 8　ARUP
- 9　ARUP
- 12　10,500㎡
- 13　6,541㎡

106　House I
- 1　Chiba, Japan / 千葉県、日本
- 2　2014.09 –
- 4　Private House / 専用住宅
- 6　Steel Frame / 鉄骨造
- 7　1 storey / 地上 1 階
- 11　3707㎡
- 12　340.5㎡
- 13　295㎡

107　Skyscraper/Forest
- 2　2015.01 -

Profile
略歴

Sou Fujimoto

1971	Born in Hokkaido, Japan
1994	Graduated from The University of Tokyo, Faculty of Engineering Department of Architecture (Bachelor)
2000	Established Sou Fujimoto Architects in Tokyo

藤本壮介（ふじもと・そうすけ）

1971	北海道生まれ
1994	東京大学工学部建築学科卒業
2000	藤本壮介建築設計事務所設立

http://www.sou-fujimoto.net/

Liget Budapest House of Hungarian Music First Prize	2014
Wall Street Journal Architecture Innovator Award 2014	2014
Invited International Competition for the Second Folly of Montpellier Winner	2014
"Grand Prize" for Fuke Kindergarden Competition	2013
2013 Marcus Prize for Architecture	2013
The Golden Lion for Best National Participation to the Japan Pavilion at the 13th International Architecture Exhibition - La Biennale di Venezia	2012
The 9th Annual Emirates Glass LEAF Awards, the Best Public Building Award(Musashino Art Museum Library)	2012
RIBA International Fellowships	2012
"1st Prize" in International Competition for Taiwan Tower in Taichung, Taiwan	2011
"1st Prize" in International Competition for Waterfront Center in Belgrade, Serbia	2011
"2nd Prize" in International Competition for Centre for Promotion of Science of Belgrade, Serbia	2011
"1st Prize" in International Competition for Dalarna Library, Sweden	2011
"2nd Prize" in International Competition for Auditorium and Art Center in Torres de Cotillas, Spain	2010
Spotlight: The Rice Design Alliance Prize	2010
Wallpaper Design Awards 2009 – Best New Private House (Final Wooden House)	2009
World Architectural Festival – Private House Category Winner (Final Wooden House)	2008
2008 Japanese Institute of Architecture Grand Prize (Residential treatment center for emotionally disturbed children)	2008
AR Awards 2007 "Highly Commended" (House O), England	2007
AR Awards 2006 "Grand Prize" (Residential treatment center for emotionally disturbed children), England	2006
AR Awards 2005 "Hightly Commended" (Dormitory for the Mentally Disabled in Date/House T), England	2006
"Gold Prize" in House Competition by Tokyo Society of Architects and Building Engineers(T house)	2005
"1st Prize" in Wooden House Competition in Kumamoto, Japan	2005
JIA New Face Award 2004(Rehabilitation Dormitory for the Mentally Disabled in Date)	2004
"1st Prize" in International Design Competition for the Environment Art Forum for Annaka, Japan	2003
"2nd Prize in Design Competition for the Aomori-prefecture Art Museum, Japan	2000
SD Review 1995, 1997, 2000, 2001, 2002, 2003	

Liget Budapest House of Hungarian Music （ハンガリー）国際設計競技 1 等受賞	2014
Wall Street Journal Architecture Innovator 2014 受賞	2014
モンペリエ国際設計競技最優秀賞受賞	2014
浮気保育園設計競技最優秀賞受賞	2013
2013 年マーカス建築賞	2013
第 13 回ベネチア・ビエンナーレ国際建築展日本館の展示で金獅子賞受賞	2012
エミレーツ ガラス・リーフ賞 公共建築部門最優秀賞受賞（武蔵野美術大学図書館）	2012
王立英国建築家協会（RIBA）インターナショナル・フェローシップ受賞	2012
台湾タワー国際設計競技（台中）1 等受賞	2011
ベトン・ハラ ウォーターフロントセンター国際設計競技（セルビア）1 等受賞	2011
Blok39 科学未来センター国際設計競技（セルビア）2 等受賞	2011
ダラーナ大学新図書館国際指名設計競技（スウェーデン）1 等受賞	2011
ラス・トレス・デ・コティラス新音楽ホール国際設計競技（スペイン） 2 等受賞	2010
Spotlight : The Rice Design Alliance Prize	2010
Wallpaper Design Awards 2009 - 個人住宅部門受賞（Final Wooden House）	2009
World Architectural Festival ー 個人住宅部門最優秀賞（Final Wooden House）	2008
JIA 日本建築大賞 (児童心理治療施設)	2008
AR AWARDS 2007 優秀賞受賞（House O）（イギリス）	2007
AR AWARDS 2006 大賞受賞（児童心理治療施設）（イギリス）	2006
東京建築士会住宅建築賞 金賞（T house）	2006
くまもとアートポリス設計競技 2005；次世代モクバン　最優秀賞	2005
AR AWARDS 2005 入賞（伊達の援護寮・T house）（イギリス）	2005
JIA 新人賞 2004（伊達の援護寮）	2004
安中環境アートフォーラム国際設計競技　最優秀賞	2003
青森県立美術館設計競技　優秀賞	2000
SD Review 1995, 1997, 2000, 2001, 2002, 2003	

Staff List
スタッフリスト

Current Staff Members
現スタッフ

Sou Fujimoto　藤本壮介
Yumiko Nogiri　野桐友美子
Naganobu Matsumura　松村永宣
Shintaro Honma　本間新太郎

- Team Leaders -
Hideto Chijiwa　千々岩秀人
Masaki Iwata　岩田正輝
Keisuke Kiri　桐圭佑
Nadine De Ripainsel
Yibei Liu　劉軼北
Marie de France

Aya Tatsuta　立田彩
Naoki Tamura　田村直己
Toshiyuki Nakagawa　中川俊之
Nobuyuki Tejima　手島伸幸
Minako Suzuki　鈴木美南子
Hugh Hsu　許昕緯
Pui Ling Luk　陸沛靈
Hitoshi Fujiita　藤井田仁
Hsin Ju Lai　賴馨儒
Marcello Galiotto
Li Qun Tang　李立群
Nicolas Gustin
Sylvia Chen　陳民嘉
Robert Fournais
Jinsun Baik　白眞善
Nikki Yukari Minemura　峯村裕加里
Izumi Osumi　大隅泉

Former Staff Members
旧スタッフ

Koji Aoki　青木弘司
Hiroshi Kato　加藤比呂史
Ayumi Motose　本瀬あゆみ
Tomoko Kosami　小佐見友子
Yasushi Yamanoi　山野泰靖
Takahiro Hata　畑貴博
Suzuko Yamada　山田紗子
Kaz Yoneda　カズ米田
Maiko Shimada　嶋田麻依子
Nao Harikae　張替那麻
Yoshihiro Nakazono　中園美博
Kosaku Matsumoto　松本光索
Takeo Minato　湊健雄
Wai Yan Chu
Victoria Diemer Bennetzen
Marc Dujon
Ryo Tsuchie　土江亮
Andy Yu
Sei Hayashi　林盛

Kanna Arita　有田かんな
Ryota Okada　岡田良太
Mai Suzuki　鈴木舞
Shingei Katsu　葛芯芸
Tim Bacheller
Haruka Tomoeda　友枝遥
Shaofeng Chiu　邱紹峰
Marcos Duffo
Angel Barreno
Yinfang Wang　王吟方
Yichen Hsieh　謝宜蓁
Helen Lung　龍翠雲
Lisa Awazu Wellman
Midori Hasuike
Vincent Hecht
Andreas Nordström
Motoko Sumitani　住谷素子
Weiwei Zhang　張微偉
Yumiko Hori　堀友美子
Marie Liesse de Rougé

Credits
クレジット

Photographs
写真

Iwan Baan
pp.77-79、pp.81-83、pp.88-91、pp.118-121
p.136、pp.148-151、pp.175-179
pp.211-213、pp.216-219、pp.245-249、
pp.252-254、p.332

Daici Ano　阿野太一
pp.36-37、pp.44-45、p.47、pp.54-57
pp.62-63、p.93、p.96、p.135、pp.138-139、p.144

Shinkenchiku-sha　新建築写真部
p.39、p.46、p.59、p.80、p.165、p.239
pp.250-251、p.255

Edmund Sumner
p.61、p.159

Shigeo Ogawa　小川重雄
pp.94-95

Yukio Futagawa　二川幸夫
pp.140-143

Naoya Hatakeyama　畠山直哉
p.221

Hiroshi Yoda　与田弘志
p.225

Vitamin Creative Space
p.232

Sebastiano Luciano
p.235

Hufton and Crow
pp.304-305

Adolf Bereuter
pp.306-307

Marc Domage
pp.330-331

Simone Bossi
p.333

photo-Yuji Ono　Courtesy of Casa BRUTUS
/Magazine House
撮影／小野祐次
写真提供／カーサ　ブルータス
p.364 bottom right

David Vintiner
p.374

Sketches, Hand Drawings
スケッチ

Sou Fujimoto　藤本壮介

Renderings and Architecture Drawings
レンダリングイメージ、図面

Sou Fujimoto Architects + NICOLAS LAISNE ASSOCIES + MANAL RACHDI OXO ARCHITECTES + FRANCK BOUTTE CONSULTANTS + Rendering by RSI-STUDIO
pp.298-303

Images/figures other than the above were provided by Sou Fujimoto Architects
上記以外は藤本壮介建築設計事務所

English Translations
英訳

Christopher Stephens
Introduction, commentaries on works (041-107), and chronology
序、作品解説文 (041-107)、藤本壮介年表

Hideto Chijiwa (Sou Fujimoto Architects)
千々岩秀人（藤本壮介建築設計事務所）
Keywords in Introduction, catchphrases for commentaries (001-040) and works (001-107)
序キーワード、作品解説文 (001-040) 作品キャッチコピー (001-107)

Book Design
ブックデザイン

Sou Fujimoto Architects
藤本壮介建築設計事務所

Design Cooperation
デザイン協力

Masahiro Eigen
榮元正博

Sou Fujimoto Architecture Works 1995-2015
藤本壮介建築作品集

2015 年 4 月 16 日　初版第 1 刷発行
2025 年 6 月 30 日　初版第 6 刷発行

著者：藤本壮介
発行者：渡井 朗
発行所：TOTO 出版（TOTO 株式会社）
〒 107-0062 東京都港区南青山 1-24-3 TOTO 乃木坂ビル 2F
[営業] TEL: 03-3402-7138　FAX: 03-3402-7187
[編集] TEL: 03-3497-1010
URL: https://jp.toto.com/publishing
印刷・製本：TOPPANクロレ株式会社

落丁本・乱丁本はお取り替えいたします。
本書の全部又は一部に対するコピー・スキャン・デジタル化等の無断複製行為は、著作権法上での例外を除き禁じます。本書を代行業者等の第三者に依頼してスキャンやデジタル化することは、
たとえ個人や家庭内での利用であっても著作権法上認められておりません。
定価はカバーに表示してあります。

© 2015　Sou Fujimoto

Printed in Japan
ISBN978-4-88706-349-5